FINANCIAL MANAGEMENT–I

[For WBUT-BBA (403)—Fourth Semester (New Syllabus)]

FINANCIAL MANAGEMENT–I

[For WBUT-BBA (403)—Fourth Semester (New Syllabus)]

Dr S Kr Paul MCom, PhD, MBIM (London)
Principal [Retd]
Reader and Head, Department of Accountancy
South City College, Kolkata

Chandrani Paul MCom, MBA (WBUT)
Faculty Member, Sikkim-Manipal University and
Asia-Pacific Institute of Hospitality Management

New Central Book Agency (P) Ltd
LONDON
DELHI KOLKATA PUNE HYDERABAD ERNAKULAM

REGD. OFFICE

8/1 Chintamoni Das Lane, Kolkata 700 009, India
email: ncbapvtltd@eth.net

OVERSEAS

27 Catherine Court, Chase Road, Southgate, London, N14 4RB

EXPORT

212 Shahpur Jat, New Delhi 110 049
email: ncbaexp@ncbapvtltd.com

BRANCHES

4262/3 1st Floor, Flat Nos. 105 & 106
Ansari Road, Daryaganj, New Delhi 110 002
email: ncbadel@ncbapvtltd.com

House No. 3-1-315, 1st Floor
Nimboliadda, Kachiguda, Hyderabad 500 027
email: ncbahydb@ncbapvtltd.com

Shop Nos. 3 & 4, Vinayak Towers
681/B Budhwar Peth, Appa Balwant Chowk
Pune 411 002
email: ncbapune@ncbapvtltd.com

GSS Shopping Complex, 1st Floor
Opposite College Post Office, Convent Road
Ernakulam 682 035
email: ncbaernk@ncbapvtltd.com

FINANCIAL MANAGEMENT— I [BBA—Fourth Semester]

First Published: January 2010

PUBLISHER AND TYPESETTER

New Central Book Agency (P) Ltd
8/1 Chintamoni Das Lane, Kolkata 700 009

PRINTER

New Central Book Agency (P) Ltd
Web-Offset Division, Dhulagarh, Sankrail, Howrah

COVER DESIGNER

Soumen Paul

COVER PRINTER

Biswanath Studio, Kolkata

TECHNICAL EDITOR

Subas Maitra

PROJECT TEAM

Prabhat Jas, Pradip Das, Ashoke Das

ISBN: 978-81-7381-618-5

Price: Rs 295.00 [Rupees Two Hundred and Ninety-five]

Dedicated to

Principal Saibal Mukherjee

JIS College of Engineering and Management

Kalyani

CONTENTS

3. COST OF CAPITAL 3.1-3.48

PREFACE

The dimension of **FINANCIAL MANAGEMENT** is rapidly changing day-by-day due to diversification in business and economic activities in the society in particular, and in the country at large. As a result, academic and professional bodies of Financial Management are also trying to incorporate such changes in their management literature. West Bengal University of Technology (WBUT) is also not lagging behind in this regard. They have prepared their syllabus for **Financial Management for the BBA** students keeping in mind the changed circumstances.

This volume has been prepared for the **Fourth Semester BBA Examinees** of WBUT. The New Syllabus prescribed by the WBUT has been followed faithfully.

We know that a major section of the students come from non-commerce streams at the Plus-Two level. Considering this aspect, the book has been presented in a easy lucid style, so that they can understand the subject without taking any assistance from anybody. Every theoretical part is explained with the help of illustrations which will, no doubt, help the students to understand the principles of financial management and its applications.

We are thankful to Prof. Atas Banerjee, Professor, Business Administration Department, Pailan College of Management and Technology who gave us the idea of preparing a book for the BBA students. This we have done promptly.

We are also thankful to Amitabha Sen, Director, New Central Book Agency (P) Ltd, for his active cooperation and support. We also express our appreciation for the cooperation of Subas Maitra, Prabhat Jas, Pradip Kr. Das and Ashok Kr. Das of New Central Book Agency (P) Ltd for bringing out the book within the shortest possible time.

In spite of out best efforts, some grey areas may have remained. If any error is found, please e-mail at **authorskpaul@gmail.com.** We also welcome constructive suggestions and criticisms from teachers and students which will help us in making the title more student-friendly in the forthcoming editions.

187B Lake Town
Block B, Kolkata 700 089
Ph. 033 2534 6405

25 December 2009

S Kr Paul
Chandrani Paul

SYLLABUS

PAPER CODE **[BBA 403] Financial Management—I**

1. **Financial Management:** Financial goals; Profit vs wealth maximisation; Financial functions—investment, financing, and dividend decisions; Financial planning.
2. **Capital Budgeting:** Nature of investment decisions, investment evaluation criteria, payback period, accounting rate of return, net present value, internal rate of return, profitability index; NPV and IRR comparison.
3. **Cost of Capital:** Significance of cost of capital; Calculating cost of debt; Preference shares, equity capital, and retained earnings; combined (weighted) cost of capital.
4. **Operating and Financial Leverage:** Measure; Effects on profit, analysing alternate financial plans, combined financial and operating leverage.
5. **Capital Structure:** Theories and determinants.
6. **Dividend Policies:** Issues in dividend policies; Walter's model; M-M Hypothesis, forms of dividends and stability in dividends, determinants.
7. **Management of Working Capital:** Nature of working capital, significance of working capital, operating cycle and factors determining of working capital requirements.

   Management of working capital—cash, receivables, and inventories.

CHAPTER 1

FINANCIAL MANAGEMENT

Introduction

The concept of Financial Management is of very recent origin. It gains considerable academic interest. Financial Management, practically, is concerned with the decision-making about the flow of funds in a firm. In other words, after procuring the funds from various sources, how the said funds are applied—that should be analysed. In short, it deals with the procurement of funds in the most economic manner and utilise the said funds in the most optimum way in order to maximise the rate of return to the shareholders. Financial Management receives a prime relevance as a functional area since the procurement of funds and its best utilisation is practically the key to success of any organisation. As each and every aspect of business relates to finance, Financial Management plays a very significant role for all financial transactions.

It may also be stated that Financial Management affects the finance functions of a firm. The Financial Manager must be careful about the effective utilisation of available resources in the best possible manner so that the ultimate rate of return is maximised. So, Financial Management deals with the procurement of funds and its proper utilisation. It may also be stated that 'Financial Management is concerned with the effective use of an important economic resource, namely Capital Funds'—**Solomon**. The definition is : "Financial Management is concerned with the managerial decisions that result in the acquisition and financing of Long-term and Short-term Credits for the firm. As such, it deals with the situation that requires selection of specific liability (or combination of liabilities) as well as the problem of size and growth of an enterprise. The analysis of these decisions is based on the expected inflows and outflows of funds and their effects upon managerial objective." —**Philipatus.**

So, from discussions made so far it becomes quite clear that Financial Management deals with the flow of funds, i.e., the procurement of funds and its effective utilisation in the best possible manner so that the rate of return is maximised after due consideration of risk, cost and control operations.

NATURE OF FINANCIAL MANAGEMENT

The nature of Financial Management refers to its functions, scope and objectives. Financial Management itself is concerned with the planning and controlling of the financial resources of the firm. As an academic discipline, it has undergone fundamental changes in relation to its scope, functions, and objectives. In the past, when it was simply a branch of economics, it was treated as the raising of funds. But, at present, it is used in a broader sense which includes the efficient use of resources in addition to procurement of funds. At the same time, the academic thinking relating to the objective of Financial Management has also undergone changes over the years. However, the object of the present study is to describe the functions and objectives of Financial Management in the academic literature in order to serve as a background to its various aspects which are very important.

Scope and Functions of Financial Management

The scope and functions of Financial Management are divided into two following broad categories, viz., (1) Old or Traditional Approach and (2) New or Modern Approach.

(1) **Old/Traditional Approach**

Financial Management, at the initial stage of its evolution, was a separate branch of academic literature and the term 'Corporation Finance' was used. At present, this term is being replaced in the academic world by 'Financial Management' which deals with the financing of corporate enterprises. According to this approach, the scope of Financial Management and the role of Financial Management are considered to be confined to the procurement of funds in a broader sense. As a result, the entire financing technique is treated as encompassing three interrelated aspects of raising and administering resources from outside:

(i) the organisation of capital market in the form of financial institution;

(ii) funds are raised from the capital markets through financial instruments along with the practices and procedural aspects of capital markets;

(iii) the legal and accounting relationships between the sources of funds and a firm itself.

Therefore, the area of corporation finance was limited to the covering of complex of capital market institutions, practices and instruments through which funds are obtained. Besides, since the problem of raising funds is more intensely felt in case of an episodic event, detailed description of the events like mergers, consolidations, reorganisation, recapitalisation etc. are contained in the field of academic story. The traditional approach to Financial Management did not allow the financial manager to take any decision regarding the allocation of the firm's funds although he was required to raise the needed funds from various sources.

The traditional approach evolved in the 1930s and 1940s which dominated the academic thinking during 40s and early 1950s. But, subsequently, the same was discarded due to the following snags: (i) since the basic conceptual and analytical framework of the definitions and scope of finance are limited and (ii) the treatment of various topics and their emphasis is not enough.

Besides, the traditional approach was criticised for the following reasons[1]:

(a) The traditional approach emphasises on raising and administering funds. The subject of finance is treated from the investor's point of view. No importance was given to the point of view of the financial decision-maker (i.e., who makes internal financial decisions). In short, the traditional view is the *other-looking-in approach.*

(b) The traditional approach is considered as the *episodic financing function* since it gives overemphasis on topics of securities and its markets, incorporation, promotion, merger, etc.

(c) Since the traditional approach gives more emphasis on the long-term financing problem, it *ignores the importance of working capital management.*

---

1 Solomon, E. : *The Theory of Financial Management* — Columbia University Press, New York, 1969, p. 5.

(d) The traditional approach plays a significant role in financing problems of *non-corporate enterprises.*

The shortcomings of the traditional approach were primarily due to the fundamental weakness other than the treatment and/or emphasis of different aspects. Its conceptual and analytical limitations arose from the fact that it recognised only the problem of procuring the external funds and ignored the dimensions of allocations of capital which Solomon described as the *central issues of Financial Management.*[1]

Of course, certain 'traditional' authors like Gerstenberg[2] and Lincoln[3] emphasised and initiated discussion on the topics of day-to-day financial operations including sales forecasting, budgeting, financial control, cost control, etc., along with the discussion on episodic financial events.

(2) Modern Approach

The traditional approach was criticised for its conceptual and analytical grounds by the proponents of modern or contemporary approach since the former neglects the problems of allocation of capital to different assets and the problems of optimum combination of finance, which omitted two important matters, as pointed out by Dewing :

(i) The traditional approach does not recognise the relationships between financing mix and the cost of capital and fails to solve the problems relating to optimum combination of finance; and

(ii) It also fails to deal with the problems relating to the valuation of the firm and the cost of capital.

It has already been stated above that the traditional approach evolved its utility during the 1940s and mid-1950s. But, after mid-1950s, an efficient and effective utilisation of a firm's resources were necessitated—as there were a number of economic and environmental factors, like the increasing pace of industrialisation, technological inventions and innovations, intense competition, government intervention, population growth, etc. Fortunately, a number of management skills and decision-making techniques were developed which facilitated implementing the optimum allocation of a firm's resources. In other words, the approach and scope of Financial Management changed, i.e., the emphasis shifted from raising of funds to the efficient and effective use of funds or from episodic financing to the managerial financial problems.

The modern approach is an analytical way of viewing the financial problems of a firm. No doubt Financial Management is an integral part of overall management.

In the words of Solomon, E. : 'In this broader view the central issue of financial policy is the wise use of funds, and the central process involved is a rational matching of advantages of potential uses against the cost of alternative potential sources so as to achieve the broad financial goals which an enterprise sets for itself.[4] Therefore, the primary finance function is to take proper decision about the expenditure and the demand for capital for those expenditures, i.e., the proper and efficient use of allocation of funds.

---

1 *Ibid.*

2 Gerstenberg, C. W. — *Materials of Corporation Finance,* Englewood Cliffs, N. J. Prentice-Hall, 1915.

3 Lincoln, E. E. — *Problems in Business Finance* — Chicago, Shaw, 1921.

4 Solomon, E. — op. cit., p. 2.

For this purpose, a financial manager should know: [1]

(i) How large should an enterprise be, and how fast should it grow?

(ii) In what form should it hold its assets?

(iii) What should be the composition of its liabilities?

The above questions actually cover the major financial problems of a firm. In short, according to the modern approach, Financial Management deals with the solution of the above three major problems relating to the financial operations, viz., investment, financing and dividend decisions. Therefore, Financial Management includes as functions of finance the three major decisions : (i) The Investment decisions, (ii) The Financing decisions, and (iii) The Dividend Policy decisions.

The new approach to Financial Management may be broadened to include profit-planning function also.[2]

OBJECTIVES OF FINANCIAL MANAGEMENT

From the discussion we have made so far, it becomes clear that a firm has to take three major decisions:

(i) Where to invest fund and by what amount? — the Investment decisions;

(ii) Where to raise funds and by what amount? — the Financing decisions;

(iii) How much to pay by way of Dividends? — the Dividend Policy decisions.

The investment and the financial policies depend on the above decisions. It should be remembered that a clear understanding of the objectives which are sought to be attained is necessary in order to make wise decisions. No doubt the objective provides a framework for optimum financial decision-making. It is generally accepted that the financial objective of the firm is to maximise the owner's economic welfare.

For this purpose, two well-established and widely-discussed criteria are:

(a) Profit Maximisation, and (b) Wealth Maximisation.

Profit Maximisation

How a private firm should behave depends on Profit Maximisation as a decision criterion. Under this concept, actions that increase the firm's profit are undertaken and those that decrease profit are avoided. Profit can be maximised either by increasing output for a given set of scarce input or by reducing the cost of production for a given output. That is, there must be efficient use of resources. According to Modern Microeconomic Theory, profit maximisation is nothing but a criterion for economic efficiency as profits provide a yardstick by which economic performances can be judged under condition of perfect competition. Besides, under perfect competition, where all prices accurately reflect true values and consumers are well-informed, profit maximisation behaviour by firms leads to an efficient allocation of resources and maximum social welfare.

There is no doubt that the Financial Management deals with the efficient use of economic resources, i.e., capital funds. Since the capital is a scarce item, it follows that the profit maximisation should serve as the primary need for the decision taken by the financial managers of private firms which, in practice, it follows. But the same has to be

---

1 Ibid.

2 Mao, C. T. : Quantitative Analysis of Financial Decisions, New York, The Macmillan Co., 1969, p. 6. The term profit-planning refers to the operating decisions in the areas of pricing, volume of output and the firm's selection of product lines. Profit-planning is, therefore, a prerequisite for optimising investment and financing decisions. — Ibid.

transformed to provide the necessary principles and guidelines to the financial managers since the profit maximisation concept does not recognise the real-world problems that we feel when we want to take actual decisions about the efficient use of capital funds. As a result, we cannot implement the fundamental idea which underlines the rationale of Adam Smith's *invisible hands*[1] by which total economic welfare is maximised.

Profit maximisation is widely preferred, but, in fact, the concept has been questioned and criticised on the following grounds :

(a) **Vague/Uncertainty**

Practically, profit maximisation as an operational criterion becomes unsuitable for the problems of uncertainty in relation to the investment and financing decisions since it considers only the size of benefits and gives no weight to the degree of uncertainty of the future benefits. For example, two alternative courses of action might have the same expected outcome, but one might be far more risky than the other. The following illustration will make the principle clear.

Let there be two investment opportunities, A and B, whose profit depends on the state of economy as illustrated in Table 1.1 :

Table 1.1 : Uncertainty about Expected Profits

State of Economy		Profit (in rupees)	
		Alternative A	Alternative B
Recession	Period I	9,000	0
Normal	Period II	10,000	10,000
Boom	Period III	11,000	20,000
		30,000	30,000

From Table 1.1, shown above, it is quite clear that the total returns related to two alternatives become equal to Rs. 30,000 in a normal economy but the range of variation is very wide in case of Alternative B. But the same is very narrow in case of Alternative A. In other words, the returns associated with the Alternative B are more uncertain and/or risky since they fluctuate widely depending on the state of economy. Similarly, Alternative A is better from the standpoint of uncertainty and risk. Here profit maximisation criterion fails to express it.

(b) **Ambiguity**

Profit maximisation concerns ambiguity since the term *'profit'* is vague and can vary widely—depending on the principles of accounting applied.

(c) **Timing**

Profit maximisation ignores timings. The money received today has a higher value than money received next year, a profit seeking organisation must consider the timing of cash flows and profits. Which is more profitable to a firm : it selects a 3-year project with a return of 20% or a 5-year project with a return of 17%? No doubt the latter project may result in greater total profits if the firm could not immediately reinvest its profits when the same was received from the 3-year project.

---

1 Adam Smith in his famous book *"Inquiry into the Nature and Causes of the Wealth of Nations" (1776)* pointed out that "(The businessman) by directing .... industry in the such a manner as its producer may be of greater value .... intends only his own gain, and he is in this as in many other case, led by an invisible hand to promote an end which was not a part of his intention ...." —Adapted from Solomon, E. and Pringle, J. J. : *An Introduction to Financial Management*, op. cit., p. 7.

The principle can be explained with the help of the following Table 1.2:

Table 1.2 : Timing of Anticipated Profit

State of Economy	Profit (in rupees)	
	Alternative A	Alternative B
Period I	500	—
Period II	1,000	1,000
Period III	500	1,000
	2,000	2,000

From Table 1.2, shown above, it is clear that the total profits shown by the Alternatives A and B are equal. Therefore, if profit maximisation is the decision-criterion, both of them should be given equal importance. But the important difference between them is that Alternative A provides a higher return in earlier years whereas Alternative B provides a higher return in the later years, i.e., they are not strictly equal. Because, we all know that the earlier the better — as benefits received sooner are more valuable than benefits received later on the ground that the former can be reinvested to earn returns. The same is due to the fact that there is a time value of money. The profit maximisation criterion does not recognise the distinction between the returns received in different period of time and treats them at par which is not true in real-world as the profits (benefits) in earlier years should be valued more highly than the profits (benefits) in the subsequent years.

Therefore, from the above discussion, it can be taken into consideration that the profit maximisation, as an operational criterion, is unsuitable and inappropriate of a firm from the standpoint of investment, financing and dividend policy. It is vague and ambiguous and does not recognise the two basic facts, viz., (a) risk; and (b) time value of money.

It can be stated that the appropriate operational-decision criterion should include:

(i) It must be precise and exact;

(ii) It should consider both quality and quantity dimension;

(iii) It should recognise the time value of money.

For the reasons shown above, value maximisation has replaced profit maximisation as an operational criterion for management decisions.

Wealth Maximisation

The Value Maximisation or Net Present Worth Maximisation — which is universally accepted as an appropriate and operationally feasible criterion in order to choose among the alternative courses of action for Financial Management — is to maximise the value of the firm over a long run.[1] It removes the limitations suffered by the earlier method — Profit Maximisation.

Under this method, the net present value or wealth of a course of action is maximised. The net present value is the difference between the gross present value of the benefits of that action and the amount of investment required to achieve those benefits.

On the other hand, the gross present value of the same is determined by discounting or capitalising its benefits at a rate which reflects their timing and uncertainty.

The operational features of wealth maximisation satisfy all the three requirements (exactness, quality of benefit, and time value of money — stated above) of a suitable operational objective of financial courses of action. Let us discuss these one by one.

1 Hampton, J. J. : *Financial Decision-making — Concepts, Problems and Cases* — Prentice-Hall of India, New Delhi, 1983, p. 10.

The value of an asset is best viewed in terms of the benefits it can produce. The worth of a course of action can be judged in terms of the value of benefits it produces, less the cost of undertaking it. The benefits of an investment or financing decision can be measured in terms of the stream of future expected cash flows generated by the decision[1], rather than the accounting profit which is the basis for the measurement of benefits in the case of profit maximisation criterion.

The next feature of the wealth maximisation criterion is that it recognises both the quantity and quality dimensions of benefits (which has already been mentioned above) along with the time value of money. The value of a stream of future cash flows must consider not only the expected value of the flows, but also their degree of uncertainty. Other things being equal, less uncertain flows are valued more highly than more uncertain flows. Besides, money has time value. That is, the sum of money received in future is less valuable than it is today. In other words, necessary adjustments must be made in the cash flow pattern in order to incorporate the risk and also to make an allowance for differences in the timing of benefits. Therefore, the value of a stream of cash flows can be calculated by discounting its elements back to the present at a capitalisation rate that reflects both time and risk.[2]

The capitalisation/discount rate is the rate which reflects both time and risk preferences of the owners of capital. Generally, capitalisation rate is expressed in decimal notation, i.e., if the rate of discount is taken as 16%, the same will be recorded as $0.16 = \frac{16}{100}$. Capitalisation rate will be higher if the risk is greater and the period is longer.

It is quite clear that net present value maximisation is, no doubt, superior than the profit maximisation criterion as an operational objective. The value maximisation decision criterion involves a comparison of value to cost. An action that has a discounted value, reflecting both time and risk that exceeds its cost can be said to create value. Such actions should be undertaken. Conversely, actions with values less than cost reduce the value of the firm and should be rejected. In the case of mutually exclusive alternatives, when only one is to be chosen, the alternative with the greatest net present value should be selected.[3]

According to E. Solomon's symbols and methods, net present worth can be ascertained as:

(i) $W = V - C$ (1.1) where, W = Net Present Worth.

V = Gross Present Worth.

C = Investment (Equity Capital) required in order to acquire the asset or to purchase the course of action.

(ii) $V = \frac{E}{K}$ (1.2) where, E = Size of future benefits available to the suppliers of the Input Capital.

K = The capitalisation/discount rate reflecting risk and timing of benefits attached to E.

---

1 Solomon, E. and Pringle, J. J. : op. cit., p. 12.

2 *Ibid.*

3 *Ibid.*

It should be remembered that, while applying value maximisation criterion, the term 'value' is used in terms of worth of the owners/equity shareholders.

(iii) $E = G-(M+I+T)$ (1.3)

where, G = Average future flow of gross annual earnings expected from the courses of action (before interest, taxes and dividends).

M = Average annual reinvestment required to maintain G at the projected level.

I = Expected flows of annual payments on account of interest, dividend and charges.

T = Expected annual outflows on account of taxes.

The operational objective of Financial Management is the maximisation of W in Equation (1.1).

W can also be money explicitly defined by short-cut method Present Value/Worth or Wealth is) :

$$W = \frac{A_1}{(1+K)} + \frac{A_2}{(1+K)^2} \cdots\cdots\cdots \frac{A_n}{(1+K)^n} - C$$

$$= \sum_{t=1}^{n} \frac{A_1}{(1+K)^t} - C$$

where, A_1, A_2 .... A_n represent the stream of benefits (cash flows) expected to occur if a course of action is adopted.

C is the cost of that action.

K is the appropriate discount rate to measure the quality of A-s.

and W is the net present worth or wealth, (which is the difference between the present worth of the stream of benefits and the initial cost).

From the above, it becomes crystal clear that value maximisation decision criterion recognises the time value of money and also tackles the risk which is ascertained by the uncertainty of the expected benefits. Moreover, it is a very precise and unambiguous concept and is, therefore, considered as an appropriate and operationally feasible decision criterion. That is why it is rightly said that maximisation of wealth is more useful than maximisation of profit as a statement of the objective of most business firms. It properly points out that the profit factor should be considered from a long-term point of view. At the same time, it balances this single factor with related goals, such as growth, stability, risk avoidance and the market price of the firm's stock.[1]

Goals of Financial Management

There are a number of classifications which can be used to define the specified goals of Financial Management. Two of them are discussed in the present chapter : viz., (i) Profit-Risk Approach to Financial Goals, and (ii) Liquidity-Profitability Approach to Financial Goals.

---

1 Hampton, J. J. : op. cit., p. 12.

(i) Profit-Risk Approach to Financial Goals

Under this approach, in order to maximise profits at a given level of risk, finance deals with creating the proper framework. For this purpose, the firm must develop controls over flows of funds which allows sufficient flexibility to respond to change in the operating environment.[1]

This approach, however, recognises:

(a)	Maximise Profits	:	Generally, finance strives for a high level of long-term profit and, at the same time, a short-term profit.
(b)	Minimise Risk	:	Finance seeks a course of action which avoids unnecessary risk and anticipates problem areas and ways of overcoming difficulties.
(c)	Maintain Control	:	Funds which are flowing in and out should always be monitored in order to assure that they are safeguarded and properly utilised.
(d)	Achieve Flexibility	:	We all know that a firm has to deal with an uncertain future. Flexibility can be maintained provided there is careful management of funds and activities. Where there is a sufficient source of funds in advance of needs, it is flexible when actual requirement is made.

Liquidity-Profitability Approach to Financial Goals

There are two goals which are to be achieved by a financial manager, viz., liquidity and profitability. Liquidity means one's ability to meet claims and obligations as and when they become due. In other words, the firm can pay all its bills as soon as they become due and have to meet certain contingencies. On the other hand, profitability of a firm is represented by the rate of return on its capital employed (which is measured by Net Profit to Capital Employed). It requires the firm's operation to yield a long-term profit for Shareholders as part of the overall goal of maximising the present value of common stock.

However, the above two classifications are to some extent similar and overlapping. Under the former, an element in minimising risk is the achieving of liquidity, whereas, under the latter, achieving liquidity requires the maximisation of risks. Therefore, the financial manager must understand the firm's goal and the goals of the finance function.

FINANCE FUNCTIONS

The financing decisions play a very important role of a corporate body whenever the question of finance comes. Financing decisions affect all financial matters of a firm. Thus, the areas of financial management are : *(i) Need for funds; (ii) Investment Decision; (iii) Financing Decisions and (iv) Dividend Decisions.* These are depicted as :

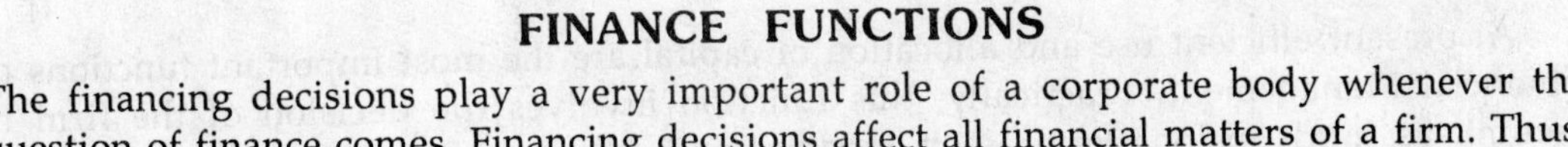

1 *Ibid.*

These are explained below one by one:

(i) **Need for Funds**

We all know that funds are required by a firm for different purposes. Naturally, how much fund is required depends on the nature and type of business enterprise.

Generally, two well-known classifications are:

(a) ***Investment in fixed assets***, and

(b) ***Investment in current asset*** (i.e., in Working Capital)

Fixed assets (e.g., Land and Building, Plant and Machinery, Furniture and Fixtures etc.) are required not for sale and they are usually owned. They help to continue the production function for goods and services in order to earn revenue. Investment in fixed assets must be made in such a way that they are properly utilised, i.e., must not be idle. So, investments in fixed assets need the following further considerations:

(i) Provision to be made for adequate planned capital expenditure;

(ii) Proper evaluation of the project to be made before the actual execution; and

(iii) Estimates and schedules are made for approved capital projects, and so on.

Here, we are to remember that investment in fixed assets must be made either from own source or from long-term sources. Otherwise, if fixed assets are financed from short-term sources, Working Capital would be found to be ***'negative'*** which will invite a lot of financial troubles.

Similarly, current assets (e.g., Stock, Debtors, Cash, Bank etc.) are required for Working Capital purposes. The funds for investment in Working Capital must also be properly utilised since idle Working Capital will increase cost. We are also to remember that investment in current assets are usually financed from short-term sources which usually do not create any problem. But there must be a synchronisation of cash, (cash receipts and cash payments) for maintaining liquidity position of the enterprise. On the contrary, if current assets are financed from own sources or long-term sources, no problem will appear. In that case, net Working Capital position of the firm would be always ***'positive'*** having sufficient liquid sources in the hands of the firm.

Since the financial resources are always limited proper allocation and utilisation of funds are necessary. Moreover, limited financial resources compelled a firm to consider the alternative courses of action. viz., (i) Rental—as the alternative to ownership; (ii) Buying—as an alternative to manufacturings.

(ii) **Investment Decisions**

At present efficient use and allocation of capital are the most important functions of Financial Management. Practically, this function involves the decision of the firm to commit its funds in long-term assets together with other profitable activities. However, the decision of the firm to invest funds in long-term assets needs considerable importance as the same tends to influence the firm's wealth, size, growth, and also affects the business risk. No doubt the primary consideration of all types of investment decisions is the rate of earning capacity, i.e., rate of return. But there are other considerations as well, e.g., risk factor. In short, risk factor also plays a significant role in investment decisions.

Generally, investment decisions fall under two broad categories:

(i) Investment in own business; and

(ii) Investment in outside business, i.e., in securities and other companies.

We all know that the primary sources of supplying capital are: (i) owners; and (ii) lenders/outsiders. It is also known to us that there is a cost of capital in all types of capital investment in the business. Therefore, investment in own business is justified only when the return for the same will be at least equal to the estimated return resulting from the investment by way of relevant cost of capital. In other words, investment in own business is desirable provided the return from such enterprise is higher than the estimated return on the relevant cost of capital. The primary purpose, of course, of investment funds in business assets is to produce future economic benefits in such a manner which will cover not only the cost of capital and operating expenses but also will leave a sufficient margin in order to cover the risk which is involved in it.

Investment Involves Risk

The values of invested capital can, no doubt, be affected due to the following factors:

(a) Advancement in technology leads to an improved and efficient machine which may prove existing machinery worthless.

or, (b) A change in pattern and design which involves the scrapping of parts or materials or tools lying in stock and which can no longer be used in future.

or, (c) If the consumers' tastes and preferences are changed, it is nothing but a loss of value to a company.

or, (d) Investments made in receivables may prove bad and irrecoverable, and so on.

Therefore, adequate consideration relating to investment of capital should always be made since investments involve risk.

(iii) Financing Decisions

Financing decisions deal with the composition of capital structure of a firm i.e., the proportion of debt/borrowed capital and equity capital. In other words, these two sources are the primary sources of funds. Debt or borrowed capital means the funds supplied by the outsiders against fixed rate of interest. Although debt capital bears a fixed rate of Interest payment, it is cheaper than the cost of equity capital. Moreover, it has tax advantages. ***Trading on equity*** can be made possible by the application of debt capital which again gives a better return to the equity shareholders. But it possesses a risk element in it i.e., the payment of fixed rate of interest to the bondholders or others. If a firm is unable to pay the interest on such bondholders, it may bring insolvency of a firm. Moreover, when debt capital will mature for payment a huge amount of liquid sources of funds will be required which adversely affect the liquidity position of an enterprise. In spite of having such limitations every firm takes the risks of having borrowed/debt capital just to enjoy the benefit of '*Trading on Equity*'.*

On the other hand, equity financing does not involve neither the committed amount of paying return on investment nor the question of repayment will arise. So question of outflow of funds does not arise—neither for paying fixed amount of return or for the repayment of capital contributed by the shareholders. But it does not enjoy the benefit of tax advantages. It must be remembered that preference share capital is just like the debt/borrowed capital, which needs fixed rate of dividend and needs funds for repayment in future.

In real-world situation, however, we find that every firm employs both debt or borrowed capital as well as equity capital i.e, the composition of debt capital and equity

---

* Moreover, when debt capital will mature for payment a huge amount of liquid sources of funds will be required which adversely affect the liquidity positions of an enterprise.

capital. However, from the standpoint of long-term solvency of a firm, proportion of equity or owned capital should be higher than the borrowed capital i.e., Debt-Equity ratio must be normal.

(iv) **Dividend Decisions**

Another important criterion is the dividend decision. The shareholder who has acquired the shares expects always a better return on his investment by way of dividend. Declaration of dividend depends on the earning capacity of the company together with the cash position (as dividend can never be paid in kind). Moreover, certain legal restrictions are there before declaring and paying dividend to shareholders. It is an appropriation of profit. The Directors in the general meeting decides to pay the rate of dividend considering all other financial aspects. The market value of a share goes up if the rate of paying dividend is very high and vice versa in the opposite case. So, dividend decision play a very important role in finance functions. There are many factors which affect the dividend policy of a firm viz., (a) External factors (e.g., General state of economy; Capital Market considerations, legal, contractual, Constraints and Restrictions, Tax policy; Inflation; Stability of Dividend etc.) and (b) Internal factors (e.g., Liquidity position, Growth Rate, $\frac{D}{P}$ Ratio etc.)

FUNDAMENTAL CONSIDERATIONS: RISK AND RETURN

It is needless to mention that the market value of the shares are largely affected by the risk and return of the firm which, again, depends on the financial decision. In order to maximise the firm's shares a balance must be maintained between risk and return which is called *'Risk-Return Trade off'*. Fig. 1.1 shows the relationship among market value financial decision and *risk-return trade off*.

In order to maximise the owner's wealth it is the duty of the financial manager to maximise the return at the cost of minimum risk. He must take the necessary steps so that unnecessary risks can be avoided. For this purpose, sources and applications of funds must be monitored to see that they are properly utilised. If necessary, financial reporting system should be introduced which will predict the trade pictures of the firm.

RESPONSIBILITIES OF FINANCIAL MANAGEMENT IN FIRM

An efficient and sound organisation must be set up for the finance functions as the financial decision of a firm is very important. As we know, the top management (viz., Treasurer, Controller, etc.) is absolutely liable to carry out the decision taken for finance functions. For this purpose a separate department may be introduced under the direct control of the Board of Directors to control and organise the financial activities of the firm. At the same time, such department may be headed either by a committee or an official who will consider the financial policy matter and other routine activities may be assigned to others.

Practically, the following reasons advocate why the finance functions should be handed over to the top management:

(i) It is the pivot for a firm. Survival and development of a firm depend on it.

(ii) Liquidity and Solvency position are largely affected by it.

(iii) Financial functions should always be centralised which result in economies.

(iv) Financing Current Assets is also affected by it.

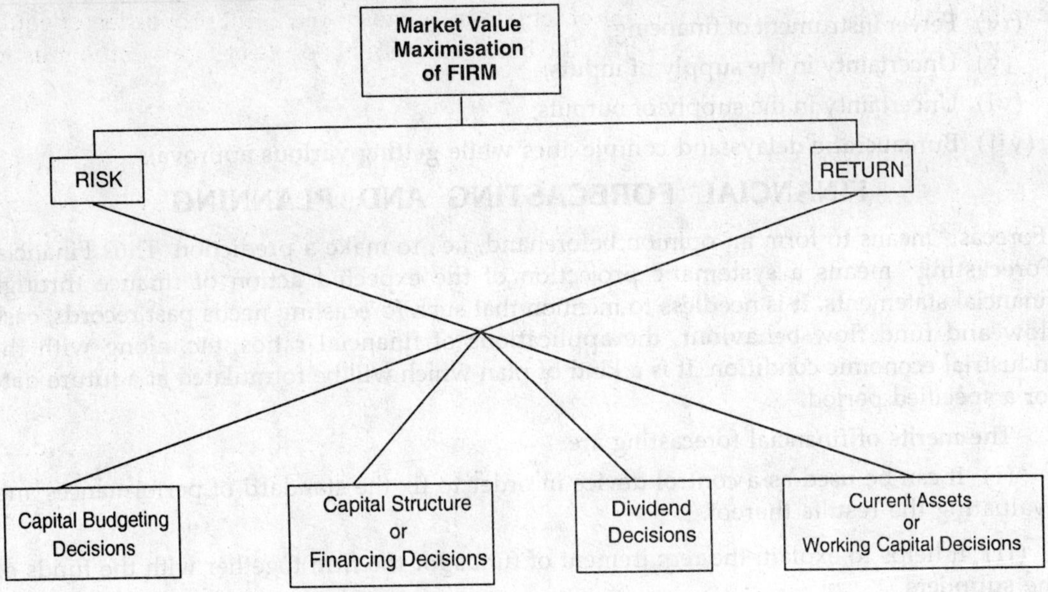

Fig. 1.1 : Relationship of Market Value, Financial Decisions and Risk-return Trade Off

Needless to mention that the organisation structure differs from firm to firm. It depends on many factors, viz., size, types, nature, types of financial operation, financial employees/officers, financial health of the firm. Similarly, the designation also differs from firm to firm, some are called financial controller, some are called financial manager or vice-president for finance or director of finance, etc. In our country, two other officers are usually appointed under the control of the above personnel — Treasurer and Controller.

The functions and duties of the Treasurer and Controller are:

Treasurer	Controller
1. Securing finance (both long and short-term)	1. Financial accounting and control
2. Banking and custody	2. Management accounting and control
3. Cash management	3. Taxation
4. Collection of credit	4. Reporting and interpreting
5. Investment	5. Economic appraisal
6. Contract with investment community	6. Reporting to government

Financial Management in India

In India, financial system and activities of a firm are, to some extent, controlled by government rules and regulations although it has an underdeveloped Capital Market. So, in India, a financial manager, in order to perform his duties effectively and efficiently, must be acquainted with:

(i) Capital structure restrictions;

(ii) Control of credit by commercial banks;

(iii) Restrictions/Control on investment opportunities;

(iv) Fewer instrument of financing;

(v) Uncertainty in the supply of inputs;

(vi) Uncertainty in the supply of outputs;

(vii) Bureaucratic delays and complexities while getting various approvals.

FINANCIAL FORECASTING AND PLANNING

'Forecast' means to form an opinion beforehand, i.e., to make a prediction. Thus Financial Forecasting means a systematic projection of the expected action of finance through financial statements. It is needless to mention that such forecasting needs past records, cash flow and fund flow behaviour, the applications of financial ratios, etc. along with the industrial economic condition. It is a kind of plan which will be formulated at a future date for a specified period.

The merits of financial forecasting are:

(i) It can be used as a control device in order to fix the standard of performances and evaluating the results thereof.

(ii) It helps to explain the requirement of funds for the firm together with the funds of the suppliers.

(iii) It also helps to explain the proper requirements of cash and their optimum utilisation is possible and so surplus/excess cash, if any, invested otherwise.

Financial planning, on the other hand, is nothing but one part of a larger planning process within an organisation. 'A complete planning system begins at the highest level of policy with the firm's basic goals or purpose, usually stated in qualitative, mission-oriented terms. From this it is derived the firm's commercial strategy, defining the product or services it will produce and the markets will serve. Supporting policies are developed in production, marketing, research and development, accounting and finance. The extent to which the system is formulated with detailed planning and budgeting system in each area depends in part on the firm's size and the complexity of its operation'. — **E. Solomon and J. S. Pringle.**

Thus, in a broader sense, financial planning can be viewed as the representation of an overall plan for the firms in terms of finance and, similarly, in a narrower sense, it may refer to the process of determining the financial requirements which is needed in order to support a given set of plans in other areas.

ELEMENTS OF FINANCIAL FORECASTING AND PLANNING

Financial forecasting involves preparation of proforma financial statements and also the preparation of Cash Budget. Therefore, it includes the preparation of:

A. Proforma Income Statement;

B. Proforma Balance Sheet; and

C. Cash Budget.

A. Proforma Income Statement

This statement is a projection of income for a period of time in future which, in other words, is to furnish a fair and reasonable estimate of expected revenue, cost, profits, taxes, dividends and other financial items. It is prepared around the estimate of the expected sales for the forecast period. The sales may be estimated on the basis of market research and economic surveys. On the contrary, production schedule can be formulated and estimates may be made for the cost of production. The most accurate forecast may be made available with the help of a detailed analysis of purchases, productive wages and overhead costs. Sometimes, cost of goods sold are estimated on the basis of past ratios of cost of goods sold to sales.

Next, the estimate is made for administrative and selling expenses. Since both of them are generally budgeted in advance, their estimates are seldom accurate. Further estimates are made for other income and expenses along with interest in order to ascertain the net income before taxes. Income-taxes are to be deducted at the prescribed rate for ascertaining the net estimated income after taxes. At last, dividend payments have to be predetermined at the appropriate level which are also to be deducted from the estimated net income/profit—after tax.

A typical form of Proforma Income Statement is presented (with imaginary figures):

Proforma Income Statement

for the year ending 31st Dec. 2007

		Rs.	Rs.
Revenues			
	Sales		8,00,000
Expenses			
	Cost of Goods Sold :		
	Raw Materials	2,00,000	
	Direct Wages	3,00,000	
	Factory Overheads	50,000	
			5,50,000
	Gross Profit		2,50,000
	Administrative Expenses	40,000	
	Depreciation	20,000	
	Interest	10,000	
	Selling and Distribution Expenses	30,000	
			1,00,000
	Operating Profits/Net Income before Tax		1,50,000
Less:	Taxes 50%		75,000
	Profit after Tax/Net Income		75,000
Add:	Retained Earnings b/d		25,000
			1,00,000
Less:	Dividend		50,000
	Retained Earnings c/d		50,000

Therefore, the Proforma Income Statement helps us to analyse the composition of expected future income statement and Balance Sheet with the help of different Financial Ratios. These ratios along with the raw figures may be compared with the present and past Balance Sheets. The financial manager, with the help of this information, realises the changes in the financial position together with the performances of the firm over the past, present and future.

If estimates are made accurately, the preparation of Proforma Income Statement and Cash Budget help to proceed rapidly. Continuous reversion of the estimates helps the firm to tackle the changed circumstances of the business.

B. Proforma Balance Sheet

This Balance Sheet depends on the information available in the Proforma Income Statement together with different schedules and budgets. Preparation of a Proforma Balance Sheet is based on:

(a) the Net Worth of the company — calculated after adjusting the projected income;
(b) the comparison of the projected assets with the total sources of fund — i.e., if assets exceed the total expected liabilities, the difference will represent additional sources which must be accounted for and, in the opposite case, the excess will indicate the additional cash;
(c) the liabilities which are based on past indications;
(d) the net investment in each component of the assets of the company in order to achieve the planned levels of production.

Interpretation of Proforma Balance Sheet Items

Assets:

(a) *Fixed Assets:* In order to acquire, replace or disposal of Fixed Assets over a number of years, Capital Budget plan is to be drawn up and adjustments have to be made accordingly. Depreciation on assets should also be considered before arriving at the values of Fixed Assets for preparing the projected Balance Sheet. Other assets will remain as they are unless specially mentioned.

(b) *Current Assets:* (i) *Sundry Debtors*

It depends on the number of days' credit allowed to customers which can be ascertained either:

(i) $\dfrac{\text{Credit Sales}}{\text{Average Debtors}}$

or, (ii) $\dfrac{\text{Debtors}}{\text{Credit Sales}} \times 365$

(ii) *Inventories*

The inventory level in relation to production programme which is to be maintained is an important item in this regard. As soon as the level is fixed by the management, the same will be an item of the Proforma Balance Sheet. These are ascertained as:

$$\text{Stock Turnover Ratio} = \frac{\text{Cost of Goods Sold/Sales}}{\text{Average Inventories}}$$

(iii) *Cash*

A minimum amount of cash is to be maintained in hand for different purposes. But where the flexible bank borrowing is available, the cash balance will represent the difference between the assets and the liabilities.

Liabilities:

(a) *Shareholders' Fund/Net Worth:* It represents the amount of Share Capital and Reserves and Surplus (Fixed Assets plus Current Assets minus Current and Long-term Liabilities). But for this purpose, fresh issue of Shares, redemption of Preference Shares, a retained earnings from profit should also be taken into consideration.

(b) *Creditors:* It depends on the number of days the credit is allowed by suppliers. This can be ascertained for the purpose of Proforma Balance Sheet by either:

$$(i) \quad \frac{\text{Credit Purchase}}{\text{Average Creditors}}$$

$$\text{or,} \quad (ii) \quad \frac{\text{Creditors}}{\text{Credit Purchase}} \times 365$$

(c) *Outstanding Liabilities:* These are ascertained on the basis of the pattern of wages payment, tax payment, etc. For this purpose past and future data relating to them are also to be taken into consideration while preparing a Proforma Balance Sheet.

(d) *Provision for Tax and Dividends:* Proper provisions for Taxes and Dividends should also be made for the Proforma Balance Sheet. They also depend on past and future data of the rate of Tax and Dividend, etc.

Once we estimate/ascertain all the components of Proforma Balance Sheet, they are combined and presented in a Balance Sheet. Moreover, all the Balance Sheet items can be estimated by projecting financial ratios for the future.

C. Cash Budget

A Cash Budget method is an available way for preparing a Proforma Statement. Where such budget is not available, Bills (Receivable and Payable), Debtors and Creditors, Accrued Wages and Expenses are based on historical relationship between production and sales.

ASSIGNMENT MATERIALS

THEORETICAL

Short Answer-type Questions

1. Discuss the nature of financial management.
2. Define : (a) Profit maximisation
   (b) Wealth maximisation.
3. What is traditional approach of financial management?
4. What is modern approach of financial management?
5. What are the objectives of financial management?
6. What are the goals of financial management?
7. Discuss the Liquidity-Profitability approach to financial goals.
8. Define :
   (a) Investment Decisions; (b) Financial Decisions; (c) Dividend Decisions.
9. Explain the relationship between Risk and Return.
10. What are the elements of financial forecasting?

Long Answer-type Questions

11. Explain the various elements of financial forecasting.
12. Explain in details the scope and functions of financial management.
13. What are the objectives of financial management?
14. Explain : (a) Profit Maximisation; (b) Wealth maximisation.
15. What are the goals of financial management?
16. What are the elements of financial forecasting?
17. Explain the relationship between Investment Decisions and Dividend Decisions.

CHAPTER 2

CAPITAL BUDGETING

Introduction

It has been pointed out earlier (Chapter 1) that financial management is concerned with the planning and controlling of the financial resources of the firm. That is, in other words, it expresses the procurement of funds along with their efficient use in order to maximise the firm's benefit. Therefore, question of allocation of funds rises before us. We all know that the allocation depends on the commitment of funds to various assets and activities which is also known as *'Investment Decision'*. In short, it is a choice of assets where funds will be invested. It is also known to us that assets have two broad classifications : viz. (i) short-term or current assets, and (ii) long-term or fixed assets.

As such, there will be two types of investment decisions also. The first one is known as current assets investment decision or working capital management (which has been explained in detail in Chapter 3) and the second one is the long-term investment decision which is widely known as capital budgeting or capital expenditure decision. It should be noted that the term 'capital budgeting' is used interchangeably with capital expenditure decision or capital expenditure management, or long-term investment decision etc.

The present chapter is devoted to an in-depth and comprehensive discussion of capital expenditure management decisions which includes the general principles and basic concepts of capital budgeting/capital expenditure budget including various aspects, importance, types, process etc.

Definition and Meaning

Economics is concerned with the allocation of scarce resources between alternative uses in order to the obtain best objectives. Capital expenditure/budgeting, on the other hand, concentrates on these allocations over time; on decisions which involve current outlays in return for expectations of future benefits, i.e., a return for an anticipated flow of future benefits. In other words, it is applied in order to evaluate expenditure decisions which involve current outlays but the benefits are likely to be produced in future, i.e., over a longer period of time. The said benefits may be earned either in the form of reduction in cost or in the form of increased revenues. And that is why it includes addition, alternation, modification, disposition and replacement of fixed assets.

Therefore, the salient features of capital budgeting are:

(i) potentially large anticipated benefits;
(ii) a relatively high degree of risk; and
(iii) a relatively long time period between the initial outlay and the anticipated 'return'.[1]

---

1 Osteryoung, J.— *Capital Budgeting : Long-term Assets Selection,* Columbus, Ohio, Grid, 1974, p. 4.

However, capital budgeting decision seeks to provide a body of analyses giving answers to the following three questions :

(i) What specific investment projects should the firm accept?

(ii) How much of capital expenditure should the firm undertake?

(iii) How should this portfolio of projects be financed?

Obviously, the above three decisions are closely related to each other. The problem is not simply to decide which investments should be financed with a given amount of funds for the amount of borrowings and the volume of shares issued are variables with the firm's control. As such, the two problems must be tackled simultaneously. So, capital budgeting covers all the three questions.

It may be noted that a capital budgeting decision is a two-sided process. The first one is that the analyst must evaluate a proposed project to forecast the likely or expected return from the project. The said return may be calculated with the help of two methods :

(i) Internal Rate of Return, and

(ii) Net Present Value.

The other side of a capital budgeting decision is to determine the required return from a project.[1]

From the discussion made so far, it may be summarised that capital budgeting decision is the firm's decision to invest its funds most efficiently in long-term activities against an anticipated flow of future benefits over a number of years.

Importance of Capital Budgeting

Capital Budgeting decisions have given the primary importance to financial decision-making since they are the most crucial and critical business decisions as they have significant impact on the profitability aspect of the firm. As the capital budgeting/expenditure decision affects the fixed assets only which are the sources of earning revenue, i.e., the profitability of the firm, special attention must be given to their treatment.

Capital budgeting decisions have placed greater emphasis due to:

(a) *Capital budgeting has long-term implications*

The most significant reason for which capital budgeting decisions are taken is that they have long-term implications, i.e. their effects will extend into the future, and will have to be endured for a longer period than the consequences of current operating expenditure.[2] Because, a proper investment decision can yield spectacular returns, whereas a wrong investment decision can endanger the very survival of the firm. That is why it may be stated that the capital budgeting decisions determine the future destiny of the firm. Moreover, it also *changes the risk complexion* of the enterprise. When the average benefits of the firm increase as a result of an investment proposal which may cause frequent fluctuations in its earnings that will become a risky situation.

(b) *Capital budgeting requires large amount of funds*

Capital investment decisions require large amount of funds which the majority of the firms cannot provide since they have scarce capital resources. As a result, the investment decisions must be thoughtful, wise and correct. Because, a wrong/incorrect decision would result in losses and the same prevents the firm from earning profits from other investments as well due to scarcity of resources.

---

1 Hampton, J. J., *Financial Decision Making—Concepts, Problems and Cases*—Prentice-Hall of India Ltd., New Delhi, 1983, p. 350.

2 Quirin, G. David, *The Capital Expenditure Decision*—Richard D. Irwin, Inc., Illinois, 1977, p. 2.

(c) *Capital budgeting is not reversible*

Once the capital budgeting decisions are taken, they are not easily reversible. The reason is that there may neither be any market for such second-hand capital goods nor is there any possibility of conversion of such capital assets into other usable assets, i.e., the only remedy is to dispose-off the same sustaining a heavy loss to the firm.

(d) *They are actually the most difficult decisions*

Capital investment decisions are, no doubt, the most significant since they are very difficult to make. It is because of the fact that their assessment depends on the future uncertain events and activities of the firm. Similarly, it is practically a difficult task to estimate the accurate future benefits and costs in terms of money as there are economical, political and technological forces which affect the said benefits and costs.

Kinds of Capital Budgeting Decisions

Since capital budgeting includes the process of generating, evaluating, selecting and following-up on capital expenditure alternatives, allocation of financial resources should be made by the firm to its new investment projects in the most efficient manner.

A firm may adopt three types of capital budgeting decisions:

(i) *Mutually Exclusive Projects*

It means if a firm accepts one project, it may rule out the necessity for others i.e., the alternatives are mutually exclusive and only one is to be chosen. For example, if there is a need to transport supplies from a loading dock to the warehouse, the firm may adopt two proposals, viz., (a) fork lifts to pick up the goods and move them, or, (b) a conveyor belt may be connected between the dock and the warehouse. If one proposal is accepted it will eliminate the other.

(ii) *Accept-Reject Decisions or Acceptance Rule*

The proposals which yield a higher rate of return in comparison with a certain rate of return or cost of capital are accepted and, naturally, the others are rejected. For example, if the minimum acceptable return from a project is, say, 10%, after tax, and an investment proposal which shows a return of 12% may be accepted and another project which gives a return of 8% only may be rejected. In other words, using Net Present Value Method Criterion, an investment opportunity will be accepted if NPV > 0, or, the same will be rejected if NPV < 0. That is, all independent projects are accepted under this criterion. It is to be noted that independent projects are those which do not compete with one another, i.e., the acceptance of one precludes the acceptance of the other. At the same time, those projects which will satisfy the minimum investment criterion should be taken into consideration.

(iii) *Capital Rationing Decision*

Capital rationing is normally applied to situations where the supply of funds to the firm is limited in some way. As such, the term encompasses many different situations ranging from that where the borrowing and lending rates faced by the firm differ, to that where the funds available for investments are strictly limited. In other words, it occurs when a firm has more acceptable proposals than it can finance. At this point, the firm ranks the projects from highest to lowest priority and, as such, a cut-off point is considered.

Naturally, those proposals which are above the cut-off point will be accepted and those which are below the cut-off point are rejected, i.e., ranking is necessary to choose the best alternatives.

Illustration 2.1

Minimum acceptable rate of return (after-tax) is 10%.

Investments to be made Rs. 12,00,000.

Four alternative investment opportunities are there—A, B, C, and D :

A—8%, B—11%, C—13%, and D—12%.

Solution

Since alternative A shows a return which is less than the standard return laid down by the firm, it should be totally rejected. Among the remaining three, ranking is done on the basis of profitability which is shown as :

Proposal	Expected Rate of Return	Rank
C	13%	1
D	12%	2
B	11%	3

Proposal C is the most profitable project and, hence, it may be accepted.

Planning Period for the Decisions

The future time period for which the capital expenditure budget is prepared is determined in the decision programme.

The time period should be determined in the context of the following major considerations[1] :

(a) **Type of Industry** : For example, a pharmaceutical firm is to make plans for a shorter period since its equipments are short-lived; whereas a mining firm has to make a plan for a longer period.

(b) **General Economic Conditions** : At the time of prosperity, the planning time gets longer whereas, at the time of crisis, the same is shorter.

(c) **Degree of Faith the Executives have in Long-range Planning** : If they believe in it, there will be longer time period and, in the opposite case, it will be reversed.

However, there are some authors who prefer to classify the time horizon in Investment Decisions into two following groups:

(i) Long period : which may include a period from 5 to 20 years.

(ii) Short period : which is considered for inclusion in the next annual budget period.

Generally, investments in long-term assets require a plan for several years ahead for a number of reasons[2] :

(a) Long-term investment expresses a framework for the future development of the firm which must be visualised in advance;

(b) A long gestation period lies between the time of planning the project and the actual operation of the plant;

(c) Arrangement must be made for the required fund from different sources in advance which needs careful planning.

---

1 National Association of Accountants, Financial Analysis, Techniques for Equipment Replacement Decision, 1956, p. 8.

2 *Ibid.*

Short-term budgets, on the other hand, may be influenced by the financial resources. Of course, in case of an emergency need, the funds are to be procured/arranged from different sources so that the project may be taken up.

Kinds of Investment

Generally, two types of investments are made :

(i) the replacement of existing assets; and

(ii) the purchase of completely new assets for expansion.

It may also be mentioned that there may be other types of investment as well which are considered as a matter of policy. They are :

(a) *Welfare Projects*	:	Investment is made in order to promote the morale of the employees and/or staff.
(b) *Educational and Training Projects*	:	Investment is also to be made for educational and training projects for improving the efficiency of the employees, although it is very difficult to evaluate the results from it.
(c) *Research and Development Projects*	:	The research projects may be successful but it is very difficult to measure the benefits which are derived in future.
(d) *Projects to be Complied with Statutory Requirements*	:	According to the Factories Act, 1948, every employer should make proper provisions for accidents, fire-fighting devices, rest-room etc., which are obligatory on the part of the employer.
(e) *Prestige-value Projects*	:	In order to create a favourable image among the public, this type of investment is to be made, e.g., to construct a guesthouse.

Capital Expenditure Budget

This budget indicates the estimated outlay on fixed assets during the budget period. It may be long-term or short-term. But, it is usually prepared for a long period, say, 5 to 10 years. If it is prepared for a longer period, it will have to be broken down into short periods. Since there is a high degree of inflexibility, recovery of cost will take a long period of time because of the investment in fixed assets. That is why this budget should be coordinated with other budgets, viz., Cash Budget, Factory Overhead Budget, Balance Sheet Budget etc. This budget is normally prepared by the Accountant. However, separate budgets may be prepared for each individual item of fixed assets. It is prepared for:

(i) the purchase of additional assets, either required for increased production or for starting a new type of product;

(ii) the replacement of existing assets;

(iii) the installation of improved types of assets due to technological development.

The advantages of such budget are :

(i) It reveals the estimated capital expenditure;

(ii) It helps to control the capital expenditure; and

(iii) It facilitates the preparation of budget summaries.

Process of Capital Budgeting

The process of capital budgeting is not so simple rather, the same is a complex one as the selection of the proposals for investments depends on a number of factors—considering the available funds and benefits to be desired therefrom. Thus, one should carefully study the process of capital budgeting before selecting and implementing the same. However, we are highlighting here the process of capital budgeting as:

(a) *To identify the proposals*

At first, one should identify the proposals for the capital expenditure to be incurred. The proposals which are received from various angles should carefully be analysed by the experts and the same should be referred to the top management (e.g. Capital Expenditure Planning Committee) for final decision and approval. While identifying the proposals the various available opportunities should also be taken into consideration.

(b) *To analyse the proposals*

After receiving the proposals from various sources/departments, the top management or executive committee will analyse and screen the proposals from various angles to see that these proposals do not make any conflict with the corporate strategies and which will not go against the policy of the firm.

(c) *To evaluate/scrutinise the proposals*

After analysing and screening the proposals the same must be evaluated and scrutinised carefully considering the profitability of the proposal with the help of various capital budgeting techniques (e.g., IRR, NPV, Pay Back Method etc.). The proposal which will give the highest return will be selected.

(d) *To select proposals on priority basis*

The next step is to select the proposals on priority basis as all the proposals do not present the same results, the proposal which will give the highest return/profitability and less risky, the same should be selected first. In other words, the unprofitable proposals should be rejected and profitable project should be selected. But, in case of more than one proposal, ranking method should be applied as it may not always be possible for a firm to take all the proposals at a time due to scarcity of funds.

(e) *To approve the final proposals*

The proposal which will meet the criteria for selection is finally approved. The selected proposal is included with the Capital Expenditure Budget which will highlight the estimated amount of expenditures.

(f) *To implement the proposal at last*

It must be remembered that it does not necessarily mean that, if a proposal is included in the budget, the same will be implemented at once. There may be some additional formalities. Projects will be implemented only when the same has finally been approved by the Capital Expenditure Committee or top executive committee—fulfilling all the necessary formalities.

(g) *To review the performance*

The process of capital expenditure will be completed after evaluating the same with the comparison of expenditure between the budgeted figure and the actual amount and also to compare the expected return from the investments and the actual return of the same. The variance, if any, should carefully be studied and analysed for making necessary corrections to be made at a subsequent date to avoid repetition.

Taxation Effect Due to Depreciation on Cash Flows

Net cash flows are calculated after tax but before charging depreciation. Depreciation is calculated due to normal wear and tear of the assets on its original cost and the same is charged against profit as per accounting procedures. Depreciation is an expenses which does not require any cash payment i.e., it is a non-cash item. As depreciation is charged against profit, the profit of the firm is reduced to that extent and, consequently, it affects tax as the taxable incomes depend on the profit. Thus, it has a direct bearing on income-tax. In short, depreciation allows a firm to retain cash as a result of tax shield and increases the amount of cash flows of a firm.

As such, it requires explanation about the relevant provisions for depreciation and other allowances/charges which are contained in the Income Tax Act, 1961. They are:

Normal Depreciation [Section 32]

(i) Such depreciation is allowed at prescribed rates on actual or written-down value (WDV) of building machinery, plant or furniture u/s 32, (ii) and on actual cost of ship. Where the actual cost of any machine or plant does not exceed Rs. 5,000, the actual cost thereof shall be allowed as a deduction. No normal depreciation will be allowed on asset sold or discarded or destroyed after using a part of the year. Normal depreciation will be allowed on an asset in full on the basis of Diminishing Balance Method at prescribed rates even if it worked only for the last day of the year. But it should be remembered that, whatever method is followed, the amount of depreciation is to be added back to the profit after tax in order to ascertain the net cash flow for a specific period.

Terminal Depreciation [Section 41(2)]

According to Section 31(2), in the case of any building, machinery, plant or furniture which is sold, discarded, demolished or destroyed, the amount by which the money payable in respect of such asset together with the amount of scrap value, if any, fall short of the written-down value thereof, as reduced by initial depreciation, if any, shall be deductible by way of terminal depreciation or allowance provided such deficiency is actually written-off in the books of the assessee. Terminal depreciation cannot be claimed if the asset is not used for the purpose of business or profession.†

Balancing Charge

It applies, where any depreciated asset, such as building, machinery, plant or furniture, which are used for the purpose of business or profession, is sold, discarded, demolished or destroyed and the money paid or payable in respect of such asset together with the scrap value, if any, exceeds the written-down value, so much of the excess as does not exceed the difference between actual cost and the written-down value, i.e., the total depreci-ation (including initial depreciation, if any) allowed uptodate, shall be chargeable to income-tax by way of Balancing Charge, and the remaining surplus, if any, as taxable as capital gains. It may be mentioned here that where the insurance company replaces the asset lost or discharge the liability in respect of claim for asset lost under conditions of the policy, question of Balancing Charge will not arise in that case as there is no payment of money. ***The rules laid down by explanation 2 to Section 41(2) in respect of terminal depreciation are applicable in case of Balancing Charge.***

Practically, the amount of balancing charge will bring down the amount of net cash flow or the amount realised on sale by the amount of tax payable on such Balancing Charge. In order to encourage the development of industries, development rebate was also introduced by the Finance Act, 1955 (Section 33) in respect of certain machinery or plant, apart from the provisions already discussed above.

---

† Note : Terminal depreciation cannot be claimed in respect of an asset bought and sold in the same year. The net result will be treated as short-term capital gain or capital loss. Where an asset is discarded in one year and sold in another year, the assessee must claim this allowance in the year in which the asset is discarded without waiting for the sale of assets.

Working Capital

Requirement of additional working capital in the various components of additional current assets, viz. Inventory (raw materials, work-in-progress and finished goods), as well as to pay off wages and other bills, is needed in addition to the investment in fixed asset on a project. Therefore, while determining total amount of investment, requirement of additional working capital should also be taken into consideration. Similarly, when the project comes to an end, the amount of working capital (in full or in part) so realised, should also be considered along with the scrap value of fixed assets, if any. Sometimes a run down of working capital investment may so happen before the project actually comes to an end. In that case, the release of funds must be considered in the respective years during the life of the project carefully. The following illustration will, however, make the principle clear:

Illustration 2.2

Initial Outlay	Rs. 20,000
Life	5 years
Profit before tax and depreciation	Rs. 8,000
Requirement of additional working capital	Rs. 4,000
Rate of tax	40%
Rate of depreciation on diminishing balance method	10%
Initial depreciation	20%
Scrap value of the investment will fetch	Rs. 3,122
Cost of capital is	10% p.a.

Advise management as to the profitability of the project, assuming that the working capital can be recovered in full at the end of the project life.

Solution

Workings :

Statement of Depreciation and Terminal Allowance

	Rs.			Rs.
Cost of the Project	20,000	Written-Down Value at the end of 4th year		20,000
Year 1. Dep. @ 10%	2,000	Cost of Project		
	18,000	*Less :* Total Dep.		
Year 2. Dep. @ 10%	1,800	Initial @ 20% on Rs. 20,000	4,000	
	16,200	Normal Dep.		
Year 3. Dep. @ 10%	1,620	(2,000 + 1,800 + 1,620 + 1,458)	6,878	10,878
	14,580			9,122
Year 4. Dep. @ 10%	1,458	*Less :* Scrap Value		3,122
	13,122	Terminal Allowance		6,000

Profitability Statement

Years	Profit before Tax and Depreciation	Depreciation and Allowance	Taxable Profit	Tax @ 40% on (c)	Profit after Tax	Profit after Tax but before Depreciation	P.V. Factor at 10%	Present Value
	(a)	(b)	(c) = (a) – (b)	(d)	(e) = (c) – (d)	(f) = (b) + (e)	(g)	(h) = (f) × (g)
	Rs.	Rs.	Rs.	Rs.	Rs.	Rs,	Rs.	Rs.
1	8,000	6,000	2,000	800	1,200	7,200	0.909	6,555
2	8,000	1,800	6,200	2,480	3,720	5,520	0.827	4,565
3	8,000	1,620	6,380	2,552	3,828	5,448	0.751	4,091
4	8,000	1,458	6,542	2,617	3,925	5,383	0.683	3,676
5	8,000	6,000	2,000	800	1,200	7,200	0.621	4,471
								23,348
	Scrap Value					3,122	0.621	1,939
	Working Capital (recovery)					4,000	0.621	2,484
								27,771

Thus the total amount of discounted cash flow, Rs. 27,771, exceeds the total cost of investment (both fixed capital and working capital, i.e., Rs. 20,000 and Rs. 4,000) = Rs. 24,000. Hence, the project should be accepted. If, however, the Profitability Index (PI) is considered, the same is found to be 1.16 $\left(\text{i.e.} \dfrac{\text{Rs. } 27{,}771}{\text{Rs. } 24{,}000}\right)$.

Components of Cash Flow

The components of cash flows are of the following three types:

(a) Cash Inflow;

(b) Terminal Cash Inflow; and

(c) Initial Cash Outlay.

(a) Cash Inflow

Needless to say that annual cash inflows generate after meeting up the cash outflows for which capital expenditures are incurred. It must be remembered that such cash inflows are considered always at after tax basis. Now, these cash flows are of two types viz.,

(i) ***even or equal amount of cash flows, and***

(ii) ***uneven or unequal amout of cash flows.***

In other words, in case of former, even or equal amount of cash flows will generate throughout the effective life of the assets but, in case of latter, unequal or uneven amount of cash flows will generate throughout the effective life of the assets annually.

Now, these cash flows may generate from two elements viz.,

(i) From Revenue Generating Projects;

(ii) From Earnings as a result of reduction of cost.

(i) From Revenue Generating Projects

It means net cash inflows i.e., excess of cash inflows over cash outflows from operating activities which may be computed in the following manner:

Ascertainment of Cash Inflows

		Rs.
	Sales	* * *
Less :	Variable Cost	* * *
	Contribution	* * *
Less :	Fixed Cost (excluding non-cash items like dep.)	* * *
	Earning before depreciation	* * *
Less :	Depreciation	* * *
	Earnings before Tax	* * *
Less :	Tax	* * *
	Earnings after tax	* * *
Add-back :	Non-cash items (like Dep.)	* * *
	Net Cash Inflows after tax	* * *

(ii) **From earnings as a result of reduction in cost**

This happens when revenues of a firm are increased as a result of reduction in cost (i.e., variable cost in the form of material, labour and variable overhead) in operating activities due to replacement of an improved machine. It is ascertained in the following manner:

Ascertainment of Cash Inflows
(applicable in case of Replacement of Assets)

		Rs.
	Earnings/Saving in variable cost	* * *
Less:	Incremental or Additional Depreciation (New Machine – Old Machine)	* * *
	Earnings before Tax	* * *
Less :	Tax	* * *
	Earnings after Tax	* * *
Add-back :	Incremental or Additional Dep.	* * *
	Cash Inflows	* * *

(b) **Terminal Cash Inflow**

Terminal cash inflows are nothing but the scrap value or salvage value of machine which is realised after the expiry of effective life of the assets. This should be added to cash inflows in the last year.

It is computed as under:

Ascertainment of Terminal Cash Inflows

		Rs.
	Additional/Requirement of working capital	* * *
Add :	Scrap value/Salvage value of the asset	* * *
	Terminal Cash Flow	* * *

(c) **Initial Cash Outlay**

Initial cash outlay means the cost of acquisition of assets along with the cost of installation. It reveals the amount of all cash outlays/outflows, at zero time period. It is needless to mention here that, at the time of computing initial cash outflow one important point should also be taken into consideration i.e., the amount of (Net) working capital. (it has been explained here in a subsequent paragraph). Initial cash outlay is ascertained as:

Ascertainment of Initial Cash Outlay	Rs.
Initial cost of the assets	* * *
Add : Cost of Installation	* * *
Add : Requirement of Working Capital	* * *
Initial Cash Outlay	* * *

Illustration 2.3

P Ltd. presented the following particulars from which you are asked to ascertain (i) Annual Cash Inflow, (ii) Terminal Cash Inflow in the 5th year and (iii) Initial Cash Outlay:

	Rs.
Cost Price of the Machine	10,00,000
Installation expenses	2,00,000
Scrap Value of the machine	1,00,000
Estimated life of the machine 5 years	
Profit (before depreciation and tax)	2,50,000
Rate of IncomeTax @ 40%	

Solution

(i) **Computation of Annual Cash Inflow**

	Rs.
Profit (before Dep. and Tax)	2,50,000
Less : Depreciation $\left(\frac{\text{Rs.}10,00,000 + \text{Rs.}2,00,000 - \text{Rs.}1,00,000}{5}\right)$	2,20,000
Profit (before Tax)	30,000
Less : Tax @ 40%	12,000
Profit (after Tax)	18,000
Add back : Depreciation	2,20,000
Annual Cash Inflow after Tax	2,38,000

(ii) **Computation of Terminal cash Inflow in the 5th year**

It is nothing but the scrap value of the machine, i.e. Rs. 1,00,000

(iii) **Computation of Initial Cash Outlay**

	Rs.
Cost price of the machine	10,00,000
Add : Installation expense	2,00,000
	12,00,000

Illustration 2.4

P Ltd. describe to replace it old machine. Two improved machines are available in the market. They are : Model LX, Model VX. You are asked to ascertain the annual cash flows from the particulars given below:

	Model LX	Model VX
	Rs.	Rs.
Initial Investment	10,000	15,000
Effective life	5	6

Contd.

	Rs.	Rs.
Additional Cost of maintenance	1,000	1,500
Additional Cost of other expenses	1,500	1,800
Estimated Saving in Cost	800	1,200
Estimated Savings in Wages	4,000	6,000

Solution

Ascertainment of Annual Cash Flows

		Model LX		Model VX
Estimated Savings:		Rs.		Rs.
—In Cost		800		1,200
—In Wages		4,000		6,000
Less: Additional Cost:		4,800		7,200
—for Maintenance	1,000		1,500	
—for other Expenses	1,500		1,800	
		2,500		3,300
Annual Cash Inflow		2,300		3,900

Ascertainment of Incremental Cash Flow

Illustration 2.5

Philips India Ltd. desires to replace an old machine by a new one. The cost price of the new machine is Rs. 2,50,000. The old machine was purchased for Rs. 1,20,000 before two years and depreciation was charged on it under Straight Line method over its useful life of 10 years which can be sold for Rs. 80,000. Installation expense of the new machine would be Rs. 50,000 and effective life would be 5 years and scrap value of the new machine would be Rs. 25,000 at the end of its effective life of 5 years. Additional Working Capital would be required for Rs. 50,000. Rate of tax assumed to be @ 50%.

Expected earning before depreciation and tax for the next 5 years with old and new machines are:

Year	Old Machine Rs.	New Machine Rs.
1	5,00,000	5,50,000
2	4,00,000	4,50,000
3	4,50,000	5,50,000
4	6,50,000	7,00,000
5	7,00,000	8,00,000

Ascertain incremental or additional Cash Inflow and incremental Cash Outflow.

Solution

(*a*) **Ascertainment of Incremental Cash Inflow**

	Years 1 Rs.	2 Rs.	3 Rs.	4 Rs.	5 Rs.
Earnings (before Dep. and Tax)					
New Machine	5,50,000	4,50,000	5,50,000	7,00,000	8,00,000
Less : Old Machine	5,00,000	4,00,000	4,50,000	6,50,000	7,00,000
Incremental Earnings (before Dep. & Tax)	50,000	50,000	1,00,000	50,000	1,00,000

Contd.

			Rs.	Rs.	Rs.	Rs.	Rs.
Less : Incremental Depreciation :							
	New Machine $\frac{[\text{Rs.}2,50,000 + \text{Rs.}50,000 - \text{Rs.}25,000]}{5}$	Rs. 55,000					
Less:	Old Machine (Rs. $\frac{1,20,000}{10}$)	Rs. 12,000					
			43,000	43,000	43,000	43,000	43,000
	Incremental Profit		7,000	7,000	57,000	7,000	57,000
Less:	Tax @ 50%		3,500	3,500	28,500	3,500	28,500
	Incremental earning after tax		3,500	3,500	28,500	3,500	28,500
Add-back :	Incremental Depreciation		43,000	43,000	43,000	43,000	43,000
	Incremental Cash Inflow after tax		46,500	46,500	71,500	46,500	71,500

(*b*) **Ascertainment of Incremental Cash Outflow**

		Rs.	Rs.
	Cost Price of New Machine		2,50,000
Add :	Installation Expense	50,000	
	Requisite of working capital	50,000	
			1,00,000
			3,50,000
Less :	Scrap value of old machine		80,000
			2,70,000

Incremental Operating Cash Flow and Effect of Taxes

Needless to say that the cash flows are measured in terms of incremental analysis in capital budgeting decisions. In other words, we should consider only those cash flows which differ from accepting a particular project. The incremental or relevant cash flows relate to those cash flows that are related to the particular proposal/project. For this incremental cash flows the following points are relevant:

(a) **Cost of Overhead**

The costs of overhead are not directly associated with the product, rather, they are distributed on the basis of some logical reasoning. The costs of overhead that are incurred for the existing product are not related to the new project. However, if existing cost of overhead is distributed to the new project, the same cannot be taken as the cost of the new project. But it must be remembered that if the costs of overheads are increased as a result of implementing the new project, in that case only, the incremental cost of overhead should be taken into consideration. For example, as a result of implementing the new project, office and administration expenses are increased (e.g., for recruiting additional staff).

(b) **Co-existence with the Proposals**

It appears when the incremental cash flows co-exist with the proposal. For example, X Ltd. is evaluating Project I, & Project II. The Project I, however, needs repair amounting to Rs. 50,000 at the end of the 5th year, but Project II needs an annual services charge of Rs. 12,500 p.a. In the case of former Rs. 50,000 is relevated to Project I whereas Rs. 12,500 p.a. is related to Project II as an annual cash outflow. Naturally if Project I is implemented service contract for repairs is not required whereas if Project II is undertaken, the repair cost amounting to Rs. 50,000 is not required.

(c) **Product Cannibalization**

It appears when a new product is introduced in the market for which the sales of the existing product of the same firm is reduced. In other words, it relates to the sales appeared by a product at the cost of some other product. It may be stated that this is nothing but a negative aspect of incremental effect for which the existing product looses its cash flow stream and the same may be treated as costs of the new product.

It is, no doubt, difficult to understand the principles of incremental cash flows in the analysis of capital budgeting. At the time of evaluating a proposal, the financial manager must consider whether a particular cash flow is incremental or not. It is needless to say that for the decision in capital budgeting, only incremental cash flow is to be taken into consideration. In short, the cash inflows/outflows which is directly or indirectly recognised should be taken into consideration.

Effect of Taxation

We know that cash flows which are associated with capital budgeting are the after-tax cash flows. It has already been stated above that the so-called after-tax cash flows which arise from a project are referred to incremental cash flows. As such, it is needless to say that this incremental cash flows will not come if the project is not implemented. The annual cash flow will, however, increase the amount of taxable profit. As it is taxable profit, tax liability will accrue and increase in tax liability must be equal to the cash inflow multiplied by the rate of tax. In other words, net cash inflow must be equal to cash inflow (before the appropriation of tax) which is multiplied by (I–tax rate). That is why, in capital budgeting, decisions/ analysis must be expressed in after-tax term which reveals that all items that would affect taxes, non- cash items (e.g. Depreciation) etc. should be taken into consideration.

Accounting Profit vs Cash Flows

Accounting Profit

The success or failure of a capital expenditure proposal is usually tested on the basis of accounting profit. Although the accounting profit is a sound technique for increasing the efficiency of firm, the same may not be prove to be a really sound one to estimate the benefits to be derived from a proposal. The same is ignored for the following reasons:

(a) **Accounting Policy**

It is needless to say that the accounting profit is largely affected by our accounting policies. The so-called accounting policies differ from firm to firm, industry to industry as well e.g., Methods of depreciation, Inventory valuation etc. As such, accounting profit practically does not convey the real picture.

(b) **Non-Cash Items**

We know that accounting profit is greatly affected by non-cash items (e.g. depreciation, write-off losses etc.). As such, the balance of profit does not show the true measure of benefits.

(c) **Accrual Concept**

Accounting profit is computed on accrual basis.

(d) **Measurement of Accounting Profit**

The accounting profit exhibits the profit for a specified year in terms of money value of that year also. But we know that the expenses and benefits may continue over a period of time. Thus, the benefit that we receive in terms of accounting profit cannot effectively be compared over a period of time due to inflation or interest factor. At the same time, it may also be stated that if there are two mutually exclusive projects having different useful lives, the same cannot be compared on the basis of accounting profit.

Cash Flows

In capital budgeting technique, expense or cost and profit or benefits of a particular project is measured on the basis of cash flow. Hence, the cash flow means the amount of cash generated by way of return from project. Accurate measurement, in this manner, is not possible but on the basis of accounting data an approximation is possible. It may be mentioned in this respect that the benefits are termed as cash inflows whereas costs are termed as cash outflows.

From the above discussion it may be suggested that there is a wide difference between accounting profit and cash flow. Accounting profit is ascertained on the basis of established accounting principles. There are certain cost which are deducted from computing accounting profit and do not require any cash payment, e.g. depreciation writing-off losses etc. On the other hand, in case of a capital expenditure which requires cash payment can not deduct from revenue for ascertaining accounting profit as the same is not treated as cost for the purpose. So, the difference which appears between accounting profit and cash flow is due to the non-cash items and presence of capital expenditure.

The following illustration will help us to understand the difference between accounting profit and cash flow:

Income Statement

Accounting Profit		Rs.	*Cash Flow*	Rs.
Sales		4,00,000	Sales	4,00,000
Less : Cost of goods sold	2,60,000		*Less :* Cash of goods sold	2,60,000
Depreciation	40,000			1,40,000
		3,00,000	*Less :* Tax	50,000
Profit before Tax		1,00,000	Profit after Tax	90,000
Less : Tax @ 50%		50,000		
Profit after Tax		50,000		

Thus, the difference between accounting profit and cash flow is Rs. 40,000 (Rs. 90,000 – Rs. 50,000) which happened due to depreciation.

Thus, *Cash flow = Profit after Tax + Non-Cash Items*

On the contrary, if there is any capital expenditure, accounting profit will not be affected but there will be an outflow of cash.

Thus, *Cash flow = Profit after Tax + Non-Cash Items – Capital Expenditure*

Illustration 2.6

P Ltd. presented the following particulars:

Cost Price of Plant and Machinery	Rs.	1,00,000
Installations Expenses	Rs.	10,000
Scrap Value	Rs.	10,000
Useful Life		10 years
Net Profit (before Depreciation & Tax)		Rs. 40,000
Income-Tax Rate @ 50%		

You are asked to ascertain the amount of cash flow.

Solution

$$\text{Depreciation} = \frac{\text{Cost Price + Installation Expenses} - \text{Scrap Value}}{\text{Useful life}}$$

$$= \frac{1{,}00{,}000 + \text{Rs. } 10{,}000 - \text{Rs. } 10{,}000}{10}$$

$$= \text{Rs. } 10{,}000$$

	Ascertainment of Cash Flow	Rs.
	Net Profit (before depreciation and tax)	40,000
Less :	Depreciation	10,000
	Profit before Tax	30,000
Less :	Tax @ 50%	15,000
	Profit after Tax	15,000
Add :	Depreciation (Add-back)	10,000
	∴ Cash Flow p.a.	25,000

Note :

From the above illustration it becomes clear that the initial outlay (cash flow) was Rs. 1,10,000 (Cost price + Installation Expenses) and its annual inflow was Rs. 25,000 for 10 years = Rs. 2,50,000 + Scrap Value amounting to Rs. 10,000 = Total cash flow were Rs. 2,60,000 at the end of 10th year.

Accounting Profit vs Cash Inflow

To sum up, the difference between the two concepts are noted below:

Points of Difference	Accounting Profit	Cash Flow
1. **Time Value of Money:**	Accounting profit does not recognise the time value of money.	Cash flow recognised the concept of time value of money.
2. **Policy:**	Ascertainment of Accounting profit differs from one accounting policy to another accounting policy or methods.	Ascertainment of cash flow technique does not make any difference.
3. **Non-Cash Expenses:**	It recognises non-cash expenses while calculating net profit.	It does not recognise non-cash items as it does not involve any outlay.
4. **Capital Expenditure:**	It does not recognise any capital expenditure while calculating profit.	It recognises capital expenditure as there is a cash outlay.
5. **Applicability:**	This method is applicable in traditional financial statement.	This method is applicable in modern financial statement.

CAPITAL BUDGETING — METHODS OF APPRAISAL

(Investment Criteria)

It has been highlighted in the present chapter that capital expenditure decisions require a current investment the benefits of which are received in future/after one year, i.e., it involves a long-term commitment. This decision actually is a very significant one since the future development and the competitive power of the firm depends on it which, in other words, has a direct impact on the future earning and growth of the firm. For this purpose, a sound appraisal method should be adopted in order to measure the economic worth of each investment project.

But the investment criteria which are to be used must possess the following features :

(a) It must provide a ranking of projects according to desirability;

(b) It must provide a way of distinguishing between unacceptable and acceptable projects;

(c) It must be a criterion which may be applicable to any investment project;

(d) It must choose the right one among alternative projects, if any; and

(e) It should recognise that early benefits are considered than the latter ones.

However, there are a number of investment criteria which are widely used. The methods of appraising capital expenditure decisions can be classified into two broad categories, viz. (A) ***Traditional or Unsophisticated,*** and (B) ***Time-Adjusted or Sophisticated.*** The first category includes (i) Accounting or Average Rate of Return Method, and (ii) Pay Back Period Method. The latter categories are popularly known as Discounted Cash Flow Techniques or Criteria which includes : (i) Net Present Value Method; (ii) Internal Rate of Return Method; (iii) Profitability Index or Benefit-Cost-Ratio; and (iv) Net Terminal Value Method. All the above criteria may be represented as:

CAPITAL BUDGETING TECHNIQUE/INVESTMENT CRITERIA

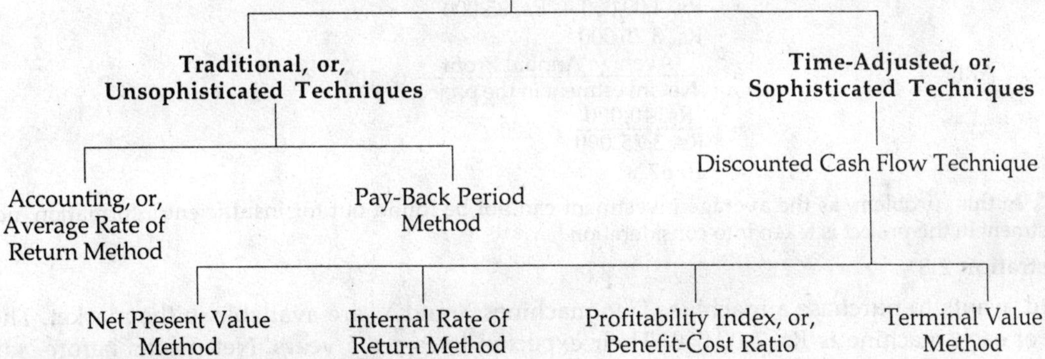

Traditional or Unsophisticated Techniques

Project Evaluation and Selection

ACCOUNTING ON AVERAGE RATE OF RETURN METHOD

The Average Rate of Return (ARR) method is used in order to measure the profitability of the investment proposals. This is practically an accounting method and it incorporates the expected return which may be obtained from the project. Under this method, average annual profit (after tax) is expressed as a percentage of investment. There are a number of alternatives for calculating ARR. Although there is no unanimity regarding its definition, the most common usage of the ARR which is found out ***by dividing the average annual profit or, income after tax by the average investment.*** In this connection, it may be noted that the average investment must be equal to the original investment plus salvage value, if any, divided by two. Moreover, the ARR can also be found out by dividing the total book value of investment (after depreciation) by the life of the project. Therefore, this is nothing but an average rate which is expressed as a percentage and can be determined with the help of :

$$\text{ARR} = \frac{\text{Average Annual Profit after Tax}^{\dagger}}{\text{Average Investment}} \times 100$$

Where, Average Annual Profit after Tax

$$= \frac{\text{Total Profit (after depreciation and Tax) for the entire life of the project}}{\text{Total Profit lives in years}}$$

$$\text{Average Investment} = \left(\frac{\text{Initial Cost + Installation Expenses} - \text{Scrap Value}}{2}\right) + \text{Salvage Value + Additional Working Capital}$$

Under this method, the investment which will give the highest rate of return will be accepted. Sometimes, a firm may fix a standard rate or cut-off rate of return and, as such, investments which will not produce this rate will be excluded.

Illustration 2.7

A project requires an investment amounting to Rs. 4,00,000 which has a scrap value of Rs. 25,000 after 5 years. Annual cash flow (after depreciations and taxes) Rs. 20,000, Rs. 30,000; Rs. 40,000; Rs. 50,000 and Rs. 60,000, respectively, during the five years.

Calculate ARR.

Solution

$$\text{Average Annual Profit} = \frac{\text{Rs. } 20{,}000 + \text{Rs. } 30{,}000 + \text{Rs. } 40{,}000 + \text{Rs. } 50{,}000 + \text{Rs. } 60{,}000}{5}$$

$$= \text{Rs. } 40{,}000$$

$$\text{Net Investment in the project} = \text{Initial Investment} - \text{Scrap Value}$$

$$= \text{Rs. } 4{,}00{,}000 - \text{Rs. } 25{,}000$$

$$= \text{Rs. } 3{,}75{,}000$$

$$\therefore \quad \text{ARR} = \frac{\text{Average Annual Profit}}{\text{Net Investment in the project}} \times 100$$

$$= \frac{\text{Rs. } 40{,}000}{\text{Rs. } 3{,}75{,}000} \times 100$$

$$= 10.67\%$$

* In this problem, as the average investment can not be found out for insufficient information, net investment in the project is taken into consideration.

Illustration 2.8

A Ltd. wants to purchase a machine. Two machines X and Y, are available in the market. The cost of each machine is Rs. 1,00,000. Their expected lives are 5 years. Net profits before tax during the expected life of the machines are:

Years	Machines X Rs.	Machines Y Rs.
I	10,000	7,000
II	15,000	13,000
III	13,000	15,000
IV	20,000	25,000
V	17,000	20,000
Total	75,000	80,000

Note : The average rate of tax is 50%.

† *Average Annual Profit after tax is determined by adding the after-tax expected profits for each year of the life of the project and dividing the same by the number of years.*

From the above information, ascertain which one is more profitable.

Solution

Comparative Profitability Statement

	Machine X	Machine Y
Cost Price	Rs. 1,00,000	Rs. 1,00,000
Estimated Life (years)	5	5
Total Net Profit	Rs. 75,000	Rs. 80,000
Average Annual Profit (before tax)	Rs. 15,000 (75,000 ÷ 5)	Rs. 16,000 (80,000 ÷ 5)
Average Annual Profit (after tax)	Rs. 7,500	Rs. 8,000
Average Investment	Rs. 50,000 $\frac{(1,00,000)}{2}$	Rs. 50,000 $\frac{(1,00,000)}{2}$
ARR $\left(\frac{\text{Average Annual Profit after tax}}{\text{Average Investment}}\right)$	15%	16%

Hence, Machine Y is more profitable since it gives the higher return.

Illustration 2.9

Determine the average rate of return from data of two machines A and B :

	Machine A	Machine B
Cost	Rs. 56,125	Rs. 56,125
Annual estimated income after depreciation and income tax		
	Rs.	Rs.
1st year	3,375	11,375
2nd year	5,375	9,375
3rd year	7,375	7,375
4th year	9,375	5,375
5th year	11,375	3,375
	36,875	36,875
Estimated life in years	5	5
Estimated Salvage Value	Rs. 3,000	Rs. 3,000
Average Income-tax rate	55%	55%

Depreciation has been charged on Straight Line basis.

[Delhi, M.Com.]

Solution

$$\text{Average Investment} = \left(\frac{\text{Initial cost} - \text{Instllation Exp.} - \text{Scrap Value}}{2}\right) + \text{Scrap Value} + \text{Additions Working Capital}$$

$$\textbf{Machine A} = \left(\frac{\text{Rs.}56{,}125 - \text{Rs.}3{,}000}{2}\right) + \text{Rs.}3{,}000 + \text{Rs.}4{,}000$$

$$= \text{Rs. } 26{,}563 + \text{Rs. } 7{,}000 = \text{Rs. } 33{,}563$$

$$\textbf{Machine B} = \left(\frac{\text{Rs.}56{,}125 - \text{Rs.}3{,}000}{2}\right) + \text{Rs.}3{,}000 + \text{Rs.}5{,}000$$

$$= \text{Rs. } 26{,}563 + \text{Rs. } 8{,}000 = \text{Rs. } 34{,}563$$

Computation of ARR

(i) Machine A $= \dfrac{\text{Rs. } 7{,}375}{\text{Rs. } 33{,}563} \times 100 = 21.97\%$ (Approx)

(i) Machine B $= \dfrac{\text{Rs. } 7{,}375}{\text{Rs. } 34{,}563} \times 100 = 21.34\%$ (Approx)

Advantages of ARR

(i) It is very simple and easy to calculate.

(ii) It supplies the readily available accounting information.

Disadvantages of ARR

(i) The significant demerits of the method is that it does not recognise the timings of cash inflows and outflows since it is based on accounting income instead of cash flows.

(ii) Moreover, competing projects generally have a varying length of life. In order to find out the average earnings, additional years' earnings of a project which has a longer life are compared with the earnings of a project which has a comparatively short life. This is unfair. As such, that system will be taken into consideration which will satisfy both the factors, viz. timing of income and varying length of life.

Additional Rate of Return

It is the average additional profit expressed as percentage of investment. Under the circumstances, if it is found that the return is satisfactory in comparison with what is available, the replacement may be made. Before discussing the principles, it becomes necessary to explain the related terms in that respect, viz. (a) Investment, and (b) Average additional profit.

(a) *Investment* : (i) The original cost of investment

(ii) Average investment.

We know that the original cost of an asset gradually diminishes from year to year over its effective life since the capital cost is recovered by way of depreciation charges. As such, if the Straight Line Method of depreciation is followed, the average investment will be half of the depreciable part plus whole of the non-depreciable (remaining) part of the cost of the investment. It should be mentioned that the depreciation portion is divided by two, since the uncovered investment declines from the original cost of the asset to zero.

Illustration 2.10

Initial cost of asset (investment)	Rs. 20,000
Estimated life	5 years
Scrap value	Rs. 5,000
Depreciation : Under Straight Line Method	

Find out the Average Investment.

Solution

Average Investment $= \dfrac{\text{Rs. } 20{,}000 - \text{Rs. } 5{,}000}{2} + 5{,}000$

$= \text{Rs. } 12{,}500$

(b) *Average Additional Profit*

It is simply the difference between the profit which arises out of the sale proceeds of output produced by the new machine and those which are produced by the machine which is proposed to be replaced. It may be taken (for the purpose of calculating return on investment) as the profit either before-tax or after-tax.

Illustration 2.11

ABC Co. has a machine which has been in operation for 6 years. The management is considering a proposal to purchase an improved model of a similar machine which gives an increased output.

Give your opinion as a Cost Accountant in regard to the proposal from the following data:

	Old Machine	New Machine
(1) Purchase price of machine (Rs.)	60,000	1,20,000
(2) Expenditure p.a. (Rs.) on account of :		
(i) Power consumption	7,000	8,000
(ii) Consumable stores	4,000	5,000
(iii) Repairs and maintenance	5,000	4,000
(3) Labour cost per running hour (Rs.)	2	2.25
(4) Units of output per hour	40	60
(5) Machine running hours p.a.	2,000	2,000
(6) Material cost per unit (Paise)	40	40
(7) Selling price of output per unit (Re.)	1	1
(8) Estimated life (years)	10	10

[I.C.W.A. Final]

Solution

Compare profitability statements of both the machines:

Comparative Profitability Statement

	Old Machine			New Machine		
	Amount	Amount	Amount	Amount	Amount	Amount
	Rs.	Rs.	Rs.	Rs.	Rs.	Rs.
Purchase Price	60,000			1,20,000		
Estimated life (years)	10			10		
Units produced p.a.	80,000			1,20,000		
Sales (80,000 @ Re. 1)			80,000			1,20,000
Less : *Cost of Production*						
Materials (80,000 × .40) (1,20,000 × .40)	32,000			48,000		
Wages (2,000 × Rs. 2) (2,000 × Rs. 2.25)	4,000			4,500		
Prime Cost		36,000			52,500	
Variable Overheads						
Power Consumptions		7,000			8,000	
Consumable Stores		4,000			5,000	
Repairs & Maintenance		5,000			4,000	
Depreciation :		6,000			12,000	
Total Cost			58,000			81,500
Profit before tax			22,000			38,500
Tax (say, @ 50%)			11,000			19,250
Profit (after tax)			11,000			19,250

Average Additional Profit per annum

(i) Before tax (Rs. 38,500 – Rs. 22,000) = Rs. 16,500

(ii) After tax (Rs. 19,250 – Rs. 11,000) = 8,250

$$\therefore \text{ Profitability } \left(\frac{\textit{Average Additional Profit}}{\textit{Average Additional Investment}} \times 100\right)$$

$$\therefore \text{ Before tax } = \frac{\text{Rs. } 16{,}500}{\text{Rs. } 60{,}000} \times 100 = 27.5\%$$

$$\text{After tax } = \frac{\text{Rs. } 8{,}250}{\text{Rs. } 60{,}000} \times 100 = 13.75\%$$

Hence, if the proposed project is undertaken, there will be an additional return on capital invested @ 27.5% before tax and 13.75% after tax, which may be considered as satisfactory. Therefore, the new project may be taken into consideration.

Acceptance Rule

From the foregoing discussion it becomes clear that the financial decision-maker can decide whether a particular project will be undertaken or not with the help of the ARR, i.e., whether a project will be accepted or rejected. The accept-reject criterion, on the basis of the ARR, is followed by the management.

In other words, those projects will be accepted whose ARR is higher than the minimum established rate/standard rate and those projects will be rejected whose ARR is less than the said minimum established rate/standard rate. Ranking method may also be used here. That project will be given rank *one* which has highest ARR and, on the contrary, *lowest* rank will be assigned if the ARR is lowest.

Evaluation of ARR

Before evaluating ARR, its merits and drawbacks should carefully be considered. Its advantages are :

(i) The most significant attribute of ARR is that it is very simple to understand and easy to calculate.

(ii) It can be easily computed on the basis of accounting data which is furnished by the financial statements.

(iii) It recognises the entire stream of income while calculating the accounting rate.

Even ARR is not free from snags:

(i) The principal shortcoming of ARR is that it recognises only the accounting income instead of cash flows.

(ii) It does not recognise the time value of money.

(iii) It does not take into consideration the length of lives of the projects.

(iv) It does not consider the fact that the profits may be reinvested.

PAY BACK PERIOD

The Pay Back Period Method is the second unsophisticated method of capital budgeting and is widely employed in order to overcome some of the shortcomings of ARR method. It recognises that recovery of the original investment is an important element while appraising capital expenditure decisions. It may be stated that it is simply an application of 'break-even' concept to investment. Practically, this method gives the answer about the question. 'How many years will it take for the cash benefits to pay the original cost of an investment?'

It is defined as the number of years required to cover the original cash outlay which are invested in a project. In other words, Pay Back Period is the period required for the savings in costs or net cash flow after tax but before depreciation, to recover the cost of investment.[1] Thus, Pay Back Period is computed when

(i) Cash flow accrues at even rate, i.e., where there is equal cash inflow:

$$\textit{Pay Back Period (P.B.P.)} = \frac{\textit{Cost of the Investment Cash Outlay}}{\textit{Annual Net Cash Inflow}}$$

(ii) Where there is unequal cash inflow :

— the P.B.P. can be found out by adding up the cash inflows until the total is equal to the initial cash investment.

Illustration 2.12

Where there is equal cash inflow

A project requires an investment of Rs. 1,00,000 with a life of 10 years which yields an expected annual net cash inflow of Rs. 25,000. Compute the pay back period.

Solution

$$\text{Pay Back Period (P.B.P.)} = \frac{\textit{Cost of the Investment (projects)}}{\textit{Annual Net Cash Inflow}}$$

$$= \frac{\text{Rs. } 1,00,000}{\text{Rs. } 25,000} = 4 \text{ years}$$

Illustration 2.13

X Ltd. presented the following particulars:

Project Cost Rs. 10,00,000

Annual Profit (after depreciation @ 10% p.a. but before tax @ 50%) Rs. 2,00,000

Calculate Pay Back Period.

Solution

Computation of Pay Back Period

		Rs.
	Profit (before tax but after depreciation)	2,00,000
Less :	Tax @ 50%	1,00,000
	Profit after Tax	1,00,000
Add-back :	Depreciation @ 10% on Rs. 10,00,000	1,00,000
	Annual Net Cash Flow (or Profit before depreciation but after tax)	2,00,000

$$\therefore \text{ Pay Back Period} = \frac{\text{Cost of Project/Investment}}{\text{Annual Net Cash Flow}}$$

$$= \frac{\text{Rs. } 10,00,000}{\text{Rs. } 2,00,000} = 5 \text{ years}$$

Illustration 2.14

X Ltd. presented the following particulars:

	Two Machines			
		X		Y
Cost of Machine	Rs.	1,00,000	Rs.	2,00,000
Scrap Value	Rs.	10,000	Rs.	20,000

1 *Banerjee, B.*, Financial Policy and Management Accounting, *op. cit., p.* 624.

Estimated Life	4 years	5 years
Additional Cost of Maintenance	Rs. 7,000	Rs. 10,000
Additional Cost of Operation	Rs. 8,000	Rs. 15,000
Estimated Savings in Overhead	Rs. 40,000	Rs. 60,000

Calculate Pay Back Period and comment which machine should be recommended.

Solution

Profitability Statement

		Machine X		Machine Y
		Rs.		Rs.
Estimated Savings p.a.				
Estimated Savings in Overhead		40,000		60,000
Add : Scrap Value		10,000		20,000
		50,000		80,000
Less : **Additional Cost**				
Cost of Operation	8,000		15,000	
Cost of Maintenance	7,000		10,000	
		15,000		25,000
Annual Cash Flow/Net Savings		35,000		55,000

$$\therefore \text{Pay Back Period} = \frac{\text{Cost of Investment}}{\text{Annual Cash Flow}} = \frac{\text{Rs. } 1,00,000}{35,000} = \frac{\text{Rs. } 2,00,000}{\text{Rs. } 55,000}$$

$$= 2.86 \text{ years} \qquad = 3.64 \text{ years}$$

Comment

Since Pay Back Period is less in case of Machine X, Machine X, should be recommended.

Ascertainment of Pay Back Period for mutually exclusive projects where there is even cash flows.

Illustration 2.15

ITC Ltd. has decided to purchase a machine to augment the company's installed capacity to meet the growing demand for its products. There are three machines under consideration of the management. The relevant details including estimated yearly expenditure and sales are given:

	Machine 1	Machine 2	Machine 3
	Rs.	Rs.	Rs.
Initial investment required	3,00,000	3,00,000	3,00,000
Estimated annual sales	5,00,000	4,00,000	4,50,000
Cost of Production (estimated) :			
Direct Materials	40,000	50,000	48,000
Direct Labour	50,000	30,000	36,000
Factory Overheads	60,000	50,000	58,000
Administration Costs	20,000	10,000	15,000
Selling and Distribution Costs	10,000	10,000	10,000

All sales are on cash. Corporate Income Tax rate is 40%.

The economic life of Machine 1 is 2 years, while it is 3 years for the other two. The scrap values are Rs. 40,000, Rs. 25,000 and Rs. 30,000, respectively.

You are required to find out the most profitable investment based on 'Pay Back Method'.

[I.C.W.A. Inter]

Solution

Statement Showing the Computation of Pay Back Period

	Machine No. 1	2	3
	Rs.	Rs.	Rs.
Annual Cash Inflows			
Estimated Annual Sales	5,00,000	4,00,000	4,50,000
Estimated Costs:			
—Direct Materials	40,000	50,000	48,000
—Direct Labour	50,000	30,000	36,000
—Factory Overhead	60,000	50,000	58,000
—Depreciation $\left(\frac{\text{Cost Price} - \text{Scrap Value}}{\text{Estimated life}}\right)$	1,30,000	91,667	90,000
—Administration Cost	20,000	10,000	15,000
—Selling and Distribution Costs	10,000	10,000	10,000
Total Cost...........	3,10,000	2,41,667	2,57,000
Profit/Earnings before Tax (EBT)	1,90,000	1,58,333	1,93,000
Less : Tax @ 40%	76,000	63,333	77,200
Profit after Tax (PAT)	1,14,000	95,000	1,15,800
Add-back : Depreciation	1,30,000	91,667	90,000
Annual Cash Inflow after Tax	2,44,000	1,86,667	2,05,800
Initial Investment	3,00,000	3,00,000	3,00,000
$\therefore$ Pay Back Period (Years) = $\frac{\text{Initial Investment}}{\text{Annual Cash Inflow}}$	1.23	1.61	1.46
Rank	1st	3rd	2nd

Since Machine 1 has the lowest pay back period, hence it should be treated as most profitable investment.

Where there is unequal cash inflow

Illustration 2.16

Calculate the pay back period for a project which requires a cash outlay of Rs. 40,000 but the same generates a cash inflow of Rs. 16,000; Rs. 12,000; Rs. 10,000 and Rs. 6,000.

Solution

If we add the cash inflows for the first three years, we find that Rs. 38,000 are recovered against the total cash outlay of Rs. 40,000, leaving an unrecovered part of Rs. 2,000. But, in the fourth year, generation of cash inflow is Rs. 6,000 and over Rs. 2,000 of the original outlay remains to be recovered. If cash inflows occur at an even rate during the year, the time required to cover Rs. 2,000 will be $\left(\frac{\text{Rs. } 2{,}000}{\text{Rs. } 6{,}000} \times 12\right)$ 4 months. Thus, the Pay Back Period is 3 years plus 4 months.

Alternative Approach

Year	Cash Flows	Cumulative Cash Flows
	Rs.	Rs.
1	16,000	16,000
2	12,000	28,000
3	10,000	38,000
4	6,000	44,000

In 3rd year Cumulative Cash Flows are Rs. 38,000 and in 4th year Rs. 44,000; i.e., pay back period lies in between them. Thus, the Pay Back Period will be $= 3 \text{ years} + \frac{\text{Rs. } 2{,}000}{\text{Rs. } 6{,}000} \times 12$

$$= 3 \text{ years} + 4 \text{ months}$$

$$= 3 \text{ years } 4 \text{ months.}$$

Under the Pay Back Period Method, the time period which is necessary in order to recover its capital cost is calculated and that project will be treated as best which will take the shortest pay back period. This principle is based on the understanding that the original outlay must be returned if the enterprise continues its operation. It should be remembered that if the estimated productive period does not exceed the estimated pay back period, a part of the invested capital may be lost and, hence, such project is rejected. This method is particularly applicable where (i) the cost of the project is comparatively small and which is completed in a short period; (ii) the project is productive immediately after the investment is made.

Advantages

1. It is simple to operate and easy to understand. Since it is very easy the same is used in many advanced countries, viz., U.K., U.S.A.
2. It shows how soon the cost of purchasing an asset will be recovered. In other words, it considers the liquidity aspect of working on the ground that a project with short pay-off period is better than those with long pay-off periods.
3. Short-term approach reduces the loss through obsolescence, particularly when there is any rapid technological development.
4. It considers risks as well which may arise due to :
   (i) Political instability;
   (ii) Nature of the product; and
   (iii) Introduction of a new product.
5. It acts as a yardstick in comparing the profitability of two projects.
6. In some cases, Pay Back Period is closely related to ARR and, as such, it enjoys the benefit of ARR. This is particularly applicable where the projects have substantially longer lives than their pay back periods and annual savings on cash inflows are comparatively uniform.[1]

Disadvantages

1. It recognises only the recovery of purchase costs, not profits earned during the working life of the asset.
2. It gives much stress on converting capital into cash, which is not important in case of those assets which have longer working life.
3. It does not recognise the time value of money.
4. It does not take into consideration that profits from different projects may accrue at an uneven rate.
5. It ignores the basic fact that actual profitability depends on the number of years it will continue to operate after the pay back period. Thus, Profitability = Net Cash Flow, or Saving × (Expected life of the project – Pay Back Period).

[1] *Return on Capital as a Guide of Managerial Decisions* — N.A.A. Research Report, 35, 1959, Ch. 9.

Overcoming the Limitations of Pay Back Period

The limitations or disadvantages of Pay Back Period which have been explained above, can be overcome by three improved methods = viz.

(a) Pay Back Profitability;

(b) Pay Back Reciprocal; and

(c) Discount Pay Back Period.

(a) **Pay Back Profitability**

This is a modified version of Pay Back Period Method. It recognises the fact that the total cash flow remains after recovering the cost of investment as the ordinary Pay Back Period Method totally ignores the cash flows that are earned after the said period for which profitability can not be ascertained. Therefore, project will be selected on the basis of profitability after pay-off period or, post pay back period.

Profitability is calculated as:

Profitability = Net Cash Flow or Savings/Earning × (Expected life of the project – Pay Back Period)

However, the following illustration will make the above principle clear :

Illustration 2.17

There are two alternative machines. You are asked to compute the profitability of investment on the basis of pay back profitability :

	Machine X	**Machine Y**
Purchase Price	Rs. 25,000	Rs. 42,000
Estimated life (years)	8	10
Net earnings p.a. (after tax but before depreciation)	Rs. 5,000	Rs. 6,000

Solution

Profitability Statement

	Machine X	**Machine Y**
Cost of Investment	Rs. 25,000	Rs. 42,000
Estimated life	8	10
Net earnings p.a. (after tax but before depreciation)	Rs. 5,000	Rs. 6,000
Pay Back Period	5 years $\left(\frac{25,000}{5,000}\right)$	7 years $\left(\frac{42,000}{6,000}\right)$
Profitability (Net Savings × Expected Life – Pay Back Period)	Rs. 15,000	Rs. 18,000

It is evident from the above statement that, while calculating profitability, Machine Y is, no doubt, a profitable investment. But if the pay back period, which has been discussed earlier, is considered, Machine X appears to be more profitable since its pay back period is shorter, i.e., 5 years, in comparison with Machine Y which has a payback period of 7 years. As the machine Y contributes Rs. 3,000 more (Rs. 18,000 – Rs. 15,000) after recovering its capital cost, hence, it is more profitable to invest in Machine Y than in Machine X.

(b) **Pay Back Reciprocal**

It has already been explained that pay back period expresses the profitability in terms of year and it does not reveal any return as a measure of investment. And, this pay back reciprocal is utilised in order to rectify the said situation. It is useful where the cash flow/earning is relatively consistent and the life of the asset is at least double the pay back period. It may also be expressed as a percentage. If the pay back period is same as the life of the asset, the reciprocal would be one. As such, it is useful for long-term projects and it is also used as a guide to ascertain the discount factor in discounted cash flow calculations (which has been discussed in the next part of the present chapter).

The Pay Back Reciprocal is computed as :

$$\text{Pay Back Reciprocal} = \frac{\textit{Annual Earnings}}{\textit{Cost of Investment}} \times 100$$

$$\text{Or, Pay Back Reciprocal} = \frac{1}{\textit{Pay Back Period}} \times 100$$

Considering the previous illustration, the pay back reciprocal is computed as :

(1) **Pay Back Reciprocal**

$$\text{for Machine X} = \frac{\text{Rs. } 5{,}000}{\text{Rs. } 25{,}000} \times 100 = 20\%$$

$$\text{for Machine Y} = \frac{\text{Rs. } 6{,}000}{\text{Rs. } 42{,}000} \times 100 = 14.29\%$$

Or, (2) **Pay Back Reciprocal**

$$\text{for Machine X} = \frac{1}{\text{Pay Back Period}} = \frac{1}{5} \text{ or, } 0.20$$

$$\text{for Machine Y} = \text{do} = \frac{1}{7} \text{ or, } 0.143$$

Acceptance Rule

The Pay Back Period may also be used as an accept-or-reject criterion along with a method of ranking projects for an investment proposal. In other words, if Pay Back Period is less than the maximum Pay Back Period which is set up by the management, it would be accepted; on the contrary, it would be rejected. Similarly, as a ranking method, the project which has the shortest Pay Back Period will be assigned to the highest rank, and the lowest rank is assigned to the highest Pay Back Period. Naturally, the project with the shorter Pay Back Period will be selected between the two.

Illustration 2.18

Following are the details of three projects A, B and C :

	A	B	C
Cost (Rs.)	50,000	70,000	70,000
Life (years)	10	12	14
Estimated Surplus (Rs.)	5,000	10,000	7,000
Annual Profit (Less Tax) (Rs.)	5,000	6,000	5,500

Select the best one using :

(a) Pay Back Period;

(b) Surplus life over pay back period; and

(c) Surplus Cash flow, as decision-criteria.

[A.C.S. Final]

Solution

(a) **Pay Back Period**

		Projects A	B	C
	Annual Profit (less tax)	5,000	6,000	5,500
Add :	Depreciation $\left(\frac{50,000-5,000}{10}\right)$ and so on	4,500	5,000	4,500
	Annual Net Cash Inflow	9,500	11,000	10,000
		50,000	70,000	70,000
	Pay Back Period = $\frac{\text{Cost of Investment}}{\text{Annual Net Cash Inflow}}$ =	9,500	11,000	10,000
		= 5.26 yars	6.36 years	7 years
	Rank	1	2	3

The best is Project A since it secures the highest rank i.e., shortest Pay Back Period.

		A	B	C
(b)	**Surplus life over pay back period (years)**	4.74	5.64	7
		(10 – 5.26)	(12 – 6.36)	(14 – 7)
	Rank	3	2	1

∴ The best is project C.

(c) **Surplus Cash Flows**

		A	B	C
	Total Cash Flow	95,000	1,32,000	1,40,000
		(9,500 × 10)	(11,000 × 12)	(10,000 × 14)
Less :	Cost of Investment	50,000	70,000	70,000
		45,000	62,000	70,000
Add :	Scrap Value	5,000	10,000	7,000
	Surplus Cash Flow	50,000	72,000	77,000
	Rank	3	2	1

∴ Best one is Project C.

Illustration 2.19

X Ltd. is considering the purchase of a new machine which will carry out some operations at present performed by labour. Two alternative models — A and B — are available for the purpose.

From the information, prepare a profitability statement for submission to management :

	Machine A	Machine B
Estimated life (years)	5	6
Cost of Machine (Rs.)	80,000	1,50,000
Estimated additional Cost (Rs.) :		
Maintenance (p.m.)	500	750
Indirect Material (p.a.)	2,000	3,000
Supervision (per quarter)	3,000	4,500
Estimated saving in scrap (p.a.) (Rs.)	8,000	12,000
Estimated savings in direct wages (p.a.) :		
Employees not required	10	15
Wages per employee (Rs.)	7,200	7,200

Depreciation is calculated using Straight Line Method. Taxation may be taken at 50% of profit (net savings).

[C.U. M.Com.]

Solution

Profitability Statement

		Machine A Rs.		Machine B Rs.
Estimated Annual/Cash Inflow:				
In scrap		8,000		12,000
In Direct Wages				
(7,200 × 10)		72,000		1,08,000
(7,200 × 15)		—		—
		80,000		1,20,000
Less : Additional Costs:				
Maintenance	6,000		9,000	
Indirect Material	2,000		3,000	
Supervision	12,000		18,000	
Depreciation	16,000			
$\left(\frac{\text{Rs. } 80,000}{5}\right)$	—			
$\left(\frac{\text{Rs. } 1,50,000}{6}\right)$			25,000	
		36,000		55,000
Net Annual Cash Inflow		44,000		65,000
Less: Tax @ 50%		22,000		32,500
Net Annual Cash Inflow		22,000		32,500
Add back: Depreciation		16,000		25,000
Net Annual Cash Inflow after tax but before depreciation		38,000		57,500
Pay Back Period $\left(\frac{\text{Cost of Investment}}{\text{Annual Net Cash Inflows}}\right)$		$\frac{\text{Rs. } 80,000}{\text{Rs. } 38,000}$ = 2.11 years		$\frac{\text{Rs. } 1,50,000}{\text{Rs. } 57,000}$ = 2.61 years
Rank		1		2
Pay Back Profitability				
[Net Cash Flow × (Expected life of the project – Pay back Period)]		Rs. 38,000 × (5 – 2.11) = 1,09,820		Rs. 57,500 × (6 – 2.61) = Rs. 1,94,925
Rank		2		1

(c) Discounted Pay Back Period

This method actually recognises the time value of money by combining pay back with Net Present Value (Discounted Cash Flow). Generally, the NPV are added in a cumulative manner from the beginning of the project till the same becomes a positive one. And the turning point is known as the Discounted Pay Back Period of a project which is defined as the time when the capital so invested has been coming back with the interest cost of funds related to it.

Illustration 2.20

Calculate the pay back period from the following particulars using (i) the traditional method, and (ii) the discounted pay back method.

Cost of the Project	Rs. 40,000
Life	5 years
Cost of Capital	10%
Year (N.C.F. — Rs.)	

Years	**Rs.**	**P.V. of Re. 1 at 10%**
1	7,000	0.909
2	7,000	0.826
3	7,000	0.751
4	7,000	0.683
5	7,000	0.621
6	8,000	0.564
7	10,000	0.513
8	15,000	0.467
9	10,000	0.424
10	4,000	0.386

Solution

(i) **Pay Back Period** (under traditional method)—

Years	**N.C.F.**	**Cumulative N.C.F.**
	Rs.	Rs.
1	7,000	7,000
2	7,000	14,000
3	7,000	21,000
4	7,000	28,000
5	7,000	35,000
→ Time required to cover the original investment of Rs. 40,000 ←		
6	8,000	43,000
7	10,000	53,000
8	15,000	68,000
9	10,000	78,000
10	4,000	82,000

Therefore, the pay back period is $5 + \left(\frac{5,000}{8,000}\right)$ years or $5 + .62 = 5.62$ years

(ii) **Discounted Pay Back Period**

Years	**N.C.F.**	**Discount Factor**	**P.V. of Cash Inflow**	**Cumulative P.V. of Cash Inflow**
	Rs.	Rs.	Rs.	Rs.
1	7,000	0.909	6,363	6,363
2	7,000	0.826	5,782	12,145

Contd.

	Rs.	Rs.	Rs.	Rs.
3	7,000	0.751	5,267	17,412
4	7,000	0.683	4,781	22,193
5	7,000	0.621	4,347	26,540
6	8,000	0.564	4,512	31,052
7	10,000	0.513	5,130	36,182
8	15,000	0.467	7,005	43,187

Thus, the discounted pay back period lies between 7th and 8th year from the beginning of the project. Thus, the payback period lies in between two years, i.e. Rs. 36,182 and Rs. 43,187.

$$\text{So, the Pay Back Period} = 7 \text{ years} + \frac{\text{Rs. } 3{,}818 \text{ (Rs. } 40{,}000 - \text{Rs. } 36{,}182)}{\text{Rs. } 7{,}005}$$

$$= 7 \text{ years} + .55 \text{ years} = 7.55 \text{ years}$$

Illustration 2.21

Compute : (a) Traditional Pay Back Period; (b) Discounted Pay Back Period from the following particulars:

	Rs.
Initial Outlay	1,60,000
Estimated Life	5 years
Profit after Tax:	
End of Year 1	12,000
End of Year 2	28,000
End of Year 3	48,000
End of Year 4	32,000
End of Year 5	Nil

Depreciations has been calculated under Straight Line Method. The cost of capital may be taken at 20% and P.V. of Re. 1 at 20% is given:

Year	1	2	3	4	5
P.V. Factor	0.83	0.69	0.58	0.48	0.40

Solution

(a) Computation of Traditional Pay Back Period

Computation of Cash Flows

Year	Profit (after Tax) PAT	Depreciations $= \frac{\text{Rs. } 1{,}60{,}000}{5}$	Cash Flow (PAT + Dep.)	Cumulative Cash Flow
	Rs.	Rs.	Rs.	Rs.
1	12,000	32,000	44,000	44,000
2	28,000	32,000	60,000	1,04,000
3	48,000	32,000	80,000	1,84,000
4	32,000	32,000	64,000	2,48,000
5	—	32,000	32,000	2,80,000

Traditional Pay Back Period

In 2nd year cumulative cash flow is Rs. 1,04,000 and in 3rd year Rs. 1,84,000. i.e, pay back period lies in between 2nd year and 3rd year as the initial investment is Rs. 1,60,000 lie in between them. Thus, the Pay Back period will be $= 2 \text{ years} + \frac{\text{Rs. } 56{,}000}{\text{Rs. } 80{,}000}$

$= 2 \text{ years} + 0.7 \text{ years}$

$= 2.7 \text{ years}$

(b) Computation of Discounted Pay Back Period

Computations of Present Value of Cash Flow

Year	Cash Flows	Discount Factor at 20%	Present Value of Cash Inflow	Cumulative P.V. to Cash Inflow
	Rs.	Rs.	Rs.	Rs.
1	44,000	0.83	36,520	36,520
2	60,000	0.69	41,400	77,920
3	80,000	0.58	46,400	1,24,320
4	64,000	0.48	30,720	1,55,040
5	32,000	0.40	12,800	1,67,840

It becomes quite clear that Rs. 1,60,000 lie in between the cumulative P.V. of Cash Inflows of 4th year and 5th year i.e., Rs. 1,55,040 and Rs. 1,67,840. Thus the pay back period lies in between the said two years.

So, Pay Back Period $= 4 \text{ years} + \frac{4{,}960 \text{ (i.e. Rs. } 1{,}60{,}000 - \text{Rs. } 1{,}55{,}040)}{\text{Rs. } 12{,}800}$

$= 4 \text{ years} + 0.4 \text{ years}$

$= 4.4 \text{ years}$

Advantages

The significant merit of this method is that it incorporates the usual requirement to make some return on an investment. Secondly, the method of calculation helps in the selection of project risk. For example, in case of foregoing illustration, if nationalisation or takeover in any form is expected within 7.55 years, the project itself proves a highly risky one which will never becoming a profitable one.

TIME ADJUSTED/SOPHISTICATED,/OR DISCOUNTED CASH FLOW TECHNIQUES

The earlier two methods, viz.—ARR method and Pay Back Period method, discussed so far for the purpose of appraising the investment proposals, do not consider the basic fact, i.e. timing of cash flows. Because the Accounting or Average Rate of Return method recognises cash proceeds to the original or average cost of investment whereas Pay Back Period method considers all each flows received before the Pay Back Period. Thus, both methods fail to recognise the basic fact that the sum of money received in future is less valuable than it is today, i.e., the time value of money. There are three reasons for this: (a) Reinvestment opportunities, (b) Uncertainty, and (c) Inflation.

In order to overcome the shortcomings of ARR and Pay Back Period described earlier, Discounted Cash Flow (DCF) methods are recognised since they actually provide a more realistic basis. The distinguishing feature of the DCF is that it recognises the time value of money. Moreover the commendable characteristic of these techniques is that they consider all benefits and costs occurred during the life of the project. Attempt has been made in the present chapter to discuss the DCF evaluation method. At first, the DCF technique, viz., Net Presented Value (NPV), has been discussed. This is followed by the Internal Rate of Return (IRR) method. There are two variations of the NPV method : (a) the Profitability Index or Benefit Cost Ratio, and (b) Terminal Value method, which are subsequently discussed.

Before discussing the NPV method, we are going to explain the two concepts. viz., Compounding (Interest), and Discounting (Present Value). It is known to all that interest rate is a rate at which one will be compensated for exchanging value now than it is later. The original amount/price is known as 'principal'. Here, the word 'compound' refers to add interest to principal at periodic intervals for the purpose of establishing a new basis for subsequent interest computations. In other words, under this method, the interest of the first year is computed on the amount of principal, but the interest of the next (2nd) year will be computed on the principal plus the interest of the first year, and so on. This process continues till the end of the final year.

The following illustrations will make the principle clear:

Illustration 2.22

Suppose, the principal is Rs. 100. Rate of interest (compound) is 10% for five years. The compound interest will be calculated as under (calculation to be made to the nearest rupee). Prove it.

Years	Principal (P)	Interest (I)	Total Amount = (P + I)
1	100	10	110
2	110	11	121
3	121	12	133
4	133	13	146
5	146	15	161

Solution

By using the following compound interest formula the same (i.e., Rs. 161) can be computed as :

$A = P(1 + I)^n$ where, A = Principal + Interest

or, $A = 100(1 + 10)^5$ P = Principal

or, $A = 161$ i = Rate of interest

(with the help of log table) n = No. of years

Thus, each years (P + I) can be computed as :

$$A_1 = P_1(1 + i)^1 = \text{Rs. } 110$$
$$A_2 = P_2(1 + i)^2 = \text{Rs. } 121$$
$$A_3 = P_3(1 + i)^3 = \text{Rs. } 133$$
$$A_4 = P_4(1 + i)^4 = \text{Rs. } 146$$
$$A_5 = P_5(1 + i)^5 = \text{Rs. } 161$$

It should be remembered that when the period *'n'* is small, application of logarithms is not necessary. The same can be found out by simple arithmetical calculation. However, the same result can also be ascertained with the help of discounting. ***Discounting*** is just the opposite of ***compounding***. In this case, we are to compute the *present value* which is to be received of a future period. From the above example, if we want to find out the present values at the beginning of the respective years 1, 2, 3, 4 and 5 Rs.110, Rs. 121, Rs. 133, Rs. 146 and Rs. 161, respectively, at 10% p.a., the result will be Rs. 100 in each case with the help of the said formula:

$$A = P(1+i)^n$$

$$\text{or,} \quad P = \left(\frac{A}{(1+i)^n}\right)$$

$$\text{or,} \quad P_1 = \left(\frac{A_1}{(1+i)^1}\right) = \left(\frac{\text{Rs. } 110}{(1+10)^1}\right) = \text{Rs. } 100$$

$$P_2 = \left(\frac{A_2}{(1+i)^2}\right) = \left(\frac{\text{Rs. } 121}{(1+10)^2}\right) = \text{Rs. } 100$$

and so on.

NET PRESENT VALUE (NPV) METHOD

The Net Present Value (NPV) method is the time value of money approach to evaluate the return from an investment proposal. Under this method, we discount a project using the required return as the discount factor. In other words, a stipulated compound interest rate is given and, by the use of this percentage, net cash flows are discounted to present values. The present value of the cost of the project is subtracted from the sum of present values of various cash inflows. The surplus is the net present value. If the NPV is positive, the proposal's forecast return exceeds the required return the proposal is acceptable. But if the NPV is negative, the forecast return is less than the required return, the proposal is not acceptable. Thus, the decision rule for a project under NPV is to ***accept the project if the NPV is positive*** and ***reject if the NPV is negative.***

So, (1) NPV > zero = Accept

(2) NPV < zero = Reject.

Conversion of Net Cash Flow (NCF) into Present Value (PV)

1. *By the use of Logarithms*

In case of uneven Net Cash Flow (NCF), the present value of a future sum may be computed with the help of the following formula :

$$V = \frac{A}{(1+i)^n}$$

where,

V = Present Value

A = Annual Net Cash Flow (after tax but before depreciation)

i = Rate of Interest

n = Number of years

Where there are a number of years, annual net cash flows, the above formula may be continued to :

$$V = \frac{A_1}{(1+i)^1} + \frac{A_2}{(1+i)^2} + \frac{A_3}{(1+i)^3} + \ldots\ldots\ldots + \frac{A_n}{(1+i)^n}$$

However, if there is uneven net cash flows, the PV of various NCF must be computed separately which will result in tedious calculation.

But, if there is an even rate, the following annuity formula may be used :

$$V = \frac{A}{i}\left\{1-(1+i)^{-n}\right\}$$

Note : PV of 1st, 2nd and nth cash flows are :

$$\left(\frac{A}{(1+i)}\right) + \left(\frac{A}{(1+i)^2}\right) + \left(\frac{A}{(1+i)^3}\right) + \left(\frac{A}{(1+i)^n}\right)$$

V represents the sum of the present values of all NCF.

$$V = \frac{A}{(1+i)} + \frac{A}{(1+i)^2} + \frac{A}{(1+i)^3} + \ldots\ldots\ldots + \frac{A}{(1+i)^n}$$

$$\text{or, } \frac{A}{i}\left\{1-\frac{A}{(1+i)^n}\right\} = \frac{A}{i}\,\frac{(1+i)^n-1}{(1+i)^n} = \frac{A}{i}\left\{1-(1+i)^{-n}\right\}$$

Therefore, any of the above three forms may be accepted.

The following illustration will make the principle clear :

Illustration 2.23

The management of a firm desires to purchase a machine. Two machines are available in the market—Machine A and Machine B. You are asked to advise the management which of the two alternatives will be more profitable under the NPV method from the following particulars :

	Machine A	Machine B
Initial outlay	Rs. 40,000	Rs. 50,000
Annual net earnings (after tax but before depreciation)	Rs. 20,000	Rs. 15,000
Estimated Life	4 years	8 years

The rate of interest may be taken at 10% p.a.

Solution

Before taking decisions it is necessary to find out the present value of net cash flows from the alternative investments with the help of the following annuity formula:

$$V = \frac{A}{i}\left\{1-(1+i)^{-n}\right\}$$

Machine A

$$V = \frac{20,000}{0.1}\left\{1-(1+.1)^{-4}\right\}$$

$= 2,00,000\ \{1 - 0.6829\}$

$= 2,00,000 \times 0.3171$

$=$ Rs. 63,420

Let $x = (1 + .1)^{-4}$

or, $\log x = -4 \log 1.1$

$= -4 \times 0.0414$

$= -.1656$

$= \bar{1}.8344$

or, $x =$ antilog of $\bar{1}.8344$

$= 0.6829$

Machine B

$$V = \frac{15,000}{0.1}\left\{1-(1+.1)^{-8}\right\}$$
$$= 1,50,000\ \{1 - 0.4665\}$$
$$= 1,50,000 \times 0.5335$$
$$= \text{Rs. } 80,025$$

Let $x = (1+.1)^{-8}$

or, $\log x = -8 \log 1.1$

$= -8 \times 0.0414$

$= -.3312$

$= \bar{1}.6688$

or, $x = \text{antilog of } \bar{1}.6688$

$= 0.4665$

Profitability Statement

	Machine A	Machine B
	Rs.	Rs.
Present Value of Net Cash Flows	63,420	80,025
Less : Initial Outlay	40,000	50,000
Net Present Value	23,420	30,025

It is evident from the above that Machine B will be the more profitable investment since the NPV of earnings in Machine B is greater than that of Machine A.

2. *By the use of Discount Tables*

Sometimes net cash flows (NCF) can be converted into NPV with the help of the Discount Table which reveals the present value of Re. 1 receivable at different intervals of time together with wide range of interest rates. It should be noted in this respect that when there is expected uneven cash flows each year's NCF will have to be discounted separately in order to find out the NPV. But if there is even NCF, a general Present value table is sufficient for the purpose.

Illustration 2.24

Calculate the NPV for project 'A' which initially costs Rs. 3,000 and generates annual cash inflow of Rs. 1,000, Rs. 900, Rs. 800, Rs. 700 and Rs. 600 in five years. The discount rate is assumed to be @ 10%.

Solution

Net Present Value of Project A

Years	Net Cash Flow	Discounting Factor at 10% (as per Table 1 shown in Appendix)	Present Values of Cash Inflows (2) × (3)
(1)	(2)	(3)	(4)
	Rs.		Rs.
1	1,000	.909	909
2	900	.826	743
3	800	.751	601
4	700	.683	478
5	600	.621	373
	4,000		3,104
	Less : Initial Outlay		3,000
	Net Present Value		104

Thus, it is possible to calculate the NPV for any series of future cash flows with the help of the above procedure.

It is needless to mention that if NCF accrues at even rate the procedure is quite simple. For example the future cash flows is Rs. 400 in a series which is to be received at the end of the next three years.

The above procedure may be neglected but the same is computed as:

	Re.
P.V. of Re. 1 to be received at the end of year 1	0.909
P.V. of Re. 1 to be received at the end of year 2	0.826
P.V. of Re. 1 to be received at the end of year 3	0.751
	2.486

This discount factor, i.e. 2.486, can be applied directly.

Therefore, the P.V. of Rs. 400 to be received annually for 3 years would be —

Rs. 400 × 2.486 = Rs. 994 (approx.)

Illustration 2.25

Your company can make either of the following two investments at the beginning of 2008. The following particulars are available in this respect:

	Project I	Project II
Estimated cost (to be incurred initially)	Rs. 20,000	Rs. 28,000
Estimated life (years)	4	5
Scrap value at the end of estimated life	Nil	Nil
Estimated Net Cash Flow (Rs.)		
End of 2008	5,500	5,600
End of 2009	7,000	9,000
End of 2010	8,500	9,000
End of 2011	7,500	9,000
End of 2012	—	9,000

It is estimated that each of the alternative projects will require an additional working capital of Rs. 2,000 which will be received back in full after the expiry of each project life. In estimating net cash flow, depreciation has been provided under straight line method.

Cost of finance to your company may be taken at 10% p.a. The present value of Re. 1 to be received at the end of each year at 10%:

Year	1	2	3	4	5
P.V.	0.91	0.83	0.75	0.68	0.62

[I.C.W.A. Final]

Solution

Net Present Value Method

Project I				Project II			
End of Year	N.C.F.	P.V. Factor @ 10%	Present Value	End of Year	N.C.F.	P.V. Factor @ 10%	Present Value
(1)	(2)	(3)	(4) = (2) × (3)	(1)	(2)	(3)	(4) = (2) × (3)
2008	5,500	0.91	5,005	2008	5,600	0.91	5,096
2009	7,000	0.83	5,810	2009	9,000	0.83	7,470

Contd.

2010	8,500	0.75	6,375	2010	9,000	0.75	6,750
2011	7,500	0.68	5,100	2011	9,000	0.68	6,120
				2012	9,000	0.62	5,580
Working Capital to be received back at the end of life	2,000	0.68	1,360		2,000	0.62	1,240
Total			23,650				32,256
Less :							
Estimated Cost	20,000				28,000		
Working Capital	2,000				2,000		
			22,000				30,000
Net Present Value			1,650				2,256

Hence Project II is more profitable since its N.P.V. is higher.

Illustration 2.26

A company whose cost of Capital is 12% p.a. is considering two projects A and B. The following data are available:

		Project A	Project B
		Rs.	Rs.
Original Investment			
Cash Flow		1,40,000	1,40,000
	Year 1	20,000	1,00,000
	Year 2	40,000	80,000
	Year 3	60,000	40,000
	Year 4	1,00,000	20,000
	Year 5	1,10,000	20,000

Work out their NPVs and comment which project is better.

Solution

Computation of Net Present Value

Project A				Project B			
Year	Net Cash Flow	P.V. Factor at 12%	Present Value	Year	Net Cash Flow	P.V. Factor at 12%	Present Value
	Rs.		Rs.		Rs.		Rs.
1	20,000	·8929	17,858	1	1,00,000	·8929	89,290
2	40,000	·7972	31,888	2	80,000	·7972	63,776
3	60,000	·7118	42,708	3	40,000	·7118	28,472
4	1,00,000	·6355	63,550	4	20,000	·6355	12,710
5	1,10,000	·5674	62,414	5	20,000	·5674	11,348
			2,18,418				2,05,596
Less :	Initial Investments		1,40,000				1,40,000
	Net Present Value		78,418		Net Present Value		65,596

Comment

Since the NPV of project A is greater than the NPV of project B, hence, Project A should be undertaken.

Ascertainment of NPV for mutually exclusive project

Illustration 2.27

XYZ Ltd. had decided to diversify its production and wants to invest it surplus finds on the most profitable projects. It has under consideration only two projects—A and B. The cost of project A is Rs. 100 lakhs and that of B is Rs. 150 lakhs. Both the projects are expected to have a life of 8 years only and, at the end of this period, A will have a salvage value of Rs. 4 lakhs and B Rs. 14 lakhs. The running expenses of A will be Rs. 35 lakhs per year and that of B Rs. 20 lakhs per year. In either case, the company expects a rate of return of 10%. The company's tax rate is 50%. Depreciation is charged on straight line basis.

Which project should the company take up?

[I.C.W.A. Inter]

Solution

The expected rate of return is 10%, i.e., the company will earn a return @ 10% on its investment which is taken as the cost of capital.

Ascertainment of Annual Cash Flow

		Project A Rs.	Project B Rs.
Earning/Profit (after tax) @ 10% on cost of investments		10,00,000	15,00,000
Add-back :	Depreciation $\left(\frac{\text{Cash Price} - \text{Scrap Value}}{\text{Estimated life}}\right)$		
	$\left(\frac{\text{Rs. } 1,00,00,000 - \text{Rs. } 4,00,000}{8 \text{ years}}\right) =$	12,00,000	—
	$\left(\frac{1,50,00,000 - \text{Rs. } 14,00,000}{8 \text{ years}}\right) =$	—	17,00,000
	∴ Annual Cash Flow	22,00,000	32,00,000

Computation of Net Present Value

Project A				Project B			
Year	Annual Cash Flow Rs.	Discount Factor at 10%	P.V. of NCF Rs.	Year	Annual Cash Flow Rs.	Discount Factor at 10%	P.V. of NCF Rs.
1 to 8 years	22,00,000	5.335	1,17,37,000	1 to 8 years	32,00,000	5.335	1,70,72,000
	4,00,000 (Salvage Value)	0.467	1,86,800		14,00,000 (Salvage Value)	0.467	6,53,800
			1,19,23,800				1,77,25,800
Less :	Initial Investments		1,00,00,000	*Less :*	Initial Investments		1,50,00,000
	Net Present Value		19,23,800				27,25,800

Since the Project B presents a higher NPV in comparison with Project A, Project B should be undertaken.

Illustration 2.28

P Ltd. desires to acquire a plant costing Rs. 2,00,000. The life of the plant is 5 years. The expected outputs from the plant during the project life are:

Year	1	2	3	4	5
Output (in units)	10,000	8,000	12,000	14,000	10,000

Selling Price p.u. is Rs. 10 variable cost is @ 50%. Scrap Value of the plant is after the period of 5 years Rs. 20,000. Cost of capital is @ 10%. Fixed cost Rs. 10,000, Rate of Tax is 50%.

Evaluate the proposal under the NPV method.

Solution

Ascertainment of Annual Cash Flow (after tax)

	Year I	Year II	Year III	Year IV	Year V
	Rs.	Rs.	Rs.	Rs.	Rs.
Sales (units × Rs. 10)	1,00,000	80,000	1,20,000	1,40,000	1,00,000
Less : Variable Cost (@ 50%)	50,000	40,000	60,000	70,000	50,000
Contribution	50,000	40,000	60,000	70,000	50,000
Less : Fixed Cost	10,000	10,000	10,000	10,000	10,000
Profit—before dep. and tax	40,000	30,000	50,000	60,000	40,000
Less : Depreciation $\left(\frac{2,00,000 - \text{Rs. } 20,000}{5}\right)$	36,000	36,000	36,000	36,000	36,000
Profit before Tax	4,000	(–) 6,000	14,000	24,000	4,000
Less : Tax @ 50%	2,000	—	7,000	12,000	2,000
Profit (after tax)	2,000	—	7,000	12,000	2,000
Add-back: Depreciation	36,000	36,000	36,000	36,000	36,000
	38,000	30,000	43,000	48,000	38,000
Add : Scrap Value	—	—	—	—	20,000
Annual Cash Flow (after tax)	38,000	30,000	43,000	48,000	58,000

Computation of NPV

Year	Annual Cash Flow	P.V. Factor at 10%	P.V. of NCF
	Rs.		Rs.
1	38,000	0.909	34,542
2	30,000	0.826	24,780
3	43,000	0.751	32,293
4	48,000	0.683	32,784
5	58,000	0.621	36,018
			1,60,417
	Less:	Initial Investments	2,00,000
		Net Present Value (Negative)	(–) 39,583

The proposal should be rejected as the NPV is found to be negative.

Illustration 2.29

National Electronics Ltd., an electronic goods manufacturing company, is producing a large range of electronic goods. It has under consideration two project X and Y, each costing is Rs. 120 lakhs.

The projects are mutually exclusive and the company is considering the question of selecting one of the two. Cash flows have been worked out for both the projects and the details are given below. X has a life of 8 years and Y has a life of 6 years. Both will have zero salvage value at the end of their operational lives. The company is already making profit and its tax rate is 50%. The cost of capital of the company is 15%.

(Rs. in lakhs)

At the end of year	Net Cash Flow Project X	Net Cash Flow Project Y	Present Value of rupee at 15%
1	25	40	0.870
2	35	60	0.756
3	45	80	0.685
4	65	50	0.572
5	65	30	0.497
6	55	20	0.432
7	35		0.376
8	15		0.327

The company follows Straight Line Method of depreciating assets.

Advise the company regarding the selection of the project.

[I.C.W.A. Inter, June 1996]

Solution

Calculation of Net Present Value of Project X and Project Y

Project X

End of the year	Cash Flow	Dep.	Profit before Tax	Tax @ 50%	Profit after Tax	Net Cash Flow (Profit after Tax + Dep.)	Discount Factor	Present Value of NCF
1	25	15	10	5	5	20	0.876	17.40
2	35	15	20	10	10	25	0.756	18.90
3	45	15	30	15	15	30	0.658	19.74
4	65	15	50	25	25	40	0.572	22.88
5	65	15	50	25	25	40	0.497	19.88
6	55	15	40	20	20	35	0.432	15.12
7	35	15	20	10	10	25	0.376	9.40
8	15	15	—	—	—	15	0.327	4.91
						P.V. of Cash Inflow		128.23
						Less: Initial Investment		120.00
						Net Present Value		8.23

Project Y

End of the year	Cash Flow	Dep.	Profit before Tax	Tax @ 50%	Profit after Tax	Net Cash Flow (Profit after Tax + Dep.)	Discount Factor	Present Value of NCF
1	40	20	20	10	10	30	0.870	26.10
2	60	20	40	20	20	40	0.756	30.24
3	80	20	60	30	30	50	0.658	32.90

Contd.

4	50	20	30	15	15	35	0.572	20.02
5	30	20	10	5	5	25	0.497	12.43
6	20	20	—	—	—	20	0.432	8.64
							P.V. of Cash Inflow	130.33
							Less: Initial Investment	120.00
							Net Present Value	10.33

Since the Net Present Value of Y is higher than Project X, Project Y is to be undertaken.

Evaluation of NPV Method

Advantages of the NPV method:

(i) It recognises time value of money.

(ii) It also recognises all cash flows throughout the life of the project.

(iii) It helps satisfy the objectives for maximising the firm's values.

Disadvantages

The NPV method has the following drawbacks:

(i) It is difficult.

(ii) It does not present a satisfactory answer when there are different amounts of investment for the purpose of comparison.

(iii) It does not present a correct picture in case of alternative projects or where there are unequal lives of the project with limited funds.

(iv) The NPV method of calculation is based on discount rate which, again, depends on the firm's cost of capital. The latter is difficult to understand as well as difficult to measure in actual practice.

INTERNAL RATE OF RETURN OR YIELD METHOD

The Internal Rate of Return (IRR) method is the second discounted cash flow or time adjusted method for appraising capital investment decisions. It was first introduced by Joel Dean.[1] It is also known as ***yield on investment, marginal efficiency of capital, rate of return over cost, time-adjusted rate of return,*** and so on. Internal rate of return is a rate which actually equates the present value of cash inflows with the present value of cash outflows. It is the rate of return which is earned by a project, i.e., it is a rate at which the NPV of investment is zero. This method also recognises the time value of money like NPV method by discounting the cash streams. Since it exclusively depends on the initial outlay and cash proceeds of the projects, and not by any rate determined outside the investment, it is appropriately called Internal Rate of Return. Under this method, the IRR should be compared with a required rate of return which is the out-off or hurdle rate.* A project is profitable only when the IRR is not less than the required rate, i.e., a firm is to undertake any project whose internal rate of return exceeds required rate. In the opposite case, it is rejected. In other words, where there are a number of alternative proposals, the acceptances criterion can be considered after analysing:

(i) IRR to be found out in each alternative case.

(ii) Compare the IRR with cut-off rate and those projects are rejected whose IRR is less than the cut-off rate.

(iii) Comparing the IRR of each alternative and selecting one which produces the highest rate and is the most profitable one.

1 Dean Joel, *Capital Budgeting,* Columbia University Press, 1951.

* It is generally taken as the firm's cost of capital.

IRR can be found out by solving the following equation (mathematically). It is represented by the rate, r, such that :

$$C = \left(\frac{P_1}{(1+r)^1}\right)+\left(\frac{P_2}{(1+r)^2}\right)+\left(\frac{P_3}{(1+r)^3}\right)+\ldots\ldots\ldots\ldots+\left(\frac{P_n}{(1+r)^n}\right)$$

where C = Initial cash outlay;

P_1, P_2, P_3 = Stream of future net cash flows.

The main shortcoming of this method is to ascertain the IRR which equates P.V. or NCF with that of initial cash outlay. In most cases, the rate is chosen at the first attempt and, consequently, one has to resort to trial and error (that is why this method is sometimes called *'Trial and Error'* method):

$$C = \left(\frac{P_1}{(1+r)^1}\right)+\left(\frac{P_2}{(1+r)^2}\right)+\left(\frac{P_3}{(1+r)^3}\right)+\ldots\ldots\ldots\ldots+\left(\frac{P_n}{(1+r)^n}\right)$$

$$= \frac{P}{r}\left\{\left(1-(1+r)^{-n}\right)\right\}$$

Here, C. P. and n are all known and, as such, r can be found out by solving the equation. But the problem arises since the value of log $(1 + r)^{-n}$ cannot be determined.

Naturally, after applying three or four trial runs, an area can be noticed where the actual rate lies and simple interpolation or graph may be used in order to approximate the actual rate. The above principles may be explained with the help of the following illustration under two conditions:

(a) **Where there is even series of Net Cash Flows**

Under the circumstances, initial cash outlay should be divided by the NCF per annum and locating the nearest discount factors. And choosing that discount rate which corresponds to the approximate rate of return. For this purpose, simple interpolation may be used for accuracy. The following illustration will, however, make the principle clear:

Illustration 2.30

Initial Outlay Rs. 40,000

Annual Net Cash Flow (NCF) Rs. 12,000

Estimated life 5 years

Calculate the Internal Rate of Return (r) of the project.

Solution

In order to find out IRR, we are to calculate the rate which will actually equate the original investment (Rs. 40,000) with the present value of Rs. 12,000 received annually for five years.

Suppose, we start with 14% rate of interest. The present value of Re. 1 received annually for 5 years at 14% is Rs. 3.4331, which is the discount factor. At the same time, the total present value of Rs. 12,000 received annually for 5 years becomes Rs. 60,000 (Rs. 12,000 × 5), which actually comes to Rs. 41,197.2. The present value of future cash streams exceeds the initial investment (i.e. Rs. 40,000).

Alternatively, it can be stated that the NPV > zero. As such, this rate is naturally not the IRR. As the NPV > zero we are to search for a higher rate of interest in order to have a lower NPV.

Let us try again on the assumption that the discount rate is 16%. Thus, the discount factor is 3.2743 which, multiplied by Rs. 12,000, presents a total present value of Rs. 39,291.6. As a result, the present value of cash stream falls short of the outlay (by Rs. 708.4) and, as such, the NPV < zero.

Therefore, the IRR lies between 14% and 16%.

We consider again 15% rate of interest which is 3.3522. In that case, the present value of Rs. 12,000, after five years, will be Rs. 40,226.4, i.e., slightly more than the original outlay.

So, the IRR will be slightly more than 15% but not more than 16%.

However the exact figure can be obtained by the application of the following interpolation formula:

$$\text{IRR} = \text{LR} + \left(\frac{\text{PVC} - \text{PVL}}{\text{DCP.}}\right) \times \text{DR}$$

where,

LR = Lower rate of discount;
PVC = Calculated present value of cash inflows;
PVL = Present Value of cash outlay;
DCP = Difference in present value so calculated;
DR = Difference in rate of interest.

Substituting the above values, we get

$$\text{IRR} = 15\% + \left(\frac{40,226.4 - 40,000}{40,226.4 - 39,291.6}\right) \times 1\%$$

$$= 15\% + \left(\frac{226.4}{934.8}\right) \times 1\%$$

$$= 15\% + .24\%$$

$$= 15.24\%$$

Therefore the IRR is 15.24%.*

From the above, it is evident that the said principle is particularly applicable if there is a constant annual cash flow. But, in actual practice, that is not always possible. The calculation in such a case is more difficult. This principle is explained below.

(b) **Where there is uneven series of Net Cash Flow**

It has already been stated above that if there is any uneven series of net cash flow, calculation is comparatively difficult. In this case, in order to reduce the number of trial runs, the first trial rate should be carefully selected.

It should be remembered that if net cash flow is not too uneven, selection of first rate may be considered as:

$$\text{IRR} = \text{HR} - \left(\frac{PVL - PVC}{DCP}\right) \times DR$$

$$= 16 - \left(\frac{40,000 - 39291.6}{934.8}\right) \times 1\%$$

$$= 16\% - .76\%$$

$$= 15.24\%$$

$$\frac{\text{Average excess Cash Flow over Cost of Investment}}{\text{Average Investment}} \times 100$$

Note: Average excess cash flow = $\frac{\text{Total Net Cash Flows minus Cost of Investment}}{\text{Projected Life}}$

* It can alternatively be calculated considering the higher rate.

When the first trial rate is applied for converting net cash flows to present values, the next trial rates can be selected on the basis of:

(i) When the present value of NCF is < the cost of the project = the second trial rate will be less than the first trial rate;

(ii) When the present value of NCF is > the cost of the project = the second trial rate will be more than the first one.

In this matter, there will be a place where the exact discount rate will lie and the same can be ascertained with the help of simple interpolation.

The following illustration will help to make the principle clear:

Illustration 2.31

A Co. Ltd. desires to purchase a new machine in order to increase its present level of production. Two alternative machines, Machine X and Machine Y, are available in the market.

The details of the machines are:

	Machine X	Machine Y
Initial outlay	Rs. 1,00,000	Rs. 1,20,000
Estimated life	5	5
Net Cash Flows after tax		
Years		
1	25,000	15,000
2	35,000	35,000
3	55,000	55,000
4	30,000	45,000
5	17,500	30,000
	1,62,500	1,80,000

You are asked to ascertain the more profitable machine (assume that the minimum rate of return laid down by the management is 16% p.a.).

Solution

The first rate is selected on the basis of the following Guide Rate:

Project X

$$\text{Average excess cash flows} = \frac{(\text{Rs. } 1{,}62{,}500 - \text{Rs. } 1{,}00{,}000)}{5} = \frac{\text{Rs. } 62{,}500}{5} = \text{Rs. } 12{,}500$$

$$\text{Average Investment} = \frac{\text{Rs. } 1{,}00{,}000}{2} = \text{Rs. } 50{,}000$$

$$\therefore \text{Guide Rate} = \frac{\text{Rs. } 12{,}000}{\text{Rs. } 50{,}000} \times 100 = 25\%$$

Profitability Statement

for Project X

Years	Net Cash Flow	Trial No. 1 Discount Rate 25% p.a.		Trial No. 2 Discount Rate 20% p.a.		Trial No. 3 Discount Rate 15% p.a.	
		P.V. of Re. 1	P.V. of N. C. F.	P.V. of Re. 1	P. V. of N. C. F.	P. V. of Re. 1	P. V. of N. C. F.

Contd.

	Rs.		Rs.		Rs.		Rs.
1	25,000	0.800	20,000	0.833	20,825	0.870	21,750
2	35,000	0.640	22,400	0.694	24,290	0.756	26,460
3	55,000	0.512	28,160	0.579	31,845	0.658	36,190
4	30,000	0.410	12,300	0.482	14,460	0.572	17,160
5	17,500	0.328	5,740	0.402	7,035	0.497	8,698
	1,62,500		88,600		98,455		1,10,258

Therefore from the above statement it becomes quite clear that actual rate will be between 15% and 20% which may be found out with the help of the following interpolation:

(Following the earlier method but by a different approach)

Discount Rate	P.V. of N.C.F.
%	Rs.
15	1,10,258
20	98,455
5	11,803

$$\therefore \text{ Actual Rate } = 15\% + \frac{\{10{,}258\ (1{,}10{,}258 - 1{,}00{,}000)\}}{\text{Rs. } 11{,}803} \times 5\%\ (20\% - 15\%)$$

$$= 15\% + 4.35\%$$

$$= 19.35\%$$

Project Y

The first trial rate is calculated as:

$$\text{Average excess cash flows} = \frac{(\text{Rs. } 1{,}80{,}000 - \text{Rs. } 1{,}20{,}000)}{5} = \text{Rs. } 12{,}000$$

$$\text{Average Investment} = \frac{\text{Rs. } 1{,}20{,}000}{2} = \text{Rs. } 60{,}000$$

$$\therefore \text{ Guide Rate} = \frac{\text{Rs. } 12{,}000}{\text{Rs. } 60{,}000} \times 100 = 20\%$$

Profitability Statement for Project Y

Years	Net Cash Flow	Trial No. 1 Discount Rate 25% p.a.		Trial No. 2 Discount Rate 20% p.a.		Trial No. 3 Discount Rate 15% p.a.	
		P.V. of Re. 1	P.V. of N.C.F.	P.V. of Re. 1	P.V. of N.C.F.	P.V. of Re. 1	P.V. of N.C.F.
	Rs.		Rs.		Rs.		Rs.
1	15,000	0.833	12,495	0.870	13,050	0.909	13,635
2	35,000	0.694	24,290	0.756	26,460	0.827	28,945
3	55,000	0.579	31,845	0.658	36,190	0.751	41,305
4	45,000	0.482	21,690	0.572	25,740	0.683	30,735
5	30,000	0.402	12,060	0.497	14,910	0.621	18,630
	1,80,000		1,02,380		1,16,350		1,33,250

Thus, the actual rate will be between 10% and 15% which is calculated as:

Discount Rate	P.V. of N.C.F.
%	Rs.
10	1,33,250
15	1,16,350
5	16,900

$$\therefore \quad \text{Actual Rate} = 10\% + \left(\frac{13{,}250}{16{,}900}\right) \times 5\% \; (15\% - 10\%)$$

$$= 10\% + 3.92\%$$

$$= 13.92\%$$

Comments

Project X is to be undertaken by the management since it satisfies the norms prescribed by the latter (i.e., 16%) and the rate of return is also higher than the project Y.

Acceptance Rule

It has already been highlighted in the present context that a project is profitable only when the IRR is not less than the required rate (which is also known as the firm's cost of capital or cut-off or hurdle rate), i.e., when IRR is higher than or at least equal to the minimum required rate. Similarly, in the opposite case, that is, if the IRR is less than the cost of capital, the project shall be rejected. For example, if the required rate of return were 12% and this criterion is used, the investment proposal considered above would be accepted. If the required rate of return is the return the investors expect the firm to earn on the project, accepting a project with an internal rate of return in excess of the required rate of return should result in an increase in the market price of the stock. Because, the firm accepts a project with a return greater than that required to maintain the present market price per share.[1]

Evaluation of IRR

The Internal Rate of Return Method has few advantages:

(a) It recognises the time value of money like Net Present Value Method;

(b) It also takes into account the cash flows throughout the life of the project;

(c) This method also reveals the maximum rate of return and presents a fairly good idea about the profitability of the project even if the firm's cost of capital is absent since the latter is not a precondition for use of it;

(d) The percentage which is calculated under the method is more meaningful and justified and that is why it is acceptable to the users since it satisfied them in relation to cost of capital.

Although the IRR method is theoretically sound, even it is not free from snags. Some of them are:

(a) The method of calculation is, no doubt, complicated and it is difficult to use and understand.

(b) This method does not present unique answers under all circumstances and situations. It may even present a negative rate or multiple rates under certain circumstances.

(c) This method recognises the fact that intermediate cash inflows which are generated by the project are reinvested at the internal rate, whereas the NPV method recognises

[1] Van Horn, J. C. — *Financial Management and Policy* — op. cit., p. 84.

that cash inflows are reinvested at the firm's cost of capital, which is more appropriate and justified in comparison with the IRR method.

(d) It may present inconsistent result with the NPV method when the projects actually differ from their expected life or cash outlays or timing of cash flows.

Illustration 2.32

X Ltd. has currently under examination a project which will yield the following returns over a period of time:

Years	Gross Yield
	Rs.
1	80,000
2	80,000
3	90,000
4	90,000
5	75,000

Costs of machinery to be installed works out at Rs. 2,00,000 and the machine is to be depreciated at 20% p.a. on WDV basis. Income tax rate is 50%.

If the average cost of raising capital is 11%, would you recommend accepting the project under the Internal Rate of Return Method?

Present value of money at rates of interest is as under:

Years	at 10%	at 14%
1	.91	.88
2	.83	.77
3	.75	.67
4	.68	.59
5	.62	.52

[C.A. Final]

Solution

Before ascertaining the IRR with the help of a profitability statement, the following statement for computing cash flows is prepared:

Cash Flow Statement

Year	Gross Yield	Depreciation on WDV basis at 20% on Investment	Profit before Tax	Tax @ 50%	Profit after Tax	Cash Flow (Profit after Tax + Dep.)
(a)	(b)	(c)	(d) = b – c	(e) = d × 50%	(f) = d – e	(g) = f + c
	Rs.	Rs.	Rs.	Rs.	Rs.	Rs.
1	80,000	40,000	40,000	20,000	20,000	60,000
2	80,000	32,000	48,000	24,000	24,000	56,000
3	90,000	25,600	64,400	32,200	32,200	57,800
4	90,000	20,480	69,520	34,760	34,760	55,240
5	75,000	81,920 *(bal. fig.)*	(–) 6,920	(–) 3,460	(–) 3,460	78,460
Total	4,15,000	2,00,000				3,07,500

Profitability Statement

Year	Cash Flow Rs.	P.V. Factor at 10%	P.V. Rs.	P.V. Factor at 14%	P.V. Rs.
1	60,000	0.91	54,600	0.88	52,800
2	56,000	0.83	46,480	0.77	43,120
3	57,800	0.75	43,350	0.67	38,726
4	55,240	0.68	37,563	0.59	32,592
5	78,460	0.62	48,645	0.52	40,799
			2,30,638		2,08,037

Cost of machinery, i.e., investments, Rs, 2,00,000. From the above statement it is found that IRR is higher than 14%. Since IRR is higher than the average cost of raising capital, which is 11%, the project may be undertaken.

Practically, IRR comes between 15% and 16%, i.e., 15.6% (calculations are not shown).

Illustration 2.33

The particulars relating to two alternative capital projects are:

	Project X	Project Y
Life of the project	4 years	6 years
	(Rupees in lakhs)	
Estimated Cash Outflow	15	15
Estimated Cash Inflow		
1st year	8	7
2nd year	10	8
3rd year	7	8
4th year	3	6
5th year	—	5
6th year	—	4

Compute internal rate of projects X and Y and state which project you would recommend. You may use the present value table given on next page:

P.V. of Re. 1

After	20%	25%	30%	35%	40%	45%	50%
1st	0.833	0.800	0.769	0.741	0.741	0.690	0.677
2nd	0.694	0.640	0.592	0.549	0.510	0.476	0.444
3rd	0.579	0.512	0.455	0.406	0.364	0.328	0.296
4th	0.482	0.410	0.350	0.301	0.260	0.226	0.198
5th	0.402	0.328	0.269	0.223	0.186	0.156	0.132
6th	0.335	0.262	0.207	0.165	0.133	0.108	0.088

[A.C.S. Final]

Solution

Profitability Statement
for Project X

Years	Discount Rate at 35%		P.V. of N.C.F.	Discount Rate at 40%	
	Cash Inflow	P.V. of Re. 1		P.V. of Re. 1	P.V. of N.C.F.
	Rs.		Rs.		Rs.
1	8,00,000	0.741	5,92,800	0.714	5,71,200
2	10,00,000	0.549	5,49,000	0.510	5,10,000

Contd.

	Rs.		Rs.		Rs.
3	7,00,000	0.406	2,84,200	0.364	2,54,800
4	3,00,000	0.301	90,300	0.260	78,000
			15,16,300		14,14,000

Estimated Cash Outflows = Rs. 15,00,000

Thus from the above statement, it becomes clear that actual rate will be between 35% and 40% which may be found out with the help of:

Discount Rate	P.V. of N.C.F.
	Rs.
35%	15,16,300
40%	14,14,000
5%	1,02,300

$$\therefore \text{ Actual Rate} = 35\% + \left(\frac{16,300}{1,02,300}\right) \times 5\% \ (40\% - 35\%)$$

$$= 35\% + .80\%$$

$$= 35.80\%$$

$$\therefore \text{ IRR} = 35.80\%$$

Profitability Statement

for Project Y

Years	Discount Rate at 40%		P.V. of N.C.F.	Discount Rate at 45%	
	Cash Inflow	P.V. of Re. 1		P.V. of Re. 1	P.V. of N.C.F.
	Rs.		Rs.		Rs.
1	7,00,000	0.714	4,99,800	0.690	4,83,000
2	8,00,000	0.510	4,08,000	0.476	3,80,000
3	8,00,000	0.364	2,91,200	0.328	2,62,400
4	6,00,000	0.260	1,56,000	0.226	1,35,600
5	5,00,000	0.186	93,000	0.156	78,800
6	4,00,000	0.133	53,200	0.108	43,200
			15,01,200		13,83,000

Estimated Cash Outflow = Rs. 15,00,000

∴ IRR lies between 40% and 45%.

Actual Rate will be:

Difference in Rate (40% – 45%) = 5%. Difference in P.V. (15,01,200 – 13,83,000) = 1,18,200

$$\text{IRR} = 40\% + \left(\frac{1,200}{1,18,200}\right) \times 5\%$$

$$= 40\% + .05\%$$

$$= 40.05\%$$

Therefore, Project Y is recommended since its IRR is higher in comparison with Project X.

Net Present Value vs Internal Rate of Return

The Net Present Value and the Internal Rate of Return methods are closely related and time-adjusted investment criteria for measuring investment proposals. They do not, however, lead to the same decision. Because, under the NPV method already stated earlier, cash flows are converted into their present value with the help of a discount rate which represents the firm's cost of capital and, as such, those proposals which result in negative NPV are rejected. But, under the IRR method, also highlighted above, it has to be selected in such a manner that the present value of capital outlay must be equal to the present value of net cash flow (NCF). Here, there is no discount rate like NPV method. This method expresses the fact that the best investment will be one which will produce the highest rate of return at the time of equating the PV of capital outlay and PV of NCF.

The NPV and IRR methods are to some extent similar in certain respects. For example, they would present the same accept-reject decisions in some circumstances. But they differ in the sense that the results about the selection of an asset are mutually contradictory under certain conditions.

As such, a comparison is needed between the two methods when

(i) there are similarities (between NPV and IRR methods) and (ii) there are differences (between NPV and IRR methods). These are discussed below:

(ii) **NPV and IRR : Similarities (i.e. in case of Independent Project)**

It has been explained above that the NPV and IRR methods actually lead to the same acceptance or rejection decision rule where there is a single project. That is due to:

(a) the discount rate which is greater than the IRR and, as such, the NPV becomes negative;

(b) the required rate which is greater than the IRR and, as such, the project is rejected.

Therefore, the situation where the two methods will present a concurrent accept/reject decision will be in respect of conventional and non-conventional investment projects.

Conventional Investment

A Conventional investment is one whose cash flow takes the pattern of an initial cash outlay followed by cash inflows. It has only one change in sign, e.g. – + + + ...[1]

Non-conventional Investment

A non-conventional investment is one of the cash outflows which are not restricted to the initial period but are interspersed with cash inflows throughout the life of the project.[2] It has more than one change in sign e.g. – + + + – ....

The NPV and IRR methods will result in the same accept-reject decision rules where conventional investments are economically independent and where there are no constraints in accepting all profitable projects and same projects become profitable by both of them, viz., NPV and IRR. The reason is very simple. Because, it may be recalled that, under NPV, a project will be accepted only when it has positive NPV, i.e. NPV exceeds zero (NPV > 0) whereas, under IRR a project may be accepted when IRR, is higher than the required rate of return (i.e. $r > k$) i.e. cost of capital.

It there is only one project there is actually no scope of conflict between NPV and IRR since they are used simultaneously for the purpose of measuring the investment. The principle followed by a diagram will help to make it clear.

---

1 Bierman, H. and Smidt, S.—*The Capital Budgetary Decisions*, New York, Macmillan Publishing Co., 1975, pp. 7-8.

2 *Ibid.*

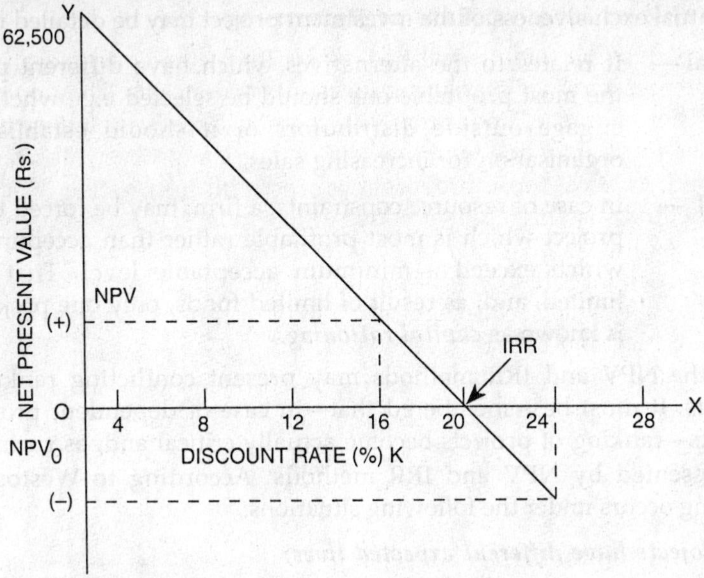

Fig. 2.1: Relationship between NPV and IRR — Single Project

By taking the figures of Project X from the previous Illustration No. 2.31, a graph is plotted (Fig. 2.1). The Net Present Value (NPV) of the project would be maximum, i.e. Rs. 62,500 i.e., difference between total NCF — Initial outlay (Rs. 1,62,500 – Rs. 1,00,000) if the discount rate is assumed to be zero, although it is an unreal situation. When the discount rate increases, NPV starts decreasing. That is, at 19.35%, the NPV is found to be zero. IRR is calculated in this case which is also 19.35%. It is to be noted that two points—one representing the highest NPV and the other by IRR—are joined. It is interesting to note that if the cost of capital is assumed to be 16%, the project may be accepted under the IRR method since IRR is greater than k, i.e., IRR > k or, 19.35% > 16%.

From Fig. 2.1 it is noticed (from the vertical axis) that at 16% cost of capital, i.e., discount rate, NPV is positive (which is represented by NPV value in the graph). Therefore, under NPV method, the project may also be accepted. On the other hand, when cost of capital is taken 25%, the project is rejected since IRR < k, i.e. 19.35% < 25%. The NPV is also found to be negative at 25% which is represented by NPV_O in the group. Therefore, the same is also rejected.

Thus, Fig. 2.1 portrays NPV as (i) positive, (ii) zero, and (iii) negative, corresponding to three situations, viz., (i) IRR > k, (ii) IRR = k, and (iii) IRR < k.

Thus, it can be stated that the two approaches lead to identical result about the accept-reject decision.

NPV and IRR: ***Difference (i.e. in case of Ranking Dependent Projects)***

From the foregoing discussion we have seen that the NPV and IRR methods present the concurrent result in case of independent conventional investments. Sometimes they present contradictory result, particularly when there are alternative ways for achieving an objective — i.e. in case of mutually exclusive investment project. Mutually exclusive means acceptance of one investment completely eliminates the expected proceeds of the other investment, or, in short, acceptance of an investment precludes the acceptance of others.

Now, the mutual exclusiveness of the investment project may be detailed into two groups:

(i) **Technical** — It relates to the alternatives which have different profitabilities and the most profitable one should be selected e.g., whether a firm should engage outside distributors or it should establish its own sales organisation for increasing sales.

(ii) **Financial** — In case of resource constraints, a firm may be forced to accept only one project which is most profitable rather than accepting all the projects which exceed a minimum acceptable level. That is, if funds are limited, and, as result of limited funds, only one project is accepted, it is known as ***capital rationing.***

Here, both the NPV and IRR methods may present conflicting rankings to mutually exclusive projects. It must be remembered that—in case of dependent projects or mutually exclusive projects—ranking of projects become actually critical and, as such, we are to tackle the problem presented by NPV and IRR methods. According to Weston and Brigham,[1] conflicting ranking occurs under the following situations:

(i) ***The projects have different expected lives;***

(ii) ***The cash outlay of one project is larger than that of the other; and***

(iii) ***The cash flow pattern of the projects may differ.***

Project Lives

Where the lives of the projects are unequal the NPV and IRR, methods present a conflicting ranking to mutually exclusive projects.

The following example will help to make the principle clear:

	Project X	Project Y
Initial Cash Outlay	Rs. 20,000	Rs. 20,000
Net Cash Flow generates	Rs. 24,000	Rs. 40,200
	(at the end of one year)	(at the end of fifth year)
Required Rate of Return (RRR)(k)	10%	10%
Net Present Value (NPV)*	Rs. 181.6	Rs. 4,990
Internal Rate of Return (IRR)**	20%	15%

Thus, from the above, it is found that the ranking given by two methods, NPV and IRR, is different. In other words, IRR method suggests Project X while NPV method recommends Project Y.

Cash Outlay

Another situation where the IRR and NPV methods present contradictory ranking is when there is different sizes of initial cash outlay, i.e. if cash outlay of some projects is larger than that of others. Consider the following example which will make the principle clear:

---

1 Weston, J. F. and Eugene, F. Brigham — *On Capital Budgeting Technique* — An Issue in Managerial Finance, Ed., E. F. Brigham and R. E. Johnson, The Dryden Press, Illinois, 1976, p. 108.

* Calculations are not shown.

** Calculations are not shown.

	Project X	Project Y
Initial Cash Outlay	Rs. 10,000	Rs. 10,00,000
Net Cash Inflows (at the end of one year)	Rs. 15,000	Rs. 12,00,000
Required Rate of Return (k)	10%	10%
Therefore,		
Net Present Value (NPV)	Rs. 635.00	Rs. 90,800
Internal Rate of Return (IRR)	50%	20%

Thus, the two projects are ranked in a different manner. In short, NPV method recommends the Project Y whereas IRR method will suggest the Project X.

Cash Flow Timings

The next contradictory ranking presented by NPV and IRR methods is the cash flow timings although the initial outlay of the projects may be the same, i.e. the mutually exclusive proposals may differ simply on the basis of cash flows generated. No doubt, it is a conflict in ranking of proposals presented by the NPV and IRR methods since they have different patterns of cash flows.

That is, in other words, if there are two or more investment proposals which are mutually exclusive, they may present contradictory results and, hence, ranking would vary according to the method followed. The following example, will, however, help to understand the principle:

	Proposals I	Proposals II
Initial outlay (Rs.)	70,000	70,000
Net cash flow (Rs.)		
Year end 1	10,000	50,000
2	20,000	40,000
3	30,000	20,000
4	45,000	10,000
5	60,000	10,000
	1,65,000	1,30,000
Thus		
Internal Rate of Return	27.33%	37.62%
Net Present Value (Rs.) (assuming a discount rate of 10% p.a.)	46,135	36,550

Note: Calculations of IRR and NPV are not shown.

From the above, it becomes quite clear that if IRR is used, the decision will go in favour of Proposal I since it has the higher returns. On the other hand, if NPV is used as decision criterion, it will go in favour of Proposal II since it has the higher NPV. Naturally, if one of them is to be selected, there will be a clear conflict between the two.

In order to suggest a remedy for resolving the conflict and also to explain the nature of the problems, the above illustration can also be graphically presented as:

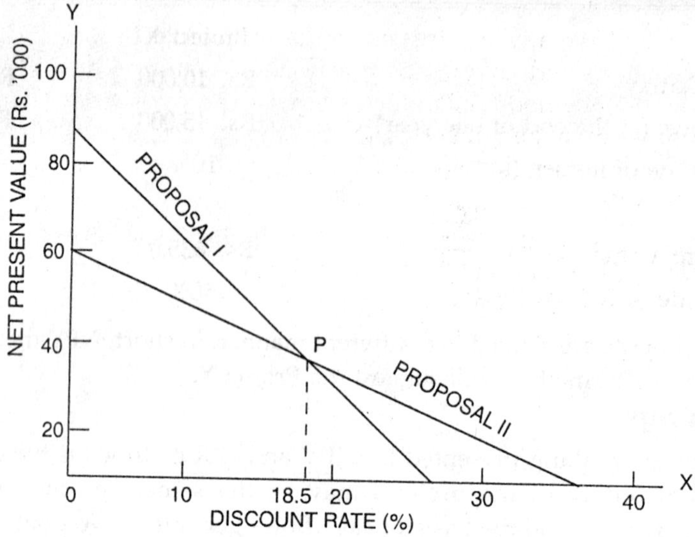

Fig. 2.2 : Relationship between NPV and IRR — Mutually Exclusive Projects

Fig. 2.2 portrays that, when discount rate is assumed to be zero, the NPV will be Rs. 95,000 (Rs. 1,65,000 – Rs. 70,000) and Rs. 60,000 (Rs. 1,30,000 – Rs. 70,000), respectively, for Proposals I and II, the IRRs are 23.33% and 37.62% respectively. In the above diagram, IRR is plotted on X-axis whereas NPV is plotted on Y-axis.

It is seen from the above that, when the discounting rates are increased, NPV starts to decline and, as such, NPV is zero corresponding to 27.33% (IRR) in case of Proposal I whereas, in case of Proposal II, it is 37.62%.

Similarly, Proposal II (at zero discount rate) shows highest NPV in Y-axis corresponding to an IRR of 27.33% in X-axis. These two points are joined to form a straight line. Same procedure is also to be adopted in case of Proposal II. Then, the two lines intersect at a certain point, viz. P. Hence, this discounting rate corresponding to intersection point is above 18.5%. Naturally, if there is any discounting rate which is below 18.5%, the two methods would rank them in a different manner. For example, the NPV of Proposal I is higher in comparison with Proposal II (if discounting rate is 10%) and, hence, it is preferable to use NPV method. On the contrary, IRR of Proposal I is 27.33% as against 37.62% of Proposal II. That is, there is a clear conflict. But, if discounting rate exceeds 18.5%, here will be no conflict between them.

The general principle about the conflict between NPV and IRR is that, if the IRR is greater than the rate at which the NPV of mutually exclusive projects are equal, both of them will present the compatible result, i.e., if there is a higher IRR in any project, there will also be a higher NPV. On the other hand, if the IRR is less than the rate at which the NPV of mutually exclusive projects are equal, both of them will present a contradictory result. In other words, the projects with lower IRR will have higher NPV, or higher IRR with lower NPV.

Ranking Conflict between NPV and IRR and Reinvestment Rate Assumption

The foregoing discussions have already highlighted that the NPV and IRR methods would rank projects in a different manner in case of mutually exclusive projects provided that there is (a) initially different cash outlays, (b) different patterns of cash flow, and (c) unequal service life of the projects, although ranking given by NPV is theoretically more sound.

Practically, the conflicts between the two methods are primarily due to the different assumptions about the reinvestment rates. IRR method is deficient since it attempts to find an interest rate which will equate the present value of a project's proceeds with that of its investment outlays, i.e. to find an average yearly rate of return which just equates the two. Therefore, using the IRR method for ranking is equivalent to assuming that any intermediate cash flows from a project will be reinvested to earn the projected internal rate of return, while the NPV method hypothesises that such cash flow streams will earn only interest equal in value to the discount rate.

The reinvestment assumptions of the NPV method, on the other hand, seem to make economic sense where everyone can borrow or lend at the going rate of interest. Under the circumstances, any project which offers a return higher than the market rate of interest will always be accepted. This reinvestment assumption is merely a specific application of the NPV model's general assumption that the discount rate reflects the opportunity cost of capital.

As such, discounting at the going rate of interest recognises that with a perfect capital market, the sacrifices of accepting any specific project are measured either by the cost of, borrowed funds or by the interest foregone if internal funds are used.

Again, extra emphasis is imposed on IRR since, under this method, different cash flow streams for each investment proposal will constitute the different investment rates. As such, there will be as many rates of reinvestment as there are investment proposals which are to be measured.

This reinvestment rate and IRR method can be demonstrated with the help of hypothetical examples[1]:

Example

Projects	Initial Outlay	Cash Inflows	
		Year I	Year II
A	Rs. 100	Rs. 200	0
B	Rs. 100	0	Rs. 400

According to IRR method, both the projects A and B have a rate of return @ 100% (i.e. if Rs. 100 are invested for one year @ 100%, it will amount to Rs. 200; similarly, if investment is made for two years, it will grow Rs. 400). As both the projects present the same IRR, the firm may accept any one of them or, it should be indifferent about their acceptability. In order to be true it must be necessary that Rs. 200, received at the end of first year, must be Rs. 400 at the end of the second year, i.e. the rate of earning must be the same i.e. at 100%. If the rate of earning is not the same, i.e. 100%, Rs. 200 will not be Rs. 400 at the end of the second year. And, in that case, if Rs. 200 is not transformed to Rs. 400 at the end of the second year we cannot give the equal rank to the two projects. Of course, the fact that a firm may find other investment opportunities at the required rate is ignored.

However, the present value method is free from the said snag. The principle is explained here by taking the same example to be prepared under NPV method assuming that the cost of capital (k) is @ 10%:

	Project A			Project B		
Years	Cash Flow	P.V. Factor	P.V. of N.C.F.	Cash Flow	P.V. Factor	P.V. of N.C.F.
	Rs.		Rs.	Rs.		Rs.
1	200	0.909	182	0	—	0

Contd.

1 The example has been taken from Pollach, G. A. — *The Capital Budgeting Controversy : Present Value vs Discounted Cash Flow Method*, Nov. 1961 — quoted from Khan and Jain — *Financial Management*, op. cit., p. 265.

	Rs.		Rs.	Rs.		Rs.
2	0	—	0	400	0.826	330
			182			330
Less :	Initial outlay		100			100
	Net Present Value		82			230

From the above, it becomes crystal clear that, according to NPV method, Project B is more profitable than Project A—since the latter has a higher NPV in comparison with the former. It is needless to mention that the reinvestment rate, here, is more realistic, reasonable and dependable.

The reinvestment rate assumption about the cash flow generation is theoretically more correct and appropriate under NPV method than the IRR method since the rate itself is consistent in case of NPV itself; while, in case of IRR, it is widely varied. Moreover, the IRR method also suffers from computational problem, i.e., it is difficult to calculate.

Illustration 2.34

A company is considering as to which of two mutually exclusive projects it should undertake. The Financial Director thinks that the project with the higher NPV should be chosen whereas the Managing Director thinks that the one with the higher IRR should be undertaken—specially as both projects have the same initial outlay and length of life.

The company anticipates a cost of capital of 10% and the net after-tax cash flows of the projects are as follows:

(Rs. '000)

Year	0	1	2	3	4	5
Cash Flows :						
Project X	(200)	35	80	90	75	20
Project Y	(200)	218	10	10	4	3

Required :

(a) Calculate the NPV and IRR of each project.

(b) State, with reasons, which project you would recommend?

(c) Explain the consistency in the ranking of two projects.

The discount factors are:

Year	0	1	2	3	4	5
Discount Factor:						
10%	1	0.91	0.83	0.75	0.68	0.62
20%	1	0.83	0.69	0.58	0.48	0.41

[C.A. Final]

Solution

(a) ***Computations of NPV and IRR***

For Project X

Computation of NPV

	Discount Factor at 10%			Discount Factor at 20%		
Year	**Cash Flows**	**P.V. Factor at 10%**	**P.V. of N.C.F.**	**Cash Flows**	**P.V. Factor at 20%**	**P.V. of N.C.F.**
	Rs.		Rs.	Rs.		Rs.
1	35,000	0.91	31,850	35,000	0.83	29,050
2	80,000	0.83	66,400	80,000	0.69	55,200

Contd.

	Rs.		Rs.	Rs.		Rs.
3	90,000	0.75	67,500	90,000	0.58	52,200
4	75,000	0.68	51,000	75,000	0.48	36,000
5	20,000	0.62	12,400	20,000	0.41	8,200
			2,29,150			1,80,650
Less:	Initial Investment		2,00,000	*Less :* Initial Investment		2,00,000
	Net Present Value		29,150	Net Present Value (Negative)		(–) 19,350

Computation of IRR

From the above NPV table it is quite clear that there is 10% discount factor Total PV is Rs. 2,29,150 whereas when there is 20% discount factor P.V. is Rs. 1,80,650. Thus, IRR lies in between 10% and 20%. Actual rate will be:

Discount Rate	P.V.
	Rs.
10%	2,29,150
20%	1,80,650
10%	48,500

$$\text{Actual Rate} = 10\% + \frac{\text{Rs. } 29{,}150 \text{ (i.e. } 2{,}29{,}150 - \text{Rs. } 2{,}00{,}000)}{\text{Rs. } 48{,}500} \times 10\%$$

$$= 10\% + 6.01\%$$

$$= 16.01\%$$

For Project Y

(b) Computation of NPV

	Discount Factor at 10%			Discount Factor at 20%		
Year	**Cash Flows**	**P.V. Factor at 10%**	**P.V. of N.C.F.**	**Cash Flows**	**P.V. Factor at 10%**	**P.V. of N.C.F.**
	Rs.		Rs.	Rs.		Rs.
1	2,18,000	0.91	1,98,380	2,18,000	0.83	1,80,940
2	10,000	0.83	8,300	10,000	0.69	6,900
3	10,000	0.75	7,500	10,000	0.58	5,800
4	4,000	0.68	2,720	4,000	0.48	1,920
5	3,000	0.62	1,860	3,000	0.41	1,230
			2,18,760			1,96,790
Less:	Initial Investment		2,00,000	*Less:* Initial Investment		2,00,000
	Net Present Value		18,760	Net Present Value (Negative)		(–) 3,210

Computation of IRR

From the above NPV table it is quite clear that when there is 10% discount factor, total PV of cash flows are Rs. 2,18,760, whereas, when there is 20% discount factors total PV of cash flows are Rs. 1,96,790. Thus, IRR lies in between 10% and 20% discount factor. So, actual rate will be:

Discount Rate	PV
%	Rs.
10	2,18,760
20	1,96,790
10	21,970

$$\text{Actual Rate} = 10\% + \frac{\text{Rs. } 18{,}760}{\text{Rs. } 21{,}970} \times 10\%$$
$$= 10\% + 8.54\%$$
$$= 18.54\%$$

Rank	Project X	Project Y
NPV	1st	2nd
IRR	2nd	1st

Recommendation

Considering NPV—It reveals from the above that as per NPV method Project X is superior than Project Y as, in case of former, the NPV is higher. It is also interesting to note that in both the cases NPV is positive.

Considering IRR

If IRR method is considered Project Y is superior to Project X as, in case of former, the IRR is greater than the latter. Thus, the conflict arises between the two i.e. which one should be taken into consideration. Under the circumstances, we should recommend Project X as its NPV is higher than Project Y as it is possible to maximises the wealth of the proprietor's fund.

(c) The inconsistency happens due to the

(i) different cash flow pattern; and

(ii) reinvestment rate assumption.

Analysis

In case of Project X, major cash flow come in 2nd, 3rd and 4th year, respectively, but, in case of Project Y, major cash flow comes out in 1st year. Moreover, IRR of Project Y is higher in comparison with Project X as a result of re-investment rates.

Incremental Method

The previous section gives an idea as to how the IRR method can be used to select correctly between the mutually exclusive projects. It should be remembered that the correct comparison between Proposal I and Proposal II (shown earlier) must not be in terms of average yearly yields but the same should be in terms of cash flow differences between the two projects. In other words, using Proposal II as base, the incremental investment in order to obtain Proposal I should be compared with the consequent incremental cash flows. The question is : After having accepted Proposal II, may we realise a better return from Proposal I ? Consider the following table for the purpose:

Incremental Yield Method

	Proposal I	Proposal II	Differences
Initial Outlay	Rs. 9,000	Rs. 9,000	
Net Cash Flow			
Year End	Rs.	Rs.	Rs.
1	3,000	6,000	– 3,000
2	5,000	4,000	+ 1,000
3	6,000	3,000	+ 3,000
Internal Rate of Return (Calculations are not shown)			18%

Thus, the switch to Proposal I entails foregoing Rs. 3,000 in year 1 as against extra cash flows of Rs. 1,000 and Rs. 3,000 in years 2 and 3, respectively. The IRR in this case is 18%, which is greater than the cost of capital. Therefore, Proposal I is better than Proposal II, and, hence, it should be accepted despite the fact that its IRR is 22.5% in comparison with Proposal

II which has an IRR of 24%. Thus, the modified method of IRR will actually lead to the same conclusion as arrived at under NPV method.†

Problems of Multiple/Dual Rates

Another serious difficulty associated with IRR method is that it can yield multiple internal rates of return, i.e. the projects which have non-conventional cash flow patterns may have multiple rates of return. For example, the cash flow series — Rs. 1,000 + Rs. 2,550, — Rs. 1,575 has IRR of 5% and 50%. This is shown in Fig. 2.3 where NPV *curve intersects the horizontal axis twice* shown below.

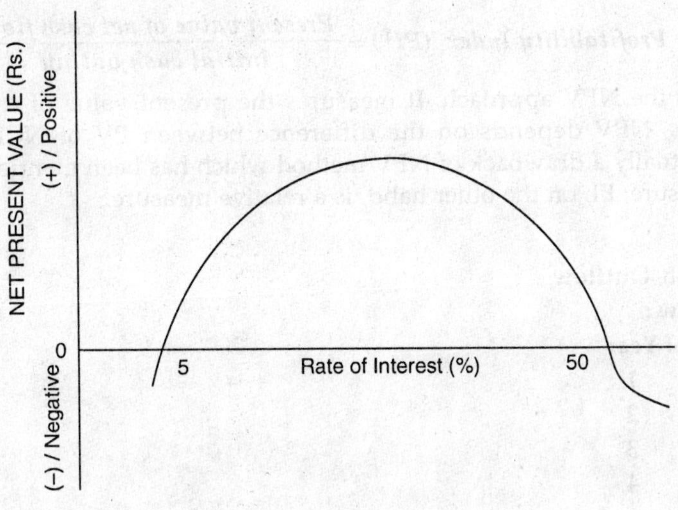

Fig. 2.3: Multiple Rates of Return

It should be remembered that multiple rates arise since several different interest rates may equate the present value of cash inflow of a project to the present value of its initial outlay. This happens simply because different interest rates may present different values to each and every component of a project's cash flows, i.e., very high rate of interest will give a low value to all but a project's near cash flows and, on the contrary, very low rate of interest presents all cash flow almost nearly of equal value. As such, since the interest rate tends to zero, the P.V. of a project will approach the algebraic sum of its undiscounted cash flows and will be negative if this is negative.

In Fig. 2.3, it is shown that at all interest rates below 5%, the negative third term of the project, exceeds the weight of its positive middle term and produces a negative (–) P.V., and, with a cost of capital higher than 5%, the positive second term in the cash flow pattern will be less sensitive to change in discount rate than the third term. The P.V. of cash inflows, with these rates of interest, will exceed the weight of the two negative cash flows and give the project a positive (+) NPV. Similarly, if the rate of discount rises continuously, the negative (–) third term of the project will not be significant but the positive (+) cash flows will fall in value comparatively faster than the negative (–) first term. Therefore, the value of the negative (–) terms will exactly offset, at some specific rate of interest, that of the positive (+) second term and, as a result, the NPV curve will intersect the horizontal axis again.

G. D. Quirin has rightly said in his book *(The Capital Expenditure Decision)* that when multiple rates of return exist there seems to be no mathematical or economic grounds for

† The correct procedure when IRR is used for selecting between mutually exclusive projects is to compute the incremental rate of return between the projects. That is, no doubt, a complex procedure for pairs of projects for comparison.

specifying any one of them having value of more than 100% as the IRR for all are the roots of a single polynomial equation.

PROFITABILITY INDEX (PI) OR BENEFIT-COST RATIO ($\frac{B}{C}$ RATIO)

Another time-adjusted technique for evaluating investment proposals is the Profitability Index (PI) or Benefit-Cost Ratio ($\frac{B}{C}$ Ratio).* It is the relation between present value of future net cash flows and the initial cash outlay, i.e., this ratio is computed by dividing the present value of net cash flows by the initial cash outlay. It is computed as :

$$\textit{Profitability Index } (PI^{\dagger}) = \frac{\textit{Present value of net cash flows}}{\textit{Initial cash outlay}}$$

It is similar to the NPV approach. It measures the present value of return of per rupee invested. Whereas, NPV depends on the difference between PV of NCF and PV of cash outflow. This is actually a drawback of NPV method which has been mentioned above since it is an absolute measure; PI, on the other hand, is a relative measure.

Illustration 2.35

Initial Cash Outflow	Rs. 50,000
Cash Inflow :	
End of Year	Rs.
1	20,000
2	15,000
3	25,000
4	10,000

Calculate the NPV and PI of the project assuming that the discount factor is 10%.

Solution

Calculation of Profitability Index

Year	Cash Inflow	Discount Factor	P.V. of N.C.F.
	Rs.	@ 10%	Rs.
1	20,000	0.909	18,180
2	15,000	0.826	12,390
3	25,000	0.751	18,775
4	10,000	0.683	6,830
			56,175
Less : Initial Outlay			50,000
		N.P.V.	6,175

$$\therefore \text{Profitability Index } (PI^{\dagger}) = \frac{\text{PV of NCF}}{\text{Initial Cash Outlay}} = \frac{\text{Rs. } 56{,}175}{\text{Rs. } 50{,}000} = 1.12$$

* This is known as $\frac{B}{C}$ ratio since the numerator measures benefits and denominator measures costs.

† $PI = \dfrac{\sum_{t=1}^{n} \frac{A_t}{(1+k)^t}}{A_0}$

Under this method it should be remembered that an investmental proposal may be accepted when the Profitability Index (PI) is greater than one. However, in case of mutually exclusive proposals, the acceptance criterion will be — the higher the index, the more profitable is the proposal, and vice versa.

Example: (Data taken from the previous Illustration)

	Machine A	Machine B
Initial Outlay (Rs.)	40,000	50,000
P.V. of N.C.F. (Rs.)	63,420	80,025
Profitability Index	$\left(\frac{63,420}{40,000}\right) = 1.59$	$\left(\frac{80,025}{50,000}\right) = 1.60$

Thus, Investment in Machine B will be more profitable. It may also be done with the help of ranking. That is, the highest rank will be given to that prospect which has highest PI.

Acceptance Rule (Accept-Reject Decision)

It has been mentioned earlier that an investment proposal is accepted when the PI is greater than one. When PI equals 1 the firm is indifferent to the project. Similarly, where PI is greater than, less than, or equal to 1, the NPV is greater than, less than, or equal to 0, respectively, i.e.

NPV will be positive = PI > 1

NPV will be negative = PI < 1

Therefore, NPV and PI present the same result about the investment proposals.

Evaluation of Profitability Index

Like other DCF techniques, PI is, no doubt, conceptually sound since it satisfies almost all the requirements of appraising an investment project, viz., time value of money, totality of benefit etc.

Although it involves more calculations than the traditional methods (viz. ARR or Pay-Back Period Methods) it is less than the IRR method. According to this method, it has already been stated that ranks are assigned to the projects on the basis of PI and, naturally, higher ranks will be given to the project which has highest PI.

Illustration 2.36

M/s L. & Co. has Rs. 2,00,000 to invest. The following proposals are under consideration. The cost of capital for the company is estimated to be 15%:

Project	Initial Outlay Rs.	Annual Cash Rs.	Life of Project (Years)
A	1,00,000	25,000	10
B	70,000	20,000	8
C	30,000	6,000	20
D	50,000	15,000	10
E	50,000	12,000	20

Rank the above projects on the basis of (i) NPV Method, and (ii) Profitability Index Method.

Present value of annuity of Re. 1 received in steady stream discounted @ 15%:

8 years = 4.6586

10 years = 5.1790

20 years = 6.3345

[A.C.S. Final—Adapted]

Solution

(i) **Calculation under Net Present Value Method**

Project	Annual Cash Flow	Life of Project (Years)	P.V. at 15%	Present Value of N.C.F.	Initial Outlay	Net Present Value	Ranks
	Rs.			Rs.	Rs.	Rs.	
A	25,000	10	5.1790	1,29,475	1,00,000	29,475	1
B	20,000	8	4.6586	93,172	70,000	23,172	4
C	6,000	20	6.3345	38,007	30,000	8,007	5
D	15,000	10	5.1790	77,685	50,000	27,685	2
E	12,000	20	6.3345	76,014	50,000	26,014	3

(ii) Profitability Index $= \dfrac{\textit{P.V. of Net Cash Flows}}{\textit{Initial Cash Outlay}}$

Calculation under Profitability Index Method

Project	P.V. of N.C.F.	Initial Outlay	Profitability Index	Rank
(1)	(2)	(3)	(4) $= \frac{(2)}{(3)}$	(5)
A	1,29,475	1,00,000	1.29	4
B	93,172	70,000	1.33	3
C	38,007	30,000	1.27	5
D	77,685	50,000	1.55	1
E	76,014	50,000	1.52	2

Illustration 2.37

A firm whose cost of capital is 10% is considering two mutually exclusive projects X and Y, the details of which are:

		Project X	Project Y
		Rs.	Rs.
Investment		70,000	70,000
Cash Flow			
Year	1	10,000	50,000
	2	20,000	40,000
	3	30,000	20,000
	4	45,000	10,000
	5	60,000	10,000
		1,65,000	1,30,000

Compute the NPV at 10% Profitability Index for the two projects.

Discount Factors

Year	10%	15%	20%	25%	30%	35%	40%
1	.909	.870	.833	.800	.769	.741	.744
2	.826	.756	.694	.640	.592	.549	.510
3	.751	.658	.579	.512	.455	.406	.364
4	.683	.572	.482	.410	.350	.301	.260
5	.621	.492	.402	.328	.269	.223	.186

Solution

Net Present Value (at 10% discount factor)

Years	P.V. Factor at 10%	Project X		Project Y	
		Cash Inflow	P.V of N.C.F.	Cash Inflow	P.V. on N.C.F.
		Rs.	Rs.	Rs.	Rs.
1	.909	10,000	9,090	50,000	45,450
2	.826	20,000	16,520	40,000	33.040
3	.751	30,000	22,530	20,000	15,020
4	.683	45,000	30,735	10,000	6,850
5	.621	60,000	37,260	10,000	6,210
			1,16,135		1,06,550
Less : Investment (Initial Outlay)			70,000		70,000
∴ Net Present Value			46,135		36,550

Profitability Index $= \frac{\text{Rs. } 1,16,135}{\text{Rs. } 70,000} = 1.66$ $\qquad = \frac{\text{Rs. } 1,06,550}{\text{Rs. } 70,000} = 1.52$

TERMINAL VALUE (TV) METHOD

Under this method, it is assumed that each cash inflow is reinvested in another asset at a certain rate of return and calculating the terminal value of net cash flow at the end of project life. In short, the NCF and the outlay are compounded forward rather than backward by discounting which is used by NPV method.

The following illustration will make the principle clear:

Illustration 2.38

Initial Outlay	Rs. 20,000
Project Life	5 years
Net Cash Inflow	Rs. 8,000 each for 5 years
Cost of Capital	@ 10% (k)

Expected interest rates

End of the Year	Percentage
1	6%
2	6%
3	6%
4	8%
5	8%

Solution

Before preparing the table we are to know that we will reinvest Rs. 8,000 (which is received) at the end of year 1 for 4 years @ 6%. The NCF of year 2 will also be reinvested for 3 years. Similarly, the NCF of year 3 will be reinvested for 2 years, and so on. Naturally there will be no reinvestment at the end of the 5th year. Therefore, the total sum of these compound NCFs is then discounted back to the present at *(k)* in order to compare the PV of cash outflow which, in this case, is Rs. 20,000.

PV of Terminal Sum is shown below under consideration that the cost of capital is 10% :

Years	N.C.F. (– Rs. 20,000) Rs.	Internal Rate	Years for Investment	Compounding Factor	Compound Sum Rs.
1	8,000	6 %	4	1.262	10,096
2	8,000	6 %	3	1.191	9,528
3	8,000	6 %	2	1.166	9,328
4	8,000	8 %	1	1.080	8,640
5	8,000	8 %	0	1.000	8,000
				Total	45,592

* As per Table shown in Appendix.

Here the discount rate represents the cost of capital *(k)* (10%). We are also to find out the PV of Rs. 45,592 which will actually be received at the end of five years.

Therefore, the PV of the total compounded sum will be calculated as:

$$PV = \frac{\text{Rs. } 45{,}592}{(1+\cdot 10)^5} = \text{Rs. } 28{,}313$$

Note : PV of Re. 1, received 5 years @ 10% discount rates, is 0.621.
The sum of the PV will be Rs. 45,592 × 0.621 = Rs. 28,313.

Since TV is positive here, the project can be accepted. Its TV is Rs. 8.313.

Acceptance Rule

From the foregoing discussion, it becomes clear that, if the value of the total compounded reinvested cash flow is greater than the present value of outflow, i.e., if NCF have a higher terminal value in comparison with the outlay, the project is accepted, and vice versa. The accept-reject rule can thus be formulated as:

(1) If there is a single project : Accept the project if the terminal value (TV) is positive.

(2) If there are mutually exclusive projects : The project will be more profitable which has the highest positive terminal value (TV).

It can also be stated that if TV is positive, accept the project and, if TV is negative, reject the project.

It should be remembered that TV method is similar to NPV method. The only difference is that, in case of former, values are compounded while, in case of latter, values are discounted. Of course, both of them will present the same result provided the rate is same (i.e., discounting and compounding).

Capital Rationing

From the foregoing discussion it may be recalled that the profitability of a project can be measured by any one of the DCF techniques (viz., IRR, NPV and PI), particularly the two theoretically sound methods IRR and NPV. Practically, the firm may accept all those projects which give a rate of return higher than the cost of capital or which have positive NPV. And, in case of mutually exclusive projects, the projects having the highest NPV or giving the highest rate of return may be accepted. In other words, a firm should accept that investment proposal which increases maximum the firm's value.

In actual practice, however, every firm prepares its annual capital expenditure budget which depends on the availability of funds with the firm or other considerations. In that case, a firm has to select not only the profitable investments opportunities but also it has to rank the projects from the highest to lowest priority, i.e., a cut-off point is selected. Naturally, the proposal which is above the cut-off point will be funded and which is below the cut-off point will be rejected. It should be remembered that this cut-off point is determined on the basis of the number of projects, funds available for financing capital expenditure, and the objectives of the firm.

That is, in other words, question of Capital Rationing appears before us. It is normally applied to situations where the supply of funds to a firm is limited in some way. It actually encompasses many different situations ranging from that where the borrowing and lending rates faced by the firms differ to that where the funds available for investment by the firm are strictly limited. In short, it rejects a situation where the firm is constrained, for external or self-imposed reasons, to obtain necessary funds to invest in all profitable investment projects, i.e. a situation where a constraint is placed on the total size of capital investment during a particular period. In the circumstances, the firm has to select a combination of investment proposals which provides the highest NPV, subject to the budget constraint.

Selection Process under Capital Rationing

Under capital rationing a firm cannot accept all the projects even if all of them are profitable. In order to select or reject the projects, a comparison must be made among them.

Selection of project depends on two steps:

(i) Ranking the projects according to the Profitability Index (PI) or Net Present Value (NPV) method;

(ii) Selecting projects in descending order of profitability (until the funds are exhausted).

The projects can be ranked by any one of the DCF techniques, viz., IRR, NPV and PI. But PI method is found to be the more suitable and reliable measure of profitability since it determines the relative profitability, while NPV method is an absolute measure of profitability.

Illustration 2.39

Funds available for capital expenditure in a year are estimated at Rs. 2,50,000 in a firm. The profitability index (PI) with mutually exclusive investment proposals are:

Projects	Initial Outlay (in Rs. '000)	Profitability Index (PI)
P_1	25	1.12
P_2	40	1.20
P_3	50	1.15
P_4	70	1.30
P_5	60	1.25
P_6	20	0.98
P_7	30	1.19
P_8	20	0.95

Which of the above projects should be accepted?

Solution

It has already been pointed out that the projects should be selected on the basis of profitability under PI method and rank is assigned accordingly, subject to maximum utilisation of available funds showing:

Projects	Initial Outlay Rs.	Profitability Index (PI)	Rank
P_4	70,000	1.30	1
P_5	60,000	1.25	2
P_2	40,000	1.20	3
P_7	30,000	1.19	4
P_3	50,000	1.15	5
	2,50,000		
P_1	25,000	1.12	6
	2,75,000		

From the above, it becomes clear that the first projects should be selected as the optimum mix since they will completely utilise the available funds amounting to Rs. 2,50,000. Projects P_6 and P_8 are not included in above as their PI is less than unity (1) and, hence, are to be rejected.

Illustration 2.40

The following investment proposals along with their profitability index (PI) are:

Proposals	P_1	P_2	P_3	P_4
Initial outlay (in '000 rupees)	60	30	40	35
PI	1.13	1.12	1.12	1,09

Budgeted funds are Rs. 75,000

Select the most profitable project.

Solution

Profitability Statement on the Basis of PI Method

Proposals	PI	Rank
P_1	1.13	1
P_2	1.12	2
P_3	1.12	3
P_4	1.09	4

Here P_1 ranks first. But it does not utilise fully the available funds. If P_3 is selected alone, it will be worse than P_1. P_3 cannot be selected since its total requirements become Rs. 1,00,000 (Rs. 60,000 + Rs. 40,000) which is more than the available funds, viz. Rs. 75,000. Therefore, if P_3 and P_4 are selected available funds can completely be utilised. As such, the mix (P_3 and P_4) will be the most profitable projects and they will maximise the present value shown:

Mix	Proposals	Initial Rs.	Net Present Value	
1	P_1	60,000.	(1.13 - 1)	Rs. 7,800
2	P_2	40,000	(1.12 - 1)	Rs. 4,800
3	P_3	40,000	(1.12 - 1)	Rs. 4,800
	P_4	35,000	(1.09 - 1)	Rs. 3,150
				Rs. 7,950

Thus, the total NPV of proposal 3 is highest in comparison with Proposals 1 and 2. As such, the firm, in this case, will be able to utilise its scarce resources for optimum use.

Project Indivisibility

It has been highlighted above that selection of project must be in such a manner so as to maximise profitability, subject to the budget ceiling. Naturally, if this is strictly followed, then it is better to accept many lower order smaller projects (according to ranking) than to accept a single large project. Therefore, under capital rationing, a possibility of trade-off arises between the two types of projects. In other words, if a single large project is accepted, a series of small projects are rejected due to this indivisibility, i.e., a project is an entity to be accepted or rejected as a whole. It should be remembered that the problem of indivisibility may prove to be serious and make the entire selection process quite unwidely. The most efficient way for solving the same is the integer programming.[1]

Ranking-Error Problem

We know that any one of the DCF techniques can be used for ranking. Since there are different cash flow timings the three DCF techniques—viz., IRR, NPV and PI—present conflict in ranking as to the project which is known as ***'Ranking-Error Problem'***. The following illustration will make the principle of ***'Ranking-Error Problem'*** clear.

Illustration 2.41

From the information presented below, rank the projects after applying IRR, NPV and PI when each of them are as under:

Projects	IRR (%)	NPV (Rs.)	PI
P_1	12.25	1,00,000	1.25
P_2	11.02	– 80,000	0.94
P_3	18.50	75,000	1.15
P_4	16.26	90,000	1.12
P_5	15.50	40,000	1.18
P_6	13.25	25,000	1.07

Solution

Ranking by IRR, NPV and PI is:

Projects	Rank IRR	NPV	PI
P_1	5	1	1
P_2	6	6	6
P_3	1	3	3
P_4	2	2	4
P_5	3	4	2
P_6	4	5	5

From the above, it becomes clear that the DCF criteria rank the different projects in different ways. If there are no limit of funds, all the projects (excluding P_2) could be accepted by all the criteria. But if capital is rationed, different decisions are reached by each criterion.

That is, the IRR would suggest to accept projects P_3 and P_4 whereas the NPV would suggest to accept projects P_1 and P_4, and the PI would suggest to accept projects P_1 and P_5, respectively. Naturally, the question arises before us which one is the 'Correct Criterion'. The problem

1 Weingartner, H. M. — *Mathematical Programming and the Analysis of Capital Budgeting Problems* — Englewood Cliffs, N. J., Prentice-Hall, 1963.

arises due to the differing timing of the cash flow. However, the problem can be tackled if a common reinvestment rate is considered.[1]

Capital Rationing Using Graph

Sometimes funds for investment are strictly limited in the current period. After that the same are freely available at the prevailing rate of interest. Of course, if there is any liquidity crisis in a firm it will find out some financing sources even if the rate of interest becomes very high although the financing sources are limited. The effect of limits on funds can be portrayed with the help of a diagram (Fig. 7.4), where amount of capital in a period is shown on the horizontal axis whereas (average) cost of capital is shown on the vertical axis.

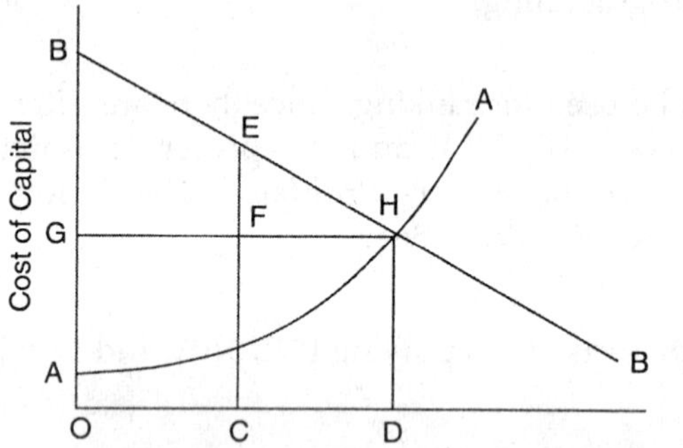

Fig. 2.4 : The Demand and Supply of Capital under Capital Rationing

The supply of capital at different costs of capital/prices is shown by AA curve. The increasing slope of the said curve (AA) reflects the higher marginal cost of each extra increment of funds. Curve BB represents the usual demand curve for funds. Here projects are ranked inversely in order to diminish profitability. As such, any point on this line shows the funds which are needed to finance those projects which have positive (+) NPV. (Where discounted at the cost of capital shown horizontally opposite on the Y axis, i.e. OD funds will be demanded when average cost of finance is OG).

Under the situation, the firm will try to utilize that amount of funds which are indicated by the intersection of the demand curve (BB) and supply curve (AA).

In the present case, the firm must raise OD funds and finance those projects which are represented by the BH segment of BB. It will give the greatest increment in net present worth. That is, such project to the left of H has a positive (+) NPV of discounted at OG and, at this rate of interest, the marginal project has a zero (O) NPV.

Therefore, from the above, it may be stated that the marginal project which is accepted simply covers its cost and all other projects which are accepted, yield a return over and above their financing which are indicated by the area covered by the line GHB in the diagram. If, on the other hand, investments cannot exceed, say, OC, the shareholders (equity) will forgo the NPV from those projects represented by EC. In that case, cost to equity shareholders is represented in Fig. 2.4 by the area covered by EFH which reveals the excess returns over the average cost of capital.

GENERAL ILLUSTRATIONS

Illustration 2.42

A company has an investment opportunity costing Rs. 40,000 with the following expected net cash flow (i.e., after tax and before depreciation):

Year	Net Cash Flow Rs.
1	7,000
2	7,000
3	7,000

Contd.

[1] Solomon, E. — *'The Arithmetic of Capital Budgeting Decision'* — Journal of Business, XXIX(2), April 1956.

	Rs.
4	7,000
5	7,000
6	8,000
7	10,000
8	15,000
9	10,000
10	4,000

Using 10% as the cost of capital (rate of discount) determine:

(i) Pay-Back period; (ii) Net present Value at 10% discounting factor; (iii) Profitability index at 10% discounting factor; (iv) Internal Rate of Return with the help of 10% discounting factor, and 15% discounting factor.

[C.A. Final]

Solution

(a) **Pay Back Period**

Year	Net Cash Flow
	Rs.
1	7,000
2	7,000
3	7,000
4	7,000
5	7,000
	35,000

From the above it is clear that Rs. 35,000 is recovered in 5 years and balance Rs. 5,000 (Rs. 40,000 – Rs. 35,000) to be recovered in $\frac{\text{Rs. } 5{,}000}{\text{Rs. } 8{,}000} = \frac{5}{8}$ years, or .62 years. Then, the Pay Back period is 5.62 years.

(b) **Net Present Value**

Year	Net Cash Flow	P.V. Factor at 10%	P.V. of N.C.F.
	Rs.		Rs.
1	7,000	0.909	6,363
2	7,000	0.826	5,782
3	7,000	0.751	5,257
4	7,000	0.683	4,781
5	7,000	0.621	4,347
6	8,000	0.564	4,512
7	10,000	0.513	5,130
8	15,000	0.467	7,005
9	10,000	0.424	4,240
10	4,000	0.386	1,544
			48,961
	Less: Initial Outlay		40,000
	Net Present Value		8,961

(c) **Profitability Index (PI)**

$$PI = \frac{\text{P.V. of N.C.F.}}{\text{Initial Cash Outlay}} = \frac{\text{Rs. } 48,961}{\text{Rs. } 40,000} = 1.22$$

(d) **Internal Rate of Return**

10% discount rate has already been calculated above. Now, at 15% discount rate, NPV is calculated:

Year	Net Cash Flow	P.V. Factor at 5%	P.V. of N.C.F.
	Rs.		Rs.
1	7,000	0.897	6,090
2	7,000	0.756	5,292
3	7,000	0.658	4,606
4	7,000	0.572	4,004
5	7,000	0.497	3,479
6	8,000	0.432	3,456
7	10,000	0.376	3,760
8	15,000	0.327	4,905
9	10,000	0.284	2,840
10	4,000	0.247	988
			39,420
	Less: Initial Outlay		40,000
	Net Present Value		(–) 580

From the above date, it becames clear that the NPV at 10% discount rate is positive which is in excess of Rs. 8,961. But, at 15% discount rate, the NPV is found to be negative. So the actual IRR will be slightly less than 15%. As per simple interpolation technique, the exact rate can be determined which is calculated as:

5% difference in rate of discount is equal to the sum of difference Rs. 9,541 (i.e., Rs. 48,961 – Rs. 39,420). As such, Rs. 580 difference would amount to 0.30% (Rs. 580 ÷ Rs. 9.541) × 5%.

Thus, the actual IRR = 15% – .30%

= 14.70%

Illustration 2.43

Calculate the 'Pay Back Period', 'Average Rate of Return', and 'Net Present Value' for a project which requires an initial outlay of Rs. 10,000 and generates year-ending cash flows of Rs. 6,000; Rs. 3,000; Rs. 2,000; Rs. 5,000 and Rs. 5,000 from the end of the first year to the end of the fifth year. The required rate of return is 10% and pays tax at 50% rate.

The project has a life of five years and is depreciated on straight line basis:

Year	Discounting Factor at 10%
1	.909
2	.826
3	.751
4	.683
5	.621

Solution

It is assumed that year-ending cash flow represents the cash flow before depreciation and tax.

Pay Back Period

Statement of Cash Flow

Year Ending	Cash Flow before Dep. and Tax	Depreciation	Profit before Tax	Tax @ 50%	Profit after Tax	Cash Flow (Profit after Tax and Dep.)
	Rs.	Rs.	Rs.	Rs.	Rs.	Rs.
1	6,000	2,000	4,000	2,000	2,000	4,000
2	3,000	2,000	1,000	500	500	2,500
3	2,000	2,000	—	—	—	2,000
4	5,000	2,000	3,000	1,500	1,500	3,500
5	5,000	2,000	3,000	1,500	1,500	3,500
	21,000				5,500	15,500
∴ Average ÷ 5	4,200				11,000	31,000

Pay Back Period = Rs. 4,000 + Rs. 2,500 + Rs. 2,000 = Rs. 8,500 for 3 years.
(since there is unequal cash inflow)

Balance (Rs. 10,000 – Rs. 8,500) = Rs. 1,500

∴ For the year $= \frac{\text{Rs. } 1,500}{\text{Rs. } 3,500} = \frac{3}{7}$

So, Pay Back Period is $= 3 + \frac{3}{7} = \frac{24}{7}$ or 3.43 years

Average Rate of Return

$$\text{ARR} = \frac{\text{Average Annual Profit after Tax}}{\text{Average Investment}} \times 100$$

$$= \frac{\text{Rs. } 1,100}{\text{Rs. } 5,000 \ (\text{Rs. } 10,000 \div 2)} \times 100$$

$$= 22\%$$

Net Present Value

Year	Cash Flow	Discount Factor @ 10%	P.V. of N.C.F.
	Rs.		Rs.
1	4,000	.909	3,636
2	2,500	.826	2,065
3	2,000	.751	1,502
4	3,500	.683	2,391
5	3,500	.621	2,174
			11,768
Less:	Initial Outlay		10,000
	Net Present Value		1,768

Illustration 2.44

B. Industries Ltd. purchased a machine five years ago. A proposal is under consideration to replace it by a new machine. The life of the machine is estimated to be 10 years. The existing machine can be sold at its written-down value.

As a cost accountant of the company you are required to submit your recommendations based on the following information:

	Existing Machine Rs.	New Machine Rs.
Initial Cost	25,000	50,000
Machine hours p.a.	2,000	2,000
Wages per running hour	1.25	1.25
Power per hour	0.50	2.00
Indirect Material p.a.	3,000	5,000
Other expenses p.a.	12,000	15,000
Cost of materials per unit	1	1
Number of units produced per hour	12	18
Selling prices per unit	2	2

Interest to be paid at 10% on fresh Capital invested.

[I.C.W.A. Final]

Solution

Comparative Profitability Statement

		Existing Machine Rs.		New Machine Rs.
Sales				
24,000 (2,000 × 12) × Rs. 2		48,000		—
36,000 (2,000 × 18) × Rs. 2		—		72,000
		48,000		72,000
	Rs.		Rs.	
Less: Cost of Materials	24,000		36,000	
Wages (2,000 × 1.25)	2,500		2,500	
Power (2,000 × 0.50)	1,000			
(2,000 × 2)			4,000	
Indirect Materials	3,000		5,000	
Other Expenses	12,000		15,000	
Depreciation	2,500		5,000	
Interest on Capital @ 10% on (50,000 – 12,500)	—		3,750	
		45,000		71,250
Profit		3,000		750
Selling Price per unit		2.00		2.00
Cost Price per unit (45,000 ÷ 24,000)		1.88		1.98
(71,250 ÷ 36,000)				
Profit per unit		0.12		0.02

Hence, the existing machine should be continued since its per unit profit is more than the new machine.

Illustration 2.45

A company has to select one of the two alternative projects whose particulars are:

	Project E	Project F
	Rs.	Rs.
Initial outlay	11,872	10,067
Net Cash Flow :		
End of year 1	10,000	1,000
" " " 2	2,000	1,000
" " " 3	1,000	2,000
" " " 4	1,000	10,000

The company can arrange necessary funds at 8%. Compute Net Present Value and Internal Rate of Return of each project and comment on the results.

Is there any contradiction in the above results? If so, state the reasons for such contradiction.

The P.V. of Re. 1 to be received at the end of the each year at different costs of capital is given:

Year	8%	10%	12%	14%
1	0.926	0.909	0.893	0.877
2	0.857	0.826	0.797	0.770
3	0.794	0.751	0.712	0.675
4	0.735	0.683	0.636	0.592

Solution

(a) Computation of Net Present Value

Project E				Project F			
Year	**Net Cash Flow**	**P.V. Factor at 10%**	**Present Value**	**Year**	**Net Cash Flow**	**P.V. Factor at 10%**	**Present Value**
1	10,000	0.926	9,260	1	1,000	0.926	926
2	2,000	0.857	1,714	2	1,000	0.857	857
3	1,000	0.794	794	3	2,000	0.794	1,588
4	1,000	0.735	735	4	10,000	0.735	7,350
			12,503				10,721
Less :	Initial Outlay		11,872	*Less :*	Initial Outlay		10,067
	Net Present Value		631		Net Present Value		654

Comment

Since NPV of Project F is higher than NPV of Project E, Project F should be undertaken although both the projects have positive NPV.

Yes, there is a contradiction in the result. The contradiction is that by investing lesser amount i.e., Rs. 10,000, in case of Project F, NPV is higher than project E although investment in Project E is more.

Moreover, Net Cash Flow in case of Project E is gradually decreasing whereas, in case of Project F, the same is gradually increasing.

(b) Computation of Internal Rate of Return

For Project E **Discount 12%**

Discount Rate at 10%

Year	Cash Flow	P.V. Factor at 10%	P.V. of NCF	P.V. of Re. 1	P.V. of NCF
	Rs.		Rs.		Rs.
1	10,000	0.909	9,090	0.893	8,930
2	2,000	0.826	1,652	0.797	1,594
3	1,000	0.751	751	0.712	712
4	1,000	0.683	683	0.636	636
			12,176		11,872

Since, exact amount of Rs. 11,872 comes out, i.e., as per initial outlay, IRR will be 12%

For Project F **Discount 10%**

Discount Rate at 12%

Year	Cash Flow	P.V. Factor at 12%	P.V. of NCF	P.V. Factor at 10%	P.V. of NCF
	Rs.		Rs.		Rs.
1	1,000	0.893	893	0.909	909
2	1,000	0.797	797	0.826	826
3	2,000	0.712	1,424	0.751	1,502
4	10,000	0.636	6,360	0.683	6,830
			9,474		10,067

Since, exact amount of initial outlay comes out, i.e., 10,067 at 10% discount factor, hence, IRR will be @ 10%.

Illustration 2.46

Z Ltd. are thinking of investing in a project costing Rs. 20 lakhs. The life of the project is 5 years and the estimated salvage value of the project is zero. Straight line method of charging depreciation is followed. The tax rat is 50%. The expected cash flows before tax are as follows:

Year	—	1	2	3	4	5
Estimated cash flow before depreciation and tax (Rs. in lakhs)	—	4	6	8	8	10

You are required to determine the: (i) Pay back period for the investment; (ii) Average Rate of Return on the Investment; (iii) Net Present Value at 10% Cost of Capital; (iv) Benefit-Cost Ratio; (v) Internal Rate of Return.

[I.C.W.A. Final—Adapted]

Solution

(i) Pack Back Period

Computations of Annual Cash Flows (after tax)

Year	Cash Flow (before Dep. and Tax)	Depreciation $\left(\frac{\text{Rs. 20,00,000}}{\text{5 years}}\right)$	Profit before Tax	Tax @ 50%	Profit after Tax	Net Cash Inflow	Cumulative Cash Inflow
Col (1)	(2)	(3)	(4)	(5)	(6)	(7) = (3)–(6)	(8)
	Rs.	Rs.				Rs.	Rs.
1	4,00,000	4,00,000	—	—	—	4,00,000	4,00,000
2	6,00,000	4,00,000	2,00,000	1,00,000	1,00,000	5,00,000	9,00,000

Contd.

	Rs.	Rs.				Rs.	Rs.
3	8,00,000	4,00,000	4,00,000	2,00,000	2,00,000	6,00,000	15,00,000
4	8,00,000	4,00,000	4,00,000	2,00,000	2,00,000	6,00,000	21,00,000
5	10,00,000	4,00,000	6,00,000	3,00,000	3,00,000	7,00,000	28,00,000
					8,00,000		

In 3rd year cumulative cash flows are Rs. 15,00,000 and in 4th year Rs. 21,00,000 i.e. pay back period lies in between 2nd and 3rd year as the initial investment of Rs. 2,00,000 lie in between item.

Thus, the Pay Back Period will be $= 3 \text{ years} + \dfrac{\text{Rs. } 5{,}00{,}000 \text{ (i.e. Rs. } 20{,}00{,}000 - \text{Rs. } 15{,}00{,}000)}{\text{Rs. } 6{,}00{,}000 \text{ (Rs. } 21{,}00{,}000 - \text{Rs. } 15{,}00{,}000)}$

$= 3 \text{ years} + .83 \text{ years}$

$= 3.83 \text{ years}$

(ii) **Average Rate of Return (ARR)**

$$\text{ARR} = \frac{\text{Average Annual Profit (After Tax)}}{\text{Average Investments}} \times 100$$

$= \text{where, Average Annual Profit} = \dfrac{\text{Rs. } 8{,}00{,}000}{5} = \text{Rs. } 1{,}60{,}000$

$\text{Average Investment} = \dfrac{\text{Rs. } 20{,}00{,}000}{2}$

$= \text{Rs. } 10{,}00{,}000$

$= \dfrac{\text{Rs. } 1{,}60{,}000}{\text{Rs. } 10{,}00{,}000} \times 100$

$= 16\%$

(iii) **Net Present Value** (at 10% cost of Capital)

Year	Cash Inflow (after Tax)	Discount Factor at 10%	P.V. of NCF
	Rs.		Rs.
1	4,00,000	0.9091	3,63,640
2	5,00,000	0.8264	4,13,200
3	6,00,000	0.7513	4,50,780
4	6,00,000	0.6830	4,09,800
5	7,00,000	0.6209	4,34,630
			20,72,050
	Less: Initial Investment		20,00,000
	Net Present Value		72,050

(iv) **Benefit Cost Ratio, i.e. Profitability Index (PI)**

$$\text{PI} = \frac{\text{P.V. of NCF}}{\text{Initial Cash Outlay}}$$

$= \dfrac{\text{Rs. } 20{,}72{,}050}{\text{Rs. } 20{,}00{,}000}$

$= 1.036$

(v) **Internal Rate of Return (IRR)**

10% discount rate has already been calculated above which presents a reasonable amount of positive figure. Now it may be suggested that the rate must lie in between 11% and 12% i.e., Trial and Error method should be followed as there were unequal Cash flows.

Profitability Statement

Year	Cash Inflows Rs.	Discount Rate at 11% P.V. on Re. 1	P.V. of NCF Rs.	Discount Rate at 12% P.V. of Re. 1	P.V. of NCF Rs.
1	4,00,000	0.901	3,60,400	0.893	3,57,200
2	5,00,000	0.812	4,06,000	0.797	3,98,500
3	6,00,000	0.731	4,38,600	0.712	4,27,200
4	6,00,000	0.659	3,95,400	0.636	3,81,600
5	7,00,000	0.593	4,15,100	0.567	3,96,900
			20,15,500		19,61,400

Thus, from the above statement it becomes clear that the actual rate will be in between 11% and 12% which may be found out with the help of the following:

Discount Rate	P.V. of NCF
11%	20,15,500
12%	19,61,400
1%	54,100

$$\therefore \quad \text{Actual Rate} = 11\% + \frac{(\text{Rs. } 15{,}500 \text{ i.e. Rs. } 20{,}15{,}500 - \text{Rs. } 20{,}00{,}000)}{\text{Rs. } 54{,}100} \times 1\% \ (12\% - 11\%)$$

$$= 11\% + 0.286\%$$

$= 11.286\%$ or 11.29% (i.e. at this rate Initial Investment and P.V. of NCF will be equal or NPV will be zero.)

Illustration 2.47

A company is contemplating to purchase a machine. Two machines A and B are available, each costing Rs. 5 lakhs. In comparing the profitability of the machines, a discount rate of 10% is to be used and the machine is to be written-off in 5 years by straight line method at depreciation with nil residual value.

Cash flow after tax are expected as:

Year	Machine A Rs.	Machine B Rs.
1	1,50,000	50,000
2	2,00,000	1,50,000
3	2,50,000	2,00,000
4	1,50,000	3,00,000
5	1,00,000	2,00,000

Indicates which machine would be profitable using the following methods of ranking investments proposals:

(i) Pay Back Method; (ii) Net Present Value Method; (iii) Profitability Index Method; and (iv) Average Rate of Return Method.

The discounting factors at 10% are:

Year	—	1	2	3	4	5
Discounting factor	—	0.990	0.826	0.751	0.683	0.621

[C.S. Final]

Solution

(i) Pay Back Period

Computation of Annual Cash Flow

Machine A				Machine B	
Year	Annual Cash Flow Rs.	Cumulative Cash Flow Rs.	Year	Annual Cash Flow Rs.	Cumulative Cash Inflow Rs.
1	1,50,000	1,50,000	1	50,000	50,000
2	2,00,000	3,50,000	2	1,50,000	2,00,000
3	2,50,000	6,00,000	3	2,00,000	4,00,000
4	1,50,000	7,50,000	4	3,00,000	7,00,000
5	1,00,000	8,50,000	5	2,00,000	9,00,000

For Machine A

In 2nd year cumulative cash flows are Rs. 3,50,000, and in 3rd year Rs. 6,00,000, i.e. pay back period lies in between 2nd and 3rd as the initial investment of Rs. 5,00,000 lies in-between them.

$$\text{Thus, the Pay Back Period will be} = 2 \text{ years} + \frac{1,50,000}{\text{Rs. } 2,50,000}$$

$$= 2 \text{ years} + .6 \text{ years}$$

$$= 2.6 \text{ years.}$$

For Machine B

In 3rd year cumulative Cash flows are R. 4,00,000 in a 4th year Rs. 7,00,000 i.e. pay back period lies in between 3rd and 4th year as the initial investment of Rs. 5,00,000 lies in between them.

$$\text{Thus, the Pay Back Period will be} = 3 \text{ years} + \frac{1,00,000}{\text{Rs. } 3,00,000}$$

$$= 3 \text{ years} + .33 \text{ years}$$

$$= 3.33 \text{ years.}$$

∴ Rank : Machine A = First
Machine B = Second

Hence, Machine A should be purchased as its pay back period is less than the pay back period of machine B.

(ii) Net Present Value Method

Computation of Net Present Value of Machine A and Machine B

Year	Annual Cash Flow Rs.	Discount Factor 10%	P.V. of NCF Rs.	Annual Cash Flow Rs.	Discount Factor at 10%	P.V. of NCF Rs.
1	1,50,000	0.909	1,36,350	50,000	0.909	45,450
2	2,00,000	0.826	1,65,200	1,50,000	0.826	1,23,900
3	2,50,000	0.751	1,87,750	2,00,000	0.751	1,50,200
4	1,50,000	0.683	1,02,450	3,00,000	0.683	2,04,900
5	1,00,000	0.621	62,100	2,00,000	0.621	1,24,200
			6,53,850			6,48,650
Less :	Initial Investment		5,00,000	*Less :* Initial Investment		5,00,000
	Net Present Value		1,53,850			1,48,650

Since, Machine A has more NPV in comparison with Machine B, Machine A is recommended.

∴ Rank: Machine A = First

Machine B = Second

(iii) **Profitability Index Method**

Machine A $= PI = \dfrac{\text{P.V. of NCF}}{\text{Initial Cash Outlay}} = \dfrac{\text{Rs. } 6{,}53{,}850}{\text{Rs. } 5{,}00{,}000} = 1.31;$ Rank = First

Machine B $= PI = \dfrac{\text{P.V. of NCF}}{\text{Initial Cash Outlay}} = \dfrac{\text{Rs. } 6{,}48{,}650}{\text{Rs. } 5{,}00{,}000} = 1.30;$ Rank = Second

∴ Machine A is profitable to purchase.

(iv) **Average Rate of Return (ARR)**

$$ARR = \frac{\text{Average Annual Profit after Tax}}{\text{Average Investment}} \times 100$$

		Machine A	Machine B
		Rs.	Rs.
	Average Annual Profit =	8,50,000	9,00,000
Less :	Depn. for 5 years (Rs. 1,00,000 × 5)	5,00,000	5,00,000
	Profit after Depreciation	3,50,000	4,00,000
∴	Average Profit	$= \frac{3{,}50{,}000}{5}$	$= \frac{4{,}00{,}000}{5}$
		= Rs. 70,000	= Rs. 80,000
	Average Investment	= Rs. 5,00,000 ÷ 2	= Rs. 5,00,000 ÷ 2
		= Rs. 2,50,000	= Rs. 2,50,000
∴	PI	$= \frac{\text{Rs. } 70{,}000}{\text{Rs. } 2{,}50{,}000} \times 100$	$\frac{80{,}000}{\text{Rs. } 2{,}50{,}000} \times 100$
		= 28%	= 32%

Hence, Machine B is more profitable.

Rank— Machine B = First

Machine A = Second

Illustration 2.48

EEC Ltd. is considering the purchase of a machine—Two machines LM and RM are available, each costing Rs. 1,00,000. Both machines will last for 5 years with no residual value. In comparing the profitability of the machinery a discount rate of 10% is to be used.

Earnings after taxation @ 40% and charging depreciation on straight line are expected to be as:

Year	LM	RM
	Rs.	Rs.
1	10,000	(10,000) Loss
2	20,000	1,00,000
3	30,000	20,000
4	10,000	40,000
5	Nil	20,000

Indicate which machine would be a more profitable investment under the various methods of ranking investment proposals, viz., ARR, Pay Back, NPV and PI.

Note : Present value interest factor @ 10% p.a.

Period	0	1	2	3	4	5
Factory	1,000	0.909	0.826	0.751	0.683	0.621

[C.S. Final]

Solution

(a) **Computation of ARR**

$$\text{ARR} = \frac{\text{Average Annual Profit after Tax}}{\text{Average Investment}} \times 100$$

Average Annual Profit		**Machine LM**		**Machine RM**
		Rs.		Rs.
Total Profit after depn. and tax:				
(Rs. 10,000 + Rs. 20,000 + Rs. 30,000 + Rs. 10,000)		70,000		—
(– Rs. 10,000 + Rs. 10,000 + Rs. 20,000 + Rs. 40,000 + Rs. 20,000)		—		80,000
		70,000		80,000
∴ Average Profit	=	$\frac{\text{Rs. } 70,000}{5}$	=	$\frac{\text{Rs. } 80,000}{5}$
	=	Rs. 14,000	=	Rs. 16,000
Average Investment =	=	$\frac{\text{Rs. } 1,00,000}{2}$	=	$\frac{\text{Rs. } 1,00,000}{2}$
	=	Rs. 50,000	=	Rs. 50,000
∴ ARR	=	$\frac{\text{Rs. } 14,000}{\text{Rs. } 50,000} \times 100$	=	$\frac{\text{Rs. } 16,000}{\text{Rs. } 50,000} \times 100$
	=	28%	=	32%
∴ Rank		2nd		1st

Thus, Machine RM is more profitable than machine LM.

(b) **Pay Back Method**

Computation of Cash Flows

Year	Machine LM Cash Flow	Dep.	Cash Inflow	Cumulative Cash Inflow	Machine RM Cash Flow	Dep.	Cash Inflow	Cumulative Cash Inflow
	Rs.	Rs.	Rs.	Rs.	Rs.	Rs.	Rs.	Rs.
1	10,000	20,000	30,000	30,000	(–)10,000	20,000	10,000	10,000
2	20,000	20,000	40,000	70,000	10,000	20,000	30,000	40,000
3	30,000	20,000	50,000	1,20,000	20,000	20,000	40,000	80,000
4	10,000	20,000	30,000	1,50,000	40,000	20,000	60,000	1,40,000
5	Nil	20,000	20,000	1,70,000	20,000	20,000	40,000	1,80,000

For Machine LM

In 2nd year Cumulative Cash flows are Rs. 70,000 and in 3rd year Rs. 1,20,000, i.e., pay back period lies in-between 2nd and 3rd year as the initial investment of Rs. 1,00,000 lies in-between them.

$$\text{Thus, the Pay Back period will be} = 2 \text{ years} + \frac{\text{Rs. } 30,000}{\text{Rs. } 50,000}$$

$$= 2 \text{ years} + .6 \text{ years}$$

$$= 2.6 \text{ years.}$$

For Machine RM

In 3rd year cumulative cash flows are Rs. 80,000 and in 4th year Rs. 1,40,000; i.e. pay back period lies in between 2nd year and 3rd year as the initial investment of Rs. 1,00,000 lie in-between them.

$$\text{Thus, the Pay Back Period will be} = 3 \text{ years} + \frac{\text{Rs. } 20{,}000}{\text{Rs. } 60{,}000}$$

$$= 3 \text{ years} + .33 \text{ years}$$

$$= 3.33 \text{ years.}$$

Rank— Machine LM = First

Machine RM = Second

Hence, it is more profitable to purchase Machine LM since the pay back period is comparatively short.

(c) **Computation of NPV**

Machine LM				Machine RM			
Year	**Cash Flow**	**Discount Factor at 10%**	**P.V. of NCF**	**Year**	**Cash Flow**	**Discount Factor at 10%**	**P.V. of NCF**
	Rs.		Rs.		Rs.		Rs.
1	30,000	0.909	27,270	1	10,000	0.909	9,090
2	40,000	0.826	33,040	2	30,000	0.826	24,780
3	50,000	0.751	37,550	3	40,000	0.751	30,040
4	30,000	0.683	20,490	4	60,000	0.683	40,980
5	20,000	0.621	12,420	5	40,000	0.621	24,840
			1,30,770				1,29,730
Less: Initial Investment			1,00,000	*Less:* Initial Investment			1,00,000
Net Present Value			30,770	Net Present Value			29,730
Rank			1st				2nd

Hence, it is more profitable to purchase Machine LM as its NPV is greater than Machine RM as per NPV method.

(d) **Profitability Index (PI) Method**

$$\text{PI} = \frac{\text{P.V. of NCF}}{\text{Initial Cash Outlay}}$$

$$\text{Machine LM} = \frac{\text{Rs. } 1{,}30{,}770}{\text{Rs. } 10{,}00{,}000} \qquad \text{Machine RM} = \frac{\text{Rs. } 1{,}29{,}730}{\text{Rs. } 1{,}00{,}000}$$

$$= 1.31 \qquad = 1.30$$

Rank 1st 2nd

Hence, it is more profitable to purchase Machines LM than to purchase Machine RM as per PI method.

Illustration 2.49

Gama & Co. wants to replace its old machine with new automatic machine. Two models Zee and Chee are available at the same cost of Rs. 5,00,000 each. Salvage value of the old machine is Rs. 1,00,000. The utilities of the existing machine can be used if the company selects Zee. Additional cost of utilities to be purchased in that case are Rs. 1,00,000. If the company purchases Chee then all the existing utilities will have to be replaced with new utilities costing Rs. 2,00,000. The salvage value of the old utilities will be Rs. 20,000.

The cash flows are expected to be:

Year	Zee Rs.	Chee Rs.
1	1,00,000	2,00,000
2	1,50,000	2,10,000
3	1,80,000	1,80,000
4	2,00,000	1,70,000
5	1,70,000	40,000
Salvage value at the end of 5 years	50,000	60,000

The targeted return on capital is 15%.

You are required to compute, for two machines separately, (a) Net Present Value, (b) Discounted Pay Back Period, (c) Desirability Factor, and (d) Advise which of the machines is to be selected.

Solution **[C.A. Final]**

Computation of Net Cash Outlay

	Model Zee Rs.	Model Chee Rs.
Cost of Machine	5,00,000	5,00,000
Add: Additional Cost of Utilities	1,00,000	2,00,000
	6,00,000	7,00,000
Less: Salvage Value	1,00,000	1,00,000
	5,00,000	6,00,000
Less: Salvage Value of old utilities	—	20,000
Net Cash Outlay	5,00,000	5,80,000

(a) **Computation of Net Present Value**

Model Zee				Model Chee			
Year	Cash Flow Rs.	P.V. Factor at 15%	P.V. of NCF Rs.	Year	Cash Flow Rs.	P.V. Factor at 15%	P.V. of NCF Rs.
1	1,00,000	0.870	87,000	1	2,00,000	0.870	1,74,000
2	1,50,000	0.756	1,13,400	2	2,10,000	0.756	1,58,760
3	1,80,000	0.658	1,18,440	3	1,80,000	0.658	1,18,440
4	2,00,000	0.572	1,14,400	4	1,70,000	0.572	97,240
5	1,70,000	0.497	1,09,340	5	40,000	0.497	49,700
			5,42,580				5,98,140
Less: Initial Investment			5,00,000	*Less:* Initial Investment			5,00,000
Net Present Value			42,580	Net Present Value			98,140

(b) **Computation of Discounted Pay Back Period**

Model Zee			Model Chee		
Year	P.V. of NCF Rs.	Cumulative P.V. of NCF Rs.	Year	P.V. of NCF Rs.	Cumulative P.V. of NCF Rs.
1	87,000	87,000	1	1,74,000	1,74,000
2	1,13,400	2,00,400	2	1,58,760	3,32,760
3	1,18,440	3,18,440	3	1,18,440	4,51,200
4	1,14,400	4,33,240	4	97,240	5,48,440
5	1,09,340	5,42,580	5	49,700	5,98,140

For Model Zee

In 4th year, the cumulative PV of Cash flows are Rs. 4,33,240 and in 5th year Rs. 5,42,580; i.e. the pay back period lies in between 4th and 5th years as the initial investment of Rs. 5,00,000 lie in between them.

$$\text{Thus, the Pay Back Period will be} = 4 \text{ years} + \frac{\text{Rs. } 66{,}760}{\text{Rs. } 1{,}09{,}340}$$

$$= 4 \text{ years} + .61 \text{ years}$$

$$= 4.61 \text{ years}$$

For Model Chee

In 4th year, the cumulative PV of cash flows are Rs. 5,48,490 and in 5th year Rs. 5,98,140; i.e. the pay back period lies in-between 4th and 5th years as the initial investment of Rs. 5,80,000 lie in-between them.

$$\text{Thus, the Pay Back Period will be} = 4 \text{ years} + \frac{\text{Rs. } 31{,}560}{\text{Rs. } 49{,}700}$$

$$= 4 \text{ years} + .64 \text{ years}$$

$$= 4.64 \text{ years}$$

(c) **Computation of Desirability Factor or Profitability Index**

$$PI = \frac{\text{PV of NCF}}{\text{Initial Cash Outlay}}$$

$$\text{Model Zee} = \frac{\text{Rs. } 5{,}42{,}580}{\text{Rs. } 5{,}00{,}000} = 1.09 \qquad \text{Model Chee} = \frac{\text{Rs. } 5{,}98{,}140}{\text{Rs. } 5{,}80{,}000} = 1.03$$

(d) On the basis of the above information; conclusions may be drawn as:

				Rank
Model Zee	=	N P V	Rs. 42,580	1st
Model Chee	=	N P V	Rs. 18,140	2nd

Model Zee	=	Discount Pay Back Period	= 4.61	1st
Model Chee	=	"	= 4.64	2nd
Model Zee	=	PI	= 1.09	1st
Model Chee	=	"	= 1.03	2nd

Comment

It becomes quite clear from the above that Model Zee is better after testing the three different methods of capital budgeting techniques. As such, Model Zee should be purchased.

Illustration 2.50

A company is considering the replacement of its existing machine which is obsolete and unable to meet the rapidly rising demand for its product. The company is faced with two alternatives : to buy Machine A which is similar to the existing machine or to go for Machine B which is more expensive and has much greater capacity. The cash flows at the present level of operations under the two alternatives are:

Machine	Immediate Cash Outlay (Rs. in lakhs)	Cash Flows (in lakhs) 1st yr.	2nd yr.	3rd yr.	4th yr.	5th yr.
Machine A	25	—	5	20	14	14
Machine B	40	10	14	16	17	15

The company's cost of capital is 10%. The finance manager tries to appraise the machine by calculating the following: (i) Net Present Value; (ii) Profitability Index; (iii) Pay Back Period; and (iv) Discounted Pay Back Period.

At the end of his calculation, however, the finance manager is unable to make up his mind as to which machine to recommend.

You are required to make these calculations and, in the light thereof, to advise the finance manager about the proposed investments.

Present value of Re 1 at 10% discount rates are:

Year	0	1	2	3	4	5
PV	1.00	0.91	0.83	0.75	0.68	0.62

[C.A. Final]

Solution

(i) **Net Present Value**

Machine A				Machine B			
Year	**Cash Flow** Rs.	**P.V. Factor at 10%**	**P.V. of NCF** Rs.	**Year**	**Cash Flow** Rs.	**P.V. Factor at 15%**	**P.V. of NCF** Rs.
1	—	0.91	—	1	10,00,000	0.91	9,10,000
2	5,00,000	0.83	4,15,000	2	14,00,000	0.83	11,62,000
3	20,00,000	0.75	15,00,000	3	16,00,000	0.75	12,00,000
4	14,00,000	0.68	9,52,000	4	17,00,000	0.68	11,56,000
5	14,00,000	0.62	8,68,000	5	15,00,000	0.62	9,30,000
			37,35,000				53,58,000
Less: Initial Investment			25,00,000	*Less:* Initial Investment			40,00,000
Net Present Value			12,35,000	Net Present Value			13,58,000
Rank			1st				2nd

(ii) **Profitability Index (PI)**

$$PI = \frac{\text{P.V. of NCF}}{\text{Initial Outlay}}$$

Machine A $= \frac{\text{Rs. } 37,35,000}{\text{Rs. } 25,00,000} = 1.49$ Machine B $= \frac{\text{Rs. } 53,58,000}{\text{Rs. } 40,00,000} = 1.34$

Rank: Machine A — 1st; Machine B — 2nd

(iii) **Pay Back Period**

Machine A			Machine B		
Year	**Cash Flow** Rs.	**Cumulative Cash Flows** Rs.	**Year**	**Cash Flow** Rs.	**Cumulative Cash Flows** Rs.
1	—	—	1	10,00,000	10,00,000
2	5,00,000	5,00,000	2	14,00,000	24,00,000
3	20,00,000	25,00,000	3	16,00,000	40,00,000
4	14,00,000	39,00,000	4	17,00,000	57,00,000
5	14,00,000	53,00,000	5	15,00,000	72,00,000

It is interesting to note that in both the cases the pay back period is 3 years. In case of Machine A initial investment was Rs. 25,00,000 against the cash flows of 3 years and same in case of Machine B also, i.e., initial investments of Rs. 40,00,000.

(iv) **Discounted Pay Back**

Machine A			Machine B		
Year	PV of NCF	Cumulative PV of Cash Flows	Year	PV of NCF	Cumulative PV of Cash Flows
	Rs.	Rs.		Rs.	Rs.
1	—	—	1	9,10,000	9,10,000
2	4,15,000	4,15,000	2	11,62,000	20,72,000
3	15,00,000	19,15,000	3	12,00,000	32,72,000
4	9,52,000	28,67,000	4	11,56,000	44,28,000
5	8,68,000	37,35,000	5	9,30,000	53,58,000

For Machine A

In 3rd year, Cumulative PV of cash flows were Rs. 19,15,000 and in 4th year of Rs. 28,67,000, i.e. the pay back period lies in between 3rd and 4th year as the initial investments of Rs. 25,00,000 lie in-between them.

Thus, the Discounted Pay Back Period will be $= 3 \text{ years} + \frac{\text{Rs. } 5{,}85{,}000}{\text{Rs. } 9{,}52{,}000}$

$= 3 \text{ years} + .61 \text{ years}$

$= 3.61 \text{ years}$

For Machine B

In 3rd year, cumulative PV of cash flows were Rs. 32,72,000 and in 4th year Rs. 44,28,000, i.e. the pay back period lies in between 3rd and 4th year as the initial investment of Rs. 40,00,000 lie in between them.

Thus, the Discounted Pay Back Period will be $= 3 \text{ years} + \frac{\text{Rs. } 7{,}28{,}000}{\text{Rs. } 11{,}56{,}000}$

$= 3 \text{ years} + .63 \text{ years}$

$= 3.63 \text{ years}$

Comment (on the basis of the following result)

Method	Machine A	Machine B	Rank 1st	Rank 2nd
NPV	Rs. 12,35,000	Rs. 13,58,000	Machine B	Machine A
PI	1.49	1.34	Machine A	Machine B
PB	3 years	3 years	No difference	
DPB	3.61 years	3.63 years	Machine A	Machine B

From the above, apparently it is better to purchase Machine A since its PI, PB and DPB are better than Machine B. But, since there is a demand of the product and it is rising rapidly it is advisable to purchase Machine B.

Illustration 2.51

The following statements give quantitative considerations relevant for the ranking of Projects A and B:

Criteria	Project A	Project B
Investment	Rs. 400	Rs. 300
Internal Rate of Return	Nearly 18%	Nearly 20%
Net Present Value at 6% discount factor	Rs. 542.7	Rs. 421.2
Net Present Value at 6% discount factor	Rs. 142.7	Rs. 121.2
Net Present Value at 12% discount factor	Rs. 60.5	Rs. 60.5

Project A required an investment of Rs. 400 and was expected to have cash inflow of Rs. 110, Rs. 120, Rs. 130, Rs. 140 and Rs. 150 over its 5-year economic life. Project B involved an investment of Rs. 300 and was expected to have cash inflows of Rs. 100 each year over its five year economic life.

Which of the two projects will you select if cost of capital is (i) 10%, (ii) 12%, and (iii) 15%?

Give reasons in support of your decisions.

(*Note:* PV Table may be consulted for PV factors.)

[C.A. Final]

Solution

Before giving decision, we are to calculate the profitability index (PI) which is one of the best among DCF criteria, of the two projects together with the consideration of IRR.

Project A:

Years	Cash Flows	Discount Rate 10%		Discount Rate 12%		Discount Rate 15%	
		P.V. Factor	P.V. of N.C.F.	P.V. Factor	P.V. of N.C.F.	P.V. Factor	P.V. of N.C.F.
	Rs.		Rs.		Rs.		Rs.
1	110	0.909	99.99	0.893	98.23	0.870	95.70
2	120	0.826	99.12	0.797	95.64	0.756	90.72
3	130	0.751	97.63	0.712	92.56	0.658	85.54
4	140	0.683	95.62	0.636	89.04	0.572	80.08
5	150	0.621	93.15	0.567	85.05	0.497	74.55
	650		485.51		460.52		426.59

Profitability Index

$$= \frac{\text{P.V. of N.C.F.}}{\text{Initial Cash Outlay}} \qquad = \frac{485.51}{400} = 1.21 \qquad = \frac{460.52}{400} = 1.15 \qquad = \frac{426.59}{400} = 1.07$$

Project B :

Years	Cash Flows	Discount Rate 10%		Discount Rate 12%		Discount Rate 15%	
		P.V. Factor	P.V. of N.C.F.	P.V. Factor	P.V. of N.C.F.	P.V. Factor	P.V. of N.C.F.
	Rs.		Rs.		Rs.		Rs.
1	100	0.909	90.9	0.893	89.3	0.870	87.0
2	100	0.826	82.6	0.797	79.7	0.756	75.6
3	100	0.751	75.1	0.712	71.2	0.658	65.8
4	100	0.683	68.3	0.636	63.6	0.572	57.2
5	100	0.621	62.1	0.567	56.7	0.497	49.7
			379.0		360.5		335.3

Profitability Index

Profitability Index	$= \frac{379.0}{300}$	$= \frac{360.5}{300}$	$= \frac{335.3}{300}$
	= 1.26	= 1.20	= 1.12

Thus, the results are:

	Project A	Project B
Investment	Rs. 400	Rs. 300
IRR	Nearly 18%	Nearly 20%
Profitability Index		
at 10%	1.21	1.26
at 12%	1.15	1.20
at 15%	1.07	1.12

ASSIGNMENT MATERIALS

THEORETICAL

Multiple Choice Questions

1. (a) Traditional method of investment criteria is:

(i) NPV Method (ii) IRR Method
(iii) ARR Method (iv) None of these

(b) DCF techniques is:

(i) ARR Method (ii) NPV Method
(iii) Pay Back Method (iv) None of these

(c) IRR comes under:

(i) Traditional Method (ii) DCF Method
(iii) Old Method (iv) None of these

(d) ARR is computed as:

(i) $\frac{\text{Average Annual Profit}}{\text{Average Investment}}$ (ii) $\frac{\text{Average Investment}}{\text{Average NCF}}$

(iii) $\frac{\text{Average NCF}}{\text{Initial Outlay}}$ (iv) None of these

(e) Pay Back Period is computed as:

(i) $\frac{\text{Cost of Investment}}{\text{Annual Net Cash Flow}}$ (ii) $\frac{\text{Initial Outlay}}{\text{Average Investment}}$

(iii) $\frac{\text{PV of NCF}}{\text{Average Investment}}$ (iv) None of these

(f) NPV is positive when:

(i) NPV < 0 (ii) NPV > 0
(iii) NPV = 0 (iv) None of these

(g) PI is found out as:

(i) $\frac{\text{PV of NCF}}{\text{Initial Outlay}}$ (ii) $\frac{\text{Initial Outlay}}{\text{Average Investment}}$

(iii) $\frac{\text{Initial Outlay}}{\text{PV of NCF}}$ (iv) None of these

(h) NPV is positive when:

(i) PI >1 (ii) PI < 1

(iii) PI = 0 (iv) None of these

[Ans. (a) (iii); (b) (ii); (c) (ii); (d) (i); (e) (i); (f) (i); (g) (i); (h) (i)]

Short Answer-type Questions

2. What are capital expenditures? Discuss the importance of capital budgeting.
3. How do you ascertain the 'planning period for the decisions'?
4. What are the various types of investment decisions?

   Define 'Accept-Reject Decisions' in this respect.
5. Define and explain with their respective merits and demerits:
   (a) Average Rate of Return;
   (b) Pay Back Period; and
   (c) Discounted Pay Back Method.
6. (a) Explain the concept of 'average investment' as used in connection with ROI.

   (b) Why Pay Back Period Method of project evaluation is considered to be conceptually unsound?

   [C.U. M.B.M.]
7. Account for the extensive use of the 'Pay Back Period' in capital budgeting decisions in spite of certain irrationalities inherent in it.

   [C.U. M.Com.]
8. Explain the salient features of the 'Present Value Method' of project evaluation and examine its rationality.
9. Explain how the 'Present Value Method' and 'Internal Rate of Return' differ as a criteria for evaluating capital expenditure projects.

   [C.U. M.Com.]
10. Discuss briefly the following statements giving suitable illustrations with imaginary figures:

    (a) "Pay back method attempts to measure the period of time it takes for the original cost of a project to be recovered from the additional earnings of the project itself."

    (b) "The real profitability of an investment depends on the number of years it will continue to operate after the pay-off period."

    [C.U. M.Com.]
11. Discuss the reasons for popularity of *Pay-Back Period* and *Accounting Rate of Return* method followed in appraising capital expenditure decisions in India.

12. Explain the term 'Risk' and 'Uncertainty' and also explain how risk analysis helps the management's investment decisions.
13. What are the basic components of capital budgeting analysis? Explain the differences between IRR and NPV methods.

[Delhi, M.Com. & C.A. Final]

14. "Capital expenditure decisions are by far the most important decisions in the field of financial management."—Illustrate.

[Madurai, M.Com.]

15. What do you understand by the term IRR? Is it the same as the value determined under the NPV method? —Discuss.

[C.A. Final]

16. "Pay back method is a test of liquidity and not profitability." —Discuss.
17. What is a Capital Expenditure Budget? Why is it necessary? What are its essential features?

[Calicut, M.Com.]

18. Discuss briefly the NPV method vs IRR method of evaluation of projects.

[C.A. Final, Delhi M.Com.]

19. Explain the salient features of the "Present Value Method" of project evaluation and examine its rationality.

[C.U. M.Com.]

20. Outline the financial management technique of capital investment in fixed assets.

[Meerut, M.Com.]

Long Answer-type Questions

21. Explain briefly the following methods of ascertaining the profitability of capital expenditure project bringing out merits and demerits of each:
    (a) Pay Back Method, and
    (b) Return on Investment Method. [Kerala, M.Com.]
22. List out the important methods of ranking investment proposals and discuss the conflicting opinions on the fundamentals of these different basic approaches.

[Annamalai, M.Com.]

23. "If the economic life of a project is long relative to its pay-back period, the reciprocal of pay-back period gives a reasonable estimate of a project's rate of profit."— Analyse this statement and give the situations where this argument holds good.

[Delhi, M.Com.]

24. Show that the pay-back reciprocal is a close approximation of the IRR.

[Gauhati, M.Com.]

25. What are the distinct categories of investment decisions? Discuss the basic factors on which investment decisions depend.

[I.C.W.A. Final]

26. Discuss some of the problems that financial managers in a developing country like India have to grapple with.

[Bharthiar, M.B.A.]

27. Discuss briefly the NPV method and state its merits in evaluating capital expenditure.

[Bharthiar, M.Com.]

28. The principal yardsticks for measuring the financial characteristics of investment proposals are:

    (a) Pay-Back Period;

    (b) Rate of Return on Capital Employed;

    (c) Discounted Cash Flow Method.

    Discuss the comparative merits and limitations of the above method.

[I.C.W.A. Final]

29. Compare and contrast IRR and NPV techniques. Which method will you recommend for evaluating investments? —Explain.

[C.S. Final]

30. Discuss the method used for evaluating and ranking of investment proposals. Compare the IRR method with the NPV method.

[Madurai, M.Com.]

31. What is the distinguishing feature of Present Value Technique over the other methods of Investment Appraisals? Is the former superior to the latter in all cases?

[Madurai, M.Com.]

32. What is Terminal Value Method? Give its acceptance rule.
33. Write notes on Sensitivity Analysis.
34. What is Decision Tree? Discuss the steps to construct a Decisions Tree.
35. What is Capital Rationing? Explain the selection process under Capital Rationing.

PRACTICAL

Pay Back Method

1. The cost of a project is Rs. 40,00,000, yielding an annual return (profit) of Rs. 6,00,000 after charging depreciation @ 12.5% but before tax at 50%.

Calculate its pay back period.

[Ans. 5 years]

2. X Ltd. is considering an investment proposal to install new milling control at a cost of Rs. 50,000. The facility has a life expectancy of 5 years and no salvage value. The tax rate is 35%. Assume the firm uses straight line method of depreciation and the same is allowed for tax purpose. The estimated cash flows before depreciation and tax (CFBT) from the investment proposals are:

Year	CFBT
	Rs.
1	10,000
2	10,692

Contd.

	Rs.
3	12,769
4	13,462
5	20,385

Compute the Pay Back Period.

[Ans. 4.328 years]

3. Delhi Machinery Manufacturing Company wants to replace the manual operations by a new machine. There are two alternative models X and Y of the new machine.

Using pay back period, suggest the most profitable investment. Ignore taxation.

	Machine X	Machine Y
Original Investment (Rs.)	9,000	18,000
Estimated life of the machine (years) (Rs.)	4	5
Estimated saving in scrap (Rs.)	500	800
Estimated saving in wages (Rs.)	6,000	8,000
Additional cost of maintenance (Rs.)	800	1,000
Additional cost of supervisors (Rs.)	1,200	1,800

[C.S. Final]

[Ans. The lowest pay-back period is 2 years in case of Machine X; Most profitable investment is to invest on Machine X]

4. The following projects require a cash outlay of Rs. 10,000.

You are required to suggest which one should be accepted if the standard pay back period is 5 years:

Year	Cash Inflows		
	Project A	Project B	Project C
	Rs.	Rs.	Rs.
1	2,500	4,000	1,000
2	2,500	3,000	2,000
3	2,500	2,000	3,000
4	2,500	1,000	4,000
5	2,500	—	—

[Ans. Pay back period is 4 years. Project B is best as its cash inflows are higher in the earlier years]

5. The two following mutually exclusive Project X and Project Y require an equal investment of Rs. 50,000 and are expected to generate net cash flow as:

Years	Project X	Project Y
	Rs.	Rs.
Year I	25,000	10,000
Year II	15,000	12,000
Year III	10,000	18,000

Contd.

	Rs.	Rs.
Year IV	—	25,000
Year V	12,000	8,000
Year VI	6,000	4,000

The cost of capital is 10%. The following are the present value factor at 10% p.a.:

Year	I	II	III	IV	V	VI
P.V. factor at 10% p.a.	0.909	0.826	0.751	0.683	0.621	0.564

Compute the Pay Back period and comment which project is preferred.

[Ans. Project X pay back period is 3 years and Project Y is 3.4 years. So, Project X is preferred since it has a shorter period]

6. From the following particulars compute the Pay Back Period:

Investment	Rs. 4,00,000
Rate of Depreciation	20% p.a.

Net Cash Flow before charging depreciation and after all other expenses are:

Year	I	II	III	IV	V
Amount (Rs.)	1,00,000	1,00,000	80,000	80,000	40,000

[Ans. Remember that net cash flow here is the normal income before depreciation but after all charges as their is no tax. Pay Back Period is 2 year]

Profitability Index

7. Jolly commenced business as an investment opportunity costing Rs. 40,000 with the following expected cash inflows (i.e. after tax and before depreciation):

Years	Inflow Rs.	PVF (10% p.a.) Rs.
1	7,000	0.909
2	7,000	0.826
3	7,000	0.731
4	7,000	0.653
5	7,000	0.621
6	8,000	0.564
7	10,000	0.513
8	15,000	0.467
9	10,000	0.424
10	4,000	0.386

Using 10% as the cost of capital (rate of discount) determine the (1) Net Present Value, (2) Profitability Index.

[C.S. Final]

[Ans. (i) 8.611; (ii) 1.215]

8. A firm whose cost of Capital is 10% is considering two projects X and Y, the details of which are:

Years		Project X Rs.	Project Y Rs.
Investments		70,000	70,000
Cash Flow :			
	Year I	10,000	50,000
	Year II	20,000	40,000
	Year III	30,000	20,000
	Year IV	45,000	10,000
	Year V	60,000	10,000
		1,65,000	1,30,000

Compute the Net Present Value at 10%, Profitability Index and Internal Rate of Return for the two projects.

[C.A. Final]

[Ans.	Project X Rs.	Project Y Rs.
N.P.V.	46,135	36,550
Profitability Index	1.659	1.522
IRR	27.326%	37.56%]

Internal Rate of Return (IRR)

9. The estimated cost of a project is Rs. 32,400. Its expected life is 3 years which generates a cash flow of Rs. 6,000, Rs. 14,000 and Rs. 12,000, respectively, Calculate the IRR.

[Ans. 15%]

10. Calculate the IRR from the following data:
Investment required Rs. 12,000;
Annual Cash Flow is expected Rs. 4,000 for 5 years. [Ans. 20%]

11. From the following data, comment which project should be chosen following the IRR method:

Years		Project X Rs.	Project Y Rs.
Investments		33,000	30,000
Cash Flow:			
	Year I	18,000	3,000
	Year II	6,000	3,000
	Year III	1,000	2,000
	Year IV	5,000	10,000
		30,000	18,000

[Ans. Project X should be chosen as its IRR is higher i.e. 10.24% as compared to Project Y which was only 11.3%]

12. X Ltd. has currently under examination a project which will yield the following returns over a period of time:

Year	I	II	III	IV	V
Gross Yield (Rs.)	80,000	80,000	90,000	90,000	75,000

Cost of the machinery to be installed works out to Rs. 2,00,000 and the machine is to be depreciated at 20% WDV basis. Income-Tax rate is 50%.

If the average cost of raising capital is 11% would you recommend accepting the project under IRR method?

[C.A. Final]

[Ans. IRR 14%, the project may be accepted]

13. Compute the IRR from the following data and suggest whether the project should be accepted or not:

	Rs.
Investment	2,77,000
Cost of Capital	12%

Net Cash Flows:

Year	I	II	III	IV	V
Amount (Rs.)	60,000	1,00,000	1,20,000	60,000	40,000

[Ans. IRR 10%, the project should not be accepted]

Discounted Cash Flow Method

14. The relevant data on three projects are given below using different methods (Return on investments, Discounted Cash Flow etc.).

Choose the best project and justify your answer (Use an interest of 20%):

Items	Projects A Rs.	B Rs.	C Rs.
Investment	60,000	60,000	60,000
Return at the end of 1st year	30,000	20,000	25,000
Return at the end of 2nd year	20,000	30,000	25,000
Return at the end of 3rd year	20,000	19,000	25,000

[I.C.W.A. Final]

[Ans.		**A**	**B**	**C**
Return on Investment:	**(ROI)**	**5.56%**	**5%**	**8.33%**
Pay Back Period:		**2.5**	**2.53**	**2.4**
Discounted Cash Flow (DCF):		**– Rs. 9,537**	**– 11,505**	**– 3,338**

Comment: No project should be taken since all of them show negative NPV. But if any project is to be taken, Project C may be considered as negative NPV is lowest]

15. Compute the Pay Back Period under (1) Ordinary Pay Back Period Method; (2) Discount Pay Back Method which require Rs. 1,60,000 as investments and estimated life is 5 years and suggest on the performance. Depreciation is calculated under Fixed Instalment Method.

	Year I	Year II	Year III	Year IV	Year V
Profit (after tax) (Rs.)	12,000	28,000	48,000	32,000	Nil
Cost of Capital 20%					
P.V. of Re. 1 given below					
P.V. Factor	.83	.69	.58	.48	.40

[Ans. (a) 2.7 years; (b) 4.39 years]

16. Comment which project should be accepted and why from the following data:

	Project A Rs.	Project B Rs.
Initial Investment	26,000	38,000
Cost of Capital	12%	

PV of Re. 1 at 12%

Year	I	II	III	IV	V	VI	VII	VIII	IX	X
	0.893	0.797	0.712	0.636	0.567	0.507	0.452	0.404	0.361	0.322
Cash Inflow										
Project A (Rs.)	9,000	7,000	6,000	5,000	4,000	4,000	3,000	3,000	3,000	3,000
Project B (Rs.)	8,000	10,000	12,000	14,000	8,000	2,000	10,000	—	—	—

[Ans.
NPV Project X Rs. 3.981
Project Y Rs. 7.344
Project Y may be preferred]

17. From the following data presented by X Ltd. suggest the most attractive proposal on the basis of NPV method, bearing in mind that future incomes are discounted at 12%:

	Proposal X Rs.	Proposal Y Rs.
Investments	9,500	20,000
Estimated Income:		
Year I	4,000	8,000
Year II	4,000	8,000
Year III	4,500	12,000

[Ans. NPV in Proposal X Rs. 467; Proposal Y Rs. 2,064; hence Proposal Y is accepted]

18. Y Ltd. furnished the following data. You are asked to suggest whether the project should be accepted or not, assuming that the cost of capital is 10% and investment required Rs. 50,000:

Year	1	2	3	4	5
Cash Inflows (Rs.)	18,000	16,000	14,000	12,000	10,000
P.V. of Re. 1 at 10%	0.909	0.826	0.751	0.683	0.621

[Ans. NPV is Rs. 4,498]

Miscellaneous

19. The Philips Corporation, which has a 50% tax rate and a 10% after-tax cost of capital, is evaluating a project which will cost Rs. 1,00,000 and will require an increase in the level of inventories and receivable of Rs. 50,000 over its effective life. The project will generate additional sales of Rs. 1,00,000 and will require cash expenses of Rs. 30,000 in each year of its 5-year life. It will be depreciated on a straight-line basis.

What are the Net Present Value and Internal Rate of Return for the project?

[Delhi, M.Com.]

[Ans. NPV is Rs. 51.645; IRR 21.27%]

20. X Ltd., having cost of capital 10%, is considering two mutually exclusive projects X and Y, the details of which are:

Cost of invstment Rs. 70,000 —both in Project X and Project Y.

Cash Flows	Year 1	Year 2	Year 3	Year 4	Year 5
Project X (Rs.)	10,000	20,000	30,000	45,000	60,000
Project Y (Rs.)	50,000	40,000	20,000	10,000	10,000

Compute the NPV at 10% Profitability Index, and IRR for the two projects.

[Ans.		Project X	Project Y
	PI	= 1.659	1.522
	NPV	Rs. 46,130	Rs. 36,550
	IRR	27%	37%]

21. The management of a company has two alternative projects under consideration. Project A requires a capital outlay of Rs. 1,20,000 but Project B needs Rs. 1,80,000. Both are estimated to provide a cash flow for five years : A Rs. 40,000 per year and B Rs. 58,000 per year. The cost of capital is 10%.

Show which of the two projects is preferable from the viewpoint of (i) NPV, and (ii) IRR.

[Delhi, M.Com.]

[Ans. (i) Project B; (ii) Project A]

22. X Ltd. is considering to instal a capital project which needs a capital outlay of Rs. 4,00,000. Estimated annual income (after charging depreciation but before charging tax) is:

Year	1	2	3	4	5
Amount (Rs.)	2,00,000	2,00,000	1,60,000	1,60,000	80,000

Depreciation may be considered as 20% on original cost and taxation @ 50% of net income.

Compute:

(a) Pay Back Method; (b) Rate of Return on Original Investment Method; (c) Rate of Return on Average Investment Method; (d) Discounted Cash Flow Method (assume cost of capital is @ 10%); (e) Net Present Value Index Method; (f) Internal Rate of Return.

[Ans. (a) 2.25 years; (b) 20%; (c) 40%; (d) Rs. 1,08,130; (e) 154%; (f) 30%]

23. A company is considering two mutually exclusive projects. Both require an initial investment of Rs. 50,000 each and have a life of 5 years. The cost of capital of the company is 10% and tax rate is 50%. The depreciation is charged on straight line method.

The estimated net cash inflows (before depreciation and tax) of the two projects are:

Year	Project A	Project B
1	20,000	30,000
2	22,000	27,000

Contd.

3	28,000	22,000
4	25,000	25,000
5	30,000	20,000

What project should be accepted as per NPV and IRR method?

[Delhi, M.Com.]

[Ans.

		Project A	Project B
NPV	=	Rs. 15,492	Rs. 16,744
IRR	=	21%	23%

Project B has higher NPV as well as higher IRR, hence, Project B is preferred]

24. X Ltd. considers the two following projects. The details are:

	Project A	Project B
Investment (Rs.)	10,00,000	15,00,000
Estimated Life	4 years	6 years
Scrap Value	10%	10%
Tax Rate	50%	50%
Working Capital (Rs.)	5,00,000	5,00,000
Estimated Income		
(before depreciation and tax)		
1	8,00,000	15,00,000
2	8,00,000	9,00,000
3	8,00,000	15,00,000
4	8,00,000	8,00,000
5	—	6,00,000
6	—	3,00,000

Compute Accounting Rate of Return and suggest which project is to be preferred.

[Ans.

ARR— Project X: $\frac{\text{Rs. 2,87,500}}{\text{Rs. 15,00,000}} = 19.1\%$

Project Y: $\frac{\text{Rs. 3,54,166}}{\text{Rs. 20,00,000}} = 17.75\%$**]**

25. Bright Metals Ltd. is considering two different investment proposals. The details are:

	Project A	Project B
	Rs.	Rs.
Investment	9,500	20,000
Estimated Income at the end of the year:		
Year I	4,000	8,000
Year II	4,000	8,000
Year III	4,500	12,000

(a) Suggest the most attractive proposal on the basis of excess present value mehod considering future incomes are discounted at 12%.

(b) Also find out IRR of the two proposals.

The present value of Re. 1 receivable at the end of each period on various rates of discount are:

Years	10%	11%	12%	13%	14%	15%	16%	17%	18%
1	.9091	.9009	.8929	.8850	.8772	.8696	.8621	.8547	.8475
2	.8265	.8116	.7972	.7832	.7695	.7561	.7432	.7305	.7182
3	.7513	.7312	.7118	.6931	.6750	.6575	.6407	.6244	.6086

[I.C.W.A. Final]

[Ans.	**Proposal A**	**Proposal B**
NPV	**464**	**2063**
IRR	**14.76%**	**17.5%**

Most attractive is Proposal B since both its NPV and IRR are higher]

CHAPTER 3

COST OF CAPITAL

Introduction

In the next chapter (Chapter 4) we have highlighted the sophisticated capital budgeting techniques for the purpose of evaluating capital projects under the conditions of certainty, risk, and uncertainty. The earlier sections of the chapter also shows unmistakably that a certain discount rate or required rate of return is an important element while evaluating the same. This discount rate is used as acceptance-rejection criterion. It will also be observed (earlier, in that chapter) that the discount rate or required rate of return is actually the cost of capital i.e., the cost of capital as given. The purpose of the present study is to develop the concept, of cost capital and suggest its measurement. It may be mentioned that the cost of capital is probably one of the most difficult, disputed and controversial topic in financial management. There are widespread differences among financial experts as to how this can be computed and measured. In view of the crucial operational significance of the concept, the discussions that follow are within the general framework for the computation of cost of capital. At first the significance, importance and definition of the cost of capital in general terms are presented which have been followed by a detailed account of the measurement of the same.

Relevance, Significance and Importance of Cost of Capital

The cost of capital is the most significant concept in capital budgeting decisions since it is used as a decision criterion. Under DCF techniques, if NPV method is followed as a decision criterion, the cost of capital is used as a discount rate in evaluating the desirability of the projects in order to calculate the NPV and, if there is a positive (+) NPV, the project will be accepted; and vice versa. Similarly, if IRR method is adopted, the computed IRR is compared with the cost of capital, i.e., if the project has greater/higher rate of return (IRR) in comparison with the cost of capital, the same will be accepted and vice versa. At the same time, Profitability Index (B. C. Ratio) may be applied for the purpose while determining the present value of future cash flow. Thus, it plays a significant role in investment decisions and supplies a yardstick to measure the value of investment proposals. In short, it is referred to as the minimum required rate of return, cut-off rate, hurdle or target rate, standard return etc., which implies the crucial significance of the same. In this context, the accept-reject rules desire that, if the rate of return is higher than the cost of capital, a firm may undertake such investment opportunities. On the contrary, if the rate of return is lower than the cost of capital, the firm is advised not to undertake such investment proposals. In other words, if a project is accepted which will yield a higher return than the cost of capital, the same will increase the prices of shares along with the shareholders' wealth and, in the opposite case, the prices of the shares will go down, i.e., the shareholders' wealth will decline. Thus, the cost of capital presents a rational technique for the purpose of making optimum investment decisions. Apart from the above, it is important from the standpoint of both capital budgeting and capital structure planning decisions which are:

(i) **Capital Budgeting Decisions**

It has already been explained earlier that cost of capital is used as a discount rate and, in order to find out the present value, the firm's cash flows are discounted by the rate, i.e. it is the most significant basis for financial appraisal of the new capital expenditure decisions.

(ii) **Capital Structure Decisions**

The cost of capital, no doubt, is an important consideration in designing the firm's capital structure. At the time of raising finance from different sources, the firm should optimise the risk and cost factors. Needless to mention that the sources of funds which are less costly involve greater degree of risk. Therefore, a firm should always aim at minimising the cost of capital and maximising the market value after considering the risk factors.

Moreover, the framework of cost of capital can be applied in order to evaluate financial performance of the top management.[1] This evaluation depends on a comparison between the actual profitability of the projects that are undertaken and the overall cost of capital including the cost of raising funds.

Definition and Concept of Cost of Capital

Cost of Capital may be defined according to the following two terms : (a) ***under operational terms,*** and (b) ***under economic terms.*** Under operational terms, it is defined as the minimum rate of return which a firm must earn on its investment, i.e., it refers to the discount rate which is used while determining the present value of estimated future cash flows. But, under economic terms, however, there are two formulations. First, it is the cost of raising funds required in order to finance the proposed project, i.e., it is the borrowing rate of the firm. Secondly, it refers to the opportunity cost of the funds, in terms of the lending rate, i.e., the expected earnings by investing funds outside. Here, we prefer to use the term 'Cost of Capital' as a borrowing rate since it is impracticable on the part of the firm which is going to take any capital budgeting decision to invest outside. Thus, this approach is very much realistic as well as practicable. Of course, under economic terms, the cost of capital is defined as the weighted average cost of each type of capital.[2]

There are three basic aspects about the concept of cost:

(i) **It is not a cost as such :**

Practically, the cost of capital of a firm is the rate of return which it requires on the projects. That is why, it is a 'hurdle' rate. Although such rate may be computed on the basis of actual cost of different components of capital. The term 'component' means the different sources from which funds are actually raised since each sources of fund or each component of capital has its own cost, i.e. equity capital has a cost followed by preference share capital, and so on.

1 Bhattacharya. S. K. — *'A Cost of Capital Framework for Management Control' : Economic and Political Weekly,* Vol. 35 (29.8.1970).

2 Here, weight is the ratio of the market value of securities which represents the sources of capital to the market value of all securities. 'Security' includes equity and preference shares, debentures and other fixed interest-bearing securities, retained earnings. At the same time, sale of assets is to be included as a source of funds —Poterfield J. T. S. —*Investment Decision and Capital Costs* — Englewood Cliffs, Prentice-Hall, 1965, pp. 42-63.

(ii) **It is the minimum rate of return :**

Cost of capital represents the minimum rate of return (already stated above) which is required in order to maintain the market value of equity shares.

(iii) **It includes the following components :**

(a) ***The riskless cost of the particular type of financing or return at zero risk level, r_0 :***

It relates to the expected rate of return when a project involves no risk, whether business or financial, i.e., the firm's business and financial risks are unaffected by the acceptance and financing of the project.[1]

(b) ***The Business Risk Premium, b :***

Business risk measures the variability in operating profit (Earning before interest and taxes) as a result of changing sales. If the project which is accepted is found to be more risky than the average or normal, the supplier of funds, naturally, will expect a higher rate of return than the normal or average rate, i.e. the cost of capital, in that case, will go up. Therefore, the business risk premium is determined by the capital budgeting decisions for investment proposals.

(c) ***The Financial Risk Premium, f :***

Financial risk depends on the capital structure pattern of the firm, i.e., debt-equity mix. Because, if a firm has higher debt-content (debt-equity ratio) in its capital structure in comparison with a firm where the said content is low, the same is more risky simply because the former must have a higher operating profit in order to cover the periodic interest payment and repayment of principal at the time of maturity as well. In other words, possibility of cash insolvency exists in case of such firms. As a result, the suppliers will expect a higher rate of return from such firms for carrying a higher degree of risk as compared to the latter.

Thus, the above three components of cost of capital may be written in the form of the following equation :

$$K_0 = r_0 + b + f$$

where,

K_0 = Cost of Capital;

r_0 = Return at zero risk level;

b = Premium for business risk;

f = Premium for financial risk.

It should be noted that the business and financial risks are assumed to be constant, and, as such, the changing cost of each type of capital over time should be affected by the demand and supply of each type of funds as well.

Classification of Cost of Capital

Cost of Capital can broadly be classified as:

(a) Explicit Cost and Implicit Cost;

(b) Future Cost and Historical Cost;

---

1 *Gitman, L. J., Principles of Managerial Finance* — Harper & Row, New York, 1976, p. 33.

(c) **Specific Cost;**

(d) **Average Cost and Marginal Cost; and**

(e) **Overall Cost or Composite or Combined Cost.**

(a) Explicit Cost and Implicit Cost

The explicit cost of any source of capital may be defined as the discount rate that equates the present value of the cash inflows that are incremental to the taking of the financing opportunity with the present value of its incremental cash outflow.[1] When a firm raises funds from different sources, it involves a series of cash flows. At its first stage, there is only a cash inflow by the amount raised which is followed by a series of cash outflows in the form of interest payments, repayment of principal or repayment of dividends. Therefore, if a firm issues 1,000, 8% debentures of Rs. 100 each, redeemable after 10 years at par, there will be an inflow of cash to the extent of Rs. 1,00,000 (1,000 × Rs. 100) at the beginning, but the annual cash outflow will be Rs. 8,000 (Rs. 1,00,000 $\times \frac{8}{100}$) in the form of interest. There will also be an outflow of Rs. 1,00,000 at the end of the 10th year when the debentures will be redeemed. We know that a firm can raise its funds by issuing equity or preference shares, or debentures, or by selling assets etc., which are known as sources of funds. The cash outlays for this purpose may be in the form of interest/dividends, repayments of principal.

The equation used in general in order to calculate the explicit cost of capital is:

$$I_0 = \frac{C_1}{(1+k)^1} + \frac{C_2}{(1+k)^2} + \frac{C_3}{(1+k)^3} + \dots\dots\dots\dots + \frac{C_n}{(1+k)^n}$$

where,

I_0 = Net funds received by the firm at time 0;

C_1 = Outflow in the respective period;

k = Explicit Cost of Capital;

n = Period for which funds are provided.

It is evident from the above equation that I_0 is the internal rate of return of the cash flow of financing opportunity.[2] Therefore, if a firm takes any non-interest bearing loan, there will be no explicit cost since there is no outflow of cash by way of interest payment although the principal must be repaid.

From the above, it becomes clear that the explicit cost will arise when capital is raised and which is also the IRR of the financial opportunity. Implicit cost of capital, on the other hand, arises when a firm considers alternative uses of the funds raised.[3] That is, it is the opportunity cost. In other words, it is the rate of return which is available on other investment in addition to what is being considered at present. To sum up, the implicit cost may be defined as the rate of return associated with the best investment opportunity for the firm and its shareholders that will be foregone if the project presently under consideration by the firm was accepted.[4] In this respect it may be mentioned that if earnings are retained by a firm, the implicit cost is the income which the shareholders could have earned if such earnings would have been distributed and invested by them.[5]

1 Porterfield, J. T. S. — op. cit., p. 45.
2 *Ibid.*
3 *Ibid.*
4 *Ibid.*
5 Brigham, E. F. — *Financial Management — Theory and Practice,* The Dryden Press, Illinois, 2nd Edn., p. 567.

Therefore, *explicit cost will arise only when funds are raised, whereas implicit cost will arise when they are used.*

(b) **Future Cost and Historical Cost**

Future Costs are the expected costs of funds for financing a particular project. They are very significant while making financial decisions. For instance, at the time of taking financial decisions about the capital expenditure, a comparison is to be made between the expected IRR and the expected cost of funds for financing the same, i.e., the relevant costs here are future costs. Historical costs are those costs which have already been incurred in order to finance a particular project. They are useful while projecting future costs. In short, historical costs are very important by the amount they keep in predicting the future costs. Because, they supply an evaluation of performance in comparison with standard and/or predetermined costs.

(c) **Specific Cost**

The cost of each component of capital, viz., equity shares, preference shares, debentures, loans etc. are termed specific or component cost of capital which is the most appealing concept. While determining the average cost of capital, it requires consideration about the cost of specific methods for financing the projects. This is particularly useful where the profitability of the project is evaluated on the basis of the specific source of funds taken for financing the said project. For instance, if the estimated cost of equity capital of a firm becomes 12%, that project which is financed by the equity shareholders' fund will be accepted provided the same will yield a return of 12%.

(d) **Average Cost and Marginal Cost**

Average Cost

The average cost of capital is the weighted average cost of each component of the funds invested by the firm for a particular project, i.e., percentage or proportionate cost of each element in the total investment. The weights are in proportion to the shares of each component of capital in the total capital structure or investment.

But average cost has the following three computational problems :

(i) It refers to the measurement of cost of each specific source of capital;

(ii) It also requires the assignment of proper weights to each component of capital;

(iii) Is the overall cost of capital (discussed subsequently) affected by the changes in the composition of the capital?

Marginal Cost

According to the Terminology of Cost Accountancy (ICMA, Para 3.603), *Marginal Cost is the amount at any given volume of output by which aggregate costs are changed if the volume of output is increased or decreased by one unit.* Same principle is being followed in cost of capital. That is, marginal cost of capital may be defined as the *cost of obtaining another rupee of new capital.*[1] Generally, a firm raises a certain amount of fund for fixed capital investment. But marginal cost of capital reveals the cost of additional amount of capital which are raised by a firm for current and/or fixed capital investment. When the firm procures additional capital from one particular source only, i.e., not from the different sources in given proportion, the marginal cost, in that case, is known as specific or explicit cost of capital. In other words, marginal cost of capital may be more or may be less than the average cost of capital of a firm.

---

1 Brigham, E. F. — *Financial Management — Theory and Practice*, The Dryden Press, Illinois, 2nd Edn., p. 567.

Illustration 3.1

A firm presents the following information relating to cost of capital:

Sources	Amount Rs.	After-tax Cost of Capital
Equity	50,000	12%
Debt	50,000	4%

The firm wants to raise a fund of Rs. 25,000 for the purpose of an investment proposal. It also decides to take the same from a financial institution at a cost of 10%.

Compute the marginal cost of capital and compare the same with average cost of capital before and after additional financing, assuming that the corporate rate of tax is 50%.

Solution

It becomes clear from the above problem that the marginal cost is Rs. 25,000 which is 10% before tax and 5% after tax (i.e. 10% – 50% of 10%). The same is also known as specific or explicit cost of financing Rs. 25,000 since the source is only one, i.e., financial institution. But the same also differs from the average cost calculated as:

Before Additional Financing	Proportion	Cost After-tax	Weighted Average Cost (%)
Equity	0.5	12	6.0
Debt	0.5	4	2.0
	1.0		8.0

After financing Rs. 25,000

	Proportion*	Specific Cost after Tax	Weighted Average Cost (%)
Equity	0.4	12	4.8
Debt			
Old	0.4	4	1.6
New	0.2	5	1.0
	1.0		7.4

Thus, it is evident from the above that the weighted average cost comes down from 8% to 7.4%. The cost of new debt is higher than the cost of old debt. Again, the cost of new debt is lower than the cost of equity capital. Therefore, the average cost of capital reduces since there is an increase in the proportion of debt capital to total capital invested.

---

* Proportion :

Equity 50,000

Debt :

Old 50,000

New 25,000

∴ Ratio :

Equity : Debt (New) : Debt (Old) =	50,000 :	50,000 :	25,000
	2	2	1
or,	4	4	2

While raising additional capital a firm must concentrate on the optimum capital structure and should use the different sources of financing proportionately for the purpose of maintaining the optimum capital structure. In the circumstance, the present book value may be considered as weight in order to compute the average cost of capital. If the capital is raised from different sources at a given proportion, it needs a computation of average cost of capital to know the cost of the total additional amount raised.[1] So, in this case, marginal cost of capital may also be known as weighted average cost for the same. There will be no difference between the two provided there is no change in specific cost.

Consider the following illustration.

Illustration 3.2

In Illustration 3.1, it is considered that the additional amount of Rs. 25,000 will be raised by the firm from equity and debt at the existing specific cost, there will be no difference between the weighted average cost and the marginal cost of capital as both of them will be one or the same as presented:

Solution

Sources	Amount Rs.	Proportion (%)	Specific Cost after Tax (%)	Marginal Cost (%)
Equity	12,500	0.5	12	6.0
Debt	12,500	0.5	4	2.0
		1.0		8.0

Therefore, the cost of raising Rs. 25,000 is only 8% which is the marginal cost. The same should be measured with the help of weighted average cost for raising the additional fund of Rs. 25,000.

It has already been highlighted above that, if the specific cost changes, there will be a difference between the marginal cost of capital and the average cost of capital of a firm even if additional capital is procured at a given proportion. It should be remembered that the marginal cost of capital will continue to be the weighted average cost of new capital for a firm.

The following illustration will, however, make the principle clear:

Illustration 3.3

If it is assumed that cost of debt is 10% (before tax) and rate of tax is 50% and the firm prefers to raise Rs. 25,000 proportionately, compute the marginal cost of capital and the average cost of capital.

Solution

(a) **Marginal Cost of Capital**

Sources	Amount Rs.	Proportion (%)	Specific Cost after Tax (%)	Marginal Cost (%)
Equity	12,500	0.5	12	6.0
Debt	12,500	0.5	5	2.5
		1.0		8.5

1 Banerjee, B — *Financial Management and Policy* — op. cit., p. 395.

(b) **Average Cost of Capital**

Sources	Amount Rs.	Proportion (%)	Cost after Tax (%)	Weighted Average Cost (%)
Equity	62,500	0.5	12	6.0
Debt :				
Old	50,000	0.4	4	1.6
New	12,500	0.1	5	0.5
		1.0		8.1

It becomes clear from the above that overall cost of capital is raised upward as there is an increase in the cost of new debt capital. The same actually differs from the marginal cost of 8.5% for raising additional capital of Rs. 25,000 to 8.1%.

The relationship between marginal cost and average cost of capital may be presented with the help of a graph given by Brigham:*

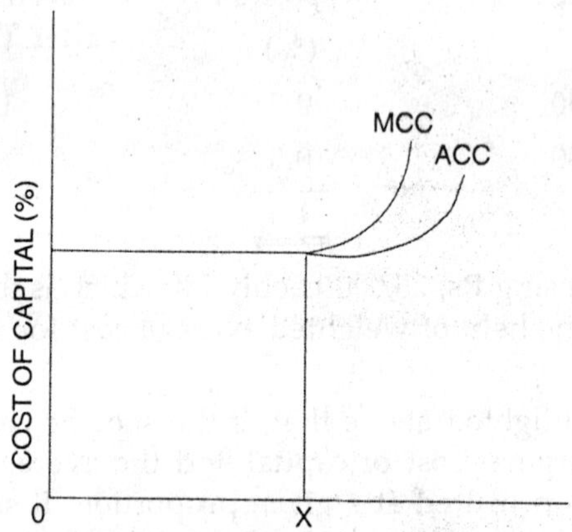

Fig. 3.1 : Relationship between Marginal Cost and Average Cost of Capital

From Fig. 3.1, it becomes clear that if additional capital is raised up to the amount X, the marginal cost of capital (MCC) and also the average cost of capital (ACC) are identical. Therefore, both of them are rising although the ACC rises at a lesser rate than the MCC.

(e) **Overall Cost or Composite or Combined Cost**

It may be recalled that the term 'cost of capital' has been used to denote the overall composite cost of capital or weighted average of the cost of each specific type of fund, i.e., weighted average cost. In other words, when specific costs are combined in order to find out the overall cost of capital, it may be defined as the composite or weighted average cost of capital. Thus, the weighted average is used on the ground that the proportions of various sources of funds are different in the total capital structure of a firm. That is why overall cost of capital recognises the relative proportions of different sources and, as such, the weighted average and not the simple average.

---

* Brigham, E. F. — op. cit., p. 574.

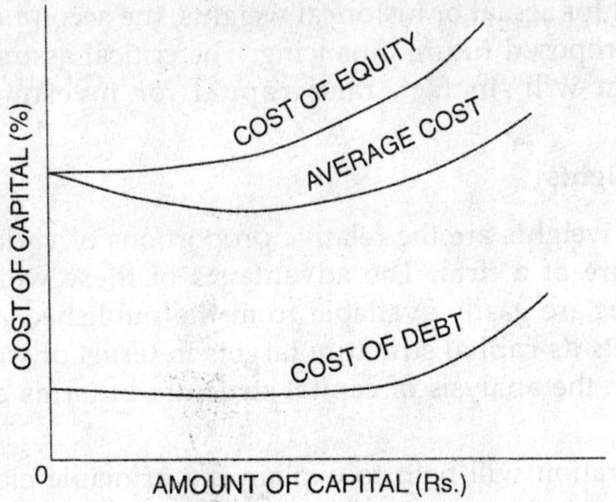

Fig. 3.2 : Relationship between Specific Cost and Average Cost of Capital

Overall cost of capital is used for the following justifications:

(i) The firm can increase the market price per share after accepting projects which yield more than the average cost.

(ii) It recognises the fact that it is better to use different sources of finance instead of a single one.

(iii) It also provides a basis for comparison among projects as a standard or a cut-off rate. One point in this respect is to be noted, that is, if specific costs are taken as the cost of financing, proper comparison is not possible. In that case, specific costs will reveal shifting standard at certain intervals. This particular attention has been depicted in the graph (Fig. 3.2) which expresses the relationship between the specific cost and the average cost of capital.

Computation of Overall Cost of Capital

The computation of overall cost of capital involves the following steps:

(i) Compute specific cost for each individual project;

(ii) Assign proper weights to specific costs;

(iii) Multiply the cost of each of the sources by the appropriate weight;

(iv) Divide the total weighted cost by the total weights in order to get the overall cost of capital.

Needless to mention that the weighted cost of capital may be changed due to (i) change in the cost of each component, or (ii) change in weight, or (iii) both.

We have explained the overall cost of capital or weighted average cost of capital after applying appropriate weights. Now the crucial part, i.e., selection of weights with its related aspects, should be highlighted. We would like to illustrate the relevant aspects of the selection of the weights.

Selection/Assignment of Weights

The following three possible weights may be assigned for the purpose:

(i) Using **'Book-value Weights'**;

(ii) Using **'Market-value Weights'**;

(iii) Using **'Marginal-value Weights'**.

The first one is used for actual or historical weights, the second one for 'current weights' and the third one for 'proposed future' financing. The critical assumption in any weighting system is that the firm will, in fact, raise capital for investment in the proportions specified.[1]

(i) Book-value Weights

Under this method, weights are the relative proportions of various sources of capital to the total capital structure of a firm. The advantages of these weights are operational in nature since book-values are easily available from the published annual report of a firm. Moreover, every firm sets its capital structure targets in terms of values rather than market value. At the same time, the analysis of capital structure in terms of debt-equity ratio also depends on book value.

The following illustration will help to explain the principle clearly:

Illustration 3.4

The cost of capital (after tax) of a firm of the specific sources is:

Cost of Debt	4.50%
Cost of Preference Shares	10.50%
Cost of Equity Capital	15.60%
Cost of Retained Earnings	15.00% (assuming external yield criterion)

Capital Structure are :

Sources	Amount Rs.
Debt	2,00,000
Preference Share Capital	3,00,000
Equity Share Capital	4,00,000
Cost of Retained Earnings	1,00,000
	10,00,000

Calculate the weighted average cost of capital using 'Book-Value Weights'.

Solution

Computation of Weighted Average Cost of Capital Under Book-value Weights

Sources	Amount	Proportion		After-tax	Weighted
(a)	(b) Rs.	(c)		(d)	(e) = (c) × (d)
Debt	2,00,000	0.2	(20%)	0.0450	0.0090
Preference Share Capital	3,00,000	0.3	(30%)	0.1050	0.0315
Equity Share Capital	4,00,000	0.4	(40%)	0.1560	0.0624
Retained Earnings	1,00,000	0.1	(10%)	0.1500	0.0150
	10,00,000	1.0	(100%)		0.1179

∴ Weighted Average Cost of Capital = 11.79%.

[1] Van-Horn, J. C. — op. cit., p. 210.

Alternative Approach

An alternative method is to compute the total cost of capital and then divide the figure by the total capital which actually avoids fractional calculations as calculated above.

Computation of Weighted Average Cost of Capital

Sources	Amount	Cost	Weighted Average Cost
(a)	(b)	(c)	(d) = (b) × (c)
	Rs.		Rs.
Debt	2,00,000	4.50%	9,000
Preference Share Capital	3,00,000	10.50%	31,500
Equity Share Capital	4,00,000	15.60%	62,400
Retained Earnings	1,00,000	15.00%	15,000
	10,00,000		1,17,900

$$\therefore \text{ Weighted Average Cost of Capital} = \frac{\text{Rs. } 1,17,900}{\text{Rs. } 10,00,000} = 11.79\%$$

(ii) Market-value Weights

Theoretically, the use of market value weights for calculating the cost of capital is more appealing due to the following reasons:

(a) The market value of the securities are closely approximate to the actual amount to be received from the proceeds of such securities.

(b) The cost of each specific source of finance which constitutes the capital structure is calculated according to the prevailing market price.

But there are some practical difficulties for using market value weights:

(a) The market value of securities may frequently fluctuate.

(b) Market value of securities are not readily available like book value since the latter can be taken from the published annual report of the company.

(c) The analysis of capital structure in terms of debt-equity ratio is based on book value and not on the market value.

Therefore, although market value weights are operationally inconvenient in comparison with book-value weights—particularly the market value of retained earnings the former is theoretically consistent and sound and, as such, may be used as a better indicator about the cost of capital of a firm.

Illustration 3.5

From the data contained in Illustration 3.4, calculate the weighted average cost of capital, bearing in mind that the market value of different sources of funds are:

Sources	Market Value
	Rs.
Debt	1,75,000
Preference Shares	3,50,000
Equity and Retained Earnings	7,25,000
	12,50,000

Solution

It has been stated above that market value weights are operationally inconvenient, particularly market value of retained earnings. But market value of retained earnings can indirectly be estimated as suggested by Gitman.[1] According to him, as retained earnings are treated as equity capital for calculating cost of specific sources of funds, the market value of equity shares may be considered as the combined market value of both equity shares and retained earnings. Individual market value (Equity Share and Retained Earnings) may also be determined by allocating each of the percentage share of the total market value equal to their respective percentage share of the total values.

Thus, according to Gitman, the sum of Rs. 7,25,000 may be allocated between equity share capital and retained earnings as:

Sources	Book-value	Percentage (%) of Book-value	Market Value
(a)	(b)	(c)	(d)
Equity Shares	4,00,000	$\left(\frac{\text{Rs.}4,00,000}{\text{Rs.}5,00,000}\times 100\right)=80\%$	7,25,000 × 80% = 5,80,000
Retained Earnings	1,00,000	$\left(\frac{\text{Rs.}1,00,000}{\text{Rs.}5,00,000}\times 100\right)=20\%$	7,25,000 × 20% = 1,45,000

Therefore, after determining the market value, weighted average cost of capital is calculated:

Computation of Weighted Average Cost of Capital (Market-value Weights)

Sources	Market-value	Cost	Weighted Average Cost
(a)	(b)	(c)	(d) = (b) × (c)
		Rs.	Rs.
Debt	1,75,000	4.50%	7,875
Preference Shares	3,50,000	10.50%	36,750
Equity Share Capital	5,80,000	15.60%	90,480
Retained Earnings	1,45,000	15.00%	21,750
	12,50,000		1,56,855

$$\therefore \text{ Weighted Average Cost of Capital} = \left(\frac{\text{Rs.}1,56,855}{\text{Rs.}12,50,000}\right) = 12.55\%$$

Thus, one significant point can be noticed from the above table. That is, average cost of capital under market value weight is higher than the average cost of capital under book value weight since the former has considerably increased due to the fact that market value of equity and preference shares are greater than their respective book values. In the present case, the overall cost is increased as these sources of finance have higher specific cost.

(iii) **Marginal Weights**

When weights are assigned to specific costs by the proportion of each type of fund to the total funds that are raised, it is known as marginal weights. In short, weights correspond to

1 Gitman, L. J. — *Principles of Managerial Finance*, Harper & Row, 1976, p. 353.

the proportions of financing inputs a firm intends to employ to finance a proposed investment proposal.[1] In this context, it may be mentioned that here new or incremental capital is considered rather than capital raised in the part of current market values.[2]

Illustration 3.6

Data are taken from Illustration 3.4. The firm desires to raise Rs. 5,00,000 for the purpose of extending its plant capacity. It also estimates that Rs. 1,00,000 may be utilised from retained earnings and the balance Rs. 4,00,000 may be raised as:

	Rs.
Long-term Debt	1,00,000
Preference Shares	3,00,000

Compute the weighted average cost of capital after applying marginal weight.

Solution

Weighted Average Cost of Capital (Marginal Weights)

Sources	Amount	Proportion		Cost	Weighted Average Cost
(a)	(b)	(c)		(d)	(e) = (c) × (d)
Debt	1,00,000	0.20	(20%)	4.50%	0.9000
Preference Share	3,00,000	0.60	(60%)	10.50%	6.3000
Retained Earning	1,00,000	0.20	(20%)	15.00%	3.0000
	5,00,000	1.00	(100%)		10.20%

∴ Weighted Average Cost of Capital 10.20%.

Needless to mention that this weighted average cost of capital (i.e., under marginal weights) is substantially lower than the above two methods, viz., book-value and market value. This is simply due to the fact that preference shares has been used by a large amount. It is interesting to note that the above computed average cost of capital would have even been lower than the present one if 'debt' is being used as a large amount since its interest rate is very low.

However, marginal weight system does not recognise the long-term implications on the current financing of a firm as capital expenditure decisions are long-term investments. Long-term implications of financing strategy should be implemented, i.e., it does not take into consideration the fact that today's financing affects tomorrow's cost. If only a single source is being employed instead of a number of sources, application of marginal weights for the purpose of computation of weighted average cost will be of no use.

Impact of After-Tax while calculating Weighted Average Cost of Capital

The Weighted Average Cost of Capital can be computed in two ways—viz., Before-Tax, or After-Tax. Needless to mention here that *After-Tax Weighted Average Cost* is more applicable and meaningful than the *Before-Tax Weighted Average* Cost as:

(i) We know that the measurement of Cost of Capital is used for decision criterion where it is considered as the discounting rate or the cut-off rate in every investment decision. We also know that dividend (which is the relevant factor to the shareholders) is

1 Banerjee, B. — *Financial Policy and Management Accounting*, op. cit., p. 391.

2 *Ibid.*

declared and paid out of after-tax profit. Thus, cost of capital should be ascertained on the basis of after-tax profit. Moreover, cost of capital is used while computing discounted cash flow technique. And as NCFs (Net Cash Flows) are computed after deducting appropriate tax, that is why overall cost of capital should be measured on the basis of after-tax profit.

(ii) It is known to us that after combining all the specific costs of capital, average cost of capital is determined. Thus, cost of debt capital is ascertained before or after-tax profit whereas cost of equity and cost of preference shares are ascertained on the basis of after-tax profit. Thus, it is preferable to follow after-tax profit basis to make an uniformity among the different components of cost of capital when various sources of overall cost of capital are combined.

MEASUREMENT OF COST OF CAPITAL

Generally, we know that the use of share capital has no accounting cost and, as such, the use of the same by a firm does not involve any outlay which an accountant would normally call costs. That is, however, not true since equity capital certainly involves a cost. But equity shareholders expect a dividend and/or capital gains against their investment and such expectations give rise to an opportunity cost of capital. (The market value of a share is a function of the return which a shareholder expects.) It may be mentioned that equity funds should be used only when the return from a project covers this cost. Equity financing arises from two major sources, viz. (a) New Issues, (b) Retained Earnings.

Conceptually speaking, the cost of equity capital is comparatively the highest among all other sources of funds. It has been stated above that the equity shareholders always expect a certain rate of return which, again, depends on, *inter alia*, the business risk and financial risk of a firm. The equity shareholders take the highest degree of financial risk, i.e., they receive dividend after paying off all the business obligations and, since they take the highest degree of risk, naturally, they expect a higher return and, as such, highest costs are related to them.

Cost of equity capital may be defined as the minimum rate of return that a firm must earn on the equity-financed portion of an investment project in order to leave unchanged the market prices of its stock.[1] For instance, if the required rate of return (RRR) is 15% and cost of debt is $12\frac{1}{2}$%, and if the company has the policy to finance with 80% equity and 20% debt, the RRR of the project would be computed as:

.80 × 15%	=	12.0%
.20 × $12\frac{1}{2}$%	=	2.5%
		14.5

It indicates that if the company requires Rs. 20,000 for a project which gives an annual return of Rs. 4,000, the rate of return on equity financed portion can be computed as:

	Total Return	=	4,000
Less :	Interest to debt (4,000 × $12\frac{1}{2}$%)	=	500
	Amount available for equity shareholders		3,500

$$\text{Rate of Return on Equity Shares} = \frac{\text{Rs. } 3,500}{\text{Rs. } 16,000} \times 100 = 21.88\%$$

1 Van Home, J. I.— op. cit., p. 198.

Therefore, the expected rate of return is 21.88%, which is above the IRR and, as such, the project may be undertaken. In other words, the market value of shares will go up. But if the project earns a return which is less than Rs. 2,400 (16,000 × 15%), it will provide a less return to the investors and, as a result, market value of share will go down.

Conceptually, this rate of return may be considered as the cost of equity capital which is determined by the following two (already mentioned) categories:

(i) New Issues, (ii) Retained Earnings.

(i) New Issues

The computation on cost of equity share capital is, no doubt, difficult and controversial task since different authorities have conveyed different explanations and approaches to it. At the same time, it is also very difficult to know the expected rate of return which the shareholders as a class expect from their investment as they differ among themselves in order to predict or quantify the said return.

However, some of the approaches by which the cost of equity capital may be computed are:

(a) Dividend Price $\left(\frac{D}{P}\right)$ Approach

This approach is based on dividend valuation model. Under this approach, the cost of equity capital is calculated against a required rate of return in terms of future dividends. Accordingly, cost of capital (K_O) is defined as the rate that equates the present value of all expected future dividends per share with the net proceeds of the sale (or the current market price) of a share.[1] In short, it will be that rate of expected dividends which will actually maintain the present market price of equity shares.

As such, the cost of equity is measured by

$$K_e = \frac{D}{P} \quad \text{where}$$

K_e = Cost of Equity Share Capital

D = Dividend/Earnings per share

P = Net proceeds per share/current market price per share.

This approach gives due importance to dividends but it ignores one basic aspect, i.e., retained earnings also has an impact on the market price of equity shares.[2]

This approach, however, assumes that:

(i) market price of shares is influenced only by variations in earnings of the firm;

(ii) future earnings, which can be expressed as an average, will grow at a constant rate.

Illustration 3.7

A company issues equity shares of Rs. 10 each for public subscription at a premium of 20%. The company pays @ 5% as underwriting commission on issues price. Expected rate of dividend by equity shareholders is 25%.

You are required to compute the cost of equity capital.

Will your answer be different if it is calculated on the basis of present market value of equity share which is only Rs. 16?

---

1 *Ibid.*

2 Banerjee, B. — op. cit., p. 383.

Solution

The cost of capital is computed as:

$$K_e = \frac{D}{P} \text{ where}$$

K_e = Cost of Equity Share Capital
D = Dividend/Earnings Per Share
P = Net Proceeds Per Share

$$K_e = \frac{\text{Rs. } 2.5}{\text{Rs. } 11.40^*} \qquad {}^*\text{Rs. } 10 + \text{Rs. } 2 \left(\text{Rs. } 10 \times \frac{20}{100}\right) - 5\% \text{ com.}$$

$$K_e = 0.22 \text{ or } 22\% \qquad = \text{Rs. } 12 - \text{Re. } 0.60$$

$$= \text{Rs. } 11.40$$

However, in case of existing equity shares, it is better to calculate cost of equity shares on the basis of market price which is computed as

$$K_e = \frac{D}{MP}$$

K_e = Cost of Equity Capital
D = Dividend Per Share
MP = Market Price Per Share

$$= \frac{\text{Rs. } 2.5}{\text{Rs. } 16}$$

$$= 0.1563 \text{ or } 15.63\%.$$

(b) Dividend Price Plus Growth $\left(\frac{D}{P}+g\right)$ Approach

Under this approach, cost of equity capital is determined on the basis of the expected dividend rate plus the rate of growth in dividend, i.e., this method substitutes earnings per share by dividend and recognises the growth in it.[1]

Symbolically,

$$K_e = \frac{D}{P} + g$$

K_e = Cost of Equity Share Capital
D = Dividend Per Share
P = Net Proceeds Per Share
g = Growth Rate in Dividend

Illustration 3.8

Calculate the cost of equity capital from the following particulars presented by X Ltd.:

The current market price of an equity share of the company is Rs. 0.80. The current dividend per share is Rs. 6.40. Dividends are expected to grow @ 8%.

Solution

$$K_e = \frac{D}{P} + g$$

$$= \frac{\text{Rs. } 6.40}{\text{Rs. } 80} + 8\%$$

$$= 8\% + 8\%$$

$$= 16\%$$

1 In case of existing equity shares, however, the cost of equity capital can also be determined by the same formula, only, instead of (P) (net Proceeds of Shares), MP (Market Price) should be used.

Illustration 3.9

X Ltd. wants to issue 10,000 new equity shares of Rs. 100 each at par. The flotation costs are 5% of the price of shares. X Ltd. pays dividend initially @ Rs. 10 per share. Dividends are expected to grow 6%. Compute : (i) the cost of new issue of equity shares.

(ii) What will be the cost of existing equity shares if the current market price of an equity share is Rs. 200?

Solution

(a) $K_e = \frac{D}{P} + g$

$= \frac{\text{Rs. }10}{(\text{Rs. }100 - \text{Rs.}5)} + 6\%$

$= 10.53\% + 6\%$

$= 16.53\%$

where, K_e = Cost of Equity Share Capital

D = Dividend Per Share = Rs. 10

P = Net Proceeds Per Share, (Here Net Proceeds = Rs. 100 – Rs. 5 floating cost) = Rs. 95

g = Growth Rate in Dividend = 6%

(b) $K_e = \frac{D}{MP} + g$

$= \frac{\text{Rs. }10}{\text{Rs. }200} + 6\%$

$= 5\% + 6\%$

$= 11\%$

MP = Market Price Per Share

Illustration 3.10

Determine the cost of equity shares of company X from the following particulars:

(i) Current Market Price of a share is Rs. 140.

(ii) The underwriting cost per share on new shares is Rs. 5.

(iii) The following are the dividends paid on the outstanding shares over the past five years:

Year	Dividends per Share
1	10.50
2	11.00
3	12.50
4	12.60
5	13.40

(iv) The company has a fixed dividend payout ratio.

(v) Expected dividend on the new shares at the end of 1st year is Rs. 14.10 per share.

Solution

For calculating the cost of funds raised by equity share capital, we are to estimate the growth rate of dividends. During the five years the dividends have increased from Rs. 10.50 to Rs. 13.40 presenting as compound factor of 1.276 i.e., $\left(\frac{\text{Rs.}13.40}{\text{Rs.}10.50}\right)$. After applying the "compound sum of one rupee table" we know that a sum of Re. 1 would accumulate to Rs. 1.276 in five years @ 5% interest. Therefore, substituting the values in the above formula we get

$$K_e = \frac{D}{P} + g$$

$$= \frac{\text{Rs. } 14.10}{\text{Rs. } 135 \text{ (Rs. } 140 - \text{Rs. } 5)} + 5\%$$

$$= 10.44\% + 5\%$$

$$= 15.44\%$$

(c) Earning Price $\left(\frac{E}{P}\right)$ Approach

Under this approach, earning per share will actually determine the market price per share. In other words, the cost of equity capital is equivalent to the rate which must be earned on incremental issues of ordinary shares so as to maintain the present value of investment intact, i.e. the cost of equity capital is measured by the earning price ratio.[1]

Symbolically:

$$K_e = \frac{E}{P} \quad \text{where}$$

K_e = Cost of Equity Capital
E = Earnings Per Share
P = Net Proceeds of an Equity Share

This approach recognises both dividends and retained earnings. But there is difference of opinion among the supporters of the approach about the applicability of both earnings and market price figures. Some prefer to use the current earning rate and current market price while some others recognise average rate of earning (which is based on the earnings of past few years) and the average market price of equity shares (which is based on market price for the last few years).[2]

Illustration 3.11

The capital structure of a company is 1,00,000 equity shares of Rs. 100 each.

Its current earnings are Rs. 10,00,000 per annum. The company desires to raise an additional fund of Rs. 20,00,000 on the issue of new equity shares. The flotation costs are expected @ 10% on face value.

What will be the cost of equity capital if it is assumed that earnings of the company are stable?

Solution

By earning price ratio, the cost of equity capital is:

$$K_e = \frac{E}{P} \quad \text{where } E = \text{Earning per share} = \frac{\text{Rs. } 10,00,000}{\text{Rs. } 1,00,000} = \text{Rs. } 10 \text{ per share.}$$

$$= \frac{\text{Rs. } 10.00}{\text{Rs. } 90}$$

P = Net Proceeds of shares, i.e.

$= 11.1\%$ = Face Value – Flotation Cost

= Rs. 100 – Rs. 10

= Rs. 90

1 Solomon, E. — *Theory of Financial Management* — New York, Columbia University Press, 1969, p. 59.
2 In case of existing equity shares it is better to apply Market Price (MP) instead of Net Proceeds (P).

(d) Realised Yield Approach

Under this approach, cost of equity capital is determined on the basis of actual realised return by the investors on their investment, i.e., on equity shares. In other words, cost of equity capital is computed on the basis of dividends (which are taken from the past records) and the actual capital appreciation in the value of equity shares which are held by them. This approach is particularly applicable in those companies where the dividends are stable and the growth rate is almost constant. In short, this approach assumes that past behaviour will be repeated in future at a reasonable degree of certainty.

Illustration 3.12

Mr. X, a shareholder of P & Co., purchased 5 shares at a cost of Rs. 260 on 1.1.2003. He retained the shares for 5 years and sold them on 1.1.2008 for Rs. 325.

The dividend which he received for the last five years are as under:

Years	Dividends
	Rs.
2003	15
2004	15
2005	16
2006	16
2007	16

Calculate the cost of equity capital.

Solution

Before calculating the cost of equity capital, we are to compute the Internal Rate of Return (IRR) which can be calculated with the help of **"Trial and Error Method"** (discussed subsequently). The rate comes to 10% which is shown as:

Years	Dividends	Sale Proceeds	Discount Factors at 10%	Present Value
	Rs.	Rs.		
2003	15	—	0.909	13.63
2004	15	—	0.826	12.39
2005	16	—	0.751	12.02
2006	16	—	0.683	10.93
2007	16		0.621	9.94
2008	—	325	0.621	201.82
				260.73

Thus, the present value of cash flow as on Jan. 2008 amounts to Rs. 260.73 as against the purchase price of 5 shares of 1st Jan. 2003 which was Rs. 260. Therefore, at 10%, the PV of cash inflow will be equal to an outflow over a period of 5 years in the year 2003. As such, the cost of equity capital will be considered at 10%.

(ii) Retained Earnings

Generally, the companies do not distribute the entire profits by way of dividend among their shareholders. A part of such profits is retained for further expansion and development. It may lead to growth in both cash flow earnings and in dividends. Retained earnings, like equity funds, have no accounting cost but do have an opportunity cost. The opportunity cost of retained earnings is the dividend foregone by the shareholders. In other words, if the company retains cash flow, the equity shareholder foregoes the return he could have obtained if these funds were paid out. He receives higher dividends in future. Those projects which expected that extra future dividends at least cover these foregone opportunities should be financed by retained earnings. As such, the cost of equity reflects the return which shareholders would receive if cash flows were paid out by way of dividends. Thus, the cost of retained earnings is the earnings foregone by the shareholders, i.e., it is equal to the income that a shareholder could have earned otherwise by investing the same in an alternative investment. For instance, if a shareholder could have invested the said funds in an alternative way he could have a return of, say, 12%. This return is actually foregone by him simply due to the fact that the company does not distribute the entire profits by way of dividend. In this case, the cost of retained earnings may be taken at 12%.

It can alternatively be explained as:

Suppose the profits/earnings are not retained by the company and distributed by way of dividend to the shareholders which are invested by the shareholders in purchasing shares of the same company. Now, their expectation about the return on such new equity shares may be reconsidered as the opportunity cost of retained earnings. In short, if earnings/profits were distributed by way of dividend, and, at the same time, if an offer is made for right issue, the shareholders would have subscribed the right issues with the expectation of a certain return which is taken also as the cost of retained earnings.

The example that we have presented above reveals that the shareholders could have invested the dividends in the firms of similar risk and earned a return at least equal to the cost of equity if the dividends would have been paid to them, i.e., it ignores the effect of personal taxation, brokerage and flotation costs of the new issues. Because, in actual practice, they have to pay tax, brokerage commission etc. Therefore, the funds which are available to the shareholders should be less than what they would have been if the same had been retained by the company. Thus, the cost of retained earnings should always be less than the cost of new equity shares issued by the company.

However, the following adjustments are to be made in order to determine the cost of retained earnings:

(i) *Adjustment for Income-tax*

Needless to mention that the dividends which are received by the shareholders are subject to income-tax. The dividend that the shareholders receive is the net dividend (i.e., gross dividend minus income-tax) and not the gross dividend.

(ii) *Adjustment for Brokerage, Commission etc.*

Generally, when a shareholder wants to purchase new shares against the dividend that he receives, he is to incur some expenses by way of brokerage, commissions, etc. i.e., they cannot utilise the entire amount of dividends so received for the purpose of investment since he is to pay such expenses.

It should be remembered in this respect that the opportunity cost of retained earnings is the rate of return that a shareholder can obtain by investing net dividends against alternative investment.

The cost of retained earnings after making proper adjustments for income-tax and brokerage cost can be measured with the help of the following formula:

$K_r = K_e (1 - T)(1 - C)$

where

K_r = Cost of Retained Earnings

K_e = Cost of Equity Share Capital

T = Marginal Tax Rate applicable to the shareholders

C = Commission and Brokerage costs etc. in terms of percentage.

Illustration 3.13

Annual Net Profit earned by a company amounted to Rs. 50,000. Shareholders' required rate of return is 10%. It is expected that retained earnings can be invested by the shareholders against a similar type of company is 10%, if the same are distributed among the shareholders. Shareholders also have to incur by way of brokerage and commission @ 3% of the net dividends. Rate of tax is @ 40%.

Calculate the cost of retained earnings.

Solution

Before calculating the cost of retained earnings it becomes necessary to calculate the net amounts which are available for investment by the shareholders and their expected rate of return which is calculated as:

		Rs.
	Dividend Received	50,000
Less :	Personal tax (income-tax @ 40%)	20,000
	After-tax dividends	30,000
Less :	Brokerage Costing @ 3%	900
	Net amount available for investment	29,100

$$\text{Earnings of Investment Rs. } 29{,}100 \times \frac{10}{100} = \text{Rs. } 2{,}910$$

Now, if the net earnings has not been distributed by the company among the shareholders, the company could reinvest the full Rs. 50,000 instead of Rs. 29,100. The rate of return to be earned on the retained earnings to the shareholders will be:

$$\frac{\text{Rs. } 2{,}910}{\text{Rs. } 50{,}000} \times 100 = 5.82\%$$

Therefore, the rate of return expected by the shareholders on retained earnings is only 5.82%. The same can also be calculated with the help of the above formula:

$$\begin{aligned} K_r &= K_e (1 - T)(1 - C) \\ &= .10(1 - .40)(1 - .03) \\ &= 5.82\% \end{aligned}$$

The fundamental difficulty in the above approach is to determine the marginal tax rate of all the shareholders which will correctly reflect the opportunity cost of retained earnings to every shareholder. There are some authorities who prefer to use another approach known as **'External Yield Criterion'.** Under this approach, the opportunity cost of retained earnings is the rate of return which can be earned by investing the funds in outside securities, i.e., cost of retained earnings is the return on direct investment of funds and not the amount that the shareholders are able to receive on their investment. That is, this approach reveals the justifiable opportunity cost which can consistently be applied.

Besides, computation of marginal tax rate does not arise under this approach. However, this method may not be universally accepted. As such, many accountants prefer to compute the cost of retained earnings at par with equity share capital.

Cost of Debt (K_d)

Cost of debt is the rate of return which is expected by lenders. This is actually the interest rate which is specified at the time of issue. Debt may be issued at par, at a discount, or at a premium. It may be perpetual, or redeemable.

Method of Computation

(i) Debt Issued at Par

The method of computation for ascertaining cost of debt which is issued at par is comparatively an easy task. It is nothing but the explicit interest rate adjusted again for the tax liability.[1] Symbolically,

$$K_d = (1-T)R$$

where K_d = Cost of debt
T = Marginal tax rate
R = Interest Rate Payable

Example :

A company has issued 8% debentures and the tax rate is 50%, the after-tax cost of debt will be 4%. It may be calculated as:

$$\begin{aligned} K_d &= (1-T)R \\ &= (1-.5)8 \\ &= .5 \times 8 \\ &= 4\% \end{aligned}$$

Since interest is treated as an expense while calculating the firm's income for income-tax purpose, the tax is deducted out of the interest payable. This tax-adjusted interest rate is used only where the EBIT (Earnings/Profits before Interest and Tax) is equal to or exceed the interest. EBIT is found to be negative, the cost of debt should be considered before adjusting the interest rate of tax, i.e., in the above case, the cost of debt (before adjusting rate of tax) will be 8% only.

(ii) Debt Issued at a Premium or at a Discount

In many cases, bonds or debentures may be issued at a premium (when it is more than the face value) or at a discount (when it is less than the face value). In that case, the cost of debt must not be equal to the coupon rate of interest. Moreover, if discounts or premiums are amortised for income-tax purpose, it should also be considered. However, the appropriate formula for calculating cost of debt where discounts or premiums and flotation cost are involved, is:

$$K_d = \frac{C}{P}(1-T)$$

where K_d = Cost of debt
C = Annual Interest Payments
P = Net Proceeds
T = Applicable Tax rate

---

1 Solomon, E. — *The Theory of Management*— op. cit., pp. 53-55.

Illustration 3.14

A company issues 10% Debentures for Rs. 2,00,000. Rate of tax is 55%.

Calculate the cost of debt after tax if the debentures are issued (i) at par, (ii) at a discount of 10%, and (iii) at a premium of 10%.

Solution

Cost of debt is calculated as:

$$K_d = \frac{C}{P}(1-T)$$

where K_d = Cost of debt
C = Annual Interest Payments
P = Net Proceeds
T = Tax rate

(i) **Issued at Par**

$$= \frac{\text{Rs. } 20{,}000}{\text{Rs. } 2{,}00{,}000}(1 - .55)$$

$$= \frac{1}{10} \times .45$$

$$= 4.5\%$$

(ii) **Issued at a Discount of 10%**

$$= \frac{\text{Rs. } 20{,}000}{\text{Rs. } 1{,}80{,}000}(1 - .55)$$

$$= \frac{1}{9} \times .45$$

$$= 5\%$$

(iii) **Issued at a Premium of 10%**

$$= \frac{\text{Rs. } 20{,}000}{\text{Rs. } 2{,}20{,}000}(1 - .55)$$

$$= \frac{1}{11} \times .45$$

$$= 4.1\%$$

Illustration 3.15

A company raises Rs. 90,000 by the issue of 1,000, 10% Debentures of Rs. 100 each at a discount of 10%, repayable at par after 10 years.

If the rate of company's tax is 50, what is the cost of debt capital to the firm?

[C.U. M.Com.]

Solution

Here C = 10% of Rs. 1,00,000 = Rs. 10,000
P = Net Proceeds = Rs. 90,000
T = .5

$$\text{where } K_d = \frac{\text{Rs. } 10{,}000}{\text{Rs. } 90{,}000}(1 - .5)$$

$$= \frac{1}{9} \times .5$$

$$= 5.5\%$$

(iii) Cost of Redeemable Debt

If debt and/or debentures are redeemed after the expiry of a period the effective cost of debt before tax can be calculated with the help of the formula:

$$K_d \text{ (before tax)} = \frac{C + \left(\frac{D-P}{n}\right)}{\frac{(D+P)}{2}}$$

where C = Annual Interest Payments
D = Par Value of Debentures
n = Number of years to maturity
P = Net Proceeds

Illustration 3.16

A company issues 10,000, 10% Debentures of Rs. 10 each and realises Rs. 95,000 after allowing 5% commission to brokers. The debentures are redeemed after 10 years.

Calculate the effective cost of debt before tax.

Solution

$$K_d \text{ (before tax)} = \frac{C + \left(\frac{D-P}{n}\right)}{\frac{(D+P)}{2}}$$

where, C = Rs. 10,000 (10% of 1,00,000)
P = Rs. 95,000
D = Rs. 1,00,000
n = 10

$$= \frac{\text{Rs.}10{,}000 + \left(\frac{\text{Rs.}1{,}00{,}000 - \text{Rs.}95{,}000}{10}\right)}{\frac{(\text{Rs.}1{,}00{,}000 + 95{,}000)}{2}}$$

$$= \frac{\text{Rs. } 10{,}000 + \text{Rs. } 500}{\text{Rs. } 97{,}500}$$

$$= 10.77\%$$

However, in the present case, if the tax rate is considered @ 55%, the cost of debt after tax may be computed as:

$$K_d \text{ (before tax)} = K_d \text{ (before tax)} \times (1 - T)$$
$$= 10.77 \times (1 - .55)$$
$$= 10.77 \times .45$$
$$= 4.85\%$$

Cost of Preference Share Capital

The procedure for measuring the cost of preference share capital creates some conceptual problems. We have seen from the previous explanations that in case of a debt/borrowing, there is a legal obligation to pay interest at a specified fixed rate while, in case of a preference share, there is no such legal obligation. It may be argued by some others that since the preference dividend is not legally binding on the part of the company (even if such dividends are paid) it cannot be treated as a charge on the earnings. On the contrary, according to them, it is a distribution or appropriation of earnings to a class of owners and, as such, preference dividends do not constitute cost.

However, this is not correct, because, although it is not legally binding on the part of the company to pay preference dividend, the same is paid as and when the company earns sufficient profits. If the preference dividends are not paid it will create a dangerous situation from the standpoint of equity shareholders. If the preference dividends are not regularly paid, the preference shareholders will enjoy the right to take part in the general meeting with equity shareholders under certain conditions which is not desired by the equity shareholders. Moreover, the accumulation of arrears preference dividend may adversely affect the right to equity shareholders. As such, the cost of preference shares should be computed at par with cost of debentures. The method of computation is:

$$K_p = \frac{D_p}{P}$$ where

K_p = Cost of Preference Shares

D_p = Fixed Preference Dividend

P = Net Proceeds of Preference Shares

Illustration 3.17

A company issues 1,000, 10% Preference Shares of Rs. 100 each.

Calculate the cost of preference share capital when they are issued at (i) 10% premium, and (ii) at 10% discount.

Solution

(i) **When preference shares are issued at a premium of 10%.**

$$K_p = \frac{D_p}{P}$$ where, D_p = Rs. 10,000 (@ 10% on Rs. 1,00,000)

$$K_p = \frac{D_p}{P}$$ P = Rs. 1,10,000 (Rs. 1,00,000 + Rs. 10,000)

$$= \frac{\text{Rs. } 10{,}000}{\text{Rs. } 1{,}00{,}000}$$

$$= 9.09\%$$

(ii) **When preference shares are issued at a discount of 10%**

$$K_p = \frac{D_p}{P}$$

$$= \frac{\text{Rs. } 10{,}000}{\text{Rs. } 90{,}000 \text{ (Rs. } 1{,}00{,}000 - \text{Rs. } 10{,}000)}$$

$$= 11.11\%$$

Cost of Redeemable Preference Shares

In this case, the cost of capital is the discount rate which equates the net proceeds of sale of preference shares with the present value of future dividend and repayment of principal. The method of computation will be similar to the method of computation for Redeemable Debentures stated earlier. It is interesting to note that the cost of preference share capital is not adjusted for taxes since it is not a charge against profit but an appropriation of profit.

GENERAL ILLUSTRATIONS

Illustration 3.18

Book value of Capital structure of X Ltd. were:

Securities	Amount Rs.	Cost after Tax
Equity Share Capital (Rs. 100 each)	10,00,000	—
12% Pref. Share Capital	5,00,000	12%

Contd.

	Rs.	
Retained Earnings	5,00,000	—
10% Debentures	2,00,000	10%
12% Term Loan	3,00,000	12%

Calculate the Weighted Average Cost assuming that expected rate of dividend was @ Rs. 20 per share.

Solution

Workings :

(i) Cost of Equity Share Capital $= \frac{\text{Dividend}}{\text{Face Value}} \times 100$

$= \frac{\text{Rs. } 20}{100} \times 100$

$= 20\%$

(ii) Cost of retained earnings is also 20%.

Computation of Weighted Average Cost

Securities	Amount	Proportion	Cost after Tax	Weighted Average Cost
	Rs.			
Equity Share Capital	10,00,000	40%	·20	8.00
Pref. Share Capital	5,00,000	20%	·12	2.40
Retained Earnings	5,00,000	20%	·20	4.00
Debentures	2,00,000	8%	·10	0.80
Term Loan	3,00,000	12%	·12	1.44
	25,00,000	100%		16.64

Hence, Weighted Average Cost is 16.64%.

Illustration 3.19

X Ltd. presented the following capital structure and after-tax costs for the use of different sources of funds.

Sources of Funds	Amount	Proportion	After Tax Cost
	Rs.	(%)	(%)
Debt	30,00,000	25	6
Pref. Share Capital	24,00,000	20	12
Equity Share Capital	36,00,000	30	15
Retained Earnings	30,00,000	25	14
	1,20,00,000	100	

Compute Weighted Average Cost of Capital.

Solution

Computation of Weighted Average Cost of Capital

Sources of Funds (a)	Amount Rs. (b)	Proportion (%) (c)	Cost (%) (d)	Weighted Average Cost (e) = (c) × (d)
Debt	30,00,000	25	6	1.50
Pref. Share Capital	24,00,000	20	12	2.40
Equity Share Capital	36,00,000	30	15	4.50
Retained Earnings	30,00,000	25	14	3.50
	1,20,00,000	100		11.90

∴ Weighted Average Cost of Capital 11.90%.

Illustration 3.20

The following items have been extracted from the liabilities side of the Balance sheet of ABC Co. Ltd. as on 31st March 2009:

	Rs.
Paid up Capital	
4,00,000 equity shares of Rs. 10 each	40,00,000
Reserve and Surplus	60,00,000
Loans	
15% Debentures	20,00,000
14% Institutional Loans	60,00,000

Other Information

Year ended 31st March	Dividend per Share Rs.	Earning per Share Rs.	Average Market Price per Share Rs.
2009	4.00	7.50	50.00
2008	3.00	6.00	40.00
2007	4.00	4.50	30.00

You are required to calculate the weighted average cost of capital using book value as weights and $\frac{E}{P}$ ratio as the basis of cost of equity. Assume 50% tax-rate.

[P.C. College, Test]

Solution

Computation of Weighted Average Cost of Capital

Capital Structure (a)	Book-value Rs. (b)	Basis of Cost (c)	After Tax Rate (d)	Cost after Tax Rs. (e) = (d) × (b)
Equity Fund (Rs. 40,00,000 + Rs. 60,00,000)	1,00,00,000	$\frac{E}{P}$ Ratio = $\frac{\text{Rs. } 7.50}{\text{Rs. } 50} \times 100$ =	15%	15,00,000
15% Debentures	20,00,000	Interest after Tax 15% × 50% =	7.5%	1,50,000
14% Institutional Loans	60,00,000	Interest after Tax 14% × 50% =	7.0%	4,20,000
	1,80,00,000			20,70,000

$$\therefore \text{ Weighted Average Cost of Capital} = \frac{\text{Rs. } 20,70,000}{\text{Rs. } 1,80,00,000} \times 100 = 11.5\%$$

Illustration 3.21

X Ltd. has the following capital structure:

	Rs.
Equity Share Capital (20,000 Shares)	40,00,000
10% Preference Shares	10,00,000
14% Debentures	30,00,000
	80,00,000

The shares of the company sells for Rs. 20 each. It is expected that the company will pay next year a dividend of Rs. 2 per share which will grow at 7% for ever. Assume a 50% tax rate.

(a) Compute the weighted average cost of capital base on the existing capital structure.

(b) Compute the new weighted average cost of capital if the company raise an additional Rs. 20,00,000 debt by issuing 15% Debentures. This would increase the expected dividend toRs. 3 and leave the growth rate unchanged, but the price of share will fall to Rs. 15 per share.

[B.U. M.B.A.—Adapted]

Solution

Working = Cost of Equity $= \frac{D}{P} + g = \frac{\text{Rs. } 2}{\text{Rs. } 20} + .07 = .17$ or 17%

Cost of Debt = (14% – Tax) = 14% – 50% of Rs. 14 = 7% or .07

(a) **Computation of Weighted Average Cost of Capital**

Securities	Amount	Cost (after Tax)	Weights	Weighted Average Cost
	Rs.			
Equity Share Capital	40,00,000	.17	·500*	·085
Preference Share Capital	10,00,000	.10	·125	·013
Debentures	30,00,000	.07	·375	·026
				0.124

∴ Weighted Average Cost of Capital = 12.4%

	Rs.		Rs.		Rs.
* Proportion	= 40,00,000	:	10,00,000	:	30,00,000
	= ·500	:	·125	:	·375

(b) **Computations of Weighted Average Cost of Capital**

Securities	Amount	Cost (after Tax)	Weights	Weighted Average Cost
	Rs.			
Equity Share Capital	40,00,000	·270*	·40	·108
Preference Share Capital	10,00,000	·010	·10	·001
14% Debentures	30,00,000	·070	·30	·021
15% Debentures	20,00,000	·075	·20	·015
				·145

∴ Weighted Average Cost of Capital = 14.5%

*Cost of Equity $= \frac{D}{P} + g = \frac{\text{Rs. } 3}{\text{Rs. } 15} \times \cdot 07 = 0.27$ or 27%

Illustration 3.22

A firm has the following capital structure and after tax cost for the different sources of funds used:

Sources of Funds	Amount	Proportion	After Tax Cost
	Rs.	%	%
Debt	4,50,000	30	7
Preference Share Capital	3,75,000	25	10
Equity Share Capital	6,75,000	45	15
	15,00,000	100	

(a) Calculate the weighted average cost of capital using book-value weights.

(b) The firm wishes to raise further Rs. 6,00,000 for the expansion of the project as:

	Rs.
Debt	3,00,000
Preference Share Capital	1,50,000
Equity Share Capital	1,50,000

Assuming that specific costs do not change, compute the weighted marginal cost of capital.

[P.C. College, Test]

Solution

(a) **Computation of Weighted Average Cost of Capital**

Sources of Funds	Amount	Proportion	After Tax Cost	Weighted Average Cost
	Rs.	(%)	(%)	
(a)	(b)	(c)	(d)	(e) = (c) × (d)
Debt	3,00,000	30	7	2.10
Preference Share Capital	1,50,000	25	10	2.50
Equity Share Capital	1,50,000	45	15	6.75
		100		11.35%

∴ Weighted Average Cost of Capital 11.35%.

(b) **Computation of Weighted Marginal Cost of Capital**

Sources of Funds	Amount	Marginal Weight Proportion	After Tax Cost	Weighted Marginal Cost
	Rs.	(%)	(%)	
(a)	(b)	(c)	(d)	(e) = (c) × (d)
Debt	3,00,000	50%	7	3.50
Pref. Share Capital	1,50,000	25%	10	2.50
Equity Share Capital	1,50,000	25%	15	3.75
	6,00,000	100%		9.75%

∴ Weighted Marginal Cost of Capital 9.75%.

Illustration 3.23

In considering the most desirable capital structure for a company, the following estimates of the debt and equity capital (after-tax) have been made at various levels of debt-equity mix. :

Debt as a percentage of Total Capital Employed	Cost of Debt (%)	Cost of Equity (%)
0	5.00	12.00
10	5.00	12.00
20	5.00	12.50
30	5.50	13.00
40	6.00	14.00
50	6.50	16.00
60	7.00	20.00

You are required to determine the optimal debt-equity mix for the company by calculating composite cost of capital.

[P.C. College, Test]

Solution

Statement Showing the Computation of Composite Cost

Debt (%)	Equity (%)	Cost of Debt (%)	Cost of Equity (%)	Composite Cost of Capital (%)	
0	100	5.00	12.00	$5 \times 0 + 12 \times 1$	= 12%
10	90	5.00	12.00	$5 \times \cdot10 + 12 \times \cdot90$	= 11.30%
20	80	5.00	12.50	$5 \times \cdot20 + 12\cdot50 \times \cdot80$	= 11.00%
30	70	5.50	13.00	$5\cdot5 \times \cdot30 + 13 \times \cdot70$	= 10.75%
40	60	6.00	14.00	$5 \times \cdot40 + 14 \times \cdot60$	= 10.80%
50	50	6.50	16.00	$6\cdot5 \times \cdot50 + 16 \times \cdot50$	= 11.25%
60	40	7.00	20.00	$7 \times \cdot60 + 20 \times \cdot40$	= 12.20%

It becomes quite clear from the above statement that the lowest composite cost will arise only when there will be 30% debt and 70% equity and, as such, optional debt-equity mix will be 30% debt and 70% equity.

Illustration 3.24

Excel Industries Ltd. has assets of Rs. 1,60,000 which has been financed with Rs. 52,000 of debt and Rs. 90,000 of equity and a General Reserve of Rs. 18,000. The firm's total profits after interest and taxes for the year ended 31st March 2005 were Rs. 13,500. It pays 8% interest on borrowed funds and is in the 50% tax bracket. It has 900 equity shares of Rs. 100 each selling at a market price of Rs. 120 per share.

What is the weighted average cost of capital?

[Delhi Univ., M.Com.]

Solution

At first we are to compute each source of specific costs. Therefore, weighted average cost can be determined after applying proper weights.

(a) **Determination of Specific Costs**

(i) Cost of Debt (K_d) :

$$K_d = (1 - T)R$$
$$= (1 - .5)\ .08$$
$$= 4\%$$

(ii) Cost of Equity (K_e) :

$$K_e = \frac{\text{Earnings per Share (EPS)}}{\text{Present Market Price}} \times 100$$
$$= \frac{\text{Rs. } 15^*}{\text{Rs. } 120} \times 100$$
$$= 12.5\%$$

[*Note = Earnings per Share = $\frac{\text{Profit after Tax}}{\text{No. of Shares}} = \frac{13{,}500}{900}$ = Rs. 15]

(iii) Reserve — Here, the cost of retained earnings is taken at par with equity share capital (assumed **'External Yield Criterion'** is considered)

(b) **Weighted Average Cost of Capital**

Sources	**Amount**	**Capital Structure Proportion**	**After Tax Cost**	**Weighted Average Cost**
	Rs.		(%)	(%)
Equity	90,000	0.56	12.5	7.00
Reserve	18,000	0.11	12.5	1.38
Debt	52,000	0.33	4	1.32
	1,60,000	1.00		9.70

Notes :

1. Since Cost of Equity and Reserve are same, i.e., 12.5%, they are to be shown at a consolidated figure, i.e., Rs. 1,08,000 and weighted average cost may be ascertained although there will not be any change.

2. There is no difference between the market values and book values of equity and reserves. It will be clear from the following:

Total market value : 900 Shares @ Rs. 120 = Rs. 1,08,000—which may be allocated between equity and reserve in the ratio 90 : 18.

Therefore, the market value will be:

$$\text{Equity} = \text{Rs. } 1{,}08{,}000 \times \frac{90}{108} = \text{Rs. } 90{,}000$$

$$\text{Reserve} = \text{Rs. } 1{,}08{,}000 \times \frac{18}{108} = \text{Rs. } 18{,}000$$

That is, they are identical with book values. In the opposite case, weighted average cost can be interpreted in both ways.

Illustration 3.25

Your company's share is quoted in the market at Rs. 20 currently. The company pays a dividend of Re. 1 per share and the investor expects a growth rate of 5% per year. Compute:

(a) the company's cost of equity capital;

(b) if the anticipated growth rate is 6% p.a., calculate the indicated market price per share;

(c) if the company's cost of capital is 8% and the anticipated growth rate is 5% p.a., calculate the indicated market price if the dividend of Re. 1 per share is to be maintained.

[I.C.W.A. Final]

Solution

We know the relationship between cost of capital, dividend, price, and expected growth, which are expressed by the following formula:

(a) Cost of Equity Capital $= \dfrac{\text{Dividend per Share}}{\text{Current Market Price}} \times 100 + \text{Growth Rate (\%)}$

$= \dfrac{\text{Re. 1}}{\text{Rs. 20}} \times 100 + 5\%$

$= 5\% + 5\%$

$= 10\%$

(b) Market Price $= \dfrac{\text{Dividend per Share}}{\text{Cost of Equity Capital} - \text{Growth Rate (\%)}}$

$= \dfrac{\text{Re. 1}}{10\% - 6\%} = \dfrac{\text{Re. 1}}{4\%} = \text{Rs. } 25$

(c) Market Price $= \dfrac{\text{Re. 1}}{8\% - 5\%} = \dfrac{\text{Re. 1}}{3\%} = \text{Rs. } 33.33$

Illustration 3.26

X Ltd. has the following capital structure:

	Rs.
Equity Share Capital (20,000 shares)	4,00,000
6% Preference Shares	1,00,000
8% Debentures	3,00,000
	8,00,000

The market price of equity share is Rs. 20. It is expected that the company will pay a current dividend of Rs. 2 per share which will grow at 7% for ever. Rate of tax may be taken at 50%.

You are required to compute :

(a) A weighted average cost of capital based on existing capital structure.

(b) The new weighted average cost of capital if the company desires to raise a fund of an additional Rs. 2,00,000 debt by the issue of 10% Debentures. This would result in increasing the expected dividend to Rs. 3 and level the growth rate unchanged but the price of the share will fall to Rs. 15 per share.

(c) The cost of capital if, in (b) above, growth rate increases to 10%.

Solution

(a) Weighted Average Cost of Capital

Sources	Amount	Capital Structure Proportion (weights)	After-tax Cost	Weighted Average Cost
	Rs.		(%)	(%)
Equity Share Capital	4,00,000	0.500	.17*	0.0850
6% Preference Share Capital	1,00,000	0.125	.06	0.0075
8% Debentures	3,00,000	0.375	.04+	0.0150
	8,00,000	1.000		0.1075

∴ Weighted Average Cost of Capital is 10.75%

* Cost of Equity Share = $\frac{\text{Rs. 2}}{\text{Rs. 20}}$ + .07 = .1 + .07 = .17 or 17%.

+ It has a tax effect.

(b) **Weighted Average Cost of Capital**

Sources	Amount	Capital Structure Proportion (weights)	After-tax Cost	Weighted Average Cost
	Rs.		(%)	(%)
Equity Share Capital	4,00,000	0.40	.27*	0.108
6% Preference Share Capital	1,00,000	0.10	.06	0.006
8% Debentures	3,00,000	0.30	.04	0.012
10% Debentures	2,00,000	0.20	.0.5	0.010
	10,00,000	1.00		0.136

∴ Weighted Average Cost of Capital is 13.6%

* Cost of Equity Share = $\frac{\text{Rs. 3}}{\text{Rs. 15}}$ + .07 = .27%

(c) **Weighted Average Cost of Capital**

Sources	Amount	Capital Structure Proportion (weights)	After-tax Cost	Weighted Average Cost
	Rs.		(%)	(%)
Equity Share Capital	4,00,000	0.40	.30*	0.120
6% Preference Share Capital	1,00,000	0.10	.06	0.006
8% Debentures	3,00,000	0.30	.04	0.012
10% Debentures	2,00,000	0.20	.05	0.010
	10,00,000	1.00		0.148

∴ Weighted Average Cost of Capital is 14.8%.

* Cost of Equity Share = $\frac{\text{Rs. 3}}{\text{Rs. 15}}$ + .10 = 30%.

Illustration 3.27

The shares of a chemical company are selling at Rs. 20 per share. The firm has paid dividend @ Rs. 2 per share last year. The estimated growth of the company is approximately 5% per year.

(i) Determine cost of equity capital of company;

(ii) Determine the estimated market price of the equity share if the anticipated growth rate of the firm (a) rises to 8%, and (b) falls to 3%.

[C.S. Final]

Solution

(i) $K_e = \frac{D}{P} + g$

where K_e = Cost of Equity Capital

D = Dividend Per Share (DPS)

P = Market Price Per Share

g = Growth Rate

or, $\frac{2}{20} + 50\% = 0.10 + 0.05 = 0.15$ or, 15%

∴ Cost of Equity Capital is 15%

(ii) (a) $g = 8\%; D = \text{Rs. } 2; K_e = 15\%$

$$K_e = \frac{D}{P} + g$$

$$15\% = \frac{2}{P} + 8\%$$

or, $15\% - 8\% = \frac{2}{P}$ or, $7\% = \frac{2}{P}$ or, $P = \frac{100}{3.5} = \text{Rs. } 28.57$

∴ Market Price of Equity Share Rs. 28.57

(b) $g = 3\%, D = \text{Rs. } 2; K_e = 15\%$

$$K_e = \frac{D}{P} + g$$

or, $15\% = \frac{2}{P} + 3\%$

or, $15\% - 3\% = \frac{2}{P}$ or, $12\% = \frac{2}{P}$ or, $P = \frac{100}{6} = \text{Rs. } 16.67$

∴ Market Price of Equity Share Rs. 16.67

Illustration 3.28

The following is an extract from the financial statements of KPN Ltd.:

		Rs. (Rs. in '00,000)
	Operating Profit	105
Less :	Interest on Debentures	33
		72
Less :	Income-Tax	36
	Net Profit	36

Equity Share Capital (shares of Rs. 10 each)	200
Reserves and Surplus	100
15% Non-Convertible Debentures (Rs. 100 each)	220
	520

The market price per equity share is Rs. 12 and per debenture Rs. 93.75.

(i) What is the earning per share?

(ii) What is the percentage cost of capital to the company for the debenture funds and the equity?

[C.A. Final]

Solution

(i) We know

$$EPS = \frac{\text{Profit after tax} - \text{Pref. Dividend}}{\text{No. of Equity Shares}}$$

$$= \frac{\text{Rs. } 36{,}00{,}000 - \text{Nil}}{20{,}00{,}000}$$

$$= \text{Rs. } 1.80$$

(ii) (a) **Cost of Debentures**

		Rs.
	Interest on Debentures (15% of Rs. 220 lakhs)	33,00,000
Less :	Tax, say 50%	16,50,000
		16,50,000

$$K_d = \frac{\text{After-tax interest}}{\text{Amount of Debenture at cost}} \times 100 = \frac{\text{Rs. } 16{,}50{,}000}{\text{Rs. } 2{,}20{,}00{,}000} \times 100 = 7.5\%$$

(b) **Cost of Equity**

$$K_e = \frac{D}{P} \qquad D = \text{Earning per share i.e., Rs. } 1.80$$

$$K_e = \frac{1.8}{12} \qquad P = \text{Market Price per share i.e., Rs. } 12$$

$$K_e = 0.15 \text{ or, } 15\%$$

Illustration 3.29

The following information is available from the balance sheet of a company:

	Rs.
Equity Share capital — 20,000 shares of Rs. 10 each	2,00,000
8% Debentures	1,70,000
Reserves and Surplus	1,30,000

The rate of tax for the company is 50%; current level of equity dividend is 12%.

Calculate the Weighted Average Cost of capital using the above figures.

[I.C.W.A. Final]

Solution

Composition of Capital Structure	Amount	Percentage
Equity Share Capital	2,00,000	40
Reserves & Surplus	1,30,000	26
Net Worth	3,30,000	66
8% Debentures	1,70,000	34
	5,00,000	100

Weighted Average Cost of Capital

Capital Structure	Amount	Per-centage	Cost before Tax	Cost after Tax	Weighted Average Cost	
	Rs.					
Equity	2,00,000	40	12%	12%	4.80	(12% × 40%)
Reserves & Surplus	1,30,000	26	12%	12%	3.12	(12% × 26%)
	3,30,000	66			7.92%	
8% Debentures	1,70,000	34	8%	4%	1.36%	(4% × 34%)
Total	5,00,000	100			9.28%	

Illustration 3.30

The following particulars about the existing structure of Co. X are:

	Amount	Before-tax Cost
	Rs.	(%)
Equity Share Capital	4,00,000	12
Preference Share Capital	50,000	7
Long-term Debt	3,00,000	8

The company wants to undertake an expansion project costing Rs. 2,50,000 which can be taken from a financial institution at 10%. The minimum acceptable rate of return from the new project is based on the company's cost of capital.

What is the minimum acceptable rate of return to the company in case of the proposed expansion projects? You may assume a 50% tax rate.

Solution

We know that the minimum acceptable rate of return should be based on the company's cost of capital. In this case, we are to compute the weighted average cost of capital shown as under:

Weighted Average Cost (after tax)

Weighted Average Cost

Sources	Amount	Capital Structure Proportion (weights)	Before-tax Cost	Before-tax	After-tax
	Rs.		(%)	(%)	(%)
Equity Share Capital	4,00,000	0.40	12	4.80	4.80
Preference Share Capital	50,000	0.05	7	0.35	0.35
Long-term Debt (Existing)	3,00,000	0.30	8	2.40	1.20
New	2,50,000	0.25	10	2.50	1.25
	10,00,000	1.00		10.05	7.60

∴ Minimum acceptable rate of return from the new project would be 7.6%.

Illustration 3.31

Given below is the summary of the Balance Sheet of B. Ltd. as at 1st January 2007:

Balance Sheet

Liabilities	Rs.	Rs.	*Assets*	Rs.	Rs.
Share Capital			Premises (at cost)		1,70,000
Divided into 20,000 equity shares of Rs. 10 each, fully paid		2,00,000	Plant etc. (at cost)	1,18,000	
			Less : Depreciation	50,000	68,000
Revenue Reserve		1,30,000			

Contd.

	Rs.	Rs.		Rs.
7% Debentures		50,000	Trade Investment	85,000
(Redeemable 2014)			*Current Assets*	
Current Liabilities			Stock	70,000
Short-term Loans	25,000		Debtors	21,000
Trade Creditors etc.	12,000		Cash	3,000
		37,000		
		4,17,000		4,17,000

You are required to calculate the firm's weighted average cost of capital using balance sheet valuations. The following additional information are provided:

(i) 7% debentures were issued and are redeemable at par.

(ii) The short-term loans carry interest at 16% p.a.

(iii) The rate of tax may be assumed at 50%.

(iv) The shares and debentures are all quoted on the stock exchange and current market price are:

Equity Shares	Rs. 12.50
7% Debentures	Rs. 95

(v) All interest payments are up-to-date and equity dividend is currently 12%.

[C.U. M.Com.]

Solution

While computing the weighted average cost of capital, Balance Sheet Values are taken into consideration and, as such, market values are irrelevant. At first, we are to calculate the effective cost of capital to equity in order to compute the average cost :

		Rs.
	Equity Share Capital	2,00,000
Add :	Revenue Reserve for 20,000 shares	1,30,000
		3,30,000

$\therefore$ Value per share $= \dfrac{3,30,000}{20,000} = \text{Rs. } 16.5$

Hence, Effective cost of equity $= \dfrac{1.2}{16.5} \times 100 = 7.27\%$

Weighted Average Cost (after tax)

Sources	Amount	Capital Structure Proportion (weight)	Before-tax Cost	After-tax Cost	Weighted Average Cost (after tax)
	Rs.		(%)	(%)	(%)
Equity	3,30,000	0.87	7.27	7.27	6.32
Debenture	50,000	0.13	7.00	3.50	0.46
	3,80,000	1.00			6.78

$\therefore$ Weighted Average Cost of Capital 6.78%.

But, if current liabilities are treated as a part of capital structure, they are also to be given due importance. As such, if short-term loans are taken into consideration, the weighted average cost may be revised as:

Weighted Average Cost (after-tax)

Sources	Amount	Capital Structure Proportion (weight)	Before-tax Cost	After-tax Cost	Weighted Average Cost (after tax)
	Rs.		(%)	(%)	(%)
Equity	3,30,000	0.82	7.27	7.27	5.96
Debenture	50,000	0.12	7.00	3.50	0.42
Short-term Loans	25,000	0.06	16.00	8.00	0.48
	4,05,000	1.00			6.86

∴ Weighted Average Cost of Capital 6.86%

Note : Cost of trade creditors is not considered here.

Illustration 3.32

A company has the following capital structure:

	Rs.
Ordinary Shares of Rs. 10 each, fully paid	40,00,000
7.5% Cumulative Preference Shares of Rs. 100 each, fully paid	2,00,000
Reserve & Retained Profits	45,00,000
11% Long-term Loan	6,00,000
Total	93,00,000

In addition, the company has a bank overdraft for working capital and this averages to Rs. 10 lakhs. Interest thereon is 15%. You are required to :

Calculate the company's overall rate of return on capital employed in order to ensure :

(i) Payment of all interest;

(ii) Dividend Pay-out Ratio of 60%;

(iii) Payment of Preference Dividend;

(iv) Ordinary Shareholders' Dividend is 12%.

Assume the tax rate to be 50%.

[I.C.W.A. Final]

Solution

Calculation of Profit (Before Tax and Interest)

	Rs.	Rs.
Interest on Bank Overdraft		
$\left(\text{Rs. } 10,00,000 \times \frac{15}{100}\right)$	1,50,000	
Interest on Long-term Loans		
$\left(\text{Rs. } 6,00,000 \times \frac{11}{100}\right)$	66,000	2,16,000

Contd.

	Rs.	Rs.
7.5% Dividend on Cumulative Pref. Shares		
$\left(\text{Rs. } 2,00,000 \times \frac{7.5}{100}\right)$	15,000	
Ordinary Shareholders' Dividend		
$\left(\text{Rs. } 40,00,000 \times \frac{12}{100}\right)$	4,80,000	
Reserves & Retained Profits		
$\left[(\text{Rs. } 4,80,000 + 15,000)\, 4,95,000 \times \frac{100}{60} = 8,25,000\right]$		
(8,25,000 – 4,95,000)	3,30,000	
		8,25,000
Tax @ 50% of Net Profit before tax		
= Net Profit after tax will be 100% i.e.		8,25,000
Profit before Tax and Interest		18,66,000

Capital Employed

(Rs. 93,00,000 + Rs. 10,00,000) = 1,03,00,000

∴ Overall Return on Capital Employed $= \frac{\text{Profit}}{\text{Capital Employed}} \times 100$

$= \frac{\text{Rs. } 18,66,000}{\text{Rs. } 1,03,00,000} \times 100$

= 18.12%

Illustration 3.33

(a) Z Ltd. is currently paying annual dividends of 8 pence per share on its ordinary share, which have a market price of £ 1.60. Advance Corporation Tax is 30%.

It is believed that the average shareholder is looking for a return on his investment of 15% after suffering personal tax of 25% on grossed up dividends and 10% on capital gains (assumed to raise from retained earnings).

Given these assumptions, what do you estimate to be cost of equity capital (or the rate of return required to be earned) for this company?

(b) The cost of equity capital to a company can alternatively be calculated as the yield on long term risk-free investments, plus a market risk premium (adjusted for personal taxation) multiplied by the beta risk factor, for the company in question.

Given the following data, and assuming the same personal tax rates as above, you are required to calculate the average shareholder's required rate of return from Z Ltd. Also, you are required to explain the nature of the beta risk factor.

Gross yield to redemption.

Gross Yield on Govt. Securities	15%
Market Risk Premium	4%
Beta Risk factor for Z Ltd.	1.2%
Dividend Cover traditionally expected	2.0

[I.C.W.A. London —Adapted]

Solution

(a)	**Shareholder's required return on his investment**		15%
Less :	Net Return		
	Dividend 8 pence per share of £ 1.60 (market price)		
	$\frac{8 \text{ Pence}}{160 \text{ Pence}} \times 100 = 5\% \times \frac{100}{70}$ (grossing up) =	7.14%	
Less :	Personal tax suffering by shareholders		
	25% i.e. $\left(7.14\% \times \frac{25}{100}\right)$ =	1.78%	
			5.36%
			9.64%
	Capital Gains Tax at 10% = $9.64 \times \frac{100}{90}$		10.71%
	Hence Cost of equity or rate of return required to be earned =		
	[Net Return + Capital Gains Tax (5.36% + 10.71)]		16.07%
(b)	**Gross yield on Govt. Securities**		15%
Add :	Market risk premium		4%
			19%
Less :	Traditionally expected dividend cover : 2.0		
	∴ Dividend = $\frac{19\%}{2}$ = 9.5%		
	Tax @ 30% = 9.5% × 30%	2.85	
	Capital Gained @ 10% of 9.5%	0.95	
			3.80%
	Net Return to Shareholders		15.20%

Adjusted market price premium

= 15.20 – (15.00 – 30%)

= 15.20 – 10.50

= 4.70%

Beta risk factor for the Company Z Ltd. : 1.20

Here, 1.20 × 4.70% = 5.64%

Average shareholder's required rate of return is 15.20 + 5.64% = 20.84%

Beta risk is the measurement of share's rise or fall in comparison with the market's rise or fall.

$$\text{So, Z Ltd.} = \frac{\text{Share's rise or fall}}{\text{Market's rise or fall}} = \frac{12\%}{10\%} = 1.2\%$$

In other words, Z Ltd.'s share is 1.2% risky as compared to an average share.

Illustration 3.34

Your company is negotiating a technical collaboration with a foreign company for a patented component which is incorporated in its products :

Forecast of royalties payable in the first five half-years of the projects is:

			Rs.
H. Y. to	December	1999	23,000
	June	2000	14,600
	December	2000	47,800
	June	2001	95,600
	December	2001	47,800

There are three alternatives available to your company as:

(a) A single commuted payment in December 1997.

(b) Two equal payments in December 1997 and December 1998.

(c) Three equal payments in December 1997, 1998 and 1999, respectively.

The marginal cost of capital to the company is 10%, while opportunity cost is 20%.

Calculate from the above the higher and lower limits for the commuted payments.

Use Present Value Table.

[I.C.W.A. Final]

Solution

(a) Since royalties are payable half-yearly, they are to be discounted at 5% (i.e. $\frac{1}{2}$ of 10%) and 10% (i.e. $\frac{1}{2}$ of 20%) for marginal cost and opportunity cost, respectively.

Present Value in December 1997

Half-year ended		No. of half-years from Dec. 1999	Royalties Payable	Marginal Per Rupee	Cost at 5% Amount	Opportunity Per Rupee	Cost at 10% Amount
(a)		(b)	(c)	(d)	(e)= (c) × (d)	(f)	(g) = (c) × (f)
			Rs.		Rs.		
Dec.	1999	4	23,000	0.8227	18,922	0.6830	15,709
June	2000	5	14,600	0.7835	11,439	0.6209	9,065
Dec.	2000	6	47,800	0.7462	35,668	0.5645	26,983
June	2001	7	95,600	0.7107	67,943	0.5132	49,062
Dec.	2001	8	47,800	0.6768	32,351	0.4665	22,299
Single Commuted Payment in Dec. 1997					1,66,323		1,23,118

(b) If two equal payments are made in Dec. 1997 and Dec. 1998, the amount which is not paid in Dec. 1997 will accrue interest for one year up to Dec. 2000. In that case the formula to be used:

$$I = \frac{1 + r}{2 + r} \times P$$

where I = Instalment

r = Rate of Interest

P = Commuted Present Value

When Marginal Cost is 10%

$$I = \frac{1 + .1}{2 + .1} \times \text{Rs. } 1,66,323$$

= Rs. 87,122

When Opportunity Cost is 20%

$$I = \frac{1 + .2}{2 + .2} \times \text{Rs. } 1,23,118$$

= Rs. 67,155

(c) In case of three equal instalments in Dec. 1997, 1998 and 1999 the following formula may be used:

$$I = \frac{(2r + 1 + r^2)}{3 + 3r + r^2} \times P$$

When Marginal Cost is 10%

$$I = \frac{(2 \times .1 + 1 + 0.1)}{3 + (3 \times .1) + (.01)} \times \text{Rs. } 1{,}66{,}323$$

$$= \frac{(.2 \times 1 + .01)}{3 + .3 + .01} \times \text{Rs. } 1{,}66{,}323$$

$$= \frac{1.21}{3.31} \times \text{Rs. } 1{,}66{,}323$$

$$= \text{Rs. } 60{,}801$$

When Opportunity Cost is 20%

$$I = \frac{(.4 + 1 + .04)}{3 + .6 + .04}) \times \text{Rs. } 1{,}23{,}118$$

$$= \frac{1.44}{3.64} \times \text{Rs. } 1{,}23{,}118$$

$$= \text{Rs. } 48{,}706.$$

Illustration 3.35

By the judicious use of the following estimates of the after-tax cost of debt and cost of equity capital at different levels of debt-equity mix in the capital structure of a company, ascertain the level at which the capital structure of the company will be at its optimum :

1 **Debt as % of Total Capital Employed**	2 **Cost of Debt (%)**	3 **Cost of Equity (%)**
0	6	10
10	6	10
20	6	11
30	7	12
40	8	14
50	9	16
60	10	20

[C.U. M.Com.]

Solution

Statement of Composite Cost of Capital under Different Capital Structures

	% of Total	Specific Cost	Composite Cost
Debt	0	6	0
Equity	100	10	10
	100		10
Debt	10	6	0.60
Equity	90	10	9.00
	100		9.60
Debt	20	6	1.20
Equity	80	11	8.80
	100		10.00

Contd.

Debt	30	7	2.10
Equity	70	12	8.40
	100		10.50
Debt	40	8	3.20
Equity	60	14	8.40
	100		11.60
Debt	50	9	4.50
Equity	50	16	8.00
	100		12.50
Debt	60	10	6.00
Equity	40	20	8.00
	100		14.00

From the above statement it becomes clear that composite cost of capital is minimum at 9.60, i.e. at 10% debt ratio. Hence, optimum capital structure in this case would be 10% Debt and 90% Equity.

ASSIGNMENT MATERIALS

THEORETICAL

Multiple Choice Questions

1. (a) Dividend plus growth for K_e is:

(i) $\frac{D}{P}-g$ (ii) $\frac{D}{P}+g$

(iii) $\frac{D}{MP-T}$ (iv) None of these

(b) K_e is equal to:

(i) $\frac{D}{P}$ (ii) $\frac{P}{D}$

(iii) $\frac{D}{P-T}$ (iv) None of these

(c) In case of $\frac{E}{P}$ approach, K_e is:

(i) $\frac{E}{P}$ (ii) $\frac{P}{E}$

(iii) $\frac{E}{P-T}$ (iv) None of these

(d) Cost of Debt is:

(i) (T – I) R (ii) (R – I) T

(iii) (I – T) R (iv) None of these

(e) Cost of Debt issued at Premium is:

(i) $\frac{C}{P}(I-T)$ (ii) $\frac{P}{C}(I-T)$

(iii) $\frac{T}{P}(C-I)$ (iv) None of these

(f) Cost of Redeemable Debt is:

(i) $\frac{C+\frac{(D-P)}{n}}{\frac{(D+P)}{2}}$ (ii) $\frac{D+\frac{(C-P)}{n}}{\frac{(C+P)}{2}}$

(iii) $\frac{C-D}{n}$ (iv) None of these

(g) Cost of Retained Earning is:

(i) $K_e(T-1)(1-c)$ (ii) $Ke(1-T)(1-c)$

(iii) $K_e(1-T)(1-c)$ (iv) None of these

(h) Weighted Average Cost of Capital is:

(i) Proportion × after-tax cost (ii) Proportions × before-tax cost

(iii) Proportion × specific cost (iv) None of these

[Ans. (a) (ii); (b) (i); (c) (i); (d) (iii); (e) (i); (f) (i); (g) (iii); (h) (i)]

Short Answer-type Questions

2. Examine critically the different approaches to the calculation of cost of equity. Discuss the merits and demerits of each.

[Delhi, M.Com.]

3. What is cost of capital? What is meant by explicit and real cost of capital?

[C.U. M.Com.]

4. Explain the various approaches for computing the cost of equity. Discuss the merits and demerits of each.

[C.A.]

5. Examine the problems faced in determining the cost of capital. How is the cost of capital relevant in capital budgeting decisions and capital structure planning?

[C.A.]

6. What is weighted average cost of capital? Examine the rationale behind the use of weighted average cost of capital.

[Delhi, M.Com.]

7. 'Cost of Capital is essentially a time cost.' —Discuss. **[C.U. M.Com.]**

8. What is meant by cost of capital of a firm and what relevance does it have in decision-making? How is it calculated for different types of sources of capital fund? Why is the Cost of Capital most appropriately measured on the 'After-tax Basis'?

[C.A.]

9. What is meant by Cost of Capital? What are the components of the Cost of Capital? What is the Cost of Retained Earnings? How is the cost of new equity issues determined?

[C.A.]

10. Identify the areas in Financial Management where the concept of 'Cost of Capital' has relevance. What do you understand by the term 'Marginal and Average Cost of Capital'? Are these concepts above criticism?

[C.U. M.B.M.]

11. Define the concept of 'Cost of Capital'. State how you would determine the weighted average cost of capital of a firm.

[C.U. M.Com.]

12. Explain the concept of 'Cost of Capital'. Also explain different types of costs.

[Meerut, M.Com.]

13. Write Notes on:
    (a) Marginal Cost of Capital **[C.A. Final]**
    (b) Weighted Average Cost of Capital. **[C.S. Final]**

Long Answer-type Questions

14. How can you determine the cost of equity capital in a growing company?

[C.A. Final]

15. Explain the concept of 'Cost of Capital' as a device for establishing a cut-off point of capital investment proposals.

[Delhi, M.Com.]

16. Explain briefly the different approaches to the computation of the cost of the equity capital.

[C.A. Final]

17. Why is it that 'debt' is the cheapest source of finance for a profit-making company?

[Delhi, M.Com.]

18. Examine the problems in the determination of composite cost of capital.

[C.S. Final]

19. What is meant by cost of capital? What are the components of cost of capital? What is cost of 'Retained Earnings'? How is the cost of new equity issue determined?

[C.A. Final]

20. What do you understand by cost of capital? How is it ascertained?

[Calicut, M.Com.]

21. Discuss the underlying logic of the cost of capital. **[C.U. M.Com.]**

PRACTICAL

1. The Xavier Corporation, a dynamic growth firm which pays no dividends, anticipates a long-term level of future earning of Rs. 7 per share. The current price of Xavier's share is Rs. 55.45; flotation costs for the sale of equity shares would average about 10% of the price of the shares.

What is the cost of new equity capital to Xavier Corporation? **[Delhi, M.Com.]**

[Ans. $\frac{7}{49.90}$ **or, 14.03%]**

2. X Ltd. desires to issue fresh equity shares. The market price of its share at present is Rs. 125 per share. Payment of dividend in the past was:

2000	—	10.75%
2001	—	11.45%
2002	—	12.25%
2003	—	13.11%
2004	—	14.03%

The flotation costs are estimated at 3% of the current selling price of the shares.

Calculate :

(i) Growth rates in dividends,

(ii) Cost of funds raised by issue of equity shares, assuming that the growth rate as calculated under (a) above will continue for ever.

Cost of new Equity Shares.

[Ans. (i) 7%; (ii) 19.01%; (iii) 19.38%]

3. Mr. X is a shareholder in Y Ltd. Although earnings for the Y Ltd. have varied considerably, Mr. X has determined that the long-term average dividend for the firm have been Rs. 2 per share. He expects a similar pattern to prevail in the future. Giving the volatility of dividends, Mr. X had decided that minimum rate of 20% should be earned on the share.

What prices should Mr. X be willing to pay for the shares?

[Delhi, M.Com.]

[Ans. Rs. 10]

4. Aries Ltd. wishes to raise additional finance of Rs. 10 lakhs for meeting its investment plans. It has Rs. 2,10,000 in the form of retained earnings available for investment purposes.

The following are the further details :

(1)	Debt/Equity Mix	30%/70%
(2)	Cost of Debt up to Rs. 1,80,000	10% (before Tax)
	beyond Rs. 1,80,000	16% (before Tax)
(3)	Earning per share	Rs. 4
(4)	Dividend pay out	50% of earnings
(5)	Expected growth rate in dividend	10%
(6)	Current market price per share	Rs. 44
(7)	Tax Rate	50%

You are required :

(a) To determine the pattern for raising the additional finance.

(b) To determine the post-tax average cost of additional debt.

(c) To determine the cost of retained earnings and cost of equity; and

(d) Compute the overall weighted average, after tax, cost of additional finance.

[C.A. Final]

[Ans. (a) Rs. 10,00,000; (b) 6.2%; (c) 15%; (d) 12.36%]

5. X Ltd. finances its investment pattern as : 60% in equity and 40% in debt. Rate of return on equity (expected) is 20% after tax and that of debt is 8% after tax. The firm is considering an investment proposal costing Rs. 40,000 with an expected return that will last for ever.

What amount (in Rs.) must the proposal yield per year so that the market price of the share does not change?

[Ans. Rate of Return on Equity After-tax 0.20]

6. A mining company's iron-ore reserves are being depleted and its cost of recovering and declining quantity of iron-ore are rising each year. As a consequence, the company's earnings and dividends are declining at a rate of 8% per year.

If the previous year's dividend was Rs. 10 and the required rate of return is 15% what would be the current price of the equity shares of the company?

[Ans. Rs. 40]

7. P Ltd. is foreseeing a growth rate of 12% p.a. in the next 2 years. The growth rate is likely to fall to 10% for the third year and the fourth year. After that, the growth rate is expected to stabilise at 8% p.a.

If the last dividend was Rs. 1.50 per share and the required rate of return is 16%, find out the intrinsic value per share of P. Ltd.

[Ans. Rs. 22.43 (Rs. 5.44 + Rs. 16.99)]

8. Messers Efficient Corporation has capital structure of 40% debt and 60% equity. The company is presently considering several alternative investment proposals costing less than Rs. 20 lakhs. The corporation always raises the required fund without disturbing its present debt-equity ratio.

The cost of raising the debt and equity are:

Project Cost	Cost of Debt	Cost of Equity
Up to Rs. 2 lakhs	10%	12%
2 lakhs—5 lakhs	11%	13%
5 lakhs—10 lakhs	12%	14%
10 lakhs—20 lakhs	13%	14.5%

Assuming the tax rate at 50%

Calculate :

(i) Cost of capital of two projects X and Y whose fund requirements are Rs. 6.5 lakhs and Rs. 14 lakhs, respectively.

(ii) If a project is expected to give after-tax return of 10%, determine under what conditions it would be acceptable?

[C.S. Final]

[Ans.

	Project	Fund Requirement	Cost of Capital
(i)	**X**	**Rs. 6.5 lakhs**	**10.8%**
	Y	**Rs. 14 lakhs**	**11.3%**

(ii) roject cost does not exceed Rs. 5 lakhs. Acceptance criterion After-tax return must be more than or at least equal to weighted average cost of capital]

9. In considering the most desirable capital structure for a company, the following estimates of the cost of debts and equity capital (after-tax) have been made at various levels of debt-equity mix:

Debtor's Percentage of Total Capital Employed	Cost of Debt (%)	Cost of Equity (%)
0	7.0	15.0
10	7.0	15.0
20	7.0	15.5
30	7.5	16.0
40	8.0	17.0
50	8.5	19.0
60	9.5	20.0

You are required to determine the optimal debt-equity mix for the company by calculating composite cost of capital.

[C.S. Final]

[Ans. Composite Cost of Capital 13.4%; Optimal Debt-Equity Mix. : Debt, 40%, Equity 60%]

10. A paper company has the following specific cost of capital along with the indicated book and market value weights:

Types of Capital	Cost (%)	Book Value Weights (%)	Market Value Weights (%)
Long-term Capital	5	30	25
Preference Shares	10	20	17
Equity Shares	12	40	46
Retained Earnings	12	10	12
		100	100

(a) Calculate the weighted average cost of capital using book-value and market value weight. Which of them do you consider better and why?

(b) Calculate the weighted average cost of capital using material weights if the company intends to raise the needed fund using 50% long-term debt, 35% Pref. Shares, and 15% retained earnings?

[Ans. (a) 9.5%, 9.9%; (b) 7.8%]

CHAPTER 4

LEVERAGES

Introduction

From the discussion made so far in Chapter Two it becomes clear that a firm can use various sources of finance although the cost for the same varies. It is to be noted that the sources may be classified into two : viz., (i) the sources which carry a fixed rate of return, and (ii) the sources which do not carry a fixed rate of return, i.e., variable. It is also interesting to note that the fixed return has an effect on those who enjoy variable return. As debts/loans require the payments of fixed rate of interest, the yield or return to the shareholders is affected by the like amount in the capital composition also. Thus, the financing decisions of a firm depends on the principles and types of leverage. In the present study we are going to highlight the various aspects of leverages while planning the capital structure.

According to the *Concise Oxford Dictionary*, 'lever' means a bar resting on pivot and used to raise heavy or firmly fixed object, or a mechanical device consisting of straight bar or other rigid structure of which one point (fulcrum) is fixed, another is connected with the force (weight) to be resisted or acted upon, and a third is connected with the force (power) applied.[1] Similarly, leverage means action of or 'way of applying lever'. In other words, the function of a lever is to raise a heavy object with a minimum force.

Same principle is also applied in business. Leverage may be defined, here, as the employment of an asset or funds for which the firm pays a fixed cost for fixed return. These fixed costs/returns may be assumed as the fulcrum of a lever. That is why when revenues less variable cost (Earning before Interest and Tax—EBIT) exceeds fixed cost/return, there is positive or favourable leverage. In the opposite case, there is negative for unfavourable leverage. In short, it may be stated that a small change in sales brings a greater change in income (EBIT). Leverage happens in varying degrees, i.e., the greater the degree of leverage the greater is the risk although it brings an additional return to the equity owners.

Practically, if we want to know that how EPS (Earning Per Share) is affected by changes in output or revenues, the answer lies in the analysis of leverage presented in financial statement. It may be expressed as:

$$\frac{LA}{LB} = \frac{\Delta \text{ (Delta which expresses change at the margin) } A/A}{\Delta B/B}$$

where $\frac{LA}{LB}$ = Leverage of A with B

ΔA = (the dependent variable) change in A

ΔB = (the independent variable) change in B

[1] *The Concise Oxford Dictionary*—O.U.P.—7th Edn., p. 577.

$\Delta A/A$ = Percentage change in A

$\Delta B/B$ = Percentage change in B

Thus, from the above, it becomes clear that leverage measures the relationship between two variables.

Types of Leverage

There are three types of Leverage :

(a) *Operating Leverage* — associated with investment (assets acquisition) activities

(b) *Financial Leverage* — associated with financing activities and

(c) *Total/Composite/ Combined Leverage* — combination of operating leverage and financial leverage.

Operating Leverage

Operating leverage arises when the operating profit varies disproportionately with the amount of sales, i.e., it appears from the existence of fixed operating expenses. We know operating cost consists of

(i) Fixed Cost — remains fixed irrespective of the quantity that is produced

(ii) Variable Cost — varies directly with the quantity produced or with the volume of sales

(iii) Semi-Variable — partly fixed and partly variable.

Thus, the operating leverage is the firm's ability to use fixed operating costs to magnify the effect of changes in the sales or its earning before interest and tax (EBIT). That is, with fixed costs, the percentage changes in profits accompanying a change in volume is greater than the percentage change in volume.[1] Needless to mention here that there will be no operating leverage, if there is no fixed operating cost.

Operating leverage exists when a firm has to pay fixed cost irrespective of volume of output or sales. A firm is said to have a high degree of operating leverage if it employs a greater amount of fixed cost and a smaller amount of variable cost. On the contrary, if the firm incurs greater amount of variable cost and a smaller amount of fixed cost, it produces a low degree of operating leverage.

Ascertainment of EBIT where operating cost includes fixed operating expenses

Illustration 4.1

X Ltd. presents the following particulars:

Units Produced and Sold	20,000 units
Fixed Operating Cost	Rs. 50,000
Variable Operating Cost	Rs. 40 per unit
Selling Price per Unit	Rs. 80

Determine the effect of EBIT if (i) sales increase by 25%, and (ii) if sales decreased by 25% and comment on them.

---

[1] Khan & Jain—*Financial Management*—Tata McGrawHill Publishing Co. Ltd., 1987, p. 434.

Solution

Ascertainment of EBIT and Different Levels of Activity

	Present activity	At 25% increase	At 25% decrease
Level of Activity (in Units)	20,000	25,000	15,000
	Rs.	Rs.	Rs.
Sales @ Rs. 80 per unit	1,60,000	2,00,000	1,20,000
Less : Variable Operating Cost @ Rs. 40 p.u.	80,000	1,00,000	60,000
Contribution	80,000	1,00,000	60,000
Less : Fixed Operating Expenses	50,000	50,000	50,000
EBIT	30,000	50,000	10,000
Increase/Decrease in EBIT	—	(+) 20,000	(–) 20,000
∴ % Change in EBIT	—	(+) 67%	(–) 67%

Comment

It is evident from the above that if sales are, increased by 25%, there will be a corresponding increase in EBIT by 67% (i.e., Rs. 30,000 to Rs. 50,000) on the contray, if volume of sales are decreased by 25% in that case, their will be a corresponding decrease in EBIT by 67% (i.e. Rs. 30,000 – Rs. 10,000).

Moreover, if volume of sales increases, the fixed operating cost p.u. will obviously be lower which will increase the EBIT.

25%, increase in sales volume has increased the amount of EBIT due to the effect of fixed operating expenses.

Where operating cost includes variable cost only

Illustration 4.2

Consider the previous illustration and ascertain the changes in EBIT assuming that there was no fixed operating expenses.

Solution

Ascertainment of EBIT at Different Levels of Activities

	Present activity	At 25% increase	At 25% decrease
Level of Activity (in Units)	20,000	25,000	15,000
	Rs.	Rs.	Rs.
Sales @ Rs. 80 per unit	1,60,000	2,00,000	1,20,000
Less : Variable Cost @ Rs. 40	80,000	1,00,000	60,000
Contributions	80,000	1,00,000	60,000
Less : Fixed Operation Expenses	—	—	—
EBIT	80,000	1,00,000	60,000
Increase/Decrease in EBIT —	—	(+) 20,000	(–) 20,000
∴ % Change in EBIT	—	(+) 25%	(–) 25%

Comment

It becomes clear from the above that 25% increase in volume of sales will lead to 25% increase in EBIT and vice versa in the opposite case, although there was no fixed operating expenses and will remain till both the variable cost as well as the selling price will not make any change.

It is interesting to note that impact of leverage appears at favourable or unfavourable one (this aspect has been explained in a subsequent paragraph), but the quotient must be a positive one. Favourable leverages appear when there is a positive impact of EBIT as a result of increase in sales, and vice versa in the opposite case.

It is needless to say that if the operating leverage is higher there will be a higher EBIT followed by higher operating risk.

Effect of fixed overhead in operating leverage

Illustration 4.3

Y Ltd. presented the following particulars:

No. of units produced and sold	5,000 units
Selling Price per unit	Rs. 100
Variable Cost per unit	Rs. 80

Compute the operating leverages and comment on the role of fixed overhead under the following conditions:

(a) if fixed overhead amounts to Rs. 25,000;

(b) if fixed overhead amounts to Rs. 30,000;

(c) if fixed overhead amounts to Rs. 40,000.

Solution

Computations of EBIT at Different Levels of Fixed Overhead

	a	b	c
	Rs.	Rs.	Rs.
Sales (5,000 units × Rs. 100)	5,00,000	5,00,000	5,00,000
Less : Variable Cost (5,000 × Rs. 80)	4,00,000	4,00,000	4,00,000
Contribution	1,00,000	1,00,000	1,00,000
Less : Fixed Overhead	25,000	30,000	40,000
EBIT	75,000	70,000	60,000
Operating Leverage = $\frac{\text{Contribution}}{\text{EBIT}}$ =	1.33	1.43	1.67

Comment

It becomes clear from the above that with the increase in fixed overhead, there is a corresponding increase in operating leverage. In other words, in case of condition (c), where sales increase by 100%, operating leverage will increase by 167%. Thus, increase in fixed overhead will increase the operating leverage also.

***Effect of operating* leverage**

Illustration 4.4

Firms	A	B	C
	Rs.	Rs.	Rs.
Selling Price	10	10	10
Fixed Costs	90,000	2,00,000	3,15,000
Variable cost per unit	7	6	5

Ascertain

(a) BEP (Break-even points) for all the firms.

(b) Profit earned by the firms if each of them sells 1,00,000 units.

(c) What will be the impact of profit if

(i) sales increases by 25%?

(ii) sales decreases by 25%?

Solution

(a) BEP for each firm :

$$\text{BEP} = \frac{\text{Fixed Costs}}{\text{Contribution (Sales – Variable Costs)}}$$

For **Firm A** $= \frac{\text{Rs. } 90,000}{\text{Rs. } 10 - \text{Rs. } 7} = \frac{\text{Rs. } 90,000}{\text{Rs. } 3} = 30,000 \text{ units}$

Firm B $= \frac{\text{Rs. } 2,00,000}{\text{Rs. } 10 - \text{Rs. } 6} = \frac{\text{Rs. } 2,00,000}{\text{Rs. } 4} = 50,000 \text{ units}$

Firm C $= \frac{\text{Rs. } 3,15,000}{\text{Rs. } 10 - \text{Rs. } 5} = \frac{\text{Rs. } 3,15,000}{\text{Rs. } 5} = 63,000 \text{ units}$

(b) Ascertainment of Profit if the firms sell 1,00,000 units :

Comparative Profitability Statement

	Firms A	Firms B	Firms C
Units Sold	1,00,000	1,00,000	1,00,000
Contribution (S – V)	(Rs. 10 – Rs. 7) = Rs. 3	(Rs. 10 – Rs. 6) = Rs. 4	(Rs. 10 – Rs. 5) = Rs. 5
Total Sales (Units × Per Unit)	Rs. 10,00,000	Rs. 10,00,000	Rs. 10,00,000
Less: Variable Cost	7,00,000	6,00,000	5,00,000
Contribution	3,00,000	4,00,000	5,00,000
Less: Fixed Cost	90,000	2,00,000	3,15,000
Profit	2,10,000	2,00,000	1,85,000

(i) Impact of Profit when sales increase by 25%

	A	B	C
Units Sold (1,00,000 + 15%)	1,25,000	1,25,000	1,25,000
Contribution	Rs. 3	Rs. 4	Rs. 5
Total Sales	12,50,000	12,50,000	12,50,000
Less: Variable Cost	8,75,000	7,50,000	6,25,000
Contribution	3,75,000	5,00,000	6,25,000
Less: Fixed Cost	90,000	2,00,000	3,15,000
Profit	2,85,000	3,00,000	3,10,000
Increase in Profit	75,000	1,00,000	1,25,000
Percentage Increase in Sales	25%	25%	25%
Percentage Increase in Profit	$= \frac{\text{Rs. } 75,000}{\text{Rs. } 2,10,000} \times 100$ $= 35{\cdot}71\%$	$= \frac{\text{Rs. } 1,00,000}{\text{Rs. } 2,00,000} \times 100$ $= 50\%$	$= \frac{\text{Rs. } 1,25,000}{\text{Rs. } 1,85,000} \times 100$ $= 67{\cdot}57\%$

(ii) Impact of Profit when sales decrease by 25%

		A	B	C
	Units Sold (1,00,000 – 25%)	75,000	75,000	75,000
		Rs.	Rs.	Rs.
	Contribution	3	4	5
	Total Sales	7,50,000	7,50,000	7,50,000
Less :	Variable Cost	5,25,000	4,50,000	3,75,000
	Contribution	2,25,000	3,00,000	3,75,000
Less :	Fixed Cost	90,000	2,00,000	3,15,000
	Profit	1,35,000	1,00,000	60,000
Percentage	decrease in Sales	25%	25%	25%
Percentage	decrease in Profit	$= \frac{\text{Rs. } 1,50,000}{\text{Rs. } 2,10,000} \times 100$	$= \frac{\text{Rs. } 2,00,000}{\text{Rs. } 2,00,000} \times 100$	$= \frac{\text{Rs. } 2,50,000}{\text{Rs. } 1,85,000} \times 100$
		= 71·4285%	= 100%	= 135·14%

From the above, it becomes crystal clear that the firm C, which has the highest amount of fixed overhead in comparison with the other firms, is most vulnerable as a result of change in sales. We also find from the above table that when sales increase from 1,00,000 units to 1,25,000 units, profit increased by 67·57% as compared to 50% and 35·71% of firms B and A, respectively. Again, when the sales decrease, the percentage decrease in profit is also highest.

Degree of Operating Leverage

It has already been explained earlier that the degree of operating leverage depends on the fixed overhead in the total cost structure of firm. The same is the function of:

(a) The volume of sales;

(b) The margin contribution;

(c) The amount of fixed overhead.

Method of Computation

Operating leverage can be calculated with the help of

$$\text{Operating Leverage} = \frac{\text{Contribution}}{\text{EBIT}} \text{ or } \frac{C}{\text{EBIT*}}$$

*[*EBIT = Earning before Interest and Tax. Here, Earnings = Operating Profit]*

It may be mentioned here that operating leverage may be favourable or unfavourable. In other words, favourable operating leverage arises when contribution (Sales – Variable Cost) exceeds fixed cost; and vice versa in the opposite case.

Degree of Operating Leverage

The Degree of Operating Leverage (DOL) is the percentage change in profit which arises from percentage change in sales. It may be computed as:

$$\textit{Degree of Operating Leverage (DOL)} = \frac{\textit{Percentage change in Profit (EBIT)}}{\textit{Percentage change in Sales volume}}$$

In the previous illustration, for firm C, if we calculate the DOL, the same will be represented as:

$$\text{DOL} = \frac{\dfrac{(\text{Rs. } 3{,}10{,}000 - \text{Rs. } 1{,}85{,}000) = \text{Rs. } 1{,}25{,}000}{\text{Rs. } 1{,}85{,}000} \times 100 = 67{\cdot}57\%}{\dfrac{(\text{Rs. } 12{,}50{,}000 - \text{Rs. } 10{,}00{,}000) = \text{Rs. } 2{,}50{,}000}{\text{Rs. } 10{,}00{,}000} \times 100 = 25\%}$$

$$= 2{\cdot}70 : 1$$

Thus, it becomes clear from the above that if amount of sales changes by 1, the profit will be changed by 2·7. This relationship is measured by DOL.

Alternatively, DOL can be measured (if only Break-even relationship is linear) at a level of output Q, with the help of

$$\text{DOL} = \frac{Q(S - V)}{Q(S - V) - F} > 1$$

where Q = Quantity of Units Sold;
S = Per Unit Selling Price;
V = Per Unit Variable Cost;
F = Fixed Cost

Above equation can also be used for ascertaining DOL (taking the figures from the previous illustration for firm C) as :

$$\text{DOL} = \frac{Q(S - V)}{Q(S - V) - F}$$

$$= \frac{1{,}00{,}000\ (\text{Rs. } 10 - \text{Rs. } 5)}{1{,}00{,}000\ (\text{Rs. } 10 - \text{Rs. } 5) - \text{Rs. } 3{,}15{,}000}$$

$$= \frac{\text{Rs. } 5{,}00{,}000}{\text{Rs. } 5{,}00{,}000 - \text{Rs. } 3{,}15{,}000} = \frac{\text{Rs. } 5{,}00{,}000}{\text{Rs. } 1{,}85{,}000} = 2{\cdot}70$$

Thus, it has been proved that both the methods present the same result.

The formula is nothing but a modified form of the original:

$$\text{i.e., DOL} = \frac{\text{Contribution}}{\text{EBIT}} = \text{i.e., } \frac{\text{Rs. } 5{,}00{,}000}{\text{Rs. } 1{,}85{,}000} = 2{\cdot}70.$$

Operating Leverage and CVP Analysis

From the foregoing discussion it becomes clear to us that operating leverage is applied for ascertaining profit planning although the CVP analysis or Break-even analysis is used for the same purpose. It is interesting to note that the reciprocal margin of safety is expressed by operating leverage whereas Break-even analysis reveals the loss or profit at different levels of output. We know that a low margin of safety is the product of high operating cost which reveals that the firm is unable to take the risk-bearing capacity due to sales variation. Similarly, high operating cost creates high degree of operating leverage which, ultimately, invites more operating risk in the field. On the contrary, a low operating leverage presents sufficient indication by providing a high margin of safety when the volume of sales vary. As a result of the above effect, we showed the various aspects of Cost-Volume Profit (CVP) analysis, in short, for further understanding and details.

Cost-Volume Profit

We know that profit is one of the most important factors while measuring business/firm's performances. Microeconomic theory tells us that profit is a signal for the allocation of resources and a yardstick for measuring managerial efficiency in a market economy. Moreover, we know that the primary objective of running a business enterprise is to earn profits which not only determine liquidity and solvency position but also the financial position as a whole. Thus, profit planning is the fundamental part of management function. And, in order to realise the goals, the management prepares the budgets which will actually help them to realise the same. The same is possible only when the information about the cost (both fixed and variable) and the selling price of the product is available in the hands of management. Because, the profit is affected by many factors, such as: (i) Variable Cost per unit; (ii) Total Fixed Cost; (iii) Volume of Sales; (iv) Selling prices per unit of the product; and (v) Sales mix.

The Cost-Volume Profit (CVP) is nothing but practically a management accounting tool to show the relationship between these ingredients of profit planning. Thus, the whole gamut of profit planning is related to Cost-Volume Profit (CVP) relationship in Break-even analysis through Marginal Costing.

Financial Leverage

Financial leverage may be expressed when the residual net income (earnings after interest and taxes and preference dividend) varies not in proportion with operating profit (EBIT). This leverage reveals the changes in taxable income in comparison with the changes in operation. In other words, a major part is played by interest on debt financing, debenture interest, preference dividend (i.e., fixed interest bearing securities) in the entire capital structure of the firm. This leverage actually refers to the mix of debt and equity used to finance the firm's activities. The firm which uses a lot of debt (in various forms) is said to be highly levered. In short, when the debt capital (debenture, preference share, long-term financing etc.) is more in comparison with equity capital it is high levered and, in the opposite case, it is said to be low levered. Thus, it is the firm's ability to use fixed financial charges in order to measure the effect of changes in EBIT on the EPS of the firm.

Measurement of Financial Leverage

The Financial Leverage is measured through the following ratios which are properly used for the purpose:

(a) Debt Ratio,

(b) Debt-Equity Ratio, and

(c) Interest Coverage Ratio.

(a) Debt Ratio

The ratio measures the relationship between debt and capital of a firm, i.e., the proportion of debt and capital, which is very significant for understanding the measurement of financial leverage by an analyst:

$$\text{Leverage } (L_1) = \frac{D}{D+E} = \frac{D}{C}$$

where D = Value of Debt

E = Value of Equity and

C = Value of Total Capital

However, D and E is usually measured as per market value or book-value.

(b) Debt-Equity Ratio

This ratio measures the relationship between debt and equity:

$$\text{Leverage } (L_2) = \frac{D}{E}$$

where D = Value of Debt

E = Value of Equity

The above two are used as per market value or book-value. Although, market value of financial leverage is more practical than the book-value as it recognises the present behaviour of the so-called investors.

But it is very difficult to collect this market value information in real world situation. Market value fluctuates frequently which is not applicable in the case of book value. There is no basic difference between the above two measures of financial leverage.

(c) **Interest Coverage Ratio**

This ratio measures the relationship between operating income, EBIT, and interest charges:

$$\text{Leverage } (L_3) = \frac{\text{EBIT}}{\text{Interest}}$$

Comment

The first measure (i.e., $L_1 = \frac{D}{D+E} = \frac{D}{C}$) is found to be quite specific since its value varies from 0 (zero) to 1. However, the second measure (i.e., $\frac{D}{E}$) varies from 0 to any large number. The second measure (i.e., Debt-Equity Ratio) is widely accepted in the corporate sector for assessing the measurement of financial leverage as there is an industry norm which is compared with any existing firm by the analyst. Obviously, if the debt equity ratio of a firm exceeds its normal level industry standard, it may be considered as risky. In our country, while granting financial assistance by commercial banks and financial institutions, this ratio is commonly used.

This ratio also helps to measure capital gearing.

The last method to measure the financial leverage is Coverage Ratio. The ratio highlights the ability of a firm to pay off its fixed interest charges against borrowings i.e., it is also a method of income/earning as it is $\frac{\text{EBIT}}{\text{Interest}}$. After analysing this ratio an analyst can compare the same with the industry standard to find out the variation and the possibility of financial risk which may be covered.

Relationship between Financial Leverage and the Return of Equity Shareholders

It has already been pointed out in an earlier chapter (Capital Structure) that the primary objective of a firm is to supply the maximum return to the equity shareholders through *Trading on Equity* (i.e., ROI must be higher in comparison with the fixed income bearing charges). As fixed charge funds are generated at a lower cost of finance than the cost of equity finance, i.e., rate of return on capital employed. When the surplus created by the aforesaid application (i.e., difference between earnings accrued by assets that are acquired by fixed interest funds and the cost of the funds the same is distributed by way of dividend to the equity shareholders. EPS increases. Naturally, if a firm procures fixed-interest funds at a higher cost than rate of return, EPS will fall; and vice versa in the opposite case. Thus, the role of EPS, and ROI are quite significant in financial leverage analysis.

Trading on Equity and Financial Leverage

Trading on Equity

Sometimes Financial Leverage is called 'Trading on Equity'.

This is a device by which the equity shareholders enjoy a large amount of profit at the cost of other fixed interest-bearing securities. The rate of dividend of the equity shares can substantially be increased by the issue of more Debentures and Preference Shares with fixed rates of interest and dividend. The following example will make the principle clear:

Suppose the total requirement of capital of a company is Rs. 20,00,000 and the expected rate of return is 12%. If the entire capital consist of Equity Shares only, there will be no Trading on Equity, but will simply be a return @ 12% on Rs. 20,00,000 by way of dividends.

Now, suppose, the capital structure of the company is:

	Rs.
10% Debentures	8,00,000
8% Preference Shares	4,00,000
Equity Shares	8,00,000

In the above case, the profit @ 12% on Rs. 20,00,000 will be 2,40,000 (Rs. 20,00,000 × $\frac{12}{100}$) out of which :

	Rs.
Preference Dividend will be (Rs. 4,00,000 × $\frac{8}{100}$)	32,000
Debenture Interest will be (Rs. 8,00,000 × $\frac{10}{100}$)	80,000
Equity Dividend will be *(bal. fig.)*	1,28,000
	2,40,000

Hence, Percentage of return on Equity Capital becomes $\frac{\text{Rs. } 1{,}28{,}000}{\text{Rs. } 8{,}00{,}000} \times 100 = 16\%$

Therefore, by the issue of Debentures and Preference Shares, Trading on Equity is possible and, as a result, the rate of equity dividend is increased from 12% to 16%.

***Note :** Trading on Equity is profitable only when the profit is earned at a higher rate than the rates payable to the holders of Debentures and Preference Shares.*

Thus, the debt-equity mix will be in such a manner that the earning per share (EPS) is increased. We also know that fixed financial charges do not vary as per earnings of the firm before EBIT. So, financial leverage expresses the results of earnings after the application of fixed interest bearing securities in the total capital structure. We can now propose that financial leverage results when fluctuation in EBIT is accompanied by disproportionate fluctuation in the firm's earning per share.[1] So, if EBIT changes, there must be a corresponding change in EPS, provided the firm does not use fixed interest bearing securities.

The following illustration will make the principle clear:

Illustration 4.5

Capital Structure	Rs.
10,000 equity shares of Rs. 10 each	1,00,000
Debentures	—
EBIT	2,00,000
Tax rate	@ 50%
Change in EBIT	(±) 20%

Show the effect(s) of proposed change in EBIT on EPS.

1 Banerjee. B.—*Financial Policy and Management Accounting*—World Press, 1984, p. 429.

Solution

		Present Level	Proposed Level (+) 20%	Proposed Level (–) 20%
		Rs.	Rs.	Rs.
	EBIT	2,00,000	2,40,000	1,60,000
Less:	Tax @ 50%	1,00,000	1,20,000	80,000
	Earning for Equity Shareholders	1,00,000	1,20,000	80,000
	No. of Shares	10,000	10,000	10,000
	∴ EPS	10	12	8
	Changes in EPS	—	(+) 20%	(–) 20%

From the above, it becomes clear that if EBIT changes, there will be a corresponding change in EPS.

In the above illustration we exclude debt financing. But, in practice, there must be a mix between debt and equity to take the advantage of trading on equity which has already been explained in the earlier paragraphs. Because, such a mix produces a better result and increases the EPS due to:

(i) debt financing is comparatively cheap than the equity capital;

(ii) it does not affect the voting rights among the existing equity shareholders;

(iii) debt financing increases the yield for equity shareholders till the same does not exceed the explicit cost of such investment; and,

(iv) debt-financing invites the degree of flexibility in the total capital structure of a firm.

Thus, there must be a mix between debt and equity. The following illustration will show how the effect of debt financing affects a disproportional change in EPS from a change in EBIT.

Illustration 4.6

Capital Structure

	Rs.
10,000 Equity Shares of Rs. 10 each	1,00,000
8%, 1,000 Debentures of Rs. 100 each	1,00,000
Change in EBIT	20%
Tax Rate	50%

Show the effect of proposed change in EBIT on EPS.

Solution

		Present Level	Proposed Level (+) 20%	Proposed Level (–) 20%
		Rs.	Rs.	Rs.
	EBIT	2,00,000	2,40,000	1,60,000
Less :	Debenture Interest	8,000	8,000	8,000
	EBIT	1,92,000	2,32,000	1,52,000
Less :	Tax @ 50%	96,000	1,16,000	76,000
	Earnings for Equity Shareholders	96,000	1,16,000	76,000
	No. of Equity Shares	10,000	10,000	10,000
	∴ EPS	9·60	11·60	7·6
	Change in EPS	—	(+) 20·83%	(–) 20·83%

From the above illustration it becomes quite clear to us that if EBIT changes, there must be a disproportionate change in EPS. So, we can say that financial leverage depends upon the debt-financing in the corporate capital composition. It can be remembered here that if the amount of debt-financing is proportionately greater in comparison with the equity capital, the degree of financial leverage also will be higher; and vice versa in the opposite case.

Illustration 4.7

Capital Structure *(under various financial plans)*

	Plan I	Plan II	Plan III
	(1 : 1)	(1 : 3)	(1 : 4)
Equity Share Capital	1,00,000	50,000	40,000
8% Debentures	1,00,000	1,50,000	1,60,000
	2,00,000	2,00,000	2,00,000

EBIT Rs. 2,00,000

Tax Rate @ 50%

Compute EPS if the various plans are implemented.

Solution

	Plan I	Plan II	Plan III
	Rs.	Rs.	Rs.
EBIT	2,00,000	2,00,000	2,00,000
Less: Debenture Interest	8,000	12,000	12,800
	1,92,000	1,88,000	1,87,200
Tax @ 50%	96,000	94,000	93,600
Earnings for Equity Shareholders	96,000	94,000	93,600
No. of Equity Shares	10,000	5,000	4,000
∴ EPS	9·6	18·8	23·4
Increase in EPS	—	96%	144%

From the above illustration it is proved that if the amount of debt financing is increased; there must be a corresponding increase in EPS. This is nothing but the effect of trading on equity which has been explained earlier. Thus, it can safely be said that if the ratio of debt financing is greater, there will be a corresponding greater increase in EPS as long as the rate of return exceeds the financing cost.

Favourable and Unfavourable Financial Leverage

When the EPS increases as an impact of debt-financing in the corporate capital structure, it is called favourable or positive financial leverage. The same happens only when the return on capital employed is more than the cost of debt-financing.

The following illustration shows the favourable financial leverage:

Illustration 4.8

The Balance Sheets of the firms X and Y are :

Liabilities	X	Y	*Assets*	X	Y
	Rs.	Rs.		Rs.	Rs.
10,000 Equity Shares, Rs. 10 each	1,00,000	—	Sundry Assets	1,00,000	1,00,000
5,000 Equity Shares, Rs. 10 each	—	50,000			
8% Debentures	—	50,000			
	1,00,000	1,00,000		1,00,000	1,00,000
EBIT	20,000	20,000			

Ascertain the amount of EPS for both the firms X and Y.

Solution

Favourable Financial Leverage

		Firm X	Firm Y
		Rs.	Rs.
	EBIT	20,000	20,000
Less :	Debenture Interest	—	4,000
		20,000	16,000
Less :	Tax @ 50%	10,000	8,000
	EBIT or earnings for Equity Shareholders	10,000	8,000
	No. of Equity Shares	10,000	5,000
	EPS	1·00	1·60

From the above, it becomes clear that favourable or positive financial leverage appears in the case of firm Y for which EPS has been increased from Re. 1·00 to Rs. 1·60, although the EBIT for both the firms are same. The same happened due to the following :

(i) Firm Y borrowed 50% of its fund by issuing debentures whose cost is lower than its return on capital employed. The most significant point is this—it paid 8% interest on debenture whereas it earned a return of 16%.

(ii) From the illustration presented above, it is found that firm Y issued only 5,000 equity shares of Rs. 10 as compared to 10,000 equity shares of Firm A. Since, Firm B raised its funds not only by issuing equity shares but also by issuing debt financing. As a result, the EBIT for both the firms change and so also the change occurs in EPS. The same was changed from Re. 1 to Rs. 1·60. Thus, a firm can raise its EPS by maximum use of its debt financing in its capital structure.

Now, the opposite side of the picture can also be pointed out, i.e., unfavourable financial leverage.

Unfavourable financial leverage arises only when the company's return on capital employed is lower than the cost of debt-financing. In short, unfavourable or negative financial leverage appears when EPS is decreased as a result of using debt-capital. Consider the following illustration.

Illustration 4.9

Take the data contained in the previous illustration and assume that EBIT was Rs. 5,000 in both the cases instead of Rs. 20,000.

Solution

Unfavourable Financial Leverage

		Firm X Rs.	Firm Y Rs.
	EBIT	5,000	5,000
Less:	Debenture Interest	—	4,000
		5,000	1,000
Less:	Tax @ 50%	2,500	500
	Earnings for Equity Shareholders	2,500	500
	No. of Shares	10,000	5,000
	EPS	0·25	0·10

Thus, from the above illustration we can easily experience an example of negative financial leverage. Because, after using debt-capital in the capital structure, EPS is reduced to Re. 0·10 in case of Firm Y as compared to Firm X which had Re. 0·25 without having any debt capital. The only reason here is that the cost of debt capital is higher than the return on capital employed, i.e., on equity capital.

Degree of Financial Leverage

It has been pointed out in an earlier paragraph that the degree of financial leverage is the percentage change in taxable profit as a result of percentage change in operating profit, i.e., the ability of the firm to utilise fixed financial charges in order to magnify the effect of changes in EBIT on EPS of the firm.

Degree of Financial Leverage (DFL) is computed as:

$$\text{DFL} = \frac{\text{Percentage change in EPS}}{\text{Percentage change in EBIT}} > 1$$

Alternative Approach

$$\text{DFL} = \frac{\text{EBIT}}{\text{EBIT} - 1} > \text{I}$$

where, I = Fixed Interest charges

$$\text{DFL} = \frac{\text{EBIT}}{\text{EBT}}$$

In case of Preference Dividend and Income-Tax—

where, P = Pref. Dividend,

T = Rate of Tax

$$\text{DEL} = \frac{\text{EBIT}}{\text{EBIT} - \text{I} - \dfrac{\text{P}}{(1-\text{T})}}$$

The above equation can better be represented with the help of the following illustration:

Illustration 4.10

Capital Structure

	Rs.
10,000 Equity Shares of Rs. 10 each	1,00,000
10%, 500 Debentures of Rs. 100 each	50,000
EBIT	40,000

Ascertain DFL.

Solution

$$\text{DFL} = \frac{\text{EBIT}}{\text{EBIT} - \text{I}} = \frac{\text{Rs. } 40{,}000}{\text{Rs. } 40{,}000 - \text{Rs. } 5{,}000} = \frac{\text{Rs. } 40{,}000}{\text{Rs. } 35{,}000}$$

$$= 1{\cdot}14$$

It becomes clear from the above illustration that if EBIT increases by 100% there will be a corresponding increase in EPS by 114%. Thus, DFL shows to what extent a firm can magnify the effect on EPS as a result of a change in EBIT after using fixed financial charges.

Illustration 4.11

MMC Company has currently an equity share captial of Rs. 40 lakhs consisting of 40,000 equity shares of Rs. 100 each. The mangement is planning to raise another Rs. 30 lakhs to finance a major programme of expansion through one of the four possible financing plans.

The options are:

(i) Entirely through equity issues.

(ii) Rs. 15 lakhs in equity shares of Rs. 100 each and the balance in 8% Debenture.

(iii) Rs. 10 lakhs in equity shares of Rs. 100 each and the balance through long-term borrowing at 9% interest p.a.

(iv) Rs. 15 lakhs in equity shares of Rs. 100 each and the balance through preference shares with 5% dividend.

The company's expected earning before interest and taxes (EBIT) will be Rs. 15 lakhs.

Assuming corporate tax rate of 50%, you are to determine the EPS and comment on the financial leverage that will be authorised under each of the above schemes of financing.

[C.U. M.Com.]

Solution

MMC Company

Statement Showing the EPS and Financial Leverage under Different Levels of Financing

(Rs. in lakhs)

Financial Plan	Equity Existing	Shares Fresh Issue	8% Debenture	9% Long Term Debt	5% Pref. Share Capital	% Total Capital
	Rs.	Rs.	Rs.	Rs.	Rs.	Rs.
I	40	30	—	—	—	= 70
II	40	15	15	—	—	= 70
III	40	10		20	—	= 70
IV	40	15	—		15	= 70

Financial Plans at Different Levels of Financing

(Rs. in lakhs)

	I	II	III	IV
	Rs.	Rs.	Rs.	Rs.
EBIT	15	15	15	15
Less : Interest on Debenture	—	1·2	—	—
Interest on Long-term Loans	—	—	1·8	—
EBT	15	13·8	13·2	15
Less : Tax @ 50%	7·5	6·9	6·6	7·5
Earning after Tax	7·5	6·9	6·6	7·5

Contd.

	Rs.	Rs.	Rs.	Rs.
Less : Pref. Dividend	—	—	—	0·75
Earning for Equity Shareholders	7·5	6·9	6·6	6·75
No. of Shares	70	55	50	55
EPS	10·71	12·55	13·20	12·27
DFL $\left(\frac{EBIT}{EBT}\right)$	1·00	1·09	1·14	1·00

Comment

Since the Plans I and IV do not use the technique of debt financing, DFL does not exceed unity. However, out of the remaining two alternatives, DFL is higher in case of Plan III. As such, Plan III should be accepted as it is the most profitable debt-equity mix in case of MMC company.

EBIT-EPS Analysis

In order to examine and analyse the effect of financial leverage on the behaviour of EPS (a) with various levels of EBIT, and (b) under alternative financing plans; EBIT-EPS analysis is very useful. We have already explained earlier that a firm can raise its funds from various sources in different proportions. Needless to mention here that when this analysis is applied in order to determine the debt-equity mix, the same is given on the value of EPS and, at the same time, the alternative which will yield the highest value should be selected as the most profitable financing plan and, as such, the same is recommended. As the DFL is the highest at this level no dispute arises between the two, viz., EBIT-EPS analysis and financial leverage. For decision-making purposes, both of them can be used at the same time. The effect of EPS with varying levels of EBIT under various sources of financing can better be presented with the help of the following illustration:

Illustration 4.12

Taking the data from the previous illustration (Illustration 4.11) ascertain the effect of EPS under various levels of EBIT using under alternative financing plans. Assume the EBIT is:

(i)	5% return on capital employed	i.e., Rs.	3·5	lakhs
(ii)	10% return on capital employed	i.e., Rs.	7	lakhs
(iii)	15% return on capital employed	i.e., Rs.	10·5	lakhs
(iv)	20% return on capital employed	i.e., Rs.	14	lakhs

Solution

Statement Showing the EBIT-EPS Analysis for Various Levels of EBIT Under Various Alternative Financing Plans

(i) **When EBIT is Rs. 3,50,000**

	Financing Plans			
	I	II	III	IV
	Rs.	Rs.	Rs.	Rs.
EBIT	3,50,000	3,50,000	3,50,000	3,50,000
Less : Interest on Debentures/Loans	—	1,20,000	1,80,000	—
	3,50,000	2,30,000	1,70,000	3,50,000
Less : Tax @ 50%	1,75,000	1,15,000	85,000	1,75,000
	1,75,000	1,15,000	85,000	1,75,000
Less : Pref. Dividend	—	—	—	75,000
Earning for Equity Shareholders	1,75,000	1,15,000	85,000	1,00,000

Contd.

	Rs.	Rs.	Rs.	Rs.
No. of Shares	70,000	55,000	50,000	55,000
EPS (Rs.)	2·50	2·09	1·70	1·82
Return on Equity Capital	25%	21%	17%	18%

(ii) **When EBIT is Rs. 7,00,000**

	Financing Plans			
	I	II	III	IV
	Rs.	Rs.	Rs.	Rs.
EBIT	7,00,000	7,00,000	7,00,000	7,00,000
Less : Interest on Debentures/Loans	—	1,20,000	1,80,000	—
	7,00,000	5,80,000	5,20,000	7,00,000
Less : Tax @ 50%	3,50,000	2,90,000	2,60,000	3,50,000
	3,50,000	2,90,000	2,60,000	3,50,000
Less : Pref. Dividend	—	—	—	75,000
Earning for Equity Shareholders	3,50,000	2,90,000	2,60,000	2,75,000
No. of Shares	70,000	55,000	50,000	55,000
EPS (Rs.)	5·00	5·27	5·20	5·00
Return on Equity Capital	50%	53%	52%	50%

(iii) **When EBIT is Rs. 10,50,000**

	Financing Plans			
	I	II	III	IV
	Rs.	Rs.	Rs.	Rs.
EBIT	10,50,000	10,50,000	10,50,000	10,50,000
Less : Interest on Debentures/Loans	—	1,20,000	1,80,000	—
	10,50,000	9,30,000	8,70,000	10,50,000
Less : Tax @ 50%	5,25,000	4,65,000	4,35,000	5,25,000
	5,25,000	4,65,000	4,35,000	5,25,000
Less : Pref. Dividend	—	—	—	75,000
Earning for Equity Shareholders	5,25,000	4,65,000	4,35,000	4,50,000
No. of Shares	70,000	55,000	50,000	55,000
EPS (Rs.)	7·50	8·45	8·70	8·18
Return on Equity Capital	75%	85%	87%	82%

(iv) **When EBIT is Rs. 14,00,000**

	Financing Plans			
	I	II	III	IV
	Rs.	Rs.	Rs.	Rs.
EBIT	14,00,000	14,00,000	14,00,000	14,00,000
Less : Interest on Debentures/Loans	—	1,20,000	1,80,000	—
	14,00,000	12,80,000	12,20,000	14,00,000
Less : Tax @ 50%	7,00,000	6,40,000	6,10,000	7,00,000
	7,00,000	6,40,000	6,10,000	7,00,000
Less : Pref. Dividend	—	—	—	75,000
Earning for Equity Shareholders	7,00,000	6,40,000	6,10,000	6,25,000

Contd.

	Rs.	Rs.	Rs.	Rs.
No. of Shares	70,000	55,000	50,000	55,000
EPS (Rs.)	10·00	11·64	12·20	11·36
Return on Equity Capital	100%	116%	122%	114%

The entire picture can be depicted with the help of the following summarised statement relating to EPS-Return on Equity Analysis at a glance:

EBIT	Rs. 3·50 lakhs		Rs. 7 lakhs		Rs. 10·50 lakhs		Rs. 14 lakhs	
Finacial Plans	EPS (Rs.)	Return on Equity (%)	EPS (Rs.)	Return on Equity (%)	EPS (Rs.)	Return on Equity (%)	EPS (Rs.)	Return on Equity (%)
I	2·50	25	5·00	50	7·50	75	10·00	100
II	2·09	21	5·27	53	8·45	85	11·64	116
III	1·70	17	5·20	52	8·70	87	12·20	122
IV	1·82	18	5·00	50	8·18	82	11·36	114

From the above table, when EBIT is expected to be Rs. 3·50 lakhs, Rs. 7 lakhs, Rs. 10·50 lakhs and 14 lakhs, the highest EPS is Rs. 2·50, Rs. 5·27; Rs. 8·70 and Rs. 12·20 in case of Financial Plan Nos. I, II, III and IV, respectively. Thus, the management must consider the variations in EPS in case of varying levels of EBIT.

The above statement can also be summed up as under for further information:

EBIT

Financial Plans	Rs. 3·50 lakhs	Rs. 7 lakhs	Rs. 10·50 lakhs	Rs. 14 lakhs	Mean $(\overline{X})$	Standard Deviation (δ)	Coefficient of Variation CV $=\left(\frac{\sigma}{X}\right)\times 100$
I	2·50	5·00	7·50	10·00	6·25	2·80	44·8%
II	2·09	5·27	8·45	11·64	6·86	3·56	51·99%
III	1·70	5·20	8·70	12·20	6·95	3·91	56·26%
IV	1·82	5·00	8·18	11·36	6·59	3·55	53·87%

From the above summarised tables it is found that if simple average $(\overline{X})$ is considered, Plan III seems the highest position followed by also the coefficient of variation which is 56·26%, i.e., the greater variability in EPS.

Conclusion

Equity shareholders will earn maximum benefit from the Financing Plan III since it possesses relatively high degree of financial leverage.

Illustration 4.13

Y Ltd. presented the following information:

Equity share capital Rs. 10,00,000 (10,000 equity share of Rs. 100 each)

It decides to raise further Rs. 6,00,000 for its expansion and development.

Following financing schemes are available :

(a) All through equity shares.

(b) Rs. 2,00,000 in equity shares and balance in 10% Debentures.

(c) All from long-term loans @ 10% p.a.

(d) Rs. 2,00,000 in equity shares and Rs. 4,00,000 in 8% Pref. Shares.

EBIT Rs. 3,00,000

Corporate Tax @ 50%

Determine EPS in each case and comment of financial leverage.

Solution

Statement Showing the EPS under Different Levels on Financing

	Plan I	Plan II	Plan III	Plan IV
	Rs.	Rs.	Rs.	Rs.
EBIT	3,00,000	3,00,000	3,00,000	3,00,000
Less : Interest on Debentures	—	40,000	60,000	
EBT	3,00,000	2,60,000	2,40,000	3,00,000
Less : Tax @ 50%	1,50,000	1,30,000	1,20,000	1,50,000
	1,50,000	1,30,000	1,20,000	1,50,000
Less : Pref. Dividend	—	—	—	32,000
Earnings for equity shareholders	1,50,000	1,30,000	1,20,000	1,18,000
No. of shares	16,000	12,000	10,000	12,000
EPS (Rs.)	9·38	10·83	12·00	9·83

Comment

Of the four financing plans, Plan III was the best one as EPS in this case is highest in comparison with other options i.e., entire additional financing should be made through 10% long-term loans followed by Plan II where ratio for equity shares and Debentures was 1 : 2. Plan I was the worst one as EPS was the lowest as entire financing was made by equity shares.

It becomes clear from the above table that EPS for equity shareholders was improved due to financial leverage. Thus it may be stated that if debt-equity ratio is higher, there will be higher return for equity shareholders of the firm.

Illustration 4.14

ABC Ltd. has currently an equity share capital of Rs. 40 lakhs consisting of 40,000 equity shares of Rs. 100 each. The management is planning to raise another Rs. 30 lakhs to finance a major programme of expansion through one of four possible financing plans. The options are:

(i) Entirely through equity shares

(ii) Rs. 15 lakhs in equity shares of Rs. 100 each and the balance in 8% Debentures.

(iii) Rs. 10 lakhs in equity shares of Rs. 100 each and the balance through long-term borrowings at 9% interest p.a.

(iv) Rs. 15 lakhs in equity shares of Rs. 100 each and the balance through preference shares with 5% dividend.

The companies expected earnings before interest and tax (EBIT) will be Rs. 25 lakhs. Assume corporate tax rate of 50%.

You are required to determine the earning per share and comment on the financial leverage under each of the above schemes of financing.

Solution

Statement Showing the Computation of EPS and Financial Leverage

	Plan I	Plan II	Plan III	Plan IV
	Rs.	Rs.	Rs.	Rs.
EBIT	25,00,000	25,00,000	25,00,000	25,00,000
Less: Interest on Debentures	—	1,20,000	—	—
Interest on long-term loans	—	—	1,80,000	—
EBT	25,00,000	23,80,000	23,20,000	25,00,000
Less: Tax @ 50%	12,50,000	11,90,000	11,60,000	12,50,000
EAT	12,50,000	11,90,000	11,60,000	12,50,000
Less: Pref. Dividend	—	—	—	75,000
Earning for equity shareholders	12,50,000	11,90,000	11,60,000	11,80,000
No. of equity shares	70,000	55,000	50,000	55,000
EPS (Rs.)	17.86	21.64	23.20	21.45
DFL = $(\frac{EBIT}{EBT})$	1	1.05	1.08	1

Comment

Plant III is the best financing plan as both EPS and DFL are highest at this plan, and, as such, the same should be accepted. In other words, the company should raise Rs. 10,00,000 by way of using equity shares and balance through long-term borrowings at 9% interest p.a. i.e., Debt-Equity mix.

Indifference Point

The Indifference Point arises only at EBIT level at which EPS or ROE are the same regardless of the debt-equity combination, i.e., it is the level of EBIT beyond which the benefits of financial leverage start operation relating to EPS. In short, it is that point at which the after-tax cost of acquisition of outside funds (viz., debt and preference shares) is equal to the rate of return from the investment.

Thus, if the expected EBIT level exceeds the indifference EBIT level, the use of debt financing would be advantageous which will lead to an increase in the EPS. On the other hand, if it is less than the indifference point, the benefits of EPS will come out from the equity capital or shareholders' fund.

Indifference point can also be depicted graphically in (Fig. 4 that follows.). But before its preparation we are to assume the following data:

Illustration 4.15

	Financial Plans	
	X	Y
	Rs.	Rs.
Equity Share Capital	1,00,000	50,000

Contd.

	Rs.	Rs.
(Shares of Rs. 100 each)		
10% Long-term Loan	—	50,000
	1,00,000	1,00,000
EBIT	5,000	12,000
Tax Rate @ 50%		

Solution

Now, we are to calculate the EPS at different EBIT levels:

EBIT Level

(i) **At Rs. 5,000 :**

$$\text{We know, EPS} = \frac{(I - R)\,(1 - t)}{N}$$

where, I = EBIT
R = Interest charges
t = Rate of tax
N = Total number of equity shares

EPS

$$\text{Plan X} = \frac{(\text{Rs. } 5{,}000 - 0)\,(1 - .5)}{1{,}000} = \text{Rs. } 2.50.$$

$$\text{Plan Y} = \frac{(\text{Rs. } 5{,}000 - 5{,}000)\,(1 - .5)}{500} = 0.$$

(ii) **EBIT level at Rs. 12,000 :**

EPS

$$\text{Plan X} = \frac{(\text{Rs. } 12{,}000 - 0)\,(1 - .5)}{1{,}000} = \text{Rs. } 6.$$

$$\text{Plan Y} = \frac{(\text{Rs. } 12{,}000 - \text{Rs. } 5{,}000)\,(1 - .5)}{500} = \text{Rs. } 7.$$

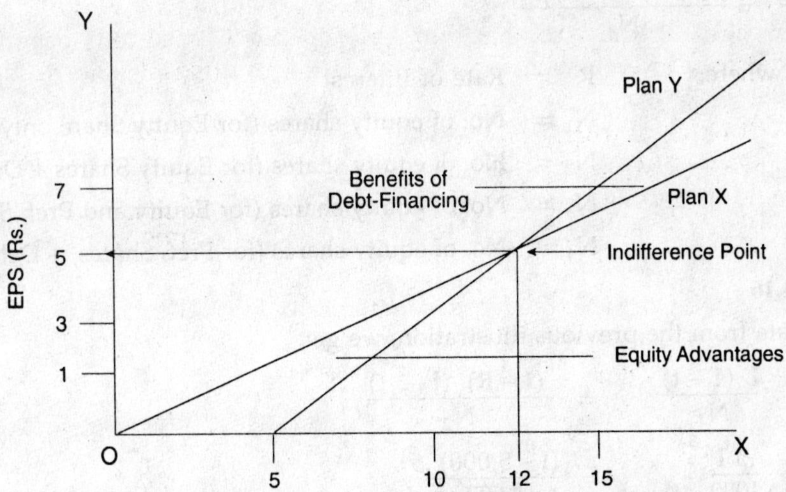

Fig. 4.1: EBIT-EPS Analysis with Indifference Point

From the above, we find that OX axis represents EBIT whereas OY axis represents EPS. It is plotted with different values of EPS corresponding to Rs. 5,000 and Rs. 12,000 at EBIT levels, respectively, which are Plan X and Plan Y, respectively. Needless to mention that the point of intersection is the *'Indifference Point'* in the graph. Naturally, if a perpendicular is drawn to the X-axis, it reveals the EBIT level at Rs. 12,000 corresponding to Y-axis, Rs. 5 in EPS. Thus, at the said Rs. 12,000 EBIT level with EPS Rs. 5, the firm attains its indifference point, and, naturally, below this level, financing on equity proves to be more advantageous to the firm.

Method of Computation of Indifference Point

The indifference point can be computed with the help of the following mathematical approach:

For an Existing Company

For existing outstanding Debentures:

For example, say R_1 = Interest changes on outstanding debentures;

R_2 = Interest charges on additional debentures, or debts. The indifference point, in that case, will be :

$$\frac{(I - R_1)\ (1 - t)}{N_1} = \frac{(I - R_1 - R_2)\ (1 - t)}{N_2}$$

For a New Company

The indifference point can be computed on the basis of the following:

(a) **When there are Equity Shares vs Debentures**

$$= \frac{I\ (1 - t)}{N_1} = \frac{(I - R)\ (1 - t)}{N_2}$$

(b) **Where that are Equity Shares vs Preference Shares**

$$= \frac{I\ (1 - t)}{N_1} = \frac{(I - 1)\ (1 - t) - P}{N_3}$$ where, P = Preference Dividend

(c) **Where there are Equity Shares vs Debentures and Preference Shares**

$$\frac{I\ (1 - t)}{N_1} = \frac{(I - 1)\ (1 - t) - P}{N_4}$$

where, R = Rate of Interest

N_1 = No. of equity shares (for Equity Share only)

N_2 = No. of equity shares (for Equity Shares + Debentures)

N_3 = No. of equity shares (for Equity and Pref. Shares)

N_4 = No. of equity shares (for Pref. Shares + Debenture)

Illustration 4.16

Taking the data from the previous illustration, we get:

$$\frac{I\ (1 - t)}{N_1} = \frac{(I - R)\ (1 - t)}{N_2}$$

or, $$\frac{.5\ I}{1000} = \frac{(I - 5{,}000)\ .5}{500}$$

or, $.5\ I \times 500 = 1{,}000 \times .5\ I - 2{,}500 \times 1{,}000$

or, $250\ I = 500\ I - 25{,}00{,}000$

or, $250\,I = 25{,}00{,}000$

$$I = \frac{25{,}00{,}000}{250} = \text{Rs. } 10{,}000.$$

On EBIT-EPS Analysis with indifference point

Illustration 4.17

A new project under consideration requires a capital outlay of Rs. 300 lakhs. The required fund can be raised either by fully paid equity shares of Rs. 100 each or by equity shares of the value of Rs. 200 lakhs and by loan of Rs. 100 lakhs at 15% interest.

Assuming a tax rate of 50%, calculate the figure of profit before tax that would keep the equity investors indifferent to the two options. Verify your answer by calculating the EPS.

[C.A. Final, May 1995]

Solution

Indifference point of the two finance plans are shown as :

$$\frac{I\,(1-t)}{N_1} = \frac{(I - R)\,(1-t)}{N_2}$$

where

I = EBIT

t = Rate of tax

R = Interest

N_1 = No. of equity shares under first plan (or when there was only equity shares)

N_2 = No. of equity shares under second plan (or when there were equity shares and debt)

Or, $$\frac{(1 - 0.50)}{3{,}00{,}000} = \frac{(I - \text{Rs. } 15{,}00{,}000)\,(1 - 0.50)}{2{,}00{,}000}$$

Or, $$\frac{0.50I}{3} = \frac{0.50I - \text{Rs. } 7{,}50{,}000}{2}$$

By cross multiplication, we get,

$1.50\,I - \text{Rs. } 22{,}50{,}000 = I$

Or, $0.50\,I = \text{Rs. } 22{,}50{,}000$

$$\therefore \quad I = \frac{\text{Rs. } 22{,}50{,}000}{0.50} = \text{Rs. } 45{,}00{,}000$$

Thus, it becomes clear that the firm is indifferent relating to finance the project at EBIT level of Rs. 45,00,000.

Confirmation Table

	Financing by equity shares only	Financing by equity shares and debt
	Rs.	Rs.
EBIT	45,00,000	45,00,000
Less: Interest	—	15,00,000
EBI	45,00,000	30,00,000
Less: Tax @ 50%	22,50,000	15,00,000
Earnings available to equity shareholders	22,50,000	15,00,000
No. of equity shares	3,00,000	2,00,000
EPS	7.50	7.50

Comment

It is interesting to note that EPS, at indifferent point, is equal in both the cases.

Illustration 4.18

MC Ltd. is planning an expansion programme which will require Rs. 30 crores and can be funded through one of the three following options:

(I) Issue further equity shares of Rs. 100 each at par.
(II) Raised @ 15% loan, and;
(III) Issue 12% Pref. shares.

The present paid up capital is Rs. 60 crores and the annual EBIT is Rs. 12 crores. The tax rate may be taken at 50%. After the expansion plan is adopted, the EBIT is expected to be Rs. 15 crores.

Calculate the EPS under all the three financing options indicating the alternative giving the highest return to the equity shareholders.

Also determine the indifference point between the equity share capital and the debt financing i.e., the option (a) and option (b) above.

Solution **[I.C.W.A. Final, Dec. 1995]**

Statement Showing the Financial Leverage under Different Levels of Financing

Financing Plan	Existing Equity Shares Rs.	First Issue	15% Loan	12% Pref. Shares	Total Rs.
I	60,00,000	30,00,000	—	—	90,00,000
II	60,00,000	—	30,00,000	—	90,00,000
III	60,00,000	—	—	30,00,000	90,00,000

Computations of EPS under Different Financing Plans

	I Rs.	II Rs.	III Rs.
EBIT	15,00,00,000	15,00,00,000	15,00,00,000
Less: Interest (15% on Rs. 30,00,00,000)	—	4,50,00,000	—
EBI	15,00,00,000	10,50,00,000	15,00,00,000
Less: Tax @ 50%	7,50,00,000	5,25,00,000	7,50,00,000
	7,50,00,000	5,25,00,000	7,50,00,000
Less: Pref. Dividend (12% on Rs. 30,00,00,000)	—	—	3,60,00,000
Earnings for Equity Shareholders	7,50,00,000	5,25,00,000	3,90,00,000
No. of Shares	90,00,000	60,00,000	60,00,000
EPS	8.33	8.75	6.50

It is needless to say that the maximum EPS comes under financing option II. i.e. Rs. 8.75 per shares which is the highest return. Now, we are to calculate the Indifference Point between the option I and option II as:

$$\frac{I(1-t)}{N_1} = \frac{(I-R)(1-t)}{N_2}$$

$$= \frac{0.50I}{90,00,000} = \frac{(I - \text{Rs. } 4,50,00,000)(1-0.50)}{60,00,000}$$

or, $$\frac{0.50I}{9} = \frac{0.50\,I - \text{Rs. } 2,25,00,000}{6}$$

where,
I = EBIT
t = Rate of Tax
R = Interest charges
N_1 = No. of equity share under 1st option
N_2 = No. of equity shares under second option

or, $4.5I - Rs.\ 20{,}25{,}00{,}000 = 3I$

or, $I = \frac{Rs.\ 20{,}25{,}00{,}000}{1.5} = Rs.\ 13{,}50{,}00{,}000.$

Comment

The indifference point between equity and debt financing comes to Rs. 13,50,00,000.

On EPS and Financial Break-Even Point

Illustration 4.19

S Ltd. is considering three financial plans.

Financial plans	Equity	Debt	Preference
A	100%	—	—
B	50%	50%	—
C	50%	—	50%

Total funds to be raised	Rs. 20,00,000
Rate of Interest on debt	12%
Corporate Tax Rate	35%
Dividend on Pref. Shares	9%

Face Value of equity shares Rs. 10 each. These shares will be issued at a premium of Rs. 10, Expected EBIT Rs. 8,00,000.

Determine

(i) EPS and financial break-even point for each plan.

(ii) Indifference points between financial plans A and B, and A and C.

[C.S. Final, June 2000—Adapted]

Solution

Statement Showing the Financial Leverage under Different Levels of Financing

Financing Plan	Existing Equity Shares Rs.	Fresh Issue Rs.	Debt Rs.	9% Pref. Shares Rs.	Total Rs.
A	—	20,00,000	—	—	20,00,000
B	—	10,00,000	10,00,000	—	20,00,000
C	—	10,00,000	—	10,00,000	20,00,000

(i) **Computation of EPS under Different Levels of Financing**

	Financing Plans A Rs.	B Rs.	C Rs.
EBIT (Expected)	8,00,000	8,00,000	8,00,000
Less: Interest @ 12%	—	1,20,000	—
EBT	8,00,000	6,80,000	8,00,000
Less: Tax @ 35%	2,80,000	2,38,000	2,80,000
EAT	5,20,000	4,42,000	5,20,000
Less: Pref. Dividend	—	—	90,000
Earning for Equity Shareholders	5,20,000	4,42,000	4,30,000
No. of Shares	1,00,000	50,000	50,000
EPS	5.20	8.84	8.60

Financial Break-Even Point

Financial break-even point appears when EPS will be zero at EBIT level under various financing plans.

Thus, for financing Plan A = Zero, since plan A does not include any debt, as such, there is no fixed amount of interest

For financing Plan B = Total amount of interest on debt @ 12% on Rs. 10,00,000 i.e. Rs. 1,20,000

Confirmation

$$\text{EPS} = \frac{(I - R)(1 - t)}{N}$$

$$= \frac{(I - \text{Rs. } 1{,}20{,}000)(1 - 0.35)}{50{,}000} = 0$$

or, $0.65\,I - \text{Rs. } 78{,}000 = 0$

$$\therefore \quad I = \frac{\text{Rs. } 78{,}000}{0.65} = \text{Rs. } 1{,}20{,}000$$

For financing Plan C

$$= \frac{\text{Pref. Div. (P)}}{(1 - t)} = \frac{\text{Rs. } 90{,}000}{(1 - 0.35)} = \frac{90{,}000}{0.65} = \text{Rs. } 1{,}38{,}462 \text{ (approx.)}$$

(ii) Indifference point between financial Plans A and B; and A and C.

Indifference point between financial Plans A and B

$$\frac{I(1 - t)}{N_1} = \frac{(I - R)(1 - t) - P}{N_2}$$

$$= \frac{I(1 - 0.35)}{1{,}00{,}000} = \frac{(I - \text{Rs. } 1{,}20{,}000)(1 - 0.35)}{50{,}000}$$

where,

I = EBIT

t = Rate of Tax

R = Interest charges

P = Pref. Dividend

N_1 = No. of equity shares under first Plan

N_2 = No of equity shares under second Plan

or, $\frac{0.65\,I}{2} = \frac{0.65\,I - \text{Rs. } 78{,}000}{1}$

or, $1.30\,I - \text{Rs. } 1{,}56{,}000 = 0.65\,I$

or, $1.30\,I - 0.65\,I = \text{Rs. } 1{,}56{,}000$

or, $I = \frac{\text{Rs. } 1{,}56{,}000}{0.65} = \text{Rs. } 2{,}40{,}000$

Indifference point between financial Plans A and C

$$\frac{I(1 - t)}{N_1} = \frac{I(1 - t) - P}{N_2}$$

or, $\frac{I(1 - 0.35)}{1{,}00{,}000} = \frac{I(1 - 0.35) - \text{Rs. } 90{,}000}{50{,}000}$

or, $\frac{0.65\,I}{2} = \frac{0.65\,I - \text{Rs. } 90{,}000}{1}$

or, $1.30\,I - \text{Rs. } 1{,}80{,}000 = 0.65\,I$

or, $1.30\,I - 0.65\,I = \text{Rs. } 1{,}80{,}000$

or, $I = \frac{\text{Rs. } 1{,}80{,}000}{0.65} = \text{Rs. } 2{,}76{,}923 \text{ (approx.)}$

Computation of EPS and ROE (Return on Equity)

Earning per share (EPS) is ascertained by dividing net earnings, i.e., earnings after interest, taxes and preference dividend by the total number of equity shares.

Thus, EPS is calculated with the help of the following formula:

$$EPS = \frac{(I - R)(I - t) - P}{N}$$

where, I = Earnings before Interest and Tax = EBIT

R = Interest charges

t = Rate of Tax

N = Total number of equity shares

P = Preference Dividend

Needless to mention here that if there is no preference share, P will be omitted from the above. Then, the same will be shown as:

$$EPS = \frac{(I - R)(1 - t)}{N}$$

When earnings after tax are divided by the net worth or shareholders' fund (i.e., Equity Share Capital plus Reserves and Surplus), ROE, in that case, will be computed in the following manner:

$$ROE = \frac{(I - R)(1 - t)}{Z}$$

where, Z = Net Worth

and, where there is preference dividend, ROE will take the following form :

$$ROE = \frac{(I - R)(1 - t) - P}{Z}$$

Illustration 4.20

Taking the data from the previous Illustration 4.11 (i.e., MMC company), calculate EPS and ROE at EBIT level of Rs. 10·50 lakhs and Rs. 14 lakhs for Financing Plans III and IV, respectively.

Solution

Plan III

$$EPS = \frac{(I - R)(1 - t)}{N} = \frac{(\text{Rs. } 10{\cdot}50 - 1{\cdot}80)(1 - {\cdot}50)}{{\cdot}50} = \frac{\text{Rs. } 4{\cdot}35}{{\cdot}50} = \text{Rs. } 8{\cdot}70$$

$$ROE = \frac{(I - R)(1 - t)}{Z} = \frac{(\text{Rs. } 10{\cdot}50 - 1{\cdot}80)(1 - {\cdot}50)}{50} = \frac{\text{Rs. } 4{\cdot}35}{50} = 0{\cdot}087 \text{ or } 8.7\%$$

Plan IV

$$EPS = \frac{(I - R)(1 - t) - P}{N} = \frac{(\text{Rs. } 10{\cdot}50 - 1{\cdot}80)(1 - {\cdot}05) - {\cdot}75}{{\cdot}55} = \frac{\text{Rs. } 4{\cdot}50}{{\cdot}55} = \text{Rs. } 8{\cdot}18$$

$$ROE = \frac{(I - R)(1 - t) - P}{Z} = \frac{\text{Rs. } 4{\cdot}50}{55^*} = 0.082 \text{ or } 8.2\%$$

* Here, shareholders' fund or net worth consists of Equity Share Capital Account only as there were no Reserves and Surplus.

COMBINED/COMPOSITE OR TOTAL LEVERAGE

While discussing the operating leverage and financial leverage we have pointed out that operating leverage measures the relationship between quantity produced and sold and EBIT, whereas financial leverage measures the relationship between EPS and EBIT. But combined/composite/total leverage measures the relationship between quantity produced and sold and EPS.

Thus, the degree of combined leverage (DCL) is computed as:

$$\text{DCL} = \text{DOL} \times \text{DFL},$$

where, DCL = Degree of Combined Leverage
DOL = Degree of Operating Leverage
DFL = Degree of Financial Leverage

Taking the value from DOL and DFL, we have,

$$\text{DCL} = \frac{\text{Percentage change in EBIT}}{\text{Percentage change in Sales}} \times \frac{\text{Percentage change in EPS}}{\text{Percentage change in EBIT}}$$

$$\text{DCL} = \frac{\text{Percentage change in EBS}}{\text{Percentage change in Sales}}$$

Alternative Approach

$$\text{DCL} = \frac{\text{Contribution}}{\text{EBIT}} \times \frac{\text{EBIT}}{\text{EBT}}$$

$$\text{DCL} = \frac{\text{Contribution}}{\text{EBT}}$$

Illustration 4.21

Calculate the degree of operating leverage, degree of financial leverage and the degree of combined leverage for the following firms and interprete the result :

	B	Q	R
Output (Units)	3,00,000	75,000	5,00,000
Fixed Cost (Rs.)	3,50,000	7,00,000	75,000
Unit Variable Cost (Rs.)	1·00	7·50	0·10
Interest Expenses (Rs.)	25,000	40,000	Nil
Unit Selling Price (Rs.)	3·00	25·00	0·50

[I.C.W.A. Final—Adapted]
[C.A. Final—Adapted]
[C.U. M.Com.—Adapted]

Solution

Statement Showing the Computation of Leverage (DOL, DFL and DCL)

		B	Q	R
	Sales	9,00,000	18,75,000	2,50,000
Less :	Variable Cost	3,00,000	5,62,500	50,000
	Contribution	6,00,000	13,12,500	2,00,000
Less :	Fixed Cost	3,50,000	7,00,000	75,000
	EBIT	2,50,000	6,12,500	1,25,000
Less :	Interest Expenses	25,000	40,000	—
	EBT	2,25,000	5,72,500	1,25,000

1. Degree of Operating Leverage: $= \frac{\text{Contribution}}{\text{EBIT}}$	2·40	2·14	1·60
2. Degree of Financial Leverage: $= \frac{\text{EBIT}}{\text{EBT}}$	1·11	1·07	1·00
3. Degree of Combined Leverage: $= \frac{\text{Contribution}}{\text{EBT}}$ (or, DOL × DFL)	2·67	2·29	1·60

Interpretation and Comments

From the above statements, the DOL reveals that if there is a variation in sales by 1%, there is a corresponding variation in EBIT by 2·4%, 2·14% and 1·6% in the case of firms B, Q and R, respectively. On the other hand, the DFL shows that if EBIT varies by 1% there will be a corresponding variation in EPS by 1·11%, 1·07% and 1% in the case of the firms B, Q and R. Similarly, DCL proves that if sales vary by 1%, there will be a corresponding variation in EBT by 2·67, 2·29 and 1·60 in the case of firms B, Q and R, respectively. It is also found from the above table that firm B possesses all the three highest leverages followed by Q and R. Moreover, the DFL is lower than DOL in all the cases. ***Combined leverage measures the total risk of the firm. Thus,*** if the two leverages are high, no doubt it is a very risky one.

Thus, if a firm enjoys low financial leverage and high operating leverage the same partly adjusts the high operating leverage which has been found in the present problem. Because, we know that a low operating leverage presents lower fixed cost and higher variable cost. A high financial leverage indicates that the firm increases its ROE after applying debt-financing in its capital structure. So, it can be concluded that a firm should always have a high financial leverage corresponding to a low operating leverage. If this is taken into consideration none of the said three firms have faithfully followed the norms.

Illustration 4.22

The following figures relate to two companies:

	P. Ltd. (Rs. in lakhs)	Q. Ltd. (Rs. in lakhs)
Sales	500	1,000
(–) Variable Cost	200	300
Contribution	300	700
(–) Fixed Cost	150	400
EBIT	150	300
(–) Interest	50	100
Profit before Tax (PBT)	100	200

Calculate the operating, financial and combined leverage of two companies and comment which firm is riskier.

Solution

Computation of Operating, Financial and Combined Leverages

		P Ltd.	Q Ltd.
(i) Operating Leverage	$= \frac{\text{Contribution}}{\text{EBT}}$	$= \frac{\text{Rs. } 300}{\text{Rs. } 150}$	$= \frac{\text{Rs. } 700}{\text{Rs. } 300}$
		= 2	= 2.33
(ii) Financial Leverage	$= \frac{\text{EBIT}}{\text{EBT}}$	$= \frac{\text{Rs. } 150}{\text{Rs. } 100}$	$= \frac{\text{Rs. } 300}{\text{Rs. } 200}$
		= 1.5	= 1.5
(iii) Combined Leverage	= Operating Leverage × Financial Leverage	$= 2 \times 1.5$	$= 2.33 \times 1.5$
		= 3	= 3.5

Comment

(a) Considering Operating Leverage

Q Ltd. has a higher degree of operating risk in comparison with P Ltd. as operating leverage of Q Ltd. is higher (i.e., 2.33) than P Ltd. (i.e., Rs. 2). It bears the greater degree of. operating risk.

(b) Considering Financial Leverage

Both P Ltd. and Q Ltd. have equal degree of financial risk as both of them have equal ratio i.e., 1.5.

(c) Considering Combined Leverage

Q Ltd. has a greater degree of combined risk as its combine leverage ratio is higher than P Ltd. Q Ltd. has greater degree of risk as its operating and compared leverage ratios are higher as compared to P Ltd. which indicates that Q Ltd. bears the greater degree of risk.

Illustration 4.23

Firms A, B and C are engaged in diverse operations. Some of their particulars for the next accounting year are:

Firms	A	B	C
Output (units)	8,000	20,000	12,000
Selling Price (p.u.) (Rs.)	10	20	2
Variable cost (p.u.) (Rs.)	4	10	1
Operating Fixed Cost p.a. (Rs.)	36,000	1,60,000	8,000
Fixed financial charges p.a. (Rs.)	10,000	20,000	Nil

You are required to make a comparative analysis of operating financial and total risks of the firm on the basis of leverage.

[C.U. M.Com.]

Solution

Statement Showing the Computation of Operating, Financial and Total/Leverage

	A	B	C
	Firms		
	Rs.	Rs.	Rs.
Sales (No. of Units × Rate p.u.)			
A = 8,000 × Rs. 10	80,000		
B = 20,000 × Rs. 20		4,00,000	
C = 12,000 × Rs. 2			24,000
Less: Variable Cost			
A = 8,000 × Rs. 4	32,000		
B = 20,000 × Rs. 10		2,00,000	
C = 12,000 × Re. 1			12,000
Contribution	48,000	2,00,000	12,000
Less: Operating Fixed Cost	36,000	1,60,000	8,000
EBIT	12,000	40,000	4,000
Less: Fixed Financial Charges	10,000	20,000	Nil
EBT	2,000	20,000	4,000

∴ **Operating Leverage** $= \dfrac{\text{Contribution}}{\text{EBIT}} = \dfrac{\text{Rs. } 48,000}{\text{Rs. } 12,000} = 4; \quad \dfrac{\text{Rs. } 2,00,000}{\text{Rs. } 40,000} = 5; \quad \dfrac{\text{Rs. } 12,000}{\text{Rs. } 4,000} = 3.$

Financial Leverage $= \dfrac{\text{EBIT}}{\text{EBT}} = \dfrac{\text{Rs. } 12,000}{\text{Rs. } 2,000} = 6; \quad \dfrac{\text{Rs. } 40,000}{\text{Rs. } 20,000} = 2; \quad \dfrac{\text{Rs. } 4,000}{\text{Rs. } 4,000} = 1.$

Total Leverage = Operating Leverage × Financial Leverage $= 4 \times 6 \quad 5 \times 2 \quad 3 \times 1$

$= 24 \quad = 10 \quad = 3$

Comment

DOL = From the above statement it is clear that the firm possesses greater degree of risk as its operating leverage is highest among the other two firms. Operating leverage presents the role of changes in sales on EBIT. It is needles to say that high degree of operating leverage not only bears greatest degree of risk but also has an effect on EBIT.

DFL = Financial Leverage appears where there is fixed financial changes and which measure the financial risk of a firm. It is interesting to note from the above table that Firm C does not have any effect on EPS since it does not have any fixed financial charges. Firm A possesses the highest degree of financial risk.

DCL = We know that firms having high operating leverage and high financial leverage bears greatest degree of risk. From the above it becomes clear that Firm C bears the smallest amount of risk among the three firms. ***The ideal situations is that when one ratio is high whereas the other is low in order to maximise profit with minimum degree of risk.*** In the present situation Firm A bears the highest degree of financial risk.

GENERAL ILLUSTRATIONS

Illustration 4.24

Zerox Ltd.

Capital Structure

20,000 Equity Shares of Rs. 10 each fully paid

10%, 1,600 Debentures of Rs. 100 each

EBIT Rs. 1,00,000

Tax Rate @ 50%

Calculate EPS.

Solution

Statement Showing the Computation of EPS

		Rs.
	EBIT	1,00,000
Less:	Debenture Interest @ 10% on Rs. 1,60,000	16,000
	EBT	84,000
Less:	Tax @ 50%	42,000
	Earning for Equity Shareholders	42,000

or, Earning after Interest & Tax (EAIT)

$$\text{Financial Leverage} = \frac{\text{EBIT}}{\text{EBT}} = \frac{\text{Rs. } 1{,}00{,}000}{\text{Rs. } 84{,}000} = 1{\cdot}19$$

$$\text{EPS} = \frac{\text{Earning after Interest and Tax (EAIT)}}{\text{Total No. of Equity Shares}} = \frac{\text{Rs. } 42{,}000}{20{,}000} = \text{Rs. } 2{\cdot}10.$$

Illustration 4.25

Calculate the Operating and Financial Leverage from the following information:

	Rs.	
Interest	5,000	
Sales	50,000	(1,000 units)
Variable Cost	25,000	
Fixed Cost	15,000	

[M.B.A. Osmania]

Solution

Computations of EBIT and EBT

		Rs.
	Sales (1,000 × Rs. 50)	50,000
Less:	Variable Cost	25,000
	Contribution	25,000
Less:	Fixed Costs	15,000
	EBIT	10,000
Less:	Interest	5,000
	EBT	5,000

Computation of Leverages

(a) Operating Leverage $= \frac{\text{Contribution}}{\text{EBIT}} = \frac{\text{Rs. } 25{,}000}{\text{Rs. } 10{,}000} = 2{\cdot}5$

(b) Financial Leverage $= \frac{\text{EBIT}}{\text{EBT}} = \frac{\text{Rs. } 10{,}000}{\text{Rs. } 5{,}000} = 2$

(c) Combined Leverage = Operating Leverage × Financial Leverage

$= 2{\cdot}5 \times 2 = 5.$

Illustration 4.26

The Balance Sheet of Well Established Company is:

	Rs.		Rs.
Equity Capital (Rs. 10 per share)	60,000	Net Fixed Assets	1,50,000
10% Long-term Debt	80,000	Current Asset	50,000
Retained Earnings	20,000		
Current Liabilities	40,000		
	2,00,000		2,00,000

The company's total assets turnover ratio is 3 : 0. Its fixed operating costs are Rs. 1,00,000 and its variable operating cost ratio is 40%. The income-tax rate is 50%.

Calculate for the company the different types of leverages and calculate the likely level of EBIT if EPS is Re. 1.

[C.S. Final—Adapted]

Solution

$$\text{Total Asset Turnover Ratio} = \frac{\text{Turnover/Sales}}{\text{Total Assets}}$$

$$3 = \frac{\text{Sales}}{\text{Rs. } 2{,}00{,}000}$$

$$\therefore \text{Sales} = \text{Rs. } 6{,}00{,}000$$

Statement Showing the Computation of EBIT and EBT

		Rs.
	Sales	6,00,000
Less :	Variable Cost @ 40%	2,40,000
	Contribution	3,60,000
Less :	Fixed Cost	1,00,000
	EBIT	2,60,000
Less :	Interest (10% on Rs. 80,000)	8,000
	EBT	2,52,000
Less :	Tax @ 50%	1,26,000
	Profit after Tax (PAT)	1,26,000

$$\text{EPS} = \frac{\text{PAT}}{\text{No. of Equity Shares}} = \frac{\text{Rs. } 1{,}26{,}000}{6{,}000} = \text{Rs. } 21$$

Computation of Leverages

(a) Degree of Operating Leverage $= \dfrac{\text{Contributions}}{\text{EBIT}} = \dfrac{\text{Rs. } 3{,}60{,}000}{\text{Rs. } 2{,}60{,}000} = 1{\cdot}385$

(b) Degree of Financial Leverage $= \dfrac{\text{EBIT}}{\text{EBT}} = \dfrac{\text{Rs. } 2{,}60{,}000}{\text{Rs. } 2{,}52{,}000} = 1{\cdot}032$

(c) Degree of Combined Leverage = Operating Leverage × Financial Leverage

$= 1{\cdot}385 \times 1{\cdot}032 = 1{\cdot}43$

Computations of EBIT if EPS is Re. 1

No. of Shares = Rs. 60,000 ÷ Rs. 10 = 6,000 shares

Total earnings (after tax) will be 6,000 × Re. 1 = Rs. 6,000 (as EPS is Re. 1)

Earnings before tax will be $= \text{Rs. } 6{,}000 \times \dfrac{100}{50}$ (as tax rate is 50%)

EBT = Rs. 12,000

Earnings before Interest and Tax will be = Rs. 12,000 + Rs. 8,000

EBIT = Rs. 20,000

Illustration 4.27

The following figures relate to two companies:

(figures in '00,000)

	P. Ltd.	Q. Ltd.
	Rs.	Rs.
Sales	500	1,000
Variable Cost	200	300
Contribution	300	700
Fixed Cost	150	400
	150	300
Interest	50	100
Profit before Tax	100	200

You are required to:

(i) Calculate the Operating, Financial and Combined leverages for the two companies, and

(ii) Comment on the relative risk position of them.

[C.A. Final]

Solution

		P. Ltd.	Q. Ltd.
(a) Operating Leverage	$= \dfrac{\text{Contribution}}{\text{EBIT}}$	$= \dfrac{300}{150} = 2$	$= \dfrac{700}{300} = 2{\cdot}33$
(b) Financial Leverage	$= \dfrac{\text{EBIT}}{\text{EBT}}$	$= \dfrac{150}{100} = 1{\cdot}5$	$= \dfrac{300}{200} = 1{\cdot}5$
(c) Combined	$= \dfrac{\text{Contribution}}{\text{EBT}}$	$= \dfrac{300}{100} = 3$	$= \dfrac{700}{200} = 3{\cdot}5$

Or

Combined Leverage	=	Operating Leverage × Financing Leverage
P Ltd.	=	$2 \times 1{\cdot}5 = 3$
Q Ltd.	=	$2{\cdot}33 \times 1{\cdot}5 = 3{\cdot}5$

Comment

(a) Operating Leverage = Since it is higher in case of Q Ltd. it has greater degree of business risk.

(b) Financial Leverage = Both the companies possess same degree of financial risk.

(c) Combined Leverage = P Ltd. is comparatively less risky in overall risk.

Illustration 4.28

T Ltd.

Capital Structure

20,000 Equity Shares of Rs. 10 each fully paid

10%, 2,000 Debentures of Rs. 100 each

12%, 500 Preference Shares of Rs. 100 each

EBIT Rs. 1,20,000; Tax Rate @ 50%

Ascertain

(a) Financial Leverage; (b) EPS; (c) What would be the effect if the EBIT is (i) Rs. 1,50,000 and (ii) Rs. 80,000?

Solution

Computation of Financial Leverage and EPS under Different Financing Plans

		Existing	Plan I	Plan II
		Rs.	Rs.	Rs.
	EBIT	1,20,000	1,50,000	80,000
Less :	Interest on Debenture	20,000	20,000	20,000
	EBT	1,00,000	1,30,000	60,000
Less :	Tax @ 50%	50,000	65,000	30,000
		50,000	65,000	30,000
Less :	Pref. Dividend	6,000	6,000	6,000
	Earning for Equity Shareholders	44,000	59,000	24,000
	Financial Leverage = $\frac{\text{EBIT}}{\text{EBT}}$ =	1·20	1·15	1·33
	No. of Equity Shares	20,000	20,000	20,000
	EPS	2·20	2·95	1·20

Comment

From the above table, it is found that an increase in EBIT by 25% DFL has been reduced from 1·20 to 1·15 which indicates lower degree of risk in capital market—which also increases EPS by ·75p. At the same time, when EBIT is reduced to Rs. 80,000, i.e. $33\frac{1}{3}$%, DFL has been increased, which ensures a high degree of risk and EPS has been reduced to 1·20.

Illustration 4.29

Capital Structure of three hypothetical companies are :

	Chawla & Co.	Chakraborty & Co.	Mitra & Co.
	Rs.	Rs.	Rs.
8% Pref. Shares	1,00,000	2,00,000	3,00,000
Equity Shares	5,00,000	3,00,000	2,00,000
6% Debentures	—	1,00,000	1,00,000
	6,00,000	6,00,000	6,00,000

Find out minimum profit (before interest and tax) that the companies must earn for enabling them to pay equity dividend of (1) 12%, and (2) 18%.

Also comment on the result. Assume a 45% taxation.

[C.U. M.Com.]

Solution

Ascertainment of EBIT

Companies	*Chawla & Co.*		*Chakraborty & Co.*		*Mitra & Co.*	
Rates of Dividend	12%	18%	12%	18%	12%	18%
	Rs.	Rs.	Rs.	Rs.	Rs.	Rs.
Minimum Profit	60,000	90,000	36,000	54,000	24,000	36,000
Add : Pref. Dividend @ 8%	8,000	8,000	16,000	16,000	24,000	24,000
EAIT (i.e., 55%)	68,000	98,000	52,000	70,000	48,000	60,000
Add : Tax @ 45%	55,635	80,180	42,545	57,270	39,270	49,090
EBT	1,23,635	1,78,180	94,545	1,27,270	87,270	1,09,090
Add : Debenture Interest	—	—	6,000	6,000	6,000	6,000
EBIT	1,23,635	1,78,180	1,00,545	1,33,270	93,270	1,15,090

Comment

As the capital structure of the three companies are quite different, the minimum EBIT are also different in order to pay dividend rates of 12% and 18%. The company which needs minimum EBIT to pay equal rates of dividend is the better one in comparison with others. In the present case, Mitra & Co. is in a better position than the other two companies as it needs minimum amount of EBIT, to pay-off its equal rates of dividend.

Illustration 4.30

(a) Calculate degree of Operating Leverage, Financial Leverage and Combined Leverage from the following data :

Sales 1,00,000 units @ Rs. 2 per unit = Rs. 2,00,000

Variable Cost per unit @ Re. 0·70

Fixed Cost Rs. 1,00,000

Interest Charges Rs. 3,668

(b) Which combinations of Operating and Financial Leverage constitute :

(i) Risky situation, and (ii) an ideal situation?

[C.A. Final]

Solution

(a) **Statement Showing the Computation of Profit before Tax (PBT)**

		Rs.
Sales		2,00,000
Less : Variable Cost		70,000
Contribution		1,30,000
Less : Fixed Cost		1,00,000
	EBIT	30,000
Less : Interest		3,668
	PBT	26,332

(i) Operating Leverage $= \dfrac{\text{Contribution}}{\text{EBIT}} = \dfrac{\text{Rs. } 1,30,000}{\text{Rs. } 30,000} = 4{\cdot}33$

(ii) Financial Leverage $= \dfrac{\text{EBIT}}{\text{PBT}} = \dfrac{\text{Rs. } 30,000}{\text{Rs. } 26,332} = 1{\cdot}14$

(iii) Combined Leverage = Operating Leverage × Financial Leverage = $4{\cdot}33 \times 1{\cdot}14 = 4{\cdot}9$

(b) (i) ***Risky situation arises only when high operating leverage is combined with high financial leverage.***

(ii) ***Normal situation arises when one leverage is high and the other is low.***

(iii) ***When both the leverages (operating and financial) are low, the same should be treated as ideal situation.***

Illustration 4.31

X Corporation has estimated that for a new product its break-even point is 2,000 units if the item is sold for Rs. 14 p.u. The Cost Accounting department has currently identified variable cost of Rs. 9 p.u.

Calculate the degree of operating leverage for sales volume of 2,500 units and 3,000 units and their differences, if any.

[C.A. Final]

Solution

Statement of Operating Leverage

	2,000	2,500	3,000
Units	Rs.	Rs.	Rs.
Sales (Rs. 14 p.u.)	28,000	35,000	42,000
Less : Variable Cost	18,000	22,500	27,000
Contributions	10,000	12,500	15,000
Less : Fixed Cost	10,000	10,000	10,000
Operating Profit/EBIT	Nil	2,500	5,000
Operating Leverage	$= \dfrac{\text{Contribution}}{\text{EBIT}}$	$= \dfrac{\text{Rs. } 12,500}{2,500} = 5$	$= \dfrac{\text{Rs. } 15,000}{\text{Rs. } 5,000} = 3$

When volume of sales becomes 3,000 units, the EBIT is 5,000 which is double EBIT of 2,500 units due to the fact that operating leverage is 5 times the sales volume of 2,500 units. In other words, the operating profit is increased by 100% (i.e., 5 times of 20%) simply by increasing 20% sales volume. Operating leverage is only 3 times in case of a sales volume of 3,000 units.

Illustration 4.32

The capital structure of a company is:

	Rs.
Equity Shares of Rs. 10 each fully paid	5,00,000
7% Pref. Shares of Rs. 100 each	2,00,000
Profit/Reserve	1,80,000
6% Debentures	1,00,000
12% Long-term Loans	5,00,000

Calculate the company's overall rate of return on capital employed in order to ensure a 15% equity dividend. The company has constantly been maintaining dividend pay-out ratio. Assume tax rate to be 50%.

[C.U. M.Com.]

Solution

Statement Showing the Overall Return

		Rs.
Earnings (Net Profit after Interest + Tax + Pref. Div.) (15% on Rs. 5,00,000)		75,000
Add : Pref. Dividend		14,000
		89,000
Add : Tax @ 50%		89,000
EBT		1,78,000
Add : Interest on debentures—	6,000	
Interest on long-term loan	60,000	66,000
EBIT		2,44,000

Capital Employed = 14,80,000

$$\therefore \text{ Overall Rate of Return} = \frac{\text{Rs. } 2{,}44{,}000}{\text{Rs. } 14{,}80{,}000} \times 100 = 16{\cdot}5\%$$

Illustration 4.33

An analytical statement of AB Company is—

	Rs.
Sales	9,60,000
Variable Cost	5,60,000
Revenue before Fixed Cost	4,00,000
Fixed Cost	2,40,000
	1,60,000
Interest	60,000
Earnings before Tax	1,00,000
Tax	50,000
Net Income	50,000

Calculate the degree of (i) Operating Leverage; (ii) Financial Leverage, and (iii) the Combined Leverage from the above data.

[C.A. Final]

Solution

Statement Showing the Computation of Leverages

(i) Operating Leverage $= \frac{\text{Contribution}}{\text{EBIT}} = \frac{\text{Rs. } 4,00,000}{\text{Rs. } 1,60,000} = 2{\cdot}50$

(ii) Financial Leverage $= \frac{\text{EBIT}}{\text{EBT}} = \frac{\text{Rs. } 1,60,000}{\text{Rs. } 1,00,000} = 1{\cdot}60$

(iii) Combined Leverage $= \frac{\text{Contribution}}{\text{EBT}} = \frac{\text{Rs. } 4,00,000}{\text{Rs. } 1,00,000} = 4$

or, (Combined Leverage = Operating Leverage × Financial Leverage)

$= 2{\cdot}50 \times 1{\cdot}60 = 4{\cdot}00$

Illustration 4.34

Calculate operating leverage and financial leverage under situations I and II and financial plans A and B, respectively, from the following information relating to the operation and capital structure of a company.

What are the combinations of operating and financial leverage which give highest and least value?

Installed capacity	2,000 units
Actual production and sales	50% of installed capacity
Selling Price per unit	Rs. 20
Variable Cost per unit	Rs. 10
Fixed Cost:	
Situation I : Rs. 4,000	
Situation II : Rs. 5,000	

Capital Structure

	Financial Plans	
	A	B
	Rs.	Rs.
Equity	5,000	15,000
Debt (Cost of Debt = 10%)	15,000	5,000
	20,000	20,000

[I.C.W.A. & C.A. Final—Adapted]

Solution

Actual Production & Sales 50% of Installed Capacity i.e., 1,000 units (2,000 × 50%)

Statement Showing the Computation of Operating, Financial and Combined Leverages

Financial Plan

	A		B	
	Situation I	Situation II	Situation I	Situation II
	Rs.	Rs.	Rs.	Rs.
Sales (1,000 × Rs. 20)	20,000	20,000	20,000	20,000
Less : Variable Cost (1,000 × Rs. 10)	10,000	10,000	10,000	10,000
Contribution	10,000	10,000	10,000	10,000

Contd.

		Rs.	Rs.	Rs.	Rs.
Less :	Fixed Cost	4,000	5,000	4,000	5,000
	EBIT	6,000	5,000	6,000	5,000
Less :	Interest	1,500	1,500	500	500
	EBT	4,500	3,500	5,500	4,500

(i) Operating Leverage $\frac{\text{Contribution}}{\text{EBIT}}$

$= \frac{10,000}{6,000} = 1.67$ $\quad = \frac{10,000}{5,000} = 2.00$ $\quad = \frac{10,000}{6,000} = 1.67$ $\quad = \frac{10,000}{5,000} = 2.00$

(ii) Financial Leverage $\frac{\text{EBIT}}{\text{EBT}}$

$= \frac{6,000}{4,500} = 1.33$ $\quad = \frac{5,000}{3,500} = 1.43$ $\quad = \frac{6,000}{5,500} = 1.09$ $\quad = \frac{5,000}{4,500} = 1.11$

(iii) Combined Leverage $= \frac{\text{Contribution}}{\text{EBT}}$

$= \frac{10,000}{4,500} = 2.22$ $\quad = \frac{10,000}{3,500} = 2.86$ $\quad = \frac{10,000}{5,500} = 1.82$ $\quad = \frac{10,000}{4,500} = 2.22$

Or, Financial Leverage = Operating Leverage × Financial Leverage

$= 1.67 \times 1.33 = 2.22$ $\quad = 2.00 \times 1.43 = 2.86$ $\quad = 1.67 \times 1.09 = 1.82$ $\quad = 2.00 \times 1.11 = 2.22$

Comment

Thus, from the above, it becomes clear that the combination of operating and financial leverage which gives highest over the least value are : highest value 2·86 in case of Financial Plan A, Situation II, whereas least value 1·82 in case of Financial Plan B, Situation I.

Illustration 4.35

The capital structure of the Progressive Corporation consists of an ordinary share capital of Rs. 10,00,000 (shares of Rs. 100 per value) and Rs. 10,00,000 of 10% Debentures. Sales increased by 20% from 1,00,000 units to 1,20,000 units, the selling price is Rs. 10 per unit; variable cost amounts to Rs. 6 per unit and fixed expenses amount to Rs. 2,00,000. The income-tax rate is assumed to be 50%.

(a) You are required to calculate:

(i) The percentage increase in earning per share;

(ii) The degree of financial leverage at 1,00,000 units and 1,20,000 units;

(iii) The degree of operating leverage at 1,00,000 units and 1,20,000 units.

(b) Comment on the behaviour of operating and financial leverage in relation to increase in production from 1,00,000 units to 1,20,000 units.

[C.A. Final]

Solution

Statement Showing the Computation of EPS, Operating Leverage and Financial Leverage

	Units	Units
No. of units sold	1,00,000	1,20,000
	Rs.	Rs.
Sales (Rs. 10 per unit)	10,00,000	12,00,000

Contd.

	Rs.	Rs.
Less: Variable Cost (Rs. 6 per unit)	6,00,000	7,20,000
	4,00,000	4,80,000
Less: Fixed Cost	2,00,000	2,00,000
EBIT	2,00,000	2,80,000
Less: Interest on Debentures @ 10% on Rs. 10,00,000	1,00,000	1,00,000
	1,00,000	1,80,000
Less: Tax @ 50%	50,000	90,000
Earnings for Equity Shareholders	50,000	90,000
No. of Shares	10,000	10,000
(i) EPS	$= \frac{\text{Rs. } 50{,}000}{10{,}000}$ = Rs. 5	$= \frac{90{,}000}{10{,}000}$ = Rs. 9

Percentage increase in EPS $= \frac{\text{Rs. 4 (Rs. 9 – Rs. 5)}}{\text{Rs. 5}} \times 100 = 80\%$

(ii) Degree of Financial Leverage $\left(\frac{\text{EBIT}}{\text{EBT}}\right)$	$= \frac{\text{Rs. } 2{,}00{,}000}{\text{Rs. } 1{,}00{,}000}$ = Rs. 2·00	$= \frac{\text{Rs. } 2{,}80{,}000}{\text{Rs. } 1{,}80{,}000}$ = Rs. 1·56
(iii) Degree of Operating Leverage $\left(\frac{\text{Contribution}}{\text{EBIT}}\right)$	$= \frac{\text{Rs. } 4{,}00{,}000}{\text{Rs. } 2{,}00{,}000}$ = Rs. 2·00	$= \frac{\text{Rs. } 4{,}80{,}000}{\text{Rs. } 2{,}80{,}000}$ = Rs. 1·71

Comment

From the above, it is quite clear that EPS has been increased from Rs. 5 to Rs. 9, i.e., 80%, in relation to increase in production and sales. But both DFL and DOL, are reduced which indicate that risks (both financial and business) are reduced which is, no doubt, satisfactory.

Illustration 4.36

A firm has a sales of Rs. 10,00,000 variable cost of Rs. 7,00,000 and fixed cost of Rs. 2,00,000 and debt of Rs. 5,00,000 at 10% rate of interest.

What are the operating, financial and combined leverage? If the firm wants to double its earning before interest and TAX (EBIT), how much of a rise in sales would be needed on a percentage basis?

Solution **[C.A. Final]**

Statement Showing the Computation of Operating Leverage, Financial Leverage and Combined Leverage

	Rs.
Sales	10,00,000
Less: Variable Cost	7,00,000
Contribution	3,00,000
Less: Fixed Cost	2,00,000
EBIT	1,00,000
Less: Interest (10% on Rs. 5,00,000)	50,000
EBT/Earnings for Equity Shareholders	50,000

(i) Operating Leverage $= \frac{\text{Contribution}}{\text{EBIT}} = \frac{\text{Rs. } 3,00,000}{\text{Rs. } 1,00,000} = 3$

(ii) Financial Leverage $= \frac{\text{EBIT}}{\text{EBT}} = \frac{\text{Rs. } 1,00,000}{\text{Rs. } 50,000} = 2$

(iii) Combined Leverage = Operating Leverage × Financial Leverage $= 3 \times 2 = 6$

Comments

From the above, we find that operating leverage is 3 times, i.e., if sales increase by 100%, operating profit will increase by 300%. Thus, if the firm wants to double (100%) EBIT sales, must be increased by $33\frac{1}{3}$ % or $\frac{1}{3}$. It can be proved from the following statements :

		Rs.
	Sales (10,00,000 + $33\frac{1}{3}$%)	13,33,333
Less:	Variable Cost (7,00,000 + $33\frac{1}{3}$%)	9,33,333
	Contribution	4,00,000
Less:	Fixed Cost	2,00,000
	EBIT	2,00,000

Illustration 4.37

The Hardware Company has to make a choice between debt issue for its expansion programme. Its current position is:

		Rs.
	Debt 5%	20,000
	Equity Capital (Rs. 10 per share)	50,000
	Surplus	30,000
		1,00,000
	Sales	3,00,000
Less:	Total Cost	2,69,000
	Income before Interest and Tax	31,000
Less:	Interest	1,000
		30,000
	Income-Tax @ 50%	15,000
	Income after Tax	15,000

The expansion programme is estimated to cost Rs. 50,000. If this is financed through debt the rate of new debt will be 7% and the price earning ratio will be 6 times. If the expansion programme is financed through equity shares, the new shares can be sold netting Rs. 25 per share and the price earning ratio will be 7 times. The expansion will generate additional rates of Rs. 1,50,000 with a return of 10% on sales before interest and taxes.

If the company is to follow a policy of maximising the market value of its shares which form of financing should it choose?

[Delhi, M.Com.]

Solution

Before taking any decision we are to prepare the following statement in order to find out the market value of shares under various financial plans:

	Financial Plans		
	7% Debt Issue		Equity Issue
	Rs.		Rs.
EBIT (Rs. 31,000 + 10% of Rs. 1,50,000)	46,000		46,000
Less: Interest	4,500	(3,500 + 1,000)	1,000
	41,500		45,000
Less: Income-Tax @ 50%	20,750		22,500
Earning for Equity Shareholders	20,750		22,500
No. of Shares	5,000		7,000
∴ EPS	$=\frac{20,750}{5,000}$ = Rs. 4·15		$=\frac{22,500}{7,000}$ = Rs. 3·21
Price Earning Ratio	6 times		7 times
Market Value of Share (EPS × Price Earning Ratio)	= (Rs. 4·15 × 6) = 24·90		= (Rs. 3·21 × 7) = Rs. 22·50

Comment

From the above statement, it is quite clear that the market value of the share will be higher if '7% Debt Issue' is chosen since the value comes to Rs. 24·90 in comparison with the 'Equity Issue' of Rs. 22·50. Thus, in order to raise the additional funds for expansion programme, the firm should choose 7% Debt Issue for Rs. 50,000.

Illustration 4.38

Zee Company's capital structure shows the following information as on 31.03.2011:

	Rs./lakhs
Equity Share Capital (10,000 shares of Rs. 100 each)	10.00
Retained Earnings	5.00
9% Debentures	15.00
Current Liabilities	5.00
	35.00

During the year 2010-11, the company produced and sold 1,00,000 units. Costs and selling price per unit were:

Selling Price per unit	Rs. 10
Variable Cost per unit	Rs. 4
Fixed Cost per unit	Rs. 3

The normal level of activity is 1,00,000 units and the authorised share capital of the company comprises 16,000 shares of Rs. 100 each.

On 01.04.2011 the company decided to undertake a new project involving a capital expenditure of Rs. 5.0 lakhs to meet part of increased demand for its product. It is expected that production will increase by 20% and fixed costs by 10% of project cost. Expansion will not have any impact on variable cost and selling price. The possible alternative sources of finance for the new project would be:

1. Entirely by Equity Share Capital.
2. Rs. 2.50 lakhs by Equity and the balance by 8% Bonds of Rs. 100 each.
3. Entirely by 8% Bonds of Rs. 100 each.

Assuming tax rate of 40%, which of the alternative schemes of financing the project do you recommend with reference to the risk involved?

[C.U. M.Com.]

Solution

Statement Showing the Computation of EPS

		Financing Plans		
		1	2	3
		Rs.	Rs.	Rs.
	Sales	12,00,000	12,00,000	12,00,000
	(No. of Units × Rate p.u. 1,20,000[1] × Rs. 10)			
Less:	Variable Cost (1,20,000 × Rs. 4)	4,80,000	4,80,000	4,80,000
	Contribution	7,20,000	7,20,000	7,20,000
Less:	Fixed Operating Costs	3,50,000[2]	3,50,000	3,50,000
	EBIT	3,70,000	3,70,000	3,70,000
Less:	Interest (Rs. 15,00,000 × 9%)	1,35,000		
	[Rs. 1,35,000 + Rs. 20,000] (i.e. 8% on Rs. 2,50,000)		1,55,000	
	[Rs. 1,35,000 + Rs. 40,000] (i.e. 8% on Rs. 5,00,000)			1,75,000
	EBT	2,35,000	2,15,000	1,95,000
Less:	Tax @ 40%	94,000	86,000	78,000
	EAT or Earnings for Equity Shareholders	1,41,000	1,29,000	1,17,000
	No. of Equity Shares	15,000 (10,000 + 5,000)	12,500 (10,000 + 2,500)	10,000
	EPS	Rs. 9.40	Rs. 10.32	Rs. 11.70

Operating Leverage = $\frac{\text{Contribution}}{\text{EBIT}}$ $= \frac{\text{Rs. } 7,20,000}{\text{Rs. } 3,70,000}$ $= \frac{\text{Rs. } 7,20,000}{\text{Rs. } 3,70,000}$ $= \frac{\text{Rs. } 7,20,000}{\text{Rs. } 3,70,000}$

1.95 1.95 1.95

Financial Leverage = $\frac{\text{EBIT}}{\text{EB}}$ $= \frac{\text{Rs. } 3,70,000}{\text{Rs. } 2,35,000}$ $= \frac{\text{Rs. } 3,70,000}{\text{Rs. } 2,15,000}$ $= \frac{\text{Rs. } 3,70,000}{\text{Rs. } 1,95,000}$

= 1.57 = 1.72 = 1.90

Workings:

1. Increased output = 1,00,000 units + 20% = 1,20,000 units
2. Fixed Operating Cost

	Rs.
Existing 1,00,000 units × Rs. 3 =	3,00,000
For expansion 10% of Rs. 5,00,000 = (Project Cost)	50,000
	3,50,000

Comment

It becomes quite clear from the above that *financing plan* 3 should be taken into consideration as it presents the maximum EPS. But at the same time it involves greater degree of financial risk as both the operating leverage and the financial leverage are high. If the firm is able to pay and cover the amount of interest on 8%. Bonds, financing plan 3 should be recommended.

Illustration 4.39

P. Ltd wants to raise Rs. 100 lakhs for a diversification project. Current estimates of EBIT from the new project is Rs. 22 lakh p.a. Cost of debt will be 15% for amounts up to and including Rs. 40 lakhs, 16% for additional amounts up to and including Rs. 50 lakhs and 18% for additional amounts above Rs. 50 lakhs.

The equity shares (full value Rs. 10) of the company have a current market value of Rs. 40. This is expected to fall to Rs. 32 if debt excluding Rs. 50 lakhs are raised.

The following options are under consideration of the company:

Option	Equity	Debt
I	50%	50%
II	60%	40%
III	40%	60%

Determine EPS for each option and state which option the company should exercise. Tax rate applicable to the company is 50%.

[I.C.W.A. Inter, Dec. 1997]

Solution

Statement Showing the Computations of EPS under Different Financing Plans

		Financing Plan		
		I	II	III
		Rs.	Rs.	Rs.
	EBIT	22,00,000	22,00,000	22,00,000
Less:	Interest	7,60,000[1]	6,00,000	9,40,000
	EBT	14,40,000	16,00,000	12,60,000
Less:	Tax @ 50%	7,20,000	8,00,000	6,30,000
	EAT/PAT	7,20,000	8,00,000	6,30,000
Less:	Pref. Dividend	—	—	—
	Earning for equity shareholders	7,20,000	8,00,000	6,30,000
	No. of equity shares	1,25,000	1,50,000	1,25,000
	EPS	5.76	8.33	5.04

Comments

From the above statement it is clear that the company should go for options I, since it presents the highest EPS.

Workings:

1. **Computation of Total Interest and No. of Equity Shares**

	Financing Plan		
	I	II	III
	Rs.	Rs.	Rs.
Equity Share Capital (50%)	50,00,000	60,00,000	40,00,000
Debt Capital (50%)	50,00,000	40,00,000	60,00,000
Total Capital	1,00,00,000	1,00,00,000	1,00,00,000
Market/Issue price per share	40	40	32 (as debt exceeds Rs. 50 lakhs as per question)
∴ No. of Equity Shares will be (Rs. 50,00,000 ÷ 40) and so on.	1,25,000	1,50,000	1,25,000

Computation of Interest

Option I up to 40 lakhs @ 15% =	6,00,000	Rs. 40,00,000 × @ 15%	Up to Rs. 40,00,000 × @ 15%	= 6,00,000
Next Rs. 10,00,000 @ 16% =	1,60,000	= Rs. 6,00,000	10,00,000	= 1,60,000
	7,60,000	6,00,000	Rs. 10,00,000 × $\frac{18}{100}$ =	Rs. 1,80,000
				9,40,000

Illustration 4.40

AB Ltd. provides you the following figures:

	Rs.
Profit	3,00,000
(–) Interest on Debentures @ 12%	60,000
	2,40,000
Income Tax @ 50%	1,20,000
	1,20,000
No. of Equity Shares	40,000
EPS	3
Ruling Price in Market (Rs.)	30
PE Ratio ($\frac{\text{Price}}{\text{EPS}}$)	10

The company has undistributed reserves of Rs. 6,00,000. The company needs Rs. 2,00,000 for expansion. This amount will earn at the same rate as funds already employed. You are informed that a debt-equity ratios i.e. ($\frac{\text{Debts}}{\text{Debt + Equity}}$) will higher than 35% will push the $\frac{P}{E}$ Ratio down to 8 and raise the interest rate on additional amount borrowed to 14%. You are required to ascertain the probable price of the share.

(i) If the additional funds raised as debt; and

(ii) If the amount is raised by issuing equity shares.

[C.A. Final, May 1992]

Solution

Computation of EPS and Probable Share Price under Alternative Financing Plans

		Financing Plans	
		I	II
		Rs.	Rs.
	EBIT (20%[1] of Rs. 17,00,000)	3,40,000	3,40,000
Less:	Interest	88,000	60,000
	EBT	2,52,000	2,80,000
Less:	Tax @ 50%	1,26,000	1,40,000
	EAT for Equity Shareholders	1,26,000	1,40,000

Contd.

	Rs.	Rs.
No. of Equity Shares	40,000	—
40,000 + 6,667 (i.e. $\frac{\text{Rs. } 2,00,000}{\text{Rs. } 30}$)	—	46,667
EPS	3.15	3.00
$\frac{P}{E}$ Ratio (already given)	8	10
Share Price (Market) Market Price (EPS × $\frac{P}{E}$ Ratio)	Rs. 25.20	30.00

Workings:

1. **EBIT on Capital Employed**

$$= \frac{\text{EBIT}}{\text{Capital Employed}} \times 100 = \frac{\text{Rs. } 3,00,000}{\text{Rs. } 15,00,000} \times 100 = 20\%$$

† **Capital Employed** = Share Capital + Reserve & Surplus + 12% Debentures

Liability Approach

Financing Plan (I) = Rs. 4,00,000 + Rs. 6,00,000 + Rs. 5,00,000 (Rs. 60,000 × $\frac{100}{12}$) = Rs. 15,00,000

Financing Plan (II) = Rs. 6,00,000 + Rs. 4,00,000 + Rs. 5,00,000 = Rs. 15,00,000

Interest

Financing Plan (I) = Rs. 5,00,000 × 12% = Rs. 60,000
= Rs. 2,00,000 × 14% = Rs. 28,000
88,000

Financing Plan (II) = Rs. 5,00,000 × 12% = Rs. 60,000

Computation of Debt-Equity Ratio

$$\text{Financing Plan (I)} = \frac{\text{Debt}}{\text{Total Equity}} \times 100$$

$$= \frac{\text{Rs. } 7,00,000 \text{ (Rs. } 5,00,000 + \text{Rs. } 2,00,000)}{\text{Rs. } 17,00,000} \times 100$$

$$= 41.18 > 35\%$$

$$\text{Financing Plan (II)} = \frac{5,00,000}{17,00,000} \times 100$$

$$= 29.41\% < 35\%$$

Comment

It is found from the above that the Debt. Equity Ratio of financing plan (I) is higher than 35% and naturally will push the ratio 8 where as under financing plan (II) it is less than 35%.

Illustration 4.41

G. Company has currently an ordinary share capital of Rs. 25 lakhs, consisting of 25,000 Equity shares of Rs. 100 each. The management is planning to raise another Rs. 20 lakhs to finance a major programme of expansion through *one of four* possible financing plans. The options are :

I. Entirely through equity/ordinary shares.

II. Rs. 10 lakhs through equity shares and Rs. 10 lakhs through long-term borrowings at 8% interest per annum.

III. Rs. 5 lakhs through equity shares and Rs. 15 lakhs through long-term borrowings at 9% interest per annum.

IV. Rs. 10 lakhs through equity shares and Rs. 10 lakhs through preference shares with 5% dividend.

The company's expected Earnings before Interest and Tax (EBIT) will be Rs. 8 lakhs.

Assuming a Corporate tax rate of 50%, determine the earnings per share (EPS) in each alternative, and comment on the implications of financial leverage.

[I.C.W.A. Final]

Solution

G. Company

Statement Showing the Computation of EPS and Financial Leverage under Different Levels of Financing

Financial Plan	Existing Equity Shares	Fresh Issue	8% Long-term Borrowing	9% Long-term Borrowing	5% Pref. Share Capital	Total
	Rs.	Rs.	Rs.	Rs.	Rs.	Rs.
I.	25,00,000	20,00,000	—	—	—	45,00,000
II.	25,00,000	10,00,000	10,00,000	—	—	45,00,000
III.	25,00,000	5,00,000	—	15,00,000	—	45,00,000
IV.	25,00,000	10,00,000	—	—	10,00,000	45,00,000

Financial Plans at Different Levels of Financing

	Plan I	Plan II	Plan III	Plan IV
	Rs.	Rs.	Rs.	Rs.
EBIT	8,00,000	8,00,000	8,00,000	8,00,000
Interest on :				
Less: Long-term Borrowing	—	80,000	1,35,000	—
EBIT	8,00,000	7,20,000	6,65,000	8,00,000
Less: Tax @ 50%	4,00,000	3,60,000	3,32,500	4,00,000
EAT/PAT	4,00,000	3,60,000	3,32,500	4,00,000
Less: Pref. Dividend	—	—	—	50,000
Earnings for Equity Shareholders	4,00,000	3,60,000	3,32,500	3,50,000
No. of Shares	45,000	35,000	30,000	35,000
EPS	8.89	10.29	11.08	10.00

Comment

It is evident from the above that under financing plan III EPS is the highest i.e., Rs. 11.08 when debt-equity mix is 1 : 2. This plan should be accepted.

It has already been stated in an earlier paragraph that if proportion of debt capital is increased there will be a corresponding increase in EPS due to the interest factor which is treated as a charge against profit by I.T. Act, 1961.

But, at the same time, it must also be remembered that if debt-capital is considerately high in comparison with the owned capital, the same is considered as a very risky proposition. However, in the present study, financing plan III should be implemented.

Ascertainment of return on Equity, Degree of operating leverage where Degree of Combined leverage is given

Illustration 4.42

The following figures are available for S & Co. Ltd.:

Net Sales Rs. 15 crores.

EBIT (as a percentage of Net Sales) 12%

Capital employed : (a) Equity Rs. 5 crores; (b) Preference Shares Rs. 1 crore bearing 13% rate of dividend; (c) Debts @ 15% Rs. 3 crores.

The applicable income-tax to be taken as 40%.

You are required to calculate :

(i) The Return on Equity of the company; (ii) the Operating Leverage of the company. Given—the combined leverage is 3.

[I.C.W.A. Final, Dec. 2001]

Solution

Statement Showing the Computations of Earning for Equity Shareholders

		Rs.
	Net Sales	15,00,00,000
	EBIT @ 12% of Net Sales (i.e. Rs. 15,00,00,000 $\times \frac{12}{100}$) =	1,80,00,000
Less:	Interest on Debts (Rs. 3,00,00,000 $\times \frac{15}{100}$)	45,00,000
	EBT	1,35,00,000
Less:	Income-Tax @ 40%	54,00,000
	EAT	81,00,000
Less:	Pref. Dividend (Rs. 10,00,000 $\times \frac{13}{100}$)	13,00,000
	Net Earnings for Equity Shareholders	68,00,000

(i) ∴ **Return on Equity**

$$= \frac{\text{Net Earnings for Equity Shareholders}}{\text{Equity Share Capital}} \times 100$$

$$= \frac{\text{Rs. } 68,00,000}{\text{Rs. } 5,00,00,000}$$

$$= 13.6\%$$

(ii) **Computation of Operating Leverage**

Combined Leverage = Operating Leverage × Financing Leverage

Again, Financial Leverage $= \dfrac{\text{EBIT}}{\text{EBIT} - \text{I} \dfrac{\text{P}}{(1-\text{T})}}$

where, I = Rate of Interest on Debt
P = Pref. Dividend
T = Rate of Tax

$$= \frac{\text{Rs. } 1,80,00,000}{\text{Rs. } 1,80,00,000 - \text{Rs. } 45,00,000 - \frac{\text{Rs. } 13,00,000}{(1-0.40)}}$$

$$= 1.5882$$

$$\therefore \text{ Operating Leverage} = \frac{\text{Combined Leverage}}{\text{Financial Leverage}}$$

$$= \frac{3}{1.5882}$$

$$= 1.89$$

Illustration on back-calculation

Illustration 4.43

Prepare an Income Statement of X Ltd., Y Ltd., and Z Ltd., from the following particulars:

	X Ltd.	Y Ltd.	Z Ltd.
Financial Leverage	3 : 1	4 : 1	2 : 1
Operating Leverage	4 : 1	5 : 1	3 : 1
Interest (Rs.)	200	300	1,000
Variable cost as a percentage of Sales	$66\frac{2}{3}$ %	75%	50%
Income-Tax Rate	45%	45%	45%

[C.A. Final, Nov. 1997]

Solution

Computation of EBIT

	X Ltd.	Y Ltd.	Z Ltd.
	Rs.	Rs.	Rs.
Financial Leverage $= \frac{\text{EBIT}}{\text{EBT}}$	$\frac{3}{1}$	$\frac{4}{1}$	$\frac{2}{1}$

X Ltd.:
or, EBIT= 3 × EBT
or, EBIT – Interest = EBT
or, 3 EBT – Rs. 200 = EBT
or, 2 EBT = Rs. 200
EBT = Rs. 100
∴ EBIT = 3 × EBT
= 3 × Rs. 100
= Rs. 300

Y Ltd.:
EBIT = 4 × EBT
EBIT – Interest = EBT
or, EBIT – Rs. 300 = EBT
or, 4EBT – Rs. 300 = EBT
or, 3 EBT = Rs. 300
EBT = Rs. 100
EBIT = 4 × EBT
= 4 × Rs. 100
= Rs. 400

Z Ltd.:
EBIT = 2 × EBT
or, EBIT – Interest = EBT
or, EBIT – Rs. 1,000 = EBT
or, 2EBT – Rs. 1,000 = EBT
or, EBT = Rs. 1,000
EBIT = 2 × Rs. 1,000
= Rs. 2,000

Computation of Sales

	X Ltd.	Y Ltd.	Z Ltd.
Operating Leverage $= \frac{\text{Contribution}}{\text{EBIT}}$	$\frac{4}{1}$	$\frac{5}{1}$	$\frac{3}{1}$
EBIT (from above)	= Rs. 300	= Rs. 400	= Rs. 2,000
Contribution	4 × Rs. 300 = 1,200	5 × Rs. 400 = Rs. 2,000	3 × 2,000 = Rs. 6,000

Variable Cost (% of Sales)	$66\frac{2}{3}\%$	75%	50%
Contribution (% of Sales)	$33\frac{1}{3}\%$	25%	50%
∴ Sales =	$= \frac{\text{Rs. } 1,200 \times \text{Rs. } 300}{100}$	$= \text{Rs. } 2,000 \times \frac{100}{25}$	$= \frac{\text{Rs. } 6,000 \times 100}{50}$
	= Rs. 3,600	= Rs. 8,000	= Rs. 12,000

Income Statement

	X Ltd.	Y Ltd.	Z Ltd.
	Rs.	Rs.	Rs.
Sales	3,600	8,000	12,000
Less: Variable Cost	2,400	6,000	6,000
Contribution	1,200	2,000	6,000
Less: Fixed Cost (*bal. fig.*)	900	1,600	4,000
EBIT (we know)	300	400	2,000
Less: Interest	200	300	1,000
EBT	100	100	1,000
Less: Tax @ 45%	45	45	450
EAT	55	55	550

Illustration 4.44

ABC Corporation plans to extend assets by 50%; to finance the expansion, it is choosing between a straight 12% debt issue and ordinary shares. Its Balance Sheet and Profit and Loss Account are:

ABC Corporation

as at 31st Dec. 2012

Liabilities	Rs.	*Assets*	Rs.
11% Debentures	40,00,000	Total Assets	2,00,00,000
Ordinary Share Capital (10,00,000 shares of Rs. 10 each)	1,00,00,000		
Retained Earnings	60,00,000		
	2,00,00,000		2,00,00,000

ABC Corporation—Profit and Loss Account

for the year ended 31st Dec. 2012

	Rs.
Sales	6,00,00,000
Total Cost (excluding Interest)	5,40,00,000
Net Income before Taxes (EBIT)	60,00,000
Interest on Debentures @ 11%	4,40,000
Income before Taxes	55,60,000
Taxes @ 50%	27,80,000
Profit after Tax	27,80,000

Earning per Share $= \frac{\text{Rs. } 27,80,000}{10,00,000} =$ Rs. 2·78

Price Earning Ratio 7·5 times

Market Price (7·5 × Rs. 2·78) = Rs. 20·85

If ABC Corporation finances Rs. 1 crore expansion with debt, the rate of incremental debt will be 12% and the price-earning ratio of the ordinary share will be 5 times. If the expansion is financed by equity, the new share can be sold at Rs. 12 per share and the price earning ratio will remain at 7·5 times.

(a) Assuming that net income before interest and taxes (EBIT) is 10% of sales, calculate earning per share at sales levels of Rs. 4 crores, 8 crores and 10 crores, when financing is raised from—(i) ordinary share, and (ii) debt.

(b) At what level of earning before interest and tax (EBIT), after the new capital is acquired, would earning per share (EPS) be the same whether new funds are raised by issuing ordinary shares or raising debt?

(c) Using the P/E ratio, calculate market value per share for each sales level for both the debt and equity financing.

[C.A. Final—Adapted]

Solution

For solution (a) please see the next page.

(b) EPS can be computed with the help of the following :

$$\text{EPS} = \frac{(I - R)\,(1 - t)}{N}$$

where, I = EBIT, R = Interest charges, t = Rate of Tax, N = Total number of equity shares.

We are to ascertain the EBIT level where EPS will be same. So,

$$\frac{(\text{EBIT} - R_1)\,(1 - t)}{N_1} = \frac{(\text{EBIT} - R_2)(1 - t)}{N_2}$$

where, R_1 = Interest on debt financing; R_2 = Interest on debt financing under second alternative; N_1 = Total number of shares under debt financing; N_2 = Total number of shares under equity financing; t = Rate of tax.

By substituting the values in the formula, we get

$$\frac{(\text{EBIT} - 16{\cdot}4)\,(1 - .5)}{10} = \frac{(\text{EBIT} - 4{\cdot}4)\,(1 - .5)}{18{\cdot}33}$$

or, EBIT = Rs. 30,806 (approx).

(c) **Market Value per Share** = EPS × Price Earning Ratio

Sales Level	Rs. 4,00,00,000	Rs. 8,00,00,000	Rs. 10,00,00,000
(i) **Under Debt Financing**			
1. EPS	1·18	3·18	4·18
2. P/E Ratio	5	5	5
3. Market Price (EPS × P/E Ratio)	5·9	15·9	20·9
(ii) **Under Equity Financing**			
1. EPS	0·97	2·06	2·61
2. P/E Ratio	7·5	7·5	7·5
3. Market Price (EPS × P/E Ratio)	7·28	15·45	19·58

Solution

(a)

ABC Corporation

Statement Showing the EPS at Various Sales Levels under Alternative Methods of Financing

	12% Debt Rs. (i)	12% Debt Rs. (ii)	12% Debt Rs. (iii)	Ordinary Shares Rs. (i)	Ordinary Shares Rs. (ii)	Ordinary Shares Rs. (iii)
Sales	4,00,00,000	8,00,00,000	10,00,00,000	4,00,00,000	8,00,00,000	10,00,00,000
EBIT @ 10% of Sales	40,00,000	80,00,000	1,00,00,000	40,00,000	80,00,000	1,00,00,000
Less : Interest on Debt :						
New issue @ 12% =	12,00,000	12,00,000	12,00,000	—	—	—
Old issue @ 11% =	4,40,000	4,40,000	4,40,000	4,40,000	4,40,000	4,40,000
	16,40,000	16,40,000	16,40,000	4,40,000	4,40,000	4,40,000
EBIT	23,60,000	63,60,000	83,60,000	35,60,000	75,60,000	95,60,000
Less : Tax @ 50%	11,80,000	31,80,000	41,80,000	17,80,000	37,80,000	47,80,000
	11,80,000	31,80,000	41,80,000	17,80,000	37,80,000	47,80,000
No. of Shares	10,00,000	10,00,000	10,00,000	18,33,333*	18,33,333	18,33,333*
EPS	1·80	3·18	4·18	0·97	2·06	2·61

	Rs.
* Existing Rs.	10,00,000
Fresh Issue $\left(\frac{\text{Rs.}10,00,000}{\text{Rs.}12}\right)$	8,33,333
Total	18,33,333

Illustration 4.45

A small industrial co. has sales levels of Rs. 8,40,000 with a 10% profit margin before interest and taxes. To maintain the business, the firm maintains a fixed asset investment of Rs. 3,00,000 and Rs. 1,50,000 as current assets.

(i) Compute the asset turnover of the firm;

(ii) What is EBIT on present investment?

(iii) What will be the rate of return if current assets increased by Rs. 1,50,000?

(iv) What will it be if current assets decreased by Rs. 75,000?

[I.C.W.A. Final]

Solution

(i) Total Assets = Fixed Assets + Current Assets

= Rs. 3,00,000 + Rs. 1,50,000 = Rs. 4,50,000

$$\therefore \text{ Assets Turnover } = \frac{\text{Sales}}{\text{Total Assets}} = \frac{\text{Rs. } 8{,}40{,}000}{\text{Rs. } 4{,}50{,}000} = 1{\cdot}87$$

(ii) EBIT Rs. 84,000 (i.e., 10% of Rs. 8,40,000)

$$\therefore \text{ \% of EBIT on Investment} = \frac{\text{Rs. } 84{,}000}{\text{Rs. } 4{,}50{,}000} \times 100 = 18{\cdot}67\%$$

(iii) Rate of Return if Current Assets increased by Rs. 1,50,000

$$\text{Rate of Return} = \frac{\text{Rs. } 84{,}000}{\text{Rs. } 6{,}00{,}000 \text{ (i.e., Rs. } 4{,}50{,}000 + \text{Rs. } 1{,}50{,}000)} \times 100 = 14\%$$

(iv) Rate of Return if Current Assets decreased by Rs. 75,000

$$\text{Rate of Return} = \frac{\text{Rs. } 84{,}000}{\text{Rs. } 3{,}75{,}000} \times 100 = 22{\cdot}4\%$$

Illustration 4.46

X Company Ltd. is considering three different plans to finance its total project cost of Rs. 100 lakhs. These are:

	Plan A Rs./ lakhs	Plan B Rs./lakhs	Plan C Rs./lakhs
Equity (Rs. 100 per share)	50	34	25
Debt. 8% Debentures	50	66	75
	100	100	100

Sales for the first three years of operation are estimated at Rs. 100 lakhs, Rs. 125 lakhs and Rs. 150 lakhs and a 10% profit before interest and taxes is forecast to be achieved; corporate taxation to be taken at 50%.

Compute earning per share in each of the alternative plans of financing for the three years.

[I.C.W.A. Final (New)]

Solution

Statement Showing the Computation of EPS under Various Financing Plans

Year I

	Plan A Rs./lakhs	Plan B Rs./lakhs	Plan C Rs./lakhs
EBIT (10% of Rs. 1,00,00,000)	10,00,000	10,00,000	10,00,000
Less: Debenture Interest	4,00,000	5,28,000	6,00,000
EBT	6,00,000	4,72,000	4,00,000
Less: Tax @ 50%	3,00,000	2,36,000	2,00,000
Earning for Equity Shareholders	3,00,000	2,36,000	2,00,000
No. of Equity Shares	50,000	34,000	25,000
EPS	6	6·94	8

Year II

	Plan A Rs./lakhs	Plan B Rs./lakhs	Plan C Rs./lakhs
EBIT (10% of Rs. 1,25,00,000)	12,50,000	12,50,000	12,50,000
Less: Debenture Interest	4,00,000	5,28,000	6,00,000
EBT	8,50,000	7,22,000	6,50,000
Less: Tax @ 50%	4,25,000	3,61,000	3,25,000
Earning for Equity Shareholders	4,25,000	3,61,000	3,25,000
No. of Equity Shares	50,000	34,000	25,000
EPS	8·50	10·62	13·00

Year III

	Plan A Rs./lakhs	Plan B Rs./lakhs	Plan C Rs./lakhs
EBIT (10% of Rs. 1,50,00,000)	15,00,000	15,00,000	15,00,000
Less: Debenture Interest	4,00,000	5,28,000	6,00,000
EBT	11,00,000	9,72,000	9,00,000
Less: Tax @ 50%	5,50,000	4,86,000	4,50,000
Earning for Equity Shareholders	5,50,000	4,86,000	4,50,000
No. of Equity Shares	50,000	34,000	25,000
EPS	11	14·29	18

Illustration 4.47

A firm has Sales of Rs. 75,00,000; Variable Cost of Rs. 42,00,000 and Fixed Cost of Rs. 6,00,000. It has a Debt of Rs. 45,00,000 at 9% and Equity of Rs. 55,00,000.

(i) What is the firm's ROI?

(ii) Does it have favourable financial leverage?

(iii) If the firm belongs to an industry whose asset turnover is 3, does it have a high or low asset leverage?

(iv) What are the operating, financial and combined leverage of the firm?

(v) If the sales drop to Rs. 50,00,000 what will be the new EBIT?

(vi) At what level the EBT of the firm will be equal to zero?

[C.A. Final]

Solution

Computation of EBIT and EBT

		Rs.
	Sales	75,00,000
Less :	Variable Cost	42,00,000
	Contribution	33,00,000
Less :	Fixed Cost	6,00,000
	EBIT	27,00,000
Less :	Interest (9% on Rs. 45,00,000)	4,05,000
	EBT	22,95,000

(i) $\textbf{ROI} = \dfrac{\text{EBIT}}{\text{Capital Employed}} = \dfrac{\text{Rs. } 27{,}00{,}000}{\text{Rs. } 1{,}00{,}00{,}000 \text{ (i.e. Debt + Equity)}} \times 100$

$= 27\%$

(ii) Since the return on investment is 27% which is far higher than the interest payable to debt at 9% so the firm has a favourable financial leverage.

(iii) **Asset Turnover Ratio** $= \dfrac{\text{Turnover/Sales}}{\text{Total Asset}} = \dfrac{\text{Rs. } 75{,}00{,}000}{\text{Rs. } 1{,}00{,}00{,}000} = 0{\cdot}75$

Since the industry average is 3, the firm has a low asset leverage.

(iv) **Operating Leverage** $= \dfrac{\text{Contribution}}{\text{EBIT}} = \dfrac{\text{Rs. } 33{,}00{,}000}{\text{Rs. } 27{,}00{,}000} = 1{\cdot}222$

Financial Leverage $= \dfrac{\text{EBIT}}{\text{EBT}} = \dfrac{\text{Rs. } 27{,}00{,}000}{\text{Rs. } 22{,}95{,}000} = 1{\cdot}176$

Combined Leverage = Operating Leverage × Financial Leverage

$= 1{\cdot}222 \times 1{\cdot}176 = 1{\cdot}438$

(v) **Percentage of Decrease in Sales** $\mathbf{33\frac{1}{3}\%}$ $\left(\text{i.e., } \dfrac{\text{Rs.}25{,}00{,}000}{75{,}00{,}000} \times 100\right)$

This EBIT will be reduced by 40·73%

(Operating Leverage × % of Decrease in Sales) = $(1{\cdot}222 \times \frac{1}{3}\%)$

So, new EBIT will be Rs. 16,00,290 [i.e. Rs. 27,00,000 × (1 – 40·73%) or Rs. 16,00,000 (rounded-off)]

(vi) **EBT will be zero.** That is 100% reduction in EBT.

The combined leverage is 1·438, percentage of sales will decrease by $\dfrac{100}{1{\cdot}438}$ or 69·54%.

The new sales will be Rs. 22,84,500 [i.e., Rs. 75,00,000 × (1 – 69·54%)].

ASSIGNMENT MATERIALS

THEORETICAL

Multiple Choice Questions

1. (a) Operating Leverage is:

(i) $\frac{\text{EBIT}}{\text{Contribution}}$ (ii) $\frac{\text{Contribution}}{\text{EBIT}}$

(iii) $\frac{\text{EBIT}}{\text{EBT}}$ (iv) None of these

(b) Financial Leverage affects:

(i) Firm's Operating Profit (ii) Earning Per Share

(iii) Both of these (iv) None of these

(c) Combined Leverage is:

(i) DOL × DFL (ii) $\frac{\text{DOL}}{\text{DFL}}$

(iii) $\frac{\text{DFL}}{\text{DOL}}$ (iv) None of these

(d) Earning Per Share is:

(i) $\frac{\text{EBIT}}{\text{No. of Equity Shares}}$ (ii) $\frac{\text{EBIT}}{\text{EBT}}$

(iii) $\frac{\text{PAT}}{\text{No. of Equity Shares}}$ (iv) None of these

(e) EBIT is:

(i) Sales – Variable Cost – Fixed Cost (ii) Sales – Fixed Cost

(iii) Sales – Variable Cost (iv) None of these

[Ans. (a) (ii); (b) (i); (c) (i); (d) (iii); (e)(i)]

Short Answer-type Questions

2. Write notes on:
   (a) Operating Leverage; (b) Financial Leverage
3. What are Operating Leverage, Financial Leverage and Total Leverage?
4. What are Degree of Operating, Financial and Total Leverage?
5. Distinguish between Operating Leverage and Financial Leverage.
6. What is Degree of Operating Leverage (DOL)? How do you calculate it?
7. What is Degree of Financial Leverage? How do you calculate it?
8. How do you measure financial leverage?
9. Explain the relationship between Financial Leverage and the Return of Shareholders.

10. What is Trading on Equity?
11. What are favourable and unfavourable financial leverage? How do you ascertain it?
12. What is combined leverage? How do you calculate it?
13. Explain the relationship between Leverage and CVP analysis.
14. How do you compute DOL?
15. How do you compute DCL?

Long Answer-type Questions

16. Define the term 'Leverage'. Discuss the various types of leverage with examples.
17. Describe the relationship between operating leverage and CVP analysis.
18. Explain the significance of operating and financial leverage analysis for a financial executive in corporate profit and financial structure planning.
[C.A. Final]
19. How does break-even analysis help in profit planning and capital structure planning? Explain with suitable illustrations.
[C.A. Final]
20. What is the significance of increase in output, fixed cost, variable costs and selling price to financial management?
[C.A. Final]
21. What is an indifferent point on the EBIT-EPS analysis? How would you compute it?
[Delhi, M.Com.]
22. Define :
(a) Operating Leverage; (b) Financial Leverage; (c) Combined Leverage.
23. "The effect of price reduction is always to reduce the P/V Ratio, to raise the Break-even Point and to shorten the margin of safety." Explain and illustrate by a numerical example.
[I.C.W.A.]
24. Does financial leverage always increase the EPS? Illustrate your answer.
25. How does trading on equity relate to financial leverage?
26. Explain the concept of Operating Leverage and Financial Leverage.
[I.C.W.A. Final]
27. Which combinations of Operating and Financial Leverage constitute (i) risky situation, (ii) ideal situation?
[C.U. M.Com.]
28. Explain the different types of leverages. State their significance.
29. (a) "An increased degree of total leverage means increased risk for the share-holders. " Do you agree? Why?
(b) How would you determine the indifference points between alternative methods of financing risk mathematically?
[C.U. M.Com.]
30. "Financial Leverage acts as a lever to magnify the influence of fluctuations of operating income on EPS." Comment on this statement with suitable examples.
31. Is there any conflict between DFL and EBIT-EPS analysis? Explain how they can be used in financing decisions of a firm.
[C.U. M.Com.]

PRACTICAL

1. Calculate the degree of Operating Leverage, Degree of Financial Leverage and the Degree of Combined Leverage for the following firms and interpret the results :

	P	Q	R
Output (Units)	3,00,000	75,000	5,00,000
Fixed Cost (Rs.)	3,50,000	7,00,000	75,000
Unit Variable Cost (Rs.)	1·00	7·50	0·10
Interest Expenses (Rs.)	25,000	40,000	Nil
Unit Selling Price (Rs.)	3·00	25·00	0·50

[Ans. (i) Operating Leverage 2·40, 2·14, 1·60; (ii) Financial Leverage 1·11, 1·07, 1·1; (iii) Combined Leverage 2·67, 2·29, 1·60]

2. The particulars of three firms—X, Y and Z are given below. Calculate DOL, DFL and DCL of each firm and comment on the results:

	X	Y	Z
	Rs.	Rs.	Rs.
Sales Value	50,000	50,000	50,000
Variable Cost	30,000	20,000	15,000
Fixed Cost (Operating)	10,000	20,000	25,000
Fixed Financial Cost	3,500	2,000	1,000

[C.U. M.Com.]

[Ans.

	X	Y	Z
	Rs.	Rs.	Rs.
DOL	2.00	3.00	3.50
DFL	1.54	1.25	1.11
DCL	3.08	3.75	3.89]

3. Calculate the various leverages from:

	(Rs. in '00,000)
EBIT	1,120
EBT	320
Fixed Cost	700

Calculate percentage change in EPS if sales increase by 5%.

[Ans. Operating Leverage 1·625; Financial Leverage 3·5; Combined Leverage 5·687; Percentage Change in EPS 28% (approx.)]

4. Calculate the various leverages from the following data under situations I and II and financial plans X and Y:

	Financial Plan	
	X	Y
	Rs.	Rs.
Debt (0·20 Interest)	10,000	5,000
Equity	10,000	15,000
	20,000	20,000

Installed capacity 4,000 units.

Actual Production and Sales 75% of the capacity.

Selling Price Rs. 30 p.u.

Variable Cost Rs. 15 p.u.

Fixed Cost:

Situation I	Rs. 16,000
Situation II	Rs. 20,000

[Ans. Operating Leverage : X 1·5 and Y 1.8

Financial Leverage :	Situation I		Situation II	
	X	Y	X	Y
	1·07	1·03	1·09	1·04]

5. Calculate operating leverage and financial leverage under situations A, B and C and financial plans I, II, and III, respectively, from the following information relating to the operating and capital structure of XYZ Co. Also find out the combinations of operating and financial leverage which give the highest value and the least value.

How are these calculations useful to the financial manager in a company?

Installed Capacity	1,200 units
Actual Production and Sales	800 units
Variable Cost p.u.	Rs. 15
Fixed Cost :	
Situation A	Rs. 1,000
Situation B	Rs. 2,000
Situation C	Rs. 3,000

Capital Struture

	Financial Plans		
	Rs.	Rs.	Rs.
Equity	5,000	7,500	2,500
Debt	5,000	2,500	7,500
Cost of Debt 12%			

[C.A. Final]

[Ans.	**Situation A**	**Situation B**	**Situation C**
Operating Leverage =	**1·33**	**2**	**4**
	Plan I	**Plan II**	**Plan III**
Financial Leverage =	**2·5**	**1·43**	**10]**

6. From the following prepare Income Statement of Companies A, B and C. Briefly comment on each company's performance :

Company	A	B	C
Financial Leverage	3 : 1	4 : 1	2 : 1
Interest	Rs. 200	Rs. 300	Rs. 1,000
Operating Leverage	4 : 1	5 : 1	3 : 1

Variable Cost as a percentage of Sales	$66\frac{2}{3}\%$	75%	50%
Income-Tax Rate	45%	45%	45%

[C.A. Final]

[Ans.	Company A	Company B	Company C
	Rs.	Rs.	Rs.
EBIT	300	400	2,000
Sales	3,600	8,000	12,000]

7. An analytical statement of X Y Co. is shown :

		Rs.
	Sales	4,80,000
	Variable Cost	2,80,000
	Revenue before Fixed Cost	2,00,000
Less:	Fixed Cost	1,20,000
		80,000
Less:	Interest	30,000
		50,000
Less:	Tax	25,000
	Net Income	25,000

Calculate the degree of (i) Operating Leverage; (ii) Financial Leverage; (iii) Combined Leverage from the above information.

[Ans. (i) 2·5; (ii) 1·6; (iii) 4]

8. Calculate degree of (i) Operating Leverage; (ii) Financial Leverage, and (iii) Combined Leverage from the following particulars : Sales 50,000 units @ Rs. 2, Rs. 1,00,000, Variable Cost p.u. @ Re. 0·70.

Fixed Cost Rs. 50,000.

Interest Charges Rs. 1,834. **[Ans. (i) 4·33; (ii) 1·14; (iii) 4·99]**

9. A company has an operating leverage of 1.2 as against 1.25 during the previous year.

If the current fixed cost is 25% more than that of the previous year, to what extent has the contribution earned by the firm changed over the previous year?

[I.C.W.A.]

[Ans. 50%]

10. The Capital structure of Progressive Corporation Ltd. consists of an equity share capital of Rs. 10,00,000 (Shares of Rs. 10 par value) and Rs. 10,00,000 of 20% debentures. Sales increased by 25% from 2,00,000 units to 2,50,000 units, the selling price is Rs. 10 per unit, variable costs amounts to Rs. 6 per unit and fixed expenses amount to Rs. 2,50,000, income-tax rate is assumed to be 50%.

(a) You are required to calculate:

(i) The percentage increase in earning per share.

(ii) The degree of financial leverage at 2,00,000 units and 2,50,000 units.

(iii) The degree of operating leverage at 2,00,000 units and 2,50,000 units.

(b) Comment on the behaviour of operating and financial leverages in relation to increase in production from 2,00,000 units to 2,50,000 units.

[C.U. M.Com.—Adapted]

[C.A. Final—Adapted]

[Ans. (a) (i) 57.14%; (ii) 1.57 and 1.36; (iii) 1.45 and 1.33]

11. Calculate the operating leverage, financial leverage and combined leverage from the following data under Situations I and II and Financial Plans A and B:

Installed Capacity	4,000 units
Actual Production and Sales	75% of the capacity
Selling Price	Rs. 30 per unit
Variable Cost	Rs. 15 per unit

Fixed Cost :

Under Situation I Rs. 15,000

Under Situation II Rs. 20,000

Capital Structure :

Financial Plan	A	B
	Rs.	Rs.
Equity	10,000	15,000
Debt (Rate of Interest at 20%)	10,000	5,000
	20,000	20,000

[C.A. & I.C.W.A. Final]

[Ans. DOL of Situation I = 1.50
DOL of Situation II = 1.80
DEL of Financial Plan A under Situation I = 1.70;
DEL of Financial Plan A under Situation II = 1.09;
DEL of Financial Plan B under Situation I = 1.03;
DFL of Financial Plan B under Situation II = 1.04;
DCL of Financial Plan A under Situation I = 1.60;
DCL of Financial Plan A under Situation II = 1.96;
DCL of Financial Plan B under Situation I = 1.55;
DCL of Financial Plan B under Situation II = 1.87]

12. You are given the following particulars relating to AB Ltd. for the year ended 30 June 2012:

Output—1,00,000 units at normal capacity
Selling Price per unit—Rs. 40
Variable Cost per unit —Rs. 20
Fixed Cost per unit—Rs. 10

The Capital structure of the company as on 30th June 2012 appeared as follows:

	Rs.
Equity Share Capital — 1,00,000 shares of Rs. 10 each	10,00,000
Reserves and Surplus	5,00,000
13.5% Debentures	10,00,000
Current Liabilities	5,00,000
Total	30,00,000

In view of emerging opportunities arising out of liberalisation, AB Ltd. has decided to undertake an expansion project which will involve Rs. 10 lakhs. This will lead to increase in output by 5%, reduction in variable cost by 10% but increase in fixed cost by 50%. The additional output can be sold at the existing selling price without any unfavourable impact on the market price.

The Finance Manager has suggested the following alternative schemes for financing the proposed expansion programme:

(a) Entirely by Equity Shares of Rs. 10 each at par.

(b) Rs. 5 lakhs by issue of Equity Shares of Rs. 10 each and the balance by issue of 12% Debentures of Rs. 100 each at par.

(c) Entirely by 12% Debentures as above.

Assuming a corporate tax of 40%, which of the above-mentioned alternatives do you recommend for AB Ltd. with reference to the risk involved?

[C.U. M.Com]

[Ans. EPS of Financing Plan (a) = 2.025; Plan (b) = 2.46; Plan (c) = 3.33
Therefore, the company should go for Plan (c)]

13. Ram Entertainers Ltd. has 10,00,000 shares of Rs. 10 each with market price of Rs. 50 per share. It has also issued bonds for Rs. 4 crore @ 12% per annum. It is considering an expansion plan and needs to mobilise Rs. 5 crores.

The alternative being considered are:

(i) Issue equity at Rs. 40 per share.

(ii) Issue straight bonds at 10% per annum.

(iii) Issue preference shares @ 12% per annum.

(iv) Finance 50% with equity at Rs. 40 per share and 50% with bonds @ 10% per annum.

The company is in tax bracket of 35%.

If the company is hopeful of generating an EBIT of Rs. 2.50 crore after expansion, which method of financing is the best from shareholders, viewpoint?

What more information is required if the market price of equity shares is the criterion for decision-making?

[C.S. Final]

[Ans. EPS of Plan (i) Rs. 5.84; EPS of Plan (ii) Rs. 9.88;
EPS of Plan (iii) Rs. 7.13; EPS of Plan (iv) Rs. 7.08;
Hence Plan (ii) is the best.]

14. The capital structure of B Ltd. is extracted below:

		Rs. in lakhs
(a)	Equity Capital : 10 lakhs shares of Rs. 10 each fully paid-up	100
(b)	Reserve and Surplus	120
(c)	12% Preference shares : 3,000 shares of Rs. 100 each fully paid-up	30
(d)	14% Debentures of Rs. 100 each; 30,000 nos.	30
(e)	Long-term loan from financial Instrument at 12% p.a.	20
		300

The company is also availing a bank overdraft of Rs. 20 lakhs carrying interest at 15% per annum.

The company is now drawing up its profit plan for the year 2012. It wants to pay dividend to equity shareholders at 15% and keep the total dividend payout (equity and preference) at 60%.

What level of earnings (EBIT) should the company try to achieve to meet its commitments?

The tax rate applicable to the company is 50%.

[I.C.W.A.]

[Ans. EBIT = Rs. 71.60 lakhs]

15. The Hardware Company has to make a choice between debt issue for its expansion programmes. Its current position is:

		Rs.
	Debt 5%	20,000
	Equity Capital (Rs. 10 per share)	50,000
	Surplus	30,000
	Total Capitalisation	1,00,000
	Sales	3,00,000
Less:	Total Costs	2,69,000
	Income before Interest and Tax	31,000
Less:	Interest	1,000
	Income before Tax	30,000
	Income Tax @ 50%	15,000
	Income after Tax	15,000

The expansion programme is estimated to cost Rs. 50,000. If this is financed through debt, the rate of new debt will be 7% and the price earning ratio will be 6 times. If the expansion programme is financed through equity shares, the new shares can be sold netting Rs. 25 per share, and the price earning ratio will be 7 times. The expansion will generate additional sales of Rs. 1,50,000 with a return of 10% on sales before interest and taxes.

If the company is to follow a policy of maximising the market value of its shares, which form of financing should it choose?

[Delhi University M.Com.]

[Ans. Market value of a share under 7% debt issue = Rs. 24.90
Market value of a share under equity issue = Rs. 22.50]

16. The existing capital structure of Zenit Enterprises is:

Paid-up share capital of Rs. 10 each	Rs. 10 crores
Reserves and Surplus	Rs. 15 crores
14% Debentures	Rs. 15 crores

An expansion plan requiring Rs. 20 crores is being considered and the plan is expected to have an increase of Rs. 6 crores in EBIT from its present level of Rs. 8 crores.

The following three plans of financing have been suggested:

Option 1: To issue equity shares of Rs. 10 each at a premium of Rs. 40 per share. The share issue expenses as also the under—pricing of the issue in comparison to the current market price result in net proceeds of Rs. 40 per share for every new share issued.

Option 2: To borrow at the rate of 15% from financial institutions.

Option 3: To borrow Rs. 10 crore @ 15% and the balance to be procured by the issue of equity shares as per the terms indicated in the Option 1.

The applicable income tax rate is 40%.

Find out:

(1) The expansion plan is to be considered only if the EPS increases from its present level—indicate whether the expansion plan qualifies for consideration?

(2) At what level of EBIT the EPS will be equal to zero under each of the financing alternatives?

[I.C.W.A. Final]

[Ans. (1) Expansion proposal may be accepted as EPS is higher under all financing plans.

(2) For Option 1 → The level of EBIT is Rs. 2.10 crores at which the EPS will be zero.

For Option 2 → The level of EBIT is Rs. 5.10 crores at which the EPS will be zero.

For Option 3 → The level of EBIT is Rs. 3.60 crores at which the EPS will be zero]

CHAPTER 5

CAPITAL STRUCTURE

Introduction

We all know that funds are required by a firm for different purposes. Naturally, how much of the funds are required depends on the nature and types of business enterprises.

Generally, two well-known classifications are :

(i) Investment in Fixed Assets (Long-term Capital); and

(ii) Investment in Current Assets (Working Capital).

Fixed assets (e.g., Land and Buildings, Plant and Machinery, Furniture and Fixtures etc.) are acquired not for sale; they are usually owned. They help to continue the production function for goods and services in order to earn revenues. Investment in fixed assets must be made in such a way that they are properly utilised, i.e., they must not be idle. So, investment in fixed assets needs the following further considerations : (i) Provision to be made for adequate planned capital expenditure; (ii) Proper evaluation of the project to be made before the actual execution; and (iii) Estimate and schedules are made for approved capital projects, and so on.

Practically, one should remember that long-term capital is nothing but the long-term funds that are employed/engaged in a firm which is possible after analysing and scrutinising the various components of liabilities from a Balance Sheet. The capital contributed by the owners and the retained earnings are known as internal capital or owned capital of a firm and also known as Proprietors Fund/Equity. The other part of long-term capital is known as Borrowed Capital/Debt/Loan Capital. It comprises of debentures, long-term loans, borrowings from various financial institutions etc. Thus, long-term capital consists of owned capital plus borrowed capital other than short-term debt/borrowings etc./or current liabilities.

The concept of long-term capital may be explained from another standpoint. The fixed assets are acquired from long-term funds and a part of current assets may also be acquired. Thus, it may be considered that fixed assets plus current assets minus current liabilities (also known as capital employed) are engaged in a firm as long-term capital.

Capital Structure

Capital structure refers to the permanent financing of the company, represented by owned capital and loan/debt capital. In other words, it includes all long-term funds invested in the business in the form of Long-term Loans, Preference Shares and Debentures, including Equity Capital and Reserves. Practically capital structure is the mix of debt and equity which finance assets of a firm. As regards capital structure, the significant point to be noted is the proportion of owned capital and borrowed capital by way of different securities to the total capitalisation for raising finance. Long-term funds can be raised either by the issue of (a) Shares, or (b) Debentures or long-term loans and borrowings. However, there is an important difference between the two. If funds are raised by the issue of equity shares, it requires dividends only if there is sufficient profits, whereas, in the latter case, it requires a fixed rate of interest, irrespective of the profit or loss. Thus, the question of capital gearing arises relating to which fund a fixed rate of interest or dividend is paid.

To Sum up,

CAPITAL STRUCTURE

- **DEBT—Compries of:**
  - Long-term Debt
  - Term Loan
  - Bonds
  - Debentures
- **EQUITY—Compries of:**
  - Equity Share Capital
  - Pref. Share Capital
  - Reserves & Surplus
  - Securities Premium

From a theoretical point of view, capital structure affects either cost of capital or expected yield, or both, of a firm. On the contrary, financing-mix affects the yield per share which belongs to the equity shareholders but do not affect the total earnings, since they are determined by investment decisions of a firm. In other words, the decisions of capital structure affects the value of the firm by the returns that are made available for the equity shareholders. On the other hand, leverage affects the value of the firm by the cost of capital.

Assumptions

The relationship between the Capital Structure and the Cost of Capital can better be understood if we assume :

(i) two types of capital, viz., debt and equity, are employed;

(ii) total assets of the firms must be presented;

(iii) regularity of paying 100% dividends to the shareholders;

(iv) the operating incomes may not be expected to grow further;

(v) business risk should be constant;

(vi) there will not be any income tax;

(vii) investors should bear the same subjective probability distribution relating to future operating income;

(viii) the firm must enjoy a perpetual life.

Symbolic Expression

In order to explain the theories of capital structure we are to use the following symbols in addition to the above assumptions. They are:

S = total market value of the equity

T = total market value of the debt

V = total market value of the firm (i.e., S + T)

I = total interest payable on debt capital.

NOI/EBIT = Net operating incomes available to the equity shareholders.

$\therefore$ (a) Cost of debt $(K_d) = \frac{1}{T}$

(b) Cost of Equity $(K_e) = \frac{EBIT - 1}{S}$

or, it can be represented as under :

$$(K_e) = \frac{DPS}{MPS} + g = \frac{EPS}{P} + 0 = \frac{EPS}{P}$$

where, DPS = Dividend per share;
MPS = Market price per share;
EPS = Earnings per share;
g = Rate of growth.

Thus, Value of Equity $= S = \frac{EBIT - 1}{K_e}$

and, Value of Debt $= T = \frac{1}{T_d}$

In order to ascertain the total value of the firm, the Equity (S) and Debt (T) may be summed up as:

$$V = S + T = \frac{1}{K_d} + \frac{EBIT - 1}{K_e}$$

Similarly, to calculate Weighted Average Cost of Capital:

$$K_w = W_d\ K_d + W_e\ K_e = \left(\frac{T}{V}\right)K_d + \left(\frac{S}{V}\right)K_e$$

where, W_d = Proportion of debt to total value
W_e = Proportion of equity to total value

The above equations are used by all capital structure theories, the controversy only lies in relation to the degree of leverage of the variable cost of equity (K_e), weighted average cost of capital (K_w), and total firm's value (V).

Financial Structure and Capital Structure

The financial structure of a firm comprises of the various ways and means of raising funds.[1] In other words, financial structure includes all long-term and short-term liabilities. But if short-term (i.e., current) liabilities are excluded the same is known as net worth or capital structure. It is needless to mention that the difference between the financial structure and the capital structure lies on the treatment of current liabilities/short-term borrowings. Thus, instead of exclusion of current liabilities, if they are included which is quite justified in a broader sense of the term—there will be no difference between the two.

Classification of Capital Structure

We know that a firm obtains its requirement from various sources and invests the same also in various forms of assets. In other words, a firm has to perform a two-fold aspect for its

1 Lindsay, I. R. and Sametz, A. W. — *Financial Management — An Analytical Approach*, Richard, D. Irwin, Inc. Homewood, Illinois, 1968, p. 319.

capital structure application, viz., (i) the sources of funds, and (ii) the applications of such funds.

Thus, the classification of capital structure can be represented as:

(i) According to Sources; (ii) According to Ownership; (iii) According to Cost; (iv) According to Nature and Type.

(i) According to Sources

Sources of funds were broadly highlighted earlier. It may be recalled that the sources are of : (i) Internal, and (ii) External Capital.

SOURCES OF CAPITAL

- **INTERNAL**
  - → Share Capital
  - → Reserves & Surplus
  - → Capital Reserves
  - → Balance of P & L Appropriation Account
- **EXTERNAL**
  - → Pref. Share Capital
  - → Securities Premium
  - → Debentures
  - → Long-term and Current Liabilities

(ii) According to Ownership

According to ownership, capital is divided into (i) Owned Capital, and (ii) Borrowed Capital:

ACCORDING TO OWNERSHIP

- **OWNED CAPITAL**
  - → Equity Share Capital
  - → Reserves & Surplus (including retained earnings)
- **BORROWED CAPITAL**
  - → Long-term Loans
  - → Debentures
  - → Cash Credit
  - → Current Liabilities

(iii) According to Cost

According to cost, however, capital structure is classified into (i) Fixed Cost Capital, and (ii) Variable Cost Capital.

ACCORDING TO COST

- **FIXED COST CAPITAL**
  - → Pref. Share Capital
  - → Debentures
  - → Long-term loans

  } i.e., Fixed Interest-bearing Securities
- **VARIABLE COST CAPITAL**
  - → Equity Share Capital (only when variable rate of dividend is paid)
  - → Current Liabilities

(iv) According to Nature and Type

There are two types of capital structure according to the nature and type of the firm : (a) Simple, and (b) Complex.

(a) Simple

When the capital structure is composed of Equity Capital only or with Retained Earnings, the same is known as Simple Capital Structure.

Example

Balance Sheet

as at ....

Liabilities	Rs.	*Assets*	Rs.
Equity Share Capital	1,00,000	Fixed Assets	70,000
		Current Assets	30,000
	1,00,000		1,00,000

(b) Complex

When capital structure is composed of more than one source or identical nature, the same is known as Complex Capital Structure. In other words, if the capital structure is composed of Equity Share Capital, Preference Share Capital, Retained Earnings, Debentures, Long-term Loans and Current Liabilities etc., the same is known as complex capital structure.

Illustration

Balance Sheet

as at ....

Liabilities	Rs.	*Assets*	Rs.
Equity Share Capital	1,00,000	Fixed Assets	1,50,000
8% Pref. Share Capital	50,000	Current Assets	1,00,000
10% Debentures	50,000		
Reserves & Surplus	10,000		
Current Liabilities	40,000		
	2,50,000		2,50,000

In practice, however, the so-called *'Simple'* form is not possible. Although a firm may start with the *'Simple'* type, the same is converted into a *'Complex'* one in course of time.

Factors Affecting Capital Structure Decisions

The following factors directly or indirectly affect the capital structure decisions. They are:

(a) Minimisation of Risk;

(b) Profitability;

(c) Flexibility;

(d) Time Element; and

(e) Control.

(a) **Minimisation of Risks**

That capital structure is called an efficient one where total risk of firm is at its minimum level. Financial risk and long-term solvency can easily be assumed from the composition of a capital structure. Needless to say that more debt financing invites financial risk and affects long-term solvency as well. Thus, a firm should always avoid excessive amount of debt-equity mix in the capital structure so that the total risk would be at its minimum level i.e., within a tolerable limit. A higher business risk always results in a higher cost of capital which must be avoided by all the firms.

The composition of capital structure directly and indirectly affect the financial risks that appears from the standpoint of financial leverage. We know that financial leverage relates to EBIT (Earning before Interest and Tax) and EPS (Earning per share). If the amount of debt capital is more than equity capital a greater amount of fixed charges by way of interest payment will invite greater financial risk. Thus, every firm must reflect an appropriate capital structure by mixing debt and equity in such a manner so that the firm bears a minimum financial risk. A firm having high business risk should go for less levered capital structure.

It has been stated above that higher operating leverage invites greater degree of financial risk. Moreover, two other factors also affect the business risk i.e. revenue and cost. We know that sales/revenue depends on the demand of the product and price for the same. A firm having a stable demand and stable price tends to a low risk level. In the opposite case, i.e., firms having flexible demand for the product and unstable price invite higher degree of financial risk.

Therefore, we should remember that there must be a proper composition of debt and equity so that the firm can avoid the higher degree of financial risk.

(b) Profitability

For the interest of equity shareholders, the composition of capital structure (i.e., debt-equity mix) should be a profitable one. In order to enjoy the benefit of *Trading on Equity*, which will increase the EPS for the equity shareholders, the firm must go in for the appropriate debt financing (which is usually be cheaper). For this purpose, different alternative compositions of capital structure should also be examined. Trading on Equity is only possible where rate of return on investment is greater than the rate of interest on debt financing.

(c) Flexibility

When a firm raise additional funds for profitable investment opportunities the same is referred to as flexible capital structure as the composition of capital structure changes. A firm may need funds for various purposes, (e.g., as a result of uncertainty in capital market, for contingencies etc.) for which borrowing powers are applied. The same is possible only when there is flexibility in capital structure. If it is found that the condition of Capital market is not favourable for capital issue, the firm should go in for debt financing to meet its requirement of funds. If there is flexibility in the composition of capital structure, a firm may go in for debt or equity financing which will be more favourable to it and which depends on the conditions of the capital market.

(d) Time Element

Timing element is also an important factor which affects the decision of capital structure. A firm should raise funds by using debts or bonds or equity at the most profitable moment. For example, at the time of boom (when there is economic development in the country, business activities are expanded etc.), investors want to invest their finds in securities. So, at that moment, a firm must issue equity shares to raise funds to meet its requirements. In the opposite case, when there is economic depression, investors are risk-averters, the firm should issue bonds to raise funds for its requirements.

(e) **Control**

A firm is controlled by the equity shareholders as they are the decision-makers. Naturally, additional equity shares, if issued for raising funds for requirements, controlling powers of the existing shareholders may be affected. They prefer to issue debt financing rather than equity financing as debt capital holders do not enjoy any voting or any power to control the firm. Even if it is found that proportion of debt capital (in the form of debenture) is more than the equity capital, question of dilution of control does not arise as the debentureholders do not enjoy any power except convertible debentures which are converted into equity share at the time of redemption.

Factors Determining Capital Structure

The following factors influence/determine capital structure:

Factors Determining the Capital Structure

INTERNAL FACTORS	EXTERNAL FACTORS	GENERAL/OTHERS
(a) → Nature and size of a firm	(a) → General level of Business Activities	(a) → Size of business
(b) → Cost of Capital	(b) → Levels of Interest Rate	(b) → Operational Activities
(c) → Degree of Risk	(c) → Tax Policy	(c) → Financial Leverage
(d) → Dilution of Value	(d) → Availability of Funds	(d) → Stable Earnings
(e) → Acceptability	(e) → Attitudes of Investors	(e) → Age of a Firm
(f) → Transferability	(f) → Level of Stock Prices	(f) → Government Policies
(g) → Surrender Operational Control		
(h) → Matching Fluctuation needs against Short-term Sources		
(i) → Trading on Equity		
(j) → Flexibility		

INTERNAL FACTORS

It is interesting to note that internal factors also determine or influence the capital structure position. These are:

(a) **Nature and Size of Firm**

The nature and size of a firm determine the capital structure position. It varies from firm to firm, small firm to big firm etc. A small firm finds it very difficult to procure funds from outside for its limited creditworthiness for which it depends on its own funds. Moreover, investors do not prefer to invest in small firms as it is very risky from the standpoint of liquidity and solvency position. They always prefer big firms from the security point of view. As such, big firms may procure funds from various sources.

(b) **Cost of Capital**

The financial manager out examine the Cost of various sources of capital and the same should be estimated and compared as cost of capital directly affects the profitability of a firm as a fixed charge, that is, the target should be to minimise the overall cost of capital. For this purpose, there must be a proper composition of debt and equity mix in the total capital structure.

(c) **Degree of Risk**

It has already been explained above that debt capital is more risky than equity capital as the former claims fixed charges by way of interest payment and requires payment after the expiry of the period which are not applicable in case of equity financing. But, EPS of a firm will only increase if the same uses debt-capital as a source of finance. Thus, the firm should decide how to increase the EPS by the use of debt capital bearing the minimum level of risk.

(d) **Dilution of Value**

A firm must not issue any share that may dilute the value of shares.

(e) **Acceptability**

A firm can borrow funds only when it has acceptability in the financial market which depends on the liquidity, solvency and profitability of the firm. Investors or financial institutions will allow borrowings or grant loans only when there will not be any doubt about the repayment of principal in addition to interest.

(f) **Transferability**

Transferability of securities helps the firm to raise funds for issuing such securities. The same is possible only when they are quoted on the stock exchange.

(g) **Surrender Operational Control**

If the existing/present shareholders want to retain the operational control of the management of the company in their own hands and are not interested to leave their power/control against the firm, the funds are raised by the higher proportion of debt capital (e.g., bonds, debentures etc.) which do not bear any controlling interest with the exception of certain cases where bondholders are required to exercise certain operational control in the firm, e.g., if interest to bondholders are not paid in due time, they may appoint a person who will be a member of the Board of Directors of the company. However, the role of operational control is acutely seen in case of private limited companies where the firm is controlled by a few members. In case of public limited companies, of course, the controlling principle is neither so important nor so effective as the number of shareholders are more.

(h) **Matching Fluctuating Needs against Short-term Sources**

Under the circumstances, the position of capital structure does not make any change rather unaffected as the firm may procure additional requirements from short-term sources, say, commercial banks during its peak period (e.g., festival season). These firms do not raise their funds from long-term sources in that case. Thus, the fluctuating needs can easily be matched from such short-terms sources.

(i) **Trading on Equity**

This is a device by which the equity shareholders enjoy a large amount of profit at the cost of other fixed interest-bearing securities. The rate of dividend of the equity shares can substantially be increased by the issue of more debentures and preference shares with fixed rate of interest and dividend. But, trading on equity is profitable only when the profit is earned at a higher rate than the rates payable to the holders of debentures and preference shares. Thus, the debt-equity mix will be in such a manner that the EPS is increased.

(j) **Flexibility**

Flexibility in the capital structure should be maintained by a firm bearing in mind the future course of action to be implemented for the greater interest of the firm. There must be proper scope for raising additional funds either through debt on through equity in future.

EXTERNAL FACTORS

There are some external factors which also affect the capital structure position of a firm. Some of them are:

(a) **General Level of Business Activity**

While designing the capital structure, a firm must consider the time factor which affects both the period of depression and the period of boom. During the period of depression a firm meets its funds by the issue of bonds which is preferred by the bondholders as the return is fixed. But, in case of boom, the firm may procure its required funds by the issue of equity shares as investors, in that case, are interested to purchase shares than bonds.

(b) **Level of Interest Rates**

If the rate of interest on bonds is very high which depends on the demand and supply factors in the financial market the firm will opt for equity financing than debt-financing. Thus, interest rate also affects the capital structure position of a firm.

(c) **Tax Policy**

Since interest on bonds is a tax-deductible item from profit, the firm takes the advantage of paying less tax. But payments of dividend is not a tax-deductible item. Hence, taxation policy also affects the composition of capital structure.

(d) **Availability of Funds**

Availability of funds in the money market also affects the capital structure position of a firm. No doubt, it affects a firm as to whether funds to be procured from debt financing or from equity financing. A firm will always go for the comparatively cheap and easy source of financing.

(e) **Attitudes of Investors**

The attitude of investors influences the capital structure position. Because, if the investors are risk-averters, they will, no doubt, depend on debt financing as the rate of interest is fixed. But if the investors prefer to take risk, they will undoubtedly go for equity financing. Thus, attitude of investors also affects the capital structure position.

(f) **Level of Stock Prices**

When prices of stock are very depressed in the stock market, no firm will prefer to raise funds by the issue of equity shares. In that case, the firm will go for raising additional funds from debt financing. On the contrary, if the conditions of stock market is found to be bullish the firm will go in for larger funds by the issue of equity shares. Thus, level of stock prices also affects the capital structure position.

GENERAL OR OTHER FACTORS

(a) **Size of Business**

Whether the size of the firm is big or small, the same will influence the capital structure position. If a firm successfully operates its financial activities and grows rapidly it will prefer bonds or preference shares without diluting the interest of equity shareholders. Issuing equity shares is neither justified nor desirable if the rate of return is very low. A firm can borrow funds only when it has adequate investment in fixed assets.

(b) **Operational Activities**

Operational activities differ from firm to firm. For example, a trading concern earns a little margin of gross profit primarily with current assets investments. Manufacturing firms, on the other hand, earn a higher amount of profit as against their huge investment in fixed assets.

(c) **Financial Leverage**

If the rate of return is less than the rate of interest payable to bondholders as a result of low level of profitability for unfavourable financial leverage, borrowings are found to be more costly than the return on investments. If the rate of earning profit is low, it is not easy for a firm to raise funds by issuing shares. In that case, financial leverage must be improved.

(d) **Stable Earnings**

Only a company having a stable earning can meet the recurring fixed charges by way of interest on debt capital. Unstable earnings can not help a firm to proceed for further development. Thus, the capital structure should be more conservative in that case. Thus, in determining capital structure, earnings of a firm play a very important role.

(e) **Age of a Firm**

At its initial stage a firm raises its funds by the issue of equity shares as it is difficult for them to raise funds by issuing debt securities simply due to the fact that they are unknown to the market. In that case, their capital structure is composed of greater amount of equities than the debts. These firms must give more emphasis to the flexibility for procuring funds for further growth and developments. This is not applicable in case of an old and established firm. They can procure their required funds as per their choice as they have reputation and goodwill in the market. Thus, the age of a firm also determines the composition of its capital structure.

(f) **Government Policies**

Government policies are the factors which determine the capital structure of firms in addition to corporate tax policy (which has already been highlighted above). Monetary and fiscal policies are formulated by the Government which directly affect the capital structure position of a firm.

Objects of Sound Capital Structure

The objects of a sound capital structure are

(a) **Solvency** : Debt Capital is a risky source of finance. The same will be profitable only when the interest on debt capital will be lower than the return on capital employed. If a firm procures and depends on too much amount of debt capital, the situation may be dangerous if the firm is not able to pay its interest along with the principal, otherwise, question of solvency will be threatened by a firm.

(b) **Conservatism** : A firm may invite debt capital with its limit. Because, it has got a direct bearing on profitability position of a firm. That is why, if a conservative firm invites a limited amount of debt capital and is quite able to pay-off its interest, there is no harm in it.

(c) **Control** : We know that equity shareholders are the owners of the company and they enjoy voting rights. As such, the entire management is controlled by them and they won't allow anyone to exercise any power on them. Naturally, if more amount is procured by the issue of debt capital, their interest are not affected. Thus, control is one of the major objectives of sound capital structure.

(d) **Lower Cost of Financing** : The capital structure composition will be made in such a manner that it will reduce the cost of capital so that rate of earning profit will be high, i.e., rate of return on capital employed. Moreover, if cost of capital is low, the return, will be higher.

(e) **Flexibility** : The capital structure position of a firm will be made in such a manner that can easily be accepted, i.e., changing conditions can easily be accommodated. That is why a flexible capital structure will help a firm to make adjustments according to its needs.

(f) **Minimising Cost of Issue** : Various types of securities may be issued to raise funds from debt capital. For this purpose certain minimum amount of expenses may be incurred which are really lower than the issue of debentures, e.g., cost of issuing public deposit is comparatively lower than the issuing of other securities, viz., Debentures/Long-term Loans.

(g) **Interest of Various Interested Parties** : Interest of various interested parties are protected as their returns are assured. Debt-capital holders get interest on their capital at a fixed rate and fixed time. Similarly, equity shareholders expect a steady return on their investment. That is why a sound capital structure will help all these interested parties of a firm, e.g., investors, shareholders, debt-capital holders and others.

(h) **Perfect Trade-off between Risk and Return** Financial Leverage increases the return on equity as well as the shareholders' fund by increasing debt to an excessive level which ultimately, increases the financial risk of the stock-holders. But a sound capital structure allows leverage only on that level (i.e., perfect proportion of debt-equity mix) which will make a perfect trade-off between risk and return—although the same is not an easy task.

Optimum Capital Structure

Optimum capital structure means when the cost of capital is minimised and value of the firm i.e., shareholders' wealth is maximised. In other words, that capital structure or combination of debt and equity which leads to the maximum value of the firm is called optimum capital structure. We know that a proper use of debt and equity in capital structure can maximise the value of the firm or shareholders' wealth. But it is not an easy task to ascertain the optimum capital structure of a firm because maximisation of shareholders' wealth depends on some basic decisions.

In order to maximise the value of equity shares of the firm, the firm must choose a financing mix-capital structure which will assist in achieving the desired objectives, i.e., maximisation of shareholders' wealth or value of the firm. We know that use of debt financing has got some distinct edges over equity capital, i.e., the benefit of tax-deductibility, which increase comparatively higher profits (as interest on debt capital is a tax-deductible item). But it does not mean that the firm should increase its debt capital subsequently year after year as compared to equity capital. We know that, by the use of debt capital, EPS is also increased through *Trading on equity*.

Thus, a particular debt-equity mix is to be ascertained for optimum capital structure position. However, in real-world situation, it is not an easy task to find out the proper composition of debt-equity mix for the purpose of maximising the shareholders' wealth or value of the firm. For ascertaining optimum capital structure two ways are advocated. They are:

(i) As ascertainment of exact optimum capital structure is not practically possible, one should try to find out as far as possible the best approximisation;

(ii) The capital structure will be determined in such a manner so that the same will maximise the value of the firm.

Thus, we cannot ignore the importance of capital structure of a firm as we believe that there is a clear relationship between the value of the firm and the capital structure although some others do not accept it.

The following illustration will help us to understand the principle clearly :

Illustration 5.1

Balance Sheet

as at 31st December 2012

Liabilities	Rs.	*Assets*	Rs.
Equity Share Capital	5,00,000	Fixed Assets	7,00,000
Reserves & Surplus	3,00,000	Current Assets	4,00,000
12% Debentures	2,50,000		
Current Liabilities	50,000		
	11,00,000		11,00,000

Rate of Return @ 20%.

Solution

Capital Employed = Fixed Assets + Current Assets – Current Liabilities
= Rs. 7,00,000 + Rs. 4,00,000 – Rs. 50,000
= Rs. 10,50,000.

		Rs.
	Earning before Interest = Rs. 10,50,000 $\times \frac{20}{100}$ =	2,10,000
Less :	Interest on Debenture	30,000
	Earning to Equity Shareholders	1,80,000

$$\therefore \text{ Rate of Return on Equity Shareholders} = \frac{\text{Rs. } 1{,}80{,}000}{\text{Rs. } 5{,}00{,}000 + \text{Rs. } 3{,}00{,}000} \times 100$$

$$= 22.5\%.$$

Thus, the rate of earning on shareholders' fund is 22.5%, although the rate of return is 20%.

From the above example it becomes quite clear that the firm will be interested to use more debt capital. But it has already been mentioned above that too much use of debt capital is a risky situation as, ultimately, it increases cost. At the same time a dangerous situation may arise if the firm is not able to earn more rate of return than it pays for. Thus, debt capital financing should be used very carefully. That is why there must be a proper financing mix between debt and equity capitals for the optimum situation.

Considerations

In order to ascertain the amount of optimum capital structure, the following considerations will assist a finance manager:

(a) **Advantage of Corporate Taxes**

A finance manager may take the opportunity of utilising the financial leverage through corporate taxes. It has already been pointed out in the above paragraphs that debt financing is less costly than equity financing due to the allowances prescribed by the corporate tax authorities. Since the equity financing involves higher cost, the same can be avoided for raising finance. The ultimate benefit will be enjoyed by the equity shareholders, i.e., Trading on Equity.

(b) **Advantage of Financial Leverage**

If the return on investment is comparatively higher than fixed cost of funds, a finance manager may go for raising fund although there is a fixed cost of finance, as the equity shareholders will, ultimately, be benefited.

(c) **Avoidance of High Risk Capital Structure**

If the proportion of debt capital is more than owned capital the same will invite risk; as a result the prices of share in the open market will go down due to high risky proposition of capital structure. In other words, highly geared capital structure is always risky. Thus, a finance manager must not go for raising further finance through borrowings under such circumstances. That is, whether a firm should prefer debt-financing or equity financing, the decision depends on the optimum capital structure of a firm.

(d) **Advantages of Debt-Equity Mix**

A finance manager may take the advantage of debt-equity mix in the composition of capital structure in order to ascertain the optimum capital structure of a firm. Once the optimum capital structure is attained, a finance manager is free from financial hazards. Thus, the ultimate goal of a finance manager is to see that the proper utilisation of debt-equity mix has been attained.

Features of an Optimum Capital Structure

It has already been highlighted above that optimum capital structure appears when value of a firm or shareholders wealth is maximised and cost of capital is minimised. Practically, capital structure varies from firms to firm due to difference in size, nature, cost of risks, earnings competitive conditions etc.

However, we are giving some features of optimum capital structure. They are:

(a) **Cost of Capital**

When a firm reaches at its optimum level of capital structure, its cost of capital must be minimum which will increase the value of shares. If cost of capital increases, profit will decrease, i.e., under this stage the earnings of equity shareholders will be at its maximum level.

(b) **Profitability**

It has already been stated above that profitability of a firm is maximised when there is an effective proportion of debt-equity mix in capital structure. As cost of debt capital is less (as a result of tax deductibility) in comparision with cost of equity capital, higher amount of debt capital may be introduced in order to increase/maximise profitability.

(c) **Adequate Liquidity**

Adequate liquid assets help a firm to repay it liabilities as soon as they mature for payments. Thus, maintaining adequate liquid assets in the composition of capital structure avoid the problem of making payments for current and liquid liabilities. So sufficient amount of cash in the form of liquid assets must be kept in hand to meet or to make payment for immediate maturing liabilities.

(d) **Flexibility**

It has also been stated in the earlier paragraph that capital structure of a firm should be flexible so that it can adjust or manage the changed circumstances. In other words, in case of need, a firm may issue equity share for its requirement or may issue bonds whichever is found to be most suitable for it. Thus, the capital structure should be flexiable in nature.

(e) **Conservatism**

We know that, in order to maximise the value of the firm, or to increase the rate of earning, higher amount of debt capital may be taken. But, it must be remembered that Current Ratio, Liquid Ratio, Debt-Equity Ratio should be maintained at their normal level. Other-wise excessive amount of debt capital will lead to insolvency of a firm so firm must be conservative while ascertaining its capital structure.

(f) **Debt-Equity Mix**

In order to maximise the rate of earnings or value of the firm there must be proper proportion of debt-equity mix in capital structure. Bearing in mind the financial risk which is related to debt capital, i.e., there is a fixed charge by way of interest payment and repayment of principal at the date of maturity.

(g) **Control**

It has already been stated above that equity shareholders want to retain controlling power in their own hands. The same is possible if, instead of issuing equity share debt instruments are issued (which do not have any volting or controlling power except in some exceptional cases). That is why, shareholders always want to raise funds by the issue of debt capital for their requirements.

Pattern of Capital Structure

It has already been pointed out above while discussing the classification of capital structure, that a company may begin with the *simple* type of capital structure i.e., by the issue of equity share only, but gradually this becomes a *complex* type, i.e., along with the issue of equity share, it may make a financing-mix with debt.

The patterns of capital structure are:

(a) With the issue of equity shares only;

(b) With the issue of both equity shares and preference shares;

(c) With the issue of equity shares and debentures; and

(d) With the issue of equity shares, preference shares, and debentures.

But the best method of choosing the composition of capital structure depends on many factors, the most significant is to choose the alternative which gives the highest EPS or rates of return on equity capital.

The relationship between debt and equity has already been explained earlier. We have also explained the basic difference between debt and equity. In order to avoid repetitions we explain here only the role of debt and equity mix i.e., the proportion of debt and equity in the total capital structure of a firm. To raise funds through debt is cheaper than to raise funds through equity due to tax factor as interest on debenture is an allowable deduction. On the other hand, payment of dividend is an appropriation of profit, hence, the same is not allowed as deduction for computation of taxable income. In short, if a company having 50% tax bracket pays debenture interest @ 10% the ultimate effective cost comes to 5%. That is not applicable also in case of preference shares. If a firm raise its funds by the issue of 10% preference shares, the dividend so paid to the preference shareholders is also not allowed as deduction for income tax purposes, i.e., the cost of raising funds would be @ 10%. So, it can safely be stated that to raise funds by the issue of debt capital or borrowings is cheaper and result in a higher profit available to the equity shareholders which, in other words, increase the EPS.

However, the following illustrations will highlight the different methods of financing among the various alternative sources of finance.

Illustration 5.2

X Ltd., a widely held company, is considering a major expansion of its production facilities and the following alternatives are available:

	Alternatives		(Rs. in '00,000)
	A	B	C
	Rs.	Rs.	Rs.
Share Capital	50	20	10
14% Debentures	—	20	15
Loan from a financial institution @ 18% p.a. rate of interest	—	10	25

Expected rate of return before Tax is 25%. The rate of dividend of the company is not less than 20%. The company at present has low debt corporate taxation 50%.

Which of the alternatives would you choose?

[C.A. Final]

Solution

Statement Showing the Rate of Return under Various Financial Plans

(Rs. '00,000)

	A	B	C
	Rs.	Rs.	Rs.
EBIT			
(25% on Rs. 50,00,000)	12.50	12.50	12.50
Less : Interest on :			
Debentures	—	2.80	2.10
Loans	—	1.80	4.50
Profit before Tax	12.50	7.90	5.90
Less : Tax @ 50%	6.25	3.95	2.95
Profit after Tax	6.25	3.95	2.95
Rates of Return on Share Capital	$= \frac{\text{Rs. } 6.25}{\text{Rs. } 50.00} \times 100$	$= \frac{\text{Rs. } 3.95}{\text{Rs. } 20.00} \times 100$	$= \frac{\text{Rs. } 2.95}{\text{Rs. } 10.00} \times 100$
	= 12.5%	= 19.75%	= 29.5%

Recommendation

Since rate of return in case of alternative C is the highest, i.e., 29.5%, Alternative C should be chosen.

Illustration 5.3

A company needs Rs. 5,00,000 for purchase of a new machinery. The following three financial plans are feasible:

(a) Issue of 50,000 shares at Rs. 10 per share;

(b) Issue of 25,000 shares at Rs. 10 per share and issue of 2,500 debentures at Rs. 100 per debenture which would carry interest at 8%.

(c) Issue of 25,000 ordinary shares at Rs. 10 per share and 2,500 preference shares at Rs. 100 per share which bear dividend rates of 8%.

Assumptions

(i) Company's earnings before interest and tax (EBIT) would be Rs. 60,000 p.a. after the purchase of new machinery.

(ii) Income-tax rates at 50%.

Which alternative would you recommend and why?

Solution

Statement Showing the EPS under Different Financial Plans

	A	B	C
Plan	Rs.	Rs.	Rs.
EBIT	60,000	60,000	60,000
Less : Interest	—	20,000	—
PBT (Profit before Tax)	60,000	40,000	60,000
Less : Tax @ 50%	30,000	20,000	30,000
PAT (Profit after Tax)	30,000	20,000	30,000
Less : Pref. Dividend	—	—	20,000
Profit available to Equity Shareholders	30,000	20,000	10,000
No. of Equity Shares	50,000	25,000	25,000
∴ EPS	$=\frac{\text{Rs. } 30,000}{50,000}$	$=\frac{\text{Rs. } 20,000}{25,000}$	$=\frac{\text{Rs. } 10,000}{25,000}$
	= Re. 0.60	= Rs. 0.80	= Rs. 0.40

Recommendation

Hence, Financial Plan B is recommended as its EPS will be highest.

Illustration 5.4

X Ltd. has equity share capital of Rs. 5,00,000 (face value Rs. 100 each). To meet the expenditure of an expansion programme, the company wishes to raise Rs. 3,00,000 and has the following four alternative sources to raise the funds:

Plan A: To have full money from the equity shares.

Plan B: To have Rs. 1,00,000 from equity shares and Rs. 2,00,000 from borrowings from the financial institution @ 10% p.a.

Plan C: Full money from borrowing @ 10% p.a.

Plan D: Rs. 1,00,000 in equity shares and Rs. 2,00,000 from preference shares @ 8% p.a. dividend.

The company is having present earning of Rs. 1,50,000. The corporate tax is 50%. Suggest the suitable plan from the above four plans from raise the required funds.

Solution

Statement Showing the EPS under Different Financial Plans

	Plan A	Plan B	Plan C	Plan D
	Rs.	Rs.	Rs.	Rs.
EBIT	1,50,000	1,50,000	1,50,000	1,50,000
Less : Interest on 10%	—	20,000	30,000	—
	1,50,000	1,30,000	1,20,000	1,50,000
Less : Tax @ 50%	75,000	65,000	60,000	75,000
Profit/Earning after Tax	75,000	65,000	60,000	75,000
Less : Pref. Dividend @ 8%	—	—	—	16,000
Profit available to Equity Shareholders	75,000	65,000	60,000	59,000
No. of Equity Shares (5,000 + 3,000)	8,000	6,000	5,000	6,000
∴ EPS	$= \frac{\text{Rs. } 75,000}{8,000}$ = Rs. 9.375	$= \frac{\text{Rs. } 65,000}{6,000}$ = Rs. 10.83	$= \frac{\text{Rs. } 60,000}{5,000}$ = Rs. 12	$= \frac{\text{Rs. } 59,000}{6,000}$ = Rs. 9.83

Recommendation

Plan C is recommended since its EPS is highest. In other words, it may be suggested that the required funds should be raised in full from borrowings @ 10% p.a.

Illustration 5.5

Company A is presently having a capital structure of 10,000 ordinary shares of Rs. 500 each. The company proposes to raise additional Rs. 50,00,000 for a major expansion programme and is considering four possible financial plans:

Mode of Financing	Alternative I	Alternative II	Alternative III	Alternative IV
Equity Shares	10,000 @ Rs. 500	5,000 @ Rs. 500	—	5,000 @ Rs. 500
Preference Shares @ 10%	—	—	—	5,000 @ Rs. 500
Term Loan @ 12%	—	Rs. 25,00,000	—	—
Term Loan @ 13%	—	—	Rs. 50,00,000	—

The additional input of capital would double the company's present earning before interest and tax from the level of Rs. 6,00,000. Assume a tax rate of 30%.

You are required to calculate the impact on earning per share (EPS) for the shareholders under the four alternative plans and comment.

Solution

Statement Showing the EPS under Different Financial Plans

	Plan I	Plan II	Plan III	Plan IV
	Rs.	Rs.	Rs.	Rs.
EBIT (Rs. 6,00,000 × 2)	12,00,000	12,00,000	12,00,000	12,00,000
Less : Interest on term loan	—	3,00,000	6,50,000	—
Profit before Tax	12,00,000	9,00,000	5,50,000	12,00,000
Less : Tax @ 30%	3,60,000	2,70,000	1,65,000	3,60,000
Profit after Tax	8,40,000	6,30,000	3,85,000	8,40,000
Less : Pref. Dividend	—	—	—	2,50,000
Earnings available to Equity Shareholders	8,40,000	6,30,000	3,85,000	5,90,000

Contd.

	Rs.	Rs.	Rs.	Rs.
No. of Equity Shares (10,000 + 10,000)	20,000	15,000	10,000	15,000
	$= \frac{\text{Rs. } 8,40,000}{20,000}$	$= \frac{\text{Rs. } 6,30,000}{15,000}$	$= \frac{\text{Rs. } 3,85,000}{10,000}$	$= \frac{\text{Rs. } 5,90,000}{15,000}$
∴ EPS	= Rs. 42	= Rs. 42	= Rs. 38.50	= Rs. 39.33

Recommendation

Plan I or Plan II may be taken since the EPS is highest.

Illustration 5.6

A company's capital structure consists of:

	Rs.
Equity shares of Rs. 100 each	20,00,000
Retained Earnings	10,00,000
9% Preference Shares	12,00,000
7% Debentures	8,00,000
Total	50,00,000

The company earns 12% on its capital. The income-tax rate is 50%. The company requires a sum of Rs. 25,00,000 to finance its expansion programme for which the following alternatives are available:

(i) Issue of 20,000 Equity Shares at a premium of Rs. 25 per share;

(ii) Issue of 10% Preference Shares; and

(iii) Issue of 8% Debentures.

It is estimated that the $\frac{P}{E}$ ratio in the case of preference share and debenture financing would be 21.4, 17 and 15.7, respectively.

Which of the three financing alternatives would you recommend and why?

[C.A. & C.S.]

Solution

Statement Showing the Computation of EPS under Different Financing Plans

	Present Capacity	Plan I	Plan II	Plan III
	Rs.	Rs.	Rs.	Rs.
EBIT (12% on Rs. 50,00,000)	6,00,000	—	—	—
(12% on Rs. 75,00,000)	—	9,00,000	9,00,000	9,00,000
Less: Interest				
Old	56,000	56,000	56,000	56,000
New	—	—	—	2,00,000
Profit before Tax	5,44,000	8,44,000	8,44,000	6,44,000
Less: Tax @ 50%	2,72,000	4,22,000	4,22,000	3,22,000
Profit after Tax	2,72,000	4,22,000	4,22,000	3,22,000

Contd.

	Rs.	Rs.	Rs.	Rs.
Less : Pref. Dividend				
Old	1,08,000	1,08,000	1,08,000	1,08,000
New	—	—	2,50,000	—
Earnings for Equity Shareholders	1,64,000	3,14,000	64,000	2,14,000
No. of Equity Shares	20,000	40,000	20,000	20,000
∴ EPS	$= \frac{\text{Rs. } 1,64,000}{20,000}$	$= \frac{\text{Rs. } 3,14,000}{40,000}$	$= \frac{\text{Rs. } 64,000}{20,000}$	$= \frac{\text{Rs. } 2,14,000}{20,000}$
	= Rs. 8.20	= Rs. 7.85	= Rs. 3.20	= Rs. 10.70
$\frac{P}{E}$ Ratio (given)	—	21.4	17	15.7
MPS (EPS × $\frac{P}{E}$ Ratio)	—	167.99	54.40	167.99

Recommendation

The financing alternative which possesses the highest MPS (Market price per share) should be selected. But in this problem both Plan (I) and Plan (III) present the same MPS, so any one of the two may be selected or recommended. But, from the taxation point of view, Debenture Financing is better, as after-tax cost will be only 4% (i.e., 8% – 50% of 8%). Thus, Debenture Financing should be recommended.

Illustration 5.7

A company is considering raising of funds of about Rs. 100 lakhs by one of the two alternative methods, viz., 14% institutional term loan, and 13% non-convertible Debentures. The term loan option would attract no major incidental cost. The debentures would have to be issued at a discount of 2.5% and would involve cost of issue of Rs. 1,00,000.

Advise the company as to the better option based on the effective cost of capital in each case. Assume the tax rate is 50%.

[C.A.]

Solution

Statement Showing the Effective Cost of Capital

	Option I (14% Inst. Term Loan)	Option II (13% Non-Convertible Debentures)
	Rs.	Rs.
Effective Capital to be raised (FV)	1,00,00,000	1,00,00,000
Less: Discount	—	2,50,000
	1,00,00,000	97,50,000
Less: Cost of Issue	—	1,00,000
	1,00,00,000	96,50,000
Interest Charges on FV of Rs. 1,00,00,000	14,00,000	13,00,000
Less: Tax @ 50%	7,00,000	6,50,000
	7,00,000	6,50,000
∴ Effective Cost of Capital	$\frac{\text{Rs. } 7,00,000}{\text{Rs. } 1,00,00,000} \times 100 = 7\%$	$\frac{\text{Rs. } 6,50,000}{\text{Rs. } 96,50,000} \times 100 = 6.74\%$

Recommendation

Since the effective cost of capital is less in case of Option II, i.e., by issuing 13% Non-Convertible Debentures, the same should be considered for raising funds of Rs. 1,00,00,000.

Illustration 5.8

X Company Ltd. is considering 3 different plans to finance its total project cost of Rs. 100 lakhs. These are:

	Plan A (Rs. in lakhs)	Plan B (Rs. in lakhs)	Plan C (Rs. in lakhs)
Equity (Rs. 100 per share)	50	34	25
Debt 8% Debentures	50	66	75
	100	100	100

Sales for the first three years of operation are estimated at Rs. 100 lakhs, Rs. 125 lakhs and Rs. 150 lakhs, and 10% profit before interest and taxes is forecast to be achieved. Corporate taxation to be taken at 50%.

Compute earnings per share in each of the alternative plans of financing for the three years.

Solution

Profit before interest & tax @ 10% on sales:

	Years 1 Rs.	2 Rs.	3 Rs.
Sales	1,00,00,000	1,25,00,000	1,50,00,000
EBIT @ 10%	10,00,000	12,50,000	15,00,000

Computation of EPS under Different Financing Plans

Year 1

	Plan A Rs.	Plan B Rs.	Plan C Rs.
EBIT	10,00,000	10,00,000	10,00,000
Less : Interest on Debentures @ 8%	4,00,000	5,28,000	6,00,000
Profit before Tax	6,00,000	4,72,000	4,00,000
Less : Tax @ 50%	3,00,000	2,36,000	2,00,000
Profit after Tax	3,00,000	2,36,000	2,00,000
No. of Equity Shares	50,000	34,000	25,000
∴ EPS	$= \frac{\text{Rs. } 3,00,000}{50,000}$	$= \frac{\text{Rs. } 2,36,000}{34,000}$	$= \frac{\text{Rs. } 2,00,000}{25,000}$
	= Rs. 6	= Rs. 6.94	= Rs. 8

Year 2

	Plan A Rs.	Plan B Rs.	Plan C Rs.
EBIT	12,50,000	12,50,000	12,50,000
Less : Interest on Debentures @ 8%	4,00,000	5,28,000	6,00,000
Profit before Tax	8,50,000	7,22,000	6,50,000
Less : Tax @ 50%	4,25,000	3,61,000	3,25,000
Profit after Tax	4,25,000	3,61,000	3,25,000

Contd.

	Rs.	Rs.	Rs.
No. of Equity Shares	50,000	34,000	25,000
∴ EPS	$= \frac{\text{Rs. } 4,25,000}{50,000}$	$= \frac{\text{Rs. } 3,61,000}{34,000}$	$= \frac{\text{Rs. } 3,25,000}{25,000}$
	= Rs. 8.50	= Rs. 10.62	= Rs. 13.00

Year 3

	Plan A	Plan B	Plan C
	Rs.	Rs.	Rs.
EBIT	15,00,000	15,00,000	15,00,000
Less : Interest on Debentures @ 8%	4,00,000	5,28,000	6,00,000
Profit before Tax	11,00,000	9,72,000	9,00,000
Less : Tax @ 50%	5,50,000	4,86,000	4,50,000
Profit after Tax	5,50,000	4,86,000	4,50,000
No. of Equity Shares	50,000	34,000	25,000
∴ EPS	$= \frac{\text{Rs. } 5,50,000}{50,000}$	$= \frac{\text{Rs. } 4,86,000}{34,000}$	$= \frac{\text{Rs. } 4,50,000}{25,000}$
	= Rs. 11	= Rs. 14.29	= Rs. 18

Recommendation

Since EPS of alternative plan C is highest among the plans, the same should be selected in all the 3 years stated above.

Illustration 5.9

X Ltd. is contemplating conversion of 8% convertible debentures of Rs. 1,000 each. At present, it has 500 such debentures outstanding. The market price of the debentures is Rs. 1,080. The debenture incentive provides that one debenture will be converted for 10 shares. The price earning ratio before redemption is 20% and anticipated price-earning ratio after redemption is 25 : 1.

The number of shares outstanding prior to redemption was 10,000. Earning before interest and taxes amounted to Rs. 2,00,000. The company is in the 50% tax bracket.

Should the company convert its debentures into shares?

Solution

X Ltd.
Evaluation of Redemption Option

	Pre-Conversion	Post-Conversion
	Rs.	Rs.
EBIT	2,00,000	2,00,000
Less : Interest (8% on 500 × 1,000)	40,000	—
Profit before Tax	1,60,000	2,00,000
Less : Tax @ 50%	80,000	1,00,000
Profit after Tax	80,000	1,00,000

Contd.

No. of Shares	10,000	15,000
EPS	$= \frac{\text{Rs. } 80,000}{10,000} = \text{Rs. } 8$	$= \frac{\text{Rs. } 1,00,000}{15,000} = \text{Rs. } 6.67$
Price Earning Ratio	20 : 1	25 : 1
MPS (Market Price of a share)	Rs. 8 × 20 = Rs. 160	= Rs. 6.67 × 25 = Rs. 166.75

Recommendation

This company should convert its debentures into shares as market price of a debenture is Rs. 1,080. One debenture is converted into 10 shares. So, the market price of 10 shares will be Rs. 1,667.50 (Rs. 166.75 × 10). So, the debentureholders also will be benefited as a result of the conversion.

Illustration 5.10

The Ever Growing Company has to decide between debt fund and equity for its expansion programme. Its current position is:

		Rs.
	Debt @ 5%	40,000
	Equity Capital (Rs. 10 per share)	1,00,000
	Surplus	60,000
	Total Capitalisation	2,00,000
	Sales	6,00,000
	Less : Total Cost	5,38,000
	Income before Interest and Tax	62,000
Less :	Interest	2,000
		60,000
	Income-Tax @ 57.25%	34,350
	Income after Tax	25,650

The expansion programme is estimated to cost Rs. 1,00,000. If this is financed through debt, the rate of new debt will be 7% and the price earning ratio will be 6 times. If the expansion programme is financed through equity shares, the new shares can be sold netting Rs. 25 per share, and the price to earning ratio will be 7 times. The expansion will generate additional sales of Rs. 3,00,000 with a return of 10% on sales before interest and taxes.

If the company is to follow a policy of maximising the market value of its shares, which form of financing should it choose?

[I.C.W.A. Final]

Solution

Statement Showing the Market Value of Shares under Different Financial Plans

	Plan I (7% Debt Issue)	Plan II (Issuing 4,000 Equity Shares of Rs. 25 each)
	Rs.	Rs.
EBIT (Rs. 62,000 + 10% of Rs. 3,00,000)	92,000	92,000
Less : Interest (2,000 + 7,000)	9,000	2,000
Profit before Tax	83,000	90,000
Less : Tax @ 57.25%	47,518	51,525
Profit after Tax	35,482	38,475

Contd.

	Rs.	Rs.
No. of Shares	10,000	14,000
EPS	$= \frac{\text{Rs. } 35,482}{10,000}$ = Rs. 3.55	$= \frac{\text{Rs. } 38,475}{14,000}$ = Rs. 2.75
Price Earning Ratio	6 times	7 times
Market Price of a Share (EPS × PE Ratio)	= Rs. 3.55 × 6	= Rs. 2.75 × 7
	= Rs. 21.30	= Rs. 19.25

Recommendation

Since the market price of a share under 7% Debt Financing is higher i.e. Rs. 21.30, in comparison with equity financing of Rs. 19.25, financing for Rs. 1,00,000 should be chosen from 7% debt financing.

CAPITALISATION

It is the financial structure of the business which is represented by total par value of all Shares, Debentures, i.e. the sum total of owned capital and borrowed capital including Long-term Debts. In the words of Gerstenberg : 'Capitalisation comprises a corporation's ownership capital and its borrowed capital, as represented by its long-term indebtedness'. Therefore, capitalisation consists of all long-term funds invested in the corporation.

But it is to be remembered that the term capitalisation is used in the case of corporate enterprises only and not in any other form of organisation. It is an important aspect of company management, and the success or failure of the corporation depends on its proper assessment although capital necessary for a particular unit depends on the nature, type and volume of the unit.

Theories of Capitalisation

There are two theories which are widely used for ascertaining the amount of capital:

(i) The Earning Theory of Capitalisation, and

(ii) The Cost Theory of Capitalisation.

(i) The Earning Theory of Capitalisation

The object of this theory is to determine the amount of capital on the basis of the current rate of return on investment and also the expected or fair rate of future return on capital invested in the business. In other words, the value of capitalisation is equal to the capitalised value of profit.

It can be represented as :

$$\textit{Capitalised Value of Profit/Earning} : \frac{\textit{Profit/Earning}}{\textit{Normal/Expected rate of return}} \times 100$$

The above can also be explained with the help of an example. If the expected rate of return is 10% and the profit becomes Rs. 10,000, the capitalisation, according to this theory, will be Rs. 1,00,000 $\left(\frac{\text{Rs.}10,000}{10} \times 100\right)$.

Therefore, in order to estimate the correct amount of capital, the correct computation of fair rate of return and expected earnings are very significant.

(ii) The Cost Theory of Capitalisation

According to this theory, the amount of capital is computed by summing up the different expenses, viz., cost of fixed assets, the requirement of working capital for the continuous operation, expenses for establishment and promotion and improvement and extension. This is very important for a newly started company since the promoters can understand about the amount of funds to be raised.

But this theory suffers from certain limitations. One of them is that it recognises only the book value of the assets for the purpose of calculating capitalisation which does not, strictly speaking, indicate the net worth of the assets because the net worth can only be ascertained on the basis of market value of the assets.

Over-capitalisation

It indicates that the earnings of a company are not sufficient to enable it to sell its stocks and bonds on par value basis, i.e., the shares issued by a company are much in excess of actual needs and, as a result, the invested funds are not used properly. In other words, over-capitalisation appears when the value of stocks and shares exceeds the current value of assets. Prof. Gerstenberg defines : 'A corporation is over-capitalised when its earnings are not large enough to yield a fair return on the amount of stocks and bonds that have been issued, or when the amount of securities outstanding exceeds the current value of the assets'.

Causes of Over-capitalisation

(i) Raising Excess Capital

It is resorted to by the promoters on the expectation that more profit may be earned if more capital is invested which will increase the future rate of earnings. But, in practice, the same does not happen. In short, the capital which is not utilised properly, or remains idle, results in over-capitalisation.

(ii) Decline in the Efficiency of the Assets

The value of assets may decline owing to the inadequate provision for depreciation, obsolescence etc. which lower the profit-earning capacity of the assets, i.e., earning capacity of the assets may not be commensurate with the higher value of the assets.

(iii) Borrowing at Exorbitant Rates of Interest

Practically, this accounts for a large portion of the profit and, as such, leaves a very insufficient part for the distribution of dividend for the shareholders.

(iv) Floating of a Concern During a Period of Boom

If a company is floated under the conditions of inflation, it requires a large fund for acquiring its necessary assets. But when depression sets in, naturally, the prices of the assets fall which ultimately leads to over-capitalisation.

(v) Incurring High Promotion Expenses

Payment of expenses on elaborate establishment or promotion expenses, costly machines, plans and project, excessive preliminary expenses etc. which means a high promotional cost, may create over-capitalisation.

(vi) Payment of Dividend and Taxation

Liberal payment of dividend as well as higher rates of taxation may lead to over-capitalisation.

Evils or Disadvantages of Over-capitalisation

(i) Poor Credit-Worthiness

When a company sells its shares at less than their nominal value, i.e., less than at par, it suffers from poor credit-worthiness. Naturally, it becomes very difficult for the company to raise funds by further issue of shares as and when necessary.

(ii) Reduction in the Rate of Dividend

Since the capital is not utilised properly, i.e., the company cannot effectively use its capital employed, the rate of return must be low and, consequently, the value of shares in the market may go down.

(iii) Loss to Shareholders

The shareholders, under the condition of over-capitalisation, are victimised and put in a very awkward position. In other words, they are in a fix as to whether they should sell the shares or retain it. If they want to sell, they will have to suffer heavily because of the lower price and, again, if they retain them, they will get a very poor rate of return by way of dividend.

(iv) Loss to Employees and Labourers

The employees and labourers suffer since they cannot receive adequate salaries and wages owing to lower profit.

(v) Loss to Creditors

Creditors may have to suffer since they may have to accept a lower rate of interest, and suffer permanent loss of capital in case of liquidation.

(vi) Loss to the Society

People suffer from a poor quality of the products as well as higher prices. Besides, limited resources of the society are not utilised properly since, under conditions of over-capitalisation, the company is unable to make the best use of capital.

Under-capitalisation

It means an effective utilisation of capital and, as such, a higher rate of return on capital. It is just the opposite of over-capitalisation. In the words of Gerstenberg : 'A corporation may be under-capitalised when the rate of profits it is making on the total capital is exceptionally high in relation to the return enjoyed by similarly situated companies in the same industry, or when it has too little capital with which to conduct its business':

Evils or Disadvantages of Under-capitalisation

(i) Underestimation in the Requirement of Capital

It leads to under-capitalisation since a lesser amount of capital is raised than is actually required.

(ii) Inflationary Effect

The companies set up at the time of depression may experience inflation which sets in as a result of increase in earnings.

(iii) Issue of Minimum Share Capital

A minimum of equity shares may sometimes be issued by the promoters in order to exercise control over the management which, ultimately, leads to under-capitalisation.

(iv) Scope for Fluctuation in the Securities

Under-capitalisation provides scope for fluctuation in the securities which leads to speculation in the security market.

(v) Lower Price of the Goods or Higher Wages Precluded

Since the scale of operations may have to be restricted owing to inadequacy of working capital, neither the consumers can expect lower price of the goods nor can the labourers expect higher rates of wages.

Watered Capital

When share capital is not represented by the assets of equal value, it is called Watered Capital. In other words, it is represented by intangible assets which practically do not help directly in the profitable working of business unit. In the words of Husband and Dockerary : 'the primary test of watered stock is found in the intent of the promoters who sell the stock. If there is a deliberate attempt to milch the shareholders by the inflation of the value of the assets a watered condition is all the inevitable result'. The following illustration will make the principle clear:

Suppose a company issues 10,000 shares of Rs. 10 each to the public which are taken up by the investors for a consideration of Rs. 1,00,000 as fully paid. The said sum is spent over the establishment of the company by acquiring various types of assets. But later it is discovered that the assets' realisable value (and not the real value), i.e., the market value of the assets or the recovery price of assets, of the company is only Rs. 80,000. Therefore, the capital is watered to the tune of Rs. 20,000 (Rs. 1,00,000 – Rs. 80,000).

Over-trading and Under-trading

Over-trading arises only when the capital employed is inadequate in comparison with the volume of business. In other words, it is an expansion of sales without adequate support from capital. That is to say, the company with limited resources tries to increase the volume of business which, ultimately, suffers from acute shortage of liquid funds. This results in a Low Proprietary Ratio, Low Current Ratio and Liquid Ratio with inadequate working capital. Under this condition, the company does not maintain the adequate level of inventories and, as a result, it has to depend on regular supplies. On the other hand, payments of expenses (Wages, Salaries etc.) and Creditors including taxes cannot be made in time since there is a serious shortage of cash.

Whether or not the company is over-trading can easily be known after analysing certain ratios, viz., Current Ratio, Liquid Ratio, Debtor's Turnover Ratio, Inventory Turnover Ratio etc. In the case of over-trading, however, the Current Ratio and Liquid Ratio will be lower than their standard of normal ratios but the turnover ratios will be higher than their standard of normal ratios.

The *symptoms* of over-trading are discernible when:

(a) a company takes a comparatively long time to pay-off its creditors or the amount of creditors increases in comparison with debtors, or creditors increase more rapidly or fall more slowly than debtors.

(b) the amount of profit declines.

(c) the company increases the rate of borrowings in a way which is quite excessive in relation to the assets owned by the shareholders.

(d) a company is buying fixed or non-current assets out of short-term funds.

(e) Bills Payable are recorded which is not customary, and unaccounted reduction is made in Bills Receivable which indicates discounting.

Under-trading is a condition contrary to over-trading. It is an application of idle funds. Too much investment in current assets and smaller amount of current liabilities results in under-trading.

The *symptoms* of under-trading, however, are to show :

(a) A very high Current Ratio and Liquid Ratio,

(b) Lower Turnover Ratios.

The consequences of under-trading are :

(a) Reduction in profits.

(b) Reduction in the rates of return on capital employed.

(c) Loss of Goodwill.

(d) Fall in the prices of the shares in the market.

Assets Structure

Assets structure refers to the application of long-term and short-term funds in various component of total assets of a firm. In short, it encompasses both fixed assets as well as current assets of a firm. There are many factors which directly affect the assets structure, e.g., operating cycle, method and technology taken etc. because the ratio of fixed assets, investments and current assets investments vary from firm to firm. Sometimes it may be found that fixed asset investments are significantly high than the current asset investments in a particular type of industry, e.g., public utility service industry, e.g., Electricity etc. Similarly, in a trading concern, current asset investments are significantly high than the fixed asset investments.

One point is very significant. That is, operating fixed costs are actually determined by the assets structure of a firm. If the ratio of fixed assets investments are very high than the current assets investments, the operating fixed costs will also be very high in that case (e.g., in the form of depreciation, insurance, repairs & maintenance etc.). Thus, care must be taken while selecting the assets structure of a firm, bearing in mind that operating profit is largely affected by the application of assets structure.

To sum up:

Financial Structure = *Liabilities side of the Balance Sheet*

Capital Structure = *Total Liabilities minus Current or Short-term Liabilities*

Capitalisation = *Total Amount of Securities issued by the firm*

Assets Structure = *Assets side of the Balance Sheet*

Illustration 5.11

From the Balance Sheet presented by Amrita Ltd. for the year ended 31st December 2004, ascertain (i) Capital Structure; (ii) Financial Structure; (iii) Capitalisation; and (iv) Assets Structure.

Balance Sheet

as at 31st December 2012

Liabilities	Rs.	*Assets*	Rs.
Equity Share Capital	25,00,000	Fixed Assets	30,00,000
10% Pref. Share Capital	10,00,000	Current Assets	15,00,000
8% Debentures	5,00,000		
Reserves & Surplus	3,00,000		
Current Liabilities	2,00,000		
	45,00,000		45,00,000

Solution

(a) CAPITAL STRUCTURE

	Rs.	Proportion
Equity Share Capital	25,00,000	58%
10% Pref. Share Capital	10,00,000	23%
Reserves & Surplus	3,00,000	7%
8% Debentures	5,00,000	12%
	43,00,000	100%

or, Total Liabilities – Current Liabilities
= Rs. 45,00,000 – Rs. 2,00,000
= Rs. 43,00,000

(b) FINANCIAL STRUCTURE

	Rs.	Proportion
Equity Share Capital	25,00,000	56%
10% Pref. Share Capital	10,00,000	22%
Reserves & Surplus	3,00,000	7%
8% Debentures	5,00,000	11%
Current Liabilities	2,00,000	4%
	45,00,000	100%

or, Total Liabilities side of the Balance Sheet.

(c) CAPITALISATION
(i.e., Total number of Securities issued by a firm.)

	Rs.
Equity Share Capital	25,00,000
10% Pref. Share Capital	10,00,000
8% Debentures	5,00,000
	40,00,000

(d) ASSETS STRUCTURE
(i.e., Total Fixed Assets + Total Current Assets)

Fixed Assets	30,00,000
Current Assets	15,00,000
	45,00,000

THEORIES OF CAPITAL STRUCTURE

There are several major contributors to the theory of capital structure. Durand, Modigliani-Miller, Donaldson, Soloman and Schwartz are more important among others.

There are several theories which are used in order to explain the interrelationship of Cost of Capital, Capital Structure, and the value of the firm:

(a) **Net Income Approach;**

(b) **Net Operating Income Approach;**

(c) **Traditional Theory Approach;**

(d) **Modigliani-Miller Approach.**

(a) NET INCOME (NI) APPROACH

David Durand[1] suggested the two famous capital structure theories, viz., **Net Income Approach** and the **Operating Income Approach.** According to NI approach a firm may increase the total value of the firm by lowering its cost of capital. When cost of capital is lowest and the value of the firm is greatest, we call it the optimum capital structure for the firm and, at this point, the market price per share is maximised. The same is possible continuously by lowering its cost of capital by the use of debt capital. In other words, using more debt capital with a corresponding reduction in cost of capital, the value of the firm will increase. The same is possible only when:

(i) Cost of Debt (K_d) is less than Cost of Equity (K_e);

(ii) there are no taxes; and

(iii) the use of debt does not change the risk perception of the investors since the degree of leverage is increased to that extent.

---

1 Durand, D. — *The Cost of Debt and Equity Funds for Business* — The Management of Corporate Finance, E. Solomon, Ed., New York, The Free Press, 1959, pp. 91-116.

Since the amount of debt in the capital structure increases, weighted average cost of capital decreases which leads to increase the total value of the firm. So, the increased amount of debt with constant amount of cost of equity and cost of debt will highlight the earnings of the shareholders.

Illustration 5.12

X Ltd. presents the following particulars :

EBIT (i.e., Net Operating income) is Rs. 30,000;

The equity capitalisation ratio (i.e., cost of equity) is 15% (K_e);

Cost of debt is 10% (K_d);

Total Capital amounted to Rs. 2,00,000.

Calculate the cost of capital and the value of the firm for each of the following alternative leverages after applying the NI approach.

Leverage (Debt to total Capital) 0%, 20%, 50%, 70% and 100%.

Solution

Statement Showing the Cost of Capital and the Value of the Firm

Degree of Leverage	0	0.2	0.5	0.7	1.0
	Rs.	Rs.	Rs.	Rs.	Rs.
Equity Capital	2,00,000	1,60,000	1,00,000	60,000	—
Debt Capital	—	40,000	1,00,000	1,40,000	2,00,000
Total	2,00,000	2,00,000	2,00,000	2,00,000	2,00,000
EBIT @ 15%	30,000	30,000	30,000	30,000	30,000
Less: Interest on Debt	—	4,000	10,000	14,000	20,000
Earnings to Equity	30,000	26,000	20,000	16,000	10,000
Market Value of Debt	—	40,000	1,00,000	1,40,000	2,00,000
Market Value of Equity Earnings $\left(\frac{\text{Earnings}}{K_e}\right)$	2,00,000	1,73,333	1,33,333	1,06,667	66,667
Total Value of the firm	2,00,000	2,13,333	2,33,333	2,46,667	2,66,667
Thus,					
Cost of Debt (K_d) — given	10%	10%	10%	10%	10%
Cost of Equity (K_e) — given	15%	15%	15%	15%	15%
Average Cost of Capital $\left(\frac{T}{V}\right)$	30%	28%	25%	23%	20%

Workings :

Average Cost of Capital is computed as under (under various financing plans):

$K_w = \left(\frac{T}{V}\right)K_d + \left(\frac{S}{V}\right)K_e$, substituting the values:

(i) When leverage is 0

$K_w = 0 \times 10 + 2 \times 15 = 30\%$

(ii) When leverage is 0.2

$K_w = .4 \times 10 + .16 \times 15 = 28\%$

(iii) When leverage is 0.5

$K_w = .10 \times 10 + .10 \times 15 = 25\%$

(iv) When leverage is 0.7

$K_w = .14 \times 10 + .6 \times 15 = 23\%$

(v) When leverage is 1

$K_w = .20 \times 10 + 0 \times 15 = 20\%$

From the above table it is quite clear that the value of the firm (V) will be increased if there is a proportionate increase in debt capital but there will be a reduction in overall cost of capital. So, Cost of Capital is increased and the value of the firm is maximum if a firm uses 100% debt capital.

It is interesting to note the NI approach can also be graphically presented as under (with the help of the above illustration):

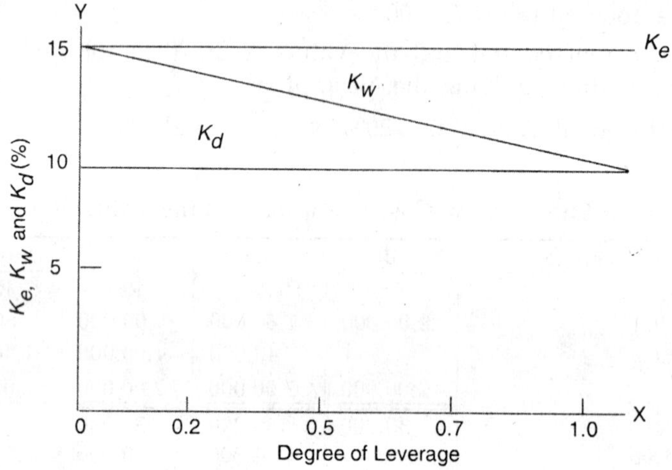

Fig. 5.1: Behaviour of K_e, K_w and K_d as per Net Income Approach

The degree of leverage is plotted along the X-axis whereas K_e, K_w and K_d are on the Y-axis. It reveals that when the cheaper debt capital in the capital structure is proportionately increased, the weighted average cost of capital, K_w, decreases and, consequently, the cost of debt is K_d. Thus, the optimal capital structure is the minimum cost of capital if financial leverage is one, in other words, the maximum application of debt capital.

The value of the firm (V) will also be the maximum at this point.

Limitations

NI approach is not free from snags. Some of them are:

(i) This method assumes that the whole amount of profit is distributed as dividend but in real world situations it is not practicable.

(ii) All investors are equally risk averters, and

(iii) This method assumes that cost of debt capital and cost of equity capital are constant but, in practice it is found that as soon as debt capital is introduced in the firm, cost of equity increases up to a certain level and, thereafter, cost of debt capital will also increase.

(b) NET OPERATING INCOME APPROACH

Now we want to highlight the Net Operating Income (NOI) Approach which was advocated by David Durand[1] based on certain assumptions.

---

[1] *Ibid.*

They are :

(i) The overall capitalisation rate of the firm, K_w, is constant for all degree of leverages;

(ii) Net operating income is capitalised at an overall capitalisation rate in order to have the total market value of the firm. Thus, the value of the firm, V, is ascertained at overall cost of capital (K_w) :

$$V = \frac{\text{EBIT}}{K_w} \quad \text{(since both are constant and independent of leverage)}$$

(iii) The market value of the debt is then subtracted from the total market value in order to get the market value of equity:

$$S = V - T$$

(iv) As the Cost of Debt is constant, the cost of equity will be:

$$K_e = \frac{\text{EBIT} - \text{I}}{\text{S}}$$

The NOI Approach can be illustrated with the help of the following diagram:

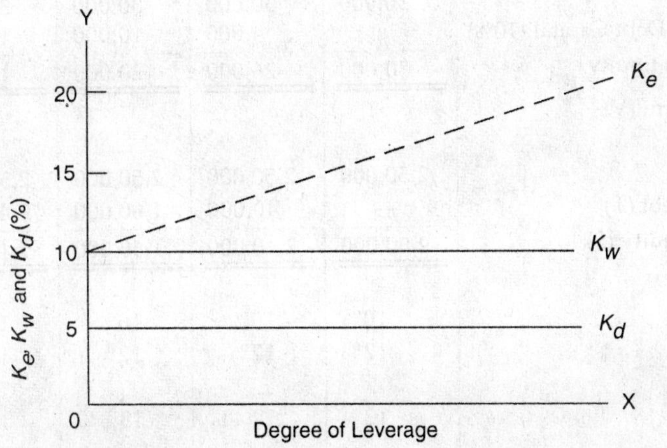

Fig. 5.2: Behaviours of K_e, K_w and K_d under Net Operating Income Approach

Under this approach, the most significant assumption is that the K_w is constant irrespective of the degree of leverage. The segregation of debt and equity is not important here and the market capitalises the value of the firm as a whole. Thus, an increase in the use of *apparently cheaper* debt funds is offset exactly by the corresponding increase in the equity-capitalisation rate. So, the weighted average Cost of Capital K_w and K_d remain unchanged for all degrees of leverage. As the firm increases its degree of leverage it becomes a more risky proposition and investors are to make some sacrifice by having a low $\frac{P}{E}$ ratio.[1]

[1] According to the Net Operating Income Approach the real cost of debt and the real cost of equity are the same — namely K_0. The Cost of Debt has two parts : the explicit cost, represented by the rate of interest, and the implicit cost or *hidden cost, which is represented by the increase in the equity-capitalisation rate that accompanies an increase in the proportion of debt to equity. Because, the cost of capital of the firm cannot be altered through leverage, the approach implies that there is no one optimal capital structure. All capital structures are optimal for market price per share does not change with leverage.'* — J. C. Vanhorne — *Financial Management and Policy,* 4th Edn., Prentice-Hall of India, New Delhi, 1979, p. 235.

Illustration 5.13

Assume:

Net Operating Income or EBIT Rs. 30,000

Total Value of Capital Structure Rs. 2,00,000.

Cost of Debt Capital K_d 10%

Average Cost of Capital K_w 12%

Calculate Cost of Equity, K_e : value of the firm V applying NOI approach under each of the following alternative leverages:

Leverage (debt to total capital) 0%, 20%, 50%, 70%, and 100%.

Solution

Statement Showing the Cost of Equity and the Value of the Firm

	Degree of Leverage	0	0.2	0.5	0.7	1.0
		Rs.	Rs.	Rs.	Rs.	Rs.
	Equity Capital	2,00,000	1,60,000	1,00,000	60,000	—
	Debt Capital	—	40,000	1,00,000	1,40,000	2,00,000
	Total	2,00,000	2,00,000	2,00,000	2,00,000	2,00,000
	EBIT	30,000	30,000	30,000	30,000	30,000
Less :	Interest on Debt Capital (10%)	—	4,000	10,000	14,000	20,000
	Earnings to Equity	30,000	26,000	20,000	16,000	10,000
	Value of Firm (V)					
	$V = \frac{EBIT}{K_w}$	2,50,000	2,50,000	2,50,000	2,50,000	2,50,000
Less :	Value of Debt (T)	—	40,000	1,00,000	1,40,000	2,00,000
	Value of Equity (S)	2,50,000	2,10,000	1,50,000	1,10,000	50,000
Thus,						
	(K_d) Given	10%	10%	10%	10%	10%
	(K_e) Given	12%	12%	12%	12%	12%
	$(K_e)\left(\frac{EBIT}{S}\right)$	12%	12.4%	13.3%	14.5%	20%

Although the value of the firm Rs. 2,50,000 is constant at all levels, the cost of equity is increased with the corresponding increase in leverage. Thus, if the cheaper debt capital is used, that will be offset by the increase in the total cost of equity K_e, and, as such, both K_e and K_d remain unchanged for all degrees of leverage, i.e., if cheaper debt capital is proportionately increased and used, the same will offset the increase of cost of equity.

Limitations

NOI approach is also not free from snags. Some of them are:

(a) Under this approach, there may not be any optimum capital structure of a firm which is impracticable.

(b) NOI Approach assumes that benefits of cheaper debt capital sets off the increase in cost of equity capital which is also not a practical proposition in real-would situation.

(c) This approach assumes that market value of the firm is not affected by the change in the composition of capital structure which is not true.

(c) TRADITIONAL THEORY APPROACH

It is accepted by all that the judicious use of debt will increase the value of the firm and reduce the cost of capital. So, the optimum capital structure is the point at which the value of the firm is highest and the cost of capital is at its lowest point. Practically, this approach encompasses all the ground between the Net Income Approach and the Net Operating Income Approach, i.e., it may be called Intermediate approach. The traditional Approach explains that up to a certain point, debt-equity mix will cause the market value of the firm to rise and the cost of capital to decline. But after attaining the optimum level, any additional debt will cause to decrease the market value and to increase the cost of capital. In other words, after attaining the optimum level, any additional debt taken will offset the use of cheaper debt capital since the average cost of capital will increase along with a corresponding increase in the average cost of debt capital.

Thus, the basic propositions of this approach are:

(a) The cost of debt capital, K_d, remains constant, more or less, up to a certain level and, thereafter, rises.

(b) The cost of equity capital, K_e, remains constant, more or less, or rise gradually up to a certain level and, thereafter, increases rapidly.

(c) The average cost of capital, K_w, decreases up to a certain level, remains unchanged more or less and, thereafter, rises after attaining a certain level.

The traditional approach can graphically be represented by taking the data from the previous illustration :

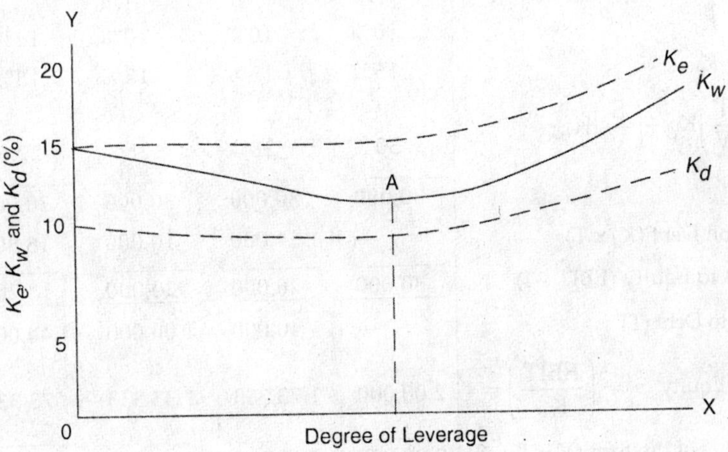

Fig. 5.3: Behaviour of K_e, K_w and K_d under Traditional Approach

It is found from the above that the average cost curve is U-shaped. That is, at this stage, the cost of capital would be minimum which is expressed by the letter 'A' in the graph. If we draw a perpendicular to the X-axis from A, the same will indicate the optimum capital structure for the firm. Thus, the traditional position implies that the cost of capital is not independent of the capital structure of the firm and that there is an optimal capital structure. At that optimal structure, the marginal real cost of debt (explicit and implicit) is the same as the marginal real cost of equity in equilibrium. For degree of leverage before that point, the marginal real cost of debt is less than that of equity; beyond that point the marginal real cost of debt exceeds that of equity.[1]

Illustration 5.14

EBIT	
Total Value	Rs. 30,000
Capital Structure	Rs. 2,00,000

Cost of Equity		Cost of Debt	
Up to Rs. 1,00,000	@ 15%	Up to Rs. 1,00,000	@ 10%
Between Rs. 1,00,000 and Rs. 1,50,000	@ 18%	Between Rs. 1,00,000 and Rs. 1,50,000	@ 12%
Between Rs. 1,50,000 and Rs. 2,00,000	@ 20%	Between Rs. 1,50,000 and Rs. 2,00,000	@ 15%

Calculate the cost of capital and the value of the firm under each of the following alternative degrees of leverage and comment on them:

$$\text{Leverage}: \left(\frac{\text{Debt}}{\text{Total Capital}}\right) = 0\%, 20\%, 50\%, 70\%, 100\%.$$

Solution

Statement Showing the Cost of Capital and the Value of the Firm

Leverage	0	0.2	0.5	0.7	1.0
Given —					
K_d	10%	10%	10%	12%	15%
K_e	15%	15%	15%	18%	20%
$K_w = \left(\frac{T}{V}\right)K_d + \left(\frac{S}{V}\right)K_e$	30%*	28%	25%	27.6%	30%
EBIT	30,000	30,000	30,000	30,000	30,000
Less : Interest on Debt ($K_d \times T$)	—	4,000	10,000	16,800	30,000
Earnings to Equity (EBIT – I)	30,000	26,000	20,000	13,200	—
Amount to Debt (T)	—	40,000	1,00,000	1,40,000	2,00,000
Value of Equity $S = \left(\frac{EBIT}{K_e}\right) =$	2,00,000	1,73,333	1,33,333	73,333	—
Total Value of the firm (V = T + S)	2,00,000	2,13,333	2,33,333	2,13,333	2,00,000

* (i) ***When financing leverage is 0***

$$K_w = \left(\frac{T}{V}\right)K_d + \left(\frac{S}{V}\right)K_e$$

$$= 0 \times 10 + 2 \times 15$$

$$= 30\%$$

[1] Vanhorne, J. C. — *op. cit.*, pp. 237-8.

(ii) *When financing leverage is .2*

= .4 × 10 + .16 × 15 = 28%

(iii) *When financing leverage is .5*

= .10 × 10 + .10 × 15 = 25%

(iv) *When financing leverage is .7*

= .14 × 12 + .6 × 18 = 27.6%

(v) *When financing leverage is 1.0*

= 2.0 × 15 + 0 × 20 = 30%

Thus, from the above table, it becomes quite clear the cost of capital is lowest (at 25%) and the value of the firm is the highest (at Rs. 2,33,333) when debt-equity mix is (1,00,000 : 1,00,000 or 1 : 1). Hence, optimum capital structure in this case is considered as Equity Capital (Rs. 1,00,000) and Debt Capital (Rs. 1,00,000) which bring the lowest overall cost of capital followed by the highest value of the firm.

Variations on the Traditional Theory

It has already been mentioned that this theory underlines between the Net Income Approach and the Net Operating Income Approach. Thus, there are some distinct variations in this theory. Some followers of the traditional school of thought suggest that K_e does not practically rise till some critical conditions arise. Only after attaining that level the investors apprehend the increasing financial risk and penalise the market price of the shares. This variation expresses that a firm can have lower cost of capital with the initial use of leverage significantly. This variation in Traditional Approach is depicted as:

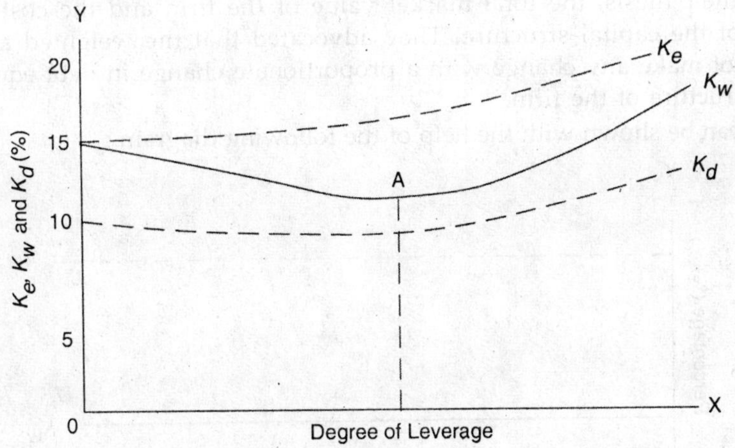

Fig. 5.4: Behaviour of K_e, K_w and K_d under variation of Traditional Approach (when K_e constant at first).

Other followers, e.g., Solomon, are of opinion the K_e is being saucer-shaped along with a horizontal middle range. It explains that optimum capital structure has a range where the cost of capital is rather minimised, and where the total value of the firm is maximised. Under the circumstances, a change in leverage has, practically, no effect on the total firm's value. So, this approach grants some sort of variation in the optimal capital structure for various firms under debt-equity mix.

Such variation can be depicted in the form of graphical representation:

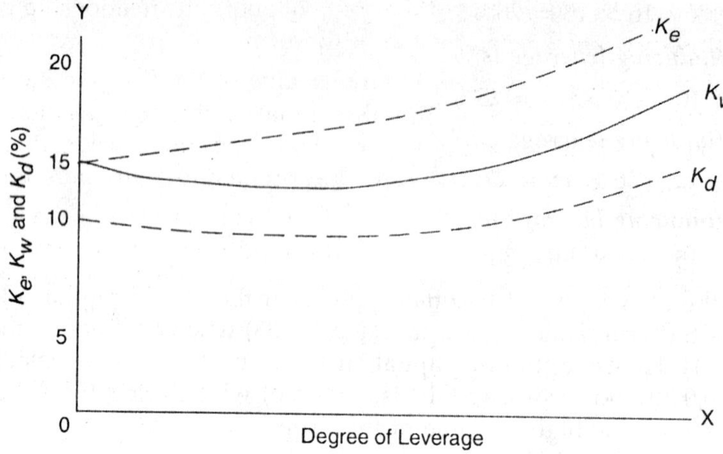

Fig. 5.5: Behaviour of K_e, K_w and K_d under Saucer-Shaped K_e Curve of Traditional Approach

(d) MODIGLIANI-MILLER APPROACH

Modigliani-Miller[1] (MM) advocated that the relationship between the cost of capital, capital structure and the valuation of the firm should be explained by NOI (Net Operating Income Approach by making an attack on the Traditional Approach. The Net Operating Income Approach, supplies proper justification for the irrelevance of the capital structure. In this context, MM support the NOI approach on the principle that the cost of capital is not dependent on the degree of leverage irrespective of the debt-equity mix. In other words, according to their thesis, the total market value of the firm and the cost of capital are independent of the capital structure. They advocated that the weighted average cost of capital does not make any change with a proportionate change in debt-equity mix in the total capital structure of the firm.

The same can be shown with the help of the following diagram :

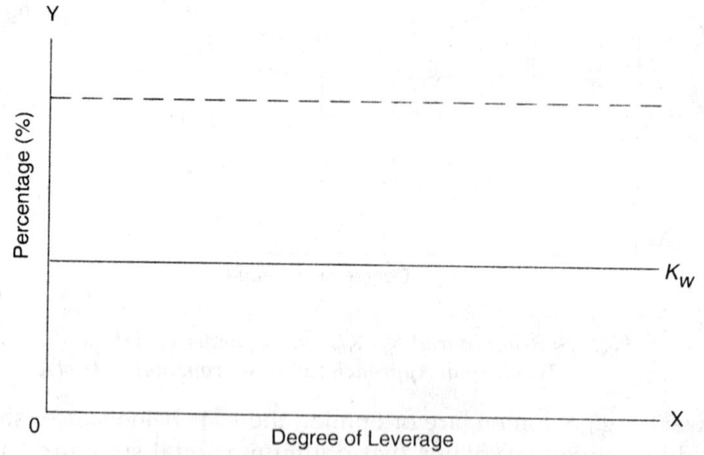

Fig. 5.6: The Weighted Average Cost of Capital does not make any change (MM Hypothesis Proposition)

1 Modigliani, Franco and Miller, Merton. H — *The Cost of Capital, Corporation Finance and The Theory of Investment*, American Economic Review, June 1958, Vol. 48, pp. 261-297.

Proposition

The following propositions outline the MM argument about the relationship between cost of capital, capital structure and the total value of the firm:

(i) The cost of capital and the total market value of the firm are independent of its capital structure. The cost of capital is equal to the capitalisation rate of equity stream of operating earnings for its class, and the market is determined by capitalising its expected return at an appropriate rate of discount for its risk class.

(ii) The second proposition includes that the expected yield on a share is equal to the appropriate capitalisation rate of a pure equity stream for that class, together with a premium for financial risk equal to the difference between the pure-equity capitalisation rate (K_e) and yield on debt (K_d). In short, increased K_e is offset exactly by the use of cheaper debt.

(iii) The cut-off point for investment is always the capitalisation rate which is completely independent and unaffected by the securities that are invested.

Assumptions

The MM proposition is based on the following assumptions :

(a) *Existence of Perfect Capital Market*

It includes:

(i) there is no transaction cost;

(ii) flotation costs are neglected;

(iii) no investor can affect the market price of shares;

(iv) information is available to all without cost;

(v) investors are free to purchase and sale securities.

(b) *Homogeneous Risk Class/Equivalent Risk Class*

It means that the expected yield/return have the identical risk factor, i.e., business risk is equal among all firms having equivalent operational condition.

(c) *Homogeneous Expectation*

All the investors should have identical estimate about the future rate of earnings of each firm.

(d) *The Dividend pay-out Ratio is 100%*

It means that the firm must distribute all its earnings in the form of dividend among the shareholders/investors, and

(e) *Taxes do not exist*

That is, there will be no corporate tax effect (although this was removed at a subsequent date).

Interpretation of MM Hypothesis

The MM Hypothesis reveals that if more debt is included in the capital structure of a firm, the same will not increase its value as the benefits of cheaper debt capital are exactly set-off by the corresponding increase in the cost of equity, although debt capital is less expensive than the equity capital. So, according to MM, the total value of a firm is absolutely unaffected by the capital structure (debt-equity mix) when corporate tax is ignored.

Proof of MM Hypothesis—The Arbitrage Mechanism

MM have suggested an arbitrage mechanism in order to prove their argument. They argued that if two firms differ only in two points viz., (i) the process of financing, and (ii) their total market value, the shareholders/investors will dispose off share of the over-valued firm and will purchase the share of under-valued firms. Naturally this process will be going on till both attain the same market value. As such, as soon as the firms will reach the identical position, the average cost of capital and the value of the firm will be equal. So, total value of the firm (V) and Average Cost of Capital, (K_w), are independent. It can be explained with the help of the following illustration:

Let there be two firms, Firm 'A' and Firm 'B'. They are similar in all respects except in the composition of capital structure. Assume that Firm 'A' is financed only by equity whereas Firm 'B' is financed by a debt-equity mix.

The following particulars are presented:

	Firm 'A'	Firm 'B'
	Rs.	Rs.
Equity Share Capital	5,00,000	3,00,000
Debt Capital	0	2,00,000
Total Capital employed	5,00,000	5,00,000
EBIT (Net Operating Income)	50,000	50,000
Interest on Debt Capital	0	10,000
Market Value of Debt (T) (Debt capitalisation rate is 5%)		2,00,000
Earnings of Equity	50,000	40,000
Equity Capitalisation Rate	10%	12%
Market Value of Equity (S)	5,00,000	3,33,333
Total Value of the Firm (V)	5,00,000	5,33,333
(T + S)	(0 + 5,00,000)	(2,00,000 + 3,33,333)
(Weighted) Average Cost of Capital K_w	10%	9.37%

From the table presented above, it is learnt that value of the levered firm 'B' is higher than the unlevered firm 'A'. According to MM, such situation cannot persist long as the investors will dispose-off their holding of firm 'B' and purchase the equity from the firm 'A' with personal leverage. This process will be continued till both the firms have same market value.

Suppose Ram, an equity shareholder, has 1% equity of firm 'B'. He will do the following :

(i) at first, he will dispose-off his equity of firm 'B' for Rs. 3,333.

(ii) he will take a loan of Rs. 2,000 at 5% interest from personal account.

(iii) he will purchase by having Rs. 5,333 (i.e. Rs. 3,333 + Rs. 2,000) 1.007% of equity from the firm 'A'.

By this, his net income will be increased as :

	Rs.
Return from the firm 'A'	533
Less : Interest @ 5%	100
Net Income	433

Obviously, this net income of Rs. 433 is higher than that of the firm 'B' by disposing-off 1% holding.

It is needless to say that when the investors will sell the shares of the firm 'B' and will purchase the shares from the firm 'A' with personal leverage, this market value of the share of firm 'A' will decline and, consequently, the market value of the share of firm 'B' will rise—and this will be continued till both of them attain the same market value.

In the earlier paragraph we have explained that the value of the levered firm cannot be higher than that of the unlevered firm (other things being equal) due to the arbitrage process. We will now highlight the **reverse direction** of the arbitrage process.

Consider the following illustration:

	Firm 'A'	Firm 'B'
Equity Earnings	50,000	40,000
Equity Capitalisation Rate	8%	12%
Market Value of Equity	6,00,000	3,33,333
Interest on Debt Capital	0	10,000
Market Value of Debt	0	2,00,000
Total Market Value (Debt + Equity)	6,00,000	5,33,333

In the above circumstances, equity shareholder of the firm 'A' will sell his holdings and, by the proceeds, he will purchase some equity from the firm 'B' and invest a part of the proceeds in debt of the firm 'B'.

For instance, an equity shareholder holding 1% equity in the firm 'A' will do the following:

(i) he will dispose-off his 1% equity of firm 'A' for Rs. 6,250.

(ii) he will buy $1\frac{11}{64}$% of equity and debt of the firm 'B' for the like amount.

(iii) as a result, he will have an additional income of Rs. 86.

Thus, if the investors prefer such a change, the market value of the equity of the firm 'A' will decline and, consequently, the market value of the shares of the firm 'B' will tend to rise and this process will be continued till both the firms attain the same market value, i.e., the arbitrage process can be said to operate in the opposite direction.

Criticisms of the MM Hypothesis

We have seen (while discussing MM Hypothesis) that MM Hypothesis is based on some assumptions. There are some authorities who do not recognise such assumptions as they are quite unrealistic, viz., the assumption of perfect capital merket. We also know that most significant element in this approach is the arbitrage process forming the behavioural foundation of the MM Hypothesis. As the imperfect market exists, the arbitrage process will be of no use and, as such, the discrepancy will arise between the market value of the unlevered and levered firms.

The shortcomings for which arbitrage process fails to bring the equilibrium condition are:

(i) *Existence of Transaction Cost*

The arbitrage process is affected by the transaction cost. While buying securities, this cost is involved in the form of brokerage or commission etc. for which extra amount is to be paid which increases the cost price of the shares and requires a greater amount although the return is same. As such, the levered firm will enjoy a higher market value than the unlevered firm.

(ii) *Assumption of borrowing and lending by the firms and the individual at the same rate of interest*

The above proposition—that the firms and the individuals can borrow or lend at the same rate of interest—does not hold good in reality. Since a firm holds more assets and credit reputation in the open market in comparison with an individual, the former will always enjoy a better position than the latter. As such, cost of borrowing will be higher in case of an individual than a firm. As a result, the market value of both the firms will not be equal.

(iii) *Institutional Restriction*

The arbitrage process is retarded by the institutional investor, e.g., Life Insurance Corporation of India, Commercial Banks, Unit Trust of India etc., i.e., they do not encourage personal leverage. At present these institutional investors dominate the capital market.

(iv) *"Personal or home-made leverage" is not the prefect substitute for "corporate leverage."*

MM hypothesis assumes that "personal leverage" is a perfect substitute for "corporate" leverage—which is not true as we know that a firm may have a limited liability whereas there is unlimited liability in case of individuals. For this purpose, both of them have different footings in the capital market.

(v) *Incorporation of Corporate Taxes*

If corporate taxes are considered (which should be taken into consideration) the MM approach will be unable to discuss the relationship between the value of the firm and the financing decision. For example, we know that interest charges are deducted from profit available for dividend, i.e., it is tax deductible. In other words, the cost of borrowing funds is comparatively less than the contractual rate of interest which allows the firm regarding tax advantage. Ultimately, the benefit is being enjoyed by the equityholders and debt-holders.

According to some critics the arguments which were advocated by MM are not valued in the practical world. We know that cost of capital and the value of the firm are practically the product of financial leverage.

MM Hypothesis with Corporate Taxes and Capital Structure

The MM Hypothesis is valid if there is perfect market condition. But, in the real world capital market, imperfection arises in the capital structure of a firm which affects the valuation. Because, presence of taxes invites imperfection. We are, now, going to examine the effect of corporate taxes in the capital structure of a firm along with the MM Hypothesis. We also know that when taxes are levied on income, debt financing is more advantageous as interest paid on debt is a tax-deductible item, whereas retained earning or dividend so paid in equity shares are not tax-deductible. Thus, if debt capital is used in the total capital structure, the total income available for equity shareholders and/or debt-holders will be more. In other words, the levered firm will have a higher value than the unlevered firm for this purpose, or, it can alternatively be stated that the value of the levered firm will exceed the unlevered firm by an amount equal to debt multiplied by the rate of tax. The same can be explained in the form of the following equation :

$V_1 = V_n + tD$ where V_1 = Value of the levered firm

V_n = Value of unlevered firm

t = Rate of corporate tax

D = Amount of debt

Illustration 5.15

Assume:

Two firms — Firm 'A' and Firm 'B' (identical in all respects except capital structure)

Firm 'A' has financed a 6% debt of Rs. 1,50,000

Firm 'B' Levered

EBIT (for both the firms) Rs. 60,000

Cost of Capital is @ 10%

Corporate rate of tax is @ 60%

Compute market value of the two firms.

Solution

The market value of the firm 'A' (unlevered)

$$V_n = \frac{\text{EBIT }(1 - t)}{K_e}$$

$$V = \frac{\text{Rs. } 60{,}000\ (1 - .6)}{.10} \quad \text{(putting the value)}$$

$$V = \text{Rs. } 2{,}40{,}000$$

The market value of the firm 'B' (levered)

$$V_1 = V_n - tD$$

$$= \text{Rs. } 2{,}40{,}000 + .6 \times \text{Rs. } 1{,}50{,}000$$

$$= \text{Rs. } 3{,}30{,}000$$

Thus, a firm can lower its cost of capital continuously due to the tax deductibility of interest charges. So, a firm must use the maximum amount of leverage in order to attain the optimum capital structure although the experience that we realise is contrary to the opinion. In real-world situation, however, firms do not take a larger amount of debt and creditors/lenders also are not interested to supply loan to highly levered firms due to the risk involved in it. Thus, due to the market imperfection, after-tax cost of capital function will be U-shaped. In answer to this criticism, MM suggested that the firm would adopt a target debt ratio so as not to violate the limits of level of debt imposed by creditors. This is an indirect way of stating that the cost of capital will increase sharply with leverage beyond some safe limit of debt[1].

[1] Pandey, I. M. — *Financial Management* — *op. cit.*, p. 249.

MM Hypothesis with corporate taxes can better be presented with the help of the following diagram :

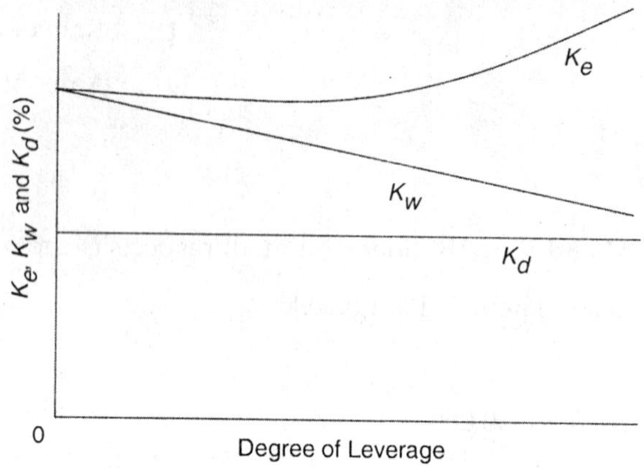

Fig. 5.7: Behaviour of Leverage on Cost of Capital under MM Hypothesis with Taxes

PLANNING THE CAPITAL STRUCTURE

In the preceding part we have highlighted the various theories of capital structure and explained that there is an optimal capital structure which minimises the cost of capital, i.e., it is one when the marginal real cost (the sum of both the explicit and implicit costs) of each method of financing is the same. Practically, the discussion made so far is theoretical.

Now we are to learn its practical application. In other words, we are to see how the financial manager may determine an appropriate capital structure for his particular firm in real-world situation. For this purpose, we are to examine the various methods with their applications which can properly be used. Truly speaking, none is found to be completely satisfactory in itself. So, a rational decision can be taken by a financial manager if he considers them collectively as they supply sufficient information. We should not think that the financial manager can easily identify the exact percentage of debt-equity mix which will maximise the price of shares. He should try, at best, to do so.

We know that planning capital structure implies selecting a desired debt-equity mix. As soon as that desire level is achieved, the same is continued over a period of years till it becomes necessary to change/amend it. Practically, it depends upon the actual need of a firm which varies from one to another. However, we are going to focus on the factors which influence the capital structure.

Factors Influencing the Capital Structure Planning

While planning the capital structure, the following important as well as significant factors are carefully to be considered:

(a) EBIT-EPS Analysis;

(b) Cost of Capital;

(c) Cash Flow Analysis;

(d) Control;

(e) Timing and Flexibility;

(f) Nature and Size of the firm; and

(g) Industry Standard.

(a) EBIT-EPS Analysis

It is needless to say that if we want to examine the effect of leverage, we are to analyse the relationship between the EBIT (earnings before interest and tax) and EPS (earnings per share). Practically, it requires the comparison of various alternative methods of financing under various alternative assumptions relating to *Earning before Interest and Taxes.*

Effect of leverage has been discussed in detail, but we will explain again its significant aspects. Financial leverage or trading on equity arises when fixed assets are financed from debt capital (including preference shares). When the same gives a return which is greater than the cost of debt capital, the excess will increase the EPS (Earnings per share) and the same is also applicable in case of preference share capital. But the former has some edges over the latter due to : (a) interest on debt capital is an allowable deduction as per Income-Tax rule while calculating profit, (b) usually the cost of preference share is more costly than the cost of debt. However, while planning capital structure of a firm, the effect of leverage, EPS, are to be given due consideration. In order to increase the shareholders' fund, a firm can effectively use its high level of EBIT against the high degree of leverage. It is already stated above that the effect of leverage can be examined if we analyse the relationship between the EBIT and the EPS.

The above principle can be illustrated with the help of the following illustration:

Illustration 5.16

Let us suppose firm X has a capital structure consisting of equity capital only. It has 50,000 equity shares of Rs. 10 each. Now the firm wants to raise a fund for Rs. 1,25,000 for its various investment purposes after considering the following three alternative methods of financing :

(i) if it issues 12,500 equity shares of Rs. 10 each;

(ii) if it borrows Rs. 1,25,000 at 8% interest; and

(iii) if it issues 1,250, 8% Preference Shares of Rs. 100 each.

Show the effect of EPS under various methods of financing if EBIT (after additional investment) is Rs. 1,56,250 and rate of taxation is @ 50%.

Solution

Effects of EPS under Various Alternative Methods of Financing

		Equity Financing	Debt Financing	Preference Share Financing
		Rs.	Rs.	Rs.
	EBIT (after additional investment)	1,56,250	1,56,250	1,56,250
Less:	Interest on debt financing @ 8% on Rs. 1,25,000	—	10,000	—
	Earnings after Interest before Tax	1,56,250	1,46,250	1,56,250
Less:	Income-Tax @ 50%	78,125	73,125	78,125
	Earning after Tax	78,125	73,125	78,125
Less:	Preference Dividend @ 8%	—	—	10,000
	Earnings for equity shareholders	78,125	73,125	68,125
	No. of Equity Shares	62,500	50,000	50,000
	EPS $\left(\frac{\text{Earnings for equity shares}}{\text{No. of equity shares}}\right)$	1.25	1.46	1.36

Thus, from the above table it becomes quite clear that the EPS is maximum when the firm uses debt-financing although the rate of preference dividend and the rate of debt financing is the same. These happened due to the most significant role played by Income Tax as preference dividend is not a deductible item from taxation while the interest on debt is a deductible item.

It has already been stated above that EPS will increase with a high degree of leverage with the corresponding increase in EBIT. But if the firm fails to earn a rate of return in its assets higher than the rate of debt financing, or preference share financing, it will have to experience an opposite effect on EPS.

This can be shown with the help of the following illustration:

Let us suppose the EBIT is Rs. 40,000 instead of Rs. 1,56,250. The EPS under various methods of financing is shown:

Effects of EPS under Various Alternative Methods of Financing

		Equity Financing	Debt Financing	Preference Share Financing
		Rs.	Rs.	Rs.
	EBIT	40,000	40,000	40,000
Less:	Interest on debt financing @ 8% on Rs. 1,25,000	—	10,000	—
	Earnings after Interest before Tax	40,000	30,000	40,000
Less:	Income-Tax @ 50%	20,000	15,000	20,000
	Earning after Tax	20,000	15,000	20,000
Less:	Preference Dividend @ 8%	—	—	10,000
	Earnings for equity shareholders	20,000	15,000	10,000
	No. of Equity Shares	62,500	50,000	50,000
	EPS $\left(\frac{\text{Earnings for equity shares}}{\text{No. of equity shares}}\right)$	0.32	0.30	0.20

Thus, if the rate of debt financing is more than the rate of earning before tax, the EPS will come down with the corresponding degree of leverage that directly affect the EPS.

Whether the debt financing should be taken into consideration by a firm or not, the financial manager must analyse the EBIT-EPS relationship which has a direct bearing on the capital structure position of a firm. Before taking any decision the financial manager must see the subsequent changes in EBIT and must scrutinise the impact of EPS under various alternative financing plans in his hands. Consequently, if he finds that the cost of debt is less or EBIT is more than that, he can suggest a large amount of debt capital in order to increase the EPS in the total capital structure of a firm which has a favourable effect on the market value of each equity share.

In the opposite case, however, i.e., when EBIT is less or cost of debt capital is more than the rate of earnings, a firm must not go for debt financing. Thus, if there is a higher level of EBIT and less possibility of fluctuation, a firm can effectively use debt as a method of financing mix in its total capital structure position.

(b) **Cost of Capital**

While explaining cost of capital we have mentioned that usually cost of equity (K_e) is greater than the cost of debt (K_d) due to the most significant advantages of income-tax among others. Actually, financing decision should be based on overall cost of capital (i.e., after considering both equity and debt). In other words, their combination will be in such a way that, either it minimises the overall cost of capital or maximises the market value of the firm. It has already been mentioned just in the earlier paragraph (while discussing EBIT-EPS analysis) that if debt financing is increased there will be a corresponding reduction in the overall cost of capital till the rate of return exceeds the explicit cost of financing. But if debt financing is continuously increased, the same will increase the cost of equity and debt capital as well which invites more financial risk and, consequently, increases the weighted average cost of capital up to a certain level of debt-equity mix. Thus, it can be stated that optimum capital structure may not always be attained by the financing decision which is based on financial leverage by allowing due importance to the cost of capital.

It can further be stated that if debt-financing is continuously taken by a firm to minimise the overall cost of capital, the debt, after attaining a certain limit, will become costly as well as a risky source of finance. Thus, if the degree of leverage increases, the creditors desire a high rate of interest for increased risk and if the debt reaches a particular point, they will not provide any further loan. Moreover, the position of the shareholders becomes risky due to such excessive debt for which cost of equity is gradually increased. So, combination of debt and equity will be in such a manner that the market value per share increases and minimises the average cost of capital of a firm. In real-world situation, however, a range of debt-equity ratio exists where cost of capital is minimum although this range varies from firm to firm—according to their nature, type and size.

We know that cost of equity capital includes cost of fresh issue of shares and cost of retained earnings as well. We also know that cost of debt is cheaper than cost of equity as also cost of retained earnings. Again, in between retained earnings and cost of equity (new issues), the former is cheaper as the personal taxes are paid by the shareholders on their dividend income but retained earnings is a tax-free source, and it also does not require any flotation cost. Thus, retained earnings are preferred between the two sources of equity funds.

(c) **Cash Flow Analysis**

In order to meet the fixed service charge of a firm, analysis of cash flow is very important. It indicates the ability of the firm to meet its various commitments including the fixed service charges, which includes fixed operating charges and interest on debt capital. Thus, the analysis of the cash flow ability of the firm to service fixed charges is no doubt an important tool while analysing financial risk in addition to EBIT-EPS analysis in capital structure planning. It has already been mentioned earlier that, if the amount of debt capital increases, there is a corresponding increase in the amount of uncertainty which a firm must face to meet its obligation in the form of fixed charges. Because, if a firm borrows more than its capacity and if it fails to meet its maturing obligation at a future date, the creditors will acquire the assets of the firm for their unsatisfied claim which brings financial insolvency. So, before taking any additional debt capital, analysis of expected future cash flows must carefully be considered as the fixed interest charges are paid out of cash. That is why analysis of cash flow presents a very significant information in this regard. If there is greater and stable expected future cash flow, a firm should go for a higher degree of debt which can be used as a source of finance. Similarly, if the expected future cash flows are unstable and smaller, a firm should avoid any fixed charge securities which will be considered a very risky proposition.

Moreover, analysis of cash flow presents the following significant advantages which help to prepare the debt-equity mix in the total capital structure of a firm:

(i) Cash flow analysis highlights the solvency and liquidity position of a firm at the time of adverse condition;

(ii) It records the various changes made in the Balance Sheet and other cash flows which do not exhibit in Profit and Loss Account;

(iii) It takes the financial trouble in a dynamic context over a number of years.

In order to judge the liquidity and solvency position through cash flows analysis, the following measures can be taken into consideration:

(i) The most effective measure is the *ratio of fixed charges to net cash inflows* as suggested by Van Horne.[1] This ratio measures the relationship between fixed financial charges and the net cash inflow of a firm, i.e., it reveals the number of times the fixed financial charges are covered by the net cash flows of a firm. The higher the ratio, the higher amount of debt can be used by the firm.

(ii) The other measure is the preparation of Cash Budget, that is, whether the expected cash flows are quite sufficient to meet the fixed-charge requirements or not. It is prepared to ascertain the possible deviation between the expected cash flows and the actual cash flow of the firm. The information so received from such budget will help us to know the ability of the firm to pay its fixed-charge obligation through the application of budget which should be prepared for a range of possible cash inflows along with their respective probability. It is interesting to note that as we know the possible probability of cash flow trend, a firm can easily decide its debt policy to cover fixed charges and work within the insolvency limit tolerable to the management.[2] Donaldson has suggested that a firm can meet its fixed obligation relating to fixed charges (interest on debt capital) together with the principal. A firm cannot meet the said obligation only during the adverse circumstances and is then considered at risk of bankruptcy. He termed it *'recession condition'*. The said recession condition can be challenged by preparing a net cash flow for such period and evaluate the result which will, no doubt, help to find out the alternative debt policy on the risk of bankruptcy.

(d) **Control**

We know that the equity shareholders, being the owner of the firm, can exercise control over the affairs of the firm. They also have the voting right. On the contrary, debenture-holders and preference shareholders do not possess such voting rights except under certain conditions for the preference shareholders only. Practically, lenders have no direct *'say'* in the management of a company. Till their interest (i.e., regarding payment of interest and dividend) is not affected legally, they can do very little against the company as they have no direct control, i.e., regarding policy matter or decision-making they have nothing to do. They do not have any voting rights for the appointment of board of directors as well. Other lenders and creditors also, like debentureholders and preference shareholders, do not have any *'say'* in the management of the company, i.e., they cannot actually take part in the management as the entire body is being controlled by the equityholders or the owners of the company. Thus, if the primary objective of the company is to control efficiently, more weight must be given to debt capital for additional requirement of capital in the total capital structure of a firm as, in that case, management does not have to make any sacrifice regarding the control of the firm.

If the firm borrows more than its repayment capacity, they (lenders and creditors) may seize the assets of the company against their claims for interest/dividend as well as for

---

1 Van Horne, J. C. — *Financial Management and Policy* — op. cit. p. 232.

2 Donaldson, D. — *Corporate Debt Capacity*, Harvard University Press, Boston, Division of Research, 1961.

principal. In the circumstances the management loses all control over the affairs of the company. Naturally, it is better on the part of the management to sacrifice a part of their control by issuing additional equity shares rather than taking the risk of losing all control to the outsiders, viz., lenders and creditors, by taking too much debt for the requirements of additional funds.[1] Thus, from the standpoint of control, issuing equity shares may be treated as a better source of financing in the hand of the company. Yet, it may also be stated that if the firm can maintain its liquidity and solvency position by earning higher profitability ratio, and the existing management prefers to keep control in its own hand, then it may encourage borrowings rather than issuing fresh equity shares as, in the case of latter, there is the possibility of losing control over the company affairs. Thus, the firm should select an appropriate debt-equity mix after considering its overall profitability.

(e) Timing and Flexibility

After determining an appropriate capital structure, a firm has to face this problem relating to timing of security issues. For procuring additional funds, a firm has to face the question of appropriate mix of debt and equity and what should be the timing of issuing such securities in order to maintain the strict proportion of debt and equity, although it is not an easy task. At the same time, which one will be issued at first, i.e., whether debt at first and equity at last, or vice versa — that also should be decided. The answer lies in the evaluation of alternative methods of financing according to the general state of the economy and the firm's expectation about it. If the existing rate of interest on debt capital is high and there is the possibility of coming down of the rate of such interest, the management will go for issuing equity shares now and will postpone debt issue. On the contrary, if the market for the company's equity issues are depressed but there is a chance in near future to improve the same, naturally, the management must go for debt issues now and will postpone equity issues. The same may be issued at a later date when there will be favourable conditions for the company, i.e., when the market for the company's equity shares will go up.

If the alternative stated is chosen, a certain amount of flexibility must be sacrificed. When the amount of debt capital will be quite substantial and things take a turn for the worse, the company may be forced to issue equity in future even in unfavourable terms. In order to preserve its flexibility in tapping the capital markets, it may be better for a firm to issue equity shares now so as to have unused debt capacity for future needs.[2] If the company's requirements of funds are unpredictable and sudden, it is better for it to preserve unused debt capacity which, in turn, presents the company financial maneuverability by leaving the option open for it. It is interesting to note that this flexibility could also be attained by maintaining excess liquidity position by avoiding the opportunity cost, if any.

However, for a developing firm, the above criterion has a snag in itself. By issuing stock now so as to have unused debt capacity, the company will properly have to issue more shares than it would if it postponed the stock issue. Consequently, there is more dilution to existing shareholders over time. The trade-off is between preserving financial flexibility and dilution in earnings per share. If the price of the stock is high, and is expected to fall, the firm can achieve both the flexibility and minimum dilution by issuing stock now.[3]

Debt financing can be quite substantial for financing equity shares, even though the benefits of good timings are limited for debt financing. Because, the value of a share can vary significantly on the effect of the general state of economy, and expectations for the

---

1 Johnson, R. W. — *Financial Management* — Allyn and Bacon, 1971, p. 227.

2 Van Horne, J. C. — *Financial Management and Policy* — op. cit., p. 272.

3 *Ibid*, p. 273.

firm as well. Thus, it is the duty of the existing management of the company to sell the shares among the existing shareholders at a favourable price. Similarly, they should consider debt capital also at a favourable rate of interest. Although both the debt and equity financing have substantial roles to play in a financing mix, the timing of issuing shares is a very important aspect which should be given due consideration.

(f) Nature and Size of the Firm

The nature and size of a firm have a significant role while procuring funds from various sources. For example, it is very difficult for a small firm to raise funds from long term sources even if its credit status is good. The same is available for it at a comparatively high rate of —interest with inconvenient repayment terms as well. For this purpose, the management of such firms cannot operate their functions normally due to various interference and, as such, their capital structure becomes very inflexible. That is why they are to depend on their own source of finance for long-term funds viz., equity shares, retained earnings/ ploughing back of profits etc. Moreover, in case of small firms, the cost of issuing equity shares is comparatively higher than that of a big firm. Besides, if equity shares are issued at frequent intervals for procuring long-term funds, there may be a possibility of losing control over the affairs of the company as a whole which may not arise in case of a big firm.

But a small firm has a distinct edge over a big one. That is, the shares of a small company are not scattered widely throughout the country and the dissident shareholders, if any, can be controlled and organised easily in an efficient manner while the same is not possible in the case of a big company as its shares are widely issued throughout the country. So it is difficult to control them. Thus, a small firm—instead of growing fast by issuing more shares—prefers to restrict the business and use its retained earnings as a source of long-term funds. But a big company has got more flexibility while designing its capital structure. For raising funds for long-term purpose, it can take loan on easy terms which are available, issue debentures and preference shares to the public for such long-term funds. Moreover, the cost of issuing shares are comparatively low than a small firm. So, appropriate capital structure depends on the nature and size of the firm.

(g) Industry Standard

Evaluation of capital structure of other similar risk-class firm is absolutely needed when designing the capital structure of a firm and also the industrial position. Because, if a firm follows a different capital structure than that of the similar firm(s) in the same industry, it may have to face a lot of problems, e.g., investors may not accept it. Lenders and creditors, always together with the investment analysts, evaluate the firm according to the industry standard. So, if a firm goes out-of-line, it must prove its justifiability in the capital market along with other firms who are in the same line. Moreover, there are certain common factors which are to be considered while designing capital structure, e.g., the general state of economy, nature, type and size of the firm etc. Besides the above, the nature and size of the firm may have a direct effect on the capital structure composition, for instance, public utility concerns (e.g., electricity) where day-to-day transactions are done primarily on cash basis. As such, those firms may undertake more risks and they may go for more debt as the liquidity and solvency and profitability position will not be adversely affected. On the contrary, a firm which has to make a heavy investment in fixed assets and a high operating leverage will, naturally, prefer less financial risk and design the capital structure in a different manner than the public utility concern. Moreover, the general state of economy affects the composition of debt and equity in the capital structure. It has been stated above that a firm having stable sales and better prospects for development may use more debt capital in its capital structure than those firms which have unstable sales and no prospect for growth.

Besides the above, one point should also be considered, i.e., conditions of the capital market. For example, reputed concerns enjoy certain favourable response from the public whereas new or less known established concerns find some difficulty. In our capital market, the position of preference shares and debentures are not popularly accepted with the exception of convertible debentures due to their conversion facility, i.e., from debentures to equity shares. These are other long-term institutional loans which are sanctioned after fulfilling certain terms and conditions (e.g., debt-equity ratio should be 2 : 1). Thus, while designing capital structure, all the above stated factors should be considered carefully.

IMPORTANT RATIOS USED IN CAPITAL STRUCTURE

A. Debt-Equity Ratio

This ratio measures the claims of outsiders and the owners, i.e., shareholders against the assets of the firm. It is also known as External-Internal Equity Ratio. It actually measures the relationship between the external debts/equity/outsiders fund and Internal equities/shareholders fund.

In short, it expresses the relation between the external equities and internal equities, or, the relationship between borrowed capital and owner's capital. It is a measure of long-term solvency. It reveals the claims of creditors and shareholders against the assets of the firm, i.e., comparative proportion of Debts and Equity. Here, Debt includes all debts, whether long-term or short-term, or in the form of Mortgage, Bills and Debentures etc. On the other hand, ***Owner's claims consist of Equity and Preference Share Capital + Reserves and Surplus + Capital Reserves + Reserves for Contingencies + Sinking Fund – Fictitious Assets viz., Preliminary Expenses etc.***

$$\text{Debt-Equity Ratio} = \frac{\text{External Equities}}{\text{Internal Equities}}$$

$$\text{or, } \frac{\text{Outsiders' Fund}}{\text{Shareholders' Fund}}$$

$$\text{or, } \frac{\text{Long-term Debts/Total Debts}}{\text{Proprietors' Equity/Shareholders' Equity}}$$

$$\text{or, } \frac{\text{Long-term and Short-term Debts + Bills + Debentures etc.}}{\text{Eq. Share Capital + Pref. Share Capital + Reserves and Surplus + Capital Reserves etc.}}$$

There are some authorities who prefer to take Long-term Debts only instead of total debts. Again, some prefer to include preference share capital in external equities and not to include the same in shareholders' fund. The reason for such opinion (i.e., inclusion of pref. share capital in external debts) is that they are entitled a fixed rate of dividend and they are also redeemed after stipulated period.

Interpretation and Significance

This ratio tells the story about the utilisation of debt financing in a firm, i.e., proportion of claims between outsiders and the shareholders against the assets of the firm—in order to give an information to the outsiders about their position while winding-up. Assets are acquired by the utilisation of both outsiders' fund and shareholders' fund. The shareholders desire to utilise more funds taken from the investors so that they will share lesser risk and, at the same time, to increase the rate of dividend after paying a smaller fixed rate of interest to outsiders. Similarly, outsiders desire that shareholders should take the greater risk. Thus, the interpretation and significance of this ratio depends on the financial policy of the firm and nature and type of business. The norm of such ratio is 2 : 1 —although there is no standard norm which is applicable for all enterprises. Sometimes more than 2 : 1 is found to be satisfactory. A high ratio indicates that claims of outsiders are more than the owner and, naturally, they will demand to take part in management and creditors do not prefer such a situation, as in case of liquidation their margin of safety will be reduced. In short, the higher the ratio, the greater will be the risk to the creditors and this indicates too much dependence on long-term debts. On the contrary, a lower ratio reveals a high margin of safety to the creditors.

B. Capital Gearing Ratio

Capital gearing stands for the determination of proportion of various kinds of securities to the total capitalisation. The gearing may be high, low, or even. When the proportion of Equity Share capital is high in comparison to other securities in the total capitalisation, it is called low geared, and, in the opposite case, it is high geared. At the same time, if the Equity Share capital is equal to the other securities it is called evenly geared.

Thus, the capital gearing ratio is the ratio between Equity Share Capital and Fixed Interest Bearing Securities :

$$\textit{Capital Gearing Ratio} = \frac{\text{Fixed Interest Bearing Securities}}{\text{Equity Share Capital}}$$

The following illustration will make the gearing principle clear:

Illustration 5.17

	Companies		
	X	Y	Z
	Rs.	Rs.	Rs.
Equity Share Capital	4,00,000	2,50,000	1,00,000
8% Preference Share Capital	25,000	1,00,000	2,00,000
6% Debentures	75,000	1,50,000	2,00,000
Capital Employed	5,00,000	5,00,000	5,00,000
∴ Capital Gearing Ratio:			
$\frac{\text{Fixed Interest Bearing Securities}}{\text{Equity Share Capital}}$ =	$\frac{\text{Rs. } 1,00,000}{\text{Rs. } 4,00,000}$	$\frac{\text{Rs. } 2,50,000}{\text{Rs. } 2,50,000}$	$\frac{\text{Rs. } 4,00,000}{\text{Rs. } 1,00,000}$
	1 : 4	1 : 1	1 : ·25
Result	Low-geared	Evenly-geared	High-geared

Thus, from the above, it is quite clear that the capital structure of Company X is low-geared, Company Y is evenly-geared, and Company Z is high-geared.

The higher the gear, the more speculative will be the character of equity shares, since, under this condition, dividend on equity shares fluctuates disproportionately with the amount of divisible profits.

Comparison between Capital Gearing Ratio and Debt-Equity Ratio

Points	Capital Gearing Ratio	Debt-Equity Ratio
(a) Similarities		
(i) Nature	This ratio highlights the long-term solvency position of a firm since it is used for the purpose of capital structure analysis.	It expresses how far the firm is solvent as it is also a very important indicator of analysing the capital structure position.
(ii) Significance	If this ratio varies, shareholders' earning and the risk of the firm may be affected.	No doubt, this ratio also affects both the risks and shareholders' return.

(b) **Dissimilarities**

(i) Basic Objectives	The basic principle of this ratio is to see that, by investing a minimum amount, the equity shareholders control the business-activities and also to increase the rate of profitability of the firm.	The dependence of the firm—other than on the owners—can be known.
(ii) Elements	In this case, current liabilities are not considered as a part of fixed income bearing securities.	Here, it is considered.
	Preference shares are considered as a numerator.	Preference shares are considered as a part of equity. But, in USA, it is considered as a part of debt-capital.

Factors Affecting Capital Gearing

(a) Trading on Equity

This is a device by which the equity shares enjoy a large amount of profit at the cost of other fixed interest-bearing securities. The rate of dividend of the equity shares can substantially be increased by the issue of more Debentures and Preference Shares with fixed rates of interest and dividend.

The following illustration will make the principle clear:

Illustration 5.18

Suppose, the total requirement of capital of a company is Rs. 20,00,000 and the expected rate of return is 12%. If the entire capital consists of Equity Shares only, there will be no *Trading on Equity*, but will simply be a return @ 12% on Rs. 20,00,000, by way of dividends. Now, suppose, the capital structure of the company is:

	Rs.
10% Debentures	8,00,000
8% Preference Shares	4,00,000
Equity Shares	8,00,000

Solution

In the above case, the profit @ 12% on Rs. 20,00,000 will be Rs. 2,40,000 (Rs. 20,00,000 $\times \frac{12}{100}$) out of which:

	Rs.
Preference Dividend will be (Rs. 4,00,000 $\times \frac{8}{100}$)	32,000
Debenture Interest will be (Rs. 8,00,000 $\times \frac{10}{100}$)	80,000
Equity Dividend will be *(bal. fig.)*	1,28,000
	2,40,000

Hence, Percentage of Return on Equity Capital becomes : $\frac{\text{Rs. } 1,28,000}{\text{Rs. } 8,00,000} \times 100 = 16\%$.

Therefore, by the issue of Debentures and Preference Shares, Trading on Equity is possible and, as a result, the rate of equity dividend is increased from 12% to 16%.

Note : Trading on Equity is profitable only when the profit is earned at a higher rate than the rates payable to the holders of Debentures and Preference Shares.

(b) Elasticity of Capital Structure

Capital Structure, if made elastic, may be expanded by the fresh issue, in case of necessity for improvement and extension of the business, or may be contracted according to necessity. Contraction of capital is not an easy matter, particularly in the case of equity capital, since it cannot be redeemed throughout the life of the company. On the other hand, Preference Shares and Debentures or Loans can be redeemed at the end of the stipulated period as they provide flexibility in the capital structure.

(c) Control of the Enterprise

Since the holders of Preference Shares and Debentures have no voting rights (except in certain cases), the promoters are more interested in issuing Preference Shares and Debentures to meet the additional requirement of capital than in issuing Equity Shares. The Equity Shares which are issued are allotted to the friends and relatives of the promoters first so that control and management of the company may be retained by the promoters.

(d) Propensity of the Investors

The company issues different types of securities for different investors. Debentures are taken by those who prefer security of the principal together with the stability of income whereas Preference Shares are taken by those who prefer to have a higher rate or regular income (than that of the Debentureholders) together with some safety of capital. Again, Equity Shares are taken by those who want to take risks and, at the same time, are desirous of exercising control over the affairs of the company.

(e) Cost of Financing

Sometimes it may be desirable to raise funds by the issue of a particular type of security. But the cost of financing such a security proves prohibitive for the company. Normally, the issue of equity shares is costly in comparison with the issue of preference shares and debentures and that is why the companies prefer to issue a part of the capital structure by the issue of debentures or preference shares.

(f) Market Sentiment

It also plays a significant role in capital gearing, debentures may be issued more easily than the equity shares at the time of slump whereas, at the time of boom, equity shares may be issued. Besides, Bank and Insurance companies prefer debentures or preference shares than equity shares as security.

C. Other Capitalisation Ratios

The following ratios are used, if necessary, in addition to Capital Gearing Ratio and Debt-Equity Ratio for the purpose of analysing the capital structure:

(i) *Equity Capital Ratio* : $\frac{\text{Equity Capital + Reserves and Surplus}}{\text{Net Worth + Debentures}} \times 100$

This ratio indicates how much is being contributed by the Equity Shareholders to the total long-term funds and expressed as a percentage. The higher the ratio, the lesser will be the dependence of the firm on the outsiders.

(ii) *Preference Share Capital Ratio* : $\frac{\text{Preference Share Capital}}{\text{Net Worth + Debentures}} \times 100$

This ratio indicates how much is being contributed by the Preference Shareholders to the total capital structure of the firm and expressed as a percentage.

(iii) *Debenture (Capital) Ratio* : $\dfrac{\text{Debentures}}{\text{Net Worth + Debentures}} \times 100$

This ratio indicates how much is being contributed by the Debentureholders to the total investments made by the Equity Shareholders and Debentureholders and expressed as a percentage. The Debentureholders can form an idea about the Debenture interest and the safety of capital from this ratio.

Illustration 5.19

The following summarised Balance Sheet is presented by X Co. Ltd. as on 31.12.1994:

Balance Sheet

as at 31.12.1994

Liabilities	Rs.	*Assets*	Rs.
Equity Share Capital		Fixed Assets	5,00,000
(Shares of Rs. 10 each)	2,00,000	Current Assets	3,00,000
8% Preference Share Capital	1,00,000		
6% Debentures	1,50,000		
General Reserve	1,00,000		
Profit and Loss Account	1,50,000		
Current Liabilities	1,00,000		
	8,00,000		8,00,000

Ascertain the following ratios and comment on the capital structure of the company : (a) Debt-Equity Ratio; (b) Capital Gearing Ratio; (c) Equity Share Capital Ratio; (d) Preference Share Capital Ratio; and (e) Debenture (Capital) Ratio.

Solution

Computation of Ratios

(a) ***Debt-Equity Ratio*** : $\dfrac{\textit{Total Debts}}{\textit{Proprietors' Fund}} = \dfrac{\textit{Debentures + Current Liabilities}}{\textit{Eq. Shareholders' Fund + Pref. Cap.}}$

$$= \frac{\text{Rs. 1,50,000 + Rs. 1,00,000}}{\text{Rs. 4,50,000 + Rs. 1,00,000}} = \frac{\text{Rs. 2,50,000}}{\text{Rs. 5,50,000}}$$

$= \quad 0.45 : 1$

(b) ***Capital Gearing Ratio*** : $\dfrac{\textit{Fixed Interest Bearing Securities}}{\textit{Equity Shareholders' Fund}}$

$$= \frac{\textit{Debentures + Pref. Capital}}{\textit{Eq. Cap. + G.R. + P \& L A/c}}$$

$$= \frac{\text{Rs. 1,50,000 + Rs. 1,00,000}}{\text{Rs. 2,00,000 + Rs. 1,00,000 + Rs. 1,50,000}}$$

$$= \frac{\text{Rs. 2,50,000}}{\text{Rs. 4,50,000}} = 1 : 1.8$$

Contd.

(c) *Equity Share Capital Ratio :*

$$= \frac{\text{Eq. Cap. + Reserves \& Surplus}}{\text{Net Worth + Debentures}} \times 100$$

$$= \frac{\text{Rs. } 2{,}00{,}000 + \text{Rs. } 1{,}00{,}000 + \text{Rs. } 1{,}50{,}000}{\text{Rs. } 5{,}50{,}000 + \text{Rs. } 1{,}50{,}000} \times 100$$

$$= 64.28\%$$

(d) *Preference Share Capital Ratio :*

$$= \frac{\text{Preference Share Capital}}{\text{Net Worth + Debentures}} \times 100$$

$$= \frac{\text{Rs. } 1{,}00{,}000}{\text{Rs. } 5{,}50{,}000 + \text{Rs. } 1{,}50{,}000} \times 100$$

$$= 14.28\%$$

(e) *Debentures (Capital) Ratio :*

$$= \frac{\text{Debentures}}{\text{Net Worth + Debentures}} \times 100$$

$$= \frac{\text{Rs. } 1{,}50{,}000}{\text{Rs. } 5{,}50{,}000 + \text{Rs. } 1{,}50{,}000} \times 100$$

$$= 21.43\%.$$

Comments

Debt-Equity Ratio of the company indicates that the company is to some extent dependent on outside liabilities. It is not a healthy sign. Capital Gearing Ratio, however, is found to be satisfactory since this ratio maintains its normal level.

Equity Share Capital Ratio indicates that more than 50% of the total long-term funds are contributed by the equity shareholders. It is a good sign since stability in the capital structure can be maintained.

Preference Share Capital Ratio reveals that only 14.28% of the total long-term funds is being contributed by the Preference Shareholders. As a result, it indicates that the controlling power remains in the hands of Equity Shareholders and there will not be any change in voting rights in the near future.

Debenture (Capital) Ratio is found to be only 21.43% which expresses that only one-sixth of the total long-term funds is being contributed by the Debentureholders. That is, the company is not so dependent on them.

Advantages and Disadvantages of Debt-Financing

Advantages

(a) The rate of equity dividend can be increased if a part of capital is collected by way of debt capital (i.e., by the issue of debentures or preference shares etc.) since the rate of return on investments by employing business resources is normally greater than the fixed rate of interest/dividend paid to debt-capital.

(b) If capital is procured by the issue of the debt capital, that (capital) can be redeemed during slack periods. As a result, the expenditure of the firm may be redeemed. Besides, flexibility in the capital structure is not possible, except in case of liquidation, if the entire capital is raised by the issue of equity shares. The same, however, is possible if the capital is financed by the issue of debt capital.

(c) The equity shareholders exercise control over the affairs of the company if capital is financed by the issue of loan/debt capital since the holders of preference shares and debentures have no voting rights and, as such, they cannot take part in the management. Therefore, if fresh issue of equity shares is made, instead of issuing preference shares or debentures, controlling power may be handed over to fresh equity shareholders. For this purpose, the equity shareholders prefer not to issue further equity shares for raising funds.

(d) Debts may be collected at a cheaper rate than by the issue of equity shares. Equity shareholders expect a minimum rate of return on their investment which is, in other words, called cost of capital in accounting. Actually, cost of capital is not the only cost which is paid by way of dividend since dividend is paid after paying taxes. That is, the cost of equity capital is the sum total of both dividends and taxes whereas this is not applicable in the case of debt capital since the firm is not to pay taxes for the payment of interest to be made for debt capital. As a result, the cost of debt is the only part of cost which is payable by way of interest only.

(e) Sometimes it may so happen that there is no way out for raising funds except the issuing of debt capital. The firm cannot issue equity shares if it has reached its prescribed limit. In that case, the firm is to depend on debt capital for raising further funds.

(f) Sometimes it may also happen that funds may not be realised by the issue of equity shares at a reasonable cost. But the firm can do so by pledging or hypothecating its assets for a short or long period.

Disadvantages

(a) Raising funds by the issue of debt capital is more risky than the issue of equity capital since the amount to be paid by way of interest/dividend—which is fixed together with the repayment of capital—does not depend on the capacity for earning profit. The risk is greater where the rate of profit which is earned fluctuates or the trend of profit is not stable.

(b) Since the debts are fixed in nature, the debt creditors impose certain conditions which are stringent in comparison with those laid down by equity shareholders and which are not at all desirable from the standpoint of the firm as economic conditions are constantly changing.

Therefore, from the above discussion, it may be further stated that the ratio between debt and equity depends on the certainty of earnings, levels of earnings and the risk performance of the directors etc.

FINANCIAL LEVERAGE

Financial leverage may be expressed when the residual net income (earning after interest and taxes and preference dividend) varies not in proportion with operating profit (EBIT). This leverage reveals the changes in taxable income in comparison with the changes in operation. In other words, a major part is played by interest on debt financing, debenture interest, preference dividend (i.e., fixed interest-bearing securities) in the entire capital structure of the firm. This leverage actually refers to the mix of debt and equity used to finance the firm's activities. The firm which uses a lot of debt (in various forms) is said to be highly levered. In short, when the debt capital (debenture, preference share, long-term financing etc.) is more in comparison with equity capital it is highly levered and, in the opposite case, it is said to be low levered. Thus, it is the firm's ability to use fixed financial charges in order to measure the effect of changes in EBIT on the EPS of the firm.

Trading on Equity and Financial Leverage

Trading on Equity

Sometimes Financial leverage is called *'Trading on Equity'*.

It has already been stated cashier that ***it is a device by which the equity shareholders enjoy a large amount of profit at the cost of other fixed interest-bearing securities.*** The rate of dividend of the equity shares can substantially be increased by the issue of more debentures and preference shares with fixed rates of interest and dividend. Illustration 5.20 will make the principle clear:

Thus, the debt-equity mix will be in such a manner that the earning per share (EPS) is increased. We also know that fixed financial charges do not vary as per earnings of the firm before EBIT. So, financial leverage expresses the results of earnings after the application of fixed interest bearing securities in the total capital structure. We can now propose that financial leverage results when fluctuation in EBIT is accompanied by disproportionate fluctuation in the firm's earning per share.[1] So, if EBIT changes, there must be a corresponding change in EPS provided the firm does not use fixed interest bearing securities.

The following illustration will make the principle clear.

Illustration 5.20

	Rs.
Capital Structure	
10,000 equity shares of Rs. 10 each	1,00,000
Debenture	—
EBIT	2,00,000
Tax rate	@ 50%
Change in EBIT	(±) 20%

Show, the effect of proposed change in EBIT on EPS.

Solution

		Present Level	Proposed Level	
			(+) 20%	(–) 20%
		Rs.	Rs.	Rs.
	EBIT	2,00,000	2,40,000	1,60,000
Less :	Tax @ 50%	1,00,000	1,20,000	80,000
	Earnings for equity shareholders	1,00,000	1,20,000	80,000
	No. of shares	10,000	10,000	10,000
	∴ EPS	10	12	8
	Change in EPS	—	(+) 20%	(–) 20%

From the above, it becomes clear that, if EBIT changes, there will be a corresponding change in EPS.

In the above illustration we exclude debt financing. But, in practice, there must be a mix between debt and equity to take the advantage of trading on equity which has already been explained in the earlier paragraphs. Because, such a mix produces a better result and increase the EPS due to:

---

1 Banerjee, B. — *Financial Policy and Management Accounting*—World Press (P) Ltd. — 1984, p. 429.

(i) debt financing is comparatively cheap than the equity capital;

(ii) it does not affect the voting rights among the existing equity shareholders;

(iii) debt financing increases the yield for equity shareholders till the same does not exceed the explicit cost of such investment; and

(iv) debt-financing invites the degree of flexibility in the total capital structure of a firm.

Thus, there must be a mix between debt and equity.

Capital Structure Trend in Private Sector in India

In order to find out the capital structure trend in private sector in India, which is expressed with the help of debt-equity ratio in different industries, the significant factors are divided into:

(a) Debt-Equity Ratio Norms,

(b) Review of such Norms, and

(c) Industry Practice.

(a) Debt-Equity Ratio Norms

We know that the norm of debt-equity ratio is 2 : 1. The same is also followed by various all-India financial institutions granting credit in the private sector although there are certain relaxations :[1]

(a) Capital intensive industries (i.e., Paper, Cement, Aluminium, Fertilizer in the private sector maintain a debt-equity ratio of 3 : 1 except Ship Building industry where the same ratio is around 6 : 1 or even higher);

(b) very high cost project in the priority seçtor;

(c) projects in backward areas, and

(d) project sponsored by technician entrepreneurs.[2]

(b) Review of the Norms

The normal Debt-Equity ratio 2 : 1 has also been suggested by various all-Indian Financial Institutions. The State Governments and the Associations of Industry requested the Central Government to relax the said debt-equity ratio norms. Accordingly, the Government requested the Management Development Institute to carry out a survey about the debt-equity ratio norms which are followed by the various all-Indian Financial Institutions, Industries, Government Agencies, among others, and to suggest a recommendation for the same. The study was carried out by Dr. B. K. Madan, Chairman, Management Development Institute, New Delhi. He submitted his report in February 1977 which was published by the Institute in January 1978.[3]

The study has revealed that the debt-equity ratio norms of 2 : 1—which has been suggested by various financial institutions—has been treated as a general guideline or broad indicator rather than as a rigid one in order to assess the capital structure composition of firms either to increase of capital or financial assistance, or for fresh issue. But the large capital intensive industries are permitted to maintain the ratio of 3 : 1, or even higher. At the same time, the small industrial projects are allowed some concessions, reliefs and aids

1 Madan, B. K. — *Report on a Study of the Debt-Equity Ratio Norms*, Adapted from Management Development Institute, New Delhi, 1978, p. 1.

2 Banerjee, B. — *Financial Management and Policy*, op. cit., p. 483.

3 *Report on the Study of the Debt-Equity Ratio Norms*, Management Development Institute, New Delhi, — made by Dr. B. K. Madan, 1978, p. 134.

which will help them to maintain very high level of debt in relation to equity for such purposes.

The following recommendations have been suggested by the study conducted by Dr. B. K. Madan, Chairman, Management Development Institute, New Delhi:

(i) The debt-equity norm of 2 : 1 should be maintained for the purpose of good order in, and for, facilitation of decision-making, although the norm is considered at present as a general indicator or a broad guideline relating to the matter for desiring long-term capital structure of a project, the same must be considered as much as practicable and not as a rigid one.

(ii) Whether the existing debt-equity ratio norm should be raised or not, the study suggested that there should hardly be a case for upward shift of the existing norm for such ratio.

(iii) The report also revealed that the application of multiple norms for various industries is neither desirable nor practicable, i.e., one norm should be applied for all.

(c) Industry Practice

The public sector enterprises (where the entire amount of equity is supplied by the Government and also major portion of the long-term debts) maintain usually a lower debt-equity ratio than the private sector enterprises as noticed by Dr. Madan.[1]

GENERAL ILLUSTRATIONS

Illustration 5.21

P. Ltd. furnished the following particulars:

		Rs.
(i)	Expected annual EBIT	2,00,000
(ii)	12% Debentures	8,00,000
(iii)	Equity Capitalisation Rate	@ 12.5%

P. Ltd. wants to redeem Debentutes amounting to Rs. 2,00,000 by the proceeds of issuing fresh equity shares of Rs. 2,00,000.

(a) Value of the firm;

(b) Overall Cost of Capital.

Solution

Statement Showing the Cost of Capital and Value of the Firm

		Rs.
	(a) Value of the Firm	
	EBIT	2,00,000
Less:	Debenture Interest (Rs. 6,00,000 × $\frac{12}{100}$)	72,000
	Earnings for Equity Shareholders	1,28,000
	Equity Capitalisation Rate (K_e)	12.5%

Contd.

1 *Ibid.*

	Rs.
Market Value of Equity:	
$= \frac{\text{Rs. } 1,28,000}{12.5} \times 100 =$	10,24,000
Market Value of Debt ($\frac{\text{Rs. } 72,000}{12} \times 100$)	6,00,000
Total Value of the Firm	16,24,000

(b) **Overall Cost of Capital**

Overall Cost of Capital $= \frac{\text{Rs. } 2,00,000}{\text{Rs. } 16,24,000} \times 100 = 12.32\%$

Illustration 5.22

E Ltd. with EBIT of Rs. 2,00,000 is evaluating a number of possible capital structures given below. The corporate tax rate is 35%.

Which of the capital structure will you recommend and why?

Capital Structure	Debt in Capital Structure Rs.	Cost of Debt before Tax %	Cost of Equity %
1	0	Nil	12.0
2	1,00,000	10.0	12.0
3	2,00,000	10.5	12.6
4	3,00,000	11.0	13.0
5	4,00,000	12.0	13.6
6	5,00,000	14.0	15.6
7	6,00,000	17.0	20.0

[C.U. M.Com]

Solution

Computation of Market Value of the Firm

	Capital Structure						
	1	**2**	**3**	**4**	**5**	**6**	**7**
	Rs.	Rs.	Rs.	Rs.	Rs.	Rs.	Rs.
EBIT	2,00,000	2,00,000	2,00,000	2,00,000	2,00,000	2,00,000	2,00,000
Less: Int. on Debt	—	10,000	21,000	33,000	48,000	70,000	1,02,000
EBT	2,00,000	1,90,000	1,79,000	1,67,000	1,52,000	1,30,000	98,000
Less: Tax @ 35%	70,000	66,500	62,650	58,450	53,200	45,500	34,300
Earning for Equity Shareholders	1,30,000	1,23,500	1,16,350	1,08,550	98,800	84,500	63,700
Cost of Capital (K_e)	12.0	12.0	12.6	13.3	13.6	15.6	20.0
Market Value of Equity ($\frac{\text{Earning}}{K_e}$) =	10,83,333	10,29,167	9,23,413	8,35,000	7,26,471	5,41,667	3,18,500
Market Value of Debt =	0	1,00,000	2,00,000	3,00,000	4,00,000	5,00,000	6,00,000
Market Value of the Firm	10,83,333	11,29,167	11,23,413	11,35,000	11,26,471	10,41,667	9,18,500

Comment

It becomes clear from the above statement that capital structure No. 4 should be recommended as in this case market value of the firm is highest, i.e., that capital structure should be recommended whose value of the firm will be maximised.

Illustration 5.23

From the particulars presented below, calculate the total market value of each of the following firms and ascertain their weighted average cost of capital (K_w) assuming that there are no corporate taxes :

Firms	EBIT (Earnings before Interest and Taxes) Rs.	I (Interest)	K_e equity (Cost of Capital)
A	50,000	5,000	12%
B	75,000	15,000	16%
C	1,25,000	50,000	15%
D	1,50,000	60,000	18%

Solution

Ascertainment of the Value of the Firm (V) and Average Cost of Capital (K_w)

		Firms			
		A	B	C	D
		Rs.	Rs.	Rs.	Rs.
	EBIT	50,000	75,000	1,25,000	1,50,000
Less :	Interest	5,000	15,000	50,000	60,000
	Earnings for Equity Shareholders	45,000	60,000	75,000	90,000
	Cost of equity	0.12	0.16	0.15	0.18
	Market value of equity (S)	3,75,000	3,75,000	5,00,000	5,00,000
Add :	Market value of debt (T)	50,000	1,50,000	5,00,000	6,00,000
	Total value of the firm (V)	4,25,000	5,25,000	10,00,000	11,00,000
	Weighted Average Cost of Capital				
	$K_W = \left(\frac{EBIT}{V}\right)$	11.76%	14.29%	12.5%	13.63%

Illustration 5.24

In considering the most desirable capital structure of a company, the following estimates of the cost of debt and equity capital (after tax) have been made at various levels of debt-equity mix:

Debts as percentage of total capital employed	Cost of Debt %	Cost of Equity %
0	5.0	12.0
10	5.0	12.0
20	5.0	12.5

Contd.

30	5.5	13.0
40	6.0	14.0
50	6.5	16.0
60	7.0	20.0

You are required to determine the optimal debt-equity mix for the company by calculating composite cost of capital.

[C.U. M.Com.—Adapted, I.C.W.A. and C.A. Final]

Solution

We know that optimal capital structure will be the point where weighted average cost of capital (K_w) will be minimum. So, we are to compute the weighted average cost of capital (K_w) for the company for each of the following alternative cases using the following formula:

$K_w = W_d K_d + W_e K_e$ where, K_w = Weighted average cost of capital

W_d = Proportion of debt to total value

W_d = Proportion of debt to total value

K_d = Cost of debt

K_e = Cost of equity

W_e = Proportion of equity to total value

K_d (%)	K_e (%)	W_e	W_d (1–W_e)	W_dK_d	W_eK_e	K_w ($W_dK_d + W_eK_e$)
5.0	12.0	—	1.0	—	12.0	12.0
5.0	12.0	.1	.9	.5	10.8	11.3
5.0	12.5	.2	.8	1.0	10.0	11.0
5.5	13.0	.3	.7	1.65	9.1	10.75
6.0	14.0	.4	.6	2.40	8.4	10.80
6.5	16.0	.5	.5	3.75	8.0	11.25
7.0	20.0	.6	.4	4.20	8.0	12.20

From the above table it reveals that cost of capital is minimum when debt-equity mix is 30% and 70%, respectively. Thus, the debt-equity mix for the company will be : Debt 30% and Equity 70%.

Illustration 5.25

From the following particulars presented by company A and company B:

(i) Compute the value of firms A and B using Net Income (NI) Approach.

(ii) Compute the value of firms A and B using Net Operating Income (NOI) Approach.

Company A and Company B are identical in all respects except their capital structure. That is, Company A uses debt whereas Company B does not. The levered firms had Rs. 4,50,000 long-term loans, carrying 10% interest.

Both the firms earn on their total assets of Rs. 7,50,000 @ 20% (before interest and taxes).

Rate of tax is @ 50%.

Capitalisation Rate @ 15%.

(Assume there are perfect capital market, rational investors and so on.)

Solution

(i) **According to NI Approach**

		Firm A Levered	Firm B Unlevered
		Rs.	Rs.
	EBIT (@ 20% on Rs. 7,50,000)	1,50,000	1,50,000
Less :	Interest on long-term loans @ 10%	45,000	—
		1,05,000	1,50,000
Less :	Taxes @ 50%	52,500	75,000
	Earnings to Equity Shareholders	52,500	75,000
	Equity Capitalisation Rate (K_e)	.15	.15
	Market Value of Equity (S)	3,50,000	5,00,000
	Market Value of Debt (T)	4,50,000	—
	Total Value of the Firm (V)	8,00,000	5,00,000

(ii) **According to NOI Approach**

We know that the value of the firms, in case of tax consideration, suggested by MM, is computed with the help of:

Value of unlevered firm $V_n = \dfrac{EBIT(1-t)}{K_e}$

Value of levered firm $V_l = V_n + tD$

Thus, value of unlevered company B $V_n = \dfrac{\text{Rs. } 1{,}50{,}000(1-.5)}{.15}$

$= \text{Rs. } 5{,}00{,}000$

Similarly, value of levered company A $V_l = \text{Rs. } 5{,}00{,}000 + .5 \times \text{Rs. } 4{,}50{,}000$

$= \text{Rs. } 7{,}25{,}000$

Illustration 5.26

The values for two firms X and Y, in accordance with the traditional theory, are:

	X	Y
	Rs.	Rs.
Expected Operating Income $(\bar{X})$	50,000	50,000
Total Cost of Debt ($K_d.D = R$)	0	10,000
Net Income $(\bar{X} - R)$	50,000	40,000
Cost of Equity (K_e)	0.10	0.11
Market Value of Shares (S)	5,00,000	3,60,000
Market Value of Debt (D)	0	2,00,000
Total Value of Firm (V = S + D)	5,00,000	5,60,000
Average Cost of Capital (K_o)	0.10	0.09
Debt-Equity Ratio	0	0.556

Compute the values for firms X and Y as per MM theories.

Assume that (i) Corporate income-tax does not exist, and (ii) the equilibrium value of K_o is 12.5%.

[Delhi, M.Com.]

Solution

Computation of the Value for the Firms under MM Hypothesis

	Firm X	Firm Y
EBIT $(\overline{X})$ (Expected Operating Income)	50,000	50,000
Less: Cost of Debt	—	10,000
Net Earnings for Equity Shareholders	50,000	40,000
Equilibrium Value of Cost of Capital (K_0)	0.125	0.125
Total Value of the Firm $\left(\frac{EBIT/\overline{X}}{K_0}\right)$	4,00,000	4,00,000
Market Value of Debt	—	2,00,000
∴ Market Value of Equity	4,00,000	2,00,000
∴ Cost of Equity $\left(\frac{\text{Earnings for Equity}}{\text{Market Value of Shares}}\right)$	12.5%	20%

Illustration 5.27

There are two firms, A and B. They are identical in all respects except the capital structure. Firm A is unlevered but Firm B is levered which has a 10% Debentures of Rs. 15,00,000.

The particulars are :

	Firm A	Firm B
	Rs.	Rs.
EBIT	3,75,000	3,75,000
Interest of Debt	—	1,50,000
Earnings for Equity Shareholders	3,75,000	2,25,000
Equity Capitalisation Rate	0.15	0.15
∴ Market Value of Equity (S)	25,00,000	11,25,000
Market Value of Debt (T)	—	15,00,000
Total Value of the Firm (V)	25,00,000	26,25,000
Over-Capitalisation Rate (K_0)	15%	14.28%
Debt-Equity Mix	0	1.33

(a) Mr. X owns 10% equity shares of the Firm B.

Show the process and the amount by which he could reduce his outlay through the application of leverage.

(b) As per MM Hypothesis, when will this arbitrage process come to an end?

Solution

(i) Market value of the firm = Market Value of Equity + Market Value of Debt
= Rs. 11,25,000 + Rs. 15,00,000
= Rs. 26,25,000

Mr. X's position

(a) **Existing position of Mr. X**

Cost of Investment Rs. 1,12,500 (i.e., 10% of Rs. 11,25,000)

Income as Dividend Rs. 22,500 (i.e., 10% of Rs. 2,25,000)

(b) He sells his shares for Rs. 1,12,500 and may create a personal leverage by taking loans/borrowings Rs. 1,50,000 (i.e., 10% of Rs. 15,00,000) debt from the Firm 'B'. Thus, the total amount will be Rs. 2,62,500. So, amount of income will be:

		Rs.
	Income from Firm 'B'	22,500
Add :	Interest on personal loans/borrowings (i.e., 10% of Rs. 1,50,000)	15,000
		37,500

(c) He purchases 10% equity share of the Firm 'A' for Rs. 2,50,000 (i.e., 10% of Rs. 25,00,000).

Thus,

	Rs.
Cost of Investment	2,50,000
Income as Dividend (10% of Rs. 3,75,000)	37,500

So, he must reduce his outlay by Rs. 12,500 through the application of leverage.

(ii) As per MM Hypothesis, the arbitrage process will come to an end when market values of both the firms become equal.

Illustration 5.28

Compute the equilibrium values and capitalisation rates of equity (K) of the companies A and B on the basis of the following data. Assume that (i) there is no income-tax, and (ii) the equilibrium value of average cost of capital (P) is 18.5%:

	Initial Disequilibrium	
	Company A	Company B
	Rs.	Rs.
Total Market Value	250	300
Debt (L)	0	150
Equity (S)	250	150
Expected Net Operating Income (X)	25	25
Interest (K.L.)	0	9
Net Income (X – K.L.)	25	16
Cost of Equity (K_e)	10%	10.7%
Leverage $\frac{L}{V}$	0	0.5
Average Cost of Capital	10%	8.33%

[Delhi, M.Com.]

Solution

We know that the equilibrium values will be determined by capitalising the net operating earnings by an equilibrium value of average cost of capital. Using the symbols, we have,

$$V = \frac{X}{P} \quad \text{where,} \quad X = \text{Rs. } 25$$

By substituting the values, we get : $P = 0.085$

$$V = \text{Rs.} \frac{25}{0.085}$$

or, $V = \text{Rs. } 294.12$

Thus, the equilibrium values (for both the firms) will be Rs. 294.12.

Now, we are going to compute, for both the firms, the equity capitalisation rates:

		Company A	Company B
		Rs.	Rs.
	EBIT (X)	25	25
Less :	Interest to Debt (K.L.)	—	9
	Earnings for Equity Shareholders	25	16
	Equilibrium Cost of Capital (P)	8.5%	8.5%
∴	Total Value of the firm $\left(\frac{X}{P}\right)$	294.12	294.12
Less :	Market Value of Debt (L)	—	150
∴	Market Value of Equity	294.12	144.12
	Cost of Equity Capital (K_e) $\left(\frac{X-K.L.}{S}\right)$	8.5%	11.1%

Illustration 5.29

X Ltd. wants to determine the optimal capital structure. From the particulars presented below, ascertain the optimal capital structure :

Condition	Equity	Debt	Cost of Debt (after tax)	K_e
	Rs.	Rs.	(%)	(%)
1	50,000	2,00,000	9	10
2	1,25,000	1,25,000	6	11
3	2,00,000	50,000	5	14

Solution

Computation of Debt-Equity Mix of X. Ltd. for Optimal Capital Structure

Condition	Cost of Debt K_d(%)	Cost of Equity K_e(%)	W_1	W_2	K_dW_1	K_eW_2	$K_0 =$ $(K_dW_1 + K_eW_2)$
1	9	10	.8	.2	7.2	2.0	9.2
2	6	11	.5	.5	3.0	5.5	8.5
3	5	14	.2	.8	1.0	14.0	12.2

where, W_1 and W_2 are proportion of debt and equity (i.e., 2,00,000 : 50,000).

It is quite clear from the above table that the optimal capital structure will be in the condition 2 where cost of capital is minimum i.e., the debt-equity mix is 50%-50%.

ASSIGNMENT MATERIALS

THEORETICAL

Multiple Choice Questions

1. (a) Capital structure means:

(i) Total Liabilities
(ii) Total Liabilities – Current Liabilities
(iii) Total Assets – Long-term Liabilities
(iv) None of these

(b) Financial structure means:

(i) Owned Capital
(ii) Borrowed Capital
(iii) Liabilities side of the Balance Sheet
(iv) None of these

(c) Asset structure means:

(i) Total Fixed Asset
(ii) Assets side of the Balance Sheet
(iii) Total Current Assets
(iv) None of these

(d) Capitalisation means:

(i) Total Securities issued
(ii) Owned Capital
(iii) Debt Capital
(iv) None of these

(e) Total value of the firm is equal to:

(i) Total Equity Capital plus total Debt Capital
(ii) Owned Capital
(iii) Borrowed Capital
(iv) None of these

(f) EPS is equal to:

(i) $\frac{\text{Earnings}}{\text{No. of shares (equity)}}$
(ii) $\frac{\text{Asset}}{\text{No of equity shares}}$
(iii) $\frac{\text{Owned Capital}}{\text{No. of equity shares}}$
(iv) None of these

(g) Debt-Equity ratio is:

(i) $\frac{\text{Equity}}{\text{Debt}}$
(ii) $\frac{\text{Total Debt}}{\text{Proprietors' fund}}$
(iii) $\frac{\text{Debt}}{\text{Equity}}$
(iv) None of these

(h) Trading on equity increases:

(i) EPS
(ii) Net Asset
(iii) Net worth
(iv) None of these

[Ans. (a) (ii); (b) (iii); (c) (ii); (d) (i); (e)(i); (f) (i); (g) (ii); (h) (i)]

Short Answer-type Questions

2. Define the term 'Capital Structure'. Name the items that are included in Capital Structure.
3. Distinguish between 'Financial Structure' and 'Capital Structure'.
4. Critically examine the Traditional Approach and the MM Approach of Capital Structure Theories.

[Delhi, M.Com.]

5. Explain the assumption of NI Approach and NOI Approach with hypothetical examples.
6. "The total value of a firm remains unchanged regardless of variation in its financing mix." —Discuss.

[Delhi, M.Com.—Adapted]

7. Explain briefly the view of traditional writers on the relationship between capital structure and the value of the firm.

[Delhi, M.Com.]

8. Define 'Simple' and 'Complex' Capital Structures of a firm. Is it possible for a firm to maintain simple capital structure for a period?

Long Answer-type Questions

9. How do you ascertain:
   (i) Cost of equity under NOI Approach?
   (ii) When EBIT, Interest and Cost of Capitalisation are given, value of equity?
   (iii) The value of levered firms under MM Hypothesis with taxes?
   (iv) The overall capitalisation rate, when EBIT, value of equity and value of debentures are given?
10. How do you ascertain the optimal capital structure of a firm?
11. Explain briefly the factors that affect the planning of capital structure of a firm.
12. Explain the factors that determine the Capital Structure of a firm.

[M. Com. & MBA, Madras, I.C.W.A. Final]

13. What do you mean by Optimum Capital Structure? **[M. Com. Osmania]**
14. What is over-capitalisation? Explain its causes and evils.

[M. Com. Kerala]

15. Explain EBIT-EPS approach for determining the Capital Structure of a Company.
16. What do you understand by balanced Capital Structure? Why should a company aim at balanced Capital Structure?
17. Explain the factors that affect capital structure decisions.

[M. Com. Rajasthan]

18. Show that in the MM hypothesis under corporate tax:

    vl = vu + td, i.e.

    Value of levered firm = Value of unlevered firm + Tax-Shield.
19. Explain the factaors which determine capital structures.

20. There is nothing like an Optimal Capital Structure for a firm. Critically evaluate this statement.
21. Explain the features of Optimum Capital Structure.

[M.Com. Madras]

22. What do you mean by over-trading and under-trading?
23. Explain the objects of sound Capital Structure of a firm.
24. What factors do you consider while planning the Capital Structure of a firm?
25. Name some important ratios that are commonly used in Capital Structure and explain them.
26. Explain the advantages and disadvantages of Debt-financing.

PRACTICAL

1. X. Ltd. has a Share Capital of Rs. 1,00,000 divided into shares of Rs. 10 each. The company needs a fund of Rs. 50,000 for its development out of the following three alternative sources of finance : (a) Issue 5,000 equity shares of Rs. 10 each; (b) Issue 2,500 equity shares and 2,500, 12% Preference share of Rs. 10 each; (c) Issue 10% Debentures of Rs. 50,000. EBIT is Rs. 40,000 p.a.

Calculate the effect of the above mode of financing when (a) EBIT will remain same even after expansion; (b) EBIT increases by Rs. 10,000.

[Ans. (a) EPS will be least in case of Debenture Issues, (b) EPS will go up by Re. 0.25 per share]

2. Alpha Co. is contemplating conversion of 500, 14% convertible bonds of Rs. 1,000 each. Market price of the bond in debenture provides that one bond will be exchanged for 10 shares. Price-earning ratio before redemption is 20 : 1, and anticipated price-earning ratio after redemption is 25 : 1. Number of shares outstanding prior to redemption are 10,000. EBIT amount to Rs. 2,00,000. The company is in the 35% tax bracket.

Should the company convert bonds, into shares? Give reasons.

[C.S.]

[Ans. Yes, because post-redemption market price of equity shares would be Rs. 216.50 than the pre-redemption market price of Rs. 169]

3. Calculate EPS of Solid Ltd. and Sound Ltd. assuming (a) 20% (before tax rate) of return on assets; (b) 10% (before-tax rate) of return on assets based on data:

	Solid Ltd. (Rs. in lakhs)	Sound Ltd. (Rs. in lakhs)	
Assets	100	100	
Debt	—	50	(12% Debentures and Loan)
Equity shares of Rs. 10 each	100	50	

Assume 50% Income tax rate in both the case.

[I.C.W.A. Final]

[Ans. (a) Re. 1.00, 0.50; (b) Rs. 1.40, Re. 0.40]

4. ABC industries has borrowed Rs. 2,00,000 at an interest rate of 18%. Tabulate the effective rate of interest if the interest is charged at (i) half-yearly intervals, and (ii) quarterly intervals.

[I.C.W.A. Final]

[Ans. Effective Rate of Interest 19.25%]

5. A company is presently earning an EBIT of Rs. 12 lakhs. Its present borrowings are:

	Rs.
11% Term Loan	40 lakhs
Borrowing from Bank at 16%	33 lakhs
Public Deposit at 12%	15 lakhs

The sales of the company is growing and, to support this, the company proposes to obtain an additional bank borrowing of Rs. 25 lakhs. The increase in EBIT is expected to be 20%.

Calculate the change in interest coverage ratio after the additional borrowings and commitment.

[A.C.S.]

[Ans. If the additional bank-borrowing is restricted to Rs. 18.25 lakhs, EBIT will be just sufficient to pay all fixed interest charges]

6. Companies X and Y are identical in all respects including risk factors except for debt equity, X having issued 10% Debentures of Rs. 18 lakhs while Y has issued only equity. Both the companies earn 20% before interest and taxes on their total asset of Rs. 30 lakhs.

Assuming a tax rate of 50% and capitalisation rate of 15% for an all equity company, compute the value of companies X and Y using (i) Net Income Approach; and (ii) Net Operating Income Approach.

[C.A. Final]

[Ans. (i) Rs. 32 lakhs and Rs. 20 lakhs; (ii) Rs. 29 lakhs and Rs. 20 lakhs]

7. From the following selected data determine the value of the firms P and Q belonging to the homogeneous risk claim under (a) the NI Approach, and (b) the NOI Approach.

	Levered Firm P	Unlevered Firm Q
	Rs.	Rs.
EBIT	2,00,000	2,00,000
Interest @ 10%	50,000	—
Equity — Capitalisation Rate	15%	—
Corporate Tax Rate	15%	—

Which of the two firms has an optimal Capital Structure under the (i) NI approach, and (ii) NOI approach?

[Ans. Firm P has optimal capital structure in both the methods]

8. Y Ltd. expects an annual EBIT of Rs. 1,00,000. The company has Rs. 400 lakhs in 10% debentures. The equity capitalisation rate is 12%. The company decides to raise Rs. 1,00,000 by issue of 10% debentures and use the proceeds thereof.

You are required to calculate the total value of the firm and also the overall cost of capital.

[Ans. To raise fund by additional debt will increase the total value of the firm and will reduce the overall cost of capital. Value of the firm will decrease (as per NI approach) if the debt is decreased by issuing additional equity shares]

9. The Calgay Company is attempting to establish a current asset policy. Fixed assets are Rs. 6 lakhs and the firm plans to maintain a 50% debt-to-assets ratio. The interest rate is 10% on all debts. Three alternative current asset policies are under consideration — 40%, 50% and 60% of projected sales. The company expects to earn 15% EBIT on sale of Rs. 30 lakhs. Calgay's effective tax rate is 40%.

What is the expected return on equity under each alternative?

[C.S. Final]

[Ans. 40% = Rs. 2,16,000; 50% = Rs. 2,07,000; 60% = Rs. 1,92,000]

CHAPTER 6

DIVIDEND POLICIES

Introduction

Dividend may be defined as divisible profit which is distributed amongst the members of a company in proportion to their shares in such a manner as is prescribed by the Memorandum and Articles of Association of a company. It is the share of profits of a company divided amongst its shareholders. In other words, it is a return that a shareholder gets from the company which is distributed out of its profits on his shareholdings, i.e., dividend is a distribution to shareholders out of profits or reserves available for this purpose.

Types of Dividend

Dividend may be classified according to:

(a) *Sources from which they are derived; e.g.,*
- (i) Retained Earnings; or
- (ii) Current Profit.

(b) *Medium in which they are distributed; e.g.,*
- (i) Cash Dividend; or
- (ii) Share Dividend (i.e., Bonus Shares);
- (iii) Bond Dividend;
- (iv) Scrip Dividend.

(c) *Regularity with which they are paid; e.g.,*
- (i) Interim Dividend; or
- (ii) Annual or Final Dividend.

Cash Dividend

According to Sec. 205(3) of the Companies Act, 1956, dividend must be paid in cash except when the company decides to capitalise profit/reserves by issuing fully paid-up bonus shares or making partly paid-up shares into fully paid-up. But before declaring and paying dividend in cash, the company must see its liquid assets in the from of cash. As payment of dividend is an outflow of cash, the company must hold adequate amount of cash in order to pay dividends in cash. The company should also consider that after paying dividend, sufficient amount of cash is to be left in hand as liquid asset to meet the working capital requirements.

Share Dividend

Sometimes a company cannot pay dividend in cash due to shortage of liquid funds, viz. cash, in spite of earning a large amount of profit for a particular period. Under the circumstances, the company issues new shares to the existing shareholders in lieu of paying dividend in cash. These shares are known as 'Bonus Shares'. Such bonus shares are to be offered to the existing shareholders in proportion to the shareholdings and dividend rights. Generally, the company issues bonus shares out of profits and/or reserve to the existing shareholders. Since the profit/reserves is being capitalised, ***it is also called capitalisation of profit/reserve.*** As the company cannot receive cash from the shareholders for the purpose of issuing bonus shares, a sum equal to the total value of bonus issue is to be adjusted against profit/reserve and transferred to Equity Share Capital Account.

Bond Dividend

If the company cannot pay dividend due to shortage of liquid funds viz., cash, it may issue bonds (with interest) for the amount of dividend, to the shareholders. It, no doubt, checks the outflow of cash. The payment will be made at the date of maturity of bonds.

Scrip Dividend

When scrips or promissory notes are issue to the shareholders for the payment of dividend in lieu of paying cash, the same is known as scrip dividend. In other words, the company promises to pay dividend to the shareholders at a future date. It may be issued with interest bearing or without interest bearing.

Interim Dividend

According to Clause 86, Table A, the Board of Directors may, from time to time, pay to the shareholders interim dividend which appears to be justified by the profits of the company. Interim dividend is a dividend which is declared between two annual general meetings, i.e., before the declaration of the final dividend. For this purpose, interim accounts are prepared. However, final dividends may or may not be inclusive of interim dividend, although, generally, the final proposed dividend is inclusive of interim dividend so paid. But the Directors will keep aside the amounts which are already paid out of the profits of the company, before recommending final dividend. But before declaring such a dividend the Directors must consider some factors which are directly related to profit, e.g., whether there is any possibility of decreasing sales or increasing operating cost, the expected rate of profitability etc. Moreover, the liquidity position should also be taken into consideration, particularly the cash position (as interim dividend is paid in cash).

Annual or Final Dividend

Every company prepares its annual accounts at the end of financial the year to ascertain the amount of net profit as well as to ascertain the financial position. The Directors after considering some factors (i.e., future prospects, possibility of increasing expenditure or decreasing sales revenue etc.) decide to recommend annual of final dividend out of the current year's profit in the annual general meeting of the company which are paid to the shareholders. Before declaring dividend, a certain amount should be transferred to General Reserve by way of retention. If more profit is retained the rate of dividend will be reduced and, if the entire profit is paid by way of dividend, the same will impair the growth of the business unit. Therefore, there must be a balance between the two. So the Directors, before declaring the annual or final dividend, should consider some essential factors which are necessary for the purpose.

Legal Provisions Regarding Payment of Dividend

It is the duty of the management to consider the legal provisions regarding the payment of dividend as per Companies Act, 1956, while designing the dividend policy of a firm. This is due to the fact that the dividend policy is frequently affected by the legal provisions. It is needless to mention here that the other factors relating to the payment of dividend (i.e., $\frac{D}{P}$

Ratio, liquidity position etc.) may be favourable even though the dividend cannot be paid if it contradicts the legal provisions. As per Companies Act, 1956, however, some restrictions have been imposed relating to payment of dividend by the companies. The provisions relating to the quantum and procedure as per Companies Act, 1956, are mentioned in the Sections 205, 205A, 206A, and 207 which are outlined below in short :

(i) Sec. 205: According to Section 205 of the Companies Act, dividend can be declared or paid only out of profits of the (i) Financial year (after providing for depreciation) or (ii) Out of the undistributed profits of the previous financial year (after providing for depreciation) or (iii) Out of both, or (iv) Out of moneys provided by the Central Government or a State Government for the payment of dividend in pursuance of the guarantee given by that government.

(ii) Section 205(3): Dividend shall be payable in cash only. But this does not prohibit capitalisation of profits or reserves for the purpose of issuing (i) fully paid-up bonus shares or (ii) partly paid bonus shares to become fully paid.

(iii) Section 205(5)(b): Dividend payable in cash may be paid by cheque or dividend warrant. This must be sent to the registered address of the shareholders who are entitled to such dividend. In the case of joint shareholders the cheque or warrant should be sent to the first named shareholder enrolled in the register. But if the joint shareholders direct in writing that the cheque on warrant may be sent to any other person or address, it should be sent accordingly.

(iv) Section 206: Dividend must be paid to the registered holder of share or his order or to his banker. In the case of share warrant, however, dividend must be paid to the bearer of such warrant or to his banker.

(v) Section 207: Where the dividend has been declared but not paid or the warrant has not been posted within 42 days from the date of declaration to the shareholder who is entitled to have such dividend, every director or the officer, shall, if he is knowingly a party to the default, be punishable with simple imprisonment for a term which may extend to 7 days and also shall be liable to fine. But no offence shall be deemed to have been made in the following cases:

(a) Where the dividend could not be paid by reason of the operation of any law;

(b) Where the shareholder has given directions to the company regarding payment of dividend;

(c) Where there is a dispute regarding the right to receive dividend;

(d) Where the dividend has been lawfully adjusted by the company against any sum due to it from the shareholders.

(e) Where the failure is not due to any default on the part of the company.

Points to Remember

Directors may recommend or declare dividends for any financial year after transferring a certain amount to Reserve (not exceeding 10% which is prescribed by the Central Government).

If the company falls to redeem its preference shares (as per Sec. 80A) it cannot declare or pay dividends to its equity shareholders (till the redemption is made).

Companies (Transfer of Profit to Reserve) Rules, 1975

As per the rule, no dividend shall be declared and paid out of current profit after providing for depreciation, as per the provisions of Sec. 205, sub-section 2, except after the transfer to reserve as per the following prescribed percentage of profit:

Where the dividend proposed		Amount to be transferred to Reserve
Up to 10%		Nil
Exceeds 10.01% but does not exceed	12.5%	2.5% of the current years Profit
" 12.51% " " " "	15%	5% " " " " "
" 15.01% " " " "	20%	7.5% " " " " "
Exceeding 20%	—	10% " " " " "

Companies (Declaration of Dividend out of Reserves) Rules, 1975

As per Rule 2, if there is inadequacy of profit or in the absence of profit in any year, dividend may be declared out of accumulated profit earned in the previous year and the same transferred to the reserve subject to the followings:

(i) 10% of paid-up capital or the rate of dividend must not exceed the average rate of dividend which was declared in last five years immediately preceding that year.

(ii) the total amount which will be drawn from the past accumulated profits and which are transferred to Reserves must not exceed $\frac{1}{10}$th of paid-up capital and free reserves and such amount first be utilised to set-off the losses, if any, before any dividend is declared either on equity or on preference shares.

(iii) the balance of such Reserves must not fall below 15% of the paid-up capital.

Moreover, ***dividend should always be payable out of revenue profits but not out of capital profits.*** Sometimes dividend may also be paid out of capital profit if the following conditions are satisfied :

(i) such capital profit has been realised in cash;

(ii) the Articles of the company so provides; and

(iii) such capital profit will remain after the revaluation of the fixed assets.

Dividend Policy

Dividend policy is the policy which concerns quantum of profits to be distributed by way of dividend. This policy implies that the companies introduce a pattern of dividend payment through their Board of Directors, which, no doubt, has an implication on the future activities. Although, in practice, this procedure is not followed by most of the companies. They simply consider each dividend decision in an independent manner. This is primarily due to the fact that the financial manager cannot do anything about it since he works at an advisory capacity. The power to recommend dividend policy and declaration of dividends vests completely on the Board of Directors.

However, we are going to discuss the determinants of dividend policy of the firm which is more practical from the standpoint of dividend itself. The factors which determine the dividend policy may be divided into (i) External Factors, and (ii) Internal Factors.

Determinants of Dividend Policy

Dividend policy of a firm determines (i) the mrket value of a share, (ii) amount paid to the shareholders by way of dividend; and (iii) re-investment in the firm by way of retention. It also determine the cash flow patterns. However, we are highlighting here the determinants of dividend policy. They depend two factor viz., External Factor and Internal factors. They are:

External Factors	Internal Factors
(i) General State of Economy;	(i) Dividend Pay-out Ratio;
(ii) Capital Market Considerations;	(ii) Owner's Contribution;
(iii) Legal, Contractual Constraints and Restrictions;	(iii) Nature of Earnings;
(iv) Tax Policy;	(iv) Liquidity Position;
(v) Inflation;	(v) Rate of Return;
(vi) Stability of Dividends	(vi) Divisible Profit;
(vii) Stability of Earnings;	(vii) Degree of Control;
(viii) Cost of Financing.	(viii) Dividend Clientele.

These are discussed below one by one in detail since they have bearings on the dividend policy of a firm:

External Factors

(i) General State of Economy

As a whole, it affects the decision of the management to a great extent whether the dividend should be retained or the same should be distributed among the shareholders. In the following cases, the business may prefer to retain the whole or part of the earnings in order to build-up reserves :

(i) where there is uncertain economic and business conditions;
(ii) if there is a period of depression (management may withhold the payment of dividends for maintaining the liquidity position of the firm);
(iii) if there is a period of prosperity (since there is large profitable investment opportunities); and
(iv) where there is a period of inflation.

(ii) Capital Market Considerations

This also affects the dividend policy to the extent to which the firm has access to the capital market. In other words, if easy access to the capital market is possible whether due to financially strong or, being big in size, the firm, in that case, may adopt a liberal dividend policy. In the opposite case, i.e., if easy access to capital market is not possible, it must adopt a low dividend pay-out ratio, i.e., they have to follow a conservative dividend policy. As such, they must rely more on their own fund, viz., retained earnings.

(iii) Legal, Contractual Constraints and Restrictions

This is one of the most significant factors which is to be taken into account (already explained in an earlier paragraph) while considering dividend policy of a firm since it has to be evolved within the legal framework and restrictions. It is not legally binding on the part of the directors to declare dividends. It has already been pointed out earlier that (according to Section 205 of the Companies Act) dividend shall be declared or paid only out of current profit or past profits after charging depreciation, although the Central Government has been empowered to allow any company for paying dividends out of *current profits* for any financial year before charging depreciation. The dividend must be paid in cash, although a company can capitalise its profits/reserves for the purpose of issuing fully paid bonus shares or making partly paid shares into fully paid. Capital profits cannot be distributed by way of dividend.[1] Sometimes a company may declare dividend out of past accumulated profits if the Central Government so permits. Moreover, the Indian Income-tax Act also prescribes certain restrictions about the payment of dividend.

From the above, it becomes clear that the directors, while declaring dividends, should consider all the relevant legal formalities prescribed by the Companies Act, Income-tax Act, etc.

Contractual restrictions, on the other hand, which are imposed by certain lenders of the firm also affect the dividend policy of a firm. Because, they impose certain conditions about the payment of dividend, particularly during the period when the firm is experiencing liquidity or profitability crisis. For instance, there may be an agreement between the firm and the lenders that the former shall not pay dividend to its shareholders more than 10% until the loan is repaid or dividend shall not be declared if the liquidity ratio is found to be less than 1 : 1.

(iv) Tax Policy/Tax Consideration

The tax policy which is followed by a Government also affects the dividend policy of a firm. Whether it is better to declare and pay dividend in cash, or by the issue of bonus shares, depends to some extent on the tax policy. Because, cash dividends are not even so attractive to the investors who are in higher tax brackets. For this purpose, a firm should follow a tax-oriented dividend policy by (i) not declaring dividends and assisting the shareholders to secure their returns by the sale of appropriated shares, (ii) following a policy of regular share dividend in lieu of cash dividend, (iii) using classified equity share dividend.[2]

(v) Inflation

Inflation may also affect the dividend policy of a firm. With rising prices, funds which are generated by way of depreciation may fall short in order to replace obsolete equipments. The shortfall may be made from retained earnings (as a source of fund). This is very significant when the assets are to be replaced in the near future. As such, the dividend pay-out ratio tends to be low during the periods of inflation.

(vi) Stability of Dividends

The various external factors affecting the dividend policy have already been explained in the earlier paragraphs, which are, no doubt, important, and, as such, they should be given due weightage for this purpose although the same may differ from one firm to another. The dividend policy, of course, should have a degree of stability, i.e., earnings/profits may fluctuate from year to year but not the dividend—since the equity shareholders prefer to value stable dividends than the fluctuating ones. In other words, the investors favour a stable dividend in as much as they do the payment of dividend. Stable dividends refer to the consistence or lack of variability in the stream of dividends payments, i.e., a certain minimum amount of dividend should be paid regularly.

The stability of dividends can be made in any of three forms:

(a) Constant Dividend Per Share;

---

1 It was held in case of Lubbock vs The British Bank of South America, that capital profit should not be distributed by way of dividend until and unless it is permitted by Articles of Association and the same has been realised in cash.

2 Banerjee, B.—*Financial Policy and Management Accounting* — op. cit., p. 500.

(b) Constant Percentage of Net Earnings (Constant $\frac{D}{F}$ ratio); and

(c) Constant Dividend Per Share Plus Extra Dividend.

(a) Constant Dividend Per Share

Under this form, a firm pays a certain fixed amount per share by way dividend. For example, a firm may pay a fixed amount of, say, Rs. 5, as dividend per share having a face value of Rs. 50. The fixed amount would be paid regularly year after year irrespective of the actual earnings, i.e., the firm will pay dividend even if there is a loss. In short, fluctuation in earnings will not affect the payment of dividend. Of course, it does not necessarily mean that the amount of dividend will remain fixed for all times in future. When the earnings of the company will increase, the rate of dividend will also increase provided the new level can be maintained in future. If there is a temporary increase, in earnings, there will not be any change in the payment of dividends. The relationship between the EPS (Earning per Share) and DPS (Dividend per Share) can better be represented with the help of Fig. 6.1 :

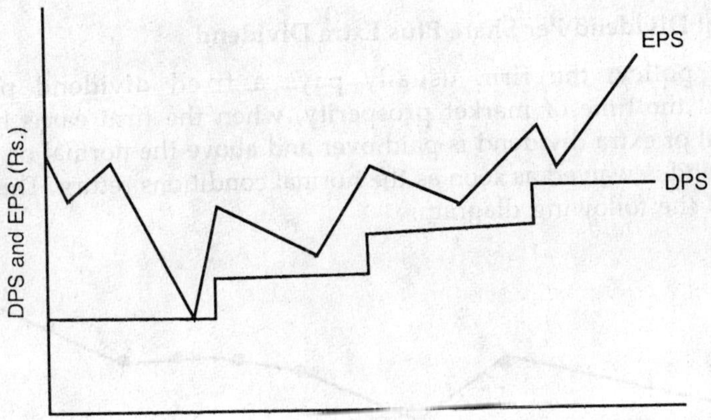

Fig. 6.1: Showing Stable Dividend Policy per Share

From the above, it becomes clear that earnings (EPS) may fluctuate from year to year but the DPS is constant. In order to formulate this policy, a firm whose earnings are not stable may have to make provisions to those years when there is higher earnings, i.e., a Dividend Equalisation Reserve Fund may be created for the purpose.

(b) Constant Percentage of Net Earnings

According to this policy, a certain percentage of the net earnings/profits is paid by way of dividend to the shareholders year after year, i.e., when a constant pay-out ratio is followed by a firm. In other words, it implies that the percentage of earnings paid out each year is fixed and, as such, dividends would fluctuate proportionately with earnings. This is particularly useful in cases where there is wide fluctuation in the earnings of a firm. This policy suggests that when the earnings of a firm decline, the dividend would, naturally, be low. For instance, if a firm adopts a 40% dividend pay-out ratio (it indicates that for one rupee earned, it will pay 40 paise to the shareholders), i.e., if a firm earns Rs. 5 per share then it will pay Rs. 2 to the shareholders by way of dividend.

The relationship under this policy between the EPS and DPS is presented below with the help of the Fig. 6.2 depicted below.

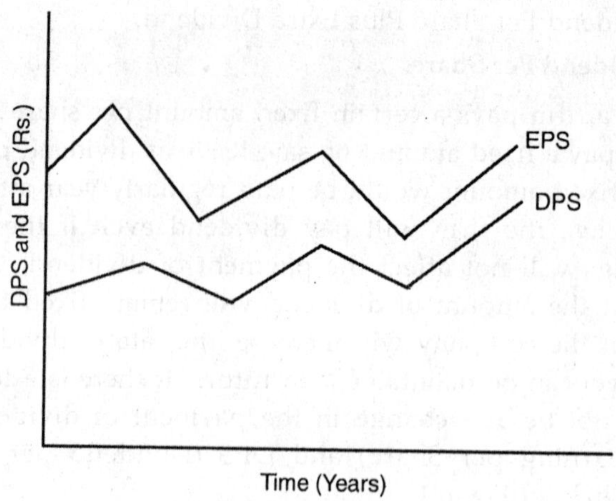

Fig. 6.2: Showing Stable Dividend Policy under Constant Pay Out Ratio

(c) Constant Dividend Per Share Plus Extra Dividend

Under this policy, the firm usually pays a fixed dividend per share to the shareholders. At the time of market prosperity, when the firm earns higher amount of profit, additional or extra dividend is paid over and above the normal or regular dividend. This extra dividend is waived as soon as the normal conditions return. The same is depicted with the help of the following diagram:

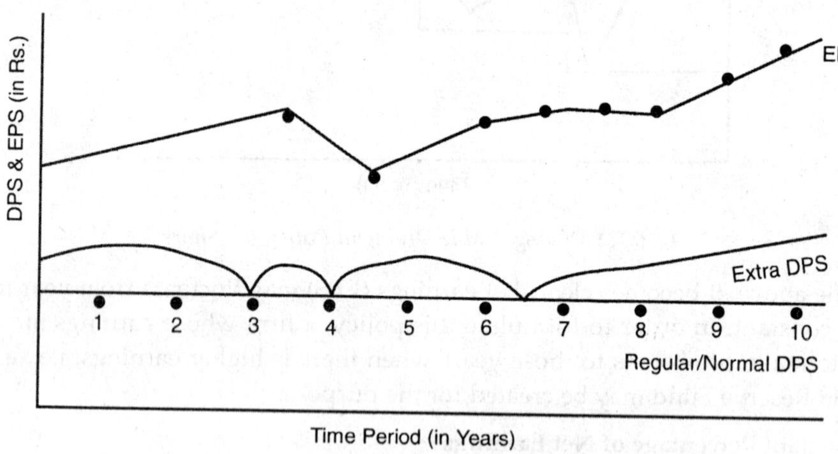

Fig. 6.3: Showing the Constant Dividend Per Share Plus Extra Dividend

Now, the questions that arise before us are which one is the most appropriate one and what is their relative suitability, or which one is most favourable to the investors, or, what are the implications to the shareholders.

Comment

The most appropriate policy may be considered as the first one, viz., *Constant Dividend Per Share*. Because, most of the investors desire a fixed rate of return from their investment which will gradually increase over a period of time. This is satisfied by the said policy.

But in case of *Constant Percentage* (*of Net Earnings*) the return actually fluctuates with the amount of earnings, and it also involves uncertainties. That is why it is not preferred by the shareholders although the same is favoured by the management since it correlates the amount of dividends to the ability of the company to pay its dividend. At the same time, in case of *Constant Dividend Per Share Plus Extra Dividend*, there is always an uncertainty about the extra dividend and, a result, it is not generally preferred by the shareholders.

A stable dividend policy is advantageous due to the following :

(i) ***Desire for Current Income***

There are investors, like old and retired persons, widows etc., who desire to have a stable income in order to meet their current living expenses since such expenses are almost fixed in nature. Such a stable dividend policy will help them.

(ii) ***Resolution of Investors' Uncertainty***

If a firm adopts a stable dividend policy, it must declare and pay dividend even if the earnings are temporarily reduced. It actually conveys to the investors that the future is bright. On the contrary, if it follows a policy of changing dividend with cyclical changes in the rate of earnings, the investors will not be confined about their return which may induce them to require a higher discount factor. The same is not desired in case of a stable dividend policy.

(iii) ***Raising Additional Finance***

If stable dividend policy is adopted by a firm, raising additional funds from external sources become advantageous on the part of the company since it will make the shares of a firm an investment. The shareholders/investors will hold the shares for a long time as it will create some confidence in the company and, as such, for further issue of shares, they would be more receptive to the offer by the company. This dividend policy also helps the company to sell preference shares and debentures. Because, past trend regarding the payment of dividend informs them that the company has been regularly paying the dividends and their interest/dividend, naturally, will be paid by the company when it will mature for repayment, together with the principal.

(iv) ***Requirements of Institutional Investors***

Sometimes the shares of a company are purchased by financial institutions like IFC, IDB, LIC, UTI etc., and educational and social institutions, in addition to the individuals. These financial institutions are the largest purchasers of shares in corporate securities in our country and every firm is interested to sell their shares to these institutions. These financial institutions are interested to buy the shares of those companies who have a stable dividend policy.

Danger of Stability of Dividends

Once this policy is being adopted by a firm, it cannot be changed with an immediate effect which will adversely affect the investors' attitude towards the financial stability of the company. Because, if a company with stable dividend policy fails to pay the dividend in any year, there will be severe financial and psychological effect on the investors than the failure to pay dividend under unstable dividend policy. That is why, in order to maintain that rate, sometimes the directors pay dividend, even if there is insufficient earnings, i.e., declaring dividend out of capital which, ultimately, if it continues year after year, invites the liquidation of a firm.

From the foregoing discussions it becomes clear that the rate of dividend should be fixed at a conservative figure which is possible to pay even in a lean period for several years.

Extra dividend can be declared out of extra earnings which, in other words, will not create any adverse effect in future.

(vii) **Stability of Earnings**

Dividend decision is also affected by stability of earnings. Future earnings of a firm can be predicted to some extent if the earnings of a firm is stable. Naturally, a firm having stable earnings may pay a higher rate of dividend than a firm having unstable earnings. As the earnings are not stable, in the case of firm having unstable earning, they prefer to retain their earnings instead of paying the same by way of dividend.

(viii) **Cost of Financing**

Cost of financing also affects the payment of dividend if the use of external funds is costlier, the firm must try to use its internal funds. In that case, the rate of payment of dividend must be lower.

Internal Factors

The following internal factors affect the dividend policy of a firm:

(i) **Dividend Pay-Out $\left(\frac{D}{P}\right)$ Ratio**

Dividend Pay-Out Ratio, $\left(\frac{D}{P}\right)$ Ratio, (i.e., percentage share of the net earnings or profits distributed to the shareholders by way of dividends*) also affects the dividend policy of a firm. It involves the decision either to pay out the earnings or to retain the same for re-investment within the firm. Retained earnings also constitute a reliable source of funds. Thus, the $\frac{D}{P}$ ratio plays a very significant role in decision-making regarding the payment of dividend.

However, the said decision should be taken into consideration after considering :

(a) **Liquidity Position**

Since dividend is paid in cash only the liquidity ratios (i.e., current ratio, liquid ratio etc.) will be reduced. as cash is a component of current/liquid assets and, in that case, it will be difficult for the firm to pay its maturing obligations. Profits cannot assure liquidity. A firm may earn sufficient profit but may not improve its cash positions or liquidity position. The question of liquidity-profitability tangle comes here (it has been discussed in details in the chapter Working Capital Management). We know that profit is the result of either increase in assets or decrease in liabilities, i.e., not necessarily the increase of cash only. Thus, the liquidity position is a very important criterion while deciding the payment of dividend.

(b) **Growth Rate**

For maintaining assets level and financing investment opportunities or expansion and development, or expanding production and sales positions, a firm should require necessary funds which may be procured either from the issue of additional equity shares or from debt and, consequently, if the firm fails to raise funds from outside, its growth rate will be adversely affected. So payment of dividend implies outflow of cash which adversely

---

* In other words, it is the ratio between dividends paid to equity shareholders and the profit (after tax) and is calculated as :

$$\frac{D}{P} \text{ Ratio} = \frac{\text{Dividend Paid to Shareholders}}{\text{Net Profit (after tax)}}$$

affects the future growth of the firms. In short, it affects the owners' wealth as well as the long-term growth of a firm. Thus, the optimum dividend policy should strike that balance between current dividends and future growth which maximises the price of the firms' share.[1] Therefore, this ratio will have to be determined in such a manner that it will maximise the firm's wealth, and, at the same time, will provide sufficient funds for the growth in future.

(c) **Control**

As a result of paying dividend in cash (it has already been stated above) the liquid funds of a firm reduces—which must be compensated either raising funds from equity or from debt. If the firm desires to raise funds by the issue of fresh equity shares, there will be a change in the composition of capital structure or, in other words, there may be a dilution of control on the part of the management. So, the existing shareholders and the management may not prefer a higher $\frac{D}{P}$ ratio. On the contrary, if the firm decides to raise funds from debt, different problems will arise since there will be a change in the composition of total external liabilities i.e., a higher Debt-Equity ratio, which is not at all desirable from the standpoint of control. Thus, a finance manager must think about the dilution of control while deciding the dividend policy of a firm.

From the discussion made so far, it becomes clear that to fix up a dividend policy may create a number of problems which, again, depends on a number of factors. If the existing shareholders are not satisfied with the company's dividend policy they may sell their shares which brings the dilution of control on the part of management. On the contrary, if the finance manager approves a higher rate of dividend to satisfy the existing shareholders and to increase the market value of shares, he will also invite a number of problems. Ultimately the firm will find itself short of funds for various investment opportunities and also to bear the burden of additional cost for raising new issues. Thus, there must be an optimum position about the liquidity affairs while deciding the dividend policy of a firm.

Effect of High $\frac{D}{P}$ Ratio

High $\frac{D}{P}$ Ratio invites the following problems :

(i) There will be a deficit in cash balance if the amount of dividend which is to be paid is more than the availables surplus of cash. Naturally, such deficit must be covered either from borrowing or from issuing securities, or otherwise.

(ii) If the dividend is not paid, the said amount could have been saved and invested otherwise in different good projects from which such higher return can be enjoyed which, ultimately, will go to the shareholders. In short, instead of paying cash dividend to the shareholders the same could have been utilised elsewhere for better investment purposes to increase the profitability.

(iii) Instead of paying cash dividend to the shareholders, the said sum could easily be utilised by the firm in the following three proposes:

---

1 Brigham, E. F. — *Readings in Managerial Finance* — New York, Holt Rinchart and Winston, 1971, p. 675.

(a) Transactions Motive; (b) Precautionary Motive, and (c) Speculative Motive.

Effect of Low $\frac{D}{P}$ Ratio

A low $\frac{D}{P}$ ratio reveals :

(i) If $\frac{D}{P}$ ratio is found to be less than its normal level, such idle cash balances increases cost.

(ii) Sometimes the idle cash is invested otherwise—which does not produce any good result, and ultimately, it is treated as bad investment.

It is interesting to note that the low $\frac{D}{P}$ ratio may be considered quite good if the firm invests such funds in particular project from which good returns for the shareholders are available, i.e., in that case, this ratio may be more positive. This is due to the fact that (i) the projects which earn greater returns than the normal rate of return on investments where such accumulation of cash invested, and (ii) poor projects are benefited from such higher returns.

(i) Owner's Considerations

The dividend policy is also to be affected by the owner's consideration of[1] :

(a) the tax status of the shareholders;

(b) their opportunities of investment; and

(c) the dilution of ownership.

(a) **The tax effect** has already been highlighted above under the head 'External Factors'.

(b) Owner's Opportunities for Investment

If the rate of return which is earned by a firm is less than the return which have been earned by the investors from outside investment, a firm should not retain such funds, which, in other words, will be detrimental to the interest of the members although it is difficult to ascertain the rate of alternative investment as well as alternative investment opportunities of its shareholders. Of course, the firm may evaluate such external rate from the firm's belonging to the same risk class. And, if it is found that the said rates is comparatively high, it should opt for a high $\left(\frac{D}{P}\right)$ ratio, or vice versa. Thus, while deciding dividend policy of a firm, external investment opportunities should also be carefully considered.

(c) Dilution of Ownership

(i) A high $(\frac{D}{P})$ ratio recognises the dilution of ownership both from the standpoint of control as well as from the viewpoint of earnings of the existing shareholders. These two aspects adversely affect the existing shareholders right. Because, in the latter case, (dilution of earnings) low retentions may compel the firm to issue first equity shares which will increase the total number of equity shares and, as such, the same will lower the earning per share (EPS) and market price will go down consequently. On the contrary, if percentage of retained earnings becomes high, dilution of earnings will be minimised.

---

1 Khan & Jain — *Financial Management*, op. cit., p. 599.

(ii) Nature of Earnings

If the income of a firm is stable it can afford a higher dividend pay-out ratio in comparison with a firm which has no such stability in its income. For instance, public utility consensus can have a higher dividend pay-out ratio since they have some monopoly rights which are not enjoyed by other companies who operate in a highly competitive market.

(iii) Liquidity Position

While deciding the dividend policy, the liquidity aspect should also be considered. Because, if dividend is paid in cash, there is an outflow of cash. It is interesting to note in this regard that a firm may have an adequate income/profit but it may not have sufficient cash to pay dividend. Thus, it is the duty of the management to see the cash position i.e., liquidity aspect—before and after the payment of dividends—at the time of taking decision about the dividend policy of a firm. If there is a shortage of cash, question of payment of dividends does not arise, even if the company makes a sufficient profit. This problem is, particularly, to be faced by new firms who are still in the process of extension and development. One particular point is to be noted by the management, i.e., to see that the liquid ratio must not be less than 1 : 1 after the payment of dividends.

(iv) Rate of Return

Dividend policy is also affected by the rate of earning profit. If the rate of return on capital employed (which is received by way of dividend) is lower than the return on outside investment, the shareholders will be interested to invest in outside securities than to invest in the existing firm.

(v) Divisible Profit

Divisible profit is that portion of profit which can legally be distributed by way of dividend to the shareholders of the company as the profit which is disclosed by a Profit and Loss Account is not the divisible profit. The Companies (Amendment) Act, 1960, contains a few specific provisions relating to divisible profit. Sec 205 provides that no dividend shall be declared or paid out of profits of the company arrived at after providing for depreciation or out of past profits or out of money provided by the Central Government or by the State Government for the payment of dividends in pursuance of the guarantee given by such Government.

Naturally, dividend policy depends on the divisible profit of a company.

(vi) Degree of Control

Usually, the shareholders do not want to sacrifice control over the company affairs for which they do not depend on internal sources of funds. As a result, they want to retain a major part of profit as retained earnings which is used for both working capital purposes as well as for long-term investment purposes. Thus, dividend policy is also affected by the degree of control over the firm.

(vii) Dividend Clientele

Dividend Clientele means a group of investors who prefer a particular type of dividend policy. Needless to say that low and zero tax payer naturally will prefer high $\frac{D}{P}$ ratio while investors who are under high-tax bracket will prefer low dividend expecting to compensate for the same from higher capital gains.

Optimum Dividend Policy

Optimum dividend policy means when market price per share reaches its maximum value at any particular $\frac{D}{P}$ ratio. This policy should be the primary objective of the firm.

Under the circumstance, the $\frac{D}{P}$ ratio is computed as:

$$\frac{D}{P} \text{ Ratio} = \frac{\text{Dividend Per Share (DPS) in Cash}}{\text{Earning per Share (EPS)}}$$

The following diagram will highlight the optimum dividend policy of a firm:

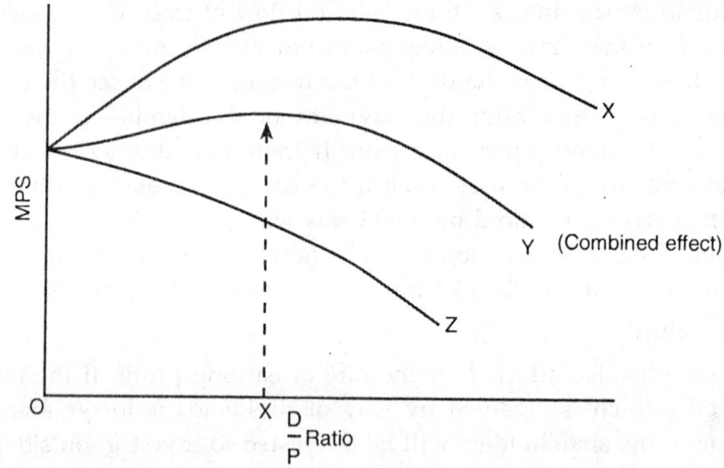

Fig 6.4: Optimum Dividend Policy

From the above diagram curve—X shows that when the $\frac{D}{P}$ ratio is high or the same increases, at first the market price of share increases, and after a certain level thereafter decreases, which indicates that higher $\frac{D}{P}$ ratio decreases retained earnings and restricts its growth. On the contrary, if the firm pays dividend out of its outside fund, the same will invite higher cost of capital. From the above, under the situation, Curve Z shows the fallings trend in market price of a share although $\frac{D}{P}$ ratio increases. And Curve Y shows the combined effect of the above factors on the market price of a share.

Thus, it becomes clear that when $\frac{D}{P}$ ratio is = X, MPS becomes maximum. It has already been stated above that every firm should try to maintain that $\frac{D}{P}$ ratio when the MPS will be maximum.

DIVIDEND THEORIES

Introduction

One of the important areas of Financial Management is the dividend decisions since a firm is to choose one between the two alternatives; viz., (i) distribute the profits to the shareholders by way of dividend, and (ii) retain them in the business, i.e., ploughing back of profit. We have already seen earlier that a cash dividend is generally welcome to a shareholder (particularly who is in low tax-bracket). But it does not necessarily mean that the firm-need is to be neglected. That is, while shaping the dividend policy of a firm the same must be considered. Formulating a dividend policy affects the retention policy of a firm as well. There is, practically, a type of reciprocal relationship between cash dividends and retained earnings—*larger retention, smaller dividends; while smaller retention, larger dividends.* Thus, the dividend policy and retention policy are competitive as well as conflicting. If dividend is paid in cash, the same will bring down the amount of retention which is also equally necessary for the growth and development of a firm. On the contrary, stable dividend policy presents a number of advantages (which have already been stated earlier).

However, we are to consider which alternative use is consistent with the object of wealth maximisation. In other words, if the payment of dividend leads to maximise the owner's wealth, the firm may use the net profit for paying dividends among the shareholders. In the opposite case, the firm is advised to retain the said profits for financing various investment opportunities. That is to say, there is a relationship between dividends and the value of the firm which should be carefully considered before taking any dividend decisions. But there are conflicting theories which affect the dividend decisions and the valuation of a firm. According to one school of thought, dividend decision does not affect the valuation of a firm since the dividends are irrelevant. On the other hand, according to another school of thought, dividend decisions affect the valuation of the firm since a firm's value may be measured in terms of market value of shares.

The viewpoints of the two school of thoughts may be classified under two groups :

(A) Irrelevance Concept of Dividend; and

(B) Relevance Concept of Dividend.

A. IRRELEVANCE CONCEPT OF DIVIDEND

This concept is supported by Franco Modigliani and Morton H. Miller and E. Solomon. According to E. Solomon, the dividend policy of the firm is a residual decision (**Residual Theory**) and dividends are a passive residual.[1] In other words, dividend policy has no effect on the prices of shares of a company and, as such, it has no significance.

According to them, dividends are irrelevant, or are a passive residual, i.e., in their opinion, investors are indifferent between dividends and capital gains. The ultimate desire of the investors is to earn higher return on their investment. If the firm has adequate investment opportunities which yields a higher rate of return in comparison with the cost of retained earnings, the investors would be content with the firm for retaining the earnings. In the opposite case, however, i.e., if the retention is less than the cost of retained earnings, the investors would prefer to receive earnings, i.e., dividends. So, it is needless to mention that a dividend decision is nothing but a financing decision. In short, if the firm has profitable investment opportunities, it will retain the earnings for investment purposes or, if not, the said earnings should be distributed by way of dividend among the shareholders/ investors.

RESIDUAL THEORY OF DIVIDEND

According to Solomon, E. and Pringle, J. J. dividend, investment and financing decision are interdependent and trade-offs must be made.[2] The firm must treat one of the following three basic decisions, viz.,

(i) the amount of new investment;

(ii) the debt-equity ratio; and

(iii) the $\frac{D}{P}$ ratio

---

1 Solomon, E. & Pringle, J. J.—*Introduction to Financial Management* — op. cit., p. 574.

2 *Ibid.*

as a residual,[1] or, it must take a policy of off-setting dividend payments by issuing fresh equity shares. In other words, the firm cannot use all the above three variables at a time unless it is interested to pay cash dividend and, simultaneously, issues fresh equity shares.

However, as a matter of policy in the long run, a firm cannot afford to:

(i) forgo alternative investments;

(ii) operate at a non-optimal debt-equity ratio/capital structure; and

(iii) finance dividend payments by selling shares.[2]

As a matter of long-run policy, none of the above is sensible and the only policy which avoids one of the above choices is to treat dividends as a long-run residual.[3] According to this theory, the equity earnings of the firm are first applied in order to provide equity finance which is required for supporting investments. The surplus (i.e., after financing all equity investments needs), if any, would be distributed among the equity shareholders as cash dividends. In other words, dividends are, practically, treated as a residual payment fulfilling equity investments needs. Similarly, if there is no surplus, naturally, no dividend will be paid. Under the circumstances, dividend policy is nothing but a financing decision.[4]

If we use dividend policy as strictly a financing decision, the payment of cash dividends is a *passive residual*.[5] We know the amount of dividend payout will fluctuate from period to period in keeping with fluctuations in the amount of acceptable investment opportunities available to the firm. It is interesting to note that if these opportunities abound, the percentage of dividend pay-out is likely to be 0. On the other hand, if the firm is unable to find profitable investment opportunities, dividend pay-out will be 100%. For situations between these two extremes, the pay-out will be a fraction between 0 and 1.[6] The treatment of dividend policy as a passive residual determined strictly by the availability of acceptable investment proposals implies that dividends are irrelevant, the investor is indifferent between dividends and capital gains (retentions).[7] This theory does not always mean that dividends may fluctuate from period to period along with fluctuations in investment opportunities. Thus, in anticipation of deficit, a firm may declare and pay dividends from its surplus funds created out of surplus over the past years.[8] If such forecasting is proved to be correct, the firm can fix up its dividend payment at a point by which accumulative distribution over the years corresponding to accumulative residual funds for such period. In short, the firm would retain earnings for investments in new projects up to the point where the marginal return on new investment equals the marginal cost of capital.[9] So whether the retained earnings would be used for investment purpose or not, the same depends upon the expected return on the available investment opportunities. If it is found that the expected return is more than the marginal cost of capital, the firm will accept the investment proposals within its limit without paying any dividend to the shareholders as the surplus/earnings are used for investment purposes, and vice versa in the opposite case. The same can be depicted with the help of the Fig. 6.5 on next page.

---

1 *Ibid.*

2 *Ibid.*

3 Ibid.

4 Van Horne, J. C.—op. cit., p. 277.

5 Solomon, E.—*The Theory of Financial Management*—Columbia University Press, New York, 1963, pp. 139-40.

6 Van Horne, J. C.—op. cit., p. 278.

7 *Ibid.*

8 Higgins, R. C.—*The Corporate Dividend—Savings Division*—Journal of Financial and Quantitative Analysis—7 March 1972, pp. 1531-38.

9 Paish, F. W. & Briston R. J.—*Business Finance*—Pitman, 5th Edn., p. 56.

Comments

Investment Schedule	X	:	indicates good investment opportunities in a year where the firm can use its retained earnings up to Rs. 50 lakhs, as, up to this point, the return exceeds the MCC.
Investment Schedule	Y	:	indicates fewer investment opportunities in a year where a firm can use its retained earnings up to Rs. 40 lakhs, when the return just exceeds MCC.
Investment Schedule	Z	:	indicates far lesser investment opportunities as it can invest only up to Rs. 30 lakhs and not more.

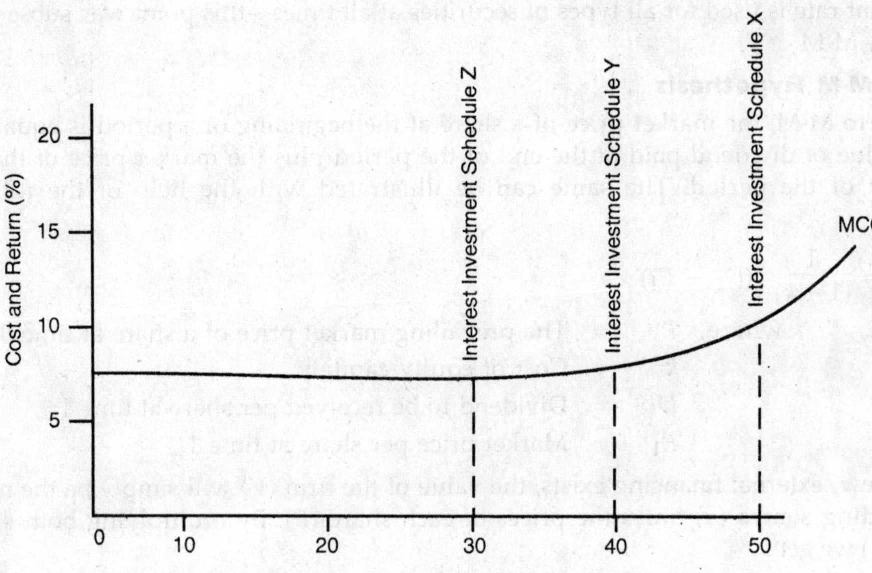

Fig. 6.5: New Investment (Rs. in 00,000)

MODIGLIANI-MILLER (M-M) HYPOTHESIS

Modigliani-Miller hypothesis provides the irrelevance concept of dividend in a comprehensive manner.[1] According to them, the dividend policy of a firm is irrelevant since it does not have any effect on the price of shares of a firm, i.e., it does not affect the shareholders' wealth. They expressed that the value of the firm is determined by the earning power of the firms' assets or its investment policy and not the dividend decisions by splitting the earnings of retentions and dividends.[†]

M-M Hypothesis—Assumptions

The M-M hypothesis is based on the following assumptions:

(i) *Existence of Perfect Capital Market*

---

1 Modigliani, F. and Miller, M. H. —*'Dividend Policy, Growth and the Valuation of Shares'*, Journal of Business, October 1961, pp. 411-33.

† According to them Under condition of perfect capital market rational investors, absence of tax discrimination between dividend income and capital appreciation given the firm's investment policy its dividend policy may have no influence on the market price of the shares"—Modigliani, F. and Miller, M. H.—*Some estimates of the cost of capital to the electricity utility industry*, 1954-57—American Economic Review, June 1966, p. 345.

It includes (a) information is available to all without cost; (b) there are no transaction costs, (c) no investor can affect the market price of shares, (d) flotation costs are neglected.

(ii) *Taxes do not exist*

That is, there is no difference in tax rates between dividends and capital gains.

(iii) ***Investors behave rationally***

It means that investors should prefer to maximise their wealth and, as such, they are indifferent between dividends and the appreciation in the value of shares.

(iv) ***Investment policy of the firm does not change, i.e., it is fixed.***

(v) ***Risk and uncertainty do not exist.***

In other words, investors may predict future prices and dividends with certainty and one discount rate is used for all types of securities at all times—this point was subsequently dropped by M-M.

Proof of M-M Hypothesis

According to M-M, the market price of a share at the beginning of a period is equal to the present value of dividend paid at the end of the period plus the market price of the share at the end of the period. The same can be illustrated with the help of the following formula :

$$P = \frac{1}{(1+k)} \cdot (D_1 + P_1) \qquad \ldots\ldots \quad (1)$$

where, P = The prevailing market price of a share at time 0;

k = Cost of equity capital;

D_1 = Dividend to be received per share at time 1;

P_1 = Market price per share at time 1.

If no new/external financing exists, the value of the firm (V) will simply be the number of outstanding shares (n) times the prices of each share (P). By multiplying both sides of equation (1) we get :

$$V = nP = \frac{n(D_1 + P_1)}{(1+k)} \qquad \ldots\ldots \quad (2)$$

If, however, the firm sells (m) number of new shares at time 1 at a price of P_1, the value of the firm (V) at time 0 will be :

$$V = nP = \frac{n(D_1 + P_1) + mP_1 - mP_1}{(1+k)}$$

$$= \frac{nD_1 + nP_1 + mP_1 - mP_1}{(1+k)}$$

$$= \frac{nD_1 + (n+m)P_1 - mP_1}{(1+k)} \qquad \ldots\ldots \quad (3)$$

It has been explained in this volume that the investment programme, at a given period of time, can be financed either from the proceeds of new issues or from the retained earnings or from both. So, the amount of new issues will be :

$$mP_1 = I_1 - (T_1 - nD_1) \qquad \ldots\ldots \quad (4)$$

$$= I_1 - T_1 + nD_1$$

where I_1 = total new investment during the period 1.

T_1 = Earnings/Profit for the period 1.

That is, total financing by the new issues is determined by the amount of investment in first period and not by retained earnings. By substituting equation (4) into equation (3), M-M revealed that the value of the firm is unaffected by the dividend policy, i.e., nD_1 term cancels out as:

$$nP = \frac{nD_1 + (n+m)\ P_1 - mP_1}{(1+k)}$$

$$= \frac{nD_1 + (n+m)\ P_1 - (I_1 - T_1 + nD_1)}{(1+k)}$$

$$= \frac{nD_1 + (n+m)\ P_1 - I_1 - T_1 + nD_1}{(1+k)}$$

$$= \frac{(n+m)\,P_1 - I_1 + T_1}{(1+k)} \quad \ldots\ldots \quad (5)$$

Thus, M-M's valuation model in equation (5) is consistent with the valuation equations (2) and (3) stated above in terms of external financing. As the value of the firm (V) can be restated as equation (5) without dividends, D_1, it proves that dividends have no effect on the value of the firm (when the external financing is being applied).

Illustration 6.1

A company has at present 1,00,000 shares. The company requires Rs. 10,00,000 to finance a new project of which Rs. 4,00,000 would be available out of profits after paying Rs. 10,00,000 as dividends. The balance amount can be raised either by issuing new shares or by new debentures. The company decides to procure finance through the issue of new shares. The market price per share at the end of the current year is expected to be Rs. 120.

If the cost of capital is 18%, determine the present value of share using M-M model.

[C.U. M.Com.]

Solution

According to M-M model, value of a share is:

$$P = \frac{D_1 + P_1}{(1+K)} \quad \text{where, } D_1 = \text{Dividend Per Share}$$

$$= \frac{\text{Total Dividend}}{\text{No. of equity shares}} = \frac{\text{Rs. } 10{,}00{,}000}{1{,}00{,}000} = \text{Rs. } 10$$

P_1 = Market Price per share = Rs. 120

K = Cost of Capital = 18% or 0.18

$$\therefore\ P = \frac{\text{Rs. } 10 + \text{Rs. } 120}{1 + 0.18} \quad \text{(putting the value in the above equation)}$$

$$= \text{Rs. } 110 \text{ (approx.)}$$

Illustration 6.2

A company currently has 1,00,000 shares. The company needs Rs. 10,00,000 to finance its new investments. The total earnings of the firm during the current year would be Rs. 10,00,000 and Rs. 5,00,000 would be paid by ways of dividends. The market price per share at the end of the current year is expected to be Rs. 110.

If the cost of capital is 15% ascertain the present value of a share under M-M model.

[C.U. M.Com.]

Solution

As per M-M model, the present value of a share is:

$P = \frac{D_1 + P_1}{(1 + K)}$ where, P = Present Value of a share

D_1 = Dividend per share

$= \frac{\text{Dividend}}{\text{No. of shares}} = \frac{\text{Rs. } 5,00,000}{1,00,000} = \text{Rs. } 5$

P_1 = Market Price per share at the end of the year = Rs. 110

K = Cost of Capital = 15% on 0.15

$\therefore \quad P = \frac{\text{Rs. } 5 + \text{Rs. } 110}{1 + 0.15}$ (putting the above values)

$P = 100$

So, Present Value of a share is Rs. 100.

Illustration 6.3

Omega Company has a cost of equity capital of 10%, the current market value of the firm *(V)* is Rs. 20,00,000 (@ Rs. 20 per share). Assume values for I (new investment), *Y* (earnings) and *D* (Dividends) at the end of the year as I = Rs. 6,80,000, *Y* = Rs. 1,50,000 and *D* = Re. 1 per share.

Show that under the M-M (Modigliani-Miller) assumptions, the payment of *D* does not affect the value of the firm.

[Delhi Univ., M.Com.]

Solution

Value of the firm (V) when dividends are paid :

(i) **Market price of the share at the end of the year :**

$$P = \frac{D_1 + P_1}{(1+k)} \quad \text{where, } \begin{cases} P = \text{Rs. } 20 \\ D_1 = \text{Re. } 1 \\ k = .10 \end{cases}$$

$$\text{or, Rs. } 20 = \frac{\text{Re.}1 + P_1}{(1+.10)}$$

$$\text{or, } P_1 = \text{Rs. } 22 - \text{Re. } 1$$

$$\text{or, } P_1 = \text{Rs. } 21$$

(ii) **Amount required for new financing :** where, $n = \frac{\text{Rs. } 20,00,000}{\text{Rs. } 20} = 1,00,000$

$$I - (Y - nD_1)$$
$$= \text{Rs. } 6,80,000 - (\text{Rs. } 1,50,000 - \text{Rs. } 1,00,000)$$
$$= \text{Rs. } 6,80,000 - \text{Rs. } 50,000$$
$$= \text{Rs. } 6,30,000$$

$$\begin{cases} \textit{And,} \\ I = Rs. 6,80,000 (given) \\ Y = Rs. 1,50,000 (given) \end{cases}$$

(iii) **Number of shares (*m*) to be issued :**

$$m = \frac{\text{Rs. } 6,30,000}{\text{Rs. } 21} = 30,000 \text{ shares}$$

(iv) **Value of the Firm :**

$$V = \frac{(n+m)P_1 - I_1 Y}{(1+k)} \qquad \text{(here, Earnings = } Y\text{)}$$

$$= \frac{(1,00,000 + 30,000) \text{ Rs. } 21 - \text{Rs. } 6,80,000 + \text{Rs. } 1,50,000}{(1.10)}$$

$$V = \frac{\text{Rs. } 27,30,000 - \text{Rs. } 5,30,000}{1.10}$$

$$= \text{Rs. } 20,00,000.$$

In order to show that the dividend payment does not affect the value of the firm (V), the value of the firm (V) is to be ascertained when dividends are not paid :

When dividends are not paid :

(i) **Market price of the share at the end of the year**

$$P_1 = P(1 + k) \qquad \text{(Since } D_1 = 0\text{)}$$

$$= \text{Rs. } 20\,(1 + .10)$$

$$= \text{Rs. } 22.$$

(ii) **Amount required for new financing**

$$I - (Y - nD_1)$$

$$= \text{Rs. } 6,80,000 - \text{Rs. } 1,50,000 \qquad \text{(here also } D_1 = 0\text{)}$$

$$= \text{Rs. } 5,30,000$$

(iii) **Number of Shares (m) to be issued**

$$m = \frac{\text{Rs. } 5,30,000}{\text{Rs. } 22} \text{ shares} = 24,091 \text{ (App) shares}$$

(iv) **Value of the firm**

$$V = \frac{(n+m)P_1 - I_1 + Y}{(1+k)}$$

$$= \frac{\left(1,00,000 + \frac{\text{Rs.}5,30,000}{22}\right)\text{Rs.}22 - \text{Rs.}6,80,000 + \text{Rs.}1,50,000}{1.10}$$

$$= \frac{\text{Rs. } 27,30,000 - \text{Rs. } 5,30,000}{1.10} = \text{Rs. } 20,00,000$$

Since the value of the firm in both the cases (i.e., when dividends are not paid, and when paid) is Rs. 20,00,000, it can be concluded that the payment of dividend (D) does not affect the value of the firm.

Criticism of M-M Hypothesis

It has already been stated in earlier paragraphs that M-M hypothesis is based on some assumptions. Under these assumptions, no doubt, the conclusion which is derived is logically sound and consistent although not well-based. For instance, the assumption of perfect capital market does not usually hold good in many countries. Since the assumptions are unrealistic in nature in real world situation, it lacks practical relevance which indicates that internal and external financing are not equivalent. The shareholders/investors cannot be indifferent between dividends and capital gains as dividend policy itself affects their perceptions, which, in other words, proves that dividend policy is relevant.

As a result, M-M hypothesis, is criticised on the following grounds :

(i) *Tax Differential*

M-M hypothesis assumes that taxes do not exist, in reality it is impossible. On the contrary, the shareholders have to pay taxes on the dividend so received or on capital gains. We know that different tax rates are applicable to dividend and capital gains and tax rate on capital gains is comparatively low than the tax rate on dividend. That is why an investor should prefer the capital gains as against the dividend due to the fact that capital gains tax is comparatively less and such capital gains tax is payable only when the shares are actually sold in the market at a profit. In short, the cost of internal financing is cheaper as compared to cost of external financing. Thus, on account of tax advantages/ differential, an investor will prefer a dividend policy with retention of earnings as compared to cash dividend.

(ii) *Existence of Flotation Costs*

M-M also assumes that both internal and external financing are equivalent. It indicates that if dividend is paid in cash, a firm is to raise external funds for its own investment opportunities. There will not be any difference in shareholders' wealth whether the firm retains its earnings or issues fresh shares provided there will not be any flotation cost. But, in reality, flotation cost exists for issuing fresh shares, and there is no such cost if earnings are retained. As a result of the flotation cost, the external financing becomes costlier than internal financing. Therefore, if flotation costs are considered, them external and internal financing, i.e., fresh issue and retained earnings, will never be equivalent.

(iii) *Existence of Transaction Costs*

M-M also assumes that whether the dividends are paid or not, the shareholders' wealth will be the same. When the dividends are not paid in cash to the shareholder, he may desire current income and, as such, he can sell his shares. When a shareholder sells his shares for current income, there remains the transaction costs which are not considered by M-M. Because, at the time of sale, a shareholder must incur some expenses by way of brokerage, commission, etc., which is again more for small sales. A shareholder will prefer dividends to capital gains in order to avoid the said difficulties and inconvenience.

(iv) *Diversification*

M-M considers that the discount rate should be the same whether a firm uses internal or external financing. But, practically, it does not happen. If the shareholders desire to diversify their portfolios they would like to distribute earnings which they may be able to invest in such dividends in other firms. In such a case, shareholders/investors will be inclined to have a higher value of discount rate if internal financing is being used, and vice versa.

(v) *Uncertainty*

According to M-M hypothesis, dividend policy of a firm will be irrelevant even if uncertainty is considered. M-M reveals that if the two firms have identical investment policies, business risks and expected future earnings, the market price of the two firms will be the same. This view is actually not accepted by some other authorities. According to them, under conditions of uncertainty, dividends are relevant because, investors are risk-averters and, as such, they prefer near dividends than future dividends since future dividends are discounted at a higher rate as dividends involve uncertainty. Thus, the value of the firm will be higher if dividend is paid earlier than when the firm follows a retention policy.

B. RELEVANCE CONCEPT OF DIVIDEND

There are some scholars (viz., *James, E. Walter, Myron, J. Jordan, John Linter, and Richardson* among others) who consider dividend decisions to be active variables while determining the firms' value, i.e., the dividend decision is assumed to be relevant. According to them, dividend policy of a firm has a direct effect on the position of a firm in a stock exchange. Because, higher dividends increase the value of shares whereas low dividend decreases its value in the market due to the fact that dividends actually present information relating to the profit earning capacity or profitability of a firm to the investors. We critically examine the two notable theories viz., (a) Walter's Model, and (b) Gordon's Model:

WALTER'S MODEL

Professor James E. Walter's model suggests that dividend policy and investment policy of a firm cannot be isolated, rather, they are interlinked; as such, choice of the former affects the value of a firm.[1] His proposition clearly states the relationship between the firm's (i) internal rate of return (i.e., r) and its cost of capital or the required rate of return (i.e., k). That is, in other words, an optimum dividend policy will have to be determined by the relationship of r and k. In short, a firm should retain its earnings if the return on investment exceeds the cost of capital and, in the opposite case, it should distribute its earnings to the shareholders. His proposition may be summed up as :

(a) **When $r > k$** *(Growth Firms)*

When $r > k$, it implies that a firm has adequate profitable investment opportunities, i.e., it can earn more what the investors expect. They are called *Growth Firms*. The optimum dividend policy, in case of those firms, may be given by a $\frac{D}{P}$ ratio (Dividend pay-out ratio) of 0. It means a firm should retain its entire earnings within itself and, as such, the market value of the share will be maximised.

(b) **When $r < k$** *(Declining Firms)*

On the contrary, when $r < k$, it indicates that a firm does not have profitable investment opportunities to invest their earnings. They are known as *Declining Firms*. In this case, rate of return from new investment (r) is less than the required rate of return of cost of capital (k), and, as such, retention is not at all profitable. The investors will be better-off if earnings are paid to them by way of dividend and they will earn a higher rate of return by investing such amounts elsewhere. In that case, the market price of a share will be maximised by the payment of the entire earnings by way of dividends amongst the investors. There will be an optimum dividend policy when $\frac{D}{P}$ ratio is 100%.

(c) **When $r = k$** *(Normal Firms)*

If $r = k$, it means there is no optimum dividend policy and it does not a matter whether earnings are distributed or retained as for all $\frac{D}{P}$ ratios ranging from 0 to 100 the market price of shares will remain constant. In other words, when the profitable investment opportunities are not available, the return from investment (r) is equal to the cost of capital (k), i.e., when $r = k$, the dividend policy does not affect the market price of a share.

---

1 Walter, J. E. — *'Dividend Policy — Its influence on the value of the enterprise'* — Journal of Finance, 18th May 1963, pp. 280-291.

Assumptions

Walter's Model is based on the following assumptions:

(i) All financing through retained earnings is done by the firm, i.e., external sources of funds, like debt or new equity capital, is not being used;

(ii) It assumes that the internal rate of return (r) and cost of capital (k) are constant;

(iii) It assumes that key variables do not change, viz., beginning earnings per share, E, and dividend per share, D, may be changed in the model in order to determine results, but any given value of E and D are assumed to remain constant in determining a given value;

(iv) All earnings are either reinvested internally immediately or distributed by way of dividends;

(v) The firm has perpetual or very long life.

Professor Walter has evolved a mathematical formula in order to arrive at the appropriate dividend decision to determine the market price of a share which is reproduced as:

$$P = \frac{D}{k} + \frac{r(E-D)/k}{k}$$

or,

$$P = \frac{D + \frac{r}{k}(E-D)}{K}$$

where, P = Market price per share
D = Dividend per share
E = Earning per share
r = Internal rate of return
k = Cost of capital or capitalisation rate

In this proposition it is evident that the optimal $\frac{D}{P}$ ratio is determined by varying 'D' until and unless one receives the maximum market price per share.

Illustration 6.4

PTS Ltd. furnished the following particulars. You are asked to compute the market price of a share using Walters' model:

Cost of Capital	12%
Rate of Return on Investment	15%
Dividend Per Share (Rs.)	5
Earning Per Share (Rs.)	10

Solution

According to Walter's model, market price of a share is calculated with the help of the following

$$P = \frac{D + \frac{r}{k}(E-D)}{K}$$

where, D = Dividend Per Share = Rs. 5
r = Rate of return on Investment = 15% or 0.15

Contd.

$$\text{or, } P = \frac{Rs.5 + \frac{0.15}{0.12}(Rs.10 - Rs.5)}{0.12}$$

$= Rs.\ 93.75$

k = Cost of Capital = 12% or 0.12

E = Earning Per shares = Rs. 10

Illustration 6.5

X Ltd. furnished the following particulars. You are asked to calculate optimum pay-out ratio using Walter's Model

Total Investmnt of Rs. 5,00,000 in 5,000 equity shares.

Rate of Profitability	25%
Cost of Capital	15%

Solution

Note: As $r > k$ (in case of growth firm) optimum dividend pay-out ratio of the company would be zero.

As per Walter's mode the market price of a share is :

$$P = \frac{D + \frac{r}{k}(E - D)}{K}$$

where,

D = Dividend Per Share = 0

r = Internal Rate of Return = 25% or 0.25

k = Cost of Capital = 15% = 0.15

E = Earning Per Share $= \frac{\text{Earning}}{\text{No. of Shares}} = \frac{25\% \text{ of Rs. } 5,00,000}{5,000} = \frac{\text{Rs. } 1,25,000}{5,000} = \text{Rs. } 25.$

$$\therefore P = \frac{0 + \frac{0.25}{0.15}(Rs.25 - 0)}{0.15}$$

$= Rs.\ 278$ (approx)

Illustration 6.6

P Ltd. furnished the following particulars, you are asked to recommend the dividend policy (using Walter's model) and asceratin the price of an equity share on the basis of your recommendation.

No of equity shares (Rs. 10 each)	10,000
Expected earnings (Rs.)	80,000
Cost of Capital	10%
Estimate Rate of return on Investment is @ 8% and	14%

Solution

Condition 1

Note: Since cost of capital (k) is 10% or 0.10 and Internal rate of return is 8% or 0.08, it is a case of declining firm and not a growth firm i.e., $r < k$. So, according to Walter's model, $\frac{D}{P}$ ratio should be 100%. Thus, on the basis of the above the market price of share (P) will be:

$$P = \frac{D+\frac{P}{k}(E-D)}{K}$$

where, k = 10% on 0.10

r = 8% on 0.08

$E = \frac{\text{Earning}}{\text{No. of Shares}} = \frac{\text{Rs. } 80{,}000}{10{,}000} = \text{Rs. } 8.00$

D = Dividend Per Share = Rs. 8 (Since $\frac{D}{P}$ ratio is 100%)

$$\therefore P = \frac{\text{Rs.}8+\frac{0.08}{0.10}(\text{Rs.}8-\text{Rs.}8)}{0.10}$$

= Rs. 88

Condition 2

When r = 14% or 0.11 and k is 10% or 0.10 i.e., r > k. Since r is greater than k it is a case of growth firm. In that case the $\frac{D}{P}$ ratio would be zero. On the basis of these information, the market price of a share as per Walter's model will be:

$$P = \frac{D+\frac{r}{k}(E-D)}{K}$$

where,

D = 0

r = 14% or 0.14

K = 10% or 0.10

E = Rs. 8.

$$\therefore P = \frac{0+\frac{0.14}{0.10}(\text{Rs.}8-0)}{0.10}$$

= Rs. 112

Illustration 6.7

Ascertain whether the dividend policy (as per Walter's model) is optimum from the following particulars presented by P. Ltd. :

No of Shares (Rs. 10 each)	1,00,000
Total Earnings	Rs. 2,50,000
Dividend Paid	Rs. 2,00,000
$\frac{P}{E}$ ratio	12

Solution

We are to calculate at first the $\frac{D}{P}$ ratio:

$$\text{Rate of Dividend} = \frac{\text{Dividend}}{\text{Total Earnings}} \times 100 = \frac{\text{Rs. } 20{,}00{,}000}{\text{Rs. } 2{,}50{,}000} = 100 = 80\%$$

$$\text{Internal rate of return (r)} = \frac{\text{Earnings}}{\text{Total Investment}} = \frac{\text{Rs. } 2{,}50{,}000}{\text{Rs. } 10{,}00{,}000\ (1{,}00{,}000 \times \text{Rs. } 10)}$$

= 0.25

$$\text{Cost of Capital (k)} = \frac{1}{\frac{P}{E}\text{ Ratio}} = \frac{1}{12} = 0.083$$

As r > k, optimum $\frac{D}{P}$ ratio should be zero, i.e., whole earnings to be retained and no dividend should be paid.

Illustration 6.8

Cost of Capital (k) = 10%.

Earning per share (E) = Rs. 10.

Assume Internal Rates of Return (r) :

(i) 15%; (ii) 10%; and (iii) 8%, respectively.

Assuming that the $\frac{D}{P}$ ratios are : 0; 40%; 75% and 100%, i.e., dividend per share is (a) Rs. 0, (b) Rs. 4, (c) Rs. 7.5, and (d) Rs. 10, the effect of different dividend policies for three alternatives of r may be shown as:

When $r > k$	When $r = k$	When $r < k$
r = .15	r = .10	r = .08
k = .10	k = .10	k = .10
E = Rs. 10	E = Rs. 10	E = Rs. 10

Solution

Dividend Policy and the Value of Shares (under Walter's Model)

When $r > k$ (At different levels of D the value of P will be as under :)	**When $r = k$** (At different levels of D the value of P will be as under :)	**When $r < k$** (At different levels of D the values of P will be as under :)
(a) D = Rs. 0 $P = \dfrac{0+\frac{.15}{.10}(10-0)}{.10}$ = Rs. 150	(a) D = Rs. 0 $P = \dfrac{0+\frac{.10}{.10}(10-0)}{.10}$ = Rs. 100	(a) D = Rs. 0 $P = \dfrac{0+\frac{.08}{.10}(10-0)}{.10}$ = Rs. 80
(b) D = Rs. 4 $P = \dfrac{4+\frac{.15}{.10}(10-4)}{.10}$ = Rs. 130	(b) D = Rs. 4 $P = \dfrac{4+\frac{.10}{.10}(10-4)}{.10}$ = Rs. 100	(b) D = Rs. 4 $P = \dfrac{4+\frac{.08}{.10}(10-4)}{.10}$ = Rs. 88
(c) D = Rs. 7.5 $P = \dfrac{7.5+\frac{.15}{.10}(10-7.5)}{.10}$ = Rs. 112.50	(c) D = Rs. 7.5 $P = \dfrac{7.5+\frac{.10}{.10}(10-7.5)}{.10}$ = Rs. 100	(c) D = Rs. 7.5 $P = \dfrac{7.5+\frac{.08}{.10}(10-7.5)}{.10}$ = Rs. 95
(d) D = Rs. 10 $P = \dfrac{10+\frac{.15}{.10}(10-10)}{.10}$ = Rs. 100	(d) D = Rs. 10 $P = \dfrac{10+\frac{.10}{.10}(10-10)}{.10}$ = Rs. 100	(d) D = Rs. 10 $P = \dfrac{10+\frac{.08}{.10}(10-10)}{.10}$ = Rs. 100

Thus, according to Walter's Model, the optimum dividend policy depends on the relationship between the internal rate of return r and the cost of capital k. The conclusion is that the firm should retain all earnings if $r > k$ and it should distribute entire earnings it $r < k$ and it will remain indifferent when $r = k$.

Criticisms

Walter's Model has been criticised on the following grounds since some of its assumptions are unrealistic in real-world situation :

(i) Walter assumes that all investments are financed only by retained earnings and not by external financing which is seldom true in real world situation and which ignores the benefits of optimum capital structure. Not only that, even when a firm reaches the optimum capital structure level, the same should also be maintained in future. In this context, it can be concluded that Walter's Model is applicable only in limited cases.

(ii) Walter also assumes that the internal rate of return *(r)* of a firm will remain constant which also stands against real-world situation. Because, when more investment proposals are taken, *r* also generally declines.

(iii) Finally, this model also assumes that the cost of capital, *k*, remains constant which too does not hold good in real-world situation. Because, if the risk pattern of a firm changes, there is a corresponding change in cost of capital, *k*, also. Thus, Walter's model ignores the effect of risk on the value of the firm by assuming that the cost of capital is constant.

GORDON'S MODEL

Another theory on relevance of dividend has been developed by Myron Gordon.[1]

Gordon's Model is based on the following assumptions :

(i) The firm is an all-equity firm;

(ii) No external financing is available or used. Only retained earnings are used to finance the investment programmes;

(iii) The internal rate of return, *r*, and the capitalisation rate or cost of capital, *k*, is constant;

(iv) The firm has perpetual or long life;

(v) Corporate taxes do not exist;

(vi) The retention ratio, *b*, once decided upon is constant. Thus the growth rate, $g = br$, is also constant.

(vii) $k > br = g$.

According to Gordon's Model, the market value of a share is equal to the present value of an infinite future stream of dividends.

Thus,

$$P_1 = \frac{D_1}{(1+k)} + \frac{D_2}{(1+k)} + \dots\dots\dots\dots + \frac{D_x}{(1+k)^x}$$

$$= \sum_{t=1}^{n} \frac{D_1}{(1+k)^t}$$

1 Gordon Myron, J. — *The Investment, Financing and Valuation of Corporation*, Homewood, llinois, Richard D. Irwin, 1962.

It can also be rewritten in a simple way as :

$$P_1 = \frac{E(1-b)}{k - br}$$

where, P = Price of shares;

E = Earnings per share;

b = Retention ratio/fraction of retained earnings;

k = Cost of Capital;

br = g = Growth rate in r;

r = Internal rate of return.

Gordon clearly states the relationship between internal rate of return, r, and the cost of capital, k. He also contends that dividend policy depends on the profitable investments opportunities. However, his proposition may be summed up as :

(a) **When $r > k$** *(Growth Firms)*

When $r > k$, the value per share P increases since the retention ratio, b, increases, i.e., P increases with decrease in dividend pay-out ratio. In short, under this condition, the firm should distribute smaller dividends and should retain higher earnings, i.e., P increases with decrease in dividend pay-out ratio. In short, under this condition, the firm should distribute smaller dividends and should retain higher earnings.

(b) **When $r < k$** *(Declining Firms)*

When $r < k$, the value per share P decreases since the retention ratio b, increases, i.e., P increases with increase in dividend pay-out ratio. It can be proved that, as the value of b increases, the value of the share continuously falls.[1] If the internal rate of return is smaller than k, which is equal to the rate available in the market, profit retention clearly becomes undesirable from the shareholders' view point. Each additional rupee retained reduces the amount of funds that shareholders could invest at a higher rate elsewhere and thus it further reduces the value of the company's share.[2]

(c) **When $r = k$** *(Normal Firms)*

When $r = k$, the value of the firm is not affected by dividend policy and is equal to the book value of assets, i.e., when $r = k$, dividend policy is irrelevant. It implies that under competitive conditions, k must be equal to the rate of return, r, available to investors in comparable shares in such a manner that any fund distributed as dividends may be invested in the market at the rate which is equal to the internal rate of return of the firm. Consequently, shareholders can neither lose nor gain by any change in the company's dividend policy and the market value of the shares must remain unchanged.[3]

Illustration 6.9

A company's total investment in asset is Rs. 1,00,00,000. It has 1,00,000 shares of Rs. 100 each. It's expected rate of return on investment is 30% and the cost of capital is 18%. The company has a policy of retaining 25% of it profits.

Determine the value of the firm using Gordon's Model.

[C.U. M.Com.]

1 Dobrovolsky, Sergeil P. — *The Economics of Corporation Finance*, New York, McGraw-Hill Book Co., 1971, p. 55

2 *Ibid.*

3 *Ibid.*

Solution

According to Gordon's model, the market price of a share

$$P = \frac{E(1-b)}{k-br}$$

where, P = Price of share;

E = Earning per share;

$= \frac{\text{Earnings}}{\text{No. of Shares}} = \frac{\text{Rs. } 1{,}00{,}00{,}000 \times 30\%}{1{,}00{,}000 \text{ share}}$

$= \frac{30{,}00{,}000}{1{,}00{,}000} = \text{Rs. } 30$

b = Retention ratio = 25% or 0.25

k = Cost of Capital = 18% or 0.18

r = Internal rate of return = 30% or 0.30

or, $P = \frac{\text{Rs. } 30\,(1-0.25)}{0.18-(0.25 \times 0.30)}$ (Putting the values in the above equations)

$= \text{Rs. } 214.29$ (app.)

Now, ∴ Market Price of a share = Rs. 214.29

Value of the firm (V) = No. of shares (n) × Market Price of a share (P)

= 1,00,000 × Rs. 214.29

= 2,14,29,000

Illustration 6.10

X Ltd. presented the following particulars from which you are asked to determine the market price of a share as per Gordon's model.

	Rs.
Total Earnings	2,50,000
Total Investment in Assets	12,50,000
Total number of shares	50,000
Pay-out Ratio	50%
Cost of Capital	15%

Solution

As per Gordon's model, market value of a share (P) is equal $= \frac{E(1-b)}{K-br}$

where, P = Price of share;

E = Earning per share;

$= \frac{\text{Total Earnings}}{\text{No. of Shares}} = \frac{\text{Rs. } 2{,}50{,}000}{50{,}000} = \text{Rs. } 5$

b = Retention ratio = 1 – 0.50 = 0.50

k = Cost of Capital = 0.15

r = Internal rate of return

$= \frac{\text{Total Earnings}}{\text{Total Investment}} = \frac{\text{Rs. } 2{,}50{,}000}{\text{Rs. } 12{,}50{,}000} \times 100 = 20\% \text{ or } 0.20$

Pay-out ratio = (1 – b) = 0.50

or, $P = \frac{\text{Rs. } 5 \times 0.50}{0.15-(0.5 \times 0.20)}$ (Pulling the above value in the equation)

$= \text{Rs. } 50$

Illustration 6.11

The following information is available in respect of the rate of return on investments *(r)*, cost of capital *(k)* and earning per share *(E)* of X Ltd. :

Rate of return of investment *(r)* :

(i) 15%; (ii) 10%, and (iii) 8%.

Cost of Capital *(k)* = 10%

Earning per Share *(E)* = Rs. 10.

Determine the value of its shares as per Gordon assuming :

	$\frac{D}{P}$ Ratio i.e. $(1-b)$	Retention Ratio i.e. $b = \frac{R}{E}$
(a)	100	0
(b)	80	20
(c)	70	30
(d)	50	50
(e)	35	65

Solution

According to the formula developed by Gordon, the value of share is given by: $P = \frac{E(1-b)}{k - br}$

Therefore, the value of shares of X Ltd. for different $\frac{D}{P}$ and retention ratios for the three alternatives of *r*, i.e., (i) $r > k$, (ii) $r = k$, and (iii) $r < k$, is presented in the table:

When $r > k$	When $r = k$	When $r < k$
$r = .15$	$r = .10$	$r = .08$
$k = .10$	$k = .10$	$k = .10$
E = Rs. 10	E = Rs. 10	E = Rs. 10.

Dividend Policy and the Value of Shares (Under Gordon's Model)

When $r > k$. Value of P at different levels of 'b'	When $r = k$ Value of P at different levels of 'b'	When $r < k$ Value of P at different levels of 'b'
(a) $b = 0 \therefore br = 0$ $P = \frac{\text{Rs. }10(1-0)}{.10-0}$ = Rs. 100	$b = 0 \therefore br = 0$ $P = \frac{\text{Rs. }10(1-0)}{.10-0}$ = Rs. 100	$b = 0 \therefore br = 0$ $P = \frac{\text{Rs. }10(1-0)}{.10-0}$ = Rs. 100
(b) $b = .20 \therefore br = .20 \times .15 = .03$ $P = \frac{\text{Rs. }10(1-.20)}{.10-.03}$ $= \frac{\text{Rs. }8}{.07}$ = Rs. 114	$b = .20 \therefore br = .20 \times .10 = .02$ $P = \frac{\text{Rs. }10(1-.20)}{.10-.02}$ $= \frac{\text{Rs. }8}{.08}$ = Rs. 100	$b = .20 \therefore br = .20 \times .08 = .016$ $P = \frac{\text{Rs. }10(1-.20)}{.10-.016}$ $= \frac{\text{Rs. }8}{.084}$ = Rs. 95

Contd.

(c) $b = .30 \therefore br = .03 \times .15 = .045$ $P = \frac{\text{Rs. } 10(1-.30)}{.10-.045}$ $= \frac{\text{Rs. } 7}{.055} = \text{Rs. } 127$	$b = .30 \therefore br = .30 \times .10 = .03$ $P = \frac{\text{Rs. } 10(1-30)}{.10-.03}$ $= \frac{\text{Rs. } 7}{.07} = \text{Rs. } 100$	$b = .30 \therefore br = .30 \times .08 = .024$ $P = \frac{\text{Rs. } 10(1-30)}{.10-.024}$ $= \frac{\text{Rs. } 7}{.076} = \text{Rs. } 92$
(d) $b = .50 \therefore br = 0.5 \times .15 = 0.75$ $P = \frac{\text{Rs. } 10(1-.50)}{.10-.075}$ $= \frac{\text{Rs. } 5}{.025} = \text{Rs. } 200$	$b = .50 \therefore br = .50 \times .10 = .05$ $P = \frac{\text{Rs. } 10(1-.50)}{.10-.05}$ $= \frac{\text{Rs. } 5}{.05} = \text{Rs. } 100$	$b = .50 \therefore br = .50 \times .08 = .04$ $P = \frac{\text{Rs. } 10(1-.50)}{.10-.04}$ $= \frac{\text{Rs. } 5}{.06} = \text{Rs. } 83$
(e) $b = .65 \therefore br = .65 \times .15 = .098$ $P = \frac{\text{Rs. } 10(1-.65)}{.10-.098}$ $= \frac{\text{Rs. } 3.5}{.002} = \text{Rs. } 1{,}750$	$b = .65 \therefore br = .65 \times .10 = .065$ $P = \frac{\text{Rs. } 10(1-.65)}{.10-.065}$ $= \frac{\text{Rs. } 3.5}{.035} = \text{Rs. } 100$	$b = .65 \therefore br = .65 \times .08 = .052$ $P = \frac{\text{Rs. } 10(1-.65)}{.10-.052}$ $= \frac{\text{Rs. } 3.5}{.048} = \text{Rs. } 73$

The above table clearly shows :

(i) When $r > k$, the market value of share, P, increases with the retention ratio b for growth firms;

(ii) When $r = k$, the market value of the share is not affected at all by dividend policy; and

(iii) When $r < k$, the market value of share P increases with the payout ratio for declining firms.

Dividend and Uncertainty

It has already been explained while defining Gordon's Model that when all the assumptions are present and when $r = k$, the dividend policy is irrelevant. If assumptions are modified in order to conform with practical utility, Gordon assumes, that even when $r = k$, dividend policy affects the value of shares which is based on the assumption that under conditions of uncertainty, investors tend to discount distant dividends at a higher rate than they discount near dividends.[1] That is, there is a twofold assumption, viz., (a) investors are risk-averse, and (b) they put a premium on certain return while they discount uncertain returns. Because, the investors are rational and risk averters; as such, they prefer near dividends than future dividends. This argument is described a *bird-in-the-hand* argument which was put forward by Krishnan in the following words[2] : "Of two stocks with identical earnings, record, prospectus, but the one paying a larger dividend than the other, the former will undoubtedly command a higher price merely because stockholders prefer present to future values. Myopic vision plays a part in the price-making process. Stockholders often act upon the principle that a bird in the hand is worth more than two in the bush and for this reason are willing to pay a premium for the stock with the higher dividend rate, just as they discount the one with the lower rate." In short, a bird in the hand is better than two in the bush on the ground that what is available in hand (at present) is preferable to what will be available in future. On the basis of this argument, Gordon reveals that the future is no doubt uncertain and, as such, the more distant the future, the more uncertain it will be. Thus, if dividend policy is considered in the context of uncertainty, the cost of capital (discount rate) cannot be assumed to be constant, i.e., it will increase with uncertainty. Since investors prefer to avoid uncertainty and they are willing to pay higher price for the share

1 Pandey, I. M.— op., cit., p. 285.

2 Krishnan, John, E. — *Principles of* Investment — New York, Mcgraw-Hill, 1933, p. 737.

which pays higher current dividend (all other things being constant), the appropriate discount rate will be increased with the retention rate which is shown in Fig. 6.6 below:

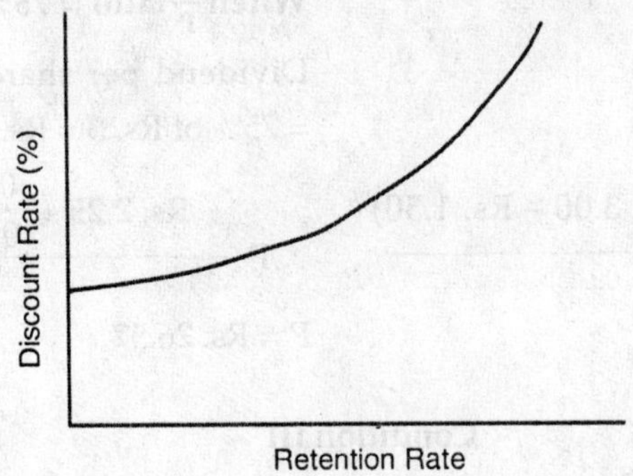

Fig. 6.6: Retention Rate and Discount Rate

Therefore, distant dividends will be discounted at a higher rate than the near dividends.

The above argument (i.e., the investors prefer current dividends to future dividends) is not free from certain criticisms. That is, this may not be proved to be true in all cases due to low capital gains tax, particularly applicable to the investors who are in high-tax brackets, i.e., they may have a preference for capital gains (which is caused by high retention) than the current dividends so available.[1]

GENERAL ILLUSTRATIONS

Illustration 6.12

The following date are available for XYZ Ltd.:

Earning per share	Rs. 3.00
Internal Rate of Return	15%
Cost of Capital	12%

If Walter's valuation formula holds, what will be the price per share when the dividend pay-out ratio is 50%; 75% and 100%?

[C.U. M.Com.—Adapted]

Solution

As per Walter, market value of a share:

$$P = \frac{D + \frac{r}{k}(E - D)}{K}$$

where, r = Internal rate of return = 15% or 0.15

E = Earning per share = Rs. 3.00

k = Cost of Capital = 12% or 0.12

D = Dividend per share

[1] Chakraborty, S. K., Bhattacharyya, K. K., Rao, N. K. & Sen, P. K. — *Financial Management and Control* — Macmillan India Ltd., 1981, p. 248.

Computation of Market Price per share

Condition I

When $\frac{D}{P}$ ratio = 50%

Dividend per share

= 50% of Rs. 3 = Rs. 1.5

$$\therefore P = \frac{\text{Rs. } 1.50 + \frac{0.15}{0.12}(\text{Rs. } 3.00 - \text{Rs. } 1.50)}{0.12}$$

P = Rs. 28.13

Condition II

When $\frac{D}{P}$ ratio = 75%

Dividend per share

= 75% of Rs. 3 = Rs. 2.25

$$\therefore P = \frac{\text{Rs. } 2.25 + \frac{0.15}{0.12}(\text{Rs. } 3.00 - \text{Rs. } 2.25)}{0.12}$$

P = Rs. 26.57

Condition III

When $\frac{D}{P}$ ratio = 100%

100% of Rs. 3 = Rs. 3.00

$$\therefore P = \frac{\text{Rs. } 3.00 + \frac{0.15}{0.12}(\text{Rs. } 3.00 - \text{Rs. } 3.00)}{0.12}$$

P = Rs. 25.00

Illustration 6.13

You are given the following information in respect of ABC Ltd.:

Earnings	Rs. 1,00,000
Equity Capital	5,000 shares of Rs. 10 each
Cost of Capital	10%

Expected rate of return (i) 9%; (ii) 10% and (iii) 12%.

Assuming that $\frac{D}{P}$ ratios are 0%, 50% and 100%, respectively, determine the effect of that different dividend policies on the share price of ABC Ltd. for the above-mentioned three alternative levels of rate of return using Gordon's model.

[C.U. M.Com.]

Solution

As per Gordon's model, the price of share is:

$$P = \frac{E(1-b)}{k-br}$$

where,

E = Earning per share

$= \frac{\text{Earnings}}{\text{No. of Shares}} = \frac{\text{Rs. } 1,00,000}{5,000} = \text{Rs. } 20$

k = Cost of Capital = 10% or 0.10

r = Internal Rate of Return = 9% on 0.09; 10% = 0.10, and

b = Retention ratio = (1 – b)

On the basis of the above, value of share at various rate of return and $\frac{D}{P}$ Ratio are:

Computation of Value of Share

When $\frac{D}{P}$ Ratio is (1 – b)%	When r = 0.09	When r = 10% or 0.10	When r = 12% or 0.12
0%	$P = \frac{Rs.\ 20 \times 0}{0.10 - (1 \times 0.09)} = 0$	$P = \frac{Rs.\ 20 \times 0}{0.10 - (1 \times 0.10)} = 0$	$P = \frac{Rs.\ 20 \times 0}{0.10 - (1 \times 0.12)} = 0$
50%	$P = \frac{Rs.\ 20 \times 0.50}{0.10 - (0.50 \times 0.09)}$ = Rs. 182 (approx)	$P = \frac{Rs.\ 20 \times 0.50}{0.10 - (0.50 \times 0.10)}$ = Rs. 200	$P = \frac{Rs.\ 20 \times 0.50}{0.10 - (0.50 \times 0.12)}$ = Rs. 250
100%	$P = \frac{Rs.\ 20 \times 1}{0.10 - (0 \times 0.9)}$ = Rs. 200	$P = \frac{Rs.\ 20 \times 1}{0.10 - (0 \times 0.10)}$ = Rs. 200	$P = \frac{Rs.\ 20 \times 1}{0.10 - (0 \times 0.12)}$ = Rs. 200

Illustration 6.14

A company has a total investment of Rs. 5,00,000 in assets and 50,000 outstanding ordinary shares at Rs. 10 per share (par value). It earns a rate of 15% on its investments, and has a policy of retaining 50% of the earnings.

If the appropriate discount rate of the firm is 10%, determine the price of its share using Gordon's model.

What shall happen to the price of share if the company has a pay-out of 80% or 20%?

[C.S. and I.C.W.A. Final]

Solution

According to Gordon's Model, the price of a share is:

$$P = \frac{E\,(1 - b)}{k - br}$$

where, P = Price of a share

E = Earning per share

$$= \frac{\text{Earning}}{\text{No. of Shares}} = \frac{15\%\text{ of Rs. }5{,}00{,}000}{50{,}000\text{ shares}} = \frac{\text{Rs. }75{,}000}{50{,}000} = \text{Rs. }1.50$$

b = Retention Rate = 50% = 0.50

k = Cost of Capital = 10% or, 0.10

r = Rate of Return = 15% = 0.15

(i) ***If Dividend Pay-out is 50%***

$$P = \frac{\text{Rs. }1.5\ (1 - 0.5)}{0.10 - (0.15 \times 0.5)} = \text{Rs. }30$$

(ii) ***If Dividend Pay-out is 80%***

$$P = \frac{\text{Rs. }1.5\ (1 - 0.8)}{0.10 - (0.15 \times 0.80)} = (-)\ \text{Rs. }15$$

(iii) ***If Dividend Pay-out is 20%***

$$P = \frac{\text{Rs. }1.5\ (1 - 0.2)}{0.10 - (0.15 \times 0.20)} = \text{Rs. }17.14$$

Comment

Cost of capital 'k' and rate of return 'r' do not make any change as a result of retention policy. If these two factors change, negative share price will not come.

Illustration 6.15

Calculate the market price of a share of ABC Ltd. under (i) Walter's formula and (ii) dividend growth model, from the following data:

Earning Per share	Rs. 5
Dividend Per share	Rs. 3
Cost of Capital	16%
Internal rate of return on Investment	20%
Retention Ratio	50%

[C.S. Final]

Solution

(a) As per Walter's Model

$$P = \frac{D + \frac{r}{k}(E - D)}{k}$$

$$\text{or, } P = \frac{\text{Rs. } 3 + \frac{0.20}{0.16}(\text{Rs. } 5 - \text{Rs. } 3)}{0.16}$$

$$P = \text{Rs. } 34.38$$

(b) **Dividend Growth Model** (i.e., Gordon's Model)

In case of growth is recorded in earnings and dividends the market value of a share will be (as per Gordon's model) as :

$$P = \frac{E(1 - b)}{k - br}$$

$$\text{or, } P = \frac{\text{Rs. } 5\ (1 - 0.5)}{0.16 - (0.5 \times 12)}$$

$$\text{or, } P = \text{Rs. } 41.67.$$

Illustration 6.16

A company has book value per share of Rs. 137.80. Its return on equity is 15% and it follows a policy of retaining 60% of its earnings.

If the opportunity cost of capital is 18%, what is the price of a share today as per (a) Walter's Model, and (b) Gordon's Model?

[C.A. Final—Adapted]

Solution

Opportunity cost of Capital	=	18% or 0.18
Return on Equity	=	15% or 0.15
Book Value per Share	=	Rs. 137.80
Earning per Share	=	15% of Rs. 137.80 = Rs. 20.67
Dividend per Share	=	40% of EPS = Rs. 20.67 × 40% = Rs. 8.27
$\frac{D}{P}$ Ratio (1 – b)	=	40% or, 0.40

(ii) Comment

A Ltd. (Growth Firm)

It becomes clear from the above that A Ltd. is a growth firm as its r > k; B Ltd. is a normal firm as its r = k and C Ltd. is a declining firm as its r < k. In the case of A Ltd. value of share is inversely related to its $\frac{D}{P}$ ratio. When $\frac{D}{P}$ ratio is increasing its market price is reducing. In this case, optimum pay-out ratio is found to be zero. When $\frac{D}{P}$ ratio is zero, the price of share becomes the highest.

B Ltd. (Normal Firm)

B Ltd. is a normal firm as its r = k. The most interesting point in this case is that the market prices of a share is Rs. 100 under all $\frac{D}{P}$ ratios. In this case, no optimum $\frac{D}{P}$ ratio or dividend policy exists.

C Ltd. (Declining Firm)

C Ltd. is a declining firm as its r < k. In this case, when $\frac{D}{P}$ ratio is 100%, market value of the share is found to be highest Optimum dividend policy, in this case, is presented by $\frac{D}{P}$ ratio which is 100% and, in this case, value of the share is found to be highest.

Illustration 6.19

E Ltd. had 50,000 Equity Shares of Rs. 10 each outstanding on Jan. 1, 2012. The shares are currently being quoted at par in the market. In the wake of the removal of the dividend restraint, the company now intends to pay a dividend of Rs. 2 per share for the current calendar year. It belongs to a risk-class whose appropriate capitalisation rate is 15%.

Using Modigliani-Miller model and assuming no taxes, ascertain the price of the company's share as it is likely to prevail at the end of the year (i) when dividend is declared; and (ii) when no dividend is declared.

Also find out the number of new equity shares the company must issue to meet its investment needs of Rs. 2 lakhs, assuming a net income of Rs. 1.1 lakhs and also assuming that dividend is paid.

[Delhi Univ., M.Com.]

Solution

Value of the Firm

(i) When dividend is paid

$$P = \frac{D_1 + P_1}{(1 + K)}$$

where, P = Rs. 10

D_1 = Rs. 2

K = .15

or, $\text{Rs. } 10 = \frac{\text{Rs.} 2 + P_1}{(1 + .15)}$

or, $\text{Rs. } 2 + P_1 = \text{Rs. } 11.5$

or, $P_1 = \text{Rs. } 11.5 - \text{Rs. } 2$

$P_1 = \text{Rs. } 9.5$

(ii) **When dividend is not paid**

$$P = \frac{P_1}{(1+K)}$$

$$\text{or,} \quad \text{Rs. } 10 = \frac{P_1}{(1+.15)}$$

$$\text{or,} \quad P_1 = \text{Rs. } 11.5$$

(iii) **When new equity shares *(m)* are issued**

$$m = \frac{1-(Y-nD_1)}{P_1}$$

$$= \frac{\text{Rs. } 2,00,000 - (\text{Rs. } 1,10,000 - \text{Rs. } 1,00,000)}{\text{Rs. } 9.5}$$

$$= 20,000 \text{ shares.}$$

Illustration 6.20

Y Ltd. belongs to a risk-class of which the appropriate capitalisation rate is 10%. It currently has 1,00,000 shares selling at Rs. 100 each. The firm is contemplating the declaration of a Rs. 6 dividend at the end of the current fiscal year, which has just begun.

Answer the following questions based on the M-M model and the assumption of no taxes:

(a) What will be the price of the shares at the end of the year, if a dividend is not declared? What will it be if it is declared?

(b) Assuming that the firm pays dividend, has net income of Rs. 10,00,000, and makes new investments of Rs. 20,00,000 during the period, how many new shares must be issued?

(c) Is the M-M model realistic with aspect to valuation? What factors might mar its validity?

[Delhi Univ., M.Com.—Adapted]

Solution

(a) **Value of the Firm**

(i) **When dividend is declared**

$$P = \frac{P_1 + D_1}{(1+K)}$$

$$\text{or, Rs. } 100 = \frac{P_1 + \text{Rs.}6}{\text{Rs.}1.10}$$

$$\text{or,} \quad P_1 = \text{Rs. } 104.$$

(ii) **When dividend is not declared**

$$P = \frac{P_1}{(1+K)}$$

$$\text{or, Rs. } 100 = \frac{P_1}{\text{Rs.}1.10}$$

$$\text{or,} \quad P_1 = \text{Rs. } 110.$$

(b) **Number of New Shares (*m*) to be issued**

$$m = \frac{1-(Y-nD_1)}{P_1}$$

$$m = \frac{\text{Rs. } 20,00,000 - (\text{Rs. } 10,00,000 - \text{ Rs. } 6,00,000)}{\text{Rs. } 104}$$

$$m = 15.385 \text{ shares to be issued.}$$

(c) No, the M-M model is not practically realistic with respect to valuation. Because, there are some factors which ignores the validity of M-M hypothesis to valuation, e.g. presence of flotation costs and transaction costs, Tax rate difference between capital gains and ordinary income etc.

Illustration 6.21

(a) The Apex Co., which earns Rs. 5 per share, is capitalised at 10% and has a return on investment of 12%.

Using Walter's dividend policy model, determine (i) the optimum pay-out; (ii) the price of share at this pay-out.

(b) The Agro Chemicals Co. belongs to a risk-class for which the appropriate capitalisation rate is 10%. It currently has 1,00,000 shares selling at Rs. 100 each. The firm is contemplating the declaration of Rs. 5 as dividend at the end of the current financial year, which has just began.

What will be the price of the share at the end of the year, if a dividend is not declared?

What will it be if one is?

Answer these on the basis of M-M model and assume no taxes.

[Delhi Univ., M.Com.]

Solution

(a) It has been pointed out while discussing Walter's Model that the optimum dividend policy may be given by a $\frac{D}{P}$ ratio (Dividend Pay Out Ratio) of 0 as $r > k$. It means that a firm should retain its entire earnings within itself and, as such, the market value of the share will be maximised. Thus:

$$P = \frac{D + \frac{r}{k}(E-D)}{k}$$

where

P = Market Price per Share

D = Dividend per Share

E = Earning per Share

r = Internal rate of return

k = Cost of Capital

$$P = \frac{12\%}{10\%} \text{ (Rs. 5)}$$

$$\text{or,} \quad P = \frac{\text{Rs. } 6}{10\%}$$

$$P = \text{Rs. } 60. \quad \text{(as D = 0)}$$

(b) (i) **When dividend is declared**

$$P = \frac{D_1 + P_1}{(1+K)}$$

or, $$\text{Rs. } 100 = \frac{\text{Rs.}5 + P_1}{(1+K)}$$

or, $$P_1 = \text{Rs. } 105.$$

(ii) **When no dividend is declared**

$$P = \frac{P_1}{(1+K)}$$

or, $$\text{Rs. } 100 = \frac{P_1}{1.10}$$

or, $$P_1 = \text{Rs. } 110.$$

Illustration 6.22

X Company earns Rs. 5 per share, is capitalised at a rate of 10%, and has a rate of return on investment of 18%.

According to Walter's formula, what should be the price per share at 25% dividend pay out ratio?

Is this the optimum pay out ratio according to Walter?

Solution

$$P = \frac{D + \frac{r}{k}(E - D)}{k}$$

Putting the values, we get,

$$P = \frac{\text{Rs.}1.25 + \frac{18\%}{10\%}(\text{Rs.}5 - \text{Rs.}1.25)}{10\%}$$

$$P = \frac{\text{Rs. } 1.25 + 1.8 \ (\text{Rs. } 3.75)}{.10}$$

$$P = \text{Rs. } 80$$

The price per share is Rs. 80 when dividend pay-out ratio is 25%, as per Walter's formula. It is not the optimum dividend pay out ratio as he suggests a 0% dividend pay-out ratio at situations where $r > k$ in order to maximise the value of the firm. Thus, it is needless to say that 0% $\frac{D}{P}$ ratio would be optimum since at this ratio the value of the share will be highest, i.e., Rs. 90, which is calculated as:

$$P = \frac{0 + \frac{18\%}{10\%}(\text{Rs.}5)}{10\%}$$

or, $$P = \frac{\text{Rs. } 1.8 \times \text{Rs. } 5}{10}$$

or, $$P = \text{Rs. } 90$$

ASSIGNMENT MATERIALS

THEORETICAL

Multiple Choice Questions

1. (a) Cash dividend refers to payment of dividend in:

(i) Cash (ii) Shares
(iii) Cash and share (iv) None of these

(b) Dividend can be paid out of:

(i) Capital Profit (ii) Current Profit
(iii) Past Profit (iv) None of these

(c) Optimum Dividend Policy is when:

(i) $\frac{D}{P}$ Ratio = $\frac{EPS}{DPS}$ (ii) $\frac{Earning}{DPS}$
(iii) $\frac{DPS \text{ in Cash}}{EPS}$ (iv) None of these

(d) As per M-M Model, market price of a share is:

(i) $P = \frac{D_1 + P_1}{(1 + K)}$ (ii) $P = \frac{(1 + k)}{D_1 + P_1}$
(iii) $P = \frac{D_1 + P_1}{1 - (1 + K)}$ (iv) None of these

(e) As per Walter's Model, market price of a share is:

(i) $P = \frac{\frac{r}{k}}{k}$ (ii) $P = \frac{\frac{r}{k}(E - D)}{K}$
(iii) $P = \frac{D + \frac{r}{k}(E - D)}{k}$ (iv) None of these

(f) As per Gordon's model, market price of a share is:

(i) $P = \frac{E(1-b)}{k - br}$ (ii) $P = \frac{k - br}{E(1 - b)}$
(iii) $P = \frac{(1 - b)}{K - br}$ (iv) None of these

(g) Interial dividend is declared in-between:

(i) Two AGM (ii) Two years
(iii) AGM (iv) None of these

(h) $\frac{D}{P}$ Ratio is calculated as:

(i) $\frac{\text{Dividend paid}}{\text{Net Profit (after tax)}}$ (ii) $\frac{\text{Earnings}}{\text{Net Profit}}$
(iii) $\frac{\text{Dividend Paid}}{\text{No. of shares}}$ (iv) None of these

[Ans. (a) (i); (b) (ii); (c) (iii); (d) (i); (e)(iii); (f) (i); (g) (i); (h) (i)]

Short Answer-type Questions

2. Explain the different types of dividend.
3. What is Dividend Policy? Explain the factors that are considered while ascertaining the dividend policy of a firm.
4. Define stability of dividend with the help of a diagram.
5. Define (i) Constant Percentage of Net Earnings, and (ii) Constant Dividend per share plus Extra Dividend.
6. Explain the danger of Stability of Dividend.
7. (a) What is $\frac{D}{P}$ Ratio? On which factors does it depend?

   (b) Write six determinants of dividend policy.
8. What are the effects of high $\frac{D}{P}$ Ratio and low $\frac{D}{P}$ Ratio?
9. Wht is Optimum Dividend Policy?
10. What is Irrelevance Concept of Dividend and Residual Theory of Dividend?
11. Discuss the factors which are relevant for determining the pay-out ratio.

Long Answer-type Questions

12. What is stable dividend policy? Why should it be followed? What are the effects of changing a stable dividend policy?
13. What is the difference between a policy of stable $\frac{D}{P}$ Ratio and a policy of stable dividend?
14. How far do you agree with the proposition that dividends are irrelevant?

    [Delhi, M.Com.]
15. What are the factors which influence management decisions to pay dividend of a certain amount ?

PRACTICAL

1. Compute the market value of the shares as per Walter's formula if the productivity of retained earnings is (i) 20%; (ii) 10%, and (iii) 8%—from the following data presented by X Ltd. :

EPS	Rs. 10
Rate of Capitalisation applicable	10%

The company has the options of adopting a pay-out of 20%, or 40%, or 80%.

[Ans. (i) Rs. 120, (ii) Rs. 100, (iii) Rs. 96]

2. Compute the market value of shares as per Walter's Model from the following particulars presented by Y Ltd.:

Earnings	Rs. 5,00,000
Dividend Paid	Rs. 3,00,000
Number of Shares Outstanding	1,00,000
Rate of Return on Investments	0.15
Price-Earning Ratio	8

[Ans. Rs. 43.20]

3. Calculate the value of an equity share of each of the following three companies viz., X Ltd., Y Ltd. and Z Ltd. as per Walter's Formula, when $\frac{D}{P}$ Ratio, is (a) 0.50; (b) 0.75; (c) 0.25:

	X Ltd.	Y Ltd.	Z Ltd.
EPS	8	8	8
Cost of Equity Capital	10	10	10
IRR	15	5	10

Draw-up the conclusions.

[Ans.

X Ltd.	**(a)**	**Rs. 100**	**(b)**	**Rs. 90**	**(c)**	**Rs. 80**
Y Ltd.	**(a)**	**Rs. 60**	**(b)**	**Rs. 70**	**(c)**	**Rs. 80**
Z Ltd.	**(a)**	**Rs. 80**	**(b)**	**Rs. 80**	**(c)**	**Rs. 80]**

4. The shareholders' fund of ABC Ltd. for the year ended 31st March 2004 are:

	Rs.
Equity Share Capital	4,00,000
12% Preference Share Capital	1,00,000
Securities Premium	40,000
Retained Earnings	3,00,000
	8,40,000

The earnings available for equity shareholders from this period's operations are Rs. 1,50,000 (included as part of retained earnings).

Required :

(a) What is the maximum dividend per share (DPS) the company can pay?

(b) If the firm has Rs. 60,000 in cash, what is the largest DPS it can pay without borrowings ?

(c) Indicate which amounts, if any, will be affected if the firm pays the dividends indicated in (b) above.

[Ans. (a) Rs. 75; (b) Rs. 15; (c) Retained Earnings and cash]

5. A company belongs to a risk-class for which the appropriate capitalisation rate is 10%. It has outstanding 25,000 shares selling at Rs. 100 each. The firm is contemplating the declaration of dividend of Rs. 5 per share at the end of the current financial year. The company expects to have a net income of Rs. 2,50,000 and has a proposal for making a new investment of Rs. 5,00,000.

Show, under M-M assumptions, that the payment of dividend does not affect the value of the firm.

[Ans.

	When Dividends are paid	When Dividends are not paid
(i) Market Price of share	**Rs. 105**	**Rs. 110**
(ii) Amount required for new financing	**Rs. 3,75,000**	**Rs. 2,50,000**
(iii) No. of additional shares to be issued	**3,571 (approx.)**	**2,273 (approx.)**
(iv) Value of the firm	**Rs. 25,00,000**	**Rs. 2,50,000]**

6. X Ltd. earns Rs. 6 per share having capitalisation rate of 10 per cent and has a return on investment at the rate of 20 per cent.

According to Walter's model, what should be the price per share at 30 per cent dividend pay-out ratio? Is this optimum pay-out ratio as per Walter?

[C.A. Final—Adapted

[Ans. P = Rs. 102, No—D/P Ratio should be zero]

7. Y Ltd. has 1,00,000 equity shares of Rs. 10 each fully paid. The company expects its earnings at Rs. 12,00,000 and cost of capital at 10% for the next financial year. Using the Walter's model, what dividend policy would you recommend when the rate of return on investment of the company is estimated at 8% and 12%, respectively?

What will be the price of equity share if your recommendations are accepted?

[C.U. M.Com. Adapted]

[Ans. D/P Ratio = 100%, Market Price = Rs. 120.00

$\frac{D}{P}$ Ratio = 0%, Market Price = Rs. 144.00]

8. The Z Ltd. which belongs to a risk-class for which the appropriate capitalisation rate is 10%. It currently has 1,00,000 shares selling at Rs. 100 each. The firm is contemplating the declaration of Rs. 5 as dividend at the end of the current financial year, which has just begun.

What will be the price of a share at the end of the year, if a dividend is not declared?

What will it be if dividend is declared? Answer these on the basis of M-M model and assume no taxes.

[D.U. M.Com.]

[Ans. Rs. 110, Rs. 105]

9. A company belongs to a risk-class for which the appropriate capitalisation rate is 10%. It currently has outstanding 25,000 shares selling at Rs. 100 each. The firm is contemplating the declaration of dividend of Rs. 5 per share at the end of the current financial year. The company expects to have a new income of Rs. 2.5 lakh and has a proposal for making a new investments of Rs. 5 lakhs.

Show that under the M-M assumptions, the payment of dividend does not affect the value of the firm.

[P.C. College Test]

[Ans. When dividends are paid, P_1 = Rs. 105.

$n_1 = \frac{3,75,000}{105}$ shares, V = Rs. 25 lakhs

When dividends are not paid, P_1 = Rs. 110,

$n_1 = \frac{2,50,000}{110}$ shares, V = Rs. 25 lakhs]

10. Bestbuy Auto Ltd. has outstanding 1,20,000 shares selling at Rs. 20 per share. The company hopes to make a net income of Rs. 3,50,000 during the year ended 31st March 2012. The company is considering to pay a dividend of Rs. 2 per share at the end of current year. The capitalisation rate or risk-class of this company has been estimated to be 15%.

Assuming no taxes, answer the questions listed below on the basis of the Modigliani-Miller dividend valuation model:

(i) What will be the price of a share at the end of 31st March 2012

—if the dividend is paid?

—if the dividend is not paid?

(ii) How many new shares should the company issue if the dividend is paid and the company needs Rs. 7,40,000 for an approved investement expenditure during the year?

[C.A. Final]

[Ans. (i) Rs. 21, Rs. 23 (ii) 30,000 shares]

CHAPTER 7

MANAGEMENT OF WORKING CAPITAL

Definition

In order to maintain flows of revenue from operations, every firm needs certain amount of current assets. For example, Cash is required by a firm either to pay for expenses or to meet obligations for service received or goods purchased etc. On the identical plane, inventories are required to provide the link between production and sale. Similarly, accounts receivables generate when goods are sold on credit.

Cash, Bank, Debtors, Bills Receivables, Closing Stock (including Raw Materials, Work-in-Progress and Finished Goods), Prepayments and certain other Deposits and Investments—which are temporary in nature—represent Current Assets of a firm. Economists like Mead, Mallot, Backer and Field are of the opinion that the whole of these current assets form the Working Capital of a firm. And this concept of Working Capital of a firm is frequently termed as Gross Working Capital in the arena of Financial Management[1]:

Gross Working Capital = *Total Current Assets*

or, " " " = *Long-term Internal Liabilities plus Long-term Debts plus the Current Liabilities minus the amount blocked in the Fixed Assets.*

There is also another opinion regarding the concept of working capital. Prof. H. G. Guthmann and H. E. Dougall, for example, define working capital as the excess of current assets over current liabilities.[2] That is, the amount of current assets that would remain in a firm if all its current liabilities are paid.[3] This concept of working capital is known as Net Working Capital in the contemporary literature on Financial Management. Of course, this aspect of working capital is a more realistic approach. than the Gross Working Capital concept.

Net Working Capital = *Current Assets minus Current Liabilities*

or, " " " = Equity plus Long-term Debts minus as much as blocked is Fixed Assets

Significance of Working Capital

(a) It is needless to emphasise the importance of working capital in a firm. It is the primary objective of any business to make profit by buying and selling transactions. In order to fulfil the basic objective it is necessary to produce goods. And that is why, without working capital, question of production does not arise. Production process is started after

---

1 Kutchal, S. C.—*Corporate Finance—Principles and Problems*—Chaitanya Publishing House, 7th Edn., p. 149.

2 Guthmann, H. G. and Dougall, H. E.—*Corporate Finance Policy*—Prentice-Hall, New York, 3rd Edn., p. 387.

3 Myer, J. N.—*Fiancial Statement Analysis*—Prentice-Hall of India Ltd., 1974, p. 99.

purchasing raw materials. Moreover, liquid cash is not always available immediately after sale. For this, a large amount of capital is blocked in different phases of production, viz., Work-in-Progress, Finished Goods, Debtors etc. which are inevitable to the firm. This multi-faceted process is not completed without working capital.

(b) A major part of the total assets of the firm is composed of working capital. A survey had been made by the Reserve Bank of India during the 1970s to show that $\frac{2}{3}$ rd of the total assets had been financed by working capital.

(c) It is not possible for a firm to acquire modern machines and equipments which are vital for the survival of the business without sufficient working capital, i.e., proper utilisation of fixed capital becomes impossible. As a result, depreciation of assets and interest on that borrowed capital which have been used are to be borne by them unnecessarily.

(d) It becomes possible to ascertain the profit-earning capacity from the application and proper utilisation of working capital.

(e) The repaying capacity of the firm can be known from the working capital. The same is possible after analysing and scrutinising the working capital position. It is not possible for a firm to repay its short term liabilities in the absence of adequate working capital. For the purpose, the importance of working capital cannot be ignored.

(f) A firm may avail of the opportunities available in the market if it has sufficient working capital. For example, bulk purchase of goods at lower prices or at a discounted price.

(g) If a firm has adequate amount of working capital, timely payment of tax and discount may be made possible to maintain the goodwill of the firm.

(h) Unforeseen contingency may also be made in the presence of sufficient working capital. At the time of depressions a huge amount of working capital is required to meet the challenge. In addition, huge loss may arise due to insolvency of customers, regular payment for wages and salaries etc.

Problems of Excess or Inadequate Working Capital

It has been stated earlier that a firm cannot continue its operation without adequate working capital. That does not mean that it must carry excess or surplus working capital—which increases cost of idle capital. On the contrary, due to lack of working capital, day-to-day operational activities may not be performed. Thus, both surplus working capital or inadequate working capital are harmful to the firm.

Snags of Surplus Working Capital

(a) Since surplus working capital increases cost of capital, overall rate of return must be lower.

(b) Surplus working capital may be utilised by the firm for hoarding stock—this is not desirable.

(c) Collection from customers may not be made possible—this may increase bad debts.

(d) Unnecessary accumulation of stock may be made by the firm—this should not be done, it increases idle cost.

Snags of Inadequate Working Capital

(a) Due to paucity of funds for working capital, day-to-day operational activities may not be made possible.

(b) Market opportunities (e.g., bulk purchase at lower prices, benefit of cash discount etc.) may not be taken.

(c) Due to lack of funds, a firm may lose its credit—worthiness since it cannot pay—off its maturing obligations as soon as it becomes due.

(d) It cannot avail of profitable investment opportunities due to insufficient working capital.

(e) The firm cannot utilise its fixed assets properly. Thus, depreciation of assets or interest on capital blocked in fixed assets increase cost.

Need for Working Capital

In order to earn sufficient profits, a firm has to depend on its sales activities apart from others. We know that sales are not always converted into cash immediately, i.e., there is a time-lag between the sale product and the realisation of cash. So, an adequate amount of working capital is required by a firm in the form of different current assets for its activities to continue uninterrupted and to tackle the problems that may arise because of the time-lag. Practically, this happens simply owing to the *'Operating Cycle'* or *'Cash Cycle'*, or *'Operating Cash Cycle'* which involves the following steps:

(a) Conversion of Cash into Inventory;

(b) Conversion of Inventory into Receivable;

(c) Conversion of Receivables into Cash.[1]

Classification of Working Capital

The working capital admits of two broad classifications:

(a) Regular or Fixed or Core or Permanent Working Capital;

(b) Variable or Seasonal or Temporary Working Capital.

(a) Regular or Fixed or Core or Permanent Working Capital

The amount of current assets which are kept by a firm in hand day-in and day-out, i.e., throughout the year, is designated as Regular or Fixed Working Capital. In other words, in order to maintain the normal day-to-day activities, a certain minimum level of working capital is required on a continuous and uninterrupted basis which will have to be met permanently. Along with other fixed assets, they are considered as fixed working capital.

On the other hand, due to seasonal variation/fluctuation, investment in raw materials, W-I-P, finished products will fluctuate or fall. In consequence, this portion of the working capital is required in order to meet such fluctuation. It can also be stated that any amount over and above the permanent level of working capital is Variable or Seasonal or Temporary Working Capital.[2] We know that both fixed and variable working capitals are required to maintain the production and sales activities. Practically, variable working capital is required to meet the liquidity requirements for short-term obligations.

The difference between the fixed and variable working capital can better be represented with the help of Figs 7.1 and 7.2.

It is quite clear from Fig. 7.1 that permanent working capital is constant but variable working capital fluctuates, i.e., it is sometimes increasing and sometimes decreasing—according to the seasonal demands of the product.

---

1 Joy, O. M.— *Introducton to Financial Management*—Richard D. Irwin, Homewood, Illinois; 1977, p. 40.

2 *Ibid.*

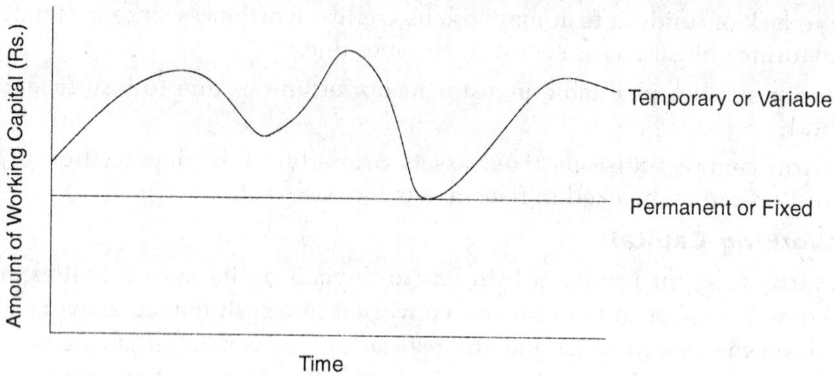

Fig. 7.1: Permanent and Temporary Working Capital

For a growing/expanding firm, the permanent working capital line may not be horizontal since demand for permanent current assets is increasing or decreasing. Thus, the difference between the permanent and temporary working capital for an expanding firm can be depicted as:

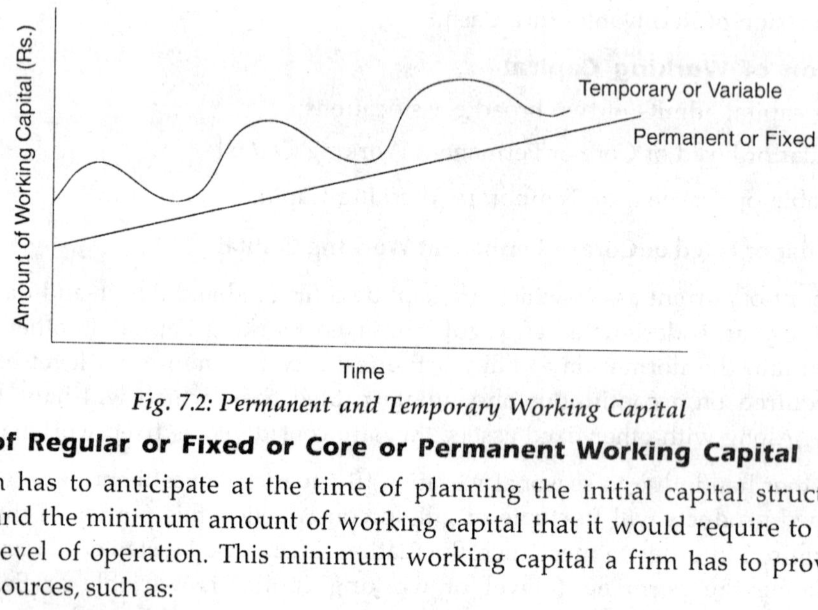

Fig. 7.2: Permanent and Temporary Working Capital

Sources of Regular or Fixed or Core or Permanent Working Capital

Every firm has to anticipate at the time of planning the initial capital structure of the company and the minimum amount of working capital that it would require to support its projected level of operation. This minimum working capital a firm has to provide out of long-term sources, such as:

(a) Issue of Shares;

(b) Issue of Debentures; and

(c) Retention in Various Forms (i.e., Ploughing-back of Profits, General Reserves etc.).

(a) Issue of Shares

Raising of funds by the issue of shares has certain distinct edges over other sources, especially the borrowed capital, which, once procured, is non-refundable except in case of liquidation and does not create any charge or encumbrance on the assets of the company, and does not impose any fixed charge for its use. It is advantageous for a firm to finance its *Fixed* or *Regular* or *Core* working capital requirements out of the proceeds of the issue of shares which, in common parlance, goes by the name of Ownership Capital.

(b) Issue of Debentures or Long-term Borrowings

Fixed or Regular or Core Working Capital may also be procured by issuing Debentures. As Debentures are fixed charge securities, besides being redeemable at the option of the company, the entire surplus after the payment of Debenture interest goes to the credit of equity shareholders—either in the form of increased rate of dividend or in the form of increased retention. Similar advantages also accrue if working capital is financed by long-term borrowings in other forms. But Debentures or long-term borrowings being non-starter,[1] it is difficult for a new firm to raise its working capital by resorting to these techniques. Besides, the redemption features of long-term loans and Debentures may create the problem of working capital finance, unless specific provision is made for their redemption and the said provision is kept invested in outside securities.

(c) Retention

Retention in the garb of free or General Reserve and/or credit balance of Profit and Loss Account may also become a source of working capital for an established company. Although it is essentially a means of financing for extension and development of a firm and its availability depends upon a host of factors—such as the rate of taxation, the dividend policy of the firm, Government policy on the payment of dividend by the corporate sector, extent of available surplus and upon the firm's appropriation policy—it is very often used to finance the working capital requirements of a firm.

Sources of Seasonal or Variable Working Capital

The firms which are seasonal in character in their business need a large amount of working capital for holding inventory during the peak period. But, as soon as the peak period is over, their working capital becomes idle. In the circumstances, such firms do not prefer to finance working capital by long-term sources as this exposes them to cost with no return therefore, during the slack session. Therefore, firms having seasonality in their business find it convenient to meet their working capital requirements by resorting to short-term sources, such as :

(a) Bank Loan;

(b) Public Deposits;

(c) Trade Credit and Other Payables;

(d) Provision for Taxation;

(e) Provision for Depreciation; etc.

(a) Bank Loan (including Cash Credit/Overdraft)

Firms usually prefer to use Bank Loan in the form of Cash Credit and/or Overdrafts by means of unsecured Promissory Notes for 90 to 180 days or against hypothecation of inventories or against endorsement of accounts receivable for financing their working capital.[2] The advantages of obtaining working capital finance by bank borrowings in the form of cash credit or overdrafts are that the borrower need not draw at once the whole amount of credit granted to him, but can do so by instalments as and when required. Secondly, he can put back any surplus amount which he may find with him for the time being. Finally, interest is payable by the borrower only on the amount to his debit at the end of each working day of business.[3] But, to what extent a firm can raise its working

1 Sur, A. K., *Principles of Corporate Finance*—Chakraborty & Chatterjee & Co., p. 37.

2 National Council of Applied Economic Research, *Structure of Working Capital*, New Delhi, p. 22.

3 Sarkar, J. B.—*An Analysis of the nature and changes of the Capital Structure of the Central Govt. Companies—1960-61 to 1969-70*. An unpublished Ph.D. dissertation (CU), p. 202.

capital by resorting to these techniques of financing depends—apart from its ability to hypothecate or pledge securities—upon the credit policy of the Government.[1]

(b) Public Deposits

Another method of procuring finance to meet the requirement of short-term or seasonal working capital is from public deposits. It has been a major source of finance for working capital in the field of cotton-textile mills of Mumbai and Ahmedabad though it did not obtain in Delhi, Chennai and in other parts of India. Further, being essentially an unsecured loan in the past, it was found to arouse temptation for over-trading by borrowers with many grave consequences in its trail. consequently, with the growth of practice of making funds available for working capital purposes in India by commercial banks, the system of inviting public deposits for financing working capital requirements went into oblivion by the 1970s.[2] After the seventies, however, there has again been resurgence of public deposits as a source of working capital finance to industries in India as the same are finding it increasingly difficult to obtain their necessary working capital finance from banks.

(c) Trade Credit and Other Payables

Trade Credit is the credit granted by the seller of raw materials and goods etc. to manufacturers and/or, wholesalers. It generally takes the form of discount for cash payment on delivery and net for future payment. The rate of discount and the period of payment may, however, vary. Among the twin objectives of trade credit and other payables, one is to serve as a source of working capital finance and is referred to as *'financial'*.[3] The trend and significance of trade credit as a source of working finance, however, depends on several factors, like the size and the rate of growth of the company, its financial resources and Bank finance. Further, since Trade Credit is costlier than Bank loans, it is used as a supplement to Bank loans for financing the short-term requirements of firms. Other payables include accrued wages and salaries, commissions and dividends. These outstanding factor payments also help to provide working capital finance, however temporary it may be.

(d) Provision for Taxation

Under the Income-Tax Act, firms are liable to pay income-tax on the assessable net profit as per rates prescribed for the same from time to time by the Finance Act. As such, once the net profit of a firm has been ascertained, it makes provisions out of the said profit for payment of Income-tax. Normally, there is a time-lag between the creation of the provision for taxes and their actual payment. And, in the period, the resources as against this provision which remain within the enterprise may be used as a source of working capital.[4]

(e) Provision for Depreciation

Short-term financing is less expensive than long-term. But, at the same time, short-term financing involves greater degree of risk. In the circumstances, the choice of sources between short-term and long-term for financing working capital of a firm has to be decided with

---

1 Recently, however, in view of the Government policy for the maintenance of higher cash reserve ratio by banks on the one hand and responsibility to provide priority and primitive sector credit, to the extent of 51% of their available funds for advances to parties, by the end of the year 1981-82, on the other hand the banks are now finding themselves extremely handicapped in providing working capital finance to industries.

2 Saha, S. N.—*Public Deposits in Retrospect and Prospect*—Business Studies., Vol. VII, No. 1, Jan. 1982, pp. 53-54.

3 The other objective of trade credit is to facilitate sales and is referred to as *'industrial'* (vide—*National Council of Applied Economic Research, op. cit.*, p. 27.).

4 Banerjee, B.—*Cash Management—A Practical Approach*—The World Press, Kolkata, 1982, p. 19.

reference to the risk-return trade-off. Generally, however, in view of lower cost and flexibility, management usually finds it more convenient to finance its working capital requirements by relying more on short-term sources than on long-term sources.

In India, the role of the Bank in relation to working capital finance to industries, among others, was reviewed in 1975 at the instance of the Reserve Bank of India by a Study Group under the chairmanship of P. L. Tandon, as an imbalance was noticed between the growth of Bank credit and industrial production within the country. The Study Group, in its Report, not only suggested three distinct methods of working out the working capital gap of firms, but also mentioned that borrowers must provide 25% of total current assets out of long-term funds, i.e., owned funds plus long-term borrowings. The said 25% is being calculated differently at the aforesaid three distinct stages.[1]

Determinants of Working Capital

There is no hard and fast formulae for ascertaining the proper requirements of working capital. Because, it varies from firm to firm, industry to industry, and even in the different seasons of the same firm. Of course, a large number of factors influence the requirement of working capital, i.e., it depends upon a host of factors.

They are discussed hereunder one by one:

(a) Nature and Size of Business

The requirements of working capital of a firm is widely related to the nature and size of the business unit. For example, trading and financial firms require a large amount of investment in working capital but a significantly smaller amount of investment in fixed assets. Similarly, a service-oriented firm, e.g., transport or electricity generation, has a modest working capital requirement since it has a very short operating cycle and sales are made on cash basis. But, in the case of a manufacturing concern, which sells its product on credit basis and has a long operating cycle, it needs a large amount of working capital. Moreover, the size of the firm is also an important factor. Because, a smaller firm needs smaller amount of Working Capital on the basis of its production activities, and vice versa in the opposite case.

We know that the ratio of Current Asset to Total Asset determines the relative requirements of working capital. The following table shows the relative proportion of Current Asset to Fixed Asset/ Total Asset investment in various industries which confirm the wide variation in working capital requirement:

Name of Industry	Current Asset Investment (%)	Fixed Asset Investment (%)
Hotel and Restaurant	10 — 20	80 — 90
Electricity—General Supply	20 — 30	70 — 80
Ship Building	30 — 40	60 — 70
Iron and Steel and Chemicals	40 — 50	50 — 60
Tea Plantation	50 — 60	40 — 50
Sugar, Cotton-Textile	60 — 70	30 — 40
Tobacco : Trading and Construction	70 — 90	10 — 30[2]

1 *The Report of the Study Group to frame guidelines for follow-up Bank Credit*—Reserve Bank of India, 1975, pp. 27-29.

2 Ramamoorty, V. E.—*Working Capital Management*—Institute of Financial Management and Research, Chennai, 1976, p. 54.

(b) Production/Manufacturing Cycle

The production cycle involves the time-lag from the initiation of manufacture of goods to the finished product. Here, time-lag includes time from the procurement of raw materials (including processing time) to the production of finished goods. Thus, funds are blocked in materials, labour and overhead till the finished products come out. In short, there is a time-lag or gap between the procurement of raw materials and the production/sale of finished goods. For this purpose, working capital is absolutely required. Thus, the longer the time-lag—either in the storage of raw material, or in the processing period or in the finished product—the more will be the requirement of working capital, and vice versa in the opposite case. It may be remembered in this respect that if there is any alternative method for manufacturing a product which requires a shorter manufacturing cycle, that should be accepted. Sometimes some firms which produce heavy machinery or capital goods take some advance from their customers in order to minimise their investment in working capital.

(c) Business Fluctuation/Cycle

The requirements of working capital of a firm are largely affected by the seasonal and cyclical fluctuations which have a direct impact, particularly on the temporary working capital. Such situation is of two types, viz., (i) where there is upward swing, and (ii) where there is downward swing.

In the case of former, the turnover will be rapidly increased and, as a result, investment in inventories and debtors will correspondingly be increased in addition to the additional investment in fixed assets for increased productivity. For the purpose of additional investment by way of fixed capital and working capital, temporary borrowings can be obtained from the market. Similarly, in case of the latter, i.e., where there is a declining trend, the opposite situation will arise. In short, the turnover will be reduced so as to reduce the investment in inventories and book-debts etc. and, as such, short-term borrowings are not required. Thus, business fluctuations affect the size of working capital requirements, and so also the seasonal fluctuations.

(d) Production Policy

The requirements of working capital are also largely affected by the production policy of the firm. Because, in the case of a seasonal product, the firm has to concentrate on the two options—, either to purchase raw materials for manufacturing finished products for certain months of the year when the market is ready for sale, or, to produce articles throughout the year. In the latter case, however, the firms have to concentrate on manufacturing varied products when there is off-season for the original product. In other words, in order to utilise the physical resource and working force, this policy is quite justified, although a greater amount of working capital is required for the purpose.

(e) Growth and Expansion

It is needless to say that if a firm extends its production capabilities, more additional funds are required by way of fixed capital investments and current asset investments as well, although it is really difficult to ascertain precisely the relationship between the production volume and the needs of working capital. The critical fact, however, is that the need for increased working capital funds does not follow growth of business activities but precedes it.[1] As such, advance planning of working capital is absolutely necessary on a continuous basis in these cases.

---

1 *Ibid*, p. 58.

(f) Credit Policy of the Firms

We know that the amount of book-debts depend on the credit period allowed by the firm to its customers. If more credit period is allowed, the more will be the requirement of working capital. From the standpoint of liquidity and financial strength, we should always grant less credit period, i.e., the firm should be prompt in making collections. Industry average norms should be followed although it may be varied from customer to customer— depending on their personal behaviour and trend. Thus, every firm should follow a rationalised credit policy depending upon the credit status of the customers and other factors. Sometimes the firm should analyse the existing credit policy and modify the same, if necessary, by reviewing the credit-worthiness of various customers. Thus, credit policy of the firm affects the requirement of working capital.

(g) Operating Efficiency

We know that the management of every firm may contribute to a great extent to the working capital position by operating efficiency in the form of efficient utilisation of existing resources, improving coordination, eliminating waste etc. This operating efficiency accelerates the pace of the cash cycle and improves the profitability of the firm and reduces the pressure on working capital. Thus, the management can effectively use its materials, labours and overheads although they have nothing to do to control the prices of materials, labours and overheads.

(h) Profit Element

The amount of net profit which has been realised in cash is a source of working capital. Such realised cash profit can be determined after adjusting non-cash items, viz., depreciation, outstanding expenses etc. from the net profit. Practically, the net cash flow from operation must not be considered as they are available for use at the end of the financial year. Even as the company's operations are in progress, cash is used up for augmenting stocks, book-debts or fixed assets.[1] So, it is the duty of the financial manager to see whether the said cash which is generated is used for the right purpose in an efficient manner. We also know that if net profits are earned in cash, the entire amount cannot be utilised by way of working capital which would be affected accordingly. Thus, the cash which is generated from operation depends on some policies of the firm, viz., on taxation, depreciation, dividend etc.

The requirements of working capital also depends on whether the profit is retained or distributed by way of dividends. Because, if dividend is paid out of profit, cash reserves of the firm is reduced to that extent for which amount of working capital is reduced by that amount. On the contrary, if the said profit is not distributed by way of dividend, but retained, no doubt the working capital position will improve. Thus, whether the profit shall be retained or distributed depends upon some factors which are to be carefully studied by the financial manager.

Besides the above factors there are some factors which have direct bearing on working capital requirements of a firm. They are Dividend Policy, Depreciation Policy, and availability of Raw Materials. Thus, from the above discussion it becomes clear that the level of working capital requirements depends upon a host of factors which are partly internal and partly external.

---

1 Paul, Dr. S. Kr.—*The Current Ratio and its Significance under Indian Conditions* — An unpublished Ph.D. dissertation, p. 60.

Effect of Inflation or Price Level Changes

It is needless to mention that the financial manager will experience a serious problem if the price level increases. He must anticipate such changes while ascertaining the requirements of working capital. We know that under changing price level, a firm must maintain a higher level of working capital with its various components. In other words, in order to maintain the same level of current asset, a firm will need increased investment in different components if price level increases. But, a firm which can immediately increase the value of each product as a result of increased prices will not experience serious problems relating to current assets investment, but vice versa in the opposite case. Moreover, the effect of increased prices will be felt by various firms in different ways since individual prices may not move in the identical manner. That is, it may so happen that some firms do not face a serious problem in working capital management as a result of inflation while the others are affected badly by it. So, the effect of inflation will not be the same in the case of all the firms, i.e., some will face a serious problem while others will not.

Components of Working Capital

There are two components of Working Capital—Current Assets and Current Liabilities.

Current Assets

An asset is termed current asset when it is acquired either for the purpose of selling or disposing-off after taking some required benefit through the process of manufacturing, or which constantly changes in form and contributes to transactions taking place with the operation of the businesses, although such asset does not continue for long in the same form. As for instance, Cash is often parted with in exchange of goods or services or in repayment of certain liability, say Creditor. Similarly, Debtors as asset yield place to Cash on realisation or Stock-in-trade is replaced by Cash or Debtors on its sale—the former in case of cash sales and the latter in case of credit sales. So, they are not only short-lived but also change their form and one type of asset can easily be converted into another, say Cash is converted into Raw Materials, Raw Materials into Work-in-Progress, Work-in-Progress into Finished Products and Finished Products into Debtors in case of Credit sales and Debtors into Cash. That is why they are also defined as *Circulating Assets*. The aforesaid conversion of one item of current asset into another in a manufacturing concern has been depicted in Fig. 7.3 :

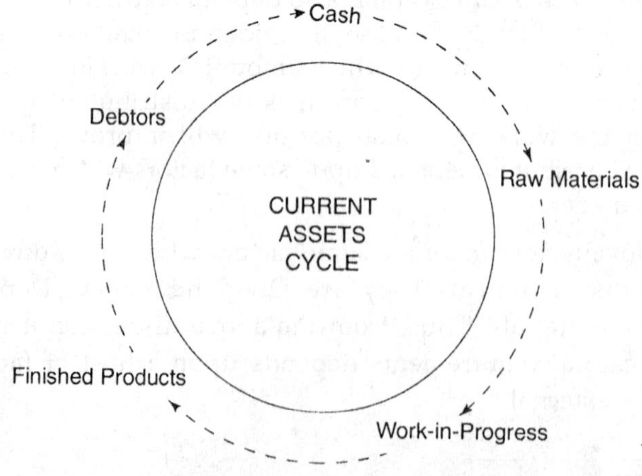

Fig. 7.3: Conversion of Current Assets or Working Capital Cycle

Time required for ultimate conversion of any component of current assets into cash is normally taken to be one year or less.[1] Nowadays, this concept has suffered a bit of change. It is not essential that current assets should always be converted into cash immediately. It may also be lost or consumed. For example, when salaries and wages are paid in cash, a part of cash is consumed and does not create any current asset through transformation directly. But when Cash is received from Debtors, Debtors are converted into Cash; Debtors here are not consumed but transformed or, rather, converted. The period of conversion in this case is also reckoned to be one operating cycle of the business instead of one year.[2]

The list of current assets comprises[3] :

Inventories (including Raw Materials, Work-in-Progress and Finished Goods and Spares), Sundry Debtors including Receivables (but net of provisions), Readily Realisable Securities and Tax Reserve Certificates, Short-term Investments, Accrued Incomes, Prepaid Expenses (not in the nature of '*deferred charge*') Cash at Bank, and Cash in hand.

Current Liabilities

Current liabilities are those which are repayable or liquidated within a short period of time by the use of the existing resources of current assets or by the creation of similar current liabilities. The short-period concerned is used to refer to a period not exceeding one year from the Balance Sheet date. But accountants at present, as in the case of current assets, are inclined to assess current liabilities also with reference to the normal operating cycle of the business so far as the time period is concerned.

Liabilities which fall due after a comparatively long period are known as *Fixed or Long-term Liabilities.* As distinguished from current liabilities, fixed liabilities are, therefore, those which are not repayable within one year of the Balance Sheet date, or normal operating cycle of the business. But a closer examination would reveal that, towards the end of their lives fixed liabilities also may be treated as current liabilities.[4] Debenture is a typical example of this type of liability, as the identification of the maturity of the same cannot be a problem in view of the legal requirements relating to the Balance Sheet of the corporate enterprise.[5]

List of current liabilities, therefore, includes Trade Creditors, Accounts Payable, Outstanding or Accrued Expenses, Bank Overdraft (of temporary nature), Outstanding Liabilities (e.g., compensation payable), short-term loans and borrowings and certain other obligations including different provisions, i.e., Provision for Taxation, Proposed Dividend etc.

---

1 Kohler, E. L.—*Dictionary for Accountants*—Prentice-Hall of India Ltd., New Delhi, 4th Edn., p. 136.

2 *Accounting Research and Terminology Bulletins*, American Institute of Certified Public Accountants, New York, 1961, p. 20.

3 Current Asset has another nomenclature as well, viz., Floating Asset. Some Floating Assets such as Cash, Bills Receivables etc. are in consideration of how rapidly they are converted into Cash, known as *Liquid Assets*. Similarly, the Floating Assets like Stock-in-trade are also known as Revenue Asset as it is directly utilised in earning revenue. (S. Sengupta, *A Textbook of Book-Keeping*, H. Chatterjee & Co., p. 8).
Liquid Investments, such as Investment in Govt. Bonds, money deposits at call etc. are sometimes treated as current assets, because it is intended to realise them at an early date. But if they are held as long-term investment, they are in the nature of fixed assets or non-current assets. (Yorston, Smyth and Brown, *Advanced Accounting*, N. M. Tripathi, Indian Reprint, Vols. 1 & 2, p. 347).
Prepaid expenses are usually shown as current assets for, if they were not paid in advance, they would require the use of current assets during the next accounting period. It may also be considered from another standpoint. Had they been not effected, cash to that extent would have remained in hand and, thereby, added to stock of current assets. But if the period covered by the prepaid expenses is more than one year, in other words, if it is in the nature of a deferred charge, it is a type of Investment and, to that extent, it cannot be classified as current assets. *Accounting Research and Terminology Bulletins —op. cit*, p. 30.

4 Holmes, Maynard, Edwards and Meier—*Intermediate Accounting*, R. D. Irwin, 3rd Edn., p. 770.

5 Chakraborty, H.—*Advanced Accountancy*, Naba Bharat Publisher, Kolkata, 2nd Edn., p. 1, 164.

In order to ascertain the real position of working capital, certain adjustments which are *abnormal* in nature are to be made against each component of current assets and current liabilities. At the same time, it is also to be looked into whether or not the current assets or current liabilities are window-dressed.

Working Capital : Positive or Negative

If current assets exceed current liabilities, it is called positive working capital, and if current liabilities exceed current assets, it is called negative working capital. If gross concept of working capital is used, there will always be positive working capital (since current liabilities are not deducted from current assets). On the other hand, if net concept of working capital is used, there may be positive, negative or nil (current asset = current liabilities) working capital. It can also be explained from another standpoint. If current assets are financed from long-term sources, working capital will always be positive. On the contrary, if fixed assets are financed from short-term sources, working capital will always be negative. The following example will make the principle clear:

Balance Sheet

as at ....

Liabilities	*Firm A*	*Firm B*	*Assets*	*Firm A*	*Firm B*
	Rs.	Rs.		Rs.	Rs.
Share Capital	10,000	6,000	Fixed Assets	12,000	12,000
Debentures (long-term)	5,000	4,000	Current Assets	8,000	8,000
Current Liabilities	5,000	10,000			
	20,000	20,000		20,000	20,000

Working Capital

Firm A = Rs. 8,000 – Rs. 5,000 = Rs. 3,000 *(Positive)*

Firm B = Rs. 8,000 – Rs. 10,000 = (–) Rs. 2,000 *(Negative)*

In Firm A, Current Assets are financed from long-term sources to the extent of Rs. 3,000 (Rs. 15,000 – Rs. 12,000); whereas, in Firm B, Fixed Assets are financed from short-term sources to the extent of Rs. 2,000 (Rs. 10,000 – Rs. 8,000).

Liquidity-Profitability Tangle

(a) ***Liquidity and its test***

Liquidity means one's ability to meet claims and obligations as and when they become due. In the context of an asset, it implies convertibility of the same ultimately into Cash and it has two dimensions in it—*time* and *risk*. The time dimension of liquidity is concerned with the speed with which an asset can be converted into Cash. Risk dimension is concerned with the degree of certainty with which an asset can be converted into Cash without any sacrifice in its book value. Viewed from this angle, all assets will have a degree of liquidity and assets that comprise of cash and *'near cash'* items are most liquid assets.[1] In the context of a firm, however, liquidity means its potential ability to meet obligations[2]. In the opinion of Solomon, E., and Springle, J., whenever one speaks of a firm's liquidity, he tries to measure the firm's ability to meet the expected and unexpected Cash requirements, to expand its assets, to reduce its liabilities or cover any operating losses.[3] Financial position a firm is considered to be solvent provided it has adequate liquidity.

1 Banerjee, B.—*Corporate Liquidity and Profitability in India*, Research Bulletin, Vol. 1, No. 2, I.C.W.A. pp. 225-26.
2 Myer, John, N.—*Practical Financial Statement Analysis*, op. cit., p. 245.
3 Solomon, E. and Springle, J.—*An Introduction to Financial Management*, Prentice-Hall of India Ltd., New Delhi, 1978, p. 97.

The liquidity is normally measured with the help of the following financial ratios :

(i) *Current Ratio;*

(ii) *Liquid Ratio;*

(iii) *Absolute Liquidity Ratio.*[1]

(i) *Current Ratio*

It is the relation between the amount of current assets and the amount of current liabilities. It is essentially a tool for measuring short-term liquidity and solvency position of firms. In other words, it may be stated that this ratio is taken to measure the margin of safety of current assets over current liabilities that the management of a firm maintains in obtaining business finance from short-term sources. Generally, a 2 : 1 ratio is considered as normal (i.e., for every two rupees of current assets there is only one rupee of current liability) and it expresses the satisfactory liquidity position. But current ratio alone cannot be accepted as an indicator of a firm's liquidity without qualification.[2] Because, there are some snags in it, e.g., the components of current assets and current liabilities may be window-dressed, or lack of common 'standard' etc. But it does not mean that it is of no use. Besides, some of the limitations may be overcome by proper action.

(ii) *Liquid Ratio*

It is the ratio between the total liquid assets to total liquid liabilities. The normal for such ratio is taken to be 1 : 1. As tool for assessment of liquidity position of firms, it is considered to be far better than that of the current ratio as it eliminates the snags in the same, since it indicates the relationship between strictly liquid assets whose realisable value is almost certain, on the one hand, and strictly liquid liabilities, on the other.

(iii) *Absolute Liquidity Ratio*

Liquid ratio measures the relationship between *cash* and *near cash* items on the one hand and immediately maturing obligations on the other. But as the composition of *cash* and *near cash* items in the calculation of liquid ratio comprises accounts receivable also, doubts have been expressed about the efficacy even of this ratio as a flawless tool for measuring liquidity position of a firm. It is argued that accounts receivable included in the denominator of liquid ratio may suffer in realisable value because of the possibility of bad debts, though, compared to inventories, accounts receivables are more liquid as an item of current asset. Therefore, a real measure of liquidity will be the ratio between cash and marketable securities to immediately maturing obligation which is known as *'Absolute Liquidity Ratio'*.[3] A firm judged by this ratio may be deemed sufficiently liquid and solvent if it is found to be in 1 : 1.

Since all current assets do not have the same liquidity and all current liabilities do not mature for payment with equal quickness, weights may be assigned on each individual current asset and current liability depending upon, however, the degree of their relative liquidity in case of current assets and relative urgency of payments in case of current

---

1 Please see the *Financial Statement Analysis* by the same author for further details.

2 According to E. W. Walker, the greatest fallacy using current ratio as a measure of solvency is that it ignores the Going Concern Concept in Accounting. To him, if all current assets are liquidated in order to meet the firm's obligations, the firm will have no Working Capital to carry on its operations and, for all practical purposes, it will be insolvent. (Walker, E. W.—*Essentials of Financial Management*—Prentice-Hall of India Ltd., New Delhi, 2nd Edn. p. 33.)

3 Joshi, N. B.—*Financial Analysis through Current Ratio—The Management Accountant*—I.C.W.A.— Vol. 14, No. 5, May 1979, p. 462.

liabilities in order to have a Weighted Current Ratio which is more dependable and reliable than the others.[1]

Again, a problem would remain — the sum of money received in future is less valuable than it is today, i.e., the problem arises from ***Time Value of Money.*** This problem can be tackled by the *Time Adjusted Current Ratio*[2] (through the process of discounting) which is much more dependable and representative for the purpose of testing short-term liquidity.

(b) ***Profitability and its test***

Profitability of a firm is represented by the rate of return on its capital employed. This is measured as:

$$\text{Profitability/Return on Capital Employed} = \frac{\textit{Net Profit}}{\textit{Capital Employed}}$$

$$= \frac{\textit{Net Profit}}{\textit{Sales}} \times \frac{\textit{Sales}}{\textit{Capital Employed}}$$

(where, Capital Employed = ***Net Fixed Assets*** + ***Working Capital)***

$$= \frac{\textit{Sales}}{\textit{Net Fixed Assets + Working Capital}}$$

[Scope of increasing efficiency of Fixed Capital being limited—as it is much of the outcome of scale of production—a firm's profitability mainly becomes a function of effective and efficient management of Working Capital.]

$$\text{The first part of the ratio} = \frac{\textit{Net Profit}}{\textit{Sales}}$$

$$= \frac{\textit{Sales} - \textit{Cost of Sales}}{\textit{Sales}}$$

It is clear from the above that the ratio between Net Profit and Sales can be increased either by reducing the Cost of Sales or by increasing the volume of Sales. Reduction in Cost of Sales is possible only when there is an effective management of working capital.

In the second alternative, increase in sales is associated with increase in variable cost. And, therefore, only an optimum use of working capital can ensure increase in profitability due to increase in sales.

Liquidity-Profitability Tangle : From what has hitherto been stated it becomes obvious that a firm, in its bid to maximise the rate of return on its investment, has first to strive for ensuring its most appropriate level of investment for working capital purposes. That is to say, its investment in working capital must be optimum—neither be in excess nor be inadequate. Secondly, once the most appropriate level of investment in working capital has been determined, the firm has to concentrate on the optimum use of the same. Where investment in working capital is much in excess of requirement, no doubt it will impair the firm's profitability. On the other hand, inadequate investment in working capital will tell upon the profitability of firms. Therefore, it may generally be assumed that there is always a negative relationship between the two. But that is, however, not true in all cases. It is only when the investment in working capital is optimum that firms can maximise their rates of return not only from the standpoint of profitability but also from the standpoint of liquidity. For existence of a linear relationship—though not continuous, between profi-

1 Roy, G. D.—*A Survey of Accounting Ideas*—Alpha Publishing Concern, 1963, pp. 454-55.

2 Pancras, U.—*Time Adjusted Current Ratio—The Management Accountant*, Vol. 16, No. 11, Nov. 1981, pp. 524-526.

tability and liquidity corresponding to the holding of current assets at least up to a certain level by firms—is not an impracticable proposition.[1]

FORECASTING WORKING CAPITAL REQUIREMENTS

It is not so easy to estimate the amount of working capital that may be required by a firm in order to maintain a particular level of operation. In other words, every firm finds it difficult to ascertain the working capital requirement which is a very practical and important problem. While inadequate working capital creates a lot of problems, an amount in excess of the requisite working capital which is not utilised properly and remains idle, can also increase the cost. Therefore, in order to avoid both these difficulties, ***a working capital requirement forecast*** is prepared after scrutinising and analysing every aspect of business activity.

1. **Trading Concern**

(a) ***Where the Balance Sheet of the earlier period is available***

The estimated requirement of working capital for the budget period can be determined on the basis of the data contained in the Balance Sheet of the earlier or previous period. The current assets and current liabilities are to be adjusted in relation to the budget period and the working capital requirement can easily be determined by deducting the estimated total value of current liabilities from the estimated total value of current assets.

Illustration 7.1

From the following information presented by X Ltd., a trading concern, you are asked to ascertain the estimated additional requirement of Working Capital:

Balance Sheet *(Extract)*
as at....................Assets side

		Rs.	Rs.	Rs.
Fixed Assets :				
	Land and Building	2,00,000		
	Plant and Machinery	1,00,000		3,00,000
Working Capital :				
Current Assets :	Stock	4,00,000		
	Debtors	3,00,000		
	Cash and Bank	1,00,000	8,00,000	
Less : Current Liabilities				
	Creditors	2,00,000		
	Taxation	60,000		
	Bank Overdraft	1,40,000		
	Outstanding Liabilities	1,00,000		
			5,00,000	
				3,00,000
				6,00,000

[1] Gentry, E. James — *Management Perceptions of the Working Capital Process.* Faculty Working Paper—College of Commerce and Business Administration. University of Illinois, 1976 (quoted from The Management Accountant, June 1981, p. 274).

Additional Information :

(a) It is estimated that the company will be able to increase sales by 25% in the following year.

(b) Maximum limit of overdraft facility granted by the Bank is Rs. 1,50,000.

(c) Credit period allowed to customers and the level of stock will remain unaltered.

Solution

Requirement of Additional Working Capital

		Current year level (as per B/S)	*Estimated increase*	*Estimated requirement*
		Rs.	Rs.	Rs.
A.	*Current Assets :*			
	Stock	4,00,000	1,00,000	5,00,000
	Debtors	3,00,000	75,000	3,75,000
	Cash and Bank	1,00,000	25,000	1,25,000
		8,00,000	2,00,000	10,00,000
B.	*Current Liabilities :*			
	Creditors	2,00,000	50,000	2,50,000
	Taxation	60,000	15,000	75,000
	Bank Overdraft	1,40,000	10,000*	1,50,000
	Outstanding Liabilities	1,00,000	25,000	1,25,000
		5,00,000	1,00,000	6,00,000
C.	*Working Capital :* (A – B)	3,00,000	1,00,000	4,00,000

D. Requirement of Additional Working Capital Rs. 1,00,000 (Rs. 4,00,000 – Rs. 3,00,000).

(b) ***Where the Balance Sheet of the earlier period is not available***

In that case, the amount of current assets and current liabilities for the budget period should be ascertained on the basis of the given data and deduct the current liabilities from current assets in order to get the estimated requirement of working capital.

Illustration 7.2

The components of Current Assets of a new trading concern are Stock. Debtors and Cash. The only component of Current Liabilities is Creditors.

Ascertain the concern's working capital requirements for the first year from the following information:

(a) Expected sales at a profit of 20% on cost	Rs. 9,00,000 (20% cash)
(b) Expected stock turnover	6 times
(c) Expected credit period to Debtors	2 months
(d) Expected credit period from Creditors	$1\frac{1}{2}$ months

(e) The concerns intends to maintain a cash balance equal to 1 months' Cash Sales

[C.U. B.Com. (Hons.)]

* Subject to the maximum limit of Rs. 1,50,000.

Solution

Ascertainment of Components of Working Capital

(a) **Stock**

Stock Turnover ratio = $\frac{\text{Cost of Goods Sold}}{\text{Average Stock}}$

$= \frac{\text{Rs. 7,50,000}}{\text{Average Stock}}$

∴ Average Stock = Rs. 1,25,000

Cost of goods sold = Sales – Gross Profit

or, = Rs. 9,00,000 – $\frac{1}{6}$ th of 9,00,000 as ($\frac{1}{5}$ th of Cost = $\frac{1}{6}$ th of Sales)

= Rs. 9,00,000 – Rs. 1,50,000

= Rs. 7,50,000

As there was no opening stock, so average stock is equal to Closing Stock.

(b) **Debtors**

Debtors Turnover Ratio = $\frac{\text{Debtors}}{\text{Credit Sales}} \times 12$ months

$2 = \frac{\text{Debtors}}{\text{80\% of Rs. 9,00,000}} \times 12$

or, Debtors = Rs. 1,20,000

(c) **Creditors**

Creditors Turnover Ratio = $\frac{\text{Creditors}}{\text{Credit Purchase}} \times 12$ months

$1\frac{1}{2}$ months = $\frac{\text{Creditors}}{\text{Credit Purchase}} \times 12$ months

[Credit Purchase = Cost of goods sold + Closing stock
= Rs. 7,50,000 + Rs. 1,25,000
= Rs. 8,75,000]

or, $\frac{3}{2}$ months = $\frac{\text{Creditors}}{\text{Rs. 8,75,000}}$

or, Creditors = Rs. 1,09,375

(d) **Cash**

Cash balance = 1 month's Cash Sales = Rs. 9,00,000 × 20% = Rs. 1,80,000 × $\frac{1}{12}$ = Rs. 15,000.

Requirements of Working Capital

	Rs.	Rs.
Current Assets		
Stock	1,25,000	
Debtors	1,20,000	
Cash	15,000	
		2,60,000
Less: ***Current Liabilities***		
Creditors		1,09,375
Working Capital Requirements		1,50,625

Illustration 7.3

EXE Ltd. is engaged in large-scale consumer retailing. From the following information, you are required to forecast their working capital requirement:

Projected Annual Sales — Rs. 65 lakhs.

Percentage of Net Profit on Cost of Sales — 25%.

Average credit period allowed to Debtors — 10 weeks.
Average credit period allowed by Creditors — 4 weeks.
Average stock carrying (in terms of sales requirement) — 8 weeks.
Add 10% to computed figures to allow for contingencies.

[C.U. M.Com.]

Solution

			Rs.
	Projected Annual Sales	Rs. 65,00,000	
∴	Projected Sales per Week	$\frac{\text{Rs. } 65,00,000}{52}$	1,25,000
Less :	Net Profit @ 25% on Cost or 20% on Sales		
	(Rs. 1,25,000 × $\frac{20}{100}$)		25,000
	Projected Cost per Week		1,00,000

Working Capital Requirements Forecast

		Rs.	Rs.
Current Assets :			
Stock (8 weeks) :	Rs. 1,00,000 × 8 =		8,00,000
Debtors (10 weeks) :	Rs. 1,00,000 × 10 =	10,00,000	
Add : Profit @ 25% on cost		2,50,000	
			12,50,000
			20,50,000
Less : Current Liabilities :			
Creditors (4 weeks) :	Rs. 1,00,000 × 4		4,00,000
	Working Capital		16,50,000
Add : 10% for Contingencies			1,65,000
∴ Total requirement of Working Capital			18,15,000

2. Manufacturing Concern

The following items are taken into consideration at the time of ascertaining the requirement of working capital:

(a) total quantity of units to be produced throughout the year;

(b) the cost of raw materials, wages and overheads for each unit;

(c) information about the period during which raw materials will remain in stock on an average before the same are issued to production—the longer the period the more will be the requirement of working capital;

(d) information about the period during which the product will be processed in the factory—the longer the period the larger will be the requirement of working capital;

(e) information about the period during which finished products will remain in warehouses, i.e., the length of sales cycle—the longer the period of stay, the more will be the requirement of working capital;

(f) information about the period of credit allowed by Debtors—the longer the period allowed to customers, the more will be the requirement of working capital;

(g) information about the period of credit allowed by suppliers—the longer the period, the less will be the requirement of working capital;

(h) information about the lag in payment of wages and overheads—the longer the period the less will be the requirement of working capital.

After ascertaining the proper requirement of working capital, a certain amount, say 10% of working capital, may be added to cover contingencies.

One is to remember that the facts which are based on estimates may not be cent per cent accurate, but by careful observation it is possible to make a reasonable assessment. The provision for contingency is made for this purpose.

To sum up, Statement of Working Capital Requirement Forecast may be computed in the following manner:

Statement of Working Capital Forecast

Current Assets :				
(a) Raw material	:	[Periodical R. M. Cost × Time lag in Stores (weekly or monthly, as the case may be)]		* * *
(b) Work-in-progress				
(i) Raw material	:	Periodical R. M. Cost × Processing time	* * *	
(ii) Wages	:	Periodical wages × Processing time	* * *	
(iii) Overhead	:	Periodical overhead × Processing time	* * *	* * *
(c) Finished goods				
(i) Raw material	:	Periodical R. M. Cost × Time-lag in warehouse	* * *	
(ii) Wages	:	Periodical wages × Time-lag in warehouse	* * *	
(iii) Overhead	:	Periodical overhead × Time-lag in warehouse	* * *	* * *
(d) Debtors				
(i) Raw material	:	Periodical R. M. Cost × Credit period allowed	* * *	
(ii) Wages	:	Periodical wages × Credit period allowed	* * *	
(iii) Overhead	:	Periodical overhead × Credit period allowed	* * *	
(iv) Profit	:	Periodical profit × Credit period allowed	* * *	* * *
		Total Current Assets		* * *
Less: ***Current Liabilities*** :				
Creditors for raw materials	:	Periodical Purchase Cost × Credit period received	* * *	
Creditors for wages	:	Periodical wages × Credit period received	* * *	
Creditors for expenses	:	Periodical expenses × Credit period received	* * *	* * *
		Working Capital		* * *

Under the second method, it is possible to know working capital requirement for each component of current assets and current liabilities. But this method cannot give information of working capital requirement for each element of cost directly as are available in the first method.

Columnar Or Matrix Method :

Statement of Working Capital Forecast

Particulars	*Time lag (Week/ Month)*	*Total*	*Raw Materials*	*Work-in-Progress*	*Finished Goods*	*Debtors*	*Creditors*
		Rs.	Rs.	Rs.	Rs.	Rs.	Rs.
1. Raw Material :							
in store	* *		* *				
in work-in-progress	* *			* *			
in finished goods	* *				* *		
Credit to Debtors	* *					* *	
	* *						
Less : Credit from suppliers	(–) * *						* *
Net Block	* *	* *					
2. Labour :							
in work-in-progress	* *			* *			
in finished goods	* *				* *		
Credit to Debtors	* *					* *	
	* *						
Less : Credit from employees	(–) * *						* *
Net Block	* *	* *					
3. Overhead :							
in work-in-progress	* *			* *			
in finished goods	* *				* *		
Credit to Debtors	* *					* *	
	* *						
Less : Credit from Creditors	* *						* *
	* *	* *					
4. Profit							
Credit to Debtors	* *	* *				* *	
		* *	* *	* *	* *	* *	* *

Problems Relating to Profit Element

Whether or not working capital is required to be raised for the profit element involved in the sale price of good—depends upon various factors. The main consideration is the policy adopted by the firm as to whether or not the said profit is retained for the purpose of reinvesting in the business. If profit is reinvested, the seasonal demand for working capital at the time of increasing demand can easily be met. But, on the contrary, if the same is distributed immediately after its creation, funds for additional working capital will be required at the time of seasonal demand.

Besides, if the profit is not retained in the business, a problem will arise, i.e., at what time it has been distributed. Here, two points are to be noted. The first one relates to the time when the sales are completed and the second is, at what time Cash is realised from Debtors. If profit is distributed immediately after the sales, no doubt Cash is required for this purpose—since Cash is not realised from customers immediately after sales.

If the policy adopted by the business is to sell goods always for cash, in that case the same may be distributed. Here, two points are to be noted. The first one relates to the time when the purpose, i.e., amount payable by debtors (towards the cost), is to be computed on the basis of cost of production of goods only. But, in most cases, it is assumed that profit is distributed immediately after sales and that is why provision should be made for dividends in this regard.

Wages and Overheads Accruing evenly

The students must remember that at the time of forecasting/assessing working capital requirements, problem may arise regarding wages and overheads for calculating the Work-in-progress. Wages and overheads are incurred during the process of production and, naturally, since these are incurred during the processing period, question arises before us that to what extent they are related to working capital. If proper or accurate estimate is to be made for them for the purpose of working capital, comprehensive records must be maintained which is not always possible for the firm during the related period of occurrence. Thus, it is usually assumed that processing is continued evenly throughout the period and, as such, wages and overheads are incurred in that manner. For this reason, it is assumed that these two elements of cost are supposed to be blocked on an average for half the processing period of the product. For instance, if processing period is 2 months, wages and overheads are to be considered for 1 month. Overheads are treated in the same manner on the assumption that they are also related to wages. Thus, they are also taken for half the processing period.

Operating Cycle (O.C.) Approach or Cash Working Capital Approach

The traditional approach towards projection of working capital requirement of a firm is the 'Balance Sheet Approach'. Under this method, the working capital requirement of a firm is sought to be determined with reference to the position of current assets and current liabilities—deducting the latter from the former. The 'Balance Sheet Approach' to working capital is now criticised on the ground that it does not indicate the exact position of working capital. A valuation put on some of the current assets items, like Finished products, Work-in-progress, Inventories and Debtors include depreciation and that on Debtors include profit element. Neither depreciation nor profit element in Debtors involve any cash payment.

Again, 'Balance Sheet Approach' to working capital includes non-circulating and non-convertible items like non-moving materials, spares, finished products, many of which become obsolete over a period of time, long-standing receivables much of which become unrecoverable, and items of almost permanent nature, like deposits with statutory authorities. Secondly, working capital derived under this approach indicates the status of a firm at a particular point of time and does not reflect the movement of value occurring in the same during the entire accounting period. Hence, the traditional 'Balance Sheet Approach' to project Working Capital requirement of a firm is now replaced by modern approach, viz., *'Operating Cycle Approach'* or *'Cash Working Capital Approach'* to Working Capital requirement.[1]

Unlike the conventional approach, consistent with the definition, this approach views working capital as a function of the volume of operating expenses. This approach suggests that actual level of working capital requirement of a firm in a period can be appropriately determined with reference to the length of Net Operating Cycle and the operating expenses needed for the period. The net duration of operating cycle is equal to the number of days

[1] Park, C. & Gladson, J. W.—*Working Capital*,—MacMillan & Co., New York, Chapter 3.

involved in the different stages of operation commencing from purchase of raw materials and ending up with collection of sale proceeds from Debtors against which the number of days credit allowed by suppliers are to be adjusted. The number of operating cycles in a period is determined by dividing the number of days in the same by the length of the Net Operating Cycle. Once the number of operating cycles has been determined, the actual working capital requirement is arrived at by dividing the total operating expenses for the period by the number of operating cycles in that period.

(a) *Length of Material Inventory Period*

This shows the average time materials remain in stores before the same is issued to production.

Method of Computation :

(i) Material consumed during the year X

(ii) Average consumption per day $= \frac{X}{365}$

The methodology of computation of the length of operating cycle and the actual working capital requirement thereunder will, therefore, be :

(iii) Average material inventory during the period, I

(iv) Number of days' consumption in stock $= I \div \frac{X}{365}$

(b) *Length of Conversion Period*

This shows the average length of production cycle.

Method of Computation :

(i) Cost of Finished Goods manufactured during the year = Opening Work-in-progress + (Material consumed + Wages + Manufacturing expenses) – Closing Work-in-progress = M

(ii) Average cost of Finished Goods manufactured per day $= \frac{M}{365}$

(iii) Average Work-in-progress during the year = L

(iv) Average conversion period $= L \div \frac{M}{365}$

(c) *Length of Finished Goods Inventory Period*

This is a period for which finished goods are held in godown before being sold to customers.

Method of computation:

(i) Cost of Finished Goods sold during the year = Opening Stock of Finished Goods + (Cost of Finished Goods manufactured during the year + Administration expenses + Selling expenses) – Closing Stock of Finished Goods = S

(ii) Average Cost of Finished Goods sold $= \frac{S}{365}$

(iii) Average Finished Goods inventory during the year = 0

(iv) Average Finished Goods inventory period $= 0 \div \frac{S}{365}$

(d) *Length of Collection Period*

This shows the average time taken in realisation of sale proceeds from the customers.

Method of Computation :

(i) Total Credit Sales during the year = P

(ii) Average daily Credit Sales during the year $= \frac{P}{365}$

(iii) Average Debtors balance = D

(iv) Average Collection period $= D \div \frac{P}{365}$

(e) ***Length of Credit Pay-off Period***

This represents the time taken on an average to pay the credit allowed by suppliers.

Method of Computation :

(i) Total Credit Purchases during the year = Q

(ii) Average Credit Purchases per day $= \frac{Q}{365}$

(iii) Average Creditors balance = Z

(iv) Average credit period allowed by suppliers $= Z \div \frac{Q}{365}$

Now, the length of Net Operating Cycle, T, is

$$= I \div \frac{X}{365} + L \div \frac{M}{365} + O \div \frac{S}{365} + D \div \frac{P}{365} - Z \div \frac{Q}{365}$$

Once the length of operating cycle has been found, Number of operating cycle, N, per annum, is then ascertained as $= \frac{365}{T}$

And, the actual working capital requirement of a firm becomes

$$= \frac{\text{Total Operating expenses}}{N}$$

Illustration 7.4

From the following Profit and Loss Account and Balance Sheet presented by Suparna Ltd., you are requested to compute the amount of working capital requirement under *Operating Cycle Approach* :

Trading and Profit and Loss Account

for the year ended ....

	Rs.	Rs.		Rs.	Rs.
To Stock :			By Sales (credit)		1,00,000
Raw Materials	10,000		" Closing Stock :		
Work-in-progress	30,000		Raw Materials	11,000	
Finished goods	5,000		Work-in-progress	30,500	
		45,000	Finished Goods	8,500	
" Purchases (credit)		35,000			50,000
" Wages and Manufacturing expenses		15,000			
" Gross Profit c/d		55,000			
		1,50,000			1,50,000
To Administrative Expenses		15,000	By Gross Profit b/d		55,000
" Selling and Distribution Exp.		10,000			
" Net Profit		30,000			
		55,000			55,000

Balance Sheet
as at ....

	Rs.		Rs.	Rs.	Rs.
Share Capital		Fixed Assets			1,00,000
(16,000 Equity Shares of Rs. 10 each)	1,60,000	Current Assets:			
Profit and Loss A/c (Balance)	30,000	Stock—			
Creditors	10,000	Raw Materials	11,000		
		Work-in-progress	30,500		
		Finished goods	8,500	50,000	
		Debtors		30,000	
		Cash and Bank		20,000	1,00,000
	2,00,000				2,00,000

Debtors (excluding profit element) and Creditors at the beginning of the year amounted to Rs. 6,500 and Rs. 5,000, respectively.

Solution

Statement Showing the Requirements of Working Capital under 'Operating Cycle Approach'

1. ***Length of Material Inventory Period :***
   (i) Material Consumed during the year = Rs. 34,000
   (Opening Raw Matrial + Purchases – Closing Raw Materials)
   (Rs. 10,000 + Rs. 35,000 – Rs. 11,000)

   (ii) Average Consumption per day $= \frac{\text{Rs. } 34{,}000}{365} = 93$ (approx.)

   (iii) Average Material inventory during the year :

Opening Inventories	Rs. 10,000
Closing Inventories	Rs. 11,000
	Rs. 21,000 ÷ 2 = Rs. 10,500

   (iv) Number of days consumed $= \frac{\text{Rs. } 10{,}500}{93} =$ 113 days (approx.) or, $3\frac{3}{4}$ months.

2. ***Length of Conversion Period :***
   (i) Cost of Finished Products manufactured during the year
   = (Opening Work-in-progress + Material Consumed + Wages and Manufacturing Expenses – Closing Work-in-progress)
   = Rs. 30,000 + Rs. 34,000 + Rs. 15,000 – Rs. 30,500.
   = Rs. 48,500.

   (ii) Average Cost of Finished Products per day $= \frac{\text{Rs. } 48{,}500}{365} = 133$ (approx.)

   (iii) Average Work-in-progress during the year:

Opening Work-in-progress	Rs. 30,000
Closing Work-in-progress	Rs. 30,500
	Rs. 60,500 ÷ 2 = Rs. 30,250

   (iv) Average Conversion period $= \frac{\text{Rs. } 30{,}250}{133} =$ 227 days or, $7\frac{1}{2}$ months.

3. *Length of Finished Products Inventory Period :*

(i) Cost of Finished Products sold during the year

(Opening Stock of Finished Products + Cost of Finished Products Manufactured + Administrative and Selling Expenses – Closing Stock of Finished Products)

= Rs. 5,000 + Rs. 48,500 + Rs. 25,000 – Rs. 8,500

= Rs. 70,000.

(ii) Average Cost of Finished Products sold per day = $\frac{\text{Rs. } 70{,}000}{365}$ = 192.

(iii) Average Stock of Finished Products sold during the year:

Opening Stock of Finished Products	Rs. 5,000
Closing Stock of Finished Products	Rs. 8,500
	Rs. 13,500 ÷ 2 = Rs. 6,750.

(iv) Average Finished Products Inventory period = $\frac{\text{Rs. } 6{,}750}{192}$

= 35 days or, $1\frac{1}{6}$ months.

4. *Length of Collection Period :*

(i) Total credit sales during the year Rs. 45,000 (excluding profit element)

Rs. 1,00,000 – Rs. 55,000 (i.e., 55%)

(ii) Average daily credit sales = $\frac{\text{Rs. } 45{,}000}{365}$ = Rs. 123.

(iii) Average Debtors balance :

Opening Debtors (excluding profit element)	Rs. 6,500
Closing Debtors (Rs. 30,000 – Rs. 16,500)	Rs. 13,500
	Rs. 20,000 ÷ 2 = Rs. 10,000.

(iv) Average collection period = $\frac{\text{Rs. } 10{,}000}{123}$

= 81 days or, $2\frac{3}{4}$ months.

5. *Length of Credit Pay-off Period :*

(i) Total credit purchases during the year Rs. 35,000

(ii) Average credit purchases per day = $\frac{\text{Rs. } 35{,}000}{365}$ = 96

(iii) Average Creditors balance:

Opening Creditors	Rs. 5,000
Closing Creditors	Rs. 10,000
	Rs. 15,000 ÷ 2 = Rs. 7,500

(iv) Average credit period allowed by suppliers = $\frac{\text{Rs. } 7{,}500}{96}$ = 78 days or, $2\frac{1}{2}$ months.

Now, the length of Net Operating Cycle, T, in the company, is

$= 3\frac{3}{4}$ months + $7\frac{1}{2}$ months + $1\frac{1}{6}$ months + $2\frac{3}{4}$ months − $2\frac{1}{2}$ months

$= 12\frac{2}{3}$ months or 378 days.

Therefore, the Number of Operating Cycle, N, per annum $= \frac{365}{T}$

$$= \frac{365}{12\frac{2}{3}} = 29 \text{ (approx.)}$$

∴ Actual Working Capital requirement becomes $= \frac{\text{Total Operating Expenses}}{N}$

$$= \frac{\text{Rs. } 70{,}000}{29} = \text{Rs. } 2{,}414.$$

Alternative Approach

The length of *Net Operating Cycle* can also be calculated in the following way:

1. ***Length of Material Inventory Period :***

$$\frac{\text{Average holding of Raw Materials}}{\text{Average daily purchases}} = \frac{\left(\frac{\text{Opening R.M.} + \text{Closing R.M.}}{2}\right)}{\frac{\text{Material Consumed}}{365}}$$

$$= \frac{\left(\frac{10{,}000 + 11{,}000}{2}\right)}{\frac{34{,}000}{365}}$$

$= 113$ days or, $3\frac{3}{4}$ months.

[Material Consumed = *Opening R.M. + Purchases of R.M. – Closing* R.M.
= Rs. 10,000 + Rs. 35,000 – Rs. 11,000
= Rs. 34,000]

2. ***Length of Production Period :***

$$\frac{\text{Average holding of Work-in-progress}}{\text{Average cost of goods produced}} = \frac{\left(\frac{\text{Opening W.I.P.} + \text{Closing W.I.P.}}{2}\right)}{\frac{\text{Cost of F.G. manufactured}}{365}}$$

$$= \frac{\left(\frac{30{,}000 + 30{,}500}{2}\right)}{\frac{48{,}500}{365}}$$

$= 227$ days or, $7\frac{1}{2}$ months.

[*Cost of F.G. Manufactured* = *Opening W.I.P. + Material Consumed*
\+ Wages and Manufacturing Expenses – Closing W.I.P.
= Rs. 30,000 + Rs. 34,000 + Rs. 15,000 – Rs. 30,500
= Rs. 48,500.]

3. ***Length of Finished Goods Inventory Period :***

$$\frac{\text{Average holding of F.G.}}{\text{Average cost of goods sold}} = \frac{\left(\frac{\text{Opening } F.G. + \text{Closing } F.G.}{2}\right)}{\frac{\text{Cost of F.G. Sold}}{365}}$$

$$= \frac{\left(\frac{5,000+8,500}{2}\right)}{\frac{70,000}{365}}$$

$$= 35 \text{ days or, } 1\frac{1}{6} \text{ months.}$$

$$\left[\begin{array}{lll} \text{Cost of F.G. Sold} & = & \text{Opening F.G. + Cost of F.G. manufactured} \\ & + & \text{Administrative and Selling Exp.} - \text{Closing F.G.} \\ & = & \text{Rs.}5,000 + \text{Rs.}48,500 + \text{Rs.}25,000 - 8,500 \\ & = & \text{Rs.}70,000. \end{array}\right]$$

4. ***Length of Collection Period :***

$$\frac{\text{Average Debtors balance}}{\text{Average Credit Sales}} = \frac{\left(\frac{\text{Opening Debtors} + \text{Closing Debtors}}{2}\right)}{\frac{\text{Credit Sales}}{365}}$$

$$= \frac{\left(\frac{6,500+13,500}{2}\right)}{\frac{45,000}{365}}$$

$$= 81 \text{ days or, } 2\frac{3}{4} \text{ months.}$$

$$\text{Total} = 113 + 227 + 35 + 81 = 456 \text{ days.}$$

5. ***Length of Credit Pay-off Period :***

$$\frac{\text{Average Creditors balance}}{\text{Average Credit Purchases}} = \frac{\left(\frac{\text{Opening Creditors} + \text{Closing Creditors}}{2}\right)}{\frac{\text{Credit purchases}}{365}}$$

$$= \frac{\left(\frac{5,000+10,000}{2}\right)}{\frac{35,000}{365}}$$

$$= 78 \text{ days or, } 2\frac{1}{2} \text{ months.}$$

$\therefore$ 456 days – 78 days = 378 days.

Another Alternative Approach

Computation of Working Capital Cycle

(a) Length of Material Inventory Period or, Raw Material Storage Period : $\frac{\text{Average holding of raw material}}{\text{Average daily consumption}}$

$$\text{or} = \frac{365}{\frac{\textit{Raw Material Consumed}}{\textit{Average Stock of Raw Material held}}}$$

(b) Length of Conversion Period Processing Period : $\frac{\text{Average holding of Work-in-progress}}{\text{Average factory cost of Production}}$

or = $\frac{365}{\frac{\text{Total Cost of Production}}{\text{Average W.I.P. held}}}$

(c) Length of F.G. Inventory Period or, Finished Goods Storage Period : $\frac{\text{Average holding of F.G.}}{\text{Average daily cost of production of goods sold}}$

or = $\frac{365}{\frac{\text{Total Cost of Sales}}{\text{Average F.G. held}}}$

(d) Period of Credit allowed to Debtors : $\frac{\text{Average Debtors}}{\text{Average daily Credit Sales}}$

or = $\frac{365}{\frac{\text{Sales for the Year}}{\text{Average total of outstanding Debtors}}}$

(e) Period of Credit allowed by Creditors : $\frac{\text{Average Creditors}}{\text{Average daily purchase}}$

or = $\frac{365}{\frac{\text{Purchase for the Year}}{\text{Average total of outstanding creditor}}}$

(f) Period of Credit allowed by employee : $\frac{\text{Outstanding Wages/Salaries}}{\text{Average Daily Wages/Salaries}}$

Illustration 7.5

From the following information extracted from the books of a manufacturing concern, compute the operating cycle in days —

	(Rs. '000)
Period covered : 365 days	
Average period of credit allowed by suppliers—16 days	
Average total of debtors outstanding	480
Raw-Material Consumption	4,400
Total Production Cost	10,000
Total Cost of Sales	10,500
Sales for the year	16,000
Value of Average Stock maintained—	
Raw Materials	320
Work-in-Progress	350
Finished Goods	260

Solution

Computation of Operating Cycle

(a) Length of Material Inventory Period : $\frac{365}{\frac{\text{Raw Materials Consumed}}{\text{Average Stock of Raw Material held}}} = \frac{365}{\frac{4,400}{320}} = 27 \text{ days}$

(b) Length of Conversion Period : $\dfrac{365}{\dfrac{\text{Total Cost of Production}}{\text{Average W.I.P. held}}} = \dfrac{365}{\dfrac{10,000}{365}} = 13$ days

(c) Length of Finished Products Inventory Period : $\dfrac{365}{\dfrac{\text{Total Cost of Sales}}{\text{Average F.G. held}}} = \dfrac{365}{\dfrac{10,500}{260}} = 9$ days

(d) Period of Credit allowed to Debtors : $\dfrac{365}{\dfrac{\text{Sales for the year}}{\text{Average total of outstanding debtors}}} = \dfrac{365}{\dfrac{16,000}{480}} = 11$ days

		60 days
Less : Period of Credit allowed by Creditor	: (Given)	16 days
∴ Total period of operating cycle		44 days

(a) Preparation of a Statement Showing Working Capital Requirements Forecast

Illustration 7.6

From the following particulars, prepare a statement showing working capital needed to finance a level of activity of 12,000 units of output per annum:

Analysis of selling price per unit :	Rs.
Raw Materials	5
Labour	3
Overhead	2
	10
Profit	2
Selling price	12

Additional Information :

(i) Raw Materials are to remain in store, on an average, 1 month.

(ii) Materials are in process, on an average, 2 months.

(iii) Finished Goods are in stock, on an average, 3 months.

(iv) Credit allowed to Debtors is 4 months.

(v) Credit allowed by suppliers is 2 months.

It may be assumed that production and overheads accrue evenly throughout the year.

Solution

Sales for the year 12,000 × Rs. 12 = Rs. 1,44,000.

Sales per month Rs. $\dfrac{1,44,000}{12}$ = Rs. 12,000.

Amounts to be blocked in Materials, Labour and Overheads per month are:

Materials Rs. 12,000 × $\dfrac{5}{12}$ = Rs. 5,000

Labour Rs. 12,000 × $\dfrac{3}{12}$ = Rs. 3,000

Overheads Rs. 12,000 × $\dfrac{2}{12}$ = Rs. 2,000

Alternatively,

Annual Production 12,000 units

Monthly Production 12,000 ÷ 12 = 1,000 units

Average cost of production per month:

Raw Material	1,000 × Rs. 5	= Rs. 5,000
Labour	1,000 × Rs. 3	= Rs. 3,000
Overheads	1,000 × Rs. 2	= Rs. 2,000.

METHOD 1

Net Block Period for Each Element of Cost

(Period in months)

	Materials	*Labour*	*Overheads*
Raw Materials in Store	1	—	—
Processing Period	2	2	2
Finished Goods in Store	3	3	3
Credit to Debtors	4	4	4
	10	9	9
Less : Credit from Suppliers	2	—	—
Net Block Period	8	9	9

Working Capital Requirements Forecast :

Raw Materials	: Rs. 5,000 × 8 =	Rs. 40,000
Labour	: Rs. 3,000 × 9 =	Rs. 27,000
Overheads	: Rs. 2,000 × 9 =	Rs. 18,000
Total requirements		Rs. 85,000

From the above, it is quite clear that the total working capital requirements would be Rs. 85,000 in order to sustain the production programme of 12,000 unit p.a. But this method fails to reveal the estimated values of current assets and current liabilities—the two components of working capital.

METHOD 2

Working Capital Requirements Forecast

Current Assets :

			Rs.	Rs.
1. Stock of Raw Materials (1 month)				
Raw Materials	Rs. 5,000 × 1	=	5,000	5,000
2. Work-in-Progress (2 months)				
Raw Materials	Rs. 5,000 × 2	=	10,000	
Labour	Rs. 3,000 × 2	=	6,000	
Overheads	Rs. 2,000 × 2	=	4,000	
				20,000
3. Stock of Finished Goods (3 months)				
Raw Materials	Rs. 5,000 × 3	=	15,000	
Labour	Rs. 3,000 × 3	=	9,000	
Overheads	Rs. 2,000 × 3	=	6,000	
				30,000

4.	Debtors (4 months)			
	Raw Materials	Rs. 5,000 × 4 =	20,000	
	Labour	Rs. 3,000 × 4 =	12,000	
	Overheads	Rs. 2,000 × 4 =	8,000	
			40,000	
	Profit Credit to Debtors ($\frac{1}{5}$th of cost or $\frac{1}{6}$th of sales)		8,000	48,000
				1,03,000
	Less : *Current Liabilities :*			
1.	Creditors (2 months)			
	Raw Materials	Rs. 5,000 × 2 =	10,000	10,000
	Requirement of Working Capital			93,000

This method, however, suggests the estimated values of current assets and current liabilities. But the difference in the requirement of working capital between the two methods is due to the profit element in Debtors, i.e., in Method 1, profit element is excluded, whereas, in Method 2, profit element is included.

METHOD 3

Or, ***Alternative Approach*** *(in a Columnar Form)*

Working Capital Requirements Forecast

Particulars	*Period in Months*	*Total*	*Raw Materials*	*Work-in-Progress*	*Finished Goods*	*Debtors*	*Creditors*
		Rs.	Rs.	Rs.	Rs.	Rs.	Rs.
1. *Materials :*							
In stores	1		5,000				
In process	2			10,000			
In Finished goods	3				15,000		
With Debtors	4					20,000	
	10						
Less : Credit from Creditors	2						10,000
	8	40,000					
2. *Wages :*							
In process	2			6,000			
In Finished goods	3				9,000		
With Debtors	4					12,000	
	9	27,000					
3. *Overheads :*							
In process	2			4,000			
In Finished goods	3				6,000		
With Debtors	4					8,000	
	9	18,000					
4. *Profit :*							
Credit to Debtors	4	8,000				8,000	
Total		93,000	5,000	20,000	30,000	48,000	10,000

∴ Total Working Capital requirement Rs. 93,000.

Illustration 7.7

You are required to prepare for the Board of Directors of Sumana Ltd. a statement showing the working capital needed to finance a level of activity of 5,200 units of output.

You are given the following information:

Elements of Cost		*Amount per unit*
		Rs.
Raw Materials		8
Direct Labour		2
Overheads		6
	Total Cost	16
	Profit	4
	Selling Price	20

Raw Materials are in stock, on average, one month.
Materials are in process, on average, half a month.
Finished Goods are in stock, on average, 6 weeks.
Credit allowed by Creditors is one month.
Credit allowed to Debtors is two months.
Lag in payment of Wages is $1\frac{1}{2}$ weeks.

Cash in hand and at bank is expected to be Rs. 7,300. You are informed that production is carried on evenly during the year and Wages and Overheads accrue similarly.

[C.U. M.Com.]

Solution

Sales for the year 5,200 × Rs. 20 = Rs. 1,04,000

$$\text{Sales per week} = \frac{1,04,000}{52} = \text{Rs. } 2,000$$

Amounts to be blocked in Materials, Labour and Overhead per week are :

Materials	$\text{Rs. } 2,000 \times \frac{8}{20}$	= Rs. 800
Labour	$\text{Rs. } 2,000 \times \frac{2}{20}$	= Rs. 200
Overhead	$\text{Rs. } 2,000 \times \frac{6}{20}$	= Rs. 600

Working Capital Requirements Forecast

Current Assets : *Period ....*

				Rs.
1. Stock of Raw Materials (4 weeks) :				
Raw Materials	Rs. 800 × 4			3,200
2. Work-in-progress (2 weeks) :				
Raw Materials	Rs. 800 × 2	=	Rs. 1,600	
Labour	Rs. 200 × 1	=	Rs. 200	
Overheads	Rs. 600 × 1	=	Rs. 600	2,400

Contd.

				Rs.
3. Stock of Finished Goods (6 weeks):				
Raw Materials	Rs. 800 × 6	=	Rs. 4,800	
Labour	Rs. 200 × 6	=	Rs. 1,200	
Overheads	Rs. 600 × 6	=	Rs. 3,600	9,600
4. Debtors (8 weeks):				
Raw Materials	Rs. 800 × 8	=	Rs. 6,400	
Labour	Rs. 200 × 8	=	Rs. 1,600	
Overheads	Rs. 600 × 8	=	Rs. 4,800	
			Rs. 12,800	
Profit : Credit to Debtors (25% on Cost)			Rs. 3,200	16,000
				31,200
Less : ***Current Liabilities*** :				
1. Creditors (4 weeks) :				
Raw Materials	Rs. 800 × 4	=	Rs. 3,200	
2. Lag in payment of wages ($1\frac{1}{2}$ weeks) :				
Labour	Rs. 200 × $1\frac{1}{2}$	=	Rs. 300	
				3,500
Net Working Capital				27,700
Add : Cash as per estimate				7,300
Estimated requirement of Working Capital				35,000

Alternative Approach

Working Capital Requirements Forecast

Particulars	*Period in Months*	*Total*	*Raw Materials*	*Work-in-Progress*	*Finished Goods*	*Debtors*	*Creditors*
		Rs.	Rs.	Rs.	Rs.	Rs.	Rs.
1. *Materials :*							
In Stock	4		3,200				
Work-in-progress	2			1,600			
In Finished Goods	6				4,800		
With Debtors	8					6,400	
	20						3,200
Less: Credit from Creditors	4						
	16	12,800					
2. *Wages :*							
Work-in-progress	1			200			
In Finished Goods	6				1,200		
With Debtors	8					1,600	
	15						
Less: Credit from employees	$1\frac{1}{2}$						300
	$13\frac{1}{2}$	2,700					

Contd.

3. *Overheads:*		Rs.	Rs.	Rs.	Rs.	Rs.	Rs.
Work-in-progress	1			600			
In Finished Goods	6				3,600		
With Debtors	8					4,800	
	15	9,000					
4. *Profit:*							
Credit to Debtors	8	3,200				3,200	
		27,700	3,200	2,400	9,600	16,000	3,500

		Rs.
	Requirement as per above statement	27,700
Add :	Cash as per estimate	7,300
	Total requirements of Working Capital	35,000

Notes:

1. **Lag in Payment of Wages :**

If the workers work evenly throughout the week, they earn wages from the beginning of the week which will increase daily till the end of the week. Therefore, the employer owes $\frac{1}{2}$ week's wages on an average. If the same is not paid at the weekend, the employer owes $1\frac{1}{2}$ weeks' wages.

2. It is assumed that wages and overhead accrue evenly during the time when the production is in progress. Processing time is given 2 weeks here, so, the total cost of labour and overheads become due for half the time of an average.

Illustration 7.8

From the following information, you are required to estimate the net working capital:

	Cost per unit
	Rs.
Raw Materials	400
Direct Labour	150
Overheads (excluding Depreciation)	300
Total Cost	850

Additional Information :

Selling Price	Rs. 1,000 p.u.
Output	52,000 units
Raw Materials in stock	average 4 weeks
Work-in-progress	average 2 weeks
(assumed 50% completion stage with full material consumption)	
Finished goods in stock	average 4 weeks
Credit allowed by suppliers	average 4 weeks
Credit allowed to debtors	average 8 weeks
Cash at bank is expected to be	Rs. 50,000
25% of purchases are made for Cash	

Assume that production is sustained at an even pace during the 52 weeks of the year. All sales are on credit basis.

Solution

Sales for the year 52,000 × Rs. 1,000 = Rs. 5,20,00,000

Sales per week Rs. $\frac{5,20,00,000}{52}$ = Rs. 10,00,000

Amounts to be blocked in Materials, Labour and Overhead per week are:

Materials Rs. 10,00,000 × $\frac{400}{1,000}$ = Rs. 4,00,000

Labour Rs. 10,00,000 × $\frac{150}{1,000}$ = Rs. 1,50,000

Overhead Rs. 10,00,000 × $\frac{300}{1,000}$ = Rs. 3,00,000

Working Capital Requirements Forecast

		Period ...... Rs.	Rs.
Current Assets			
1. Stock of Raw Materials (4 weeks):			
Raw Materials	Rs. 4,00,000 × 4	16,00,000	16,00,000
2. Work-in-Progress (2 weeks):			
Raw Materials	Rs. 4,00,000 × 2	8,00,000	
Labour	Rs. 1,50,000 × 1	1,50,000	
Overheads	Rs. 3,00,000 × 1	3,00,000	12,50,000
3. Stock of Finished Goods (4 weeks):			
Raw Materials	Rs. 4,00,000 × 4	16,00,000	
Labour	Rs. 1,50,000 × 4	6,00,000	
Overheads	Rs. 3,00,000 × 4	12,00,000	34,00,000
4. Debtors (8 weeks):			
Raw Materials	Rs. 4,00,000 × 8	32,00,000	
Labour	Rs. 1,50,000 × 8	12,00,000	
Overheads	Rs. 3,00,000 × 8	24,00,000	
		68,00,000	
Profit : Credit to Debtors		12,00,000	
(Rs. 68,00,000 × $\frac{150}{850}$)			80,00,000
			1,42,50,000
Less : Current Liabilities :			
1. Creditors (4 weeks) :			
Raw Materials	Rs. 4,00,000 × 4	16,00,000	
Less : Cash purchase @ 25%		4,00,000	12,00,000
			1,30,50,000
Add : Cash at Bank			50,000
Net Working Capital Requirements			1,31,00,000

Illustration 7.9

A proforma cost sheet of a company provides the following particulars:

Element of Cost	*Amount per unit*
	Rs.
Raw Materials	80
Direct Labour	30
Overhead	60
Total Cost	170
Profit	30
Selling Price	200

The following further particulars are available:

Raw materials are in stock on average one month. Materials are in process, on average, half a month. Finished goods are in stock, on average, one month.

Credit allowed by suppliers is one month. Credit allowed to Debtors is two months. Lag in payment of wages is $1\frac{1}{2}$ weeks. Lag in payment of Overhead Expenses is one month.

One-fourth of the output is sold against cash. Cash on hand and at Bank is expected to be Rs. 25,000.

You are required to prepare a statement showing the working capital needed to finance a level of activity of 1,04,000 units of production.

You may assume that production is carried on evenly throughout the year. Wages and Overhead accrue similarly and a time period of 4 weeks is equivalent to a month.

The company usually maintains a liability for Bills Payable for Rs. 5,000.

Solution

Sales of the year 1,04,000 × Rs. 200 = Rs. 2,08,00,000.

$$\text{Sales per week } \frac{\text{Rs. } 2{,}08{,}00{,}000}{52} = \text{Rs. } 4{,}00{,}000.$$

Amount to be blocked in Materials, Labour and Overhead per week are:

Raw Materials	$\text{Rs. } 4{,}00{,}000 \times \frac{80}{200}$ = Rs.	1,60,000
Labour	$\text{Rs. } 4{,}00{,}000 \times \frac{30}{200}$ = Rs.	60,000
Overhead	$\text{Rs. } 4{,}00{,}000 \times \frac{60}{200}$ = Rs.	1,20,000

Working Capital Requirements Forecast

Current Assets :			*Period* ....
			Rs.
1. Stock of Raw Material (4 weeks):			
Raw Materials	Rs. 1,60,000 × 4	= Rs. 6,40,000	6,40,000
2. Work-in-progress (2 weeks):			
Raw Materials	Rs. 1,60,000 × 2	= Rs. 3,20,000	
Labour	Rs. 60,000 × 1	= Rs. 60,000	
Overhead	Rs. 1,20,000 × 1	= Rs. 1,20,000	5,00,000

3. Stock of Finished Goods (4 weeks):				
Raw Materials	Rs. 1,60,000 × 4	= Rs.	6,40,000	
Labour	Rs. 60,000 × 4	= Rs.	2,40,000	
Overhead	Rs. 1,20,000 × 4	= Rs.	4,80,000	13,60,000
4. Debtors (8 weeks):				
Raw Materials	Rs. 1,60,000 × 8 × $\frac{3}{4}$	= Rs.	9,60,000	
Labour	Rs. 60,000 × 8 × $\frac{3}{4}$	= Rs.	3,60,000	
Overhead	Rs. 1,20,000 × 8 × $\frac{3}{4}$	= Rs.	7,20,000	
		Rs.	20,40,000	
Profit : Credit to Debtors Rs. 20,40,000 × $\frac{30}{170}$		Rs.	3,60,000	
				24,00,000
				49,00,000
*Less : **Current Liabilities***				
1. Creditors (4 weeks):				
Raw Materials	Rs. 1,60,000 × 4	= Rs.	6,40,000	
2. Lag in payment of Wages ($1\frac{1}{2}$ weeks):				
Labour	Rs. 60,000 × $1\frac{1}{2}$	= Rs.	90,000	
3. Lag in payment of Overhead (4 weeks):				
Overhead	Rs. 1,20,000 × 4	= Rs.	4,80,000	12,10,000
				36,90,000
Add: Cash in hand and at bank				25,000
Estimated requirement of Working Capital				37,15,000

Notes 1 . Profit on cash sales has not been considered on the assumption that the same may not be used as working capital.

2 . As Bills payable is a part of creditor, no separate treatment is required for the purpose.

Illustration 7.10

From the following details concerning a manufacturing enterprise, estimate the amount of working capital needed to finance an activity level of 50%. The capacity of the concern is to produce 2,40,000 units per annum :

Expected selling price	Rs. 10.00 per unit
Cost of raw materials	Rs. 3.00 per unit
Direct labour cost	Rs. 2.50 per unit
Annual overhead at 50% activity level (including depreciation Rs. 50,000)	Rs. 2,50,000

Raw materials are in stock, on an average, for one month. Materials are in process, on an average, for two months. Finished goods are in stock, on an average, for two months. Credit allowed to debtors is for three months and that received from suppliers of raw materials is for one month. Lag in payment of wages half a month and of overheads one month. Cash on hand and at bank 10% of net working capital. You may assume that production is carried on evenly throughout the year and wages overheads accrue similarly. One-fourth of the output is sold against cash.

[C.U. B.Com. (Hons.)]

Solution

Budgeted sale 2,40,000 units, activity level 50% of the budget, i.e., Rs. 1,20,000.

Sales for the year = 1,20,000 × Rs. 10 = 12,00,000

Sales per month = Rs. $\frac{12,00,000}{12}$ = Rs. 1,00,000

Amounts to be blocked in Material, Labour & Overhead per month are :

Material	Rs. 1,00,000 × $\frac{3}{10}$	= Rs.	30,000
Labour	Rs. 1,00,000 × $\frac{2.5}{10}$	= Rs.	25,000
Overhead	(Excluding Dep.) (Rs. 2,50,000 – Rs. 50,000) = Rs. $\frac{2,00,000}{12}$	= Rs.	16,667

Working Capital Requirements Forecast

Current Assets :			*Period................*	
			Rs.	Rs.
1. Stock of Raw Material (1 month) :				
Raw Materials	= Rs. 30,000 × 1	=	30,000	30,000
2. Work-in-progress (2 months) :				
Raw Materials	= Rs. 30,000 × 2	=	60,000	
Labour	= Rs. 25,000 × 1	=	25,000	
Overhead	= Rs. 16,667 × 1	=	16,667	
				1,01,667
3. Stock of Finished Goods (2 months) :				
Raw Materials	= Rs. 30,000 × 2	=	60,000	
Labour	= Rs. 25,000 × 2	=	50,000	
Overhead	= Rs. 16,667 × 2	=	33,333	
				1,43,333
4. Debtors (3 months) :				
Raw Materials	= Rs. 30,000 × 3	=	90,000	
Labour	= Rs. 25,000 × 3	=	75,000	
Overhead	= Rs. 16,667 × 3	=	50,000	
			2,15,000	
Less : Cash Sales @ $\frac{1}{4}$			53,750	
			1,61,250	
Add : Profit : Credit to Debtors ($\frac{1}{4}$th)			40,313	
				2,01,563
Less : ***Current Liabilities***				4,76,563

Contd.

			Rs.	Rs.
5. Creditors (1 month)				
Raw Materials	= Rs. 30,000 × 1	=	30,000	
Lag-in-payment of wages ($\frac{1}{2}$ month)	= Rs. 25,000 × $\frac{1}{2}$	=	12,500	
Lag-in-payment of overhead (1 month)	= Rs. 16,667 × 1	=	16,667	
				59,167
Working Capital requirement (subject to cash flow)				4,17,396
Add : Cash in hand for contingencies @ 10% of net working capital, i.e., $\frac{1}{9}$th				46,377
Net Working Capital required				4,63,773

Illustration 7.11

Lucky Ltd., a trading concern, provides the following information:

Annual sales during the year 1983 is Rs. 1,20,000

Analysis of sales show :

Material	60%
Expenses	15%
Profit	25%

Average credit allowed to Debtors $2\frac{1}{2}$ months.

Average credit period allowed by Creditors $1\frac{1}{2}$ months.

Raw materials are to remain in store, on average, 1 month.

Processing period, on average, 2 months.

Finished goods are to remain in warehouse, on average, 3 months.

Bank Overdraft Rs. 90,000.

10% of the total working capital (including contingencies) is to be kept in hand for contingencies.

You are required to determine the working capital requirement of Lucky Ltd. on the basis of the above information.

[C.U . B.Com. (Hons.) & C.U. M.Com.—Adapted]

Solution

Sales per month $\frac{\text{Rs. } 1,20,000}{12}$ = Rs. 10,000.

Amount to be blocked in Materials and Expenses per month are:

Materials	Rs. 10,000 × 60%	= Rs.	6,000
Expenses	Rs. 10,000 × 15%	= Rs.	1,500

Working Capital Requirements Forecast

Current Assets :			*Period* ....
			Rs.
1. Stock of Raw Material (1 month)			
Raw Materials	= Rs. 6,000 × 1	= Rs. 6,000	6,000
2. Work-in-progress (2 months)			
Raw Materials	= Rs. 6,000 × 2	= Rs. 12,000	
Expenses	= Rs. 1,500 × 2	= Rs. 3,000	15,000
3. Stock of Finished Goods (3 months):			
Raw Materials	= Rs. 6,000 × 3	= Rs. 18,000	
Expenses	= Rs. 1,500 × 3	= Rs. 4,500	22,500
4. Debtors ($2\frac{1}{2}$ months):			
Raw Materials	= Rs. 6,000 × $2\frac{1}{2}$	= Rs. 15,000	
Expenses	= Rs. 1,500 × $2\frac{1}{2}$	= Rs. 3,750	
		18,750	
Profit : Credit to Debtors ($\frac{1}{3}$rd of cost or $\frac{1}{4}$th of sales)		6,250	25,000
			68,500
Less : Current Liabilities :			
1. Creditors ($1\frac{1}{2}$ months):			
Raw Material	= Rs. 6,000 × $1\frac{1}{2}$	=	9,000
			59,500
Add : Cash required for Contingencies ($\frac{1}{9}$th of the above)			6,611
Total estimated Working Capital requirement			66,111
Less : Bank Overdraft			90,000
Requirement of Working Capital (Negative)			(–) 23,889

Illustration 7.12

From the following information presented by a manufacturing company, prepare a working capital requirement forecast statement for the coming year:

Expected monthly sales of 32,000 units at Rs. 10 per unit. The anticipated ratios of cost to selling price are:

Raw Materials	40%
Labour	30%

Budgeted Overhead Rs. 16,000 per week.

Planned stock will include raw materials for Rs. 96,000 and 16,000 units of finished goods.

Materials will stay in process for 2 weeks.

Credit allowed to Debtors is 5 weeks.

Credit allowed by Creditors is 1 month.

Lag in payment of overhead is 2 weeks.

Wages will be paid at the beginning of the week following the week of work.

Cash in hand is expected to be 10% of Net Working Capital.

Assume that production is carried on evenly throughout the year and overheads accrue similarly and a time period of 4 weeks is equivalent to a month.

[C.U . B.Com. (Hons.)—Adapted]

Solution

Elements of Cost :	Per Unit Rs.	
Materials	4	(i.e., Rs. 10 × 40%)
Labour	3	(i.e., Rs. 10 × 30%)
Overhead $\left(\frac{\text{Overhead}}{\text{No. of units}}\right)$	2	(i.e., Rs. 16,000/*8,000)
Total Cost	9	
Profit	1	
Selling Price	10	

[*Weekly production = 32,000 ÷ 4 = 8,000 units]

Cost of Materials per week	=	8,000 × Rs. 4	= Rs. 32,000
∴ Time-lag in store Rs. 96,000 ÷ Rs. 32,000	=	3 weeks	
Average staying period of finished goods in store	=	$\frac{16,000}{8,000}$ = 2 weeks	
Average Cost of Labour per week	=	8,000 × Rs. 3	= Rs. 24,000
Average Cost of Overhead per week	=	8,000 × Rs. 2	= Rs. 16,000
Average Profit per week	=	8,000 × Re. 1	= Rs. 8,000

Working Capital Requirements Forecast *Period* ....

Particulars	*Period in Weeks*	*Total*	*Raw Materials*	*Work-in-Progress*	*Finished Goods*	*Debtors*	*Creditors*
		Rs.	Rs.	Rs.	Rs.	Rs.	Rs.
1. *Materials :*							
In store	3		96,000				
In Work-in-progress	2			64,000			
In Finished Goods	2				64,000		
With Debtors	5					1,60,000	
	12						
Less : Credit from Creditors	4						1,28,000
	8	2,56,000					
2. *Wages :*							
In Work-in-progress	1			24,000			
In Finished goods	2				48,000		
With Debtors	5					1,20,000	
	8	1,92,000					

Contd.

		Rs.	Rs.	Rs.	Rs.	Rs.	Rs.
3. *Overhead :*							
In Work-in-progress	1			16,000			
In Finished Goods	2				32,000		
With Debtors	5					80,000	
	8						
Less : Credit from Creditors	2						32,000
	6	96,000					
4. *Profit :*							
Credit to Debtors	5	40,000				40,000	
		5,84,000	96,000	1,04,000	1,44,000	4,00,000	1,60,000

	Rs.
Estimated requirement of working capital as per above statement	5,84,000
Add : Expected Cash in hand @ 10% of total requirement (i.e., Rs. 5,84,000 × $\frac{1}{9}$)	64,889
∴ Total requirement of working capital	6,48,889

Illustration 7.13

Your company is operating on 60% capacity, producing 24,000 units per annum, at the following cost-price structure:

	Rs.	
Raw Materials	5	per unit
Wages	3	per unit
Overheads (variable)	2	per unit
Overheads (fixed)	1	per unit
Profit	2	per unit
Selling Price	13	per unit

On 31st December 2010 the current assets and liabilities were:

	Rs.
Raw Materials 4,000 units, at cost	20,000
Work-in-progress 1,000 units, at cost	8,000
Finished Goods 3,000 units, at cost	33,000
Sundry Debtors	78,000
Creditors for goods	30,000
Liabilities for wages	3,000
Liabilities for expenses	6,000

In view of increased demand for the product, it has been decided that, from 1st January 2011, the unit should operate at 90% capacity.

You are required to ascertain the additional working capital as would be necessary in view of additional production. The prices of materials, rates of wages and expenses and the selling price per unit will not be changed. The period of credit allowed to customers, credit allowed by suppliers and also time lag in payment of wages and expenses shall remain the same as before.

[C.U. B.Com. (Hons.)]

Solution

Statement Showing the Requirements of Additional Working Capital

	at 60% capacity, i.e., 24,000 units		at 90% capacity, i.e., 36,000 units	
Stock				
Raw Materials		20,000		30,000
Work-in-Progress		8,000		11,750
Finished Goods		33,000		48,000
Debtors		78,000		1,17,000
		1,39,000		2,06,750
Less :				
Current Liabilities :				
Creditors	30,000		45,000	
Lag in payment of wages	3,000		4,500	
Lag in payment of overheads	6,000		8,000	
		39,000		57,500
Working Capital		1,00,000		1,49,250

∴ Additional working capital required for additional 12,000 units is Rs. 49,250 (i.e., Rs. 1,49,250 – Rs. 1,00,000).

Workings : Calculation of cost and sales at 60% and 90% capacity, i.e., for 24,000 units and 36,000 units, respectively.

	at 60% capacity, i.e., 24,000 units		at 90% capacity, i.e., 36,000 units	
	C.P. per unit	Total	C.P. per unit	Total
	Rs.	Rs.	Rs.	Rs.
Raw Materials	5	1,20,000	5	1,80,000
Wages	3	72,000	3	1,08,000
Overheads				
Variable	2	48,000	2	72,000
Fixed	1	24,000	0.67	24,000
Total Cost	11	2,64,000	10.67	3,84,000
Profit	2	48,000	2.33	84,000
Selling Price	13	3,12,000	13.00	4,68,000

Now, we are to calculate the time periods which are related to different components of working capital cycle :

(i) Raw material storage period

$$\frac{4{,}000 \text{ units}}{24{,}000 \text{ units}} \times 12 \text{ months} = 2 \text{ months.}$$

(ii) Processing period

$$\frac{1{,}000 \text{ units}}{24{,}000 \text{ units}} \times 12 \text{ months} = \frac{1}{2} \text{ month.}$$

(iii) Finished goods awaiting period

$$\frac{3{,}000 \text{ units}}{24{,}000 \text{ units}} \times 12 \text{ months} = 1\tfrac{1}{2} \text{ months.}$$

(iv) Period of credit allowed to customers

$$\frac{\text{Debtors}}{\text{Sales}} \times 12 = \frac{\text{Rs. } 78{,}000}{\text{Rs. } 3{,}12{,}000} \times 12 = 3 \text{ months.}$$

(v) Period of credit allowed by suppliers

$$\frac{\text{Creditors}}{\text{Purchasers}} \times 12 = \frac{\text{Rs. } 30{,}000}{\text{Rs. } 1{,}20{,}000} \times 12 = 3 \text{ months.}$$

(vi) Lag in payment of wages

$$\frac{\text{Outstanding wages}}{\text{Total wages}} \times 12 = \frac{\text{Rs. } 3{,}000}{\text{Rs. } 72{,}000} \times 12 = \frac{1}{2} \text{ month.}$$

(vii) Lag in payment of overheads

$$\frac{\text{Outstanding overheads}}{\text{Total overheads}} \times 12 = \frac{\text{Rs. } 6{,}000}{\text{Rs. } 72{,}000} \times 12 = 1 \text{ month.}$$

Now we can calculate the requirement of working capital for 36,000 units

		Rs.	Rs.
Current Assets :			
1. Stock of Raw Materials (2 months) : 1,80,000 × $\frac{2}{12}$			30,000
2. Work-in-Progress ($\frac{1}{2}$ month) :			
Raw Materials	Rs. 1,80,000 × $\frac{\frac{1}{2}}{12}$ =	7,500	
Direct Wages	Rs. 1,08,000 × $\frac{\frac{1}{4}}{12}$ =	2,250	
Overheads	Rs. 96,000 × $\frac{\frac{1}{4}}{12}$ =	2,000	11,750
3. Stock of Finished goods ($1\frac{1}{2}$ months) : Rs. 3,84,000 × $\frac{1\frac{1}{2}}{12}$ =			48,000
4. Debtors (including profit element) : Rs. 4,68,000 × $\frac{3}{12}$ =			1,17,000
			2,06,750
*Less : **Current Liabilities :***			
1. Creditors (3 months) : Rs. 1,80,000 × $\frac{3}{12}$ =		45,000	
2. Lag in payment of wages ($\frac{1}{2}$ month) Rs. 1,08,000 × $\frac{\frac{1}{2}}{12}$ =		4,500	
3. Lag in payment of overhead (1 month) Rs. 96,000 × $\frac{1}{12}$ =		8,000	
			57,500
Requirements of Working Capital			1,49,250

Note:

It has been assumed that production is carried on evenly throughout the year and wages and overheads accrue similarly.

Preparation of Forecast Profit and Loss Account and Forecast Balance Sheet

Illustration 7.14

On 1st January, the Board of Directors of XYZ Co. Ltd. wishes to know the amount of working capital that will be required to meet the programme they have planned for the year. From the following information prepare a working capital requirement forecast and Forecast Profit and Loss Account and Balance Sheet:

Issued Share Capital :	
10,000 Equity Shares of Rs. 20 each, fully paid	Rs. 2,00,000
8% Debentures	Rs. 1,00,000
Fixed Assets on 1st January valued at	Rs. 1,10,000
Estimated production	48,000 units per annum

The expected ratios of cost to selling price are:

Materials 50%

Direct Wages and Overhead 20%

Raw materials are expected to remain in stock for an average of $1\frac{1}{2}$ months before issue to production.

Processing time 2 months.

Finished goods will stay in the warehouse awaiting despatch to customers—2 months.

Credit to Debtors — $2\frac{1}{2}$ months.

Credit from Creditors — 1 month.

Time-lag in Wage payment — $\frac{1}{2}$ month.

Lag in payment of all expenses — 1 month.

Selling price is Rs. 10 per unit. There is a regular production and sales cycle. Ignore depreciation.

[C.U . M.Com.]

Solution

Sales for the year 48,000 × Rs. 10 = Rs. 4,80,000.

Sales per month $\frac{\text{Rs. } 4,80,000}{12} = 40,000.$

Amounts to be blocked in Materials, Wages and Overhead per month are:

Materials Rs. 40,000 × 50% = Rs. 20,000.

Direct Wages and Overhead Rs. 40,000 × 20%= Rs. 8,000.

Working Capital Requirements Forecast

Period : January

Particulars	*Period in Months*	*Total*	*Raw Materials*	*Work-in-Progress*	*Finished Goods*	*Debtors*	*Creditors*
		Rs.	Rs.	Rs.	Rs.	Rs.	Rs.
1. *Raw Materials :*							
In Store	$1\frac{1}{2}$		30,000				
In Work-in-progress	2			40,000			
In Finished Goods	2				40,000		

Contd.

		Rs.	Rs.	Rs.	Rs.	Rs.	Rs.
With Debtors	$2\frac{1}{2}$					50,000	
	8						
Less : Credit from Creditors	1						20,000
	7	1,40,000					
2. *Wages and Overhead* :							
In Work-in-progress	1			8,000			
In Finished Goods	2				16,000		
With Debtors	$2\frac{1}{2}$					20,000	
	$5\frac{1}{2}$						
Less : Credit from employees and Creditors $(1 + \frac{1}{2})$	$1\frac{1}{2}$						12,000
	4	32,000					
3. *Profit:*							
Credit to Debtors	$2\frac{1}{2}$	30,000				30,000	
Total		2,02,000	30,000	48,000	56,000	1,00,000	32,000

	Rs.
Estimated requirement of working capital as per above statement	2,02,000
Add: Cash to be required as per Forecast Balance Sheet	1,24,000
∴ Estimated requirement of Working Capital	3,26,000

Forecast Profit and Loss Account

for the year ended 31st December 20.........

Dr.	Rs.		Rs. *Cr.*
To Material Consumed (50% of Rs. 4,80,000)	2,40,000	By Cost of Goods Manufactured c/d	3,36,000
" Wages Overhead (20% of Rs. 4,80,000)	96,000		
	3,36,000		3,36,000
To Cost of Goods Manufactured b/d	3,36,000	By Sales	4,80,000
" Gross Profit c/d	1,44,000		
	4,80,000		4,80,000
To Debenture Interest	8,000	By Gross Profit b/d	1,44,000
" Net Profit	1,36,000		
	1,44,000		1,44,000

Forecast Balance Sheet

as at 31st December 20...........

	Rs.		Rs.	Rs.	Rs.
Share Capital :		Fixed Assets:			1,10,000
Issued, Subscribed and Paid-up :		Working Capital:			
10,000 Equity Shares of Rs. 20 each	2,00,000	Current Assets:			
		Stock—			

Contd.

	Rs.		Rs.	Rs.	Rs.
Profit and Loss A/c (balance)	1,36,000	Raw Materials	30,000		
8% Debentures	1,00,000	Work-in-progress	48,000		
		Finished Goods	56,000		
				1,34,000	
		Debtors		1,00,000	
		Cash at Bank *(bal. fig.)*		1,24,000	
				3,58,000	
		Less :			
		Current Liabilities:			
		Creditors for Materials	20,000		
		Others	12,000	32,000	
					3,26,000
	4,36,000				4,36,000

Note : Assume Interest on debentures has already been paid.

Illustration 7.15

From the following information, you are required to prepare for the management of X Ltd.:

(a) working capital requirement statement;

(b) a Forecast Profit and Loss Account for the year ending 31st December 1999, and

(c) a Forecast Balance Sheet of the company as on that date.

	Rs.
Paid-up capital	10,00,000
8% Debentures	2,50,000
Fixed Assets on 1st January 1999	6,00,000
(Depreciation chargeable @ 10%)	

Production during the previous year was 60,000 units. It is expected that this level of activity would be maintained during the current year. The expected ratio of cost to selling price are : Raw materials 60%, Direct Wages 10%, Overhead 20%.

Raw materials are in stock on an average two months. Materials are in process (valued at cost of raw material plus 50% of direct labour and overheads) on an average one month. Finished goods are in stock, on an average, three months. Credit allowed by Creditors is two months and credit given to Debtors is three months. Selling price is Rs. 25 per unit.

You are informed that there is regular production and sales cycle. Ignore tax.

Solution

Annual Sales = 60,000 × Rs. 25 = Rs. 15,00,000.

$$\text{Sales per month} = \frac{\text{Rs. } 15{,}00{,}000}{12} = \text{Rs. } 1{,}25{,}000.$$

Amounts to be blocked in Material, Labour and Overhead per month are :

				Rs.
Raw Materials	=	Rs. 1,25,000 × $\frac{60}{100}$	=	75,000
Labour	=	Rs. 1,25,000 × $\frac{10}{100}$	=	12,500

Overhead	=	Rs. 1,25,000 $\times \frac{20}{100}$	= Rs. 25,000	
Less : Depreciation	=	Rs. 6,00,000 $\times \frac{10}{100} = \frac{\text{Rs. }60,000}{12}$	= Rs. 5,000	
				= 20,000
Profit	=	Rs. 1,25,000 × 10%	= Rs. 12,500 × 3	= Rs. 37,500

Working Capital Requirements Forecast

Current Assets : *Period* ....

				Rs.
1. Raw Material (2 months) :				
Raw Materials	= Rs. 75,000 × 2	= Rs.	1,50,000	1,50,000
2. Work-in-progress (1 month) :				
Raw Materials	= Rs. 75,000 × 1	= Rs.	75,000	
Direct Wages	= Rs. 12,500 × $\frac{1}{2}$	= Rs.	6,250	
Overheads	= Rs. 20,000 × $\frac{1}{2}$	= Rs.	10,000	
				91,250
3. Stock of Finished Goods (3 months) :				
Raw Materials	= Rs. 75,000 × 3	= Rs.	2,25,000	
Direct Wages	= Rs. 12,500 × 3	= Rs.	37,500	
Overheads	= Rs. 20,000 × 3	= Rs.	60,000	
				3,22,500
4. Debtors (3 months) :				
Raw Materials	= Rs. 75,000 × 3	= Rs.	2,25,000	
Direct Wages	= Rs. 12,500 × 3	= Rs.	37,500	
Overheads	= Rs. 20,000 × 3	= Rs.	60,000	
			3,22,500	
Add : Profit @ : Credit to Debtors			37,500	
				3,60,000
				9,23,750
Less : Current Liabilities				
Creditors (2 months) :				
Raw Materials	= Rs. 75,000 × 2	= Rs.		1,50,000
				7,73,750
Add : Cash to be required as per forecast Balance Sheet		= Rs.		71,250
Working Capital requirement				8,45,000

∴ Total (Rs. 8,45,000 + Rs. 15,000 for Dep.) = Rs. 8,60,000

Forecast Profit and Loss Account
for the year ended 31st December 1999

Dr.	Rs.		*Cr.* Rs.
To Material (@ 60% of Rs. 15,00,000)	9,00,000	By Cost of Goods Manufactured c/d	12,90,000
" Labour (10% of Rs. 15,00,000)	1,50,000		

Contd.

	Rs.		Rs.
To Overhead (20% of Rs. 15,00,000) (3,00,000 – Dep. Rs. 60,000)	2,40,000		
	12,90,000		12,90,000
To Cost of Goods Manufactured b/d	12,90,000	By Sales	15,00,000
" Gross Profit c/d	2,10,000		
	15,00,000		15,00,000
To Depreciation	60,000	By Gross Profit b/d	2,10,000
" Net Profit c/d	1,50,000		
	2,10,000		2,10,000

Forecast Balance Sheet
as at 31st December 1999

Liabilities	Rs.	*Assets*	Rs.	Rs.
Share Capital	10,00,000	Fixed Assets	6,00,000	
Profit & Loss A/c	1,50,000	*Less* : Depreciation	60,000	
8% Debentures A/c	2,50,000			5,40,000
		Working Capital :		
		Current Assets :		
		Stock		
		Raw Materials	1,50,000	
		Work-in-Progress	91,250	
		Finished Goods	3,22,500	
			5,63,750	
		Debtors	3,75,000	
		Cash at Bank *(bal. fig.)*	71,250	
			10,10,000	
		Less : Current Liabilities:	1,50,000	
		(Creditors)		8,60,000
	14,00,000			14,00,000

Note : Since depreciation is a non-cash item it does not require any provision from working capital. But in Forecast Balance Sheet debtors should be shown in full, i.e., inclusive of depreciation, i.e., Rs. 3,60,000 + 15,000 (5,000 × 3) = Rs. 3,75,000.

Illustration 7.16

From the following estimates, ascertain the amount of average working capital which may be required by a firm :

		Figures for the year
		Rs.
(a) Average amount to be blocked in Stock :		
(i) Raw Materials		8,000
(ii) Work-in-progress		6,500
(iii) Finished Goods		9,500
(b) Average period of credit allowed to Debtors :		
(i) For inland sales	8 weeks	4,16,000
(ii) For export sales	5 weeks	1,56,000
(c) Lag in payment of direct and indirect expenses :		
(i) Salaries	3 weeks	78,000
(ii) Wages	2 weeks	1,30,000
(iii) Other expenses	4 weeks	52,000

Contd.

			Rs.
(d)	Average period of credit allowed by Creditors :		
	(i) Creditors	4 weeks	2,60,000
(e)	Payment of Advance Tax (quarterly)		20,000
(f)	A fixed percentage of 10% may be provided for contingencies.		

Solution

Statement Showing the Computation of Average Working Capital

	Rs.	Rs.	Rs.
Current Assets :			
Stock: Raw Materials	8,000		
Work-in-progress	6,500		
Finished Goods	9,500		
		24,000	
Debtors:			
Inland Sales $\frac{\text{Rs. } 4,16,000}{52} \times 8 =$	64,000		
Export Sales $\frac{\text{Rs. } 1,56,000}{52} \times 5 =$	15,000		
		79,000	
Advance Tax : Rs. 20,000 ÷ 4 =		5,000	1,08,000
Less : Current Liabilities:			
Salaries (Rs. 78,000 ÷ 52) × 3		4,500	
Wages (Rs. 1,30,000 ÷ 52) × 2		5,000	
Other Expenses (Rs. 52,000 ÷ 52) × 4		4,000	
		13,500	
Creditors (Rs. 2,60,000 ÷ 52 × 4)		20,000	33,500
Net Working Capital			74,500
Add : For Contingencies @ 10% of the above			7,450
∴ Average Working Capital			81,950

Shift Working

The greatest benefit enjoyed by a firm for introducing shift working is the proper utilisation of fixed capital. Normally, production can be increased and/or doubled without any more corresponding additional investment in fixed capital to introduce double shift. But the same principle is not, however, true in the case of working capital. Because, additional amount of working capital is required for additional materials, labour and overheads for double shift working.

The impact of shift working on working capital is illustrated here in Illustration 17:

Illustration 7.17

Good Luck Ltd. operates a normal working day of 8 hours. There are 30 working days in a month.

The cost of production per month is:

	Rs.
Raw Materials	40,000
Direct Labour	16,000

Contd.

		Rs.	
Overheads :			
Fixed		8,000	
Semi-variable (50% variable)		4,000	
Variable		4,000	16,000
	Total Cost		72,000
	Profit		8,000
	Sales		80,000

Additional Information :

Raw Materials are in stock	1 month
Materials are in process	1 month
Finished goods are in warehouse	2 months
Credit allowed to Debtors	3 months
Lag in payment of wages	$\frac{1}{2}$ month
Lag in payment of overheads	1 month

The management wants to introduce double shift of work for 6 hours a day due to the acute demand of the product. It is also proposed that the workers will receive the same wages per shift as they formerly earned per day.

You are asked to ascertain the requirement of working capital under (1) Single Shift Working; and (2) Double Shift Working.

Solution

Working Capital Requirement Forecast

(Single Shift Workings)

Particulars	Period in Months	Total	Raw Materials	Work-in-Progress	Finished Goods	Debtors	Creditors
		Rs.	Rs.	Rs.	Rs.	Rs.	Rs.
1. *Materials :*							
In stores	1		40,000				
In Work-in-progress	1			40,000			
In Finished Goods	2				80,000		
With Debtors	3					1,20,000	
	7						
Less : Credit from Creditors	1						40,000
	6	2,40,000					
2. *Wages:*							
In Work-in-progress	1			16,000			
In Finished Goods	2				32,000		
With Debtors	3					48,000	
	6						
Less : Credit from Employees	$\frac{1}{2}$						8,000
	$5\frac{1}{2}$	88,000					

Contd.

		Rs.	Rs.	Rs.	Rs.	Rs.	Rs.
3. *Overheads :*							
In Work-in-progress	1			16,000			
In Finished Goods	2				32,000		
With Debtors	3					48,000	
	6						
Less : Creditors	1						16,000
	5	80,000					
4. *Profit :*							
Credit to Debtors	3	24,000				24,000	
Total		4,32,000	40,000	72,000	1,44,000	2,40,000	64,000

∴ Requirement of capital under single shift working (as per above statement) Rs. 4,32,000.

Working Capital Requirements Forecast
(Double Shift Working)

Particulars	*% Change on Single Shift*	*Total*	*Raw Materials*	*Work-in-Progress*	*Finished Goods*	*Debtors*	*Creditors*
		Rs.	Rs.	Rs.	Rs.	Rs.	Rs.
1. *Materials :*							
In Stores	$+ 33\frac{1}{3}\%$		53,333				
In Work-in-progress	—			40,000			
In Finished goods	$+ 33\frac{1}{3}\%$				1,06,667		
With Debtors	$+ 33\frac{1}{3}\%$					1,60,000	
Credit from Creditors	$+ 33\frac{1}{3}\%$						53,333
Total		3,06,667					
2. *Wages :*							
In Work-in-progress	$+ 33\frac{1}{3}\%$			21,333			
In Finished Goods	+ 100%				64,000		
With Debtors	+ 100%					96,000	
Credit from Creditors	+ 100%						16,000
Total		1,65,333					
3. *Overheads :*							
In Work-in-progress	–20.84%			12,666			
In Finished Goods	+18.75%				38,000		
With Debtors	+18.75%					57,000	
Credit from Creditors	+18.75%						
4. *Total*		88,666					19,000
Profit :							
Credit to Debtors	+ 44.91%	34,778				34,778	
		5,95,444	53,333	73,999	2,08,667	3,47,778	88,333

∴ Requirement of Working Capital under Double Shift Working (as per above statement) Rs. 5,95,444.

Workings :

1. *Materials :*

Total working hours under Double Shift 12 hours (6 × 2)

Less : Normal working hours 8

Increased by 4

∴ Percentage of increase in Double Shift $\frac{4}{12} \times 100 = 33\frac{1}{3}\%$.

So cost of materials will be increased by $33\frac{1}{3}\%$.

2. *Wages :*

Total amount to be required for wages will be increased by 100% since the workers receive the same amount of wages in Double Shift Working as they receive in Single Shift.

The effect of work-in-progress, however, is not the same. It will be calculated as :

Single Shift of Working	8	hours a day
But, Double Shift of Working	6	hours a day
Therefore, Time Saved	2	hours a day, as premium payable to workers.

Thus, the effect of working capital is to be increased by $\frac{2}{6} \times 100 = 33\frac{1}{3}\%$.

3. *Overheads :*

Under Single Shift	Rs.	Under Double Shift		Rs.	Rs.
Fixed Overhead	8,000	Fixed Overhead			8,000
Semi-Variable (50% fixed)	4,000	Semi-Variable:			
Variable	4,000	50% Fixed		2,000	
		50% Variable	2,000		
		Add : 50% of 2,000	1,000		
	16,000	(Since the production increased by 50%)		3,000	5,000
		Variable		4,000	
		Add : 50% of 4,000		2,000	
					6,000
					19,000

Amount to be increased in Double Shift (Rs. 19,000 – Rs. 16,000) Rs. 3,000.

∴ Percentage of increase = $\frac{\text{Rs. } 3,000}{\text{Rs.} 16,000} \times 100 = 18.75\%$.

But the treatment of overheads in the case of work-in-progress, however, will be different.

The same may be calculated as :

Under Single Shift	Rs.	Under Double Shift	Rs.	Rs.
Fixed Overhead	8,000	Fixed Overhead	8,000	
Semi-Variable (50% fixed)	4,000	* *Less :* $33\frac{1}{3}\%$	2,667	
Variable	4,000			5,333
	16,000			

Contd.

		Rs.	Rs.
Semi-Variable:			
Fixed	2,000		
Less : $33\frac{1}{3}\%$	667		
		1,333	
Variable		2,000	3,333
Variable Overhead			4,000
			12,666

*Total hours to be worked under Single Shift for 30 days @ 8 hours = 240 hours
The same may be covered under Double Shift 240/12 = 20 days
There is a saving of (30 – 20) = 10 days
Hence, Percentage of Savings $= \frac{10}{30} \times 100 = 33\frac{1}{3}\%$

So, decrease in overhead by Rs. 3,334 (i.e., Rs. 16,000 – Rs. 12,666)

$\therefore$ Percentage of Decrease $= \frac{\text{Rs. } 3,334}{\text{Rs. } 16,000} \times 100 = 20.84\%$.

4. *Profit* :

Cost of Sales from Debtors

	Rs.
Materials	1,60,000
Wages	96,000
Overheads	57,000
	3,13,000
Profit ($\frac{1}{9}$th of cost)	34,778
Sales	3,47,778

Profit is increased by Rs. 10,778 (i.e., Rs. 34,778 – 24,000).

$\therefore$ Percentage of Increase $= \frac{\text{Rs. } 10,778}{\text{Rs. } 24,000} \times 100$

$= 44.91\%$.

Illustration 7.18

A company has been operating on single shift basis to manufacture its product with the following cost-price structure:

	Per unit Rs.
Raw Materials	12
Wages (60% variable)	10
Overdraft (20% variable)	10
	32
Profit	4
Selling Price	36

Sales for the year ended 30th June 1997 amounted to Rs. 8,64,000.

As at 30.6.1997, the company held:

	Rs.
Stock of Raw Materials	72,000
Work-in-progress (valued at Prime Cost)	44,000
Finished Goods (valued at Total Cost)	1,44,000
Sundry Debtors	2,16,000

At present, the company receives 2 months' credit from suppliers of materials and there is a lag of payment of wages and expenses at half a month.

In view of increased market demand, it is proposed to double production by working an extra shift. It is expected that 10% discount will be available from suppliers of raw materials, in view of increased volume of production. Extra production can be sold at the existing price. There will not be any change in the credit policy. Credit from suppliers of materials and time lag in payment of wages and expenses will continue to remain at present level.

You are asked by management to ascertain the effects of working capital or introducing shift working.

Solution

Under Present Level Period : 30th June 1997

Quantity sold $= \frac{\text{Rs. } 8{,}64{,}000}{\text{Rs. } 36} = 24{,}000$ units.

Monthly Production $= \frac{24{,}000}{12} = 2{,}000$ units.

Stock of Raw Materials $= \frac{\text{Rs. } 72{,}000}{\text{Rs. } 12} = 6{,}000$ units.

$\therefore$ 6,000 ÷ 2,000 units = 3 months' requirement.

Work-in-progress $= \frac{\text{Rs. } 44{,}000}{\text{Rs. } 22\ (12 + 10)} = 2{,}000$ units = monthly by requirement.

Stock of Finished Goods $= \frac{\text{Rs. } 1{,}44{,}000}{\text{Rs. } 32\ (12 + 10 + 10)} = 4{,}500$ units

$\therefore$ 4,500 ÷ 2,000 $= 2\frac{1}{4}$ months' requirement.

Sundry Debtors $= \frac{\text{Rs. } 2{,}16{,}000}{\text{Rs. } 8{,}64{,}000} = \frac{1}{4}$ or 3 months' credit allowed to Debtors.

Sundry Creditors : 2 months' credit of Raw materials.

Lag in payment of Wages and Expenses : $\frac{1}{2}$ month.

Working Capital Requirement

Current Assets :		Rs.
1. Stock of Raw Materials		72,000
2. Work-in-Progress		44,000
3. Stock of Finished Goods		1,44,000
4. Sundry Debtors		2,16,000
		4,76,000
Less : Current Liabilities :	Rs.	
1. Sundry Creditors (2,000 × 2 = 4,000 × Rs. 12) =	48,000	
2. Lag in payment of Wages & Expenses : (2,000 × Rs. 20 (10 + 10) × $\frac{1}{2}$)	20,000	
		68,000
Working Capital Requirement		4,08,000

After introducing Shift Working (i.e., after double production)

	Rs.
Raw Materials (Rs. 12 – 10% of Rs. 12)	10.80
Wages	10.00
Prime Cost	20.80
Overheads	10.00
Total Cost	30.80

Working Capital Requirement

Current Assets :		Rs.
1. Stock of Raw Materials (12,000 units × Rs. 10.80)		1,29,600
2. Work-in-progress (4,000 units × Rs. 20.80)		83,200
3. Stock of Finished Goods (9,000 units × Rs. 30.80)		2,77,200
4. Sundry Debtors (Rs. 8,64,000 × 2 = 17,28,000 × $\frac{3}{12}$ or 2,16,000 × 2)		4,32,000
		9,22,000
Less : Current Liabilities :		
1. Sundry Creditors (4,000 × Rs. 10.80 × 2)	86,400	
2. Lag in payment of Wages & Expenses : (4,000 × 20 × $\frac{1}{2}$) or Rs. 20,000 × 2	40,000	
		1,26,400
Working Capital Requirement		7,95,600

Hence, the working capital requirement will be increased by Rs. 3,87,600 (Rs. 7,95,600 – Rs. 4,08,000).

ASSIGNMENT MATERIALS

THEORETICAL

Multiple Choice Questions

1. (a) Working Capital of a firm does not include:

(i) Its cash balance
(ii) Its balance of Sundry Debtors
(iii) Its inventory
(iv) Its immovable assets

(b) Net Working Capital means:

(i) The firms invested in Current Assets
(ii) The firm's investment in Current Assets minus Current Liabilities
(iii) The firms investment in Current Asset means Stock
(iv) The firms' Current Asset minus Stock minus Current Liabilities

(c) Sources of Fixed Working Capital are:

(i) Shares, Debentures, Retention etc.
(ii) Bank Loan, Creditors
(iii) All Current Liabilities
(iv) Short-term Liabilities

(d) Sources of Variable Working Capital are:

(i) Bank Loan, Public Deposit, Trade Credit
(ii) Pref. Shares, Debentures
(iii) Unsecured Liabilities
(iv) Short-term Liabilities

(e) Gross Working Capital is:

(i) Cash and Bank
(ii) Total Current Assets
(iii) Total Current Asset minus Total Current Liabilities
(iv) Total Assets

(f) Negative Working Capital is:

(i) When Current Assets exceed Current Liabilities
(ii) When Current Liabilities exceed Current Assets
(iii) Current Liabilities exceeds Total Assets
(iv) When total assets exceeds Current Liabilities

(g) Positive Working Capital means:

(i) When Current Assets exceed Current Liabilities
(ii) When Current Liabilities exceed Current Assets
(iii) When Fixed Assets exceeds Current Liabilities
(iv) When Current Liabilities exceeds Fixed Assets

(h) Long-term Sources of finance are:

(i) Shares, Debentures etc.
(ii) All Current Liabilities
(iii) Long-term Liabilities minus Short-term Liabilities
(iv) All Liabilities

[Ans. (a) (iv); (b) (ii); (c) (i); (d) (i); (e) (ii); (f) (ii); (g) (i); (h) (i)]

Short Answer-type Questions

2. Discuss the significance of Working Capital.
3. Define : (a) Gross Working Capital; (b) Net Working Capital.
4. Distinguish between Gross Working Capital and Net Working Capital.
5. How do you classify Working Capital?
6. Explain the sources of Core Working Capital.
7. Explain the various sources of Temporary Working Capital.
8. What is Working Capital Cycle?
9. What are the components of Working Capital?
10. What is Positive or Negative Working Capital?
11. What do you mean by Operating Cycle Concept?
12. Discuss the concept of Working Capital and Working Capital Cycle.
13. Explain the role of profit while ascertaining the requirement of Working Capital.
14. What do you mean by Liquidity-Profitability Tangle?
15. How do you estimate the requirement of Working Capital of a Trading Concern?

Long Answer-type Questions

16. Discuss the importance of Working Capital management in any typical business organisation.
17. How do you estimate the requirement of Working Capital of a manufacturing concern?
18. Explain the determinants of Working Capital.
19. Explain the various sources of Fixed and Variable Working Capital.
20. Explain the effect of inflation in Working Capital.
21. Explain the Liquidity-Profitability tangles in Working Capital requirement.
22. What is Working Capital? State the different concepts of Working Capital.
23. Discuss the different sources of Working Capital.
24. How is Working Capital determined for managing a business concern?
25. What is meant by Operating Cycle Concept in management of Working Capital?
26. Describe the need and the determinants of Working Capital in a firm.
27. What is Working Capital Cycle? How is it measured?
28. Define the term Working Capital and explain, with examples, the gross and net concept of it.
29. What is Liquidity-Profitability Tangle? What factors should be considered for solving the tangle?
30. How is Working Capital determined for managing a business concern?

[C.U. B.Com. (Hons.)]

31. Distinguish between 'Gross Working Capital' and 'Net Working Capital'.

[B.U. B.Com. (Hons.)]

32. What are the elements of Working Capital?

33. What do you mean by 'Extra Shift Work'? How should the additional working capital funds required for extra shift work be estimated?

PRACTICAL

1. From the following particulars of Sun Ltd. determine the Working Capital requirement :

(a) Monthly sales (Expected) — 16,000 units of Rs. 10 each.

(b) Analysis of Sales : Materials 40%; Labour 30%; Overhead Rs. 8,000 per week.

(c) Stock will include raw materials for Rs. 48,000 and 8,000 units of finished goods.

(d) Processing Period — 2 weeks

Credit to Debtors — 5 weeks

Credit from Creditors — 1 month

Lag in payment of overhead — 2 weeks

(e) Production is carried on evenly during the year and expenses accrue similarly.

[C.U. B.Com. (Hons.)]

[Ans. Working Capital Requirement Rs. 2,92,000; R.M. Rs. 48,000; W.I.P. Rs. 52,000; F.G. Rs. 72,000; Debtors Rs. 20,000; Creditors Rs. 80,000 (including overhead Rs. 16,000)]

2. From the following information of Sunshine Paints Ltd., you are required to determine the Working Capital Requirement:

(i)	Annual (Expected) Sales	Rs.	3,60,000
(ii)	Analysis of Sales :		
	Raw Materials	50%	
	Expenses	30%	
	Profit	20%	
(iii)	Credit allowed to Debtors		$2\frac{1}{2}$ months
	Credit allowed by Creditors		$1\frac{1}{2}$ months
	Raw Materials in Store		1 month
	Processing Period		2 months
	Finished Goods in Store		4 months
	Bank Overdraft	Rs.	1,00,000
	Cash in hand for contingencies	Rs.	6,000

Production is carried out evenly during the year and expenses accrue similarly.

[C.U. B.Com. (Hons.)]

[Ans. Working Capital Requirement Rs. 1,08,500; R.M. Rs. 15,000; W.I.P. Rs. 39,000; F.G. Rs. 96,000; Debtors Rs. 75,000; Creditors Rs. 22,500]

3. Worship Ltd., a trading concern, provides the following information:
Annual sales during the year 1993 Rs. 1,20,000
Analysis of Sales show:
Materials 60%, Expenses 15%, Profit 25%
Average credit period allowed to Debtors 3 months.
Average credit period allowed by creditors $1\frac{3}{4}$th months.
Raw Materials are to remain in Store, on average, 1 month.
Processing period, on average, 2 months.
Finished Goods are to remain in Warehouse, on average, 3 months.
Bank Overdraft Rs. 9,000.
10% of the total Working Capital is to be kept in hand for contingencies.

You are required to determine the Working Capital requirement of Worship Ltd. on the basis of above information.

[C.U. M.Com.]

[Ans. Working Capital Required Rs. 61,000; R.M. Rs. 6,000; W.I.P. Rs. 15,000; F.G. Rs. 22,500; Debtors Rs. 30,000; Creditors Rs. 10,500]

4. From the following information, prepare a statement showing the estimated working capital requirements :

(i) Projected annual sale — 26,000 units
(ii) Selling price per unit — Rs. 60.00
(iii) Analysis of selling price:
Material 40%, Labour 30%, Overhead 20%, Profit 10%
(iv) Time-lag (on average) :

Raw Materials in Stock	3 weeks
Production Process	4 weeks
Credit to Debtors	5 weeks
Credit to Suppliers	3 weeks
Lag in payment of wages and overheads	2 weeks

Finished goods are in warehouse — 2 weeks.
(v) Cash in hand is expected to be 10% of net working capital.

[C.U. B.Com. (Hons.)]

[Ans. Requirement of Working Capital Rs. 2,80,000; Cash Rs. 28,000; R.M. Rs. 36,000; W.I.P. Rs. 78,000; F.G. Rs. 54,000; Debtors Rs. 1,50,000; Creditors Rs. 36,000; Lag-in-payment of Wages Rs. 18,000; Overhead Rs. 12,000]

5. From the following information supplied by M/s Walcott & Co., prepare a working capital statement as the company will require to run its year of working :

(i) Credit allowed to Debtors against the annual sale of Rs. 9,00,000 is 2 months.
(ii) Average amount to be locked up in stocks :

(a) Finished Goods	Rs. 9,000
(b) Work-in-progress	Rs. 6,200
(c) Raw Materials	Rs. 7,800

(iii) Lag in payment of Direct and Indirect Expenses:

(a) Wages Rs. 2,04,000	2 weeks or $\frac{1}{2}$ month
(b) Raw Materials Rs. 3,60,000	8 weeks or 2 months
(c) Overheads Rs. 48,000	4 weeks or 1 month

(iv) Payment of Advance Tax (Quarterly) Rs. 20,000

(v) For contingencies and uncertainties, a fixed percentage of 10% on net working capital may be provided for.

[Ans. Average Working Capital required Rs. 1,16,050]

6. You are required to prepare for the Board of Directors of Wardha Brickworks Ltd. a statement showing the Working Capital needed to finance a level of activity of 10,400 units of output.

You are given the following information:

Elements of Cost	*Amount per Unit* Rs.
Raw Materials	4
Direct Labour	1
Overheads	3
Total Cost	8
Profit	2
Selling Price	10

Raw materials are in stock, on average, one month. Materials are in process, on average, half a month. Finished goods are in stock, on average, 6 weeks. Credit allowed by Creditors is one month.

Credit allowed to Debtors is two months.

Lag in payment of Wages is 1.5 weeks.

Cash on hand and at Bank is expected to be Rs. 22,300.

You are informed that production is carried on evenly during the year and wages and overheads accrue similarly.

[C.U. M.Com.—Adapted]

[Ans. Requirement of Working Capital Rs. 50,000]

7. From the following information available from the Books of Wonderland Toys Ltd. Prepare a statement showing the estimated Working Capital requirement (a) in total, and (b) as regards each constituent part of Working Capital.

Budget Sales Rs. 1,30,000 per annum. Analysis of cost of each unit is :

	Rs.
Raw Materials	3
Labour	4
Overheads	2
Profit	1
Total	10

It is estimated that :

(a) Pending use, raw materials are carried in stock for three weeks and finished goods for two weeks.

(b) Factory processing will take three weeks.

(c) Suppliers will give five weeks' credit and customers will require eight weeks' credit. It may be assumed that production and overheads accrue evenly throughout the year.

[C.U . M.Com.]

[Ans. Total Working Capital Requirement Rs. 27,500]

8. D. Co. Ltd. wishes to start a trading business and furnishes the following particulars:

(i) Estimated annual sales Rs. 3,60,000.

(ii) Estimated fixed expenses Rs. 2,400 p.m., of which depreciation amounted to Rs. 800 and estimated variable expenses chargeable to P & L A/c equal to 5% of sales.

(iii) Expected profit on purchases—20%.

(iv) Probable stock-turnover—5 times.

(v) The sales and purchases will occur evenly throughout the year.

(vi) All purchases will be made on credit and D. Co. Ltd. expects one month's credit for it.

(vii) One-fourth of the sales will be made against cash. Customers will be allowed two months' credit.

Calculate : (a) D. Co. Ltd.'s estimated profit for the year, and

(b) Average Working Capital Requirement.

While calculating Working Capital Requirement, provision for depreciation is not required, for cash is not required immediately for the same.

[Ans. (a) Rs. 22,800; (b) Rs. 83,100]

9. Webster & Robson Robot Manufacturing Co. Ltd. wishes to commence a new trading business and gives the following information :

(1) The total estimated sales in a year will be Rs. 12,00,000.

(2) Expenses are estimated at a fixed expense of Rs. 2,000 p.m. plus a variable expense equal to 5% of turnover.

(3) Sale price for each product will be 25% in excess of cost of purchase.

(4) Turnover to stock will be four times in the year.

(5) The sales and purchase will be evenly spread throughout the year. All sales will be for cash but one month's credit for purchases is expected.

Calculate : (a) Estimated Profit for the year;

(b) Average Working Capital Requirements.

[C.A.]

[Ans. (a) Rs. 1,56,000; (b) Rs. 1,81,000]

MANAGEMENT OF WORKING CAPITAL

The proper management policies and financing working capital have already been discussed earlier in the present chapter. Now, the impact of various components of working capital (Cash, Debtors and Inventories) are to be discussed in the present section in order to examine the optimum requirements for the same. The subsequent discussion will cover how the individual current assets are managed:

I. Management of Cash; II. Management of Debtors; and III. Inventory Management.

I. MANAGEMENT OF CASH

Introduction

Cash is the medium of exchange on the common purchasing power and the most important component of working capital. It includes coins, currency and cheques held by the firm and the balances in its bank accounts. Sometimes *near-cash* items also are included.[1] Cash is the basic input required to keep a firm running on a continuous basis. At the same time it is the ultimate output expected to be realised by selling goods and services. A firm should hold sufficient case—neither more, nor less. Excessive cash remains idle which simply increases the cost without contributing anything towards the profitability of the firm and, in the opposite case, trading and/or manufacturing operation will be disrupted.

Not only that, it largely upholds, under given condition, the quantum of other ingredients of working capital, viz., inventories and debtors, that may be needed for a given scale and type of operation.[2] Cash is, no doubt, a most important asset and that is why a firm wants to get hold of it in the shortest time possible. In the absence of sufficient quantity of cash at the proper time, payment of bills, including dividend and others, may not be made.

It is interesting to note that cash management involves three factors:

(i) Ascertainment of a minimum cash balance;

(ii) Proper arrangement to be made for collection and payment of cash in such a way that minimum balance can be maintained; and

(iii) Surplus cash to be invested to temporary investments or to be invested in fixed assets.

Similarly, cash is not productive directly like other assets, viz., it is sterile. For example, fixed assets are acquired for the purpose of earning revenue. Accounts receivables are generated by granting credit to customers, etc. Apart from the fact that it is the most liquid current asset, cash is the common denominator to which all current assets can be reduced because the other major current liquid assets, viz., receivables, inventories etc., get converted eventually into cash. It is the significance of cash management which is the key area of working capital management. Cash Management is important since it is very difficult to estimate correctly the inflow of cash. Practically, it is not so easy to make a proper synchronisation of inflows and outflows of cash.

For this purpose, the firm should develop some strategies for cash management for.[3]

(a) *Cost Planning*

A cash budget should be prepared for ascertaining the cash surplus or deficit for each period of planning through the inflows and outflows of cash.

---

1 Banerjee B.—*Cash Management—A Practical Approach*—The World Press (P) Ltd. 1982, p. 1.

2 *Ibid.*

3 Pandey. I. M.—*Financial Management*—Vikash Publishing House (P) Ltd., 1986.

(b) *Managing the Cash Flows*

The flow of cash (inflow and outflow) should properly be managed so that the synchronisation between inflow and outflow is possible.

(c) *Optimum Cash Level*

The optimum level of cash should always be maintained, i.e., the appropriate level of cash balance should be determined.

(d) *Investing Idle Cash*

The excess or idle cash should properly be invested in order to earn profit.

Motives for Holding Cash

The following motives play a very significant role for holding cash.

Keynes has identified three motives for holding cash[1] :

(a) The Transactions Motive;

(b) The Precautionary Motive; and

(c) The Speculative Motive;

(d) The Investment Motive, and

(e) Future Requirements.

These are discussed one by one.

(a) ***The Transactions Motive***

This motive refers to the holding of cash in order to meet the day-to-day transactions which a firm carries on in the ordinary course of the business. Primarily, these transactions include purchase of raw materials, wages, operating expenses, taxes, dividends etc. A firm may enter into a variety of transactions to accomplish its objectives. Similarly, there is regular inflow of cash from revenues. Thus, the receipts and payments constitute a continuous two-way flow of cash. Since the inflow and outflow of cash do not perfectly synchronise, an adequate or a minimum cash balance is required to uphold the operations if outflow exceeds the inflow. Therefore, in order to meet the day-to-day transactions, the requirement of cash is known as *Transaction Motive.* So, it refers to the holding of cash to meet anticipated obligations when timing is not perfectly synchronised with the inflow of cash. Although a major part of transaction balance is held in cash, a part may also be held in the form of marketable securities whose maturity conforms to the timing of the anticipated payments, such as payment of taxes, dividends etc.[2]

(b) ***The Precautionary Motive***

This motive for holding cash has to do with maintaining a cushion or buffer to meet unexpected contingencies. The unexpected cash needs at short notice may be the result of:

(i) uncontrollable circumstances, such as floods, strikes, droughts etc.;

(ii) bills which may be presented for settlement earlier than expected;

(iii) unexpected delay in collection of trade dues;

(iv) cancellation of some order for goods due to inferior quality; and

(v) increase in the cost of material, labour etc.

---

1 Keynes. J. M.—*The General Theory of Employment, Interest and Money*—New York, Harcourt, Brace & Jovanovich, 1936, pp. 70-74.

2 Khan, M. Y. and Jain, P. K.—*Financial Management*—op. cit., p. 664.

Precautionary balances are the cash balances which are held as reserve for random and unforeseen fluctuations in cash flows, i.e., this motive implies the need to hold cash to meet unpredictable obligations. The more predictable the cash flows, the less precautionary balances that are needed, and vice versa. Moreover, the need for this type of cash balance may be reduced if there is already borrowing power in order to meet the emergency cash outflows. Sometimes a portion of such cash balances may be held in marketable securities, i.e., near-money assets.

(c) *The Speculative Motive*

This motive refers to the holding of cash for taking advantages of expected changes in security price. In other words, when the rates of interest are expected to fall, cash may be invested in different securities so that the firm will benefit by any subsequent fall in interest rates and rise in security prices. On the other hand, when the rates of interest are expected to rise, the firm should hold cash until the rise in interest rates ceases. The precautionary motive is defensive in nature while speculative motive represents a positive and aggressive approach. The speculative motive helps to take advantages of:

(i) an opportunity to purchase raw materials at a reduced price against immediate payment, i.e., benefit of cash discounts;

(ii) a change to speculate on interest rate movements by purchasing securities when rates of interest are expected to decline;

(iii) the purchase at favourable prices.

(d) **Investment Motive**

We know that Cash is required for various investment purposes. Some of them are:

(a) to meet operational activities;

(b) to build an investment image;

(c) to maintain better relationship with banks;

(d) to provide liquidity reserves for:

(i) Major outlay;

(ii) Routine outlay;

(iii) Undesirable payment for Cash;

(iv) Taking the advantage of long-term investments.

Thus, a certain amount of cash should always be kept in hand for meeting the above expense and to take the benefits of bothlong-term and short-term investment.

(e) **Future Requirements**

The cash balance should also be maintained to meet future payments and obligations, e.g., payment for dividend and taxes, acquisition of fixed assets, repayment of loans and any contingency payments etc.

Level of Cash Balance

Adequate cash balance should always be maintained by a firm. But it does not mean that the firm should hold excessive cash balance since it is a non-earning asset. Excessive cash balance will not only impair the firm's profitability but also give a lower asset turnover ratio. Therefore, optimum cash balance should be maintained by a firm. For this purpose, two factors are to be considered, viz., (a) Compensating Balances, and (b) Self-imposed Balances.

(a) **Compensating Balances**

Banks serve different types of service to the firms, e.g., clearance of cheque, transfer of funds, against a nominal commission or fee. Generally, clients (firms) are required to maintain a minimum cash balance at the bank which cannot be utilised by them for transaction purposes.[1] The bank can use the same to earn a return. In other words, in order to compensate the services rendered by the banks, clients/firms are required to keep a balance which will be sufficient to earn a return equal to the cost of services. Such balances are known as compensating balances.[2]

Sometimes, compensating balances are also maintained when loans are granted by a bank to its customers, particularly when the supply of credit is restricted and the rate of interest is rising. In short, a borrower must maintain a minimum balance at bank in order to compensate the bank against the risk of interest rate.

Therefore, compensating balances take the following forms :

(i) An absolute minimum :

Say Rs. 10 lakhs, below which the bank balance will never be allowed to fall.

(ii) A minimum average balance :

Say Rs. 10 lakhs, over a particular period, e.g., one month.

(b) **Self-imposed Balances**

Self-imposed balance is determined in order to consider :

(i) the need for cash and its predictability;

(ii) interest rate or borrowing rate on marketable securities;

(iii) the fixed cost of effecting a transfer between cash and marketable securities.

However, some models are used for determining the self-imposed balance:

Optimum Cash Balance Using Models

Every firm should ascertain the optimum Cash balance so that there must not be any excess Cash which will remain idle and increase cost and on the other hand, there must not be any shortage of cash which adversely affect the Working Capital position. Cash budget reveals the period when a firm is expected to have a surplus or shortage of funds. If there is excess or surplus amount of cash, the excess may be utilised in profitable investment opportunities and at the same time if there is shortage or deficit of funds various ways and means should be considered. That is why every firm should maintain the optimum cash level which will indicate the trade-off between risk and return of maintaining Cash balance for a firm. There are several models developed by the scholars and researchers which deal with the problem of optimum cash balance. Some of them are highlighted below.

CASH MANAGEMENT MODELS

(a) Operating Cycle Model; (b) Inventory Model; (c) Stochastic Model; (d) Probability Model, and (e) Baumol's Model.

(a) **Operating Cycle Model**

The operating cycle concept of working capital has already been discussed earlier in the present chapter where it has been mentioned that the higher the cash turnover, the lower

---

1 In India, every current account of a firm should have a minimum balance of Rs. 5,000 at the bank.

2 Generally, the compensating balances are fixed by a bank on consideration of income from an account and cost of operation of the same—Vanhorne. J. C.—*Financial Management Policy*, Prentice-Hall of India Ltd., 1976, p. 346.

will be the requirements for cash, and vice versa. It has also been mentioned that the optimum requirement of cash needed by a firm is determined by dividing the firm's total annual expenditures by the cash-turnover rate.

The following illustration will make the principle clear:

	Case I	Case II
Total operating expenses (p.a.)	Rs. 250 lakhs	Rs. 250 lakhs
No. of working days	300	300
Length of O. C. period (days)	200	150
Cash to Working Capital (%)	$12\frac{1}{2}$	$12\frac{1}{2}$
Cash Turnover Ratio $= \left(\frac{No. of\ working\ days}{O.C.\ period}\right)$	$\frac{300}{200} = 1.5$	$\frac{300}{150} = 2$
Working Capital $= \left(\frac{Total\ Operating\ Expenses\ p.a.}{Cash\ Turnover\ Ratio}\right)$	$\frac{\text{Rs. 250 lakhs}}{1.5}$ = 166.67 lakhs	$\frac{\text{Rs. 250 lakhs}}{2}$ = 125 lakhs
Cash balance (assume $12\frac{1}{2}$% of Working Capital)	Rs. 20.83 lakhs	Rs. 15.63 lakhs

(b) **Optimum Cash Balance using Inventory Model**

The economic order quantity formula (EOQ) which is used in inventory management provides a useful conceptual foundation for the cash management problem.[1] In this model, the carrying cost of holding cash (viz., the interest forgone on marketable securities) is balanced against the fixed cost of transferring marketable securities to cash, or vice versa.

When a firm holds too small cash balance, it runs out of costs, i.e., costs of running short of cash, the elements of which are[2] :

(i) cost of passing up trade discounts;

(ii) cost of passing up quantity discounts;

(iii) cost of becoming delinquent; and

(iv) cost of failure to meet payroll on time, or to make interest and principal payment when due.

However, if there is a shortage of cash, marketable securities are liquidated or fresh borrowing can be made. Both of them require procurement costs which is inclusive of fixed costs related with the transaction. Moreover, in addition to running cost, a portion of general fixed cost may also be included. Similarly, when a firm holds too high a cash balance, it may have to incur either opportunity cost or borrowing cost. They will also arise from all other assets that have been passed up in favour of holding the cash as cash and from liabilities that continue to be outstanding because cash is not used to pay them off.[3]

---

1 It was originally applied in cash management by Baumol W. J., *The Transactions Demand for Cash : An Inventory Approach*—Quarterly Journal of Economics, 66 (Nov. 1952), pp. 545-56.

2 Banerjee. B.—*Financial Policy and Management Accounting*—op. cit., p. 155.

3 Lindsay, J. R. and Sametz. A. W.—*Financial Management—An Analytical Approach,* Richard D. Irwin. Inc. Homeword, Illinois, 1968, p. 131.

No doubt borrowing costs are the financing cost related with borrowings. Now the question arises which one is more advantageous—selling short-term securities into cash, or borrowing? Because, sometimes, it is cheaper to sell short-term securities while it may be wise to borrow from banks at times. Therefore, if the firm does not possess any short-term securities which can be sold, it can borrow from bank.

The 'cost of carrying' may be represented as opportunity/borrowing cost while 'cost of not carrying' represents transaction/short costs. It is to be remembered that the optimum cash balance is the balance where cost of carrying or opportunity cost becomes equal to the cost of not carrying or transaction cost. At this level, the total costs, i.e., the sum of opportunity cost/borrowing cost and transaction/short costs, become minimum. Thus, a firm should always maintain an optimum cash balance — neither small nor large. Fig. 7.4 shows the optimum cash balance.

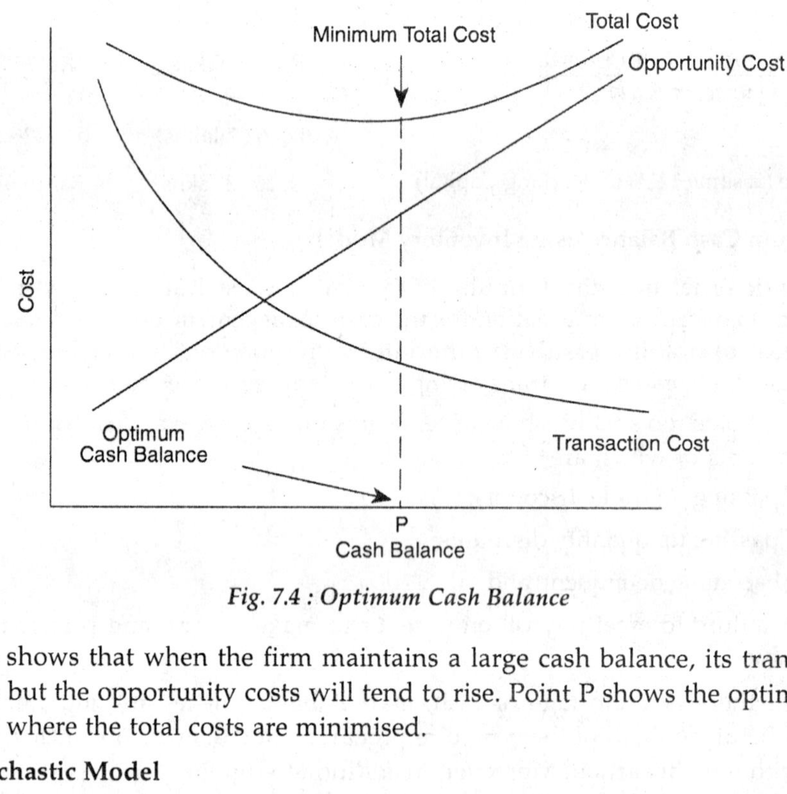

Fig. 7.4 : Optimum Cash Balance

Fig. 7.4 shows that when the firm maintains a large cash balance, its transaction costs will decline but the opportunity costs will tend to rise. Point P shows the optimum position of cash and where the total costs are minimised.

(c) **Stochastic Model**

Where the uncertainty of cash payment is large, i.e. the future is unknown with certainty, the EOQ models may not be applicable. Naturally, in order to determine optimum behaviour, other models should be used assuming that the demand for cash is stochastic and unknown in advance. Control theory can be applicable where cash balances fluctuate widely. One can set control limits such that when cash reaches an upper limit a transfer of cash to marketable securities is consummated, when it hits a lower limit a transfer from marketable securities to cash is triggered. Setting the control limits depends upon the fixed cost associated with securities transaction and the opportunity cost of holding in cash.

Miller-Orr Model[1] (1966)

There are a number of control theories to the problem. The relatively simple one is The **Miller-Orr Model**, which specifies two control limits—'h' as an upper bound and '0' (zero) amount as a lower bound. The model is illustrated as under:

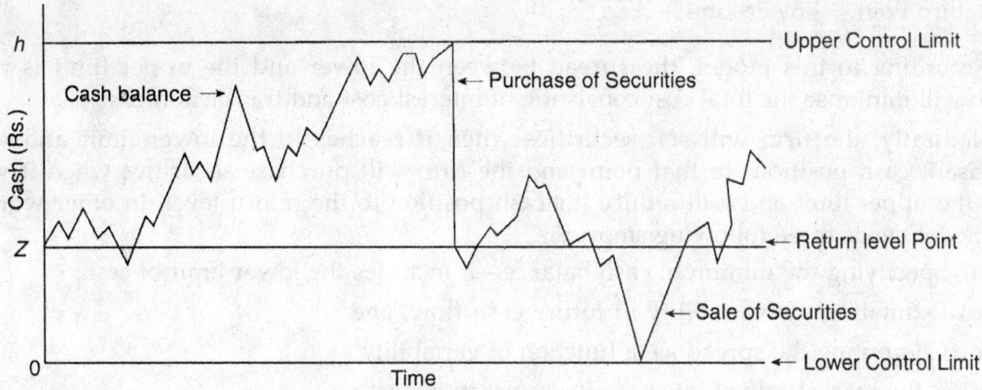

Fig. 7.5: Miller-Orr Model

It is evident that if cash balance touches the upper bound, h-Z rupees of marketable securities are purchased and as such, new balance becomes Z rupees. On this contrary, if balance touch Zero, Z rupees of marketable securities are sold and the new balance become Z again. The minimum amount can be set at some amount higher than zero, and h and z will move up in the figure accordingly. Similarly, as long as cash balance lies in between the two limits of *H* (higher) and *L* (lower), there will be no purchase and sale of securities.

In short, the model expresses the following two control limits

0 = ***Lower Control Limit*** i.e., minimum balance to be maintained by a firm.

h = ***Upper Control Limit*** i.e., beyond which the firm will not go.

Z = ***Return Level Point.***

This model gives an answer relating to minimum and maximum balance to be maintained. It should be mentioned that the solution for optimum value of *h* and *z* depends upon the fixed and opportunity cost along with the degree of likely fluctuation in cash balance.

The optimum value of *z*, the return-to-point for security transactions, is $z = \sqrt[3]{\frac{3b\sigma^2}{4i}}$

Where, b = fixed cost associated with a security transaction

σ^2 = variance of daily net cash flows

i = interest rate per day on marketable securities

The optimum value of *h* is simply 3z.

With these control limits this model minimises the total costs (fixed and opportunity) of cash management. The average cash balance cannot be determined exactly but the same is approximately $(\frac{z+h}{3})$ known. The average cash balance, according to this model, will be higher than that suggested by inventory model.

---

1 Miller, M. H. and Orr Daniel—*A Model for the Demand for Money by Firms*—Quarterly Journal of Economics—80, Aug. 1966, pp. 413-35.

Alternatively

$$\text{Spread between the control limit} = 3\left(\frac{\frac{3}{4}\times \text{Transaction Cost}\times \text{Variance of Cash Flows}}{\text{Interest Rate}}\right)^{\frac{1}{3}}$$

$$\text{Return Point} = \text{Lower Limit} + \frac{\text{Spread}}{3}$$

According to this model, the spread between the lower and the upper limit is that which will minimise the total cost consisting of interest cost and transaction cost.

Naturally, the firm will sell securities when it reaches to the lower limit and will increase it cash position to that point and the firm will purchase securities when it will cross the upper limit and will reduce it's cash position to the return level. In other words, this model needs three following steps, viz.,

(a) Specifying the minimum cash balance—it includes the lower limit of cash;

(b) Estimating the variability in future cash flow; and

(c) Computing the spread as a function of variability,
—the market rate of interest plus transaction cost.

To find out the upper cash limit the spread is added to the lower cash limit.

However, Miller-Orr Model is applicable when optimum cash balance is determined under uncertainty. Practically, this model overcomes the limitations of Baumol's model as the latter does not allow the cash flows to fluctuate. But, in real-world situation, firms neither use their cash balance uniformly nor they can predict the daily cash inflows or outflows. But Miller-Orr Model allows the daily cash variation. In short, it suggests that net cash flows are usually distributed with a 0 (zero) value of mean $(\bar{X})$ and a Standard Deviation (σ). This model is considered as a realistic one as it recognises the variation of cash balance within lower and upper control limit.

Illustration 7.19

Y Ltd. presented the following information:

Minimum Cash balance to be maintained	Rs. 3,000
Transaction Cost	Rs. 50
Rate of Interest per day	0.5%
Standard Deviation of daily cash flows	Rs. 400
(i.e., variance of Rs. 1,60,000)	

Ascertain the upper limit and the Return Point

Solution

$$\text{Spread} = 3\left(\frac{\frac{3}{4}\times \text{Transaction Cost}\times \text{Variance of Cash Flows}}{\text{Interest Rate}}\right)^{\frac{1}{3}}$$

$$= 3\left(\frac{\frac{3}{4}\times \text{Rs.}50\times \text{Rs.}1,60,000}{0.005}\right)^{\frac{1}{3}}$$

$$= \text{Rs. } 3,188 \text{ or Say Rs. } 3,200$$

Upper Limit = Lower limit + Spread

= Rs. 3,000 + Rs. 3,200

= 6,200

$$\text{Return Point} = \text{Lower Limit} + \frac{\text{Spread}}{3} = \text{Rs. } 3{,}000 + \frac{\text{Rs. } 3{,}200}{3} = \text{Rs. } 4{,}067$$

Illustration 7.20

Z Ltd. presented the following information:

Minimum Cash Balance to be maintained	Rs. 2,000
Standard Deviation (Variance Rs. 14,40,000) in daily cash flows	Rs. 1,200
Transaction Cost	Rs. 20
Rate of Interest per day	0.01%

Compute the upper control limit and lower control limit as per Miller-Orr Model.

Solution

(Following the first method)

$$Z = \sqrt[3]{\frac{3b\sigma^2}{4i}}$$

where, b = Transaction Cost of Securities = Rs. 20

δ^2 = Variance of daily cash flows = Rs. 14,40,000

i = Rate of Interest per day = 0.0001

$$\text{or, } = \left(\frac{3 \times \text{Rs.}20 \times \text{Rs.}14{,}44{,}000}{4 \times 0{,}0001}\right)^{\frac{1}{3}}$$ (Putting the values, in the above equation)

or, = Rs. 6,000

Lower Limit = Minimum balance + Z

= Rs. 2,000 + Rs. 6,000

= Rs. 8,000

Upper Limit = Minimum balance + 3Z

= 2,000 + (3 × Rs. 6,000)

= Rs. 20,000

It becomes clear from the above that as long as the cash balance will lie in-between Rs. 2,000 and Rs. 20,000, it need not worry. But if the cash balance appears below the level of Rs. 2,000, the firm must sell some securities to reach at Rs. 8,000. On the other hand, if cash balance reaches at Rs. 20,000 the firm may purchase securities till the balance comes to Rs. 8,000.

(d) **Probability Model**

The EOQ model assumes that cash flows are predictable while the Control-Limit Model assumes that they are random. But, in practice, cash flows are neither completely predictable nor stochastic. On the other hand, they are predictable within a range. In the circumstances, probability distribution may be used for a range of possible outcome and optimum cash balance may be ascertained accordingly.

(e) **Baumol's Model**

It has been stated above that the primary purpose of each model is to allow management to maintain an optimum cash level throughout the period. One sophisticated model has been developed by Baumol.[1] This model, is practically the same as EOQ (Economic Order Quantity) model of inventory management. The purpose of this model is to ascertain the balance of income forgone on cash held against the transaction cost of converting cash into marketable securities by a firm. This model explains that, to reduce the holding cost, minimum cash balances may be maintained by a firm. Thus, a firm may procure cash by disposing of some marketable securities whenever it requires cash. As a result, it must bear transaction cost and, naturally, it will try to minimise the transaction. This limitation may be overcome by maintaining a higher cash balance against higher holding cost at the same time. Thus, a firm must consider both the holding cost and the transaction cost.

It is needless to mention that an optimum cash balance may be ascertained by controlling both the costs (transaction and holding) in order to minimise the cost of holding cash by a firm. It may also be said that cash received by disposing of marketable securities will be utilised in such a manner that the transaction cost must optimally balanced with the holding of cash by a firm. The model is:

$$C = \sqrt{\frac{2BT}{i}}$$

where, C = Minimum cash balance to be maintained

B = Total cash required during a period

T = Transaction cost between cash and marketable securities

i = Interest rate which could have been earned

From the discussion made so far, it becomes clear that, according to Baumol, a firm must start with the cash balance equal to C above and will spend till the balance of cash comes to zero. When this situation will arise the firm will replenish cash by disposing of marketable securities to maintain the balance of cash.

Illustration 7.21

Compute the amount of marketable securities to be converted into cash per order using Baumol's Model assuming that the company may sell its marketable securities in any of the 5 lots viz., 75,000; 1,50,000; 3,00,000; 3,75,000 or 7,50,000.

Y Ltd. requires Rs. 15,00,000 in cash to meet its transaction cost during the next three months. It also holds marketable securities of an equal amount. Annual Yield is 20% cash of conversion into cash per transaction Rs. 1,500.

Solution

$$C = \sqrt{\frac{2BT}{i}}$$

where, B = Rs. 1,500

T = Rs. 15,00,000

i = 20% ÷ 4 = 5% or 0.05

---

1 Baumol W. J.—*The Transaction Demand for Cash : An Inventory—Theoretic Approach*, Quarterly Journal of Economics, Nov. 1952, pp. 545-56.

$$C = \sqrt{\frac{2BT}{i}}$$

$$= \sqrt{\frac{2 \times Rs.1,500 \times Rs.15,00,000}{0.05}}$$

$$= Rs.\ 3,00,000$$

Illustration 7.22

X Ltd. estimates that during the next budgeted period Rs. 12,00,000 may be required for which it decides to deposit cash to a scheduled bank against an interest rate of 10% p.a. X Ltd. may have to incur Rs. 100 for every withdrawl. Ascertain the optimal size of withdrawl.

Solution

$$C=\sqrt{\frac{2BT}{i}}$$

where, C = Minimum Cash balance to be maintained
B = Total cash required during a period = Rs. 12,00,000
T = Transaction Cost = Rs. 100
i = Rate of Interest pa = 0.10

Or, = $\sqrt{\frac{2 \times Rs.12,00,000 \times Rs.100}{0.10}}$ (Putting the value in the above equation)

= Rs. 49,000 (approx.)

∴ X Ltd. can withdraw from bank each time Rs. 49,000.

Estimation of Cash Requirements

No doubt the primary step in cash management is to estimate the requirement of Cash. For this purpose (a) Cash flows, and (b) Cash Budgets, are required to be prepared (which have been highlighted in details in the subsequent part of this volume.).

Cash Management

Synchronisation of Cash Flows

The different aspects of cash management have already been outlined earlier. Now, the various collection and disbursement methods by which a firm can increase its efficiency in cash management are discussed in the present column. Practically, these methods constitute two sides of the same coin, they exercise a joint impact on the overall efficiency of cash management. However, the efficiency of cash management depends upon:

(A) Efficient inventory management;

(B) Speeding up collections of accounts receivables; or speeding up Cash Receipts; and

(C) Slowing Down Cash Payments or, Delaying payments on accounts payable, i.e., deferring disbursements.

(A) *Efficient inventory management*

The primary elements of an efficient management of inventory are discussed in the next section of the present chapter in details.

(B) *Speeding up cash receipts and collections of accounts receivables*

In order to manage cash efficiently, the process of cash inflow can be accelerated through systematic planning and refined techniques. There are, however, two broad approaches to do this :

(a) the customers should be encouraged to pay as quickly as possible by introducing cash discounts;

(b) the payment from customers should be converted into cash without any delay, i.e., managing float to speed-up collection.

(a) **Prompt payment by customers**

Prompt billing is one of the ways for ensuring prompt payment by customers, i.e., the bill should be prepared correctly and notified to the customer concerned in advance, mentioning the date of payment. Mechanical devices for billing may be used for this purpose. The other important technique for encouraging prompt payment is the practice of introducing cash discounts which is a saving to the customer. The various aspects of introducing cash discount have been discussed in a separate paragraph that follows dealing with management of debtors.

(b) **Managing Float to speed up collection**

Where the payment is made by he customers by issuing a cheque, the procedure of collection can be expedited by prompt encashment of the same. We all know that there is a time lag between the time a cheque is prepared and mailed by the customers and the actual realisation of the same. Practically, different floats are involved for the time interval.

Float

Float is defined as the difference between the balance shown in a firm's/individual's cheque book and the balance on the bank records. The Float should properly be managed so that the length of cash cycle is reduced. The sources of floats are:

(a) **Billing Float**

Billing Float means the time taken between the sale of goods and mailing of invoice.

(b) **Postal/Mailing Float**

Postal Float is the time taken by the post office messenger service or other means of delivery to transfer the cheque from the customers to the firm, i.e., the transit or mailing time should be reduced as far as possible.

(c) **Cheque Processing Float**

The time which is taken in processing the cheque within the firm before they are deposited into bank is known as cheque processing float i.e., the time taken between the processing the cheque and receipt of cheque and deposit the same to the bank.

(d) **Bank Float/Cheque Clearing Float**

Usually, when a cheque is deposited into bank it takes 3 days to be credited to the firm's account due to clearing system. In other words, the time taken by the bank is collecting the payments i.e., (collection time within the bank) from the customer's bank is called Bank float on cheque clearing float.

Deposit Float

All the floats referred to above (i.e., postal, cheque and bank) are known as *Deposit Float*. It is defined as the sum of cheques written by customers that are not usable by the firm. No doubt, the collection of accounts receivables can be accelerated considerably by reducing the above floats, i.e., the reduction in deposit float. The same is possible only when the decentralised collection policy is being adopted by the firms.

Types of Float

Float can be divided into:

(a) Collection Float;

(b) Disbursement Float; and

(c) Net Float.

(a) Collection Float

The amount of cheques which we receive but have not yet been credited to our account is called collection float. If the collection and clearing process of the firm is more efficient than that of the recipient of its cheque, then the firm could actually show a ***negative balance*** on its own books but have a ***positive balance*** on its banker's book. For example, a firm receives cheques for Rs. 10,000 daily but it loses four days to be credited for clearance. Thus, collection float amounts to Rs. 40,000.

(b) Disbursement Float

The amount of the cheque which we have written but those are still being processed and the same have not been deducted from our accounts by the bank is known as ***Disbursement Float.*** For example, a firm issues on an average cheques amounting to Rs. 8,000 each day and it takes 3 days for the cheque to be cleared and to be deducted from the bank accounts of the firm. The difference amounting to Rs. 24,000 to be shown by our cheque book lower than the balance shown by the books of the bank. Thus, this difference is known as ***Disbursement Float.***

(c) Net Float

Net Float is the difference between the balance of our cheque book and the balance shown by the books of bank. It is the net or overall difference between the balance of firms' bank account and the balance shown by the firm's ledger accounts. When the net float is positive (i.e., when disbursement float, is more than collection float) balance of bank, in that case, exceeds the balance of firm's ledger accounts.

Management of Float

In order to overcome the difficulties discussed above—i.e., in reducing the span between the time a customer makes payment and the time such funds are available for use by a firm—two techniques are nowadays used. They are:

(a) Concentration Banking; and

(b) Lock-box System.

(a) Concentration Banking

Under this system, the firms which have a large number of branches at different places may select some of these which are strategically located as collection centres for recurring payment from different customers, i.e., multiple collection centres are established instead of a single collection centre. The purpose of this system is to speed up the time of the collection process from customers. Customers in a particular geographic area are instructed to remit their payments to the specific collection centre in that area. The establishment and the selection of collection centres, however, depends upon the volume of business and the geographic areas served. Under this system, when payments are received, they are deposited in the local account of the concerned collection centre after meeting local expenses. Surplus funds are then transferred from these local bank accounts to a central or disbursing or concentration bank. In short, a concentration bank is one in which the company has a major account—usually a disbursement account.[1] In other words, collections are decentralised but disbursements are centralised.

The transfer of surplus funds may be made either by a wire or by a mail. The choice between them, of course, depends on : (i) the amount involved, and (ii) cost of finance.

It should be mentioned that wire transfers are economical when large sums are involved and the firm earns a reasonable return on short-term, low-risk and highly liquid investment.[2]

The *advantage* of concentration banking are:

(i) The time required for mailing is reduced. Since the local collection centre prepares bills against the customers, the customer usually receives the bills earlier than if the bills were sent by the head-office directly from a distant place. At the same time, when customers pay their bills at the local collection centre instead of mailing the same to the head-office, it will also reduce time. Thus, in this way, it is estimated that there will be a saving of approximately one day in mailing time.

(ii) The time taken for collecting the cheque is also reduced. When remittances are made at the banks, the collection centre transfers immediately by computer or e-mail to the company which enables the company to have the use of the funds without delay. Naturally, the company can release nearly double the amount of average daily remittance by saving the time taken in mailing and in the collection of cheques.

(iii) Moreover, the concentration bank permits the firm to 'store' its cash more efficiently.[3]

Thus, concentration banking, as a decentralised billing and multiple collection points system, is a useful device to expedite the collection of accounts receivables.

(b) **Lock-box System**.

The alternative means of accelerating the flow of funds is a lock-box arrangement. In concentration banking, cheques are received by collection centres and deposited in the bank after processing so that mailing float is reduced. But there remains the cheque processing float. It is needless to mention that lock-box system will eliminate the cheque processing float. Under this system, the firm hires a post office box under the control of a bank at important collection centres. The customers are directed to remit their payments to the lock-box. The local banks are authorised to open the box and collect the remittances/ cheques received from the customers. Normally, the banks so authorised to collect the cheques pick up the cheques several times a day and deposits the same to the firm's accounts. The banks send a deposit slip together with the list of payments and other enclosures to the firm by way of proof record and information after crediting the respective account of the firm. After the realisation of cheques, surplus funds are transferred to the central account of the firm.

Lock-box system, in a sense, is like concentration banking since the collection is decentralised. One significant difference between the two is that, under a concentration banking system, the customers send the cheques to the collection centre, while, under lock-box system, they send them to a post office box.

Thus, lock-box system is, no doubt, an improvement over the concentration banking system since, under the former, one step in the collection process is being eliminated. In

1 Van Horne, J. C., op cit., p. 339.
2 Hampton, J. J.,—*Financial Decision Making*—Prentice-Hall of India Ltd., 2nd Edn., p. 195.
3 Solomon, E and Springle, J.—op. cit., p. 181.

short, processing time within the firm is eliminated before the actual deposit of a cheque into a bank. Therefore, extra saving in mailing time is possible as direct collection is made by bank.

The lock-box system, as an improved method of collection for accounts receivables over the concentration banking, enjoys the following advantages:

(i) The primary advantages of a lock-box system is that the time lag between cheques as received by a company and actually deposited into bank is eliminated. On the contrary, the principal disadvantage of this system is the cost, which is charged by the bank for this additional services and, as such, requires compensation for this purpose, usually preferring increased deposits. Therefore, this system is not feasible if there is unlimited remittances.

(ii) This system reduced the overhead expenses.

(iii) It also facilitates control by separating remittance from the accounts section.

(iv) It also reduced the credit losses by expediting the time at which data are posted to the ledgers.

Of course, in the present day world, it becomes less significant due to the application of Computers.

(C) ***Slowing down Cash Payment** or **Delaying Payments on Accounts Payable** or **Deferring Disbursement***

Various items of payments may be deferred till they affect the smooth running of the operation and, at the same time, damage the goodwill of the firm. There are certain items, viz., Wages, Salaries etc., which are very difficult to defer payments. But the most significant item is the payment to creditors for this purpose. Deferring disbursement (to the creditors) includes:

(a) Stretching the period of credit granted; and

(b) Using float.

The first one which is granted by the creditors is considered unfit as it affects the credit reputation of the firm. Of course, in the absence of cash discounts, there is a good possibility that such costs are hidden in the prices of the goods which may be impossible to measure.[1] If discounts are available, the said amount of discount may be compared with the benefits which may accrue if the said payments are diverted elsewhere. It is interesting to note that in the background of cash credit being heavily relied upon by the Indian firms in general for financing a part of current assets, the applicable interest rate will become one of the variables instead of opportunity cost in this decision area.[2] (Various aspects of 'floats' have already been discussed earlier in the present chapter). If the full advantage of using all kinds of floats are taken there will be a cash on hand for longer period.[3]

Other Methods of Slowing Down Cash Payment are

(a) **To pay by Draft**

Instead of issuing by cheque to the creditors, payment may be made by draft. In case of issuing a cheque the firm must have to maintain a minimum balance to the account for its clearance. But in case of a draft, the same is payable on presentation. The receiver of the draft presents it to the bank which takes a number of days before the same is credited to the

---

1 Van Horne, J. C.

2 Banerjee, B.—*Financial Policy and Management Accounting,* op. cit., p. 176.

3 Joy, O. M.—*Introduction to Financial Management*, op. cit, p. 456.

the depositor's account. The amount so saved by this method may be utilised in highly liquid but little risks securities.

(b) **To pay on last date**

Another method of delaying disbursement is the payment made on the last date of the credit period. If the last date for credit period is 30 days, payment to be made on 30th.

(c) **Inter-Bank Transfer**

To take the advantage of inter-bank transfer a company must have to open accounts at least more than one bank so that the amount may be transferred from one bank (where excess amounts were lying) to that particular bank from which the payment would be made.

(d) **To adjust payrolls**

Payrolls can be adjusted simply by reducing the frequency of payments i.e., from weekly to monthly. Moreover, the cheque may be issued to the staff for their salary on Saturday so that all cheques may not be presented on the same day or even on Monday. Money may be deposited by the firm on the basis of past experience of the finance manager so that those cheques are honoured.

(e) **Centralisation of Payment**

Payment must be made centrally by the issue of cheque or draft. In order to clear up the cheque, it takes some time to credit the party's account.

Cash Budget

The discussion of Cash Management will not be completed if we do not explain the principle and application of Cash Budget. A Cash Budget is a forecast of how much cash will be required during a specific period in future. Therefore, expected cash receipts and expected cash payments are estimated by preparing this budget. However, the estimates are prepared for weeks or months, depending upon the requirement of cash. This budget is prepared after the preparation of all the functional budgets.

This budget is intended:

(i) to see that adequate amounts of cash are available for capital as well as revenue expenditure;

(ii) to make an arrangement of cash in advance if there is any expected shortage of cash;

(iii) to see that the surplus amount of cash, if any, is employed in any profitable investment outside the business.

In reality, information is available from this budget about the sources of expected cash that will be required by the business as and when necessary. At the same time, if the synchronisation of cash between receipts and disbursements is not possible, it is impossible to earn expected profit which is shown in Budgeted Profit and Loss Account and, hence, performances of all other functional budgets will become useless.

Advantages of Preparing Cash Budget

The following advantages may be derived from the Cash Budget:

(i) The preparation of the Cash Budget gives us a clear idea of how much cash is required at what time, and necessary arrangements may be made for the purpose.

(ii) It informs how much additional cash is required during the peak period and the possible ways in which the said cash may be collected e.g., loan or overdraft taken from bank or outsiders.

(iii) Since the surplus amount of cash can be known by its preparation, benefits of Cash Discount may be derived by making payments before due date.

(iv) Cash Budget expresses either the deficit or the surplus of cash; therefore, surplus of cash, if any, should be invested properly, otherwise it will remain idle and that will increase the cost.

Difference between Cash Budget and Cash Flow Statement

A Cash Flow Statement is prepared on the basis of past data or taken from the financial accounting or estimated data of a forthcoming period. When such analysis is done from the past financial data, it is called Cash Flow Statement. But Cash Budget, on the other hand, is made when such data are taken on the basis of estimates relating to a forthcoming period. In short, Cash Budget is prepared on the basis of estimated data relating to a forthcoming period whereas Cash Flow Statement is prepared on the basis of past financial data. The differences between the two are:

Points of Difference	*Cash Budget*	*Cash Flow Statement*
Purpose	Cash Budget reveals the surplus or deficit of cash for a particular period while carrying out planned activities and shows the ways of sources of cash in case of deficit, and ways of investing the idle cash, if there is a surplus of cash.	Cash Flow Statement reveals the changes in cash position for various activities from the beginning to the end of the period by way of sources and applications.
Nature	It highlights the future cash position from the receipts and payments of cash under different heads for the budget period to indicate surplus or deficit.	It highlights the analysis of various inflows and outflows of cash on the basis of past information.
Applications	Cash Budget directly helps the management to know the estimated cash position and thereby the management may take important decisions in financial matters.	Cash Flow Statement helps the various interested per-sons relating to financial position viz., creditors, shareholders, bankers, in-vestors etc. and in various areas of management viz., operating activities, investing activities and financing activities.
Duration	Cash Budget is usually prepared for a short period, viz., daily, weekly, fortnightly, monthly, half-yearly etc.	Cash Flow Statement is prepared for a long period, usually yearly.

Contd.

Points of Difference	*Cash Budget*	*Cash Flow Statement*
Basis of Preparation	Cash Budget actually depends on various functional budgets, viz., Purchase Budget, Sales Budget, Capital Expenditure Budget, for its preparation. Moreover, some useful information are also needed for various receipts and payments.	Cash Flow Statement is prepared on the basis of opening and closing balance of cash plus funds from operations and some other useful information relating to sources and applications of cash.

Method of Preparation

A Cash Budget is prepared by any one of the following methods:

(a) Receipts and Payments Method;

(b) Adjusted Profit and Loss Method;

(c) Balance Sheet Method.

The first method (viz., Receipts and Payments Method) is very useful for the short-period Cash Budget. The inflow and outflow of cash can be estimated by a proper analysis under this method. But the second method (viz., Adjusted Profit and Loss Method) and the third method (viz., Balance Sheet Method) are, however, useful for long-period budgets, say for 2 to 5 years. Of course, it is possible to prepare the Cash Budget under the later methods if weekly or monthly Projected Profit and Loss Accounts and Projected Balance Sheets are prepared.*

(a) Receipts and Payments Method

It has already been stated that this method is useful for a short-period budget. Here, all anticipated cash receipts and payments which are expected during the budget period are taken into consideration. But accrued income and expenses are not to be considered at all in this budget. The detailed information about the inflow and outflow of cash for sales, cost of production etc., is collected from this budget. Under this method, the budget is divided into two parts—Receipts and Payments. Since the primary sources of cash are from sales,

* Generally, any one of the following two types of periods may be used for forecasting cash flows :
(a) Short Period; and (b) Long Period.
Practically, the time period which is covered by short-period cash forecast differs according to the purposes for which the data are needed. For this purpose, the following principles should be taken into consideration :
(i) **Forecasts for the immediate future (i.e., days or weeks) with receipts and disbursement:**
They are intended to determine the adequacy of the available cash balances in order to cover the disbursement and to show how much cash may be made available for day-to-day investment.
(ii) **Forecasts for the coming year by months or quarters:**
These forecasts are used where the cash position of the firm is not so critical and where the monthly/quarterly cash forecasts are considered sufficiently enough for the purpose of assuring management that sufficient cash balances are available or proper actions may be taken if there is a shortage of cash for a period.
But the long period budget covers a period of 2 to 3 years (or even 5 to 10 years) which depends on the time dimension of capital expenditure and time dimension of long-range profit plan. Naturally, the same cannot include all the detailed information like short-period cash forecast. It, of course, exhibits the major sources and applications of cash. However, Welsch mentions the following time periods in a Cash Budget :
(i) Long-range : i.e., covering up to a period of 5 years;
(ii) Short-range : i.e., equivalent to the 'Annual Profit Plan', and
(iii) Operational cash planning, i.e., for the ensuing month (week/day),
[Welsch, G. A.— *Budgeting Profit Planning and Control* — Prentice-Hall of India 1976, pp. 386-387]

the Receipts part of the budget is prepared according to the Sales Budget. On the other hand, the Payments part of the budget is prepared according to other functional budgets.

This method contains the following information :

(i) It provides information as to how much of sales is being made for cash and also about the time-lag in case of credit sales.

(ii) Information about the raw materials to be purchased from Purchase Budget is also furnished.

(iii) How much should be paid on account of wages can be known from Labour Budget and the lag in payment of wages should also be considered.

(iv) Similarly, it can also be known how much is to be paid for different overheads, and the lag in payment of overhead should also be taken into consideration.

(v) Information is also available for Capital Expenditure Budget about the cost to be incurred for acquiring fixed assets.

All other information about the receipts (viz., issue of shares, overdrafts taken from Bank, etc.) and the payments (viz., payment for dividend and taxation, repayment of loans etc.) is also available.

Illustration 7.23

From the following information prepare a monthly Cash Budget for the four months ending 31st December:

		Rs.
Expected Sales:		
	September	50,000
	October	60,000
	November	45,000
	December	80,000
Expected Purchases:		
	September	32,000
	October	60,000
	November	70,000
	December	45,000

Other Relevant Information :

(a) Wages to be paid to workers Rs. 6,000 each month.

(b) Dividend from Investments amounting to Rs. 1,000 are expected on 31st December.

(c) Income Tax to be paid (in advance) in December Rs. 2,000.

(d) Preference Share Dividend of Rs. 5,000 is to be paid on 30th November. Balance at Bank on 1st September is expected to be Rs. 6,000.

Solution

Cash Budget

Period for 4 months ending 31st December

Details	*September*	*October*	*November*	*December*
Receipts :	Rs.	Rs.	Rs.	Rs.
Balance b/d	6,000	18,000	12,000	—
Sales	50,000	60,000	45,000	80,000
Dividend	—	—	—	1,000
Deficit c/d	—	—	24,000	—
	56,000	78,000	81,000	81,000

Payments :	Rs.	Rs.	Rs.	Rs.
Deficit b/d	—	—	—	24,000
Creditors	32,000	60,000	70,000	45,000
Wages	6,000	6,000	6,000	6,000
Pref. dividend	—	—	5,000	—
Income Tax	—	—	—	2,000
Balance c/d	18,000	12,000	—	4,000
	56,000	78,000	81,000	81,000

N.B. Deficit indicates Overdraft.

(b) Adjusted Profit and Loss Method

This method is based on the assumption that profit is equivalent to cash, and both cash and non-cash transactions are taken into consideration. It is practically useful for long-term forecasting. Under this method, various non-cash charges (e.g., depreciation) are added back with budgeted net profit and deducting non-cash credit and, thereafter, adding or deducting the changes of assets or liabilities, as the case may be which ultimately affects cash.[1] Since it is started by taking the balance from Budgeted Profit and Loss Account, it is called Adjusted Profit and Loss Method. It is also called Budgeted Cash Flow Statement as the receipts and payments of cash are shown during the budget period. The adjusted profit implies the estimated cash available.

However, this method depends on:

(i) Budgeted Profit and Loss Account is to be prepared for the budget period.

(ii) Budgeted Balance Sheet, both for the current and previous periods, are also to be prepared.

The only difference between Receipts and Payments Method and Adjusted Profit and Loss Method is that the latter takes non-cash transactions into consideration and, at the same time, considers profit equivalent to cash.

Illustration 7.24

From the following information, prepare a Cash Budget:

Balance Sheet
as at 31st March 2011

Liabilities	Rs.	*Assets*	Rs.
Share Capital	15,000	Land and Building	10,000
Capital Reserve	1,500	Plant & Machinery	6,000
Profit & Loss A/c	3,000	Furniture & Fixture	1,500
Debentures	2,500	Closing Stock	1,200
Outstanding Expenses	200	Debtors	6,000
Creditors	5,000	Bank	2,500
	27,200		27,200

[1] National Association of Accountants, *Cash Flow Analysis for Managerial Control* — N.A.A. Research Report, 38, New York, 1961, p. 13.

Forecast Trading and Profit and Loss Account
for the year ended 31st March 2012

Particulars	Rs.	Rs.	*Particulars*	Rs.
To Opening Stock		1,200	By Sales	26,000
" Purchases		18,000	" Closing Stock	2,500
" Gross Profit c/d		9,300		
		28,500		28,500
To Salaries & Wages	1,800		By Gross Profit b/d	9,300
Add : Outstanding	100	1,900	" Interest Received	500
" Administrative Expenses		2,400		
" Selling Expenses		400		
" Depreciation :				
Plant & Machinery		600		
Furniture & Fixture		300		
" Net Profit c/d		4,200		
		9,800		9,800
To Dividend Paid		3,000	By Balance b/d (opening)	3,000
" Balance carried to Balance Sheet		4,200	" Net Profit b/d	4,200
		7,200		7,200

Additional Information :

(i) Issue of Shares Rs. 3,000

(ii) Issue of Debentures Rs. 2,500

(iii) On 31st March 2012 the expected Outstanding Expenses are Rs. 150; Debtors Rs. 9,000; Creditors Rs. 6,000 and Land and Building Rs. 12,500.

Solution

Cash Budget
for the year ended 31st March 2012

	Rs.	Rs.	Rs.
Opening Cash Balance			2,500
Net Profit forecast		4,200	
Add : Adjustments			
(i) Non-Cash items :			
(a) Depreciation on Plant & Machinery	600		
(b) Depreciation on Furniture & Fixtures	300		
(ii) Capital Receipts :			
(a) Issue of Share Capital	3,000		
(b) Issue of Debenture	2,500		
(iii) Increase in Sundry Creditors	1,000	7,400	
		11,600	

Contd.

	Rs.	Rs.	Rs.
Less : Deductions :			
(i) Payment of Dividend	3,000		
(ii) Increase in Current Assets :			
(a) Stock	1,300		
(b) Debtors	3,000		
(iii) Decrease in Outstanding Expenses	50		
(iv) Addition to Land & Building	2,500	9,850	
Increase in cash over the year			1,750
Expected Cash Balance in 2012			4,250

Illustration 7.25

The Balance Sheet of Sumana Ltd. as at 31st December 2005 is:

Balance Sheet

as at 31st December 2005

		Rs.			Rs.
Share Capital :			Goodwill at Cost		30,000
5,000 Equity Shares			*Fixed Assets :*		
of Rs. 10 each			Land and Building		20,000
fully paid		50,000	Plant and Machinery	50,000	
Reserves and Surplus :			*Less :* Depreciation	5,000	45,000
General Reserve		20,000	Furniture & Fixture		15,000
Capital Reserve		30,000	*Current Assets :*		
Profit and Loss Account		40,000	Stock	50,000	
Future Taxation		15,000	Debtors	40,000	
Current Liabilities :			Cash at Bank	20,000	1,10,000
Creditors	40,000				
Taxation	20,000				
Proposed Dividend	5,000	65,000			
		2,20,000			2,20,000

Information for the next twelve months ending on 31st December 2006 is:

	Rs.
Wages (Direct)	1,20,000
Wages (Indirect)	60,000
Salaries (Office)	50,000
Payments to Creditors	3,00,000
Receipts from Debtors	5,00,000
Cash Sales	2,00,000
Purchase of Land and Building	25,000
Interim Dividend	7,500
Debtors' Balance (Closing)	35,000
Creditors' Balance (Closing)	25,000

Depreciation is to be charged @ 10% on Plant and Machinery (on Straight Line Method).

Stock is expected to be valued at Rs. 70,000 at the end of the year.

Future taxation to be reserved for the following year amounted to Rs. 20,000.

Transfer Rs. 20,000 for General Reserve.

You are required to prepare a Cash Flow Statement under Adjusted Profit and Loss Method, assuming the last year's tax and dividends are to be paid. Prepare also the Forecast Balance Sheet.

Solution

Cash Flow Statement (as per Old Method)

	Rs.		Rs.
Opening Balance of Cash	20,000	*Outflow of Cash:*	
Add : Inflow of Cash :		Interim Dividend	7,500
Net Profit	1,95,000	Proposed Dividend	5,000
Depreciation on Plant & Machinery	5,000	Taxation	20,000
Decrease in Debtors	5,000	Purchases of Land & Building	25,000
		Decrease of Creditors	15,000
		Increase in Stock	20,000
			92,500
		Closing Balance of Cash	1,32,500
	2,25,000		2,25,000

Forecast Balance Sheet
as at 31st December 2006

	Rs.	Rs.		Rs.	Rs.
Share Capital		50,000	Goodwill at Cost		30,000
Reserves & Surplus:			*Fixed Assets:*		
General Reserve		40,000	Land and Building	20,000	
Capital Reserve		30,000	Additions	25,000	45,000
Profit and Loss Account		1,87,500	Plant and Machinery	50,000	
Future Taxation		20,000	*Less :* Depreciation	10,000	40,000
Current Liabilities:			Furniture and Fixture		15,000
Sundry Creditors	25,000		*Current Assets:*		
Taxation	15,000	40,000	Stock	70,000	
			Debtors	35,000	
			Cash	1,32,500	
					2,37,500
		3,67,500			3,67,500

Workings :

Debtors' Account

Dr.	Rs.		Cr. Rs.
To Balance b/d	40,000	By Cash	5,00,000
" Sales (Credit)	4,95,000	" Balance c/d	35,000
	5,35,000		5,35,000

Creditors' Account

Dr.	Rs.		Cr. Rs.
To Cash	3,00,000	By Balance b/d	40,000
" Balance c/d	25,000	" Purchase (Credit)	2,85,000
	3,25,000		3,25,000

Profit and Loss Account (Adjusted)
for the year ended 31st December 2006

Dr.	Rs.	Rs.		Rs.	Cr. Rs.
To Opening Stock		50,000	By Sales:		
" Purchase (Credit)		2,85,000	Cash	2,00,000	
" Wages:			Credit	4,95,000	
Direct	1,20,000				6,95,000
Indirect	60,000		" Closing Stock		70,000
		1,80,000			
" Gross Profit c/d		2,50,000			
		7,65,000			7,65,000
" Salaries		50,000	By Gross Profit b/d		2,50,000
" Depreciation on Plant and Machinery		5,000			
To Net Profit c/d		1,95,000			
		2,50,000			2,50,000
To General Reserve		20,000	By Net profit b/d		1,95,000
" Provision for Taxation		20,500	" Balance b/d		40,000
" Interim Dividend		7,500			
" Balance c/d		1,87,000			
		2,35,000			2,35,000

(c) Balance Sheet Method

It has already been stated that this method is useful for long-term forecasting. Under this method, a Budgeted Balance Sheet is prepared by incorporating all expected assets and expected liabilities. The excess of two sides (Liabilities or Assets) will represent either cash balance or overdraft, as the case may be. In other words, if the assets side is greater than the liabilities side, the difference will represent Bank Overdraft, or vice versa.

Illustration 7.26

Swarnali Ltd. informs the following particulars:

	Rs.
Share Capital	4,00,000
General Reserve (against Rs. 3,00,000 invested in Fixed Assets)	50,000
Stock	50,000
Debtors	1,00,000
Creditors (Trade and others)	40,000

Contd.

Additional Information :

Stock level is proposed to be increased by	100%
Additions to be made for Machinery amounted to (as per Capital Budget)	Rs. 40,000
Advance Income Tax Payment is estimated at	Rs. 50,000
Estimated Profit after charging Depreciation Rs. 30,000 and	
30% of Profit for Taxation amounted to	Rs. 80,000
6% Dividend is to be paid, also make a provision for Proposed Dividend @ 10%	
Sales Budget shows Rs. 12,00,000 Sales, and Debtors are estimated to be outstanding for 3 months.	
Creditors (Trade and others) are likely to be doubled.	

Make an estimate of cash position as at the end of the budget period.

Solution

Budgeted Balance Sheet

as at ....

		Rs.			Rs.
Share Capital		4,00,000	*Fixed Assets :*		
Reserves & Surplus :			Balance	3,00,000	
General Reserve		50,000	Additions	40,000	
Profit and Loss A/c	80,000			3,40,000	
Less : Dividend	24,000		*Less* : Depreciation	30,000	3,10,000
	56,000		*Current Assets :*		
Less : Proposed Dividend	40,000	16,000	Stock	1,00,000	
Current Liabilities :			Debtors	3,00,000	
Proposed Dividend		40,000	Advance Income Tax	50,000	
Provision for Taxation		80,000			4,50,000
Creditors (Trade & Others)		80,000			
Bank Overdraft (*bal. fig.*)		94,000			
		7,60,000			7,60,000

ILLUSTRATIONS ON CASH BUDGET

Illustration 7.27

From the following information supplied by Bright Ltd., prepare a cash budget for the period from 1st September 2008 to 31st December 2008:

Months	*Credit Purchases*	*Credit Sales*	*Wages*	*Selling Expenses*	*Overheads*
	Rs.	Rs.	Rs.	Rs.	Rs.
July	85,000	1,60,000	32,000	8,000	10,000
August	92,000	1,85,000	37,000	9,500	11,500
September	1,00,000	2,10,000	42,000	10,500	13,000
October	1,20,000	2,45,000	49,000	12,500	14,500
November	90,000	1,78,000	35,500	8,900	10,500
December	98,000	1,82,000	36,000	9,000	11,000

Additional Information :

(a) Expected cash balance on 1st September—Rs. 10,500.

(b) Period of credit allowed to debtors—2 months.

(c) Period of credit allowed by creditors—1 month.

(d) Lag in payment for wages, selling expenses and overhead—1 month.

(e) Selling commission @ 2% on sales is payable one month after sales.

(f) Expenditure on machinery worth Rs. 50,000 is payable in October.

(g) Expected cash sales per month Rs. 15,000. No commission is payable on cash sales.

[C.U. B.Com. (Hons.)]

Solution

Cash Budget

Period for 4 months ending December 2008

	September	October	November	December
	Rs.	Rs.	Rs.	Rs.
Receipts				
Balance b/d	10,500	31,800	12,100	36,200
Cash Sales	15,000	15,000	15,000	15,000
Receipts from Debtors	1,60,000	1,85,000	2,10,000	2,45,000
	1,85,500	2,31,800	2,37,100	2,96,200
Payments				
Paid to Creditors	92,000	1,00,000	1,20,000	90,000
Wages	37,000	42,000	49,000	35,500
Selling Expenses	9,500	10,500	12,500	8,900
Overheads	11,500	13,000	14,500	10,500
Selling Commission[1] (2% of previous month)	3,700	4,200	4,900	3,560
Machinery	—	50,000	—	—
Balance c/d	31,800	12,100	36,200	1,47,740
	1,85,500	2,31,800	2,37,100	2,96,200

Note : [1]Selling commission has been calculated on credit sales only.

Illustration 7.28

From the following budgeted data, forecast the cash position at the end of April, May and June 2005:

Months	*Sales*	*Purchases*	*Wages*	*Misc. Expenses*
	Rs.	Rs.	Rs.	Rs.
February	1,20,000	84,000	10,000	7,000
March	1,30,000	1,00,000	12,000	8,000
April	80,000	1,04,000	8,000	6,000
May	1,16,000	1,06,000	10,000	12,000
June	88,000	80,000	8,000	6,000

Additional Information :

(1) Sales—20% realised in the month of sale; discount allowed 2%; balance realised equally in two subsequent months.

(2) Purchase—These are paid for in the month following the month of supply.

(3) Wages—25% paid in arrears following month.

(4) Misc. Expenses—Paid a month in arrears.

(5) Rent—Rs. 1,000 p.m., paid quarterly in advances due in April.

(6) Income Tax—First instalment of advance tax Rs. 25,000 due on or before the 15th June.

(7) Income from investments—Rs. 5,000 realised quarterly—April, July, etc.

(8) Cash in hand Rs. 5,000 on 1st April 2005.

Solution

Cash Budget

Period for 3 months ending 30th June 2005

	April Rs.	May Rs.	June Rs.
Receipts:			
Balance b/d	5,000	5,680	—
Receipt from Debtors	1,15,680	1,06,736	95,648
Income from Investment	5,000	—	—
Deficit c/d	—	7,084	62,936
	1,25,680	1,19,500	1,58,584
Payments:			
Deficit b/d	—	—	7,084
Paid to Creditors	1,00,000	1,04,000	1,06,000
Wages	9,000	9,500	8,500
Rent	3,000	—	—
Misc. Expenses	8,000	6,000	12,000
Income Tax	—	—	25,000
Balance c/d	5,680	—	—
	1,25,680	1,19,500	1,58,584

Workings:

	April Rs.		May Rs.		June Rs.
1. *Receipts from Debtors:*					
80,000 × 20% =	16,000	1,16,000 × 20% =	23,200	88,000 × 20% =	17,600
Less : Discount @ 2%	320	*Less* : 2%	464	*Less* : 2%	352
	15,680		22,736		17,248
Less : 1,20,000 + 1,30,000 × 40% =	1,00,000	*Less* : 1,30,000 + 80,000 × 40% =	84,000	*Less* : 80,000 + 1,16,000 × 40% =	78,400
	1,15,680		1,06,736		95,648

2. *Wages:*

25% of 12,000 =	3,000
75% of 8,000 =	6,000 and so on.
	9,000

ASSIGNMENT MATERIALS
THEORETICAL

Multiple Choice Questions

1. (a) Motive for holding Cash:

(i) Storing black money (ii) Speculative motive

(iii) Business motive (iv) Profit motive

(b) Optimum Cash Balance is:

(i) More cash in excess of need (ii) Less cash in excess of need

(iii) Minimum Cash Balance (iv) Exact amount required

(c) As per Baumol's Model, minimum Cash Balance is ascertained by:

(i) $\sqrt{\frac{2BT}{i}}$ (ii) $\sqrt{\frac{3BT}{i}}$

(iii) $\sqrt{\frac{4BT}{i}}$ (iv) $\sqrt{\frac{5BT}{i}}$

(d) As Miller-Orr Model, Optimum Cash Balance is:

(i) $\sqrt{\frac{3b\sigma^2}{4i}}$ (ii) $\sqrt[3]{\frac{3b\sigma^2}{4i}}$

(iii) $\sqrt[4]{\frac{3b\sigma^2}{4i}}$ (iv) $\sqrt[3]{\frac{3b\sigma}{4i}}$

(e) Lock-box system:

(i) Reduces floating time (ii) Increases floating time

(iii) No effect (iv) Increases cost

[Ans. (a) (ii); (b) (iv); (c) (i); (d) (ii); (e) (i)]

Short Answer-type Questions

2. What is Cash Management?
3. How do you synchronise Cash?
4. Explain the motives for holding Cash (any three).
5. Define:

   (a) Concentration Banking (b) Lock-box System.
6. What is Optimum Cash Balance?
7. What is Cash Balance?
8. Explain the advantages of Cash Budget.

Long Answer-type Questions

9. What are the motives for holding cash?
10. What is Cash Budget? Explain its advantages and disadvantages.
11. How will you invest your surplus fund?
12. "Surplus funds should properly be invested"—Explain.
13. How do you ascertain the Optimum Cash Balance under Miller-Orr Model?
14. Explain the various motives for holding cash by a firm.
15. "A company is presently facing cash deficit. As a finance manager, what will be your strategies to deal with such situation?"
16. (a) Explain the motives for holding cash.

    (b) How can "Speeding up Cash Receipts" and "Slowing down Cash Payment" help in cash management? Explain.

PRACTICAL

1. From the following forecasts of income and expenditure, prepare a cash budget for the months January to April 1999:

		Sales (credit)	*Purchases (credit)*	*Wages*	*Manufacturing Expenses*	*Administrative Expenses*	*Selling Expenses*
		Rs.	Rs.	Rs.	Rs.	Rs.	Rs.
1998	Nov.	30,000	15,000	3,000	1,150	1,060	500
	Dec.	35,000	20,000	3,200	1,225	1,040	550
1999	Jan.	25,000	15,000	2,500	990	1,100	600
	Feb.	30,000	20,000	3,000	1,050	1,150	620
	Mar.	35,000	22,500	2,400	1,100	1,220	570
	April	40,000	25,000	2,600	1,200	1,180	710

Additional Information :

(a) The customers are allowed a credit period of 2 months.

(b) A dividend of Rs. 10,000 is payable in April.

(c) Capital expenditure to be incurred : Plant purchased on 15th of January for Rs. 5,000; a Building has been purchased on 1st March and the payments are to be made in monthly instalments of Rs. 2,000 each.

(d) The creditors are allowing a credit of 2 months.

(e) Wages are paid on the 1st of the next month.

(f) Lag in payment of other expenses is one month.

(g) Balance of cash in hand on 1st January 1998 is Rs. 15,000.

[Ans. Balance of Cash : Jan. Rs. 18,985, Feb. Rs. 28,795, March Rs. 30,975, April Rs. 28,685]

2. The estimated sales, expenses and other particulars are:

	June	July	Aug.	Sept.	Oct.	Nov.	Dec.
	Rs.	Rs.	Rs.	Rs.	Rs.	Rs.	Rs.
Sales	17,50,000	20,00,000	20,00,000	25,00,000	25,00,000	30,00,000	32,50,000
Purchases	7,00,000	8,00,000	8,50,000	10,00,000	10,00,000	12,50,000	14,00,000
Misc. Exp.	2,50,000	3,00,000	3,00,000	3,00,000	3,50,000	3,50,000	3,50,000
Wages & Salaries	6,00,000	7,00,000	7,00,000	9,00,000	9,00,000	10,00,000	11,00,000
Interest received	1,00,000	—	—	1,00,000	—	—	1,00,000
Sale of Plant			10,00,000				

Additional Information :

(i) 20% of the sales are made for cash, the balance being credit.

(ii) 1% of the credit sales are returned by the customers; 2% of the total accounts receivable constitutes bad debt losses. 50% of the goods accounts receivable are collected in the month of the sales and the rest in the next month.

(iii) The creditors are paid in the following month.

(iv) The lag in payment of miscellaneous expenses is 1 month.

(v) Similarly, wages and salaries are paid fortnightly with a time lag of 15 days.

(vi) The minimum cash balance is to be maintained at Rs. 2,50,000. Cash in excess of Rs. 3,50,000 is invested in securities in multiples of Rs. 50,000 and, at the same time, if shortfall is made in the minimum cash balance, the same should be made good by bank borrowing.

[Ans. Closing Balance : July Rs. 3,55,300; Aug. Rs. 3,57,620; Sept. Rs. 3,53,980; Oct. Rs. 3,94,380; Nov. Rs. 3,78,820; Dec. Rs. 3,54,320]

3. The income and expenditure forecasts for the months of March to August 2005 are:

Months	*Sales (Credit)*	*Purchases (Credit)*	*Wages*	*Manufacturing Expenses*	*Office Expenses*	*Selling Expenses*
	Rs.	Rs.	Rs.	Rs.	Rs.	Rs.
March	60,000	36,000	9,000	3,500	2,000	4,000
April	62,000	38,000	8,000	3,750	1,500	5,000
May	64,000	33,000	10,000	4,000	2,500	4,500
June	58,000	35,000	8,500	3,750	2,000	3,500
July	56,000	39,000	9,500	5,000	1,000	3,500
August	60,000	34,000	8,000	5,200	1,500	4,500

You are given the following further information:

(a) Plant costing Rs. 16,000 is due for delivery in July; payable 10% on delivery and the balance after 3 months.

(b) Advance tax of Rs. 8,000 is payable in March and June each.

(c) Creditors allow 2 months' credit and debtors are paying one month late. Lag in payment of expenses is one month.

(d) Opening balance of cash Rs. 8,000.

Prepare a Cash budget for the months May to July.

[Ans. Cash Balance : May Rs. 15,750; June Rs. 12,750; July Rs. 18,400]

4. Prepare a Cash Budget for the three months ending 30th June 2005 from the information :

(a)

Months	Sales Rs.	Materials Rs.	Wages Rs.	Overheads Rs.
February	14,000	9,600	3,000	1,700
March	15,000	9,000	3,000	1,900
April	16,000	9,200	3,200	2,000
May	17,000	10,000	3,600	2,200
June	18,000	10,400	4,000	2,300

(b) Credit terms are:

Sales/Debtors—10% sales are on cash, 50% of the credit sales are collected next month and the balance in the following months.

Creditors —Materials 2 months

—Wages $\frac{1}{4}$ month

—Overheads $\frac{1}{2}$ month.

(c) Cash and Bank balance on 1st April 2005 is expected to be Rs. 6,000.

(d) Other relevant information is :

(i) Plant and Machinery will be installed in February 2005 at a cost of Rs. 96,000. The monthly instalment of Rs. 2,000 is payable from April onwards.

(ii) Dividend @ 5% on Preference Share Capital of Rs. 2,00,000 will be paid on 1st June.

(iii) Advance to be received for sale of vehicles Rs. 9,000 in June.

(iv) Dividends from investments amounting to Rs. 1,000 are expected to be received in June.

(v) Income tax (advance) to be paid in June is Rs. 2,000.

[Ans. Closing Cash Balance at the end of each month Rs. 3,950; Rs. 3,000; Rs. 300]

5. From the following particulars prepare a monthly Cash Budget for the quarter ended 31st March 1999 :

Months	Sales Rs.	Purchases Rs.	Wages Rs.	Expenses Rs.
November	50,000	10,000	20,000	4,000
December	60,000	20,000	20,000	4,000
January	40,000	30,000	22,000	5,000
February	50,000	20,000	22,000	5,000
March	60,000	10,000	24,000	5,000

Other Information :

(a) 10% of sales and purchases are on cash, balance on Credit.

(b) Credit to Debtors : 1 month, on an average 50% of Debtors will make payments on the due date while the rest will make payment one month thereafter.

(c) Credit from Creditors : 2 months, 10% cash discount will be received if payments are made within one month and it is estimated that for 50% of purchases, advantage of Cash Discount will be taken.

(d) Wages : To be paid twice in a month on the 1st and 16th, respectively.

(e) Expenses generally paid within the month.

(f) Plant costing Rs. 10,000 will be installed in February on payment of 25% of the cost in addition to the installed cost of Rs. 500. Balance to be paid in three equal monthly instalments from the following month.

(g) Opening Cash Balance Rs. 20,000.

[C.U. M.Com.]

[Ans. Closing Cash Balances as on Jan., Feb. and March 1999 were Rs. 31,900; Rs. 28,750; Rs. 22,150]

6. From the following information prepare a cash budget for a period of 6 months from January to June 1999:

Months	*Sales*	*Purchases*	*Wages*	*Overheads*			
				Production	*Administration*	*Selling & Distribution*	*Research & Development*
	Rs.	Rs.	Rs.	Rs.	Rs.	Rs.	Rs.
October	60,000	40,000	4,000	3,000	1,500	1,000	600
November	50,000	30,000	3,500	2,500	1,200	1,000	600
December	70,000	40,000	4,000	3,000	1,600	1,200	800
January	80,000	50,000	4,500	3,000	1,700	1,300	800
February	80,000	45,000	5,000	3,500	2,000	1,500	900
March	90,000	60,000	5,500	4,000	2,200	1,700	900
April	1,00,000	65,000	5,000	3,000	1,500	2,000	900
May	1,00,000	55,000	5,000	4,000	2,300	1,600	1,000
June	90,000	50,000	5,500	4,500	2,500	1,500	1,000

Other Information :

(i) A new plant costing Rs. 1,00,000 will have to be installed in January. One-fourth of the price will have to be paid on the date of installation and the balance will be paid by three equal quarterly instalments.

(ii) 10% of the sales and 25% of the purchases will be made for cash at a discount of 10% in both cases.

(iii) The company allows two months' credit to customer but 50% of the customers pay after one month and the company pays to its suppliers after three months. Time lag in payment of overheads and wages are $\frac{1}{2}$ and $\frac{1}{5}$ month, respectively.

(iv) Interest on debenture and preference dividend Rs. 20,000 and Rs. 25,000 will have to be paid in the months of January and March, respectively.

(v) Bank balance as on 1st January Rs. 20,000.

Hints : Payment of overheads $\frac{1}{2}$ of last month and $\frac{1}{2}$ of current month; Payment of Wages $\frac{1}{5}$ of last month and $\frac{4}{5}$ of current month.

[Ans. Cash balances at the end of each month from January to June: (–)Rs. 16,150; Rs. 13,675; Rs. 11,525; Rs. 6,700; Rs. 41,925 and Rs. 60,175]

II. RECEIVABLE MANAGEMENT

Meaning

The previous section was devoted to an in-depth examination of one of the most important components of current assets, namely, cash. There it was observed that, in order to reduce the operating cash requirement, collection of debtors/receivables should be accelerated in such a manner that the average collection period reduces. The term 'debtor' is used to define as 'debt owed to the firm by customers arising from sale of goods or services in the ordinary course of business'. Debtors/ Receivables, as asset, represent amounts owed to the firm by customer from sale of goods or services.

A firm grants trade credit to maintain its sales from the hands of the competitors and, at the same time, to attract the potential customers to purchase its products at favourable terms. Trade credit arises only when the firm sells its product to the customers but does not receive immediate cash, i.e., at the time of credit sales. Receivables/Debtors are created out of trade credit and which are collected in the near future. Debtors have got three distinct characteristics[1]:

(i) it involves risk which should carefully be studied since cash sales are riskless whereas, at the time of credit sales, cash is yet to be received.

(ii) it is based on present economic value. At the time of sale the economic value of goods passes immediately, whereas, the seller expects an equivalent benefit at a later date.

(iii) it implies futurity. The value of goods or services received by the buyer will be payable by him at a future date.

No doubt debtors/receivables play a significant role in the total current asset composition since their position is next to inventories. In India, they form about one-third of total current asset.[2]

Objectives

It has already been stated above that accounts receivables/debtors are generated—which is collected at a future date only when the firm grants credit against an ordinary sale of goods or services without receiving cash. Credit sale is an essential part of the present competitive economic system. It is granted in order to increase the volume of sales. As such, debtors/receivables, which are created out of credit sales, are considered as a marketing tool for increasing sales. It may be mentioned in this respect that credit which is granted to the customer is done in the ordinary course of the business, i.e., on an open account. In other words, there will be no formal acknowledgement of debt obligation. But extension of credit involves cost and risk. Therefore, management should weigh the benefits against cost. As such, the objective of debtors/receivables management is 'to promote sales and profits until that point is reached (i.e., optimum point) where the return on investment in further funding of receivables is less than the cost of funds raised to finance that additional credit (i.e., cost of capital)'.[3]

---

1 In India, debtors/receivables are the major components of current assets after inventories. When credit is granted to the customers, the firm's funds are blocked. As a result, the time lag between the cost of sale and the actual realisation of the proceeds is being financed by working capital. Since substantial amounts are blocked in debtors, it requires proper management and careful analysis.

2 Ramamoorty, V. E. — *Working Capital Management*—Madras Institute of Management and Research, 1976, p. 183.

3 Bolton, S. E. —*Managerial Finance* (Boston), Houghton, Mifftin Co., 1976, p. 446.

Cost of Maintaining Debtors

The specific cost arising out of extension of credit which are related to the determination of the objectives of receivable management are:

(a) Collection Costs;

(b) Capital Costs/Cost of Financing;

(c) Delinquency Costs; and

(d) Default Costs.

(a) *Collection Costs :* These costs are those which are to be incurred by a firm in order to collect the amount on account of credit sales, i.e., these expenses would not be incurred if the firm does not sell goods on credit, e.g., additional expenses incurred for the maintenance of credit and collection department, expenses incurred for obtaining information about credit-worthiness of potential customers.

(b) *Capital Costs/Cost of Financing :* The amounts which are locked up in debtors on account of credit sales may be financed from one of the following three sources : (i) share capital; (ii) debt capital (long and short-term); and (iii) retained earnings.

Illustration 7.29

A firm sells its article at a profit of 25% on cost and the average balance of debtors amounts to Rs. 8,00,000. Investment in debtors is being financed by bank borrowings at 15%.

Ascertain the cost of financing average debtors.

Solution

$$\text{Ratio of Cost of Sales} = \frac{\text{Sales} - \text{Profit}}{100} = \frac{100 - 20}{100} \text{ (since 25\% on cost = 20\% on sales)}$$

$$= \frac{80}{100}$$

$$\text{So, Investment in Average Debtors} = \text{Debtors} \times \frac{\text{Cost}}{100}$$

$$= \frac{\text{Rs. } 8,00,000}{100} \times 80$$

$$= \text{Rs. } 6,40,000$$

Cost of Capital : 15%

Hence, cost of financiang Average Debtors :

$$\text{Rs. } 6,40,000 \times \frac{15}{100} = \text{Rs. } 96,000 \text{ annually.}$$

(c) *Delinquency Costs* : When the period of payment becomes due (i.e., after the expiry of the credit period) but is not received from the customers, the same is known as delinquency cost. It includes:

(i) blocking up of funds/cost of financing for an extended period; and

(ii) cost of extra steps to be taken to collect the overdues, e.g., reminders, legal charges etc.

(d) *Default Costs* : Sometimes the firms may not collect the overdues from the customers since they are unable to pay. These debts are treated as bad debts and are to be written-off accordingly since the amounts will not be realised in future. Such costs are termed as 'Default Costs'. Although the firms make proper provision against bad debts, the cost will increase if the amount of credit sales is increased in proportion to cash sales.

Different types of cost which are related to Receivable Management are depicted as :

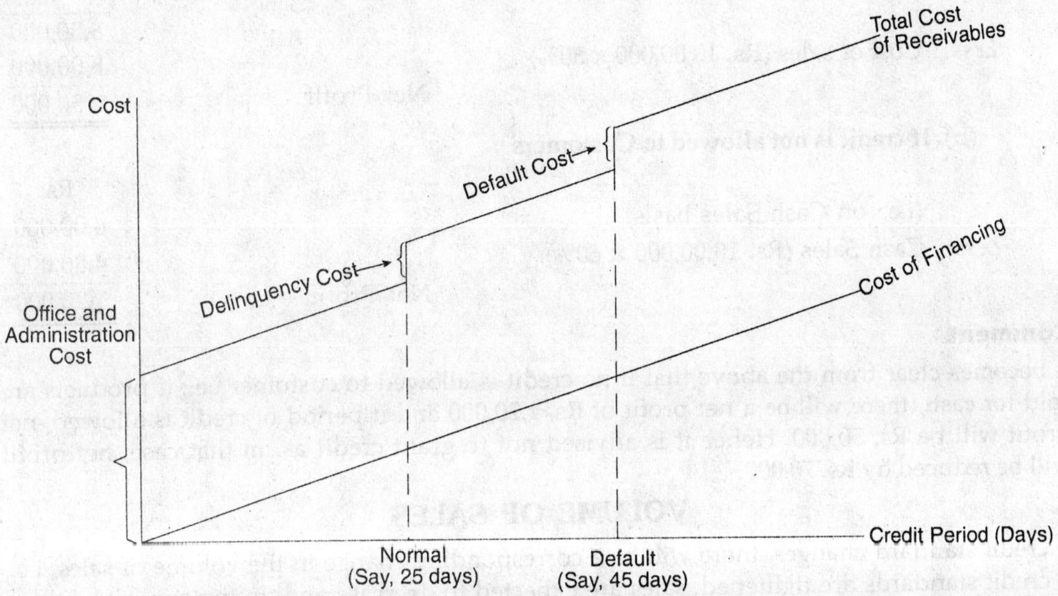

Fig. 7.6: Cost of Receivable

It becomes clear from the above that cost of receivable includes : Cost of financing + Office and Administration cost + Delinquency cost + Default Cost. These costs are related to receivables management. But, it must be remembered that receivables not only increase various types of cost but also it gives some benefits, viz, increase sales thereby increase profit.

Illustration 7.30

X Ltd. presented the following particulars:

It sells it products on credit basis (2 months).

Credit risk with customers are 10%; Cost of Sales 80% of Sales.

Expected annual turnover is Rs. 10,00,000 if credit is allowed.

Sales would be @ 60% if no credit is granted.

Advice X Ltd. whether granting credit will be profitable or not assuming that the required rate of return is 18% and Administration cost is Rs. 20,000.

Solution

Ascertainment of Net Profit

		Rs.	Rs.
(a)	**If credit is allowed to Customers**		
	Sales		10,00,000
Less:	**Cost of Credit**		
	Interest Cost (Rs. 10,00,000 $\times \frac{18}{100} \times \frac{2}{12}$)	30,000	
	Default Risk @ 10% on Sales	1,00,000	
	Administration Cost	20,000	
			1,50,000
			8,50,000
Less:	Cost of sales (Rs. 10,00,000 × 80%)		8,00,000
	Net Profit		50,000

		Rs.
(b)	**If credit is not allowed to Customers**	
	(i.e., on Cash Sales basis)	6,00,000
Less:	Cash Sales (Rs. 10,00,000 × 60%)	4,80,000
	Net Profit	1,20,000

Comment

It becomes clear from the above that if no credit is allowed to customer i.e., if products are sold for cash, there will be a net profit of Rs. 1,20,000 and if period of credit is allowed, net profit will be Rs. 50,000. Hence it is advised not to grant credit as, in that case, net profit will be reduced by Rs. 70,000.

VOLUME OF SALES

If credit standard changes, there will be a corresponding change in the volume of sales, i.e., if credit standards are tightened, sales are expected to decrease and, in the opposite case—, that is, if credit standards are relaxed—the volume of sales is expected to increase. Thus, volume of sales is affected by the the credit standard of a firm.

The following illustration will illustrate the principle clearly:

Illustration 7.31

Present selling price Rs. 20 per unit.

Present sales in units, all credit 60,000 units.

Variable Cost per unit Rs. 12

Average cost per unit is Rs. 16 (on a sales volume of 60,000 units).

[Difference between the average cost per unit and the variable cost per unit (i.e., Rs. 16 – Rs. 12) = Rs. 4 represents the contribution of each of the 60,000 units towards the fixed cost. Thus, the total fixed cost become Rs. 60,000 × 2 = Rs. 1,20,000.]

Average collection period, say, 30 days. The firm desires to relax the credit standard for which sales are expected to increase by 15%, and average collection period is increased by 15 days without, however, having any bad debt losses (Increase in collection expenses may be ignored).

Required rate of return on investment is 15%.

Suggest whether the firm should relax the existing credit standard or not.

Solution

Whether the credit standard should be relevant or not depends upon : (i) additional profit on sales, and (ii) cost of incremental investment in accounts recoverable. In other words, if additional profit on sales exceeds the cost of incremental investment in accounts recoverable, the said proposal may be accepted; the same should be rejected in the opposite case.

(i) **Additional Profit on Sale**

It can be ascertained in the following manner:

(a) by longer approach; and

(b) by shorter approach.

(a) **Longer Approach**

Under this approach, the costs and profits on existing sales and proposed sales will be determined and the difference in profit will be treated as incremental profit.

The same can be ascertained as under:

	Existing Plan			Proposed Plan	
	Rs.	Rs.		Rs.	Rs.
Sales (60,000 × Rs. 20)		12,00,000	(69,000 × Rs. 20)		13,80,000
Less : Cost :					
Variable (60,000 × Rs. 12)	7,20,000		(69,000 × Rs. 12)	8,28,000	
Fixed Cost	1,20,000			1,20,000	
		8,40,000			9,48,000
Profit		3,60,000			4,32,000

Thus, the incremental profit is Rs. 72,000 (i.e., Rs. 4,32,000 – Rs. 3,60,000).

(b) **Shorter Approach**

Under this method, the profit on sales increases by that amount which equals the product of the extra unit sold and the additional profit per unit. Thus, in the above illustration, the cost of additional unit consists of variable cost only as the fixed cost has already been absorbed by the existing level of output. Since expected increase in sales volume is 15%, i.e. 69,000 units, the marginal profit per unit will be the difference between the sale price per unit and the marginal/variable cost per unit which is Rs. 8 (i.e., Rs. 20 – Rs. 12). So the total additional profit will be 9,000 units × Rs. 8 = Rs. 72,000.

(ii) **Cost of Incremental Investment in Accounts Receivables**

The second method for relaxing the credit standards is the *Cost of Incremental Investment in Accounts Receivables* which can be ascertained by taking the difference between cost of carrying the accounts receivables before, as well as after, the proposed proposal in credit standards is taken into consideration.

The same can be computed in the following manner:

Process I

Average Investment in Accounts Receivables

$$= \frac{\text{Annual Credit Sales}}{\text{Turnover of Credit Receivables}}$$

But before computing the above two variables, the following components relating to the above is calculated as:

	Existing Plan	Proposed Plan
Annual Credit Sales	= No. of units × Selling price p.u.	= 69,000 × Rs. 20
	= 60,000 × Rs. 20	= Rs. 13,80,000
	= Rs. 12,00,000	
Turnover of Accounts Receivables	$= \frac{\text{No. of days in the year}}{\text{Average collection period}}$	
	$= \frac{360}{30}$	$= \frac{360}{45}$
	= 12	= 8
Thus, Average Investment in Accounts Receivables	$= \frac{\text{Rs. } 12,00,000}{12}$	$= \frac{13,80,000}{8}$
	= Rs. 1,00,000	= Rs. 1,72,500

Process II

$$\textit{Average Investment in Accounts Receivables} = \frac{\text{Total Cost of Goods Sold}}{\text{Turnover of Accounts Receivables}}$$

Cost of Goods Sold = unit profit × cost per unit

	Existing Plan	Proposed Plan
Cost of Goods Sold	= 60,000 × Rs. 12	= 69,000 × Rs. 12
	= Rs. 7,20,000	= Rs. 8,28,000
∴ Average Investment in Accounts Receivables	$= \frac{\text{Rs. } 7,20,000}{12}$	$= \frac{8,28,000}{8}$
	= Rs. 60,000	= Rs. 1,03,500

Process III

Cost of Marginal Investment in Accounts Receivables

= Average Investment with proposed plan – Average Investment in existing plans

= Rs. 1,03,500 – Rs. 60,000

= Rs. 43,500

In other words, the additional cost of Rs. 43,500 is the cost of marginal investment in accounts receivable.

Thus, required rate of return investment $= \text{Rs. } 43,500 \times \frac{15}{100}$

= Rs. 6,525

From the above it becomes crystal clear that the additional profit on increased rates (i.e., Rs. 72,000) is more than this cost of such incremental investment in accounts receivables (i.e., Rs. 6,525) due to relaxing of credit standard. Hence, it is justified.

Factors Affecting Size of Debtors

It has already been pointed out that debtors/receivables are the major components of total current assets. The size or level of debtors is determined by a number of factors.

Six primary factors are :

(a) Level of Sales; (b) Terms of Trade; (c) Credit Policies; (d) Credit Collection Efforts; (e) Expansion Programme; and (f) Liquidity-Profitability Aspect.

(a) *Level of Sales* : The primary factor in determining the volume of debtors/receivables is the level of credit sales. Increase in credit sales means a corresponding increase in debtors, and vice versa. No doubt the level of sales can be used to forecast changes in receivables, i.e., if a firm predicts an increase of 50% in its credit sales for the next period, it will probably experience also an increase of 50% in debtors/receivables. The following illustration will make the principle clear:

Illustration 7.32

	Year I	Year II
	Rs.	Rs.
Credit Sales	6,00,000	9,00,000
Credit to Debtors	2 months	2 months

Average Debtors $(6{,}00{,}000 \times \frac{2}{12})$ 1,00,000; $(9{,}00{,}000 \times \frac{2}{12})$ 1,50,000. Since there is an increase in sales credit (50%), there is also a corresponding equal increase (50%) in the amount of Debtors, period of credit remaining constant.

(b) *Terms of Trade* : A change in credit policy has a direct impact on debtors. Thus, if credit terms are relaxed, it will lead to increase in the amount of debtors, and vice versa. The following illustration will help to understand the principle:

Illustration 7.33

	Alternative 1	Alternative 2
Credit Sales (Rs.)	3,00,000	3,00,000
Credit to Debtors	2 months	3 months
∴ Average Debtors	$(3{,}00{,}000 \times \frac{2}{12})$	$(3{,}00{,}000 \times \frac{3}{12})$
	Rs. 50,000	Rs. 75,000

From the above, it is quite clear that since there is an increase in credit period by one month, there is a corresponding increase in the amount of debtors by Rs. 25,000 (Rs. 75,000 – Rs. 50,000) assuming that the amount of credit sales remains constant. In reality, of course, if credit period is extended credit sales increase and, at the same time, debtors' balance also will be increased in comparison with the amounts shown above.

(c) *Credit Policies* : The level of debtors/receivables balance is closely related with the collection policy of the firm. Practically, credit policy determines the amount of risk that a firm is to undertake in its sales activities.*

(d) *Credit Collection Effort:* A firm should always give emphasis to realise the dues from the customers for which periodical reminders should be given to them if they do not pay at the stipulated date. If proper attention is not given,

---

* If a firm extends its credit policy, it will experience a higher level of receivables/debtors due to:
(i) Strong customers will be less careful;
(ii) Weak customers will default.
In establishing its credit policies, the firm tries to find a satisfactory middle ground between the excessive collection costs that accompany a highly aggressive policy and the excessive defaults and bad debts that accompany a lax policy — Hampton J. J., op. cit, p. 254.

possibility of bad debts may increase gradually and it will experience a financial disaster. Thus, efforts should always be given to reduce the amount of debtors by implementing effective collection system.

(e) *Expansion Programme:* When a new firm wants to enter into a new market it must have to give some incentive to the dealers either in the form of cash discount or granting credit facilities. Gradually, the firm should reduce the credit period when it gets some dependable customers. In short, at the initial stage, liberalised credit policy is usually taken for which amount of outstanding receivables increase gradually.

(f) *Liquidity-Profitability Aspect:* It has already been stated earlier that there is an inverse relationship between liquidity and profitability which affect receivables management. More liberal credit policy will increase sales and profit but liquidity position will decrease. On the contrary, a stringent credit policy will reduce the amount of sales and profit but will increase liquidity.

Credit Procedure/Evaluation

A firm should follow some clear-cut principles and procedures for granting credit to its individual customers for effective credit management since debtors constitute an investment on the part of the firm. Generally, the credit-worthiness of a customer depends on the five Cs:

(i) Character— It relates to the willingness of the customer to honour his dues which reflects integrity. This should carefully be considered by the credit manager.

(ii) Capacity— It indicates the ability of the customer to honour his dues in time which depends on the financial position, profitability, and the working capital position.

(iii) Collateral— It reveals the security given by the firm as mortgage. i.e., hypothecation of various kinds of assets owned by the firm.

(iv) Capital— Customer should have adequate funds to pay-off there dues.

(v) Financial Conditon— Financial condition must be sound.

In short, the reputation or credit-worthiness of the customer should be examined as far as possible before granting credit. For this purpose, the collection policy of the firm will differ from customer to customer. In case of old customer, past records will tell his story but, in other cases, the credit controller should follow a channel of information. However, the following steps should be involved for the purpose:

(a) Credit information; (b) Credit investigation; (c) Credit analysis; (d) Credit limits; and (e) Collection procedures.

(a) **Credit Information** — It includes:

(i) *Banker's Enquiry*

Since the customer maintains account in a bank, necessary information can be taken if, of course, the bank so allows. Normally, banks do not provide information directly to the inquirer. The same task can be done with the help of the firm's bank. In India, practically, this source of information is not very useful because of the indifference of banks in providing information, i.e., bankers may be reluctant to disclose its customer's position.

(ii) *Trade Reference*

The firm may insist on the proposed customers to give the names of such firms as he has current dealings for the purpose of getting information about his creditworthiness. This is, no doubt, a useful source of credit information without cost. The firm should take prompt and proper steps to seek information from the references whenever the trade references have been furnished. It may be contacted personally to obtain all relevant information required by the firm.

(iii) *Credit Bureau Reports*

In advanced countries, credit bureau organisations are employed in order to get comprehensive and correct information. They are specialised in providing credit information. No doubt these are valuable sources for assessing the creditworthiness of proposed customers. There is an urgent need for such organisations in our country.

(iv) *Financial Statement*

Scrutinising the published financial statement (viz., Profit and Loss Account and Balance Sheet) of the proposed customers, the financial condition and the creditworthiness can be assessed. For example, liquidity and solvency position can be judged with the help of accounting ratios, viz., Current Ratio, Liquid Ratio, Debt-Equity Ratio, Return on Equity; EBIT to Total Assets Ratio etc. Creditors Turnover Ratio may also be tested.

(b) **Credit Investigation**

Further investigation should be made by the firm after receiving the credit information about the prospective customer.

The following factors may be advocated[1] :

(i) The type of customer, whether new or old;
(ii) The customer's business line, background and the related trade risks;
(iii) The nature of the product — perishable or seasonal;
(iv) Size of customer's order and expected future volumes of business with him;
(v) Company's credit policies and practices.

It should be remembered that a meaningful investigation can be carried out only with the help of the necessary data supplied about the proposed customers for the last four or five years.

(c) **Credit Analysis**

For granting credit, the next step is to conduct the credit analysis of the proposed customer. For this purpose, proper evaluation about the financial position of the customers should be made very carefully with the help of liquidity ratios and other ratios to be computed from the data available in the published financial statement which will indicate the repaying capacity of the customer. The performance can also be compared with industry average ratios. Besides. 'the analyst has to be alert to spot instances of imbalance in management of customer's business, marked by over-centralisation of responsibilities and authority, over-trading, shrinking margins and growing liabilities. While business failures can be distributed to a large variety of factors, the central factor is management incompetence'.[2]

---

1 Ramamoorthy, V. E. — op. cit., p. 195.
2 *Ibid.*

(d) **Credit Limit**

Whenever the decision to extend credit is being taken, the amount and duration of the same is to be decided. The decisions in this regard depend on (i) the amount of contemplated sales, and (ii) the financial strength of the customers. A line of credit can be established in case of a frequent buyer which, in other words avoids the need to investigate each order from him, i.e., a line of credit is the maximum amount of credit which can be extended by the firm at a given period. In short, it reveals the maximum risk exposure that the firm will allow itself to undergo for an account. The line of credit can be fixed on the basis of a customer's normal buying trend and depending on the regularity of payment.

(e) **Collection Procedure**

The purpose of every collection policy is to speed up the collection of dues. If collections are unnecessarily delayed, alternative sources of finance for sustaining production and sales are to be made and amount of bad debts also will increase. The collection procedures should always be well-administered and established in clear-cut terms. At the same time, special consideration should be made to some customers who are temporarily in tight financial position due to some external factors, viz., slack economic conditions.

Besides, cash discounts may be allowed to customers for the prompt payment (*This has been discussed in detail in the subsequent para).*

However, the terms of credit should be ascertained after assessing the credit-worthiness of the customers. A firm may adopt different credit policies for different customers in order to minimise the risk involved on the basis of credit reputation. **'Risk-class Approach'** established by Hampton[1] may be remembered here. According to him, a firm establishes a certain number of risk classes ranging from the strongest and most established customers to the weakest firms. A separate credit policy is developed for each class. When a customer first applies for credit, the customer is investigated and placed into one of the classes. (Of course, re-investigations are to be made at suitable intervals, and, if necessary, customers are to be re-'Classed'—up on down). This eliminates the need to make a separate discussion on extending credit each time the customer wants to make purchase.

The following table will make the principle clear:

Risk-class Approach to Receivable Management

Risk Class	*Description of Firm*	*Credit Policy*
1	Large firms whose financial position and past record indicate virtually no risk.	Open credit up to certain limit without approval required.
2	Financially sound firms not supported by a detailed past record.	Open credit with approval for purchases in excess of certain amount up to specified limit.
3	Solid firms with past record that indicate some risk.	Limited credit line with frequent checks.

[1] Hampton, op cit., p. 256.

4	Not-too-solid firms that require close watching.	Restricted credit.
5	High-risk, weak firms.	No credit.

Assessing Credit Risks

Risk is always associated with credit sales, sometimes more sometimes less or sometime no risk although the last one is very rare. Risk appears when there is a possibility of default in realisation and which ultimately proved to be Bad.

From the risk-class approach suggested by Hampton, risk can be sub-divided into the following category.

(a)	**Zero/No Risk Class**	:	Where there is practically no possibility of default or bad debts. e.g., Govt. Organisations; Big or Multinational Organisation etc.
(b)	**Usual/Normal Risk Class**	:	This includes financially sound firms but not supported by a past record.
(c)	**Small Risk Class**	:	This includes solid firms with past records but involves some degree of risk.
(d)	**Probable Risk Class**	:	This includes not financially sound firms which require close watching.
(e)	**High-Risk Class**	:	Maximum amount of bad debts appear from this class of customers who are responsible for it.

Illustration 7.34

X Ltd. extends credit facilities to the following categories of customers to boost up sales:

(i) Customer with a 10% risk on non-payment i.e., Bad Debts.

(ii) Customer with a 40% risk on non-payment i.e., Bad Debts.

Expected increase in sales in category (i) amounts to Rs. 60,000, and in (ii) Rs. 1,00,000.

The total cost is 75% of sales. Collection charges are 5% on sales in category (i) and 10% in category (ii).

Advise the firm whether extending credit facilities will be beneficial on the part of the company.

Solution

(a) **Incremental Income in Category (i) having 10% Risk**

		Rs.	Rs.
	Incremental Sales		60,000
Less:	Bad Debts Losses @ 10%		6,000
			54,000
Less:	Cost of Sales (Rs. 60,000 × 75%)	45,000	
	Collection Charges (5% of Sales)	3,000	
			48,000
	Incremental Profit		6,000

Comment

If the firm accepts the proposal, it will earn an additional income of Rs. 6,000 as it is beneficial on the part of the company.

(b) **Incremental Income in Category (ii) having 40% Risk.**

		Rs.	Rs.
	Sales		1,00,000
Less:	Bad Debts Loss @ 40%		40,000
			60,000
Less:	Cost of sales (75% of Rs. 1,00,000)	75,000	
	Collection charges (10% of sales)	10,000	
			85,000
	Net Loss		25,000

Comment

It becomes clear form the above that firm having 40% risk of non-payment will have to incur a loss amounting to Rs. 25,000. Naturally, credit should not be granted to those customers. It is not beneficial to the company.

Credit Terms

Credit terms are very significant while adopting credit policy in case of credit transactions. The credit terms will include the ***terms and time and methods*** of payments. However, while fixing up or setting up the credit terms, there are factors which are to be carefully considered, e.g., the requirements of cash and expected profit from the sale of goods etc. Usually, credit terms include terms and conditions of sale, its price, time of delivery, time of payment, allowing cash discount on prompt payment etc.

We are presenting below some credit terms:

(a) **Weekly Credit** : The goods which are supplied in this or current week must be paid in the next week on a fixed day.

(b) **Fortnight Credit** : It expresses that the goods which will be sold in the 1st half of the month must be paid in the 2nd half on a fixed day.

(c) **Monthly Credit** : The goods which will be sold in the current month must be paid on a fixed day in the following month.

(d) **Credit Period with Cash Discount for Prompt Payment** : Cash Discount is allowed to the customers for prompt settlement of account against credit sales e.g. '$\frac{3}{10}$ net 30'. It means 3% Cash Discount is allowed if payment is made within 10 days and maximum period allowed is 30 days.

(e) **Payment on a Fixed Date** : A date is fixed by the suppliers for payment of goods after-delivery. For example, net 30, which indicates that the customers are allowed 30 days credit from the date of sale/delivery for payment and naturally if any payment is made after 30 days no discount is allowed.

Illustration 7.35

ABC company's present annual sales amount to Rs. 30 lakhs at Rs. 12 p.u. Variable costs are Rs. 8 p.u. and fixed costs amount to Rs. 2.50 lakhs p.a. Its present credit period of one month is proposed to be extended to either 2 or 3 months, whichever appear to be more profitable.

The following estimates are made for the purpose :

Credit Policy	1 month	2 months	3 months
Increase in Sales (%)	—	8	30
(%) of Bad Debt to Sales	1	2	6

Fixed cost will increase by Rs. 50,000 annually after any increase in sales above 25% over the present level.

The company required a pre-tax return on investment of at least 20% for the level of risk involved.

What will be the most rewarding credit policy in case of ABC company under the above circumstances? Present your answer in a tabular form.

Solution

$$\text{We know } \frac{P}{V} \text{ ratio} = \frac{\text{Sales} - \text{Variable Cost}}{\text{Sales}} \times 100$$

$$= \frac{12-8}{12} \times 100 = 33\tfrac{1}{3}\%$$

Comparative Cost Benefit Analyses

		1 month's Rs.	2 months' Rs.	3 months' Rs.
			Credit Policy	
Amount of Sales		30,00,000	32,40,000 (30,00,000 + 8%)	39,00,000 (30,00,000 + 30%)
[∴ *Contribution = Sales* × $\frac{P}{V}$ *ratio*]		10,00,000 (30,00,000 × $33\frac{1}{3}$%)	10,80,000 (32,40,000 × $33\frac{1}{3}$%)	13,00,000 (39,00,000 × $33\frac{1}{3}$%)
Less : Fixed Cost		2,50,000	2,50,000	3,00,000
		7,50,000	8,30,000	10,00,000
Less : Bad Debts	@ 1% on 30,00,000	30,000		
	@ 2% on 32,40,000		64,800	
	@ 6% on 39,00,000			2,34,000
Profit		7,20,000	7,65,200	7,66,000
Less : Normal Profit		7,20,000	7,20,000	7,20,000
Incremental Profit		—	45,200	46,000
Debtors' Balance —				
	30,00,000 × $\frac{1}{12}$	2,50,000		
	32,40,000 × $\frac{2}{12}$		5,40,000	
	39,00,000 × $\frac{3}{12}$			9,75,000
∴ Extra Investment in Debtors		—	2,90,000 (5,40,000 – 2,50,000)	7,25,000 (9,75,000 – 2,50,000)
Pre-tax return @ 20%		—	58,000	1,45,000
Less : Incremental Profit (as calculated above)		—	45,200	46,000
Deficit		—	12,800	99,000

Hence, most rewarding credit policy is taken at 1 month since 2 months and 3 months credit policies are not at all rewarding. They are less than required pre-tax return calculated on the basis of extra debtors' balance.

Benefits of Credit Extension

If the period of credit is extended, there will be a corresponding increase in the amount of sales. Before extending credit, one has to compare additional profits with costs related with the decisions which may arise out of increased sales due to extension of credit terms.

If the period of credit is extended, that will, no doubt, increase average debtors. Additional investment in debtors should be determined first. Thereafter, the cost of additional investment in debtors is to be ascertained. For the computation of cost for additional investment in debtors, two methods are generally adopted. The first one is the appropriate ***reaquired rate of return*** for the level of risk involved in the investment of debtors. The second one is the ***cost of debt capital*** as against the cost of financial investment in debtors. This is based on the assumption that as soon as the firm expands its debtors, the same is possible usually by taking the help of long-term debt capital. However, the first one is 'superior to using the financing cost of debt.'[1]

Thus, the decision rule is that the cost of additional investment in debtors must not exceed the expected additional profit or contribution whenever there is a change in credit policy.

There are two assumptions which are to be considered before taking any decision for the extension of credit : firstly, increase in sales can be made with available capacity, and, secondly, there must not be an adverse effect on the price of articles due to increase in the volume of sales.

Illustration 7.36

Present annual sale of Company X amounts to Rs. 40,00,000 at Rs. 10 per unit.

Variable cost Rs. 6 per unit.

Fixed cost Rs. 3,00,000 annually.

The present credit period is 1 month which is proposed to be extended to 2 and 3 months, whichever appears to be more profitable.

Due to extension of credit period, sales will increase by 10% and 25%, respectively.

The company requires a pre-tax return on investment of at least 20% for the level of risk involved.

Evaluate the profitability.

[I.C.W.A. Final—Adapted]

Solution

$$\frac{P}{V} \text{ ratio} = \frac{\text{Sales} - \text{Variable Cost}}{\text{Sales}} = \frac{\text{Rs. } 10 - \text{Rs. } 6}{\text{Rs. } 10} = \frac{4}{10} = 40\%$$

Present sales Rs. 40,00,000

Selling price p.u. Rs. 10

Units sold 4,00,000 (Rs. 40,00,000 ÷ Rs. 10)

1 *Ibid.*

Proposed Sales :

When credit period is extended to

2 months = 4,00,000 units + 10% of 4,00,000 i.e., 40,000

= 4,40,000 units

3 months = 4,00,000 units + 25% of 4,00,000 i.e., 1,00,000

= 5,00,000 units

Profitability Statement

	Present Policy 1 month Rs.	Policy I 2 months Rs.	Policy II 3 months Rs.
Annual Sales	40,00,000	44,00,000	50,00,000
Additional Sales	—	4,00,000	10,00,000
Cost of Sales			
Variable Cost @ Rs. 6	24,00,000	26,40,000	30,00,000
Fixed Cost	3,00,000	3,00,000	3,00,000
Total Cost	27,00,000	29,40,000	33,00,000
Average Investment in Debtors	$\frac{\text{Rs. } 27,00,000}{12} \times 1$	$\frac{\text{Rs. } 29,40,000}{12} \times 2$	$\frac{\text{Rs. } 33,00,000}{12} \times 3$
	= Rs. 2,25,000	= Rs. 4,90,000	= Rs. 8,25,000
∴ Additional Investment in Debtors		Rs. 2,65,000	Rs. 6,00,000
A. Cost of Additional Investment @ 20% p.a.		Rs. 53,000	Rs. 1,20,000
B. Additional Contribution			
(Additional sales × $\frac{P}{V}$ ratio)		Rs. 1,60,000 (Rs. 4,00,000 × 40%)	Rs. 4,00,000 (Rs. 10,00,000 × 40%)
∴ Additional Profit (B – A)		= Rs. 1,07,000	= Rs. 2,80,000

Hence, 3 months' credit policy should be adopted by the company X since it earns more profit.

Illustration 7.37

In order to increase sales from its present level of Rs. 2.4 lakhs p.a., your marketing manager submits a proposal for liberalising the credit policy as:

Present Sales	Rs. 2,40,000
Credit Period	30 days
Proposed increase in credit Period beyond 30 days	Relevant increase in sales over Rs. 2,40,000
15 days	Rs. 12,000
30 days	Rs. 18,000
45 days	Rs. 21,000
60 days	Rs. 24,000

The $\frac{P}{V}$ ratio of the company is $33\frac{1}{3}\%$.

The company expects a pre-tax return on investment of 20%.

Evaluate the above from alternatives and advise the management (assume 360 days a year).

[I.C.W.A. Final]

Solution

Statement Showing the Result of Proposed Increase in Credit Policy

	At Present	Proposed Credit Period			
	30 days	45 days	60 days	75 days	90 days
	Rs.	Rs.	Rs.	Rs.	Rs.
Sales	2,40,000	2,52,000	2,58,000	2,61,000	2,64,000
Contribution $33\frac{1}{3}\%$	80,000	84,000	86,000	87,000	88,000
Balance of Debtors	20,000	31,500	43,000	54,375	66,000
	$\left(\frac{\text{Sales}}{360/30}\right)$	$\left(\frac{\text{Sales}}{360/45}\right)$	$\left(\frac{\text{Sales}}{360/60}\right)$	$\left(\frac{\text{Sales}}{360/75}\right)$	$\left(\frac{\text{Sales}}{360/90}\right)$
Return on investment in debtors balance 20%	4,000	6,300	8,600	10,875	13,200
A. Increase in return on investment	—	2,300	4,600	6,875	9,200
B. Increase in Contribution	—	4,000	6,000	7,000	8,000
Additional Profit (B – A)	—	1,700	1,400	125	(– 1,200)

Hence, the management is advised to extend the credit period to 45 days, as the additional profit is highest at this stage.

Illustration 7.38

Best Manufactures Ltd. sells its product in cash. Now it desires to sell its products on credit in order to increase the volume of sales.

It wants to grant credit to its customers in the following two alternative forms of which you are asked to find out the better one:

	One Month Credit Policy	Two Months Credit Policy
Increase in the volume of sales by	50%	75%
Increase in fixed expenses (Direct)	Rs. 4,000	Rs. 8,000
Cost of collection	Rs. 10,000	Rs. 15,000
Bad Debts	@ 1% on sales	@ 2% on sales
Opportunity cost of capital	@ 10%	@ 10%
Present level of activity :		
Sales	Rs. 4,00,000	
Stock	Rs. 80,000	
Profit	25% on sales	

Solution

Statement Showing the Comparative Cost Benefit Analysis

	Present Level	One Month Credit		Two Months Credit	
	Rs.	Rs.	Rs.	Rs.	Rs.
Sales	4,00,000		6,00,000		7,00,000
Working Capital:					
Debtors					
(Rs. 6,00,000 × $\frac{1}{12}$)	—	50,000			
(Rs. 7,00,000 × $\frac{2}{12}$)				1,16,667	

Contd.

	Rs.	Rs.	Rs.	Rs.	Rs.
Stock :					
$\left(\frac{\text{Rs. } 80,000}{\text{Rs. } 4,00,000}\right) = \frac{1}{5}$th of Sales	80,000	1,20,000		1,40,000	
Working Capital	80,000		1,70,000		2,56,667
Less : Existing Working Capital	80,000		80,000		80,000
Increase in Working Capital	—		90,000		1,76,667
Benefits:					
Normal Profit @ 25% on Sales	1,00,000		1,50,000		1,75,000
Less : Costs —					
Increase in Fixed Expenses	—	4,000		8,000	
Cost of Collection	—	10,000		15,000	
Bad Debt	—	6,000		14,000	
(1% on Sales)					
(2% on Sales)					
Cost of Capital @ 10%					
(on Rs. 90,000)	—	9,000		17,667	
(on Rs. 1,76,667)			29,000		54,667
Excess on Benefits	1,00,000		1,21,000		1,20,333
Existing Benefits	1,00,000		1,00,000		1,00,000
∴ Increased Benefits	—		21,000		20,333

Hence, one month's credit should be adopted by the company.

Cash Discount

Many firms offer cash discounts to their customers in order to speed up the payment of debts at a certain specified rate. The cash discount terms reveal the rate of discount and the period for which discount has been offered. As such, if a customer does not avail this opportunity, he is to make payment by the net date. Practically, credit terms include both cash discount and credit period. It indicates (i) the rate of cash discount; (ii) the period of discount, and (iii) the period of credit.

For example, credit terms are expressed as "5/15 net 30".

It expresses that a 5% discount will be granted if payment is made by the 15th day and if the offer is not availed, the payment is to be made by the 30th day.

However, the decision about the cash discount depends on the comparative study between costs and benefits. Here, costs represent the amount of discounts on credit sales which the debtors will avail of, and opportunity saving will be the benefits. In short, the average balance of debtors will come down if the cash discount is being introduced. As a result, reduction in investment in average debtors can easily be ascertained. Consequently, opportunity savings will arise by the application of required rate of return to the reduction in the investment of the debtors. Therefore, if opportunity savings is higher than the cost of cash discount, cash discount scheme will, no doubt, prove worth.

Illustration 7.39

Company X furnished the following particulars:

Credit Sales Rs. 50,00,000

Variable Cost to Sales Ratio 50%

Fixed Costs Rs. 11,00,000

Present credit policy is 2 months.

Cash discount scheme of "2/10 net 60" is to be introduced.

It is estimated that 50% of the debtors will enjoy the discount scheme. As a result, the average age of debtors would be reduced to 1 month.

Required rate of return on investment in debtors may be taken at 20% before tax.

Evaluate the proposal.

Solution

Cost of Sales/Total Cost	Rs.
Fixed Cost	11,00,000
Variable Cost (50% of Sales)	25,00,000
	36,00,000

Investment in Average Debtors

(i) Before Cash Discount $= \text{Rs. } 36,00,000 \times \frac{2}{12} = \text{Rs. } 6,00,000$

(ii) After Cash Discount $= \text{Rs. } 36,00,000 \times \frac{1}{12} = \text{Rs. } 3,00,000$

So, reduction in investment of debtors arising out of cash discount —

(Rs. 6,00,000 – Rs. 3,00,000) = Rs. 3,00,000

Opportunity Savings

= Reduction in investment of average debtors × Required rate of return
= Rs. 3,00,000 × 20%
= Rs. 60,000

Cost of Cash Discount

= Credit Sales × % of debtors accepting × discount rate

$= \text{Rs. } 50,00,000 \times \frac{50}{100} \times \frac{2}{100}$

= Rs. 50,000

Since opportunity savings exceed cost of cash discount by Rs. 10,000 (Rs. 60,000 – Rs. 50,000) the discount policy will be profitable.

However, profit or loss in cash discount decision depends on :

(1) The terms relating to discount and period offered;

(2) The rate of opportunity investment;

(3) The age of debtors who do not take the benefits of cash discount.

Cost of Cash Discount

Before allowing cash discount to customers for prompt settlement, it becomes necessary to compare the cost of discount with the benefit that is available from the reduced value of investment in Debtors. If the benefit is more than the cost of discount in that case only, cash discount may be allowed for prompt settlement. However, the cost of cash discount may be calculated in the following manner:

(a) Cost of Cash Discount = Credit Sales × % of debtors accepting the offer × Rate of Discount.

Or,

Another Approach

(b) Cost of Discount $= \left[\frac{D}{(100-D)} \times \frac{365}{(C-A)}\right]$

Where

D = Rate of Discount

C = No. of days credit offered for no discount

A = No. of days credit allowed with rate of discount

For example

Calculate the amount of Cost of Discount from the following:

Credit Sales Rs. 1,00,000

Cash Discount Allowed @ 5%

60% of the Debtors take the benefit of Cash Discount

So, Cost of Discount = Credit Sales × % of debtors accepting × $\frac{5}{100}$

$= \text{Rs. } 1{,}00{,}000 \times \frac{60}{100} \times \frac{5}{100}$

= Rs. 3,000.

Illustration 7.40

Y Ltd. furnished the following particulars:

Existing Sale (with an average period of 3 months) Rs. 3,60,000.

No discount is offered to the customers at present.

Management decides to introduce Cash Discount @ 3% on Cash Sales.

Other Information

(i) 50% of the customers take the advantage of Cash Discount;

(ii) Average collection period reduces from 3 months to 2 months;

(iii) Rate of Return on Investment @ 20%.

Suggest the company.

Solution

		Rs.
	Existing Debtors (Rs. 36,00,000 × $\frac{3}{12}$)	9,00,000
Less:	Proposed Debtors (Rs. 36,00,000 × $\frac{2}{12}$)	6,00,000
	Reduction in Investment in Debtors	3,00,000
	Increase in profit owing to decrease in Debtors	
	= (Rs. 3,00,000 × $\frac{20}{100}$)	60,000

Contd.

Less: Discount to be offered to customers — Rs.

$= (\text{Rs. } 36,00,000 \times \frac{50}{100} \times \frac{3}{100})$ — 54,000

Net Increase in Profit — 6,000

Comment

It is advised to the company that it is benẽficial on the part of the company to introduce cash discount which will reasult in an increase in profit by Rs. 6,000.

Ageing Schedule

On the basis of trend of collection from customers, it becomes necessary to prepare an ageing schedule of debtors who are divided according to outstanding period of uncollected debts. The ageing schedule of debtors supplies very important information about the collection system, efficiency or otherwise of credit collection department, etc. We can also compare the result with the previous years' of the same firm (i.e., intra-firm comparison) and with the other firms on the same industry (i.e. inter-firm comparison). We can take decisions or appropriate steps for debts which remained unpaid for a long-period of time on the basis of ageing schedule of debtors, i.e., we can ascertain the total overdue amount after analysing the ageing schedule.

Ageing schedule is drawn on the basis of number of days outstanding. For example, less than 30 days, 31-45 days, 46-60 days, and so on. This ageing schedule helps us to understand the types and nature of various customers' account and their trend of payment. This schedule also helps us to understand the good quality accounts, overdue accounts and bad quality accounts (major portion of dues out of this part becomes irrecoverable which proves bad at last).

Average Age of Debtors

It is also known as Debtors' Turnover Ratio. It indicates the speed at which the debtors are converted into cash. The same is calculated as:

$$AA = \frac{AD}{ACS}$$

where, AA = Average Age of Debtors

AD = Average Debtors

ACS = Average Credit Sales

Or, $\frac{\text{Credit Sales (CS)}}{\text{Period (P)}}$

$$\text{or, } AA = \frac{AD}{CS} \times P$$

The same is nothing but debtors' turnover ratio which can also be expressed as:

$$\text{Debtors' Turnover Ratio} = \frac{\text{Debtors (Average/Closing)}}{\text{Credit Sales}} \times 365 \text{ days or 12 months}$$

Illustration 7.41

Credit allowed by the Company X to its customers is one month. The following particulars are presented from the books of accounts for four months in an accounting year:

Months	*Credit Sale (in '000 rupees)*	*Debtors (in '000 rupees)*
1	450	800
2	550	1,000
3	600	1,200
4	700	1,500

Solution

From the figures shown above it is very difficult on the part of the management to find out any trend. On the contrary, the same is possible if the following statement is prepared:

	Months			
	1	2	3	4
Credit Sales (in '000 rupees)	450	550	600	700
Outstanding debtors (in '000 rupees)	800	1,000	1,200	1,500
Average age of debtors (days) $\left(\frac{800}{450}\times 30\right)$ and so on	53	55	60	64
Rate of increase in Credit Sales (%)	—	22.22	33.33	55.55
Rate of increase in age of Debtors (%)	—	3.77	13.21	20.75
[**Note** : 1 month = 30 days taken]				

From the above illustration, it is quite clear that the trend of credit collection period is increasing in comparison with the normal credit period of 30 days and, as such, the position is very alarming. If this position is continued the liquidity position of the firm will deteriorate and, naturally, additional funds would be required in order to continue the operation.

Besides, for the purpose of better comparison between the months, percentage increase or decrease in sales is to be compared with the percentage increase or decrease in average age of debtors. Consequently, special attention must be given when percentage of average age of debtors increases than the corresponding increases in the percentage of sales.

It is better to classify the debts according to their respective ages instead of the method of calculating the average age of debtors (so calculated above) which express an overall picture only by approximation. The classification can be represented as:

Ageing Schedule/Trade Debtor Position

as at 31st Dec. 20................

Age of Debt (in days)	*Name of Debtors*	*Months of Sales*	*Outstanding Balance Amount (in '000)*	*Percentage to total*
			Rs.	
1-30	A	December	1,200	50.0
31-60	B	November	580	24.2
61-90	C	October	360	15.0
91-120	D	September	170	7.1
121 & above	E	Earlier	90	3.7
			2,400	100.0

From the statement presented above, information like date of sales, payment received from debtors from time to time etc. can easily be known which helps the management to consult the debtors' ledger for further decision. Actually, the main purpose of the age group of classification is to ensure a stricter control on the collection of debts from individual customers. Besides, it indicates an additional information about the average age of debtors by expressing a trend for old accounts to accumulate. For example, from the above table, it is found that out of the total debts, about 50% belong to the age group of over 30 days. Again, out of the total debts, Rs. 90,000 becomes outstanding for more than the period of 120 days which may prove to be bad if the management does not take any immediate step.

GENERAL ILLUSTRATIONS

Illustration 7.42

Saurav Ltd. presents the following information for increasing sales by liberalising it's credit policy.

You are requested to state whether the company should be benefitted from the same.

Amount of Sales will be increased by liberalising credit policy amounted to Rs. 5,00,000.

Cost of collection will be @ 6%

Variable Cost will be 70% of Sales

Possibility of bad debts will be @ 10%.

Solution

		Rs.	Rs.
	Increased amount of Sales		5,00,000
Less:	Variable Cost @ 70% =	3,50,000	
	Cost of Collections @ 6% =	30,000	
	Bad Debt Losses @ 10% =	50,000	4,30,000
	Incremental Profit		70,000

Hence, the company may liberalise its policy which will earn additional revenue of Rs. 70,000.

Illustration 7.43

Arindam Ltd. presents the following particulars for a period of 12 months:

	Rs.
Sales	6,00,000
Existing credit period allowed to Customer	1 month
Selling Price per unit	Rs. 10
Total Cost (including Variable Cost Rs. 7)	Rs. 8

The company now decides to liberalise its credit policy from one month to two months, for which sales may be increased by 40% assuming that the required rate of return of the company is 20% on investments.

Should the company be benefitted from the liberalised credit policy which is extended from one month to two months?

Solution

Calculation of Average Cost if 2 months Credit is allowed

Existing No. of Units sold $= \dfrac{\text{Sales}}{\text{Selling Price Per Unit}} = \dfrac{\text{Rs. } 6,00,000}{\text{Rs. } 10} =$ 60,000

	Rs.
Existing Cost of Sales = 60,000 units × Rs. 8 =	4,80,000

Contd.

	Rs.
Add: Cost of additional units sold (40% of 60,000) = 24,000 × Rs. 8 =	1,92,000
Cost of (60,000 + 24,000) 84,000 units	6,72,000

$\therefore$ Average Cost per Unit = $\frac{\text{Rs. } 6,72,000}{84,000}$ = Rs. 8

Average Additional Investment in Debtors

	Rs.
Existing Cost of Sales	4,80,000
(*i*) Existing investment in Debtors = Rs. 4,80,000 × $\frac{1}{12}$ (Since Credit period is 1 month)	40,000
(*ii*) Proposed cost of Sales for 84,000 units =	6,72,000
Proposed investment in Debtors = Rs. 6,72,000 × $\frac{2}{12}$ = (Since credit period is 2 months)	1,12,000
$\therefore$ Additional Investment in Debtors (Rs. 1,12,000 – Rs. 40,000) =	72,000

Profit on Additional Sales

No. of additional units = Contribution per Unit

= 24,000 × Rs. 3 (Rs. 10 – Rs. 7) = Rs. 72,000

So, Return on Additional Investment $= \frac{\text{Additional Profit}}{\text{Additional Investment}} \times 100$

$= \frac{\text{Rs. } 72,000}{\text{Rs. } 72,000} \times 100$

= 100%

Comment

The company may accept the proposal as rate of return (100%) is much higher than the required rate of return of 20%.

Illustration 7.44

Prafulla Ltd. furnished the following particulars:

50,000 units are sold @ Rs. 40 per unit

Variable cost per unit is Rs. 25 per unit.

Average Cost per unit is Rs. 30 per unit.

Average collection period 60 days.

Collection charges amounted to Rs. 20,000.

Bad Debts losses are @ 5%

Proposed Policy

Average collection period is 45 days

Bad debts losses may be reduced to 2% of Sales

Collection charges would be Rs. 30,000

Volume of Sales will be reduced by 5,000 Units

The firm's required rate of return is 25%.

Should the proposed policy be accepted? Give your views.

(Assume 360 days in a year)

Solution

(i) **Savings in Losses owing to Bad Debts** — Rs.

Existing sales 50,000 units @ Rs. 40 = Rs. 20,00,000

Existing Bad Debts @ 5% on Rs. 20,00,000 = 1,00,000

Proposed Bad Debts

Proposed Sales 45,000 units @ Rs. 40 = Rs. 18,00,000

∴ Proposed Bad Debts @ 2% on Rs. 18,00,000 = 36,000

∴ Savings for Bad Debts losses 64,000

(ii) **Savings in Investments**

Existing Receivables/Debtors (Rs. 20,00,000 $\times \frac{60}{360}$) = 3,33,333

Proposed Receivables/Debtors (Rs 8,00,000 $\times \frac{45}{360}$) = 2,25,000

Reduction in Investment in Debtors 1,08,333

∴ Saving for reduction in Investment Rs. 1,08,333 × 25% = Rs. 27,083

∴ Total Savings:

	(i) Savings for Bad Debts Losses	=	64,000
Add:	(ii) Savings for Reduction in Investment	=	27,083
	Total Savings		91,083

Increased Cost and Reduction in Profit

	Rs.
Reduction of profit owing to reductions in Sales volume by 5,000 units × Rs. 15 (Rs. 40 – Rs. 25)	75,000
Increased amount of collection charges (Rs. 30,000 – Rs. 20,000)	10,000
	85,000

∴ Net Profit/Surplus (Rs. 91,083 – Rs. 85,000) = Rs. 6,083

Comment

As the proposed policy will earn an additional profit, hence, the proposal may be accepted.

Illustration 7.45

X Ltd presented the following particulars:

Selling Price per unit is Rs. 500

Expected Annual Sales is 1,000 units

Variable Cost is Rs. 250 per unit

Debtors are allowed 2 months credit

Bad Debts losses are expected to be @ 10%

Interest on Investment in Debtors is @ 15% p.a.

Y. Ltd., a credit agency, offered X. Ltd. a system which can help to identify the possible bad debts and who are to be paid Rs. 50,000 p.a. 25% of the customers are being potential bad debts. There will be no actual bad debts if these customers are rejected.

Advise the company whether the credit agency system should be implemented.

Solution

Ascertainment of Net Profit without implementing Credit Agency

			Rs.
	Sales (1,000 units × Rs. 500)		5,00,000
Less:	Bad Debts @ 10%		50,000
			4,50,000
Less:	Variable Cost (1,000 units × Rs. 250)	2,50,000	
	Interest on Investment in Debtors (Rs. 2,50,000 × $\frac{15}{100}$ × $\frac{2}{12}$)	6,250	2,56,250
	Net Profit		1,93,750

Ascertainment of Net Profit if Credit Agency System is implemented

			Rs.
	Sales (Rs. 5,00,000 × 75%)		3,75,000
Less:	Bad Debts		Nil
			3,75,000
Less:	Variable Cost (750 units × Rs. 250)	1,87,500	
	Interest on investment in Debtors (Rs. 1,87,500 × $\frac{15}{100}$ + $\frac{2}{12}$)	4,688	
	Agency Cost	50,000	2,42,188
	Net Profit		1,32,812

Comment

As the net profit is less if credit agency system is implemented by Rs. 60,938 (Rs. 1,93,750 – Rs. 1,32,812); hence it is advised not to implement the service of credit agency system. The net profit is more if the service of credit agency system is not implemented.

Illustration 7.46

Industries Ltd. has the following features:

Annual Sales	Rs.	6,00,000
Variable Cost	Rs.	4,00,000
Fixed Cost	Rs.	6,00,000

Present Credit Period = 1 month

Marketing group of the company draws up the following strategy for boosting up its sale:

	Existing	Proposed Plan	
Credit Period	1 month	2 months	3 months
Increase in Sales (%)	—	10	20
Bad Debts (% of Sales)	1	2	5

If the company has a pre-tax return of 12% p.a. on investment in receivable, work out its optimum credit period.

Solution

Comparative Cash Benefit Analysis
Credit Policy

	1 month	2 months	3 months
	Rs.	Rs.	Rs.
Sales	60,00,000	66,00,000 (10% Increase)	72,00,000 (20% Increase)
Less: Variable Cost	40,00,000	44,00,000	48,00,000
Contribution	20,00,000	22,00,000	24,00,000
Less: Fixed Cost	6,00,000	6,00,000	6,00,000
Profit	14,00,000	16,00,000	18,00,000
Less: Bad Debts (1% of Sales)	60,000 (1%)	1,32,000 (2%)	3,60,000 (5%)
	13,40,000	14,68,000	14,40,000
Less: Normal Profit	13,40,000	13,40,000	13,40,000
Incremental Profit	—	1,28,000	1,00,000

Investment in Debtors	1 month	2 months	3 months
Rs. $60,00,000 \times \frac{1}{12}$ =	5,00,000		
Rs. $66,00,000 \times \frac{2}{12}$ =		11,00,000	
Rs. $72,00,000 \times \frac{3}{12}$ =			18,00,000
Extra Investment in Debtors	—	6,00,000 (Rs. 11,00,000 – Rs. 5,00,000)	13,00,000 (Rs. 18,00,000 – Rs. 5,00,000)
Pre-Tax Return 12% p.a. =	—		
Rs. 6,00,000 × 12%		72,000	
Rs. 13,00,000 × 12%			1,56,000
Less: Incremental Profit	—	1,28,000	1,00,000
		56,000	56,000

Comment

Since incremental profit is less than pre-tax return in case of 3 month credit policy, it is not at all reward. Most rewarding credit policy is 2 month, as it is more than the pre-tax return calculated on the basis of extra debtors balance. Hence, 2 months' credit policy is most rewarding.

Illustration 7.47

From the following particulars you are asked to advise whether the following proposal should be accepted:

A good number of customers desire to make an agreement with X Ltd. to purchase goods valued Rs. 50,00,000 during the period 2009. The delivery of the goods is to be made quarterly by instalments. The price of the product is Rs. 20 per unit and is expected profit Rs. 10 per unit. If the proposal is accepted, there will be an additional recurring expenditure of Rs. 20,000 p.a.

However, the ageing schedule of accounts receivables relating to the group of customers in the past was:

Period		Percentage of Bills (against which payment received)
At the end of	30 days	15%
"	60 days	25%
"	90 days	40%
"	100 days	20%

Opportunity cost of investment in accounts receivable is 25%

Solution

Expected Profit if the Proposal is Accepted

	Rs.	Rs.
Value of contract		50,00,000
Less: Cost of Product (Rs. 50,00,000 × $\frac{10}{20}$)	25,00,000	
Additional Expenditure	20,000	25,20,000
Expected Profit		24,80,000

∴ **Opportunity cost of investment blocked in Accounts Receivables**

Quarterly Sales = Rs. 50,00,000 × $\frac{1}{4}$ = Rs. 12,50,000

The above amount shall be realised as per the following ageing schedule:

No. of Days (a)		Amount (b) Rs.	Product C = (a) × (b) Rs.
30	(Rs. 12,50,000 × $\frac{15}{100}$) =	1,87,500	56,25,000
60	(Rs. 12,50,000 × $\frac{25}{100}$) =	3,12,500	1,87,50,000
90	(Rs. 12,50,000 × $\frac{40}{100}$) =	5,00,000	4,50,00,000
100	(Rs. 12,50,000 × $\frac{20}{100}$) =	2,50,000	2,50,00,000
		12,50,000	9,43,75,000

∴ **Opportunity Cost of Investment in Account Receivables**

$$\text{Rs. } 9{,}43{,}75{,}000 \times \frac{25}{100} \times \frac{1}{365} = \text{Rs. } 64{,}641 \text{ per Quarter}$$

∴ Per year opportunity cost will be Rs. 64,641 × 4 = Rs. 2,58,562

∴ Net surplus/gain = Rs. 24,80,000 – Rs. 2,58,562 = Rs. 22,21,438.

ASSIGNMENT MATERIALS

THEORETICAL

Multiple Choice Questions

1. (a) Receivable management relates to:

(i) Stock (ii) Debtors/Accounts Receivable
(iii) Cash (iv) Cash and Accounts Receivable

(b) Delinquency Cost means:

(i) Period of payment becomes one but not received (ii) Period not due
(iii) Period matured (iv) None of these

(c) Default cost means:

(i) Bad Debts (ii) Recovery of Bad Debt
(iii) Uncollected Debts (iv) Collection expenses

(d) High Risk Class means:

(i) No possibility of default (ii) Little possibility of default
(iii) Maximum possibility of bad debts (iv) Probable risk

(e) Extended credit period increases:

(i) Sales (ii) Sales as well as bad debts
(iii) Bad Debts (iv) None of these

(f) Cash discount is allowed for:

(i) Prompt payment (ii) Delayed payment
(iii) Excess payment (iv) Timely payment

(g) Debtors' Turnover Ratio means:

(i) $\frac{\text{Debtors}}{\text{Receivable}} \times 12$ (ii) $\frac{\text{Sales}}{\text{Debtors}} \times 365$

(iii) $\frac{\text{Debtors}}{\text{Sales}} \times 365$ (iv) $\frac{\text{Debtors}}{\text{Average Sales}}$

(h) Factor means:

(i) Who undertakes to collect debts (ii) Middleman
(iii) Broker (iv) A sharebroker

[Ans. (a) (ii); (b) (i); (c) (i); (d) (iii); (e) (ii); (f) (i); (g) (iii); (h) (i)]

Short Answer-type Questions

2. What are the objectives of Receivable Management?
3. When and how volume of sales changes?
4. Define:

   (a) Delinquency Cost; (b) Default Cost; (c) Capital Cost.
5. What is optimum credit policy?

6. What are the factors that affect the size of Debtors?
7. Write Notes on:
   (a) Credit limit; (b) Credit analysis; (c) Credit investigation.
8. How do you classify risk?
9. What is Credit Term? Classify it.
10. Explain the benefits of Credit Extension.
11. How do you ascertain the cost of Cash Discount?

Long Answer-type Questions

12. How do you calculate the Average Age of Debtors? (Explain it with help of an illustrations).
13. What is ageing of debtors? How do you classify it?
14. Who is a factor? What are the characteristies of a factor?
15. Explain the Types of factoring.
16. Explain the benefits of factoring. Explain also the cost of factoring.
17. Explain the liquidity-profitability Tangle in Receivables management.
18. What is Receivable Management? Explain its objectives in details.
19. How do you control Receivables?
20. What is ageing schedule? How do you classify it?
21. Explain the role of Cash Discount in Receivable Management.

PRACTICAL

1. X Ltd. presented the following particulars:

Credit Sales Rs. 32,00,000
Selling Price Rs. 40 p.u.
Variable Cost Rs. 25 p.u.
Average Cost Rs. 32 p.u.
Average age of accounts receivables 72 days

X Ltd. is planing to tighten credit standard for which sales will be reduced to Rs. 28,00,000 and Average age of accounts receivables to 45 days.

Rate of Return @ 20%

Should the proposal be accepted?

[Ans. Proposal should not be accepted. Profit will be decreased by Rs. 1,50,000; Savings in cash Rs. 46,400]

2. Y Ltd. presented the following particulars:

It decides to increase the credit period from 30 days to 60 days.

Existing Sales Rs. 3,00,000
Selling Price p.u. Rs. 3
Bad Debts 0.5%
Variable Cost Rs. 2.30 p.u.
Average Cost Rs. 2.60 p.u.
Average age of debtors 40 days

As a result of change in credit policy sales may be increased to 3,40,000 units, Bad debts will increase to 2%.

Average collection period is 72 days.

Required rates of return on investment is @ 18%.

Should the proposal be accepted?

[Ans. Proposal should not be accepted. Expected Profit Rs. 15,900; Additional Cash Rs. 31,692]

3. As a part of the strategy to increase sales and profits, the sales manager proposes to sale goods to a group of new customers with 10% risk of non-payment. This group would require $1\frac{1}{2}$ month credit and is likely to increase sales by Rs. 1,00,000 p.a. Production and selling expenses amount to 80% of sales and the income-tax rate is 50%. The company's minimum required rate of return (after tax) is 25%.

Should the sales manager's proposal be accepted?

[Ans. The proposal should be accepted]

4. A group of customers want to enter into a contract with you to buy goods worth Rs. 20 lakhs during 2007, the deliveries to be made in four equal instalments quarterly. The price of the commodity is Rs. 20 p.u. on which you expect a profit of Rs. 10. The acceptance of this proposal would mean an additional recurring expenditure of Rs. 10,000 p.a. on your part.

The ageing schedule of accounts receivables in respect of this group of customers in the part was also:

Period	**Percentages of bills for which payment received**
At the end of 30 days	15%
" 60 days	25%
" 90 days	40%
" 100 days	20%

Assuming an opportunity cost of 20% of the funds locked up in accounts receivables, will it be desirable to accepted this proposal?

[C.A. Final]

[Ans. The proposal should be accepted. Net Profit Rs. 9,07,260; Opportunity Cost Rs. 82,740]

5. The present credit terms of P. Co. Ltd. are $\frac{1}{10}$ net 30.

Its annual sales are 80 lakhs. Its average collections period is 20 days. Its variable costs and average total costs to sales are 0.85 and 0.95 respectively, and its cost of capital is 10%. The proportion of sales on which customers currently take discount in 0.5. P Co. is considering relaxing its discount terms to $\frac{2}{10}$ net 30. Such relaxation is expected to increase sales by Rs. 5 lakhs, reduce the average collection period to 14 days and increase the proportions of discount sales to 0.8.

What will be the effect of relaxing the discount policy on company's profit? Take year as of 360 days.

[Ans. Present discount policy should not be relaxed Net decrease in profit Rs. 9,986]

6. A firm which has only credit sales allows one month credit to its customers. By changing the credit period to two months it finds that its outstanding debtors has increased to three times the previous average.

To what extent has the changes in credit period affected the sales?

[I.C.W.A. Inter, June 2004]

[Ans. 50% increase in Sales]

7. A firm has a current sales of Rs. 2,56,48,750. The firm has unutilised capacity. In order to boost up its sales, it is considering the relaxations in its credit policy. The proposed terms of credit will be 60 days' credit against the present policy of 45 days'. As a result, the bad debts will increase from 1.5% to 2% of sales. The firms' sales are expected to increase by 10%. The variable operating costs are 72% of sales. The firms corporate tax rate is 35%, and it requires an after-tax return of 15% on its investment.

Should the firm change its credit policy.

[C.A. PE II, Nov. 2003]

[Ans. for 45 days' credit period :	**Investment in Debtors**	**Rs.**	**32,06,094**
	Bad Debts	**Rs.**	**3,84,731**
for 60 days' credit period :	**Investment in Debtors**	**Rs.**	**47,02,271**
	Bad Debts	**Rs.**	**5,64,279**
Increased investment in Debtors	**= 23.40%]**		

8. High Vision Ltd. has current sales of Rs. 20,00,000. The company is planning to introduce a Cash discount policy of '$\frac{2}{10}$ net 30'. As a result, the company expects the average collection period to go down by 10 days and 80% of the sales opt for cash discount facility.

If the company required return on investments in receivable is 20%, should it introduce the new discount policy?

[CS Final 2003]

[Ans. Debtors (before introducing Cash discount policy)	**Rs.**	**1,66,666**
Debtors (after introducing Cash discount policy	**Rs.**	**1,11,111**

Net loss Rs. 20,889. Thus, it is better not to introduce Cash Discount Policy]

9. A Company has prepared the following projections for a year

Sales	21,000 Units
Selling Price p.u.	Rs. 40
Variable Cost p.u.	Rs. 25
Total Cost p.u.	Rs. 35
Credit period allowed	1 month

The company proposes to increase the credit period allowed to its customers from one month to two months. It is envisaged that the changes in the policy as above will increase the sales by 8%. The company desires a return of 25% on its investment.

You are required to examine and advise whether the proposed credit policy should be implemented or not.

[C.A. PE II, Nov. 2002]

[Ans.			
For 1 month credit period	:	**Cost of sales**	**Rs. 7,35,000**
		Investment in Debtors	**Rs. 61,250**
For 2 months credit period	:	**Cost of Sales**	**Rs. 7,77,000**
		Investment in Debtors	**Rs. 1,29,500**

Rate of Return on Increased Investment @ 36.92%]

10. The credit manager of XYZ Ltd. is re-appraising the company's credit policy. The company sells it product on terms of net 30. Cost of good sold is 85% of sales and fixed cost are further 5% of sales. XYZ classifies its customers on a scale of 1 to 4. During the past five years, the experience was as under:

Classification	Default as a % of Sales	Average collection period in days for non-defaulting accounts
1	0	45
2	2	42
3	10	40
4	20	80

The average rate of interest is 15%.

What conclusions do you draw about the company's credit policy?

What other factors should be taken into account before changing the present policy?

Discuss.

[C.A. Final, May 2000]

[Ans. Class	1	2	3	4
	Rs.	Rs.	Rs.	Rs.
Bad Debts	—	2.00	10.00	20.00
Interest	1.57	1.47	1.40	1.8
Net Profits	13.43	11.53	3.60	7.80]

11. PQR Ltd. is considering relaxing its credit policy and evaluating two proposed policies. Currently the firm has annual credit sales of Rs. 50 lakhs and Accounts Receivables is Rs. 12,50,000. The current level of loss due to bad debts is Rs. 1,50,000. The firm is required to give a return of 20% on investment in the new (additional) accounts receivables. The company's variable costs are 70% of the selling price.

The following further information is furnished:

	Present Policy	**Policy Option I**	**Policy Option II**
	Rs.	Rs.	Rs.
Annual Credit Sales	50,00,000	60,00,000	67,50,000
Accounts Receivables	1,25,000	20,00,000	28,12,500
Bad Debts Losses	1,50,000	3,00,000	4,50,000

You are the management auditor of the firms. Advise the M.D. which option should be exercised.

[I.C.W.A. Final]

[Ans. Option I is to be exercised]

III. INVENTORY MANAGEMENT

Meaning

The preceding two sections have expressed the basic considerations of the two components of working capital management, viz., Cash and Receivables. Now, the third major component of working capital—'Inventory'—will be discussed:

'Inventory' refers to the stockpile of the product a firm is offering for sale and the components that make-up the product.[1] In short, inventory is such type of assets which will be disposed-off in future in the ordinary course of the business. In other words, 'Inventory' is used to designate the aggregate of those items of tangible assets which are:

(i) held off sale in ordinary course of the business;

(ii) in the process of production for such sale; or

(iii) to be currently consumed in the production of goods or services to be available for sale.[2]

Kinds of Inventories

Thus, inventory means and includes:

(i) Raw materials & Stores (Consumable)

It contains items which are purchased by the firm from others.

(ii) Work-in-Progress (Convertible)

It consists of items which are currently used in the production process. These are semi-finished goods that are held at various stages of production in multi-stage production process.

(iii) Finished goods (Saleable)

It represents final or completed products which are available for sale.

In financial management, however, inventory is defined as the sum total of raw materials, work-in-progress, and finished products, although it depends largely upon the type of business. For example, in case of manufacturing concern, inventory will mean and include all the three groups stated above while, in case of a trading concern, it will represent only the finished goods. Manufacturing concerns hold inventories to give flexibility between production and sales. That is why it is the duty of the financial manager to see whether increase in inventories results in increased earnings and to minimise the level of inventories as well. As such, if inventories are reduced as a result of sale, the funds so generated may be used for different purposes.

Need to Hold Inventories

Holding of inventories involves tying up funds of the company and storage and handling costs. There are three general motives for holding inventories[3]:

(i) ***The Transactions motive:***

It expresses the need to maintain inventories to facilitate production and sales operation smoothly.

---

1 Bolton, S. E.—*Managerial Finance* (Boston), Houghton Mifflin & Co., 1976, p. 426.

2 Banerjee, B.—*Financial Policy and Management Accounting*—op. cit., p. 114.

3 Starr, M. K. and David, W. M.—*Inventory Control, Theory and Practice*—Englewood-Cliffs. N. J., Prentice-Hall, 1962, p. 17.

(ii) *The Precautionary motive:*

It necessitates holding of inventories to guard against the risk of unpredictable change in demand and supply forces.

(iii) *The Speculative motive:*

It influences the decision to increase or reduce inventory levels to take advantages of price fluctuation.

In order to maintain an uninterrupted flow of production it becomes necessary to hold adequate stock of materials since there is a time lag between the demand for materials and its supply due to some unavoidable circumstances. Besides, there are two other motives for holding of inventories—viz., to receive the benefit of quantity discount on account of bulk purchase and to avoid the anticipated rise in price of raw material.

The work-in-progress builds up since there is production cycle. Actually, the stock of work-in-progress is to be maintained till the production cycle is complete. Similarly, stock of finished goods has also to be held since there is a time lag between the production and sales. When goods are demanded by the customers, it cannot immediately be produced and, as such, for a continuous and regular supply of goods, minimum stock of finished goods is to be maintained. Stock of finished goods should also be maintained for sudden demands from customers and for seasonal sales.

Therefore the primary objective of holding raw materials are : (i) to separate purchase and production activities, and, for holding finished goods there should be separate production and sales activities; (ii) to obtain quantity discount against bulk purchase, and (iii) to avoid interruption in production.

At the same time, work-in-progress inventory is necessary since production is not instantaneous and finished goods should also be maintained for : (i) serving customer on a continuous basis; (ii) meeting the fluctuating demands.

Objectives of Inventory Management

Efficient inventory management should result in maximisation of the owner's wealth. For this purpose, a firm should neither hold excessive inventories nor hold inadequate inventories, i.e., it should hold the optimum level of inventory. The optimum level of inventory investment lies between the point of excessive and inadequate levels. In other words, there must not be an over-investment or under-investment in inventories. The danger of over-investment in inventories are : (i) funds of the firm are tied-up unnecessarily; (ii) it creates loss of profit; (iii) excessive carrying cost and risk of liquidity increases.

As such, the opportunity cost and carrying costs (viz., cost of storage, handling, insurance etc.) increase proportionately. No doubt these costs will impair the profitability of the firm. Excessive investment in raw materials will prove the same result except at the time of inflation and scarcity. Similar results may also be noticed for the over-investment in work-in-progress since it is very difficult to sell. Similarly, many difficulties will appear to dispose off excessive finished goods since time lengthens (viz., the goods may be sold at low price etc.). Moreover, for carrying excessive inventory, physical deterioration of the same may occur while in storage. From the above, it becomes crystal clear that there must not be an over-investment in inventories.

Similarly, inadequate level of inventories is also not free from snags. The consequences are : (i) production may shut-down; (ii) commitment for the delivery may not be possible; (iii) inadequate raw material and work-in-progress will create frequent production interruption; (iv) customers may shift to the competitor if their demands are not met up regularly, etc.

Thus, the objective of inventory management is to maintain its optimum level in the following manner :

(a) To ensure a continuous supply of materials to facilitate uninterrupted production;

(b) To maintain sufficient stock of raw materials during short-supply;

(c) To maintain sufficient finished goods for efficient customer services;

(d) To minimise the carrying cost; and

(e) To maintain the optimum level of investment in inventories.+

Cost of Holding Inventory

It has been highlighted above that the object of inventory management is to maintain the optimum level of inventory. This optimum level depends on the following costs:

(i) Ordering/Acquisition/Set-up Costs, and

(ii) Carrying Costs.

(i) **Ordering/Acquisition/Set-up Costs**

These are the variable costs of placing an order for the goods. Orders are placed by the firm with suppliers to replenish inventory of raw materials. Ordering costs include the cost of : requisiting, purchasing, ordering, transporting, receiving, inspecting and storing. The ordering costs vary in proportion to the number of orders placed. They also include clerical costs and stationery costs (That is why it is called a set-up cost.). Although these costs are almost fixed in nature, the larger the order placed, or the more frequent the acquisition of inventory made, the higher are such costs. Similarly, the fewer the orders, the lower the order cost will be for the firm. Thus, the ordering/acquisition costs are inversely related to the level of inventory.

(ii) **Carrying Cost**

These are the expenses of storing goods, i.e., they are involved in carrying inventory. The cost of holding inventory may be divided into (i) Cost of Storing the Inventory, and (ii) Opportunity Cost of Funds.

(i) **Cost of Storing the Inventory**

This include—

(a) Storage Cost (i.e., tax, depreciation, insurance, maintenance of building, etc.)

(b) Insurance (for fire and theft);

(c) Obsolescence and Spoilage;

(d) Damage or Theft;

(e) Servicing Costs (i.e., clerical, accounting costs, etc.)

(f) Cost of running out of goods.

(ii) **Opportunity Cost of Funds**

This includes the expenses in raising funds (i.e., Interest on Capital) which are used for financing the acquisition of inventory.

+ Efficient inventory management is possible by the cooperation of all departments concerned which includes : Materials Department (Purchase, Store-keeping, Material Control and Disposals), Quantity Control and Inspection, Marketing and Sales, Users' Department (e.g., Production, Maintenance, Operation etc.), Financial Accounting and Internal Audit Department, Design, Research and Development, Industrial/Standard Engineering, and Computer/Data Processing Center—Palit, A. R.—*Inventory Control is not an Isolated Function*—Lok Udyog, July 1976, p. 29.

The level of inventory and the carrying costs are positively related and move in the same direction, i.e., if inventory level decreases, the carrying costs also decrease, and vice versa.

Inventory Management Techniques

The objectives of inventory management have already been highlighted in the preceding section. In order to maximise the owner's wealth, the financial manager should aim at the optimum level of inventory on the basis of trade-off between cost and benefit.

There are two techniques which may be advocated for the purpose:

(a) Traditional Techniques of Inventory Management.

(b) Scientific Techniques of Inventory Management.

(a) Traditional Techniques of Inventory Management

Under this method, comparison may be made between firms belonging to the same industry or within the same firm for a particular period or over a period of time for establishing the standard by which efficient inventory management, or otherwise, may be determined.

For the purpose the following ratios are commonly used:

(i) Materials Turnover:

Average Materials in Stores/Average Daily Consumption

(ii) Work-in-Progress Turnover:

Average W-I-P/Average Factory Cost of Production

(iii) Finished Goods Turnover:

Average F.G. in Stores/Average Cost of Production

The above ratios are used for testing whether the raw materials are over-purchased or not, production control is effective or ineffective and finished goods are slow-moving or not. Therefore, an important indication of efficiency can be noticed with the help of these ratios. Although the rapidity of turnover depends on the nature of business, the higher the turnover ratio the shorter will be the time period. So the quicker the turnover the greater will be the profitability, and vice versa. Since the ratios are not free from snag, the next approach, i.e., Scientific Techniques of Inventory management may, be applied.

(b) Scientific Techniques of Inventory Management

The major problems comprise the heart of inventory control[1]:

(a) The Classification Problem;

(b) The Order Quantity Problem (how much to order);

(c) The Order Point Problem (when to order); and

(d) Safety Stock.

(a) The Classification Problem

ABC Analysis

This widely-used classification technique recognises different items of inventory for the purpose of inventory control which is based on the assumption that a firm should not exercise equal attention on all items of inventory since a firm has to maintain various types

---

1 Joy, O. M.—*Introduction to Financial Management*—Homewood, Illinois, Irwin, 1977, p. 469.

of inventories. It, therefore, should pay maximum attention to those items that are (i) most costly, and /or (ii) slow moving.

On the contrary, inventories which are less expensive should be given less control effort. Thus, the firm should be selective in its approach towards the inventory control management. This analytical approach is known as ABC Analysis Approach. It tends to measure the relative cost significance of each component of inventories.

According to this system, various items are grouped into three distinct categories:

(a) 'A' Items — which involve the highest/largest-investment and, as such, would be under the tightest control, i.e., the most sophisticated inventory control techniques should be applied.

(b) 'C' Items — which involves relatively least value and, as a result, need not require any special attention and control.

(c) 'B' Items — which stands in between items 'A' and 'C'. It desires less attention than A but more attention than C, or, it requires reasonable attention of the management.

Since the above items are classified according to importance of their relative value, it is also known as *Proportional Value Analysis* (PVA).

The following table—printed on the basis of physical quantities and value—will make the principle clear :

Inventory Items	% of total items	% of total value
A	15	70
B	35	20
C	50	10

The above statement can also be presented graphically as:

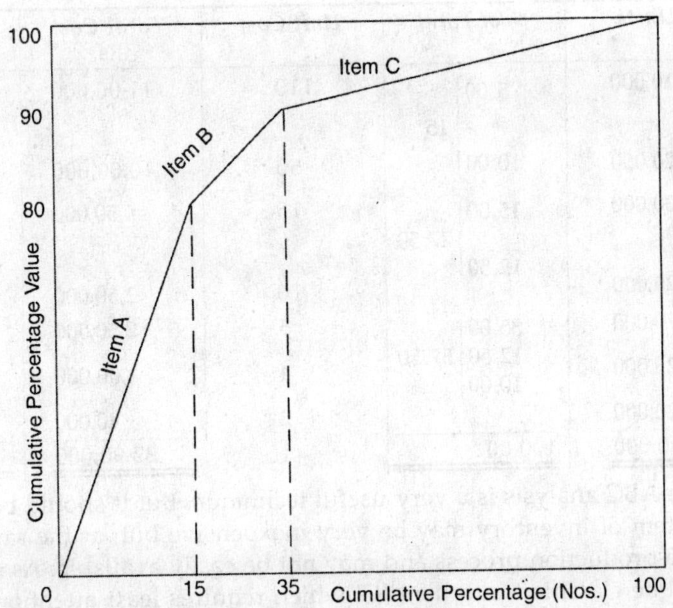

Fig. 7.7: ABC Analysis Graph

The above graphic presentation indicates that Item 'A' forms a minimum proportion but represents the highest value, viz., 70% of the cost. On the contrary, Item 'C' represents 65% of the total units but 10% of the cost. And item 'B' occupies the middle place. Thus, Item 'A' and Item 'B' jointly represent 35% of the total units but 90% of the total investment, whereas Item 'C' forms more than half of the total units against 10% of total investment.

So, the highest control should be exercised on Item 'A' for maximising profitability.

Illustration 7.48

Firm X has 7 different items in its inventory. The average number of units in inventory—together with their average cost per unit—is presented below:

Suggest a break-down of the items into ABC classification assuming that the firm wants to introduce ABC inventory system:

Item (Nos.)	Average Number of Units of Inventory Rs.	Average Cost per unit Rs.
1	10,000	110
2	20,000	50
3	30,000	15
4	25,000	10
5	70,000	5
6	25,000	4
7	20,000	2
	2,00,000	

Solution

The ABC analysis is presented with the help of the following table:

ABC Analysis

Items	*Units*	*% of Total*		*Unit Cost*	*Total Cost* Rs.	*% of Total* Rs.	
1	10,000	5.00	15	110	11,00,000	33.43	63.82
2	20,000	10.00		50	10,00,000	30.39	
3	30,000	15.00	27.50	15	4,50,000	13.68	21.28
4	25,000	12.50		10	2,50,000	7.60	
5	70,000	35.00	57.50	5	3,50,000	10.64	14.90
6	25,000	12.50		4	1,00,000	3.04	
7	20,000	10.00		2	40,000	1.22	
	2,00,000	100.00			32,90,000	100.00	

No doubt the ABC analysis is a very useful technique. But it should be used with care; for example, an item of inventory may be very inexpensive but, at the same time, may be very critical to the production process and may not be easily available. As such, as per ABC analysis, it would be classified into item 'C' which requires least attention. But because of its special importance to the production process, it deserves special attention of the management.

(b) **The Order Quantity Problem**

Economic Order Quantity (EOQ)

How much inventory should be added when inventory is replenished is a major problem in inventory management, i.e., how much to buy or produce at a time is really a problem to the management. If bulk quantities are purchased, the cost of carrying will be high and, on the contrary, if small quantities are purchased at frequent intervals, ordering cost will be high. Therefore, the quantity to be ordered at a given time should be economic, taking mainly two factors into account, viz., ordering costs, and carrying costs.† In short, it represents the most favourable quantity to be ordered at the reorder level.

EOQ is a problem of balancing the two conflicting kinds of costs—costs of carrying (arising out of balance purchases) and cost of not carrying (arising out of frequent purchases in small lots).[1] To sum up, EOQ is determined at the point where the carrying costs are approximately equal to the cost of not carrying (the ordering costs), where the total cost is minimum.

The nature of the above costs are discussed below[2] :

Cost of Carrying	Cost of not Carrying
1. Handling and transportation.	1. Extra cost of purchasing, handling and transportation.
2. Clerical	2. Frequent stockouts resulting in disruption of production schedules and, consequently, extra costs of overtime set-ups hiring and training.
3. Rent, Insurance and other Costs of storage.	3. Foregone quantity discounts and contribution margins on lost sales.
4. Interest on capital blocked.	4. Additional cost of uneconomic production runs.
5. Pilferage and normal loss of holding.	5. Loss of customer goodwill.
6. Risk of obsolescence.	

The EOQ model is illustrated below with the help of the following diagram:

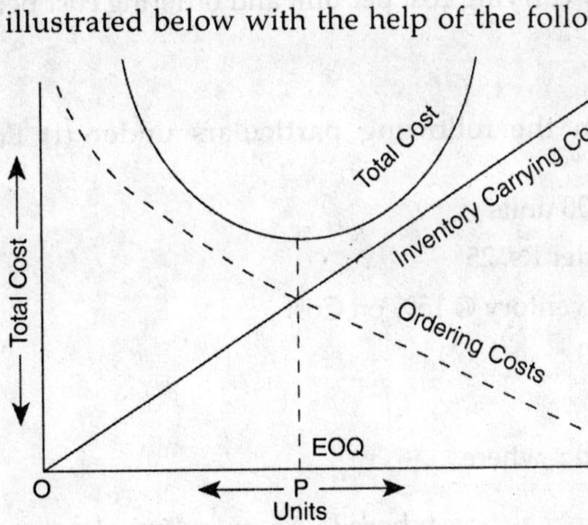

Fig. 7.8: No. of Units Per Order

---

† These costs have already been discussed earlier in the present section.

1 Banerjee, B.—*Financial Management and Policy*—op. cit., p. 123.

2 *Ibid.*

In the above diagram, the ordering costs, inventory carrying cost, and the total costs are plotted. The diagram shows that the carrying costs vary directly with the size of the order whereas ordering costs vary inversely with the size of the order. The total cost (i.e., the sum of two costs) curve at first goes downwards due to the fact that, at this stage the fixed costs of ordering are spread over many units. But, at the next stage, this curve goes upward because of the fact that at this stage, decrease in average ordering costs is more than what is offset by the additional inventory carrying costs. The point *P* denotes the optimum order where the total cost is the minimum. Therefore, *OP* units are considered as the *EOQ*.

It should be remembered that the *EOQ* is not a stock level. It lies between the Maximum Stock Level and Minimum Stock Level. However, the *EOQ* will be determined in such a way as would help in earning the advantages of bulk purchases on one side and would keep the other costs (such as interest on capital) as minimum as possible on the other.

The above principle can be illustrated with the help of the following formula :

$$EOQ \text{ or } E = \sqrt{\frac{2AO}{CS}}$$

where, A = the annual consumption, i.e., annual quantity, used in units.

O = the ordering cost/cost per purchase order.

C = carrying cost percentage.

S = cost of one unit.

The above model is based on the following assumptions:

(i) The supply position of the materials will be in such a way as will enable a firm to place as many orders as it desires;

(ii) Cost of materials or finished goods remains constant during the year;

(iii) Quantity-discount is not allowed;

(iv) Production and/or sales are evenly distributed over the period under consideration; and

(v) Variable inventory carrying cost per unit and ordering cost per order remain constant throughout the year.

Illustration 7.49

Calculate the *EOQ* from the following particulars under (i) Equation Method, and (ii) Tabular Method:

Annual Demand 300 units

Buying cost per order Rs. 25

Carrying cost of inventory @ 15% on Cost

Cost per unit Rs. 10.

Solution

Under (i) **Equation Method :** where

$$EOQ = \sqrt{\frac{2AO}{CS}}$$

$$= \sqrt{\frac{2.300.25.100}{150}}$$

where, A = Annual consumption i.e. 300 units

O = Ordering cost i.e. Rs. 25

C = Carrying cost i.e. Rs. 15%

S = Cost per unit = i.e. Rs. 10

$$= \sqrt{\frac{2 \times 300 \times \text{Rs.}25 \times 100}{15 \times \text{Rs.}10}}$$

$$= \sqrt{\frac{15,00,000}{150}}$$

$$= \sqrt{10,000}$$

= 100 units

Under (ii) **Tabular Method**

Annual Demand	*Order per Year*	*Units Order (1) ÷ (2)*	*Value per Ordered (3) × Rs. 10*	*Average Inventory Value (4) ÷ 2*	*Carrying Cost @ 15% on (5)*	*Ordering Cost Rs. 25 per Order*	*Total Cost (6) + (7)*
(1)	(2)	(3)	(4)	(5)	(6)	(7)	(8)
		Units	Rs.	Rs.	Rs.	Rs.	Rs.
300	1	300	3,000	1,500	225	25	250
	2	150	1,500	750	112.5	50	162.5
	3	100	1,000	500	75 ↔	75	150
	4	75	750	375	56.25	100	156.25
	5	60	600	300	45	125	170
	6	50	500	250	37.5	150	187.5

Hence, it is evident from the above table that 100 units per order is the most favourable one. Thus, the EOQ level is 100 units.

Illustration 7.50

From the following particulars with respect to a particular item of material of a manufacturing company, calculate the best quantity to order:

Ordering Quantities (tonnes)			Price per Tonne Rs.	Forgone Discount per Tonne
	less than	250	6.00	0.40
250	and less than	800	5.90	0.30
800	and less than	2,000	5.80	0.20
2,000	and less than	4,000	5.70	0.10
4,000	and above		5.60	—

The annual consumption for the materials is 4,000 tonnes. Stock holding costs are 20% of material cost per annum. The ordering cost per order is Rs. 6.00.

Solution

1. Annual Demand 4,000 tonnes
2. Holding Cost = 20% of materials cost
3. Ordering Cost = Rs. 6 per order

Order Size (*S*)	200	250	800	2,000	4,000
Price per tonne	Rs. 6.00	Rs. 5.90	Rs. 5.80	Rs. 5.70	Rs. 5.60
No. of orders (Annual Demand ÷ Order Size)	20	16	5	2	1
Value per order (*S* × Price)	1,200	1,475	4,640	11,400	22,400

Contd.

Average Inventory (Value per order ÷ 2)	600	738	2,320	5,700	11,200
A. Ordering Cost (Rs. 6 per order)	120	96	30	12	6
B. Carrying Costs (20% of average inventory)	120	148	464	1,140	2,240
(A + B)	240	244	494	1,152	2,246
C. Annual Cost of Materials (Annual Demand × Price)	24,000	23,600	23,200	22,800	22,400
Total Cost (A + B + C)	24,240	23,844	23,694	23,952	24,646

Therefore, it is quite clear from the above table that at 800 order quantity the total cost is the lowest one. Hence, *EOQ* is 800 tonnes.

Alternatively, the same conclusion can be drawn up if discount forgone is taken into consideration in lieu of cost of annual consumption of the components at different price. The same is shown:

Order Size (tonnes)	200	250	800	2,000	4,000
	Rs.	Rs.	Rs.	Rs.	Rs.
Cost of Ordering and Carrying as per above statement	240	244	494	1,152	2,246
Discount Forgone (Annual Demand × Rate)	1,600	1,200	800	400	—
	1,840	1,444	1,294	1,552	2,246

Hence, the *EOQ* is 800 units.

(c) **The Order Point Problem**

Reorder Point

It indicates that level of stock at which the storekeeper initiates purchase requisition for fresh supplies of the materials for replenishing the stock, i.e., when to place order for replenishment of inventories. This level is fixed somewhere between the maximum and the minimum levels. In short, this level is fixed in such a manner that sufficient quantity will remain in the stores in order to meet the normal and abnormal situations up to a certain period till the fresh supplies are received. In other words, the size of the order should be equivalent to the *EOQ*.

However, this fixation depends on : (i) the maximum delivery period, and, (ii) the maximum rate of consumption and, (iii) the minimum or safety stock level.

Reorder point may be calculated under conditions of certainty in the following manner:

(a) **With Safety Stock**

Reorder point = (Average usage of Inventory × Lead time) + Safety Stock

(b) **No Safety Stock**

Reorder point = Average usage of Inventory × Lead time

The following illustration will make the principle clear with the help of a diagram—

EOQ = 800 units

Lead Time = 3 weeks.

Average Usage = 80 units per week.

Therefore, the *EOQ* 800 units is quite sufficient for 10 weeks (800 ÷ 80). As such, if there is no lead time or the delivery of inventory is instantaneous, the new order will be placed at the end of 10th week immediately when the *EOQ* is exhausted or reaches zero level. But, since there is a lead time for 3 weeks, order should be placed at the end of the 7th week. Because, at that moment, only 240 units will remain for the next three weeks, i.e., during the lead time. So, when the lead time ends, level of inventory will reach zero and first inventory for 800 units will arrive. Thus, the reorder point is 240 units (80 × 3).

This principle is illustrated with the help of the following diagram :

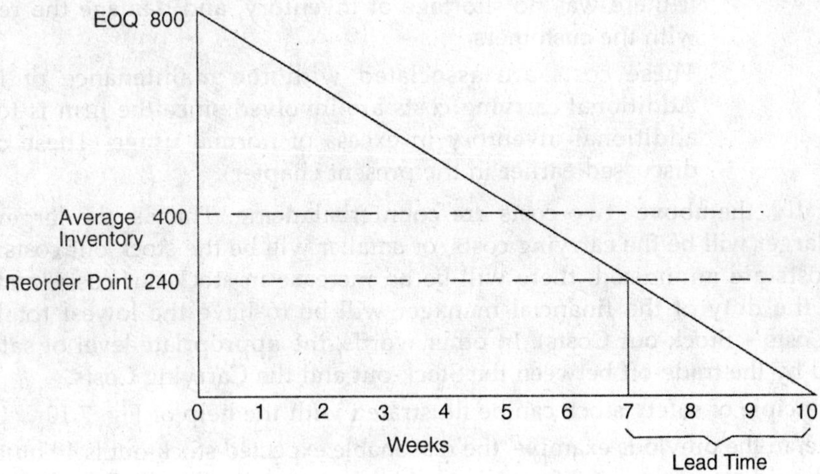

Fig. 7.9: Reorder Point under Certainty

The above diagram shows that the order should be placed at the end of 7th week where there are 240 units for the lead time. At the end of 10th week, when there is no stock, first supply of 800 units will arrive.

As such, if there is no lead time, the reorder point will be zero level of inventory.

Safety Stock

The *EOQ* and the Reorder point have been explained so far on the assumption of *certainty conditions*, i.e., on the assumption that there is constant or fixed usage/requirement of inventory and instantaneous replenishment of inventory. But, in reality, the same is not always possible since there is uncertainty. For example, the demand for inventory is likely to fluctuate from time to time, particularly, the demand may exceed the anticipated level at certain point. In short, a discrepancy may arise between the expected usage and the actual usage of inventory. Besides, the receipt of fresh inventory from the supplies may be delayed due to some abnormal situations, e.g., strikes, flood, transportation and so on, which is beyond the expected lead time. Therefore, there will be a shortage of inventory either due to increased usage or due to slower delivery, i.e., the firm will have to face a *stock-out* situation which may disrupt the production schedule. As a result, it is advantageous on the part of the firm to maintain a sufficient safety margin by having surplus additional inventory against such stock-out position. These stocks are known as Safety Stocks which will act as a buffer against the possible shortage of inventory.

The safety stock may be defined as the minimum additional inventory to serve as a safety margin or buffer or cushion to meet an unanticipated increase in usage resulting from an unusually high demand and/or an uncontrollable late receipt of incoming inventory.

Now, the question arises: How do we determine the safety stock? It should be remembered that safety stock requires two types of cost, viz., stock-out costs and carrying costs. Therefore, appropriate level of safety stocks depends on the basis of trade-off between these two costs.

Stock-out Costs : These relate to the costs which are associated with the shortage of inventory. It may be considered as an opportunity cost since the firm would be deprived of certain benefits due to the shortage of inventory, viz., the loss of profits which the firm could have earned if there was no shortage of inventory, and damage the relationship with the customers

Carrying Costs : These costs are associated with the maintenance of inventory. Additional carrying costs are involved since the firm is to maintain additional inventory in excess of normal usage (These costs were discussed earlier in the present chapter).

Practically, the above two costs are counterbalancing. That is, the larger the safety stock, the larger will be the carrying costs, or smaller will be the stock-out costs. In short, if carrying costs are minimised, there will be an increase in stock-out costs, and *vice versa.* Therefore, the duty of the financial manager will be to have the lowest total costs (i.e., Carrying Costs + Stock-out Costs). In other words, the appropriate level of safety stock is determined by the trade-off between the Stock-out and the Carrying Costs.

The principle of safety stock can be illustrated with the help of Fig. 7.10

Assume, in the previous example, the reasonable expected stock-out is 40 units per week. The firm should maintain a safety stock of (40 × 3) 120 units. So, the Reorder point will be 240 + 120 = 360 units. As such, the maximum inventory will be equal to EOQ plus the safety stock, i.e., 800 units + 120 = 920 units.

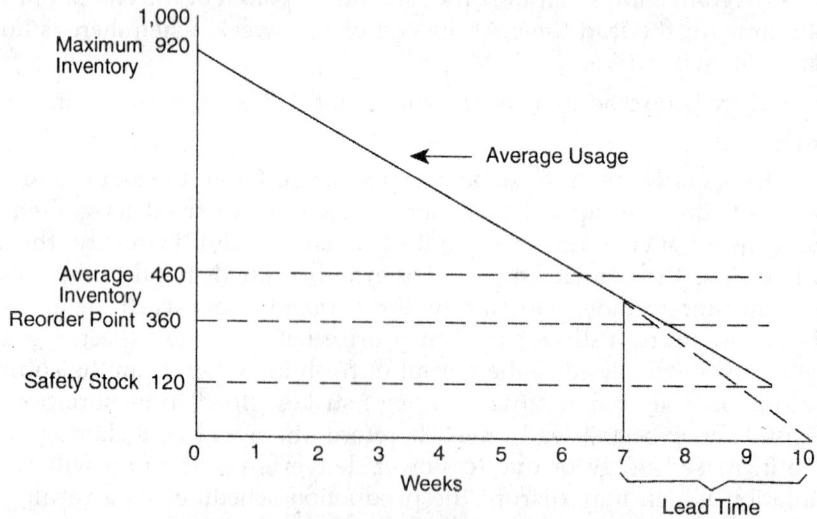

Fig. 7.10: Reorder Point under Uncertainty

Illustration 7.51

Calculate the reorder point from the following particulars:

Annual Demand 1,04,000 units.

Lead time 5 weeks.

Safety Stock may be assumed to be 1,000 units.

(Sales will be made evenly throughout the period).

Solution

$$\text{Weekly usage/sales} = \frac{1,04,000}{52} = 2,000 \text{ units}$$

Lead time 5 weeks.

Reorder Level

(i) When there is no safety stock:
2,000 units × 5 = 10,000 units.

(ii) When there is safety stock of 1,000 units
= 10,000 + 1,000
= 11,000 units

MISCELLANEOUS ILLUSTRATIONS

Illustration 7.52

Calculate:

(a) ECQ;

(b) Number of order per year; and

(c) Time Lag between two consecutive order.

The following particulars are presented by Arjun Ltd.:

Consumption	100 units per month
Cost per unit	Rs. 20
Ordering Cost	Rs. 30

Obsolescense 10% p.a. Storage and Insurance 5% and Interest on capital @ 10%.

Solution

(a) $\text{EOQ} = \sqrt{\frac{2AO}{CS}}$

where,

A = Annual consumption = 100 units × 12 = 1,200 units

O = Ordering cost Rs. 30

C = Carrying cost percentage (10% + 5% + 10%) = 25%

S = Cost per unit Rs. 20.

$$= \sqrt{\frac{2 \times 1,200 \times \text{Rs. } 30 \times 100}{\text{Rs. } 20 \times 25}}$$

= 120 units

(b) $\text{Numbers of orders per year} = \frac{\text{Annual Consumption}}{\text{EOQ}} = \frac{1,200 \text{ months}}{120 \text{ units}} = 10$

(c) $\text{Time lag between two consecutive Orders} = \frac{12 \text{ months}}{\text{No. of Orders per year}} = \frac{12 \text{ months}}{10} = 1.2 \text{ months}$

Illustration 7.53

Sachin Ltd. furnishes the following information:

(i) Consumption 300 units per quarter;

(ii) Cost per unit Rs. 40;

(iii) Cost of processing an order Rs. 600;

(iv) Obsolescense 15%;

(v) Insurance on inventory 25%

Compute:

(a) Economic Orders Quantity;

(b) No. of orders per year;

(c) Time between two consecutive orders.

A supplier offers a discount of 2% on a purchase of 600 units. Should it be accepted?

Solution

(a) $EOQ = \sqrt{\frac{2AO}{CS}}$

where,

A = Annual consumption = 300 units × 4 quarters = 1,200 units

O = Ordering cost Rs. 600

C = Carrying cost percentage 15% + 25% = 40%

S = Cost per unit Rs. 40.

$$= \sqrt{\frac{2 \times 1{,}200 \times \text{Rs. } 600 \times 100}{\text{Rs. } 40 \times 40}}$$

= 300 units

(b) Number of orders per year = $\frac{\text{Annual Consumption per year}}{\text{EOQ}} = \frac{1{,}200 \text{ units}}{300 \text{ units}} = 4$

(c) Time lag between two consecutive Order = $\frac{12 \text{ months}}{\text{No. of Orders per year}} = \frac{12}{4} = 3$ months

Computation of Total Cost as per EOQ		Rs.	**If the offer of Discount is accepted**		Rs.
Material (1,200 × Rs. 40)	=	48,000	Materials [1,200 × Rs. 39.20 (Rs. 40 – 2%)]	=	47,040
Ordering cost (Rs. 600 × 4 order)	=	2,400	Ordering cost (Rs. 600 × 2 orders)	=	1,200
Carrying Cost of Average Inventory			Carrying Cost of Average Inventory		
$\left[\text{Rs. } 16 (\text{i.e. } 40\% \text{ of Rs. } 40) \times \frac{300}{2}\right]$	=	2,400	$\left(\text{Rs. } 39.20 \times \frac{40}{100} \times \frac{600}{2}\right)$	=	4,704
Total cost		52,800			52,944

Hence : The offer of discount should not be accepted as the total cost increased by Rs. 144 (i.e. Rs. 52,944 – 52,800).

Illustration 7.54

The following particulars are presented by X Ltd:

Annual consumptions 12,000 units (in 360 days)

Ordering Cost Rs. 12 per order

Cost per unit Re. 1

Inventory carrying cost 20% (including storage cost 5% and interest on capital 5%)

Normal Lead Time 15 days

Safety Stock—30 days' consumption.

Compute

(a) EOQ;

(b) Reorder level (when should the order be placed);

(c) Ideal inventory level; and

(d) Number of Time orders for EOQ be placed in a year.

Solution

(a) $EOQ = \sqrt{\frac{2AO}{CS}}$

where,

A = 1,200 units

O = Rs. 12

C = 20%

S = Re. 1

$$= \sqrt{\frac{2 \times 12{,}000 \times \text{Rs. } 12 \times 100}{20 \times \text{Re. } 1}}$$

= 1,200 units

So, 1,200 units should be ordered each time.

(b) Reorder Level = Safety stock + Lead time

= 30 days + 15 days

= 45 days' consumption

Per day Consumption = $\left(\frac{12{,}000 \text{ units}}{360 \text{ days}}\right)$ = 33.33 unit

So, in 45 days = 33.33×45 = 1,500 units

Thus, when 1,500 units are reached, order should be placed.

(c) Ideal Inventory Level = i.e. the safety stock level which is 30 days' consumption

$= \frac{12{,}000 \text{ units}}{360} \times 30 \text{ days} = 1{,}000$ units

(d) Number of Time orders for EOQ to be placed in a year

$= \frac{\text{Annual Consumption}}{\text{EOQ}} = \frac{12{,}000 \text{ units}}{1{,}200 \text{ units}} = 10$ times

Fixation of Inventory Levels

It is the duty of the management to see that there must neither be any excess inventory maintained by the firm nor there be any inadequate inventory. The following inventory level should carefully be taken into consideration.

(a) **Reorder Level**

It has already been explained in an earlier paragraph. It is computed with the help of the following:

Reorder Level = Maximum Consumption × Maximum Reorder Period or, Maximum Consumption × Maximum Lead Time

(b) **Minimum Stock Level (Safety to Stock Level)**

It is the minimum level of stock beyond which the inventory level should never be allowed to fall. This part has also been highlighted above. It is computed as:

Minimum Stock Level = Reorder Level – (Normal Consumption × Normal or Average Reorder Period)

= Normal or Average Consumption × Average Lead Time

(c) **Maximum Stock Level**

It is just the opposite of Minimum Stock Level. Under the circumstance, the inventory level of a firm should not be allowed to rise so that the amount of working capital is blocked unnecessarily. It is computed as :

Maximum Stock Level = Reorder Level + Reorder Quantity – (Minimum Consumption × Minimum Reorder Period)

= Reorder level + EOQ —Minimum Consumption × Minimum Lead Time

(d) **Average Stock Level**

Average Stock Level is the average/mean of Maximum stock level and Minimum stock level. It is computed as:

$$\textit{Average Stock Level} = \frac{\textit{Maximum Stock Level + Minimum Stock Level}}{2}$$

$$= \textit{Minimum Stock Level} + \frac{1}{2}\textit{ of Reorder Quantity}$$

(e) **Danger Stock Level**

Danger Stock Level is that level which is fixed below the minimum stock level and it is needless to say that if inventory level reaches at this level, immediate action should be taken to replenish inventory so that stock out position can be avoided. It is computed as:

Danger Stock Level = Average Consumption/MinimumConsumption × Lead Time for Emergency Purchase

Illustration 7.55

The following particulars are given for component A in a factory:

Normal usage	50 units per week each
Minimum usage	25 units "
Maximum usage	75 units "
Reorder/Ordering quantity	300 units
Reorder/Delivery period	4 to 6 weeks

Calculate (a) Reorder Level; (b) Minimum Level; (c) Maximum Level; (d) Average Stock Level.

Solution

(a) Reorder Level = Maximum Consumption × Maximum Reorder period
= 75 units × 6
= 450 units

(b) Minimum Level = Reorder Level – (Normal Consumption × Normal Reorder period)
= 450 units – (50 units × 5)
= 200 units

(c) Maximum Level = Reorder Level + Reorder Quantity – (Minimum consumption × Minimum Reorder period)
= 450 units + 300 units – (25 units × 4)
= 750 units – 100 units
= 650 units

(d) Average Stock Level $= \text{Minimum Level} + \frac{\text{Reorder Quantity}}{2}$

$= 200 \text{ units} + \frac{300}{2}$

= 350 units

or, $= \frac{\text{Maximum Level} + \text{Minimum Level}}{2}$

$= \frac{650 \text{ units} + 200 \text{ units}}{2}$

= 425 units*

* Although answer differs, both of them are correct.

Illustration 7.56

From the details given below, calculate:

(i) Reordering level, (ii) Maximum level, (iii) Minimum level, (iv) Danger level.

Reordering quantity is to be calculated on the basis of following information:

Cost of placing a purchase order is Rs. 20.

Number of units to be purchased during the year is 5,000

Purchase price per unit inclusive of transportation cost is Rs. 50.

Annual cost of storage per unit is Rs. 5.

Details of lead time : Average 10 days, Maximum 15 days, Minimum 6 days, for emergency purchase 4 days.

Rate of consumption : Average 15 units per day, Maximum 20 units per day.

[C.A.]

Solution

Usually, Reorder Quantity is considered as EOQ which is calculated as:

(a) $$EOQ = \sqrt{\frac{2AO}{CS}}$$

where,

A = Annual consumption = 5,000
O = Ordering Cost Rs. 20
C & S = Inventory Carrying Cost (including cost per unit) = Rs. 5

$$= \sqrt{\frac{2 \times 5{,}000 \times \text{Rs. } 20}{\text{Rs. } 5}}$$

= 200 units

Minimum Consumption

Average Consumption per day $= \dfrac{\text{Maximum Consumption + Minimum Consumption}}{2}$

or, 15 $= \dfrac{20 + \text{Minimum Consumption}}{2}$

or, 10 units per day.

(i) Reorder Level = Maximum Consumption × Maximum Reorder period.

= 20 units per day × 15 days

= 300 units

(ii) Minimum Level = Reorder Level – (Normal Consumption × Normal Reorder period)

= 300 units – (15 units × 10 days)

= 300 units – 150 units

= 150 units

(iii) Maximum Level = Reorder Level + Reorder Quantity – (Minimum Consumption × Minimum Reorder period)

= 300 units + 200 units – (10 units per day × 6 days)

= 300 units + 200 units – 60 units

= 440 units

(iv) Danger Level = Average Consumption × Lead Time for emergency purchase

= 15 units per day × 4 days

= 60 units

or, = Minimum Consumption × Lead Time for emergency purchase

= 10 units × 4 days

= 40 units*

* However, both of them are correct.

Illustration 7.57

M/s Tubes Ltd. is the manufacturer of picture tube for TV. The following are the details of its operation during 1997:

Average monthly market demand	2,000 tubes
Ordering cost	Rs. 100 per order
Inventory carrying cost	20% per annum
Cost of tubes	Rs. 500 per tube
Normal usage	100 tubes per week
Minimum usage	50 tubes per week
Maximum usage	200 tubes per week
Lead time to supply	6-8 weeks

Compute from the above:

(i) Economic order quantity. If the supplier is willing to supply quarterly 1,500 units at a discount of 5%, is it worth accepting?

(ii) Maximum level of stock

(iii) Minimum level of Stock

(iv) Reorder level. [C.A.]

Solution

(a) $EOQ = \sqrt{\frac{2AO}{CS}}$ where,

A = Annual Consumption

= Normal Consumption per week × 52 weeks

= 100 units × 52

= 5,200 units

O = Ordering Cost = Rs. 100

C = Inventory carrying cost percentage = 20%

S = Cost per unit = Rs. 500

$= \sqrt{\frac{2 \times 5{,}200 \text{ units} \times \text{Rs. } 100 \times 100}{20 \times \text{Rs. } 500}}$

= 102 units (approx.)

$\text{No. of orders per year} = \frac{\text{Annual Consumption}}{\text{EOQ}} = \frac{5{,}200}{102} = 51$

Total cost if materials are purchased as per EOQ

	Rs.
Cost of Materials (5,200 units × Rs. 500)	26,00,000
Add: Ordering cost (51 orders × Rs. 100)	5,100
Add: Average Inventory Carrying cost $\left(\text{Rs. } 500 \times 20\% = \text{Rs. } 100 \times \frac{102}{2}\right) =$	5,100
Total Cost	26,10,200

If the offer of discount is accepted

Order size 1,500 tubes

$\text{No. of Orders per year} = \frac{\text{Annual usage}}{\text{Order Size}} = \frac{5{,}200}{1{,}500} = 4 \text{ (approx.)}$

	Rs.
Cost of Materials [5,200 tubes × Rs. 475 (i.e. Rs. 500 – 5%] =	24,70,000
Add: Ordering Cost (Rs. 100 × 4)	400
Add: Average Inventory Carrying Cost $\left(\text{Rs. } 20\% \text{ of Rs. } 475 \times \frac{1{,}500 \text{ tubes}}{2}\right) =$	71,250
Total Cost	25,41,650

Thus, the offer of discount should be accepted since total cost becomes Rs. 25,41,650 in place of Rs. 26,10,200, saving a Cost of Rs. 68,550 (i.e., Rs. 26,10,200 – Rs. 25,41,650).

(i) Maximum Stock Level = Reorder Level + Reorder Quantity
– (Maximum Consumption × Maximum Reorder period).
= 1,600 units (given in iv) + 102 units – (50 units × 6 weeks)
= 1,702 units – 300 units
= 1,402 units

(ii) Minimum Stock Level = Reorder Level – (Normal Consumption × Average Reorder period)
= 1,600 units – (100 units × 7 weeks)
= 1,600 units – 700 units
= 900 units

(iii) Reorder Level = Maximum Consumption × Maximum Reorder period
= 200 units × 8 weeks
= 1,600 units.

Ageing Schedule of Inventory

Inventories are classified according to ageing schedule as some inventories are slow moving while some other are going fast. Thus, inventories should be classified as per ageing schedule which helps to know the moving schedule inventories. For this purpose, it is necessary to show the date of purchase or date of manufacture of each component of inventory and they should be classified as per the following table:

Ageing Schedule of Inventory
as on 31st Dec. 2008
—A hypothetical Case

Age Classifications in terms of days	Date of Purchase	Amount Rs.	Percentage Component to Total Inventories
0—15	18.12.08	5,000	5%
16—30	3.12.08	16,000	16%
31—45	18.11.08	30,000	30%
46—60	3.11.08	4,000	4%
61—75	18.10.08	25,000	25%
75 and above	3.10.08	20,000	20%
		1,00,000	100%

From the above table it becomes clear that 30% of the total inventories lie in between the age group of 31-45 days while 25% of the total inventories the between 61-75 days followed by 20% of the inventories which take more long period i.e., 75 days and above. This information helps the management to take appropriate steps regarding the movement of inventories. The inventories which take longer time may even become obsolete which may increase cost.

GENERAL ILLUSTRATIONS

Illustration 7.58

The purchase manager of an organisation has collected the following data for one of the A Class items:

Interest on the locked up Capital	20%
Order processing cost for each order	Rs. 270
Inspection cost per lot	Rs. 50
Follow up cost for each order	Rs. 80
Pilferage while holding inventory	5%
Other holding cost	15%
Other procurement cost for each order	Rs. 170
Annual demand	1,000 units
Cost per item	Rs. 10
Discount for a minimum order quantity of 500 items	10%

What should be the ordering policy of the Purchase manager?

[I.C.W.A. Final—Adapted]

Solution

Total inventory carrying cost = (20% + 5% + 15%) = 40%

Ordering cost Rs. (i.e. Rs. 270 + Rs. 50 + Rs. 80) = Rs. 400.

(a)

$$EOQ = \sqrt{\frac{2AO}{CS}} \quad \text{where,}$$

A = Annual Consumption 1,000 units

O = Ordering Cost i.e., Rs. 400

C = Carrying Cost i.e., 40%

S = Cost per unit = Rs. 10

$$= \sqrt{\frac{2 \times 1{,}000 \times \text{Rs. } 400}{\frac{40}{100} \times \text{Rs.}10}}$$

= 447 units

Thus, the EOQ is 447 units and, as such, number of order to be placed in a year 2.24 or 3 $(\frac{1{,}000 \text{ units}}{447})$ orders. But if the firm places 3 orders the firm may place order for 334 units $(\frac{1{,}000}{3})$ only instead of 447 units.

Offer of Discount

Size of Order	Order of 500 units, say	Order based on EOQ 447 units	Order of 334 units
No. of Orders	2	3	3
Cost per order	Rs. 400	Rs. 400	Rs. 400
(a) Total Ordering Cost	Rs. 800	Rs. 1,200	Rs. 1,200
Carrying Cost p.u.	Rs. 3.60	Rs. 4	Rs. 4

Contd.

Average inventory (order size)	250	224	167
(b) Total Carrying Cost	Rs. 900	896	668
(c) Total Cost of Purchase (1,000 units @ $\frac{9}{10}$)	9,000	10,000	10,000
∴ Total Cost (a + b + c)	10,700	12,096	11,868

Comment

From the above it becomes clear when order is placed for 500 units, total cost will be the least one as such, the benefit of 10% discount is quite logical.

Illustration 7.59

Following information relating to a type of raw material is available:

Annual Demand	2,400 units
Unit Price	Rs. 2.40
Ordering Cost per order	Rs. 4.00
Storage Cost	2% p.a.
Interest Rate	10% p.a.
Lead Time	$\frac{1}{2}$ month

Calculate EOQ and total annual inventory cost in respect of the particular raw material.

[I.C.W.A. Inter]

Solution

$$\text{EOQ} = \sqrt{\frac{2AO}{CS}}$$

$$= \sqrt{\frac{2 \times 2{,}400 \times \text{Rs. } 4}{2.4 \times 0.12}}$$

$$= 258 \text{ units}$$

Computation of Total Cost of Inventory

		Rs.
Cost of Inventory	= (2,400 units × Rs. 2.40)	5,760
Add: Ordering Cost	= $(\frac{2{,}400}{258} \times \text{Rs. 4 per order})$	37
Add: Carrying Cost	= $(258 \times \text{Rs. } 2.40 \times \frac{1}{2} \times \frac{12}{100})$	37
	∴ Total Cost	5,834

Illustration 7.60

Your factory buys and uses a component for production at Rs. 10 per piece. Annual requirement is 2,000 numbers. Carrying cost of inventory is 10% p.a. and ordering cost is Rs. 40 per order. The purchase manager argues that as the ordering cost is very high, it is advantageous to place a single order for the entire annual requirement. He also says that if we order 2,000 at a time we can get a 3% discount from the supplier.

Evaluate the proposal and make your recommendation.

[I.C.W.A. Final]

Solution

Before taking any decision, we are to find out the EOQ number which is nothing but the optimum ordering quantity where the total costs are minimum. The same can be understood from the table presented:

Annual Demand	*No. of Orders*	*Ordering Quantity (1) ÷ (2)*	*Value per Order (3) × Rs. 10*	*Average Inventory Value (4) ÷ 2*	*Carrying Cost @ 10% on (5)*	*Ordering Cost Rs. 40 per Order*	*Total Cost (6) + (7)*
(1)	(2)	(3)	(4)	(5)	(6)	(7)	(8)
		Units	Rs.	Rs.	Rs.	Rs.	Rs.
2000	1	2,000	19,400*	9,700	970	40	1,010
units	2	1,000	10,000	5,000	500	80	580
	4	500	5,000	2,500	250	160	410
	5	400	4,000	2,000	200 ↔	200	400
	8	250	2,500	1,250	125	320	445
	10	200	2,000	1,000	100	400	500

(* after discount @ 3%)

Hence, it is justified to purchase 400 units at a time.

Illustration 7.61

In a factory, stock verification costs work out to about 3% on inventory values and the discrepancies revealed are about 0.6% on an average.

The following table shows a breakdown of the inventory:

	No. of Items	Value Rs. in lakhs
Unit Cost over Rs. 5	1,300	18.00
Unit Cost between Rs. 5 and Re. 1	4,000	8.00
Unit Cost Re. 1 & less	6,700	2.00
	12,000	28.00

The management feels that verification costs are excessive. Give your opinion regarding the proposed verification.

[I.C.W.A. Final]

Solution

Before taking the actual decision on verification of inventories, the cost of verification should be compared with the amount of discrepancies. (It should be remembered that verification should be done in relation to the items where the latter exceeds the former. The following table is necessary for the purpose):

No. of Items	*Cost of Verifications @ Rs. 7**	*Discrepancies Value @ 0.6% on Inventory Value*	*Remarks*
	Rs.	Rs.	
1,300	9,100	10,800	Verification is worthwhile
4,000	28,000	4,800	Verification is not worthwhile
6,700	46,900	1,200	Verification is not worthwhile

* **Notes :**

Total cost of verification : 3% on Rs. 28,00,000. i.e. Rs. 84,000 for 12,000 units.

$\therefore$ Average Cost of Verification per unit $= \dfrac{\text{Rs. } 84,000}{12,000} = \text{Rs. } 7.$

Discrepancies for 13,000 units = Rs. 18,00,000 × .006 = Rs. 10,800

(Same method of computation is, however, to be applied in case of other items)

Inventory Turnover Ratio

This ratio shows the relationship between inventory at close of the business and the overall turnover. In other words, it indicates the number of times the inventory of a firm rotates within an accounting cycle. There are, however, two formulae for ascertaining the Inventory-Turnover Ratio:

(Cost of Goods Sold = Sales – Gross Profit) (or, Opening Stock + Purchases – Closing Stock)

$$(i)\ \textit{Inventory-Turnover Ratio} = \frac{\textit{Cost of Goods Sold}}{\textit{Inventory/Average Stock}}$$

$$\textit{or,} = \frac{\textit{Sales}}{\textit{Inventory}}$$

For example, if cost of goods sold amounts to Rs. 1,00,000 and average inventory is Rs. 20,000, then Inventory Turnover Ratio will be 5 times.

It is suggested that, in the calculation of Inventory-Turnover Ratio, first Stock should be taken at the average figures [Average Stock = (Opening Stock + Closing Stock) ÷ 2] instead of ending stock figure, because, the level of inventory fluctuates over the entire year and, if average inventory figure is taken, it helps to an extent in smoothing out the fluctuation.

The application of the formula $\dfrac{\text{Sales}}{\text{Inventory}}$ is to be made by a financial analyst only where the figure of cost of goods sold is not available in the published annual statements. The normal of this ratio may be taken as 5 to 6 times.

Interpretation and Significance

Practically, this ratio tells the story by which inventory is converted into Sales. Usually a high Inventory Turnover Ratio reveals the liquidity of the inventory, i.e., how many times on an average inventory is turned-over or sold during the year. If a firm maintains minimum stock level in order to maximise sales by quick rotation of inventory no doubt the profit will be maximised since the holding cost of inventory will be minimum. A low Inventory Turnover Ratio reveals undesirable accumulation of obsolete stock.

Application of Inventory Turnover Ratio

Inventory Turnover Ratio may be applied for the purpose of making comparison between the two firms or between the two figures the different data of the same firm, i.e. both inter-firm comparison and intra-firm comparison can be made.

The so-called comparison presents the following types of inventories:

(a) Slow-moving Inventories; (b) Fast-moving Inventories; (c) Obsolete Inventories; (d) Dormant inventories.

(a) **Slow-moving Inventories**

If the Inventory Turnover Ratio is found to be low, it reveals that the inventories will slow-moving. Management should gives proper attention to improve Inventory Turnover Ratio.

(b) **Fast-moving Inventories**

If the Inventory Turnover Ratio is found to be high, it indicates that the inventories are moving fast which indicates a very healthy situation from the standpoint of liquidity of a firm. But attention must be given regarding the maintenance of inventory so that there may not be any shortage of stock which affects the production schedule.

(c) **Obsolete Inventories**

When the demand of a product falls or there is no possibility of disposing of such items due to old one they should be treated as obsolete inventories and should be sold as scrapped items.

(d) **Dormant Inventories**

Dormant inventories are those which have no demand for the time being but may be sold at a subsequent date. Adequate steps must be taken either to drop out those items or should keep the same when there is a possibility in future. The decision must be taken with the consultation of buyers, storekeepers, cost accountant etc.

INVENTORY VALUATION

Reasons for too much emphasis on Inventory Valuation

Three important reasons for too much emphasis on inventory valuation:

(i) Inventory constitutes the major bulk of current assets and it represents the major current asset investment. As such, its valuation should be made in such a way so that the profit or income is determined accurately and the Balance Sheet can exhibit a true and fair position at a particular date.

(ii) Since the inventory has direct impact on profit, proper determination of the latter depends on the proper valuation of the former. In other words, if closing inventory is undervalued, profit will be understated, or *vice versa*. Besides, if the ending inventory is overvalued and is shown in the Balance Sheet, the same amounts to a case of '*window-dressing*' which will exhibit a wrong picture about the liquidity position of a firm. Therefore, inventory should always be valued properly so that the short-term liquidity must not suffer, i.e., creditors must not be misled. If inventory is valued properly, the Balance Sheet will exhibit a true and fair view of the financial position of a firm.

(iii) The next one involves the fluctuation in commodity prices. It, again, seems to be a greater appreciation of the effects of these changes on the individual firm and the business community as a whole. In the words of Paul, Garner S. : "It became common knowledge that the income of some enterprises for specific year was tremendously influenced by the accounting procedure adopted for handling the fluctuations in the market value of the inventory consumed in operations or sold. Many firms began to indicate in their published statements the income (or loss) before and after the '*inventory adjustment*', as they called it. These adjustments were quickly impressed on the mind of the public with the result that increasing attention was devoted to the matter not only by accounts, but also by students of finance, banking credit, taxation and others".[1]

---

1 Paul, Garner S.—*Valuation of Inventories—Handbook of Modern Accountancy Theory,* Ed. by M. Backer, p. 306.

Cost Elements

The presentaiton of inventory in the annual financial statement on the basis of Historical Cost System of valuation is widely accepted although there are some other methods which are used for certain special cases.

Historical cost of inventories is the sum total of cost of purchases including costs of conversion and certain other costs which are incurred in order to be a finished product:

Cost of Purchase	:	It includes purchase price together with import duties, other purchase taxes, transport and handling costs and other costs which are directly attributable to prime cost after deducting rebate and discounts etc.
Cost of Conversion	:	It includes cost of purchases plus the production overhead (both fixed and variable overhead) which are incurred during production. But certain other costs are to be excluded from the cost of conversion, e.g., waste material of exceptional amounts, cost of idle plant etc.
Production Overhead	:	It relates to the costs of production other than the cost of direct materials and direct labours, e.g., indirect materials, indirect labours, factory expenses etc.
Other Expenses	:	It includes costs which are necessary for the inventories in order to be a finished/marketable product, e.g., expenditures which are incurred in designing product for specific customers etc.

Conventional method of valuation of inventories, of course, which is universally applicable at present is *'historical cost price or the market price value, whichever is lower'*. The term, 'market price/value' is used to designate the 'replacement price/value' and 'net realisable value'. At present, inventories are valued at the lowest of (i) historical cost, (ii) net realisable value, and (iii) replacement price/value. If this method is used as a method of valuation of inventories the Profit and Loss Account will automatically be adjusted when historical cost will be more than the net realisable or replacement value.

However, market value is to be determined on the following two bases:

1. 'Net Realisable Value' Basis, and
2. 'Replacement Value' Basis.

1. Net Realisable Value Basis

Under this concept, 'market price value' is considered as the 'net realisble value' which is equal to the estimated selling price in the ordinary course of business minus the cost of completion. This method of valuation of inventories is particularly followed where the inventories are damaged or partially obsolete. In this case, inventories are to be valued below the historical cost since the selling price of the same items will be reduced. As a result, historical cost for the items will not be realised and the difference will, however, be adjusted in Profit and Loss Account, by writing down the inventories to the net realisable value. That is why value of inventories must not be shown at a higher figure than its expected realisable value in future. It should be remembered that the estimated realisable value must not be determined on the basis of temporary fluctuations of price but on the basis of most reliable evidence.

2. Replacement Value Basis

Under this concept, the market value is considered to be the current replacement cost which is equal to the current cost of acquisition either by purchases, or by production, together with the incidental and acquisition costs. This basis usually applies more appropriately to materials or purchased merchandise since calculation of replacement cost of work-in-progress or finished goods will not be an easy task. Current cost of each element of total cost of inventory will be determined. However, current cost of raw material and labour should be determined (with tolerable precision) by incorporating current rate of wages and materials to be multiplied by actual quantity of material or labour related to finished or semi-finished product.

It may be noted that there is a difference between replacement value and realisable value. The former represents a sacrificial value whereas the latter represents a beneficial value. At the same time, historical cost represents a sacrificial value and realised value is a beneficial value. Sometimes, market value on reproduction basis should be determined on the basis of market price of raw materials, labour and overheads.

However, the AICPA has approved certain limits for inventory valuation which have been stated by the Committee on Accounting Procedure, Bulletin 29, as :[1]

'As used in the phrase *'lower of cost or market'*, the term 'market' means current replacement cost (by purchase or by production, as the case may be) except that:

(i) Market should not exceed the net realisable value (i.e., estimated selling price in the ordinary course of business, less reasonably predictable costs of completion and disposal); and

(ii) Market should not be less than net realisable value reduced by an allowance for an approximately normal profit margin'.

From the above, exception (ii) states not to reduce value until there is a clear apparent loss. The AICPA prefers to use 'market value' only to the 'replacement or reproduction value' and 'net realisable value' is treated as a separate item. But, the Institute of Chartered Accountants of England and Wales prefers to use lower of cost and net realisable value:

At the lowest of cost, net realisable value and replacement including reproduction price or 'at cost less provision to reduce the net realisable value'.

Therefore, after considering the recommendations of both the Institutes, the valuation should be made on the basis of the lowest of the three (stated above), with one exception imposed by AICPA. That is, if market price is found to be lower than the net realisable value, less normal profit, the latter should be considered.

METHODS OF VALUATION OF INVENTORY —BASED ON HISTORICAL COST

Valuation of inventory is made on a conservative basis, i.e., expected profits are not to be considered whereas possible losses are to be provided for. As such, it is valued at the lowest of (i) historical cost; (ii) net realisable value; and (iii) replacement price/value. The term 'cost' usually refers to designate the historical cost, i.e., outlay of cash or its equivalent in

1 *Accounting Research Bulletin 29.* The American Institute of Accounts Statement 3.

the acquisition of a particular item of inventory. In other words, it is the sum total of the price paid along with all expenditure and charges directly or indirectly incurred in bringing inventory to its existing condition and location.[1] Therefore, in case of materials and supplies, the price paid, including freight and carriage, represents their cost and sometimes a part of the storage expenditure is also included. In case of work-in-progress, however, cost represents the sum total of direct material cost, direct wages and direct expenses including manufacturing and factory overhead. The elements making up cost of finished goods or stock-in-trade are incurred in bringing (i) the purchase price of goods, stores, and, in case of processed stock, materials used in manufacture, (ii) all direct expenditure (e.g., direct wages, cost of tools, design etc.) incurred in bringing stock-in-trade to its existing condition and location, and (iii) indirect or overhead expenditure incidental to the class of stock-in-trade concerned.[2]

As the production and sales cycle is a continuous and repetitive process, costs which are incurred during an accounting period at different times in order to bring an article to its existing condition and location varies due to certain factors, viz., the seasonal effects, the efficiency of the workers, the attitude of management etc. This variation, no doubt, creates the difficulty of identification of cost of inventories for the purpose of their valuation. Of course, the said difficulties may be overcome by certain arbitrary assumptions and, as such, different bases are generally adopted. Some of them are enumerated:

(a) First-in-First-out

Under this method, materials which are received first are also issued first. In other words, the pricing of the issue of the first lot is done at the cost at which that lot was acquired. As such, the closing inventories are valued at latest purchase price and, thus, it will represent current condition as far as possible. That is, closing inventories are always out of the latest lots acquired or purchased or manufactured. The same leads to represent replacement price. This method is particularly applicable where prices do not fluctuate very frequently and the materials are not fast-moving.

Illustration 7.62

In a factory, stores are issued and accounted for on FIFO method. If the stock of a particular material on 1st Jan. 2012 is 1,000 units valued at Rs. 5 per unit and the particulars of purchases and issues during the month of Jan. 2012 are as follows, prepare a statement showing how the value of issues should be arrived at :

Dates				
Jan. 3	Purchase	200	units	at Rs. 5.50
9	Issue	1,000	units	
15	Purchase	1,400	units	at Rs. 6.00
17	Issue	1,000	units	
21	Purchase	800	units	at Rs. 6.50
23	Issue	1,000	units	

1 *Ibid.*

2 The Institute of Chartered Accountants of England & Wales — Recommendation 10, Para 2.

Solution

Store Ledger Account
FIFO Method

Name of Material :		Folio No. :
Specification :		Maximum level :
Code No. :	Bill No. :	Minimum level :
Unit of Measurement :	Location :	Reordering level :

Date	Receipts				Issues				Balance			
	G.R. No.	Quantity	Rate	Amount	S.R. No.	Quantity	Rate	Amount	Quantity	Rate	Amount	Remarks
2012				Rs.				Rs.			Rs.	
Jan. 1									1,000	5	5,000	
									1,000 }	5	5,000	
3		200	5.5	1,100					200 }	5.5	1,100	
9						1,000	5	5,000	200	5.5	1,100	
									200 }	5.5	1,100	
15		1,400	6	8,400					1,400 }	6	8,400	
17						200	5.5	1,100				
						800	6	4,800	600	6	3,600	
									600 }	6	3,600	
21		800	6.5	5,200					800 }	6.5	5,200	
23						600	6	3,600				
						400	6.5	2,600	400	6.5	2,600	

(b) Last-in-First-out

Under this method, it is assumed that the materials purchased are issued in the reverse order to FIFO, i.e., the last receipt is the first issued or the latest lots of inventories are exhausted first. In short, inventories are valued at earlier purchase price.

Illustration 7.63

Consider Illustration 32 and follow LIFO Method:

Solution

Store Ledger Account
LIFO Method

Name of Material :		Folio No. :
Specification :		Maximum level :
Code No. :	Bill No. :	Minimum level :
Unit of Measurement :	Location :	Reordering level :

Date	Receipts				Issues				Balance			
	GR. No.	Quantity	Rate	Amount	S.R. No.	Quantity	Rate	Amount	Quantity	Rate	Amount	Remarks
2012				Rs.				Rs.			Rs.	
Jan. 1									1,000	5	5,000	
									1,000 }	5	5,000	
3		200	5.5	1,100					200 }	5.5	1,100	

Contd.

Date	G.R. No.	Quantity	Rate	Amount	S.R. No.	Quantity	Rate	Amount	Quantity	Rate	Amount	Remarks
				Rs.				Rs.			Rs.	
9						200	5.5	1,100				
						800	5	4,000	200	5.	1,000	
15		1,400	6	8,400					200	5.5	1,100	
									1,400	6	8,400	
17						1,000	6	6,000	200	5	1,000	
									400	6	2,400	
21		800	6.5	5,200					200	5	1,000	
									400	6	2,400	
									800	6.5	5,200	
23						800	6.5	5,200				
						200	6	1,200	200	5	1,000	
									200	6	1,200	

Average Cost Method

Under this method, all items in the stores are mixed up in such a way that consumption of materials or sale of finished goods cannot be recognised from any particular lot of purchases. As a result, closing inventories are valued at the average cost of all the lots acquired under each type during a particular period.

The Average Cost may be:

(i) Simple Average Cost; and

(ii) Weighted Average Cost.

(i) Simple Average Cost

Under this method, average of different prices are only considered without having regard to the quantities involved. The Simple Average Cost is calculated by adding the different prices and, thereafter, divided by the total number of purchases. This method is applicable where there is a wide fluctuation in prices.

Illustration 7.64

Consider Illustration 61 and follow Simple Average Method.

Solution

Store Ledger Account
Simple Average Method

Name of Material :
Specification :
Code No. :
Unit of Measurement :

Bill No. :
Location :

Folio No. :
Maximum level :
Minimum level :
Reordering level :

Date	*Receipts*				*Issues*				*Balance*			
	G.R. No.	*Quantity*	*Rate*	*Amount*	*S.R. No.*	*Quantity*	*Rate*	*Amount*	*Quantity*	*Rate*	*Amount*	*Remarks*
2012				Rs.				Rs.			Rs.	
Jan. 1									1,000	5	5,000	
3		200	5.5	1,100					1,200	—	6,100	
9						1,000	5.25	5,250	200	—	850	
15		1,400	6	8,400					1,600	—	9,250	
17						1,000	5.75	5,750	600	—	3,500	
21		800	6.5	5,200					1,400	—	8,700	
23						1,000	6.25	6,250	400	—	2,450	

Notes :

1st Issue Price $= \frac{(Rs. 5 + Rs. 5.50)}{2} = Rs. 5.25$

2nd Issue Price $= \frac{(Rs. 5.50 + Rs. 6)}{2} = Rs. 5.75$

3rd Issue Price $= \frac{(Rs. 6 + Rs. 6.50)}{2} = Rs. 6.25$

(ii) Weighted Average Cost

Under this method, rate of average cost is calculated by taking into consideration both the prices and quantities acquired at such prices, i.e., the total value of materials in stock at the time of issue is divided by the total quantity of materials in stock in order to find out the weighted average rate. It is superior than the ordinary Simple Average Method since it takes into account both the prices and the quantities. This method proves very useful where there is a heavy fluctuation in the prices of inventories as it tends to smooth out fluctuations in prices by taking the average cost of different lots acquired at different time. But, under this method, cost of goods sold does not represent the actual cost.

Illustration 7.65

Consider Illustration 61 and follow Weighted Average Method:

Solution

Store Ledger Account
Weighted Average Method

Name of Material : | **Folio No. :**
Specification : | **Maximum level :**
Code No. : | **Bill No. :** | **Minimum level :**
Unit of Measurement : | **Location :** | **Reordering level :**

	Receipts				*Issues*				*Balance*			
Date	*GR. No.*	*Quantity*	*Rate*	*Amount*	*S.R. No.*	*Quantity*	*Rate*	*Amount*	*Quantity*	*Rate*	*Amount*	*Remarks*
2012				Rs.				Rs.			Rs.	
Jan. 1									1,000	5	5,000	
3		200	5.5	1,100					1,200	5.08	6,100	
9						1,000	5.08	5,080	200	5.08	1,020	
15		1,400	6	8,400					1,600	5.89	9,420*	
17						1,000	5.89	5,890	600	5.89	3,530	
21		800	6.5	5,200					1,400	6.24	8,730	
23						1,000	6.24	6,240	400	6.24	2,490	

*Notes : Due to fractions.

Base Stock Method

Under this method, it is assumed that every firm has to maintain a certain minimum amount of inventory (in the form of raw materials, work-in-progress and finished goods) throughout the year. The same will have to be maintained for meeting emergency needs, such as undue delay in supply of raw materials, excessive consumption etc. This minimum level of inventory goes by the name of Base Stock or Safety Stock. 'Base-Stock' serves as the signal below which the inventory level of a firm is never allowed to fall. (Therefore, inventory, to the extent of 'Base Stock', though basically as a class, falls within the category of current assets, assumes, for all practical purposes, the character of fixed assets.)

Generally, there may not be any wide variation between the volume of closing and opening inventory unless there is a remarkable change in the scale of operation and other factors. This 'Base Stock' level is usually created out of the first lot of the materials purchased or goods manufactured at beginning of the period and, as such, it is valued at the cost price of the first lot. Therefore, under this method, closing inventories are generally taken to be equal to the 'Base-Stock' level and, hence, they are valued at the values allotted to the respective 'Base-Stock'. However, if there is any excess (over Base-Stock level), the same should be valued either on the basis of FIFO or LIFO methods.

It should be remembered that this method is generally used with FIFO or LIFO method. There is, however, difference of opinion among the accountants as to the principles to be followed for valuation of inventories when this method is adopted. For example, Finney and Miller suggest that 'Base-Stock' may be valued at *lowest cost experienced* and valuation of closing inventory (when it goes below base-stock) should be made by deducting the value of the deficient quantity calculated at the current cost from the value of the normal quantity of Base-Stock calculated at the base price. Further, Yorston, Smyth and Brown suggest that 'the difference between the replacement price and the fixed price of the basic stock is deducted from the total value of the stock on hand computed at the base price. This method usually is operated either in conjunction with FIFO or LIFO method. It may be observed that the objective of pricing inventories on the basis of this method is to apply the current prices to issue. So, this objective will be fulfilled only when LIFO method is adopted as a method of combination'.[1]

Illustration 7.66

Consider Illustration 61 and follow Base Stock Method:

Solution

Store Ledger Account
Base Stock Method

Name of Material :
Specification :
Code No. :
Unit of Measurement :

Bill No. :
Location :

Folio No. :
Maximum level :
Minimum level :
Reordering level :

Date	*Receipts*				*Issues*				*Balance*			
Date	*G.R. No.*	*Quantity*	*Rate*	*Amount*	*S.R. No.*	*Quantity*	*Rate*	*Amount*	*Quantity*	*Rate*	*Amount*	*Remarks*
2012				Rs.				Rs.			Rs.	
Jan. 1									1,000	5	5,000	
									100* }	5	500	
									200 }			
3		200	5.5	1,100					200	5	4,500	
9										5.5	1,100	
						900	5	4,500	100 }	5	500	
						100	5.5	550	100 }	5.5	550	

Contd.

[1] Banerjee, B.—*Cost Accounting*—World Press (P) Ltd., 1981, p. 63.

2012				Rs.				Rs.			Rs.
									100	5	500
									100	5.5	550
15		1,400	6	8,400					1,400	6	8,400
17						100	5.5	550	100	5	500
						900	6	5,400	500	6	3,000
									100	5	500
									500	6	3,000
21		800	6.5	5,200					800	6.5	5,200
23						500	6	3,000	100	5	500
						500	6.5	3,250	300	6.5	1,950

* 10% of 1,000 = 100 units are considered as Base-Stock.

Specific Identification Cost/Unit Cost or Actual Cost

This method of valuation is adopted where each item of inventories and its actual cost is identifiable. It attributes certain specific costs to the identified items of inventory where each such item and its cost is identifiable. That is, this method of valuation can easily be applied where the closing inventory items can correctly be identified with specific lots. But this method suffers from the following limitations:

(i) Where there is bulk quantities of inventories, partly finished goods or finished goods, and where individual units of inventories lose their identity.

(ii) Where there is innumerable units of inventories, keeping records for each of them becomes expensive as well as time-consuming.

Other Methods of Valuation of Inventory

—Other than those based on Historical Cost

Some important methods of valuation of inventory (other than those based on historical cost) are:

(a) Standard Cost Method; (b) Inflated Cost Method; (c) Reverse Cost Method; (d) Replacement Cost Method, and (e) Realisable Market Value Method.

(a) Standard Cost Method

Under this method, closing inventories are valued at pre-fixed standard rates. This method is found suitable where the manufacturing units are engaged in production on a large scale. But this method cannot reveal the true value of inventory when production is completed after passing through several processes or where manufactured products are of different varieties. At the same time, if there is a slight error in fixing the single standard rate the same will affect the measure of all items of inventory.

Illustration 7.67

Consider Illustration 61 and follow Standard Price/Cost Method assuming that the Standard Price is fixed at Rs. 5.5 per unit.

Solution

Store Ledger Account
Standard Price Method

Name of Material :
Specification :
Code No. :
Unit of Measurement :

Bill No. :
Location :

Folio No. :
Maximum level :
Minimum level :
Reordering level :

	Receipts				Issues				Balance			
Date	*GR. No.*	*Quantity*	*Rate*	*Amount*	*S.R. No.*	*Quantity*	*Rate*	*Amount*	*Quantity*	*Rate*	*Amount*	*Remarks*
2012				Rs.				Rs.			Rs.	
Jan. 1									1,000	5	5,000	
3		200	5.5	1,100					1,200	—	6,100	
9						1,000	5.5	5,500	200		600	
15		1,400	6	8,400					1,600	—	9,000	
17						1,000	5.5	5,500	600	—	3,500	
21		800	6.5	5,200					1,400	—	8,700	
23						1,000	5.5	5,500	400	—	3,200	

(b) Inflated Cost Method

Under this method, closing inventories are valued at a cost per unit which is higher than the actual cost per unit to provide for the normal loss due to certain shortcomings inherent in them, e.g., loss due to evaporation, shrinkage etc.

(c) Reserve Cost Method

Under this method, inventories are valued at an estimated cost which is determined by deducting an amount equivalent to the normal profit margin and the estimated cost of disposal from the current selling prices. This method is also referred to as 'Adjusted Selling Price'.[1]

(d) Replacement Cost Method

Under this method, each closing item of inventory is valued at cost which is to be incurred for purchasing/procuring the said item from the open market on the date of valuation, i.e., they are valued at the replacement cost as on that date. This cost of replacement should be determined in relation to the current market price of similar items.

(e) Realisable Market Value Method

Under this method, each closing item of inventory is valued at its estimated net realisable value. The net realisable value, i.e., prospective selling price less all prospective costs to be incurred in conditioning and selling the goods, may be adopted suitably for the purpose of valuation.

Determining the Most Appropriate Method

The methods of valuation of inventory discussed so far are suitable to specific circumstances, i.e., all methods are not applicable in all cases. The method which is most suitable to the specific case should be adopted. The Recommendations of the Institute of Chartered

1 Garner, Paul. S.—op. cit., p. 306.

Accountants of England and Wales are helpful in this context. According to them, no particular basis or valuation is suitable for all types of business but, whatever the basis adopted, it should be applied consistently year after year. But before applying the same, the following points should be considered[1] :

(i) In what way does the product actually (physically) flow into production and sales, that is, are the oldest units disposed-off first, or are the newest units disposed-off first, or are the items acquired at different times mixed together in such a way as to make them indistinguishable from the standpoint of disposal priority?

(ii) Which method or methods have the tendency to 'smooth out' the reported periodic progress figures for the individual business firm?

(iii) Which method provides the most conservative (lowest in amount) inventory figure for the end-of-period Balance Sheet?

(iv) Which method provides the most useful type of cost of production and cost of sales figures for control and internal management purpose?

(v) What method provides the most useful figure for aid in determining selling price in so far as selling prices may be influenced by expired costs and expenses?

(vi) Which method comes closest to carrying out the concept of historical accounting?

Some accountants prefer to use 'Unit Cost' or 'FIFO' method for valuation while others are favouring 'LIFO' method. The 'Average Cost' method may also be suggested by some other accountants.

In making a selection between FIFO and LIFO, it becomes necessary to decide first whether current costs should be applied to the inventory (under FIFO method) or the same should be matched against current revenues (under LIFO method). That is, FIFO method places emphasis on the Balance Sheet while LIFO method places emphasis on Profit and Loss Account. During periods of changing costs and prices, more meaningful statements of profits are produced if current costs are applied to current sales, thus achieving a better matching of costs and revenues.[2] On the contrary, if LIFO method is followed, the closing inventory will be valued at replacement price. Therefore, like FIFO, it does not lead to a misstatement of working capital position in the Balance Sheet. Although the LIFO advocates contend that achieving a more appropriate matching of costs against revenues is an important objective as it offsets the 'incorrect' Balance Sheet result, the fact remains that, conceivably, inventory qualities might eventually be priced at such 'old' costs as to produce a misstatement of working capital position that would be seriously misleading.[3]

The average cost method may be applied during periods of price fluctuations and the same is most suitable where several production processes are involved in manufacturing concerns. However, whatever method a firm adopts, the same should be applied consistently year after year.

---

1 *Recommendation* 10, Para 3, The Institute of Chartered Accountants of England and Wales.

2 Finney and Miller—*Principles of Accounting Intermediate*—4th Edn., p. 363.

3 *Ibid.*

ASSIGNMENT MATERIALS

THEORETICAL

Multiple Choice Questions

1. (a) Consumable Stores means:

(i) Raw Materials and Stores (ii) W-I-P

(iii) Finished Goods (iv) None of these

(b) Work-in-Progress means:

(i) Raw Materials (ii) Semifinished Goods

(iii) Finished Goods (iv) Opening Stock

(c) EOQ is ascertained by:

(i) $\sqrt{\frac{2CS}{AB}}$ (ii) $\sqrt{\frac{2AO}{CS}}$

(iii) $\sqrt{\frac{2AOC}{S}}$ (iv) $\sqrt{\frac{2CS}{AO}}$

(d) Reorder level is determined by:

(i) Maximum Consumptions × Minimum Reorder Period

(ii) Maximum Consumption × Maximum Reorder Period

(iii) Minimum Consumption × Minimum Reorder Period

(iv) None of these

(e) Safety stock level is determined by:

(i) Normal Consumption × Reorder Level

(ii) Normal Consumption × Normal Reorder Period

(iii) Average Consumption × Reorder Period

(iv) Normal Consumption × Average Lead Time

(f) Maximum Stock level is determined by

(i) Maximum Reorder Period × Normal Consumption

(ii) Minimum Reorder Period × Normal Consumption

(iii) Maximum Reorder Period × Maximum Consumption

(iv) Reorder Level + Reorder Quantity – (Minimum Consumptions × Minimum Reorder Period)

(g) Danger Stock level is determined by:

(i) Average Consumptions × Lead Time

(ii) Average Consumptions × Lead Time for emergency Purchase

(iii) Average Consumption × Maximum Reorder Period

(iv) Average Consumption × Minimum Reorder Period

(h) Inventory Turnover Ratio means:

(i) $\frac{\text{Cost of goods sold}}{\text{Sales}}$ (ii) $\frac{\text{Cost of goods sold}}{\text{Average Stock}}$

(iii) $\frac{\text{Cost of goods sold}}{\text{Debtors}}$ (iv) $\frac{\text{Sales}}{\text{Debtors}}$

[Ans. (a) (i); (b) (ii); (c) (ii); (d) (ii); (e) (iv); (f) (iv); (g) (ii); (h) (ii)]

Short Answer-type Questions

2. Mention the different kinds of inventory.
3. Why do we hold inventories?
4. What are the objectives of inventory management?
5. Define Cost of Inventory.
6. What do you mean by ABC analysis?
7. Write Notes on:
   (i) Ordering Cost of Inventory; (ii) Carrying Cost of Inventory.
8. What do you mean by Reorder Level?
9. What is Safety Stock?
10. What is EOQ?
11. What do you mean by:
    (i) Maximum Stock Level; (ii) Reorder Level; (iii) Danger Stock Level?
12. What is Average Stock Level? How do you calculate it?
13. What is Ageing Schedule of Inventory?
14. What is Inventory Turnover Ratio?
15. What do you mean by Inventory Valuation?
16. Define:
    (i) FIFO; (ii) LIFO
17. What is Base Stock Method of Inventory?
18. Define Inflated Cost Method of Valuing Inventory.
19. Define Replacement Cost Method.
20. What is Realisable Market Value Method?

Long Answer-type Questions

21. What is EOQ? How do you calculated it? Explain with the help of an illustration.
22. What are the basic objectives of Inventory Management?
23. Should stock be valued as per Cost Price or Market Price whichever is lower? Explain.
24. Distinguish between FIFO and LIFO methods of valuing inventories.
25. 'Optimum Level of inventory is that which minimises the total cost'—Explain.

26. Define the role of ABC Analysis as a method of Inventory Control.

27. Write Notes on:

    (a) Ageing Schedule of Inventory; (b) Inventory Turnover Ratio.

28. What do you mean by EOQ? How does it help to maintain optimum level of inventory?

29. Define: (a) Safety Stock; (b) Reorder Level.

30. Explain the method of valuing inventories.

PRACTICAL

1. The following data are available in respect of a material 'MMI' used in the production of a goods of M Bright Ltd. for the year 2001:

Cost of the Materials per unit	—	Rs. 50
Weekly consumption	—	300 units
Ordering cost per order	—	Rs. 650
Stock holding cost	—	2% per month (on cost)

Compute:

(a) Economic order quantity, (b) Optimum no. of orders per year, and (c) Time lag between two consecutive orders.

[Ans. (a) 1,300 units; (b) 12; and (c) 1 month]

2. Calculate the average inventory from the following:

Annual consumption	50,000 units
Cost per unit	Rs. 1.20
Ordering cost	Rs. 45
Inventory carrying cost	@ 15% of the annual average inventory
Safety stock	500 units.

[Ans. 3,000 units]

3. The following information relating to a type of raw material is available:

Unit price	Rs. 2.40
Ordering cost per order	Rs. 4.00
Storage cost	2% per annum
Interest rate	10% per annum
Lead time	Half-month
Annual demand	2,400 units

Calculate Economic Order Quantity and Total Annual Inventory Cost in respect of the particular raw material.

[Ans. 250 unit, Rs. 5,837]

4. Following information relating to a particular type of raw materials is available:

Annual demand	16,000 units
Ordering cost per order	Rs. 200
Cost per unit of material	Rs. 50
Insurance cost per unit p.a.	7%
Obsolescence cost per unit p.a.	5%
Godown rent per unit p.a.	8%

Calculate EOQ and the number of orders to be placed.

[Ans. 800 units; 20 orders]

5. From the following particulars calculate the best quantity to be ordered:

Ordering Quantity (in kg)		Price per kg (Rs.)
Less than	500	10.00
500 to less than	1,600	9.60
1,600 to less than	4,000	9.40
4,000 to less than	8,000	9.20
8,000 and above		9.00

The annual requirement of the material is 8,000 kg. Stock holding (carrying) cost is 20% of material cost per annum. Ordering (reordering) cost per order is Rs. 10.

[C.U. B.Com. (Hons.)]

[Ans. 1,600 kg]

6. The purchase department of your organisation has received an offer of quantity discounts on its orders of materials as under:

Price per tonne Rs.	Tonnes
1,400	less than 500
1,380	500 to less than 1,000
1,360	1,000 to less than 2,000
1,340	2,000 to less than 3,000
1,320	3,000 and above

The annual requirement of the material is 5,000 tonnes. The delivery cost per order is Rs. 1,200 and the annual Stock holding cost is estimated at 20% of the average inventory.

The Purchase Department wants you to consider the following purchase options and advise which among them will be the most economical ordering quantity, presenting the relevant information in a tabular for.

The purchase quantity options to be considered are 400 tonnes, 500 tonnes, 1,000 tonnes, 2,000 tonnes and 3,000 tonnes.

[Ans. 1,000 Tonnes]

7. The quarterly production of a company's product which has a steady market is 20,000 units. Each unit of a product requires 0.5 kg of raw material. The cost of placing one order for raw materials is Rs. 100 and the inventory carrying cost is Rs. 2 per annum. The lead time for procurement of raw materials is 36 days and a safety stock of 1,000 kg of raw

materials is maintained by the company. The company has been able to negotiate the following discount structure with the raw materials supplier:

Order Quantity Kgs.	Discount Rs.
Up to 6,000	Nil
6,001-8,000	400
8,001-16,000	2,000
16,001-30,000	3,200
30,001-45,000	4,000

You are required to:

(i) Calculate the reorder point taking 30 days in a month.

(ii) Prepare a statement showing the total cost of procurement and storage of raw materials after considering the discount if the company elects to place one, two, four or six orders in the year.

(iii) State the number of orders which the company should place to minimise the costs after taking EOQ also into consideration.

[C.A.]

[Ans. (i) 5,000 kg; (ii) Total Cost for EOQ Rs. 4,000; First order Rs. 36,100; 2nd order Rs. 17,000; 4th order Rs. 8,400; 6th order Rs. 6,867; (iii) EOQ 2,000 units]

8. From the following information calculate:

(i) Reordering level; (ii) Minimum level; (ii) Maximum level; and (iv) Average stock level:

Reorder quantity	36,000
Time required for delivery	2 to 4 months
Minimum consumption	3,000 units per month
Maximum consumption	6,000 units per month
Average consumption per month	4,450 units

[Ans. (i) Rs. 24,000; (ii) Rs. 10,650; (iii) Rs. 54,000, 32,325 units]

9. Two components A and B are used as:

Minimum usage	25 units per week each
Maximum usage	75 units per week each
Maximum stock level	A 650 units; B 750 units
Reorder period	A 4 to 6 weeks; B 2 to 4 weeks

Calculate for each component:

(i) Reorder level;

(ii) Minimum level; and

(iii) Reorder quantity.

[Ans. (i) A = 450 units & 'B' 300 units; (ii) A = Rs. 200; B = Rs. 150 (iii) A = 300 units; B = 500 units]

10. The following information is available in respect of a material of Y Co. Ltd.:

Reorder quantity	12,000 units
Lead time	4 to 8 weeks
Maximum consumption	4,000 units per week
Normal consumption	3,000 units per week
Minimum consumption	1,550 unit per week

Ascertain the following from the above information:

(a) Reorder level;

(b) Minimum stock level; and

(c) Maximum stock level.

[Ans. (a) 32,000 Units; (b) 14,000 Units; (c) 37,800 Units]

11. Calculate: (a) Reorder Level, (b) Minimum Stock Level, (c) Maximum Stock Level, (d) Average Stock Level, from the following:

Delivery Period	4 to 8 weeks
Rate per Unit	Rs. 64
Ordering Cost	Rs. 400 per order
Storage Cost	50% of stock value
Usages : Yearly	3,600 units p.m.
Normal level	300 units p.m.
Minimum level	100 units p.m.
Maximum level	600 units

[Ans. (a) 4,800 Units; (ii) 3,000 Units; (iii) 4,700 Units; (iv) 3,850 Units]

12. The following details are available in respect of a consignment of 1,250 kg of Material X:

(a)	Invoice price	Rs. 20 per kg.
(b)	Excise duty	25% on invoice price
(c)	Sales tax	8% on invoice price including excise duty
(d)	Trade discount	10% on invoice price
(e)	Insurance	1% of aggregate net prices
(f)	Delivery charges	Rs. 250

(g) Cost of containers @ Rs. 60 per container for 50 kg of material. Rebate is allowed @ Rs. 40 per container if returned within six weeks; which is a normal feature.

(h) One container load of material was rejected on inspection and not accepted.

(i) Cost of unloading and handling @ 0.25% of the cost of materials ultimately accepted.

On the basis of above you are required to find out the landed cost per kg of Material X.

[I.C.W.A.]

[Ans. Total Cost Rs. 35,100; Cost per kg. Rs. 26]

13. A company uses three raw materials A, B and C for a particular product for which the following data apply:

Raw Material	Use per unit product (kgs)	Re-order quantity (kgs)	Price per kg	Delivery Period (in weeks)			Re-order level (kgs)	Minimum level (kgs)
				Minimum	Average	Maximum		
A	10	10,000	0.10	1	2	3	8,000	
B	4	5,000	3.30	3	4	5	4,750	
C	6	10,000	0.15	2	3	4		2,000

Weekly production varies from 175 to 225 units, averaging 200 units of the said product. What would be the following quantities:

(i) Minimum Stock of A?

(ii) Maximum Stock of B?

(iii) Reorder level of C?

(iv) Average stock level of A?

[C.A.]

[Ans. (i) 4,000 kg.; (ii) 7,650 kg.; (iii) 5,400 kg.; (iv) 10,125 kg]

14. A firm purchases 2,000 units of a particular item per year at an unit cost of Rs. 20. The ordering cost is Rs. 50 per order and the inventory carrying cost 25%.

Determine the optimal order quantity and the minimum total cost including purchase cost.

If a discount is offered by the supplier for purchases in lots of 1,000 or more should the firm accept the offer?

[I.C.W.A. Final, June 2000]

15. P. Ltd uses three types of materials A, B and C for production of X, the final product. The relevant monthly data for the components are:

Materials	A	B	C
Normal Usage	200	150	180
Minimum Usage	100	100	90
Maximum Usage	300	250	270
Reorder Quantity	750	900	720
Reorder periods (Months)	2 to 3	3 to 4	2 to 3

Calculate for each component (i) Reorder level, (ii) Maximum level; (iii) Minimum level, and (iv) Average stock level.

[C.S. Inter, June 1998]

[Ans. (i) A. 900, B. 1,000, C. 810 unit; (ii) A. 1,450, B. 1,600, C. 1,350 units; (iii) A. 400; B. 475; C. 360 Unit; (iv) A. 925; B. 1,038; C. 855]

Some exciting gifts are up for grabs with this book!!

FREE Gifts Rs. 1000/-

FINANCIAL MANAGEMENT—I

[WBUT-BBA—Fourth Semester]

Dr S Kr Paul and Chandrani Paul

DEAR READERS

By now you must have gone through this book in the entirety. So we invite your assessment on this title with absolute impartiality and candid observations. After all, we publishers blindly depend on your benchmarking. Friends, please fill up the open spaces below with CAPITAL LETTERS. You may add some extra sheets of paper if the space provided is not sufficient for you.

i. What are the important topics of your syllabus which are not adequately covered in this book?

ii. In which chapters and on what topics the treatment of the subject-matter by the author is not satisfactory and why?

iii. Have you come across the typos, factual inaccuracies, inconsistencies, and other forms of mistakes in the book? If yes, then please specify the mistakes and page numbers.

iv. Name top three books on the same subject, which, in your consideration, are better than this book. Could you provide some reasons?

Your 1st Preference: ....

Your 2nd Preference: ....

Your 3rd Preference: ....

v. Any suggestion to improve the quality of illustrations, diagrams, etc.?

vi. How did you like the cover design? Any suggestion on colours?

vii. Suggestions for further improvement of production-standard:

viii. Who recommended you this book:

☐ Teacher ☐ Friend ☐ Parents ☐ Bookseller ☐ Librarian

ix. Name of the person who has recommended:

Designation: ....

Address: ....

Phone No.: ....

e-mail: ....

x. Name and address of the bookseller from whom you have purchased this book:

....

....

....

xi. Name and address of the library where you would like to find the book:

....

....

xii. Name and address of your institution (Please mention the University or Board):

....

....

xiii. Your name, e-mail, and complete postal address:

....

....

....

xiv. A few other titles published by us that you would like to read:

....

....

The best assessment will be rewarded half-yearly. The award will be in the form of our publications, as decided by the Editorial and Marketing Operations Division, amounting to Rs. 1000/- (Rupees one thousand) only.

....

Please mail the filled up coupon at your earliest to :

Editorial & Marketing Operations Division

NEW CENTRAL BOOK AGENCY (P) Ltd

8/1 Chintamoni Das Lane, Kolkata 700 009

West Bengal, INDIA

Phone + Fax: 033 + 2241 8411, 2241 8573, 2241 9094

e-mail: ncbapvtltd@eth.net, ncba@cal2.vsnl.net.in

Website: www.centralgroup.com